EU Enlargement versus Social Europe?

To Mira C.

EU Enlargement versus Social Europe?

The Uncertain Future of the European Social Model

Daniel C. Vaughan-Whitehead

Edward Elgar

Cheltenham, UK • Northampton, MA, USA

Published by
Edward Elgar Publishing Limited
Glensanda House
Montpellier Parade
Cheltenham
Glos GL50 1UA
UK

Edward Elgar Publishing, Inc.
136 West Street
Suite 202
Northampton
Massachusetts 01060
USA

A catalogue record for this book
is available from the British Library

ISBN 1 84064 645 4

Printed and bound in Great Britain by MPG Books Ltd, Bodmin, Cornwall

Contents

Tables

Figures

Boxes

Preface

By voting in favour of ratification of the Nice Treaty with a comfortable majority in their referendum of 19 October 2002, the Irish people removed the last obstacle that could have seriously impeded the signing of the Nice Treaty on the institutional reforms necessary for EU enlargement.

The last formal and institutional step took place on the occasion of the European Council of Copenhagen, 12–13 December 2002; it confirmed the forthcoming accession to the EU of ten new candidate countries, eight from Central and Eastern Europe – Czech Republic, Estonia, Hungary, Latvia, Lithuania, Poland, Slovakia, Slovenia – and two Mediterranean countries (Cyprus and Malta), which should thus take place on schedule, before June 2004.

Despite the obstacles and imperfections, perhaps the most important political challenge of our century – to reunify the Western and Eastern parts of Europe – thus seems likely to be completed successfully. Such an ambitious political project required a speedy process. However, the speed of the process may lead us to question the quality of EU enlargement and to challenge the future functioning of the newly enlarged EU. In order to be able to accept former Communist countries from Central and Eastern Europe as quickly as possible, did we not risk diluting the original spirit and contents of the European Community?

It may be even more true that those most favourably disposed towards a rapid enlargement process have also been those traditionally in favour of a 'downward' reorientation of the European construction, towards just a unified single market rather than a Community with a single, strong political ambition.

At the same time, both the speed and the priority given to the political nature of this process seem to have led the EU not to take sufficient account of the specific features of the candidate countries, and in particular the significant gaps still existing in the economic and social fields. Will this not lead to serious difficulties after these countries join?

These obstacles may be even more difficult to overcome once the European Union loses the leverage of negotiating power. In other words, everything has gone forward as if the new member countries will fully conform to EU policies. However, what if the 10 – later 13 and more – new member states, motivated by a different logic, most of them emerging from 12 years of transition, will on the contrary progressively try to change EU policies from the inside?

Dilution, lack of consideration of candidate countries' difficulties and specific features, and a failure to identify the adverse implications of existing gaps, may very well be the outcome in the social field; especially since social policies have generally been recognised as not having been adequately addressed in the negotiations for EU accession, other issues – such as competition, agriculture, and structural funds – having been considered as deserving priority. This may be particularly destructive considering the important social differentials – in terms of wages, GDP per head, poverty – prevailing between candidate countries and current EU member states. In fact, these differences should have induced us to emphasise social matters in the current enlargement much more than in previous accessions.

No doubt the current EU institutional reform process represents a good opportunity to rebalance the whole process, as a sort of 'oxygen cylinder' in a context dominated by economic competition, liberalisation and globalisation. However, the current work of the Constitutional Convention seems to confirm the low priority given to social policy, which has so far not been addressed at all – even the creation of a working group on social issues, after having been initially rejected, was finally accepted only with great reluctance.

In such a context, it was important to address the issue, and to carry out an in-depth assessment of what type of Social Europe may emerge in parallel with the current EU enlargement process. In this connection, a careful analysis of the situation in the candidate countries was particularly important.

The present book has two main objectives: first, to provide a comprehensive assessment of candidate countries and their social policy areas most relevant to EU enlargement: wages, working conditions, social protection, employment, and industrial relations; and secondly, to address its most sensitive 'social dumping' aspects: capital relocation, labour migration, and redirection of trade, which may disrupt the EU enlargement process in one way or another.

All these issues are analysed systematically from two different angles: first, the characteristics of applicant countries that may influence EU social policy, and secondly, the strengths and weaknesses of the so-called 'European Social Model' with regard to EU enlargement.

The book also analyses whether the messages delivered to candidate countries in the negotiations for EU accession by both current EU member states and the European Commission have been fully appropriate to ensure the preservation of the European Social Model alongside this historic process.

This book tries in particular to identify the areas in which reform is urgently needed alongside the current enlargement – as well as other forthcoming enlargements – but also how EU social policy should be adapted to take account of the newcomers' economies and societies while trying to preserve the basic features of the European Social Model.

Given the breadth of the topics we address in this book, this volume may not always provide all the relevant data for comparative assessment, often because of a lack of comparative figures on candidate countries. A selection had to be made, the aim of this work not being to present all details on every topic, but rather to identify – from the available data – some of the problems and to draw attention to some policy issues and contribute to the debate – rather faint so far – on the social dimension of EU enlargement.

I have tried not only to present my own interpretation of the different issues under study, generally on the basis of my own experience in the field, but also to report as much as possible the views of people working in the social area, especially from candidate countries, often in the form of quotations and references, in order to make this book as lively as possible while trying to give a flavour of the general thoughts and opinions of those in the front line of these developments. I would like to take this opportunity to thank all of them – too numerous to be quoted but whose ideas are faithfully reflected in this volume – who have been providing me with continuous support and cooperation over the last ten years. I hope that they will recognise in this book some of their major concerns. I would also like to thank James Patterson for the editing and typesetting. I hope that this book will motivate many more, especially from the current EU, to tackle and investigate more deeply some of the issues presented. Others, even those not particularly concerned with social policy, will hopefully recognise the problems and their possible implications, also for the economic sphere.

The purpose of the present book is not to criticise candidate countries or current EU member states and institutions, but rather to identify the drawbacks with a view to further improvement.

At the same time, through a first assessment of the situation in the social field, this book is aimed at providing a warning signal about possible adverse routes that Social Europe may take alongside and after EU enlargement. Such routes could only generate widespread disappointment and endanger the whole process. Let us all work hard to ensure that this does not happen.

Daniel Vaughan-Whitehead

Foreword

Daniel Vaughan-Whitehead discusses the future of Social Europe with 25 and more countries, on the basis of a very detailed and well documented assessment of future member states. He rightly insists on the risks entailed by widening social and regional inequalities and the obsession with economic reforms, sometimes to the detriment of social and cohesion policies. However, he also points out that the countries of Central and Eastern Europe would benefit from a valorisation of solidarity, and that the European Union has everything it needs to boost the solidarity required to address the great imbalances that have emerged over the last decade.

This book thus properly addresses the important question of solidarity in a greatly enlarged Europe and, more fundamentally, that of the future of its social model, something virtually unique to Europe. By opening up the issue of Social Europe, this crucial 'construction site', this book will contribute to the anticipation of eventual problems, and help us to overcome obstacles, both post-enlargement and in preparation for further accessions.

The social dimension of the European construction is often little known and little understood in both current and future member states. However, it is the condition for making of the enlarged Europe not only a Europe of the economy and trade, but also a broad space combining competition, cooperation and solidarity, as well as an example of how to manage interdependencies and master globalisation.

Jacques Delors, President, Notre Europe

PART I

Candidate Countries and the Community
'Social *Acquis*': An Impossible Match?

1. The European Social Model and EU Enlargement

1.1 INTRODUCTION

Despite the fact that the European Social Model (ESM) is increasingly being invoked in a wide range of contexts, there have so far been very few attempts to explain this concept or to describe its nature precisely. At the same time, the defenders of the model have multiplied their efforts to promote it, but without giving adequate grounds. Surprisingly, the European Commission, which often refers to the concept of the European Social Model, has not provided an official definition, even in the Commission's glossary (EC 2000e). Despite this absence of a clear definition, however, during the European Summit in Lisbon in 2000 the member states took the position that 'the European Social Model, with its developed systems of social protection, must underpin the transformation of the knowledge economy'. Similarly, the Social Agenda adopted at the European summit in Nice dedicates an entire section to 'modernising and improving the European Social Model', where it usefully identifies the different ways of moving forward, simultaneously and interactively, with social development and economic growth.[1] The European Social Model was also further emphasised at the European Summit in Barcelona in 2002 (see the conclusions of the Barcelona Summit, par. 15).

On the other hand, the opponents of the European Social Model – generally also those opposed to any form of social policy – have developed a number of criticisms without giving the impression that they have really understood the various features and dimensions of this model: for instance, in an article in the *Financial Times*, the model was described as completely out of date, a criticism which is found regularly in the Anglo-Saxon press.

Our purpose is to provide here a first attempt at a definition, before describing what are the main features and contents of the European Social Model.

1. European Social Agenda, in 'Presidency Conclusions: Nice European Council Meeting, 7, 8 and 9 December 2000', EN SN 400/00, ADD1 (Annex 1, p. 4).

1.2 BASIC DEFINITION

We could define the ESM as a set of European Community and member-state legal regulations, but also as a range of practices aimed at promoting a voluntaristic and comprehensive social policy in the European Union. Beyond this, for EU policymakers and a wide range of economic and social actors, the European Social Model also represents sharing common views and principles on different social issues and their importance within the EC construction.

As emphasised in the conclusions of the Nice Summit in December 2000:

> the European Social Model, characterised in particular by systems that offer a high level of social protection, by the importance of social dialogue and by services of general interest covering activities vital for social cohesion, is today based, beyond the diversity of the member states' social systems, on a common core of values.[2]

Common Core Values

Specific core values of this model of particular interest in the context of enlargement include democracy, individual rights, free collective bargaining, equality of opportunity for all, and social welfare and solidarity. More generally, we should mention the importance attached to social protection for society as a whole, but also the belief that the social dimension is crucial for economic and social cohesion, and therefore also for political stability and economic performance.

Jacques Delors saw the European Social Model as based on three main values:

1. *Economic competition*, with a clear recognition of the adoption and development of market economies.
2. *Social cohesion and solidarity*, with a specific concern to reduce inequalities, a task carried out through the promotion of systems of redistribution and social protection; it implies a certain role left to public authorities; this solidarity is also developed at Community level, for instance by assisting the most backward regions through the structural funds, ensuring some redistribution through the promotion of appropriate social protection programmes, or guaranteeing services of general public interest (electricity, gas, transport, and so on). Protection of workers' and citizens' rights that have been enshrined in the European charters participate in spreading these values within the European Community.
3. *Responsibility*, with the involvement of all those concerned, and a particularly important role being allotted to social dialogue, at all levels, with

2. Ibid., p. 4.

Community, national, sectoral, regional, and local actors being called upon to play a role in accordance with the 'subsidiarity' principle.

Other values could be identified as part of the European Social Model, such as the notion of '*quality*' that was put forward more recently and placed on the European Commission's and individual member states' working agendas on the assumption that the competitive advantage and performance of the European Union would thereby be boosted. The notion of 'quality' is intended to apply to employment, working conditions, industrial relations, and social policy in general: 'quality' in industrial relations, for instance, reflects a society that can manage and limit its conflicts, one that generates responsible actors who can ensure transmission between local and national policies.

For some observers, common values cannot be limited to the above issues, but would encompass many other dimensions, such as culture, environment, education, and ways of living in general, the social model thus corresponding to a more general 'societal model' (Chouraqui and O'Kelly 2001). In this regard, we should emphasise that the EU member states have tended to keep areas such as education, health care, or transport under the control of the state, in contrast with the privatisation of such services under the Anglo-Saxon model, exemplified by the privatisation of the railways in the UK or by private health care in the USA. The importance given to the guarantee of 'services of general interest' is also specific to the EU, and the responsibility of the state in a number of areas important to the general public could thus certainly be ranked among the features of the European Social Model, although it also had to face virulent attacks in the 1980s and 1990s.

Among common societal values, we should also include a non-discriminatory society which gives the same opportunities and the same rights to all citizens, whatever their sex, origin, or race, although much progress is still required in this regard. We should never forget that the aim of the whole European construction since the Second World War has been to avoid similar conflicts and the xenophobia and racism that were part and parcel of it. Participation, free social responsibility, and solidarity are other fundamental values of European society.

We must add that these values and principles are not only due to Community instruments or policies, but also to those developed within individual member states. The European Community is thus not the cause of such common values, which could – and certainly would – be shared by European countries anyway. However, there is no doubt that the construction of the European Union and the willingness of EU member states to develop coordination, cooperation, interdependence, and also common rules on social policy have helped to maintain EU member states' commitment to social policy and have constrained 'free-riding' or 'social dumping' in the social area.

1.3 THE DIFFERENT ELEMENTS OF THE EUROPEAN SOCIAL MODEL

There have been many misunderstandings of the different components of the Social Model. Those against the model have a tendency to state that such a model does not exist, although quite distinctive features of social policy – including many with a statutory basis – can be identified only in the EU and not in other parts of the world; on the other hand, those in favour of the European Social Model have had the unproductive tendency to include in it almost everything, including those elements that clearly are not part – or not yet – of the Community *acquis*. It is therefore important to list some of the major elements (Box 1.1).

BOX 1.1 THE DIFFERENT ELEMENTS OF THE EUROPEAN SOCIAL MODEL

Labour law on workers' rights
Employment
Equal opportunities
Anti-discrimination
Workers' participation, information and consultation
Social partner recognition and involvement
Social dialogue and collective bargaining
Involvement of civil society
Public services and services of general interest
Decent or 'fair' wages
Social protection
Social inclusion
Fundamental working and social rights (of workers and citizens in general)
Regional cohesion
Transnational social policies and tools

1.3.1 A Comprehensive Approach to Social Matters

Beyond being based on a set of strong principles and values, the European Social Model can first be characterised by its comprehensive nature, since its aim is to encompass all important social areas and to cover the greatest number of people, something that has increasingly been achieved over the years.

Community legislation – as shown below – has progressively expanded to cover a great number of labour issues. At the same time, the European Social Model has progressively extended its coverage not only to new categories of worker, but also to other categories of people outside the labour market, notably through the development and progress of Community policy against social exclusion.

1.3.2 Increased Minimum Rights as Regards Working Conditions

It is important to remember the progressive extension of the number of issues covered by EU legislation, from labour mobility to provisions aimed at fighting distorted competition, promoting equal opportunities between men and women, and improving health and safety in the workplace. EC legislation has also been extended to cover transnational questions. At the same time, working conditions have improved for a great number of workers, particularly noteworthy being achievements in the area of gender equality, and also for workers outside regular employment, with the progressive implementation of regulations on atypical forms of contract, such as part-time and fixed-term work, or temporary jobs obtained through agencies.

1.3.3 Sustainable and Universal Social Protection Systems

Universal social protection with a strong basis in social solidarity constitutes one element of the European Social Model that the EU would like to extend and promote in both candidate and neighbouring countries (for example, in the Balkans). We shall develop this point in Chapter 3.

1.3.4 Strong and Well-Functioning Social Dialogue

For the trade unions:

> social dialogue is among the common principles behind the European Social Model, with the social partners participating in building and managing social policy, something essential to 'solidarity'. This is why it has progressively developed in a greater number of areas. For some, social dialogue clearly constitutes 'the European way to manage a market economy'.[3]

Social dialogue has been promoted in all member states, if in diverse ways, and as such constitutes a basic element of governance in the EU. At EU level, social dialogue has evolved into a shared governance process at Community

3. Speech by E. Gabaglio, Secretary General of the ETUC, Conference on 'Social Dialogue in Candidate Countries', Bratislava, 16 March 2001 (ETUC–UNICE–UEAPME 2001).

level since the Amsterdam Treaty. The other characteristic of the European social dialogue model seems to lie in the combination of different levels of negotiation (EU, national, sectoral, regional, enterprise) compared to full decentralisation to enterprise level in the US, but also Japanese systems. Some observers have not hesitated to declare this process, renamed 'multi-level regulation', as the distinctive feature of the European Social Model (Chouraqui and O'Kelly 2001).

1.3.5 Belief in Participation and Democracy in the Workplace

Democracy at the workplace (codetermination, information and consultation, financial participation, and so on) has been promoted through Community legislation but also by a number of innovative rules and practices in individual member states. It represents one important characteristic of EU enterprises, workers' participation also being developed in the Community directive on the European company statute. What is making such schemes well rooted in the EU is the commitment to it of all actors concerned. Not only trade unions, but also employers are convinced of the virtues of workers' participation and information and consultation as part of their corporate governance systems.[4]

1.3.6 Participation Extended to All Citizens

At the same time, civil society has been increasingly involved in the decision-making process. The new concept of 'European civil society' has been put forward and discussed in EU forums. Participation is thus seen as an important element of democratic life, which includes not only workers and their representatives, but also citizens and representative groups (NGOs, and so on).

1.3.7 An Inclusive Society

Guided by the principle of 'solidarity', one of the aims of European institutions and EU member states is not to leave any group of citizens out of the European construction. This implies significant social protection and social inclusion programmes for the most vulnerable, a strategy that led in 2002 to the adoption of a coordinated policy among member states to fight social exclusion, an approach currently being extended also to candidate countries.

4. See, for instance, the proceedings of the Fifth Round Table of Employers' Organisations organised in Berlin, 28–9 May 2001 (BDA 2001). On that occasion, EU employer organisations such as UNICE, but also national employer representatives – for instance, from Germany (BDA) or France (MEDEF) – promoted forms of information and consultation among their colleagues from candidate countries.

1.3.8 Decent or 'Fair' Wages and Living Standards

The fight against poverty and social exclusion is also a distinctive feature of the European Social Model, and one that has been carried out at both the European Community and national member-state levels. They are also seen as a basic condition of democracy. 'Freedom from need for the basic necessities of life – food, housing, medical care, and education – is as important to true democracy as the freedoms of speech and worship, assembly and association' (Jecchinis 2001, p. 5). Such principles of social justice have been enshrined in the European charters and other EC documents, and are supported by important programmes for social inclusion. Wages are not yet among the competencies of the European Community. They have been left to the responsibility of individual member states almost all of whom, however, have developed minimum wage regulations and other measures to ensure sustained living standards, a distinctive process which is recognised by the European employers themselves.[5] The Communication of the European Commission on 'decent wages' could be used as a useful framework in this regard, underlining the importance of ensuring a certain level of remuneration.

1.3.9 Making Employment a Priority

Employment is clearly a key priority of the European Union, and so an additional basic feature of the European Social Model. For the first time in its history, the European Council has adopted quantitative goals in active labour market policy for all member states: for example, young unemployed persons must receive, before six months of unemployment, an offer of a job, training, community work, and so on; the same rule applies to adults before they reach 12 months of unemployment.

The member states freely determine the policies they will implement in order to reach these goals, but they must achieve them within five years. Their national programmes are analysed and their results evaluated each year by the European Council. The Council has no constraining power, but can make public recommendations to states which do not fulfil the common goals. Five years after its introduction, this procedure seems to have had some effect on the members states' employment policies, although significant improvement is still possible (see Chapter 3). In any case, we must emphasise the potential shift in basic concepts introduced by the Luxembourg summit.

5. See statement by employers' representative Emmanuel Julien (from MEDEF, but also representing UNICE), according to whom the existence of the minimum wage, despite the different forms it takes in member states, is a distinctive feature of the European Social Model or what he called the European Social Identity – conference 'Which European Social Model?', Aix en Provence, 10–11 September 2001.

1.3.10 Maintaining Services of General Interest

Article 16 of the Treaty establishes the role of services of general economic interest in ensuring the European Union's social and territorial cohesion. It also recognises the important role of services of general interest – such as electricity, gas, other public utilities, and transportation – in the shared values underlying the European Social Model. The Commission revised its communication on services of general interest in September 2000. The Council then adopted a declaration on services of general interest that was endorsed by the European Summit in Nice, which also invited the Council and the Commission to continue their discussions within the framework of these guidelines and the provisions of Article 16 of the Treaty. They were also invited to report on the implementation of these guidelines to the European Council in December 2001 (p. 11 of the Nice Summit Presidency conclusions).

1.3.11 Equal Opportunities and the Fight against Discrimination

The EU has always been an engine for promoting equality between men and women. However, inequalities and discrimination persist, not only in respect of employment and social protection, but also in other respects. The notion of full employment supposes a radical redistribution of remunerated and non-remunerated work, and the paying of particular attention to measures for reconciling life at work, family life, and participation in society. Equality between men and women has become a major axis in the social agenda, in two principal ways: so-called 'mainstreaming' in order to promote equal opportunities in all Community policies, and specific measures to eliminate gender inequalities observed in particular areas of social, economic, and political life.

The EC has also implemented measures to fight against all sources of discrimination in accordance with Article 13 of the Treaty. This should also entail a similar mainstreaming approach in all Community areas, already reflected in the EC Action Plan for promoting equality of treatment for handicapped persons, ethnic minorities, and all other categories subject to discrimination.

1.4 AN EVOLVING MODEL

Before describing the different elements of the European Social Model in more detail, in particular with a view to identifying the problems that may arise with EU enlargement, I would like to provide a quick overview of the European Social Model, its main philosophy and features. It is in constant evolution: not only have there been several significant steps forward, but the instruments for social progress themselves have evolved and diversified over time.

1.4.1 The Progressive Ascent of Social Issues

We have already looked at the common elements of what can be characterised as 'European society'. Beyond this, however, European social policy can be seen as a goal to be attained, a sort of normative vision of the sort of society to which European citizens might be expected to aspire. Perhaps the main feature of this European Social Model is its constantly evolving nature. The story so far can be divided into four main periods.

The Treaty of Rome – social progress dependent on economic growth

First, we must call to mind the fact that the Treaty of Rome, which in 1956 created the European Economic Community as a 'common market', was principally a project of economic integration and did not do much to develop social considerations. The few social provisions it did contain were aimed at securing the free movement of labour between member states. It was assumed that 'economic integration . . . would in time ensure the optimum allocation of resources throughout the Community, the optimum rate of economic growth, and thus an optimum social system'. The promoters assumed that development of the social dimension would necessarily follow from the economic growth which the Treaty would unleash. At the same time, individual member states were very keen to retain this area under their own competence.

This state of affairs did not leave much room for the promotion of social policies;[6] during this first period, only the important instrument of structural funds was developed. Few social regulations were proposed, and were usually conceived in terms of a support role in the process of economic integration. One example of this is the coordination of social security systems aimed at facilitating free mobility of labour.[7] Since the Treaty of Rome had not set out a specific legal basis for the introduction of social policy measures, recourse could be made only to the general legal bases, either through Article 100 on the harmonisation of national measures, or Article 235 which provides a broad basis upon which measures may be introduced to further the objectives of the Community;[8] their use, however, was systematically blocked by the British government.

---

6. It was only under the pressure of large-scale social unrest, in 1968–9, that the 'Standing Committee on Employment' and the first 'Social Action Programme' were initiated, with very limited results.

7. At that time, fears were expressed about the risk that high social-security contributions in some countries could represent a competitive disadvantage, especially in relation to countries where very low levels of social protection and contributions prevailed.

8. Whilst the majority of measures were introduced under Article 100, the directives on sex equality – with the exception of the Equal Pay Directive of 1975 – were introduced under Article 235.

The Single Market – a new impulse for social policy
The objective of achieving a single market, confirmed by the signing of the Single European Act in 1986, despite its mainly economic emphasis, implied – even required – a new perception of social policy. More initiatives to establish social rights were taken by the European Commission – notably after Jacques Delors became President in 1985 – which called for the addition of a social dimension to the internal market or '*espace social européen*'. At that time, a number of social directives were prepared by the EC and accepted by the Council, although the fierce opposition of the UK made it difficult to fully institutionalise the framework for a stronger social policy approach.[9] This framework was able to find legal expression through the opportunities provided by Article 118a, which allowed for qualified majority voting in the area of health and safety at work. The UK, however, made sure that this framework would not be further institutionalised through its opt-out from the revised and strengthened social provisions agreed upon at Maastricht.

The limits imposed upon legislative progress on social policy led to the development of complementary measures. In 1989 the charter guaranteeing minimum social rights was drawn up and accepted by 11 member states – the UK refrained – in the form of a non-binding political declaration. It was also at this time that European social dialogue emerged as a means of making progress in the social area, notably through the promotion by the EC of autonomous social dialogue between the social partners at EU level.

Social policy alongside economic integration: the Maastricht Treaty
At the beginning of the 1990s, several member states, which were seeking to maintain a balance between the development of the single market and social progress, expressed their willingness to give a new impulse to social policy. Their concerns were reflected in the Treaty of the European Union signed in 1992 (by 11 member states, the UK once again refraining) that came into force in 1993. First, social objectives were strengthened in Article 2, in the following terms:

> to promote economic and social progress and a high level of employment and to achieve balanced and sustainable development, in particular through the creation of an area without internal frontiers, through the strengthening of economic and social cohesion and through the establishment of economic and monetary union, ultimately including a single currency in accordance with the provisions of this Treaty.

Secondly, the Treaty also instituted a new legislative framework through the social protocol (annexed to the Maastricht Treaty) which was prepared in light

---

9. It notably impeded the use of Article 235 as a means of developing a broader social dimension through Community law.

of the principles enshrined in the 1989 charter, and proposed progress in three major social areas: (i) extension of the competences of the Community on social issues; (ii) introduction of qualified majority voting in new areas (such as health and safety, working conditions, information and consultation, equal opportunities); and (iii) recognition and extension of the social partners' role and rights. This would allow European institutions to take the initiative on social issues which were hitherto the prerogative of individual member states. The European Commission will address the future of social policy within the framework of the general economic development of the EU,[10] and define the main challenges and axes of social policy.[11] At the same time, in 1994 the European Council adopted a resolution on EU social policy.[12] In this way, common and consolidated action on social policy has emerged since the mid-1990s (Quintin and Favarel-Dapas 1999).

Recognition of social priorities in the Amsterdam Treaty
Between 1994 and 1997, the growth of social problems, mainly related to the growth of unemployment and increasing social exclusion and marginalisation, led EU policymakers to go further. The Amsterdam Treaty, signed in October 1997 and entering into force in May 1999, sought to offer the citizens of EU member states a more 'social Europe' and to address their concerns on employment.

The Amsterdam Treaty incorporated the social protocol into the Treaty (Article 11), and created the title on employment (title 8, art. 125 to 130). The European Commission was given new competences in terms of industrial relations and action against exclusion (art. 136 to 145). The principle of equality between men and women was also reinforced, and a new Article 13 allowed the Council to take – by unanimous agreement – 'all the necessary measures to fight all sources of discrimination based either on sex, race or ethnic origin, on religion, convictions, handicap, age or sexual orientation'. Only on social protection and workers' participation in decision-making did decisions remain subject to unanimity.

Social policy within an ambitious programme of European integration
Through the above four identified periods, it is characteristic of the European Social Model that it has developed alongside the different steps taken towards European integration. Community social policy, as we have seen, has been

10. White Book *Growth, Competitiveness and Employment*, December 1993, European Commission (EC 1993).
11. White Book *European Social Policy. A Way to Follow for the European Union*, July 1994 (COM (94) 333), European Commission (EC 1994).
12. 'The Perspectives of European Union Social Policy: A Contribution to Economic and Social Convergence within the Union', (94/C 368/03), European Council, 1994.

strengthened from the Treaty of Rome to the Single Market. It remains also a central concern within the current ambitious policy agenda of the European Union to achieve economic and monetary union, to introduce a new common currency, and to enlarge the EU to include Central and Eastern Europe and new Mediterranean countries. This confirms how intimately this social model is related to EU economic and political integration. It also explains why the Community social policy is never static but in permanent evolution, not only in its contents but also in its tools.

1.4.2 An Increasingly Diversified Set of Instruments

This progress in social policy has also gone hand in hand with a general assessment that the sophistication of European economies, the development of knowledge societies, and the modernisation of work organisation require constant adaptation. In this evolving context, however, it became clear that it would be increasingly difficult to make progress on the sole basis of general workers' rights, given the very high levels of unemployment in some member states and significant parts of the population left without social protection. The use of financial means through the European structural funds also appeared to be insufficient. This is also the reason why European social policy has developed, and the European Social Model enriched, in a number of complementary ways.

We shall look briefly at how the major ways of developing social policy have emerged and evolved in the course of time. We can group them in five major categories:

1. extending the minimum legal rights of workers;
2. ensuring social solidarity at European level through a mechanism for the redistribution of European social funds;
3. setting up a more flexible and coordinated framework between member states (method of open coordination);
4. developing a dynamic space for social dialogue at European level;
5. extending social rights through fundamental social charters.

Some have been promoted from the start, such as social legislation and the redistributional system of social funds, although they have also benefited from progressive consolidation. Others have emerged only recently, such as the method of open coordination, or have been strengthened over time, such as social dialogue; others have emerged somewhat 'in a fit of absence of mind', as may be observed, for example, in the development of social charters with a non-binding character aimed at complementing the absence of legal regulations in given areas.

The progressive increase in the number of instruments can be explained first by the fact that further binding provisions were not possible in a number of areas (such as employment, social exclusion, social protection, working conditions, and so on), and secondly by the recognition that harmonious social and economic developments could not come from the use of merely one or two keys on the piano (legal and financial means), but from use of the entire keyboard. This would represent a more appropriate and modern form of governance imposed by a more complex and varied environment. The art of the exercise thus consists in choosing and measuring the extent to which each key should be used according to the objective pursued.

The legislative tool
On the legislative side, European social policy has been extended and diversified since the creation of the European Community. The first attempts to establish a space of free labour mobility have been complemented by new provisions in other areas. Community labour law has established a basis of approximately 70 directives or legislative instruments in four main areas: (i) free movement of workers, (ii) workers' rights, (iii) equal opportunities for women and men, and (iv) health and safety in the workplace. The new legislative instruments in these areas are aimed at establishing new social rights on transnational questions (such as free movement, European Works' Councils, detachment of workers) or at fixing new levels of minimum rights without prejudice to more favourable provisions which might exist at national level. This is an important *acquis* which in many areas has complemented or reinforced social provisions in member states. The legislative action is currently continuing in the same direction and the EC must fully exploit the new possibilities provided by the Treaty to progress on social issues, especially to provide better cover for new forms of employment, such as independent work or tele-work, and to ensure that the important principles already discussed (health and safety, non-discrimination, equal opportunities) are maintained in a context of globalisation, new technologies, restructuring and adaptation of industry and services, and of course EU enlargement.

This legal *acquis* had an important role in the pre-accession negotiations. The governments of the candidate countries, during the screening exercise, had to present and discuss their plans to bring their own legislation and practice into line with Community requirements. We shall see in Chapter 2 that such transposition efforts from candidate countries will bring results, but also continue to meet concrete problems at the local level.

The legislative method mainly responds to three aims:

1. to adopt minimum standards and prescriptions, thus progressively guaranteeing basic social rights for workers and indeed everyone living in the EU;

2. to harmonise social regulations, thus providing for the establishment of common social law in all member states. Such common social law is expected to accompany the achievement of the single market and to cover the new needs resulting from European integration and the transnational nature of many enterprises;
3. to coordinate national social rights to achieve the free movement of people.

In some areas the legislation has not gone as far as expected, something that may also cause problems in the EU enlargement process, as we shall see later.

There is therefore still progress to be made in the legislative area. What is certain is that legislation will continue to be a key instrument of social progress. In this regard, the European Commission is making full use of the provisions of the Treaty. Several proposals have recently been made, notably the anti-discrimination package on the basis of Article 13 of the Treaty, which gives the EC new competences in this area. There are two proposals of directives, and one action programme. On information and consultation, the directive on the European company statute has been passed, and has been complemented by the recent adoption of the directive on information and consultation in enterprises with more than 50 employees. A review is also being carried out to examine how current legislation can be updated, improved, and simplified.

We must also emphasise the legal role that the European Court of Justice is playing in building a Social Europe. The decisions of the Court of Justice have contributed, on the basis of common social values, to defining the coverage and extension of Community regulations in the social field. This was the case, for instance, after 1975 when it contributed to the elaboration of a directive on equal opportunities for men and women.

The European Social Fund

All structural funds have one common mission, to reduce the differences in standards of living that exist between regions of the EU. They have represented over the years a central mechanism of economic and social cohesion. In the social field, the European Social Fund (ESF), one of the EU's four structural funds, represents a particularly important instrument for the promotion of solidarity since it plays a key role not only in social but also in employment policies, especially the European Employment Strategy. The European social fund channels money to help member states to develop more and better jobs. In this regard, it helps to prevent and fight unemployment, develop the skills of the labour force, and prevent people losing touch with the labour market.

The method of open coordination

A third tool that has been developed in recent years is the 'benchmarking' or 'coordinated' method (also called by some the 'convergence' method) in areas where objectives are needed and where legislation is not possible or is undesirable. It was envisaged as an appropriate instrument in those areas of competence which are essentially national, but require concerted strategies at European level. It thus opened up new perspectives in those areas where the EU had limited competences (and prerogatives).

Recent developments in the area of employment show that it is possible to go forward in social matters in this way. The European Employment Strategy is proposing a frame of action on the basis of a combination of three different steps: (i) guidelines (employment guidelines), (ii) a method (the elaboration of national plans of action in member states), and (iii) a follow-up (the principle of multilateral monitoring). It is worth noting that the definition and implementation of common objectives with regard to employment, the comparison of national policies and practices, and finally monitoring has led to the adoption of concrete recommendations addressed to member states which are quite constraining. They are aimed at helping member states to improve their performance in this area.

This overall frame lends coherence to the whole, and will make possible a qualitative leap in European employment policy. Candidate countries are already involved in this process since they have been asked to prepare, with the EC, joint assessment papers on employment in cooperation with the social partners.

This method has recently been extended to other areas in order to establish a coordinated policy (with similar guidelines, national reports, monitoring, and so on) – for instance, against social exclusion or in favour of social protection.

Social dialogue at EU level

The fourth way is to provide a framework of dialogue; to create at European level a dynamic space in which to generate impulses for change. Social dialogue has accompanied European construction since the signing of the Treaty of Rome in 1956, but has been progressively reinforced over the years.

The social partners have progressively become key partners and have been systematically consulted on every initiative taken by the EC in the social area, with two-stage consultation early on in the process ('upstream'): first, the EC consults the social partners to find out whether an action is relevant and should be taken in a precise area and about what its general orientation should be; secondly, if it is decided to go ahead, the social partners are also consulted on the text proposed by the EC. For example, there has been consultation on European Works' Councils, information and consultation of workers, sexual harassment, flexibility of working time, and many other legal texts.

Finally, significant progress was made with the incorporation of the social protocol of the Maastricht Treaty in the Treaty of Amsterdam (as Article 138) which gave new and important responsibilities to the social partners at EU level: not only will the social partners continue to be consulted 'upstream' in order to find out whether provisions should be prepared in a specific area, but also, after this first stage of consultation, social partners can now decide to prepare such provisions not through the traditional legislative approach – that is, a legislative text prepared by EC experts and proposed to the Council – but through the negotiation among themselves of a framework agreement in the area concerned. Moreover, after such a framework agreement has been concluded, social partners can jointly decide to ask the EC to propose to the Council that the framework agreement be converted into a legislative text, that is, into a new directive. So far, this has been very stimulating and this option has often been chosen in the last few years by the social partners, who in this way have become 'legislators' themselves: they have negotiated and concluded three framework agreements, one on parental leave (1996), one on part-time work (1997), and one on fixed-term contracts (1999). The fact that all three framework agreements have since been enshrined in European legislation by the Council (at the social partners' request) is an obvious sign that social dialogue has become one of the driving forces of European social policy, and the role of social partners is one of the key features of the European Social Model. The opening of new negotiations on temporary agency work – another major form of atypical work – in June 2000 confirmed the vitality of this procedure, even if it has not led to any agreement. After the social partners had been given nine months to reach agreement, and they failed to do so, the EC took back its initial prerogative to legislate.

At the beginning of the process the social partners can take the initiative to open negotiations on a specific topic, even without prior consultation with the European Commission. Also, with its 1998 Communication on social dialogue the EC has encouraged the social partners to start a similar autonomous social dialogue process in specific sectors. This step has also met with immediate success, with the creation of 27 EC sectoral dialogue committees and the conclusion within this frame of five sectoral agreements, in agriculture and as regards working time in maritime, railway, air, and road transportation. This level of negotiation could provide many opportunities to negotiate issues and conclude agreements in areas which are more relevant for particular sectors, such as tele-work, health and safety, and working time. The progressive opening up of such committees to social partners from candidate countries may also provide opportunities to discuss new issues and help to solve several problems encountered in specific sectors as a result of impending EU enlargement.

The European Social Model will in future be increasingly developed by combining these four complementary tools. Recently, the European Commission has not hesitated to use the strong or binding method in the area of anti-discrimination policy – with two new directives – and in the area of information and consultation. At the same time, the open coordination method on employment has made it possible to go as far as politically feasible in areas such as employment, social exclusion, and social protection. European social dialogue has enabled progress on atypical working contracts.

As already mentioned, a key concept for the modernisation of the European Social Model presented by the EC is 'quality': 'quality of life for all', quality of work, quality of industrial relations, and quality of social protection.[13]

The social charters
One instrument which is often not regarded as relevant by those describing Social Europe, because not considered to be part of the legal – and thus more constraining – Community *acquis*, although it provides a series of institutional or constitutional rights, is the social charter. The social charters (see Box 1.2) have proved to be an important way of extending social rights and of having social rights accepted at the same level as human and civil rights. Further, they may well represent the basis for a future European Constitution.

There have been three major charters on social rights to complement the European Convention on Human Rights: first, the Charter of the Council of Europe of 1961, which was revised in 1996; secondly, the Community char-

---

BOX 1.2 THE EUROPEAN SOCIAL CHARTERS

– European Convention on Human Rights (1951):
  guarantees civil and political human rights
– (Revised) European Social Charter (of the Council of Europe) (signed in 1961, three protocols were added to the Charter in 1988, 1991, and 1995. In 1996, the revised Social Charter was opened for signature and has progressively replaced the first charter):
  guarantees social and economic rights
– The Charter of Workers' Rights (1989):
  first common basis of fundamental social rights
– The European Charter for Fundamental Social Rights (2000):
  puts social rights on the same level as human rights

---

13. See the Social Agenda (EC 2000d); see also the Working Document of the European Parliament on 'The New Social Agenda for the Medium Term'; Commission for Employment and Social Affairs (402946FR.doc; PE286.207), 12 May 2000.

Table 1.1 Charters ratified by the candidate countries, 30 September 2001

	European Social Charter (of Council of Europe)	Revised European Social Charter (of Council of Europe)	European Convention on Human Rights
Bulgaria	O	X	X
Cyprus	X	X	X
Czech Republic	X	O	X
Estonia	O	X	X
Hungary	X	O	X
Latvia	O	O	X
Lithuania	O	X	X
Malta	X	O	X
Poland	X	O	X
Romania	O	X	X
Slovakia	X	O	X
Slovenia	O	X	X
Turkey	X	O	X

Notes:
X: ratified
O: not ratified

ter for fundamental social rights adopted at the European Summit in Strasbourg in December 1989 (United Kingdom excluded) was drawn up with the clear objective of defining a common 'basis of fundamental social rights'; it also contributed to establishing the basic principles behind the European model of social regulation; more recently, the charter for fundamental social rights adopted at the European Summit in Nice.

There are concrete examples where social charters have constituted an important complementary tool in areas for which there are no European legislative provisions, such as wage policy and trade union rights, including the right to strike. They may not be sufficient, however. While representing an essential reference, the Charter of 1989 also has its limits since it is not integrated into the Treaties. As a result, its implementation is not guaranteed by the Court of Justice. It was for the purpose of developing a more global approach and greater visibility for civil and social fundamental rights, not only of workers but also of citizens, that a new social charter, the 'charter of fundamental rights' was prepared and adopted at the Nice Summit in

December 2000. Its non-binding nature, however, shows the need for further progress in this area. For the time being, the European Convention on Human Rights represents a sort of 'Bill of Rights' common to all European countries. The Social Charter of the Council of Europe provides a complementary tool, especially since it not only provides a list of rights, but also involves a process of supervision, with national reports being scrutinised by an experts' committee. The procedure of collective complaints adds to the constraining nature of the articles of the charter for the countries which have ratified it (see Table 1.1).

In the current negotiation process, social charters have been useful in presenting and emphasising to candidate countries particular elements of the European Social Model on which there are no EC legal provisions. 'The new charter for fundamental social rights is an element of reform crucial for enlargement, because it contributes to defining a common set of values, and thus fixes the basis of the European Social Model'.[14]

The different charters also provide new references for the Court of Justice. The 1989 charter, despite its weaknesses, was used, for example, after the closure of Renault's factory in Vilvorde. Similarly, the new social charter for fundamental social rights opens up an avenue of 'interpretation' even if it does not 'create' rights.

1.4.3 An Original 'Governance' Process: Combining Common Rules with Subsidiarity

While evolving and developing new instruments, such as the open method of coordination, which put in evidence the added value of a cooperative and concerted approach at European level, the different Community social agendas have always respected the principle of subsidiarity. The European Social Model is therefore strongly based on respective responsibilities at different levels: Community, national, regional, sectoral (both European and national), enterprise, and establishment.

While characterised by a common frame of shared social and societal values the European Social Model is thus also based on – and would seem to take its strength from – important differences between the member states (Szell 2001). We shall see that such diversity is particularly striking in industrial relations, but also welfare policies, between the Nordic, Mediterranean, and Anglo-Saxon systems. This combination of common values and rules with diversity has led to what is called by some 'multi-level regulated autonomy' (Chouraqui and O'Kelly 2001), where an important role is left to local polit-

---

14. Speech by Jean Lapeyre, Deputy Secretary General, European Trade Union Confederation, Conference of trade union legal experts 'Netlex', Riga, February 2001.

ical, economic, and social actors in adapting these common standards to the diversity of local and cultural conditions. Others have defined it as a 'multi-level governance process', with a multiplication of actors and an increased diversification of normative and institutional instruments, as well as spaces for dialogue and negotiation (Goetschy 2001). In the EU, there is a multitude of situations for which the legislator – at either Community or national level – defines objectives and general principles and calls for branch or enterprise negotiations in order to elaborate rules best adapted to the local context. Some have called it a 'freedom framed' either by objectives to be met – such as workers' involvement – or modalities to respect, such as collective bargaining (Jobert 2001).

The recent work carried out on 'governance' by the European Commission was precisely aimed at enlarging this frame even further, by investigating how the decision-making process at European level could be opened to all social and economic actors, not only social partners but also civil society and EU citizens in general.

Such a multi-level and multi-actor governance process has many advantages: it can respond more easily to the diversity of national situations, to the different contexts of individual enterprises. It can adapt more quickly to the increasing complexity of economic and industrial changes, while continuing to define common frames and principles that reinforce social cohesion. This also seems to be an easier and less conflictual way to ensure the necessary balance between two apparently contradictory objectives: the flexibility demanded by employers and the security demanded by workers. This governance process, by associating more closely all actors concerned, may help public policies to be better understood and better implemented, thus strengthening their legitimacy and efficiency. More globally, it would guarantee social democracy alongside political democracy.

At the same time, however, the model has drawbacks or weaknesses that paradoxically were also originated by the increased complexity of policy actors and tools. So far, only a limited number of actors seem to have understood and are thus using this complex model, while diversification also renders more difficult articulation between the different spaces of regulation. The poor knowledge among European citizens of the elements and functioning of the European Social Model which is revealed in every single poll is an obvious sign of the limits of a model that intends to be based – paradoxically again – on the participation of all, a situation (or a learning process) that may be progressively improved by appropriate campaigns and policies.

Finally, the respect of the principle of subsidiarity in the social field has often been used by member states to prevent new Community policies and instruments, and the adoption of binding social regulations. The coexistence of a common frame of rules and principles with the respect for diversity and subsidiarity has thus not always proved to be a successful feature of the European Social Model.

This is why in some areas, such as workers' participation, social progress could be made only after major conflicts. Binding legislation could be adopted only after a few industrial relocation and restructuring cases led to major collective protests. For instance, the Renault decision to close its establishment at Vilvorde without proper consultation of its employees led to a massive European mobilisation,[15] and gave the necessary impulse for the Directive on European Works' Councils (Quintin and Favarel-Dapas 1999).

1.5 THE MOST DISTINCTIVE FEATURE OF THE MODEL: ITS ABSENCE IN OTHER PARTS OF THE WORLD

Nothing similar to the European Social Model can be found in other parts of the world. The model is quite distinctive, rooted in shared values that have not been replicated anywhere else so far. In particular, it differs sharply from policies and developments in the United States and the United Kingdom. Whilst the USA has certainly developed a number of social policies – for instance, on social security and pensions – the system is based mainly on an individualistic approach, with little initiative being taken by the state and an increasing reliance on market forces. In particular, the American model embraces the deregulation of labour market guarantees, low wage rates for less skilled workers, lower levels of social protection (that are, moreover, based on insurance rather than guaranteed by a welfare state), and a limited role for collective bargaining and social dialogue in general. There is also a fundamental difference in respect of social protection. While the European form of 'welfare' is concerned with the social well-being of all citizens within their societies, welfare in the United States is considered to be a 'safety net' – for example, a minimum subsistence income – for those who, for whatever reason, are not employed in the mainstream economy.[16] This last vision is also the one that has been promoted by international organisations such as the IMF and the World Bank (but also by the OECD) and strongly promoted by them in Central and Eastern Europe during the first twelve years of reform, as we shall see later in this volume.

The EU model is also more concerned about reducing inequalities.

The specificity of the European Social Model is emphasised in the World Competitiveness Yearbook:

15. 50 000 workers from all over Europe joined a massive demonstration in Brussels.
16. The level of this minimum, however, has to be kept low enough not to 'demotivate' potential job-seekers, and its funding must be 'neutral' in order not to distort the allocation of resources.

Another force shaping the competitive environment of a country is the distinction between a system that promotes individual risk and one that preserves social cohesiveness. The so-called Anglo-Saxon model is characterised by emphasis on risk, deregulation, privatisation and the responsibility of the individual through a minimalist approach to welfare. In contrast, the Continental European Model relies heavily on social consensus, a more egalitarian approach to responsibilities and an extensive welfare system. (IMD 2000)

In Japan, although the paternalistic systems of industrial relations and production have given birth to a number of similar elements – such as participation at firm level – a different model of corporate governance seems to be emerging in the EU. The formal recognition of the need to involve the workers and its promotion through the generalisation of appropriate institutions – such as works' councils – contrast strikingly with the forms of workers' participation implemented on the initiative of the management (such as quality circles) that prevail in Japan, or the participation through share-ownership that characterises the American and, more generally, the Anglo-Saxon models.

Moreover, a comprehensive approach to social issues is lacking in Japan, as in the United States, with a continuing dominance of economic over social considerations. In short, the general belief is that the improvement of economic performance is the only way to afford any kind of social policy, a view in striking contrast with the one prevailing in the EU, which considers social policy first as an important element worthy of the attention of policymakers in its own right, and secondly as a potential source of improved economic performance.

The differences between the European Union and other countries cover a wide spectrum: for instance, health care, especially after (former) President Clinton's administration failed to introduce a national health care system; and also the environment: the USA's refusal to reduce pollution at the last World Environmental Summit can also be located at the opposite extreme of the ecological efforts of European industry and policy, and indeed the positions of virtually every other country in the world. American-type capitalism – that is, less committed to environmental and social issues – has already shown its limitations after its golden years of expansion in Asia and Latin America.

The financial crisis of the Asian countries is living proof of the serious weaknesses of economies not built on social partnership and democratic values (Stiglitz 2002). Similar elements of economic failure can be identified in the current economic crisis in Argentina.

If the European Social Model survives, while retaining its basic features, it may well constitute an alternative to the US capitalist model and thus represent a useful model for the rest of the world.

1.6 A MODEL UNDER CONSTANT ATTACK

1.6.1 The Neo-Liberal Vision of Social Europe

Despite a number of achievements in promoting a Social Europe at Community level and also in several member states, the importance of social matters has not been accepted by all. Several member states have repeatedly tried to undermine the social rights listed above in the belief that they would be costly for enterprises and lead to much too rigid labour markets. Among those arguing against social policies, some are ready to accept that social matters should be taken care of, but only after economic growth has been ensured. If not, there should not be any redistribution of productivity gains.

It is in this spirit that many analysts have challenged the coherence and viability of a common social model which is seen as contradicting the current logic of international economic competition and globalisation. These theories have their roots in Adam Smith (1776), who believed that individuals, by their individual endeavours, and without knowing it, contributed to the general health of the nation, a phenomenon described as the 'invisible hand'. Modern liberals have gone further, and built new theories on individualistic behaviour. They have tried to capture individuals' 'maximisation' efforts and to convert them into mathematical equations. In this way they have tried to explain – and thus predict – most economic and social phenomena according to different hypotheses on individual behaviour (individual taste, choices, initial allowances). Such neo-classical or neo-liberal theories are thus mainly founded on the abstract aggregation of individual efforts to rationally maximise profits. These theories lead to the belief that it would be possible to fully predict individuals' behaviour on the markets, and thus to better manage economies and societies, if a series of rigidities did not exist to counteract free market forces. Like the original liberals, neo-liberal theorists believe in the ability of the market to determine optimal levels of wages and employment. Labour market rigidities are the clear cause of crises. In particular, all social measures to protect individuals from the consequences of market forces have the direct effect of increasing the cost of labour and therefore act as disincentives to employment. It therefore becomes impossible for employers to lower wages to a level where excess labour supply would be restored to its 'natural' level. Moreover, social allocations by the state – such as unemployment benefits – have the effect of deincentivising work and encourage voluntary unemployment.

However, many theorists have countered that social provisions can also represent an economic incentive; for instance, social protection can be also viewed as an employment factor in the sense that it allows the job-seeker to be more efficient in his search because he does not have to concentrate on making ends meet; he may also have the opportunity to engage in further training which may turn out to be beneficial for society as a whole.

The problem is that neo-classical theory has not managed to provide a faithful image of reality, which has led an increasing number of economists (Solow, Stiglitz) to criticise its main foundation, that is, that the sum of individuals' profit maximisation leads to national economic growth. This has not yet led to any solid theoretical alternative, however.

> Conditions for having market forces guiding the economy towards efficiency are extremely restrictive: there should be perfect information and developed markets, that is never, especially in developing countries, so that "the invisible hand does not work anymore". (Stiglitz 2002, p. 108)

What is most peculiar about the neo-classical approach is that it has tried to explain the gap between its theoretical predictions and economic reality not in terms of theoretical error, but in terms of reality not behaving as it should because of market imperfections that need to be ironed out.

Moreover, the neo-classical theories developed by Anglo-Saxon economists have become widely influential in the world economy; they exerted growing influence during the 1980s and 1990s and have been advocated by dominant international monetary and economic institutions, such as the IMF, the World Bank, and the OECD, mainly as an alternative to Keynesian policies judged much too inflationary.

Paradoxically, such policies have even been imposed in many cases within the framework of very rigid macroeconomic models – for example, in the first twelve years of reform in Central and Eastern Europe – although this neo-classical policy should normally be rooted in the absence of intervention from the state or transnational organisations.

On the model of the American economy, many EU member states have started to give such an approach growing weight, and have apparently been converted to greater flexibility and less labour market regulation. The government of the UK has clearly dominated this ideological debate, first with the government of Prime Minister Margaret Thatcher in the 1980s, who successfully undermined labour market regulations while breaking the power of the trade union movement. This policy was aimed at boosting enterprise activities and so job creation. At the same time, at Community level almost all new proposals of directives in the field of labour law and social policy were fiercely opposed by the British government which managed to reject a majority of them under the veto system that allowed a single government to block any decision in the social field.

Although in a different spirit – but this time in the name of social liberalism or the 'third way' – Labour Prime Minister Tony Blair has become the most fervent and prominent advocate of neo-liberal policies, and in his firm stance against social regulations has been able to dominate the European debate. This culminated in June 1999 with the publication of a manifesto in favour of free markets and flexibility jointly prepared and signed by Tony Blair and the Chancellor of the Republic of Germany, Gerhard Schröder. In this manifesto, the belief in competition and free markets (as enshrined in the Treaty of Rome) was presented as the main recipe for economic success, with plenty of references to flexibility, free competition, and market forces:

> In a world of ever more rapid globalisation and scientific changes we need to create the conditions in which existing businesses can prosper and adapt, and new businesses can be set up and grow . . . (p. 3) a framework that allows market forces to work properly is essential to economic success and a pre-condition of a more successful employment policy . . . (p. 5) Product, capital and labour markets must be more flexible . . . To make the European economy more dynamic, we also need to make it more flexible . . . Adaptability and flexibility are at an increasing premium in the knowledge-based service economy of the future . . . companies must not be gagged by rules and regulations . . . Rigidity and over-regulation hamper our success . . . (pp. 6–7) We should make it easier for small businesses in particular to take on new staff: that means lowering the burden of regulation and non-wage labour costs (p. 8). (*Europe: The Third Way/Die Neue Mitte*, The Blair/Schröder Manifesto, 11 June 1999 www.xs4all.nl/~adampost/Archive/arc000006.html)

Social rigidities were also very much emphasised:

> Work was burdened with ever higher costs. The means of achieving social justice became identified with ever higher levels of public spending regardless of what they achieved or the impact of the taxes required to fund it on competitiveness, employment and living standards. (p. 2)

Social policy also came under attack:

> Values that are important to citizens, such as personal achievement and success, entrepreneurial spirit, individual responsibility and community spirit, were too often subordinated to universal social safeguards. (p. 2)

One year later, before the Lisbon Summit, Tony Blair prepared and signed other documents of this nature, inspired by the same ideology, with the leaders of other member states: first a report prepared by a group of Italian and British economists (Boeri et al. 2000) was distributed to the heads of the European governments with an accompanying joint letter from Tony Blair and the Prime Minister of Italy, Alessandro D'Allema, just a few days before the Lisbon summit. The report insists on the rigidities in welfare systems and labour markets as the main cause of long-term unemployment and non-participation rates in Europe, although in different ways in different countries. In

Northern Europe, including the UK, 'unemployment rates result mainly from the dysfunctional structuring of the welfare system. Huge sums are spent on long-term benefits which encourage inactivity and exclusion'. In Southern Europe, 'centralised collective bargaining institutions do not allow wages to compensate for lower productivity levels' (p. 2). The authors conclude that there is a 'close relationship' between the possibility of receiving unemployment benefits, and how long people remain unemployed. For them:

> one way to reduce long-term dependence on benefits is to make sure that benefits are used for their intended purpose – to support people who are not working and who really cannot find work . . . there must be a test of willingness to work . . . this is the policy known as 'welfare-to-work'. The phrase comes from America, where it mainly applies to lone mothers. (pp. 5–6)

A few months later, in October 2000, a common document was also jointly signed by Tony Blair with the Prime Minister of Spain, José Maria Aznar. As stressed in the title of their joint statement, 'Priorities of the Lisbon Strategic Agenda', the aim is to set out targets for reform, which the European Union was due to revise at the summit in Stockholm in spring 2001. A liberal economy is clearly the target: 'Liberalisation, openness and flexibility in product and labour markets bring about new business opportunities, the adoption of new technologies, increased competition and a larger and better supply of key inputs for the rest of the economy.' In this framework, no specific reference to social issues is made, or only as a direct implication of economic issues: 'ambitious economic reforms lead to stronger potential growth, more and better jobs, higher consumer welfare and provide the right framework for the development of a socially knowledge-based society: the goal Europe set itself at Lisbon'.[17] Tony Blair and José Maria Aznar asserted that the Lisbon summit meeting 'was a victory for the "Anglo-Saxon" approach towards a privatised and deregulated economy".[18]

Such open statements, since they are clearly aimed at pointing out the direction that EU member states should take, are obviously significant for the future of Social Europe, since they demonstrate not only the leading role played by the British government against further steps on social rights but, more importantly, the great popularity that such liberal positions have enjoyed among other European political leaders, also among industrialists and many other economic actors.

17. 'Joint Statement from Tony Blair and Jose Maria Aznar on Priorities for the Lisbon Strategic Agenda', joint press release of the British and Spanish Embassies, Berlin, 27 October 2000. See also 'The Euro is Changing the Face of Europe', by A. Blair and J.-M. Aznar, in *Financial Times* (13 June 2000).

18. 'EU Sets Goals: Surpassing America in Internet Era', *International Herald Tribune* (25 March 2000).

Tony Blair hailed the Lisbon summit as having 'developed a different set of directions for economic policy'. While also stressing the need for social protection, he maintained that the best way of preventing poverty and 'social exclusion' was to provide everyone with a job. For his spokesman Alastair Campbell, 'there was a sense of change in EU thinking away from social regulation toward a competitive, enterprise culture'.[19]

1.6.2 The Response of the Lisbon Summit

Paradoxically, the Lisbon summit, by addressing social issues within the main concerns of neo-liberal theory – that is, economic performance – managed to put such issues more strongly at the core of the policy agenda. The Lisbon summit helped to demonstrate the indissoluble link between economic performance and social progress, and to present social progress as a 'productive factor'. It notably provided a definition of new objectives and a schedule for implementing better articulation between the economy, employment, and social cohesion:[20]

> Economic and social trends can be examined [in terms of] three angles and central topics: our increasing macroeconomic interdependence, our involvement and cooperation in favour of employment, and our permanent efforts for promoting social progress within the European Union. These three factors are closely related and cannot be considered as distinct objectives. (COM(2000)82 (EC 2000f), p. 4)

On the basis of the Lisbon European Conclusions, on 28 June 2000 the Commission submitted a communication on the European Social Agenda, in which it defined, within the framework of its five-year programme, specific priorities for action for the next five years.

On this basis, on 26 October 2000 the European Parliament Resolution adopted substantial elements for deepening and enhancing the social agenda. It particularly emphasised the following points: the importance of interaction between economic, social, and employment policies; the role of the various instruments and especially the open method of coordination and legislation; and the mobilisation of all the players involved. It sought to reinforce the Agenda on a series of points and stressed the need for an annual follow-up to the Social Agenda on the basis of a 'scoreboard' drawn up by the Commission.

The Lisbon Summit also emphasised three other dimensions of the social model considered crucial for economic performance: life-long learning, the

19. *International Herald Tribune*, op. cit.
20. Considered as the three interactive and complementary angles of the same triangle, also called later the 'Lisbon triangle'.

modernisation of work organisation, and the financing of social security systems.

The EU can point to a number of good examples of interaction between social and economic progress, with many of the most successful countries – for example, in Scandinavia – also being particularly active in the social area.

It is also significant that the *World Competitiveness Yearbook* (IMD 2000), which uses 290 criteria to measure performance and covers 47 industrialised and emerging economies, clearly includes among its criteria indicators of the preservation of the social fabric – considered one of the ten golden rules of competitiveness – as well as such things as wage disparities, life-long training, investment in education, and, more globally, the preservation of value systems to which citizens are strongly attached.

On the basis of reports from the Commission and the Council and a regular 'scoreboard', the European Council will, at each spring meeting, look at how the Agenda is being implemented, something that started at the Stockholm meeting in March 2001. Social partners obviously also have a crucial role to play, both in its implementation and in monitoring.

In this context of opposing theories on the place of social policies and social standards in the European construction, EU enlargement takes on a particular importance. Existing social policies and practices in the former Communist countries after the first years of reform may well influence the future of Social Europe. At the same time, the weaknesses which still characterise the European Social Model could well become decisive within the framework of an EU enlargement process of such magnitude and with such differences in economic and social levels.

It is significant that one section of the Social Agenda adopted at the Nice European Council identifies among the main common challenges the need to 'make a success of enlargement in the social field',[21] and 'to strengthen the social policy aspects of enlargement'.[22] The document calls to mind the fact that '[n]ot only do the candidate countries face the major challenge of adjusting and changing their systems, but they are confronted with most of the problems that beset the existing Member States of the European Union'. However, this common challenge requires a careful assessment of the gap existing between candidate countries and member states in economic and social terms, and also identification of the difficulties that may emerge in every area of European social policy and the European Social Model as EU enlargement draws closer. This will be our main concern in the following chapters.

21. European Social Agenda – citation can be found in 'Presidency Conclusions: Nice European Council Meeting, 7, 8 and 9 December 2000' (EC 2000d), EN SN 400/00, ADD1 (Annex 1), p. 7.
22. Ibid., p. 17.

1.7 THE EXTENSION OF THE MODEL TO CANDIDATE AND NEIGHBOURING COUNTRIES

As already mentioned, the problems besetting Social Europe are magnified by the prospect of EU enlargement to take in Central and Eastern Europe and new Mediterranean countries.

1.7.1 Much More than 'Just Another EU Enlargement'

The current process of enlargement of the EU to more than 10 candidate countries is not just another accession process; first, because of its unprecedented scale (see Box 1.3). This process is expected to increase the EU population by 28 per cent, to more than 500 million people. It will also increase the EU's surface area by 35 per cent. However, GDP per head is expected to fall by 18 per cent and GDP as a whole not to increase much (no more than 5 per cent), mainly because of the integration of countries with significantly poorer economic performance.

At the same time, the income gaps between countries and regions will massively widen. If a Union of 27 existed today, over one-third of the population would live in countries with an income per head less than 90 per cent of the EU average, compared to one-sixth in the present EU 15 (EC Cohesion Report – EC 2001c).

At regional level, the average income per head for the bottom 10 per cent of the population living in the least prosperous regions in the enlarged Europe would only be 31 per cent of the EU 27 average. Today, the respective figure for the EU 15 is 61 per cent. In such a context, reduction of the development gap seems an unachievable task, at least in the short and medium term. We shall see that real convergence of GDP will not take place for most candidate countries for ten – in some cases as many as thirty – years, even if the best imaginable scenario is envisaged, that is, continuously higher growth rates

---

BOX 1.3 PREVIOUS EU ENLARGEMENTS

- 1951: creation of the first European Community (CECA) between the Benelux countries (Belgium, Luxembourg and the Netherlands), France, Germany and Italy
- 1973: Denmark, Ireland, and the United Kingdom
- 1981: Greece
- 1986: Spain and Portugal
- 1995: Austria, Finland, and Sweden

BOX 1.4 BRIEF CHRONOLOGY OF FORTHCOMING ACCESSIONS

Countries concerned: eight CEE countries (Czech Republic, Estonia, Hungary, Latvia, Lithuania, Poland, Slovakia, Slovenia) and two Mediterranean countries (Cyprus and Malta). Two other countries are expected to join in 2007 (Bulgaria and Romania), while the accession of Turkey will take place later. In the meantime, other countries may attain 'candidate country' status (e.g. Croatia)

Early 1990s: Signature of Europe Agreements.

Mid-1990s: Official applications for membership.

1997: Agenda 2000 published on the necessary steps for successful enlargement.

1997: Commission *avis* opening the way for the differentiation of two groups of applicants – those considered more advanced in their preparations for accession (Czech Republic, Cyprus, Estonia, Hungary, Poland and Slovenia) and those considered less advanced in meeting accession criteria (Bulgaria, Latvia, Lithuania, Malta, Romania, and Slovakia).

March 1998: pre-accession talks opened with the countries of the first group.

June 2000: Helsinki Summit confirms that the EU will not retain the 'two-groups' approach, but instead consider each applicant country case-by-case, according to its own merits and level of preparedness. It also confirms Turkey as a new applicant country.

2000: Screening exercise with all applicant countries (Turkey excluded).

December 2000: Nice Summit modifies institutional arrangements to allow the EU to accept candidate countries as new members.

2001: Report by the EC 'Making a Success of Enlargement', which names the 10 countries that could be ready by 2002 (the accession of Romania, Bulgaria and Turkey being postponed).

December 2003: The European Council of Copenhagen closes negotiations with the 10 countries, their accession date being set at 1 May 2004.

2004: First wave of candidate countries expected to become members before European Parliament elections of June 2004 (signing of accession treaties on 16 April 2003 and accession on 1 May 2004).

than in the EU (see Chapter 10). Economic convergence in itself will there-fore clearly not be enough. It should be accompanied by a progressive con-vergence in the social field. Moreover, the sacrifices requested of populations for achieving such high economic growth require also more sound social poli-cies and developments if we want to avoid the economic reforms becoming unsustainable and the political process being interrupted. At the same time, the key issue in an enlarged EU will be to continue to ensure economic and social cohesion despite greater economic and social differentials.

1.7.2 The Criteria for Accession

The above developments in the social field are also necessary to meet the membership criteria per se. The basic condition for accession to the Union is the fulfilment of the 'Copenhagen criteria'. These include: (i) establishment of democratic principles and structures; (ii) development of a functioning market economy; and (iii) acceptance and transposition into national law of the whole EU legal *acquis* (including social and employment standards, envi-ronmental and consumer protection measures).

During the negotiation process, the European Commission has insisted on the Community *acquis*. The transposition of this *acquis* in the labour area is aimed at extending improvements in workers' protection to the applicant countries and possibly to other, neighbouring countries. The extension of the European Social Model seems also to represent the best possible answer to 'excessive' differentials in the social area, which would not be acceptable in an enlarged Europe. Too large discrepancies between levels of social protec-tion or living standards would almost inevitably encourage workers in candi-date or neighbouring countries to seek more acceptable conditions in EU countries, and so make it more difficult to maintain established social rights there, initiating a kind of vicious circle. This would encourage EU enterpris-es to pursue 'social dumping' to take advantage of the situation in applicant countries. The improvement of the EU economy expected from the accession of new members should also favour a general improvement of social stan-dards. In the long term, EU actors are also convinced that such social stan-dards will turn out to be the best way of improving economic performance and also the employment situation in these new countries.

While insisting on the Community *acquis*, the European Commission has also tried to extend the coverage of the other instruments for developing the European Social Model – that is, the method of open coordination and the European Social Dialogue – to the new applicant countries. In pursuit of this, employment assessment papers have already been prepared and discussed in several applicant countries. The Commission has also requested that the gov-ernments of applicant countries reinforce their structures of social dialogue.

Different steps have thus already been taken to extend the European Social Model to applicant countries. However, without casting doubt on such necessary measures, it is important to scrutinise them in detail, and to examine, for each area covered by the European Social Model, what the implications of the different EU accession processes might be for the EU, to identify the problems that may emerge along the way, and to determine more deeply what other policy options may be advisable. The final result is far from certain, which explains the question mark in the title of this book.

In this regard, it is worth citing the *World Competitiveness Yearbook* for 2000 (IMD 2000):

> the Anglo-Saxon and the continental European models have competed for many years. It seems, however, that today the Anglo-Saxon model is prevailing. European Union legislation has moved towards more deregulation and privatisation. The Dawn of a 'New Labour' party in Britain, or the opening up of businesses in many former communist countries around the world, are just other examples of this trend.

The economies of many Central and Eastern European countries are already clearly dominated by deregulation and neo-liberal theories, although the collapse of the communist regimes did not automatically have to lead to the rejection of social and welfare policies. The advisory work of international monetary institutions, combined with the emergence of a new generation of political leaders with a strong willingness to do whatever possible to promote real capitalist economies, has already had a major impact, as we shall see in the following chapters. This only serves to emphasise even further how difficult it will be to persuade these countries of the virtues of the European Social Model, an endeavour – or even a battle, if the first years of transition are anything to go by – which is not without consequence for the maintenance of the EU's own model in the enlarged European Union of tomorrow.

The task of this book is indeed to determine whether EU enlargement may take the EU further away from its common social and societal values, as defined above, and bring about an even more intense focus on the free-trade, financial, and economic dimensions rather than on social and human values. In other words, will the European Social Model be weakened or, on the contrary, reinforced by the integration of new traditions and cultures? And will the EU after successive accession processes succeed in keeping its distinctive social features in a context of increasingly integrated global markets?

2. Wages and Working Conditions: Well below EU Standards

2.1 INTRODUCTION

As one of the criteria for accession, candidate countries have to take on board the Community *acquis*, made up of legislative and other regulatory provisions. A majority of such EC directives concern working conditions, considered as the cornerstone of workers' protection.

It is essential, however, to assess the context in which these requirements are being demanded of the candidate countries: for example, what is the local situation with regard to working conditions? Are these countries already close to or still far from EU standards? Have their governments and enterprises already started to direct their reform processes towards these Community standards, or have they taken a different, even the opposite direction in the first twelve years of transition, and if so, could the negotiation process help to change their policy before accession? At the same time, might requirements which are too strict make it impossible for these countries to implement them?

These are some of the questions that we would like to address. We understand working conditions in their larger meaning, that includes wages and other incomes from work, security at work, terms and types of labour contract, and health and safety and other conditions at work, all of which contribute to making an employee's working environment more or less acceptable.[1] This is also a good opportunity to present an overview of the Community *acquis* in this area, and to distinguish between the elements that are well covered by Community legislation, and those which continue to be left to member states' or individual actors' discretion, a discrepancy that may also influence the final outcome of the EU enlargement process.

The aims of this chapter are thus very pragmatic: first, to provide a comprehensive assessment of current working conditions in the 13 candidate countries – with a view to distinguishing between the different dynamics operating in Central and Eastern Europe and in the Mediterranean area – and

---

1. Working conditions have a narrower meaning in the British interpretation, while in France the term encompasses more elements, including remuneration. To avoid confusion we have tried – also in the title of the present chapter – to distinguish between wages and working conditions in its stricter sense, that is, employment and working conditions.

to identify country-specific experiences. This will provide a number of useful elements from which to compose a picture of the effects of the first twelve years of transition (from 1989–1990 to 2002) in this important social area. Secondly, to allow us to start testing the possible impact of the negotiation process, since full adoption of the *acquis* is expected – although sometimes unrealistically – to level the playing field between old and new member states. We shall sometimes take a somewhat critical stance in order not to miss the key issues, and to contribute to defining possible ways of improving the effectiveness – from the perspective of both EU member states and candidate countries – of the negotiations concerning current and forthcoming accessions.

2.2 WORKING CONDITIONS: AN AREA OF SIGNIFICANT EUROPEAN COMMUNITY INVESTMENT

Working conditions constitute an area in which the European Community has been particularly active and committed since the outset. The aim of a general improvement of working and living conditions was already enshrined in the Treaty of Rome.

Article 2 of the EU Treaty also lists among the goals of the Community a 'high level of employment and social protection, equality between men and women, . . . raising the standard of living and the quality of life, and economic and social cohesion and solidarity among the Member States.'[2] Article 117 of the Treaty aims at 'improved working conditions and an improved standard of living for workers'.

More recently, as part of the preparations for the inter-governmental conference leading to a revision of the treaties through the Treaty of Amsterdam, a report of a *comité des sages* in spring 1996 again emphasised the importance of workers' rights, and also advised 'incorporating "fundamental social and civic rights" into the Community legal order' (Report of the *Comité des sages*, EC 1996).

The Charter of Fundamental Social Rights adopted in Nice in December 2000 again shed light on these important principles and rights, although member states opted for a declaratory rather than a binding document.

No doubt all the above values are at the core of the Community's armoury of regulations and provisions. In fact, we can say that the adoption of legislation aimed at improving labour standards and workers' rights is one of the EU's main achievements in the social field. Its purpose is to ensure that the creation of the Single Market leads neither to a lowering of labour standards

2. Treaty of the European Union, *Official Journal* C 340, 10 November 1997, Art. 2.

nor to distortions of competition – indeed, it is considered a key element in improving competitiveness.

Since the adoption of the Single European Act, Community priorities have shifted from harmonisation to the definition of minimum requirements. The list of conditions to be fulfilled was given in the White Paper COM(95) 163 final/2 on the internal market adopted by the Essen Council in December 1994. It was progressively extended and formed the 'screening' list prepared for the pre-accession negotiations.

There are four main areas of European labour law: one concerns the free movement of workers, while the other three are more directly related to working conditions: protection of workers' rights; equal opportunities for men and women; and occupational health and safety.

There are approximately 70 directives or legislative tools in the field of social policy, the greatest number covering labour law (10 directives), equal opportunities for men and women at the workplace (10), occupational health and safety (33, including amendments), and free movement of labour (3).

2.2.1 Protection of Workers' Rights: A Basic Principle of the EU

The extension of workers' protection has taken a number of directions.

First, the social dimension of industrial change and restructuring has been integrated into Community labour law: workers' rights have been extended in the case of the closure, buyout, merger, or externalisation of the activities of their enterprise. Major progress in this regard was made after the adoption of three directives between 1970 and 1980, on *collective redundancy, transfers of undertakings*, and *employer insolvency*.

Improvements were also made with regard to labour contracts: in 1991 the Council adopted a Directive on the *employer's obligation to inform workers on the conditions applicable to the work contract*, and another on *fixed-term – that is, temporary – work*. Later on this was completed with the framework agreement between the social partners (converted into a new Directive) on *part-time work*.

Progress was also made with regard to working conditions in specific work categories or occupations: new social minima were fixed with the Directives on the *protection of pregnant women*, the *protection of young people at work*, and *the posting of workers* in the provision of services.

All these directives complement social provisions already existing in member states, always with the aim of finding a better balance between flexibility – generally demanded by employers – and security, generally the concern of workers.

The Commission has also been active in the area of working time with the general directive on the *organisation of working time* (93/104/EC), followed by complementary initiatives to cover the workers of sectors initially excluded from this directive, that is, seafarers – for whom a directive on working time was concluded in June 1999 (99/63/EC) following the signing of an agreement between the social partners in that sector – and road transport workers, who continue to be excluded from the minimum requirements on working time, however.

The Commission has also proposed a series of directives on workers' information and consultation: on the *European Company Statute, European Works Councils,* and *information and consultation* in enterprises with more than 50 employees (all three have been adopted). We shall develop this area in more detail in Chapter 6.

2.2.2 Equal Opportunities: A Significant Breakthrough

As early as 1956 in the Treaty of Rome there was a significant provision on equal pay. Over the last decade, the European Commission has successfully contributed to bring about an evolution in attitudes in the area of equal opportunities, notably by combining ambitious programmes for funding fieldwork with legislative steps to extend workers' rights.

Directives on working conditions have improved the lives of female workers significantly, including the Directive on pregnant women and the Directive on parental leave.

Since the Amsterdam Treaty (new Article 13) allowed new initiatives from the EC in this field, the European Commission decided to establish new instruments at Community level in order to improve the fight against discrimination. This led to a new communication in November 1999 and to three new proposals: a Directive forbidding discrimination with regard to employment (based on race or ethnic origin, religion or convictions, handicap, age, or sexual orientation); a Directive forbidding similar discrimination in broader areas such as employment, education, access to goods and services, and social protection; and finally an Action Programme aimed at supporting and complementing the implementation of directives, notably through exchange of information and best practice. These proposals are testimony to the EU's ambition to promote a more equal and solidarity-oriented society.

As a result, the number of women in education and their participation in the labour market has increased in the last decade. Nevertheless, they still tend to have lower pay and to be underemployed compared to men.

Discrimination is one of the areas which have to be addressed by candidate countries, as stipulated by the Copenhagen criteria: 'Membership requires that the candidate country has achieved stability of institutions guaranteeing democracy, the rule of law, human rights and respect for and protection of minorities . . .'.

2.2.3 The 'Cinderella' Status of Health and Safety

The regulation of occupational health and safety has been viewed from the inception of the European Community as a vital part of the social dimension of the Community, as enshrined in Articles 117–28 of the Treaty of Rome. For some experts 'in many ways, this area has proved to be one of the most high profile examples of an interface between the "social" as contrasted with the "economic" dimension of the single market envisaged in the 1986 Single European Act' (Neal 1998, p. 219).

Article 118 of the Treaty of Rome in particular recognised that 'the Commission shall have the task of promoting close co-operation between Member States in the social field, particularly in matters relating to . . . prevention of occupational accidents and diseases; [and] occupational hygiene . . .', aims which justified the European Commission's role of initiating, promoting, and developing a European preventive policy and later on a clearly-defined policy dealing with health and safety at work.[3]

As a result, this area today concentrates the greatest number of Community directives – two-thirds of social policy directives – and thus seems to be occupying something of a '"Cinderella" position, involving not only a wide range of important regulations, but also inspection, and policing for the safeguarding of workers' health and hygiene at work' (Neal 1998, p. 218).

It is important to stress that the Community approach seeks to cover both workers' safety and workers' health.

The importance of this area is justified of course by quality-of-life considerations, but equally important are economic interests, for two reasons in particular. First, the 'efficiency argument': more efficient health and safety and work practices are expected to bring increased productivity and better industrial relations. Secondly, the 'distortion of competition argument': the regulation of some risks needs to be harmonised at a supra-national level because of the scale of resource costs and because any disparity in the coverage and application of such provisions will produce distortions of competition and impact upon product prices.

It is recognised that the socio-economic costs of work accidents, for instance, are tremendous. In 1996 they accounted in the EU for almost 150 million lost working days, so representing one day lost per year and per worker, without taking into account all the consequences for health. The annual direct costs linked to work insurance in the EU have been roughly estimated at almost EUR20 billion. Last, the economic burden of absenteeism and of incapacity for work is estimated to be between 2.8 and 3.6 per cent of member states' GNP.

---

3. The entry into force of the Treaty of Amsterdam resulted in the disappearance of Article 118A as a specific legal basis for safety and health protection policy; it is superseded by Article 137.

This is also a matter of concern for employers, who are the main players in the prevention of occupational risks in the company, and also those ultimately responsible for the impact of their decisions on workers' safety and health: '[w]e know that the money spent on preventive measures is repaid many times over in the form of fewer operational disruptions and breakdowns.'[4]

At the same time, we must report that European employers believe that the current Community apparatus, complemented by national transposition legislation, already covers all known occupational risks. They thus recommend a legislative 'moratorium' and call for an approach designed to ensure proper application of existing legislation.[5]

At present, Community health and safety legislation can be grouped under three headings:

1. The measures taken subsequent to Framework Directive 89/391/EEC, which contains a number of basic provisions concerning the organisation of health and safety measures at work and the responsibilities of employers and workers; it has been supplemented by separate directives concerning specific groups of workers, workplaces, equipment, or substances.
2. The measures taken subsequent to Framework Directive 80/1107/EEC, which concerns the protection of workers from risks related to exposure to chemical, physical, and biological agents at work, and which has been supplemented by separate directives on specific agents.
3. The measures required under directives that contain exhaustive provisions – not linked to Framework Directives – covering occupations or particular vulnerable groups.

We shall not go into further detail here. It is nevertheless important to distinguish between general texts, concepts, or steps to be taken (as in Framework Directives) and more specific directives on technical aspects (machines directive, and so on).

The European Commission has also set up an Advisory Committee for Hygiene, Health and Safety (ACHHS). Chaired by the Commission with representatives of government and the social partners from each member state, its main aim is to support and advise the Commission in this field. Also to be noted is the existence of a European Agency for Safety and Health at Work

4. *2001: A Renaissance for Employees – Towards a More Entrepreneurial Europe*, prepared by the Swedish Employers' Confederation, Stockholm (2001), p. 13.

5. This position has been expressed on many occasions by the European Employers' Confederation UNICE; see also the discussion paper prepared by the employers' national confederations with UNICE for the Fourth Round Table of the Industrial and Employers' Federations of the EU and accession countries, Nicosia, Cyprus, 22–3 May 2000, p. 6.

located in Bilbao, which focuses its activities on collecting, compiling, and disseminating information about the working environment in the EU member states, work which is complemented by the European Foundation for the Improvement of Working and Living Conditions based in Dublin.

The provisions adopted in this area have had a direct effect, since the number of accidents at work has decreased consistently: work-related accidents involving more than three days off work fell by more than 3.3 per cent between 1994 and 1996. Even more marked is the reduction in the number of fatal accidents, with 13 per cent fewer fatal accidents between 1994 and 1996.

2.2.4 Wages: A Neglected Area

Although wages represent one of the most important elements of working conditions, both for workers and employers, Article 137 of the Treaty clearly rules out wages as an area of competence of the European Commission.

Nevertheless, in September 1993 the European Commission issued an opinion on the right of workers to an equitable wage.[6] In particular, the EC indicates that 'the Member States should give substance to the commitment given in the Social Charter to ensure the right of every worker to an equitable wage, irrespective of sex, disability, race, religion, ethnic origin or nationality'. The European Commission requested member states to take this aim into account when formulating their economic and social policies, and to take action (i) to improve the transparency of wages on the labour market, in particular by establishing better systems for the collection and dissemination of data on wages; (ii) to ensure that the right to an equitable wage is respected by protecting those groups in the labour market which are particularly vulnerable and open to discrimination; and (iii) to improve the long-term productivity and earnings potential of the workforce by increasing investment in human resources at all levels. The social partners have also been invited to address the issues raised, in particular to consider what contribution they could make to ensure the right of every worker to an equitable wage. A few years later, in January 1997, the Commission adopted a report on the progress made in this area.[7] The EC also contributes to the dissemination of data and good practice on wages (EC Industrial Relations Report 2000, EC 2000a).

It appears that many candidate countries had planned some legislation to ensure an equitable wage even before the Opinion was issued. Some have

6. Commission Opinion COM(93) 388 final, published in the *Official Journal* C 248, 11 September 1993.

7. Report of the Commission to the Council, the Economic and Social Committee and the European Parliament: 'Equitable wages – A Progress Report', COM(96) 698 final, adopted by the Commission on 8 January 1997.

extended it to the area of homeworking. Others, however, have not taken any significant measure.

Nevertheless, a legal minimum wage currently exists in eight member states, including the UK which adopted it in April 1999. In other member states, workers can enjoy statutory minimum wages for specific sectors – as in Ireland and Austria – or minimum wages fixed by collective agreements. In some cases, such minimum wages can be extended to the whole sector, as in Germany and Italy. All member states are thus applying one form of wage floor or another. At the same time, however, there has been a clear widening of wage inequalities as a result of the changes in the way wages are determined – including a decline in traditional forms of wage bargaining and growth in performance-related pay – and in the forms of work (growth in nonstandard forms of employment and in casual employment).

2.2.5 An Important Monitoring Mechanism: The Court of Justice

EU directives require transposition by member states into national law and follow-up through implementing measures. Upon transposition of a directive, each country is required to notify the European Commission. While this transposition can be carried out at national level either through legislation or through agreement between the social partners, the national authorities are responsible for their proper implementation.

The Commission attaches great importance to the implementation of Community labour law. Whenever it discovers that a Community provision has been incorrectly transposed or badly implemented in a member state, it can bring the matter to the Court of Justice of the European Communities by starting infringement proceedings. This procedure may culminate in a ruling by the European Court of Justice against the member state and in the subsequent imposition of fines.

Article 37 of the Statute of the European Court grants intervention rights. The first sentence reads: 'Member States and institutions of the Community may intervene in cases before the Court'. The Article goes on to allow intervention by others: 'The same right shall be open to any other person establishing an interest in the result in any case submitted to the Court, save in cases between Member States, between institutions of the Community or between Member States and the institutions of the Community'. Trade unions or enterprises, for example, can therefore intervene.[8]

8. Article 230 of the EC Treaty, however, which is concerned with judicial review of actions of the EC institutions, makes a distinction between actions by 'privileged' and 'non-privileged' applicants. Privileged applicants, with unconditional access to the Court, are 'Member States, the Council or the Commission'. The European Parliament has also endeavoured to become a 'privileged' applicant.

Recent cases of infringement proceedings initiated against current EU member states illustrate the vital role of the Court of Justice:

- On 12 November 1996, the UK was sanctioned for the incorrect implementation of the Working Time Directive (Case C-84/94, 1996, ECR I-5755). This judgment helped to clarify the scope of the Treaty as regards working conditions – that the British Government wanted to restrict – and consequently allowed broader perception and usage of Article 118a in this field.
- In 1998 the *Borsana* case (Case C-2/97, 1998, ECR I-8597) was a challenge by an Italian company against Italian legislation on health and safety; the Italian Court in an Opinion of 28 April applied the principle of proportionality to nullify imposing higher standards than the minimum requirements of EC health and safety directives. This opinion aroused considerable disquiet among trade unions at both EU and national level. The European Court's decision handed down on 17 November 1998 rejected the Opinion and upheld the powers of member states to introduce more stringent protection of working conditions.
- The national court in the Netherlands challenged a number of collective agreements between representatives of employers and employees. The collective agreements were said to conflict with EC rules on competition in Article 81(1) (ex 85(1)) of the EC Treaty. On 21 September 1999 the European Court declined to follow this Opinion and upheld the legality of collective agreements relying, in part, on the recognition of the EU social dialogue in the EC Treaty.

Most recently, we might mention examples of reasoned opinions issued by the Commission in 2001 to some EU member states in the field of working conditions. This is the stage before the intervention of the Court of Justice.

- For example, in 2001 the European Commission notified a reasoned opinion to Portugal regarding its failure to comply with Framework Directive 89/391/EEC on the introduction of measures to encourage improvements in the field of health and safety at work. In this case, Portugal failed to adopt rules relating to the election procedure for workers' health-and-safety representatives, which means that there can be no guarantee that such elections will take place and that the workers' representatives will be able to carry out their special functions. This example also shows the importance of social dialogue and workers' information and consultation in the implementation of legal regulations on health and safety and working conditions in general.
- Still in the health and safety area, the Commission has also decided to send a reasoned opinion on the basis of Article 226 of the EC Treaty to Ireland

and France for failing to communicate national measures – that is, laws, regulations, or administrative provisions – necessary to comply with Directive 97/42/EEC on exposure to carcinogens.

• With regard to discrimination, the Commission has also sent a reasoned opinion to Austria on the basis that Austrian legislation is discriminatory against foreigners, including those from the EU and also countries with whom the Community has concluded cooperation or association agreements. They are excluded, for instance, from eligibility to stand for elections to works councils, provisions that the Commission found contrary to the EC non-discrimination rules, notably those regarding working conditions.

In all these cases, the member states concerned have two months to reply. If they fail to do so, the Commission may bring the matter to the Court of Justice of the European Communities.

The different charters also participate in fixing the constraints on member states. In particular, the new Charter for Fundamental Social Rights signed at the European summit in Nice in December 2000 is introducing new social rights, such as the freedom of association and collective bargaining. Even if this Charter is not binding, it could be used as an important reference for the interpretative competence of the Court of Justice.

The Social Charter of the Council of Europe of 1961, revised in 1996, is also playing a role in the supervision and implementation of labour rights in individual member states, and can lead to official complaints, for instance by a trade union, an enterprise, or a non-governmental organisation against their national authorities.[9] One of the most recent complaints was introduced by the Finnish trade unions on working time and paid overtime for workers engaged in dangerous and unhealthy occupations (related to Article 2, paragraph 4 of the Charter).

It is clear that all the above monitoring processes and instruments must be taken on board by candidate countries, and thus influence their practices as regards working conditions.

2.2.6 Latest Extensions

This commitment to better working conditions has been strengthened over the years, and today they represent one of the key components of EU competitiveness. In a very competitive international and globalised context, the European Union clearly established its main aim at the European Lisbon sum-

9. Among the 13 candidate countries, however, only six had ratified the revised European Social Charter of the Council of Europe by 30 September 2001; the countries which had not ratified it are the Czech Republic, Hungary, Latvia, Malta, Poland, Slovakia, and Turkey. Of these, only Latvia and Turkey had not ratified the original charter of 1961.

mit 'to become the best performing knowledge economy in the world'. In order to achieve such a goal, it is clear that the individual – with his or her knowledge, creativity, and commitment – must be at the core of economic performance. While the proportion of repetitive and low-skill tasks and jobs is falling, the value-added of today's production is on the contrary provided by those who can innovate and take the initiative.

Greater communication and social skills are required of workers as they have to collaborate in teams and networks with suppliers and customers. This is the reason why employment relations are being radically transformed, and why social dialogue, workers' information and consultation, good working conditions, respect for the rhythms of daily – and in particular family – life, equal opportunities, and respect for differences have become central values for society and for enterprises.

This has also brought more variable forms of work, with flexible time and location, teleworking, flexible contracts, functional flexibility, outsourcing, and subcontracting, where market control replaces hierarchical control. Between 1991 and 1996, the percentage of workers with a measure of autonomy over their own pace of work increased from 64 per cent to 72 per cent (Eurostat–EC 2001, p. 56). While this variety of work possibilities gives workers more opportunities to choose their individual working time and to better combine work and family life, it can also bring more uncertainty in terms of job and income stability, especially for those categories which have fewer educational and background assets. A core–periphery labour market is emerging in which the well performing workers reap the benefits in the centre while the more poorly performing ones are sent to the periphery of production units where 'flexible working' is more associated with precariousness than with autonomy. For example, there has been an increase in the percentage of fixed-term contracts, mainly for younger workers (EC Industrial Relations Report 2000, EC 2000a).

This is why Community labour legislation has also been extended to cover atypical forms of work. It is quite significant that the directives on part-time work, fixed-term work, and working time (in transport) have been prepared by European social partners themselves through the negotiation of framework agreements that were then converted directly, on the request of the same social partners, into new EC directives. The social partners are clearly most concerned with the negotiation, introduction, and monitoring of these new and multiple forms of work. New working arrangements are also bringing forth new kinds of health and safety problems, such as stress at work – the most common work-related health problem, affecting 28 per cent of workers, together with back pain, reported by 30 per cent of them – something which is also inducing the European Commission to continue to make progress in the health and safety area.

Efforts will also continue in the future to extend workers' rights to transnational operations, following the first step represented by the Directive on European Works Councils.

The adoption of the new Charter of Fundamental Social Rights at the European Summit in Nice in December 2000 also represented an important step forward on labour issues. Not only did it mention important new labour rights, but even more significantly, it for the first time put social rights at the same level as human rights. As accession gets closer, this constitutes a strong message to the candidate countries.

Finally, the European Commission has made a special appeal to the corporate sense of social responsibility of enterprises with regard to working best practices – in terms of labour relations, social dialogue, work organisation, life-long learning, equal opportunities, social inclusion and more generally respect for fundamental rights – through its new Green Book on Corporate Social Responsibility (EC 2001i).

In short, we can say that European labour law and other Community initiatives have induced EU member states to carry out economic changes – including ambitious ones such as the achievement of the single market and the launching of Economic and Monetary Union – without moving backwards in the social field. This characteristic is certainly one part of the European Social Model that distinguishes the EU from other parts of the world, where economic and social matters have not always progressed hand in hand. It is thus important to assess developments in the same field in the candidate countries, and to identify whether their integration could create tensions in keeping the same balance between better protection at the workplace and necessary economic and market developments.

2.3 MUCH LOWER WAGES: THE RESULT OF PAST AND RECENT POLICIES

The most conspicuous gap between the current EU member states and the candidate countries is in wage levels. This is, first, the result of the previous communist regimes, which kept wages at artificially low levels, though complemented by substantial non-wage bonuses and services provided by enterprises, such as holiday facilities, transport subsidies, and free meals.

Wage levels at the beginning of the present decade, however, also reflect in great part the incomes policies implemented in the first twelve years of transition. Different studies on this issue have shown that downward rigidity of wages has represented the adjustment variable favoured by governments in the transition process, while other variables, such as prices, were allowed to fluctuate according to market forces (Vaughan-Whitehead 1998; Clarke et al.

2000). As a result, wage earners have in effect had to bear the brunt – along with those dependent on social allowances – of the burden of transition. This policy has been proved to lead to unsatisfactory outcomes on both the economic and the social level.[10] As expressed by former President of the Republic of Hungary, Árpád Göncz, the so-called 'macroeconomic stabilisation programmes often praised by international monetary institutions are imposing very strict working and living conditions on the majority of the population, with a clear risk of generating nostalgia for the past'.[11]

In this section we analyse wage trends from the perspective of the worker – that is, wage levels and their progression in real terms, as well as the minimum wage and wage differentials – while in Part II of this book we analyse wage developments from the perspective of labour costs and employers' competitiveness.

2.3.1 Paying the Price: The Burden of Transition on Wage Earners

The policy of price liberalisation launched in all countries in the region at the beginning of the reform process led to an explosive inflationary surge which had an immediate impact on wages. Restrictive incomes policies, however, were put in place with the original aim of ensuring that nominal wage increases remained well behind consumer price increases.

As shown in Figure 2.1, overall real wages fell rapidly and substantially in all the countries of the region. In 1996 all workers in Central and Eastern Europe – with the possible and very recent exception of the Czech Republic – were paid in real terms well below the wage levels which prevailed before the beginning of the transition: wages had fallen by around 26 per cent in Hungary, around 17–22 per cent in Poland, Romania, Slovakia, and Slovenia, and 50 per cent in Bulgaria. The Baltic countries have also experienced a sharp fall in real wages: 45 per cent in Estonia, 46 per cent in Latvia, and 65 per cent in Lithuania (in Russia, wages fell by over 70 per cent over the same period).

Since then, the situation has improved in most of these countries, especially in Hungary and the Czech Republic. The most recent period, however, is not rosy with regard to wage developments. Real wages have continued to deteriorate in Romania and Bulgaria. By mid-1998, wages in Bulgaria had fallen in real terms by more than 70 per cent since 1991 (Tzanov and Vaughan-Whitehead 1998). Real wages decreased again in 2000. Similarly in Slovakia, real wages started to fall again in 1999 after six years of growth, a

10. For a general assessment of the region, see Vaughan-Whitehead (ed.) (1995); for a specific example on Bulgaria, see Tzanov and Vaughan-Whitehead (1997 and 1998).
11. Preface to Vaughan-Whitehead (1998), pp. xix–xx.

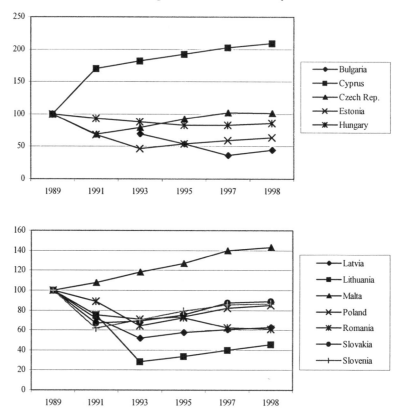

Source: TransMONEE database 2000, experts' own data, national statistical offices.

Figure 2.1 Real wages, 1989–98 (1989=100)

decrease which continued in 2000 by a further 4 per cent. Real wages, compared to 1989, were lower by 11.8 points in 1999 (Cziria 2001), a gap which
has since widened even further. Standards of living in 2001 were still below
the level achieved before the political changes and economic transformation
started in 1989 (Cziria 2001).

In the other countries, including the most economically advanced, prices
continue to increase considerably, many of them already catching up with EU
standards, while wages remain well below the EU average. Wage levels in
2000–1 continued in most candidate countries of Central and Eastern Europe to
be below their symbolic pre-transition level, which were already the result of
artificial suppression. This situation differs radically from wage developments
in Cyprus and Malta, where not only are wage levels comparable to the EU
but have been allowed to progress regularly over the same period.

2.3.2 Wage Levels Still Low in Recent Years

These very low wage levels – and so the enormous wage gap with the EU – is undoubtedly one distinctive feature of the EU enlargement process to the East; this constitutes another reason for looking at this accession from a different perspective. According to Table 2.1, average wages in all Central and East European countries continue to be much lower in euro terms than average wages in current EU member states. They are lowest – below EUR150 – in Bulgaria and Romania, above EUR200 but still below EUR300 in Latvia, Lithuania, Estonia, and Slovakia, between EUR300 and EUR400 in Hungary and the Czech Republic, and close to EUR 500 in Poland. Slovenia already has an average wage over EUR900, that is, higher than in Portugal and Greece.

Table 2.1 Average monthly gross wages, candidate countries, 2000 (euros)

Bulgaria	123
Czech Rep.	365
Cyprus	1 387
Estonia	285
Hungary	336
Latvia	267
Lithuania	236
Malta	204
Poland	480
Romania	142
Slovakia	267
Slovenia	925
Turkey	–

Source: National Statistics; Eurostat.

Other candidate countries, such as Turkey, are also characterised by very low wages. In Turkey, average wages in euro terms are well below average wages in Slovenia, and are thus more comparable to some Central and Eastern European countries than to EU standards. This is not the result of a rigid tax-based incomes policy, however, but rather of the lack of freedom to engage in autonomous collective bargaining on wage issues, and of the continuous interference of the state in this field. This is particularly the case in the public sector – in both the state administration and public enterprises – with obvious implications for employers in private enterprises. The real situation is even worse than the official statistics suggest, since they do not include the informal sector, which is particularly large in Turkey, where workers generally work for much lower, often miserable wages. According to Bayram Meral of the Confederation of Trade Unions (TURK-IS): 'Reducing competition and costs as much as possible and the emphasis on cheap labour has led to a preference for the use of clandestine workers, which is a major problem in our country. This preference has speeded the growth of the unrecorded sector.'[12]

Significantly, one of the main joint recommendations in the tripartite process pushed by the Turkish social partners, including employers' representatives, has been to 'develop a free, open collective bargaining and general wage and income policy that leads to increases in the productivity and competitiveness of enterprises, and safeguards and increases the purchasing power of workers . . . and the quality of the labour force'.[13]

2.3.3 The Minimum Wage: The Slippage of the Anchor

The minimum wage has also been kept down during the transition with the result that it has finally become more of a mechanism of destitution than one of protection (Standing and Vaughan-Whitehead 1995). On the strong advice and under the close monitoring of international monetary institutions, the minimum wage has in fact been used as a key variable by most governments in Central and Eastern Europe to keep all wages and incomes under strict control: directly in the public administration, where the whole wage scale – with different levels corresponding to a multiplier of the minimum wage – is traditionally connected to the minimum wage; and indirectly in the private sector, where new employers have tended to align their wage scales with practices prevailing in the dominant public sector, and where a low statutory minimum wage has given them the opportunity to keep all their wage scales down, especially since a large proportion of employees in most candidate countries continue to be paid at the minimum-wage level. One-third of employees in Latvia, for instance, were found to be working at the minimum wage level (EC Regular Report on Latvia 2001, p. 73).

We shall describe in Chapter 3 how the minimum wage has also been applied to restrain the increase of all types of social benefits, which were tied to it. The minimum wage thus became an easy and 'over-used' way of controlling inflationary pressures, but even more widespread has been its use to reduce budgetary expenditure. This is why the state has kept it under direct supervision, either through unilateral decisions about its increase or through controlled outcomes within the tripartite process.

12. Report 'The Social Implications of the Customs Union', presented at the fifth meeting of the EU/Turkey Joint Consultative Committee, Brussels (21 January 1998).
13. 'National Employment Policy – General Board Report', prepared by the tripartite general board, which held its first meeting on 23–4 May 2001 in Ankara, Recommendation No. 25, p. 10.

As a result, the minimum wage remains rather small compared to the average wage. Even more striking is the poor coverage by the minimum wage of basic subsistence needs. In almost all Central and East European countries – with the possible exception of the Czech and Slovak Republics, and more recently possibly also Hungary and Slovenia – the minimum wage has been allowed to fall well below the poverty line, a situation that continues today in many candidate countries. As a result, a large part of the labour force, including those with a regular job – the so-called 'working poor' – continue to work for an income below the subsistence minimum.

Table 2.2 Minimum wage, average wage, and subsistence minimum in selected candidate countries

	Gross minimum wage (MW)	Gross average wage (AW)	Subsistence min. (SM)	MW/ AW (%)	MW/ SM (%)
Bulgaria (2000) 1 000 lev=1 DEM from 1999 – in lev	75 330	238 000	245 420[1]	31.0	30.7
Cyprus (2000) – in L	287	700	–	41.0	–
Czech Republic (1998)	–	–	–	22.7	–
Estonia					
Hungary (2000) – in HUF	25 500	87 645	21 286 (1999)	29.1	105.6* 84.0**
Latvia	–	–	–	–	–
Lithuania	–	–	–	–	–
Malta – in Lm	52	81.5	28.8	63.8	180.0
Slovakia (1998)	–	–	–	30.0	–
Slovenia (1998)	–	–	–	40.0	–
Poland	–	–	–	–	–
Romania (1998)	–	–	–	23.3	–
Turkey	–	–	–	–	–

Notes:
1 Per head of household of four members (parents + two children). This is the so-called 'social minimum'. Another measure was introduced by the government, the Guaranteed Minimum Income (GMI), mainly used for the calculation of social payments and dependent on available resources.
* if gross MW.
** if net MW.

The situation may be expected to improve, however, since downward pressures on the minimum-wage level have decreased recently, for a number of reasons: first, many governments have decided to disconnect social benefits from the minimum wage, with the result that the latter variable comes to have less strategic importance; secondly, they have stepped back somewhat from the authoritarian wage policy recommended by the international monetary institutions which has not brought the expected results (Vaughan-Whitehead 1995). More regular increases in the minimum wage have also been made possible by economic growth and more favourable economic conditions. Over the last few years, governments in a number of countries have increased the minimum wage more regularly than in the earlier years of transition. More radical decisions have been taken in Hungary, where the minimum wage was increased by more than 50 per cent in 2000–01.

2.3.4 Excessive Wage Differentials – Unregulated Market Economy

Besides the fall in real wages and incomes, the period since the late 1980s has been marked by substantial growth in wage differentiation between regions, sectors, and occupational and social groups. A few people have benefited tremendously from the changes, while the majority have sunk into destitution.

The Gini coefficient, which helps to measure the distribution of income, shows much higher rates – between 30 and 42 – in some candidate countries than in the EU (25.9) (see Table 2.3). Their distribution of incomes seems to approach much more those in countries considered less egalitarian, such as the USA (34.4) and the UK (32.4, the highest among EU member states). Moreover, the situation in candidate countries worsened between the mid-1980s and the end of the 1990s, a process which seems to be continuing (Galgoczi 2002).

In Hungary as early as 1993 the average income in the highest taxation bracket was almost 18 times the average income in the lowest taxation bracket, compared to only 3–4 times in 1988; this gap has further increased since. Wage differentials in Poland increased by more than one-quarter between 1991 and 1995. Workers in the lowest grades have been seriously affected by the irregular adjustments of the minimum wage described above. Labour-force fragmentation is also particularly strong between workers in budgetary organisations – whose wages have been closely linked to the minimum wage – and those in other sectors.

In Bulgaria, between 1990 and 1997 the share of the population with incomes below 50 per cent of the average disposable income almost doubled, from 7.9 per cent to 12.2 per cent. The share of the population living below the subsistence minimum also grew, from 49.7 per cent in 1992 to 63.9 per cent in 1996. According to Tzanov and Zlatanova:

Table 2.3 Comparison of Gini coefficients measuring distribution of income in selected candidate countries, 1998

Gini coefficient	
Bulgaria (2000)	31.0
Czech Rep.	25.9
Cyprus	–
Estonia	–
Hungary	27.5
Latvia	33.6
Lithuania	34.5
Malta	–
Poland	30.0
Romania	42.2
Slovakia	–
Slovenia	30.7
Turkey	–
EU average	*25.9*
UK	*32.4*
USA	*34.4*

Source: UN Monee Database, 1998.

a large part of the population receives low incomes, a small part of the population has average incomes, and a very small part of it has high incomes. Until 1995 the inequality of households measured by the Gini coefficient indicates a tendency to increase, before decreasing in 2000 to 0.31 per cent . . . the ratio between the household incomes of marginal deciles (the lowest and highest incomes) increased from 7.8 in 1992 to 11.9 in 1995 and fell to 9 times in 2000. (2001, p. 21)

Large disparities have also opened up between regions. In Hungary, for instance, three-quarters of the rural population belong to the three lowest income quintiles, while 40 per cent of the population of Budapest is in the highest income quintile (Szamuely 1997, p. 17). This differentiation has caused widespread social discontent and it seems that the long-term danger of a fragmented labour force will be among the most serious labour and social policy questions for the next few years.

The gap between wages in the private and the public sectors was not reduced but continued to increase in many candidate countries. This was the case in the Slovak Republic in 2000 (Cziria 2001, p. 6). This led to more radical action in the education and health care sectors, as happened in the Slovak Republic and Hungary with a number of strikes in 2000–01.

Increased differentiation is also observed in Turkey: 'wage and income distribution is worsening every day. The number of low wage workers in poverty is increasing, especially those in the informal sector who do not have job or income security'.[14] The EC has emphasised the social risks of this process: 'Disparities between urban and rural areas, and upper and lower income groups, are very high in Turkey. It is likely that these disparities have further increased in the meantime, mainly due to the erosion of the purchasing power of lower income groups through chronically high inflation' (EC Regular Report on Turkey 2001, p. 38).

In the EU, wage and income inequalities are also growing, not only between member states, but also within countries. Income inequality within member states is found to be relatively high in the southern member states, the United Kingdom, and Ireland. The lowest values are to be found in Denmark, Sweden, and Austria.

Greater income inequalities within a member state tend to be related to a lower average income. It is thus obvious that the joining of the new members, especially those from Central and Eastern Europe, which have much lower incomes – with the exception of Slovenia – will lead not only to a fall in average incomes in the EU, but also to a sharp increase in wage and income differentials. By definition, this will lead to more competition based on wage and income differentials, an issue we address in Chapter 7.

2.3.5 The Non-Payment or Delayed Payment of Wages

Since official statistics on wages refer to contracted wages, not to wages actually paid, the situation is in reality even worse than we have described. In particular, the statistics on real wages can be misleading since they conceal the possible non-payment of wages. Although this phenomenon is particularly dramatic in the CIS Republics – especially Russia and Ukraine – where it has developed on a massive scale, a worrying trend is also observed in some countries of Central and Eastern Europe, especially Bulgaria and Romania.

In Bulgaria, the phenomenon is not new and had been observed on a significant scale by the end of 1996, when the amount of unpaid wages culminated at a peak of 3.6 per cent of GDP. Although this process was temporarily limited in 1997 following the introduction of the currency board and the government's decision to close unprofitable and indebted companies, it is worrying to observe that the amount of unpaid wages has started to increase again (Tzanov and Zlatanova 2001), from 1.7 per cent in 1997 to 2.5 per cent in 2000. The problem is thus far from being solved. In fact, the latest data on

---

14. General tripartite assessment in 'National Employment Policy – General Board Report', op. cit., p. 5, Ankara.

2001 confirm that the situation is worsening every day: according to Tzanov and Zlatanova (2001, p. 36), 'the worsening trend over the last several years has been alarming'.

The phenomenon is affecting all sectors of the economy, including both public and private enterprises. A similar trend may also be observed in Romania.

Unpaid wages in Bulgaria represent approximately 10–15 per cent of total wages and so affect a significant number of workers. In Romania, the non-payment of wages in 2001 affected 30 per cent of workers (Florea 2001, p. 22).

These results confirm the limitations of official wage statistics. In Romania, 'the non-payment of wages is the subject of neither statistical research nor reports of the labour inspectorate' (Florea 2001, p. 7). Unfortunately, other countries in the region generally do not carry out such investigations either, which means that we cannot exclude the possibility that this phenomenon may also be present there. As an example, the problem of non-payment of wages has also been identified in Lithuania, despite a new law imposing fines on employers which do not pay wages or which delay wage payments (ICFTU 1998).[15]

The state as an employer is also involved in the non-payment of wages. In Bulgaria, debts are increasing in the public administration, with employees in the sectors of education (60 per cent of wage arrears of municipalities), health care, and social services not being paid by municipalities. In Romania, employees in research institutes are particularly affected. Similarly, local governments in Latvia are experiencing great difficulties in paying the minimum wage and basic social benefits due to a shortage of funds (EC Regular Report on Latvia 2001, p. 73).

This situation has led to increased social tensions, with strikes being organised by teachers and health care workers in Bulgaria and Romania in 2000. Conflicts also occurred in private enterprises.

The problem of non-payment of wages is mainly due to economic conditions and the maintenance of inefficient companies, but not entirely. The causes are also of an institutional nature, with in particular the inadequate protection of workers in terms of wage payment and the absence of guarantee institutions in case of employers' insolvency. The fact that wage arrears have continued to increase in Bulgaria despite the fact that the economy has been slowly improving – higher economic growth, lower inflation rate – is a sign that it is often a basic question of priorities on the employers' and also the authorities' part. Increased unemployment places employers in a stronger position and discourages workers from finding a solution to the problem. All too rarely are penalties imposed on employers who delay payment of wages.

15. *Annual Report on Violations of Trade Union Rights*, International Free Trade Union Confederation (ICFTU/CISL), 1998.

In many candidate countries, governments have yet to put in place wage guarantee funds and to transpose the EC directive on the protection of workers in case of employer insolvency, an issue that we shall address later in this chapter.

2.4 POORER WORKING CONDITIONS: LACK OF READINESS BEFORE ACCESSION

Besides lower wage levels, workers of candidate countries are also experiencing lower standards of protection at work, especially in the two important areas of working time and health and safety.

2.4.1 Working Time: Many More Hours

Working time is an area which well reflects the tensions in operation between the need to secure certain standards for protecting workers and the need to make working time more flexible with regard to production requirements. Nevertheless, in this area as well some candidate countries seem to have preferred a more liberal approach, systematically removing or significantly reducing their previous – often more generous – provisions. This trend towards full flexibility seems to have been somehow limited by the negotiations for accession and the Community requirements in this area.

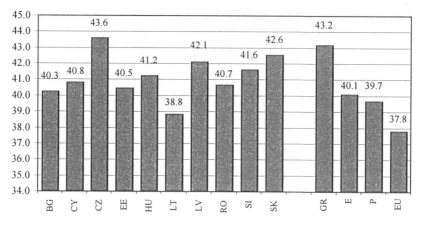

Source: Eurostat.

Figure 2.2 Average working hours in selected candidate countries and EU member states, 2000

If we compare average working hours between candidate countries and EU member states we find that employees are working many more hours in the former, and this in all sectors of the economy. In 2000 all candidate countries are above the EU average (37.8 hours a week), especially the Czech Republic (43.6, that is, nearly 6 hours more per week), Slovakia (42.6), Latvia (42.1), Slovenia (41.6), and Hungary (41.2). In the EU, comparable working time was reported only in Greece (with 43.2 hours), and the UK, which registered the highest number of average working hours, more than 45 a week. The lowest numbers are found in Belgium and Denmark. A recent survey carried out in the 12 candidate countries (Turkey excluded) in 2001 confirms their much longer working week, 44.4 hours on average, more than 6 hours above the EU average (Paoli et al. 2002).

In contrast with the EU, where women work fewer hours than men – 33 as against 41 hours on average a week in 2000 – there are no major differences in the candidate countries. In the Czech Republic, for instance, men work on average 45 hours compared to 41 hours for women. There is only a one-hour difference in Bulgaria. Only in Cyprus, where women seem to have a different status, is the difference more pronounced. Large differences by country also prevail in the EU: in the Netherlands, Austria, and Sweden the difference is less than one hour, whilst the gender gap in the United Kingdom is almost five hours (Eurostat–EC 2001, p. 80).

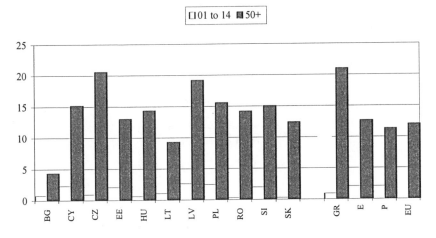

Source: Eurostat.

Figure 2.3 Proportion of employees working more than 50 hours and less than 15 hours a week, 2000

Table 2.4 Average working hours in some candidate countries and EU member states, by gender and by sector, 2000

		BG	CY	CZ	EE	HU	LT	LV	PL	RO	SI	SK	GR	E	P	EU
Women	Agriculture	35.0	32.8	42.7	48.6	41.7	38.3	43.1	–	36.6	47.2	42.0	41.2	42.1	33.8	38.3
	Industry	40.3	37.2	40.9	39.9	40.1	39.3	41.0	–	40.9	40.1	40.9	41.5	38.6	39.4	35.4
	Services	39.8	38.2	41.4	38.2	39.7	37.5	40.5	–	41.0	39.8	41.7	39.7	36.1	37.6	32.5
	Total	*39.7*	*37.8*	*41.3*	*39.2*	*39.8*	*38.0*	*40.9*	*–*	*39.6*	*40.6*	*41.5*	*40.2*	*36.8*	*37.5*	*33.1*
Men	Agriculture	38.7	48.5	46.8	44.0	44.9	40.1	42.0	–	41.3	50.4	43.9	48.2	47.5	39.7	47.3
	Industry	40.6	41.4	44.3	40.9	42.0	39.9	42.7	–	41.2	41.5	42.9	43.7	41.4	41.8	41.2
	Services	41.4	43.1	46.5	42.2	42.6	39.5	44.1	–	42.4	41.9	44.0	44.6	41.9	42	41
	Total	*40.8*	*42.9*	*45.4*	*41.8*	*42.5*	*39.7*	*43.3*	*–*	*41.6*	*42.5*	*43.5*	*44.9*	*42.1*	*41.6*	*41.3*
Total	Agriculture	37.4	42.9	45.5	45.7	44.1	39.4	42.5	–	39.0	48.9	43.3	45.2	46.1	36.7	44.3
	Industry	40.5	40.5	43.3	40.6	41.4	39.6	42.1	–	41.1	41.0	42.3	43.3	40.9	41.1	39.8
	Services	40.5	40.8	43.7	39.8	40.9	38.3	42.0	–	41.7	40.8	42.7	42.5	39.1	39.6	36.5
	Total	*40.3*	*40.8*	*43.6*	*40.5*	*41.2*	*38.8*	*42.1*	*–*	*40.7*	*41.6*	*42.6*	*43.2*	*40.1*	*39.7*	*37.8*

Source: Eurostat.

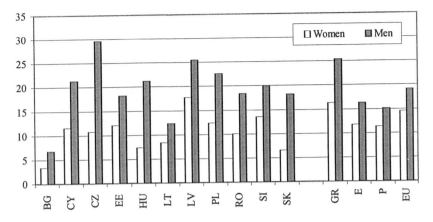

Figure 2.4 Proportion of employees working more than 50 hours a week, by gender, 2000

The picture by sector reveals that more hours are worked in agriculture, followed generally by a similar number of hours in services and in industry. In agriculture, very long hours were reported for instance for Estonian women (48.6) and for Slovenian men (50.1).

The percentage of employees working more than 50 hours a week is also much higher in candidate countries: 20 per cent in the Czech Republic, 19.2 in Latvia, and more than 15 per cent in the other candidate countries, as against the EU average of 12.1 per cent. According to Paoli et al. (2002), in 2001, 79 per cent of workers in the 12 candidate countries (Turkey excluded) – compared to 48 per cent of workers in EU member states – were found on average to work more than 40 hours a week. At the same time, the percentage of employees working less than 15 hours a week is much smaller in candidate countries: less than 2–3 per cent compared to 5 per cent in the EU.

We observe again a striking number of male workers working above 50 hours a week: in the Czech Republic (29 per cent), Latvia (23 per cent), Hungary and Cyprus (20 per cent), and Slovenia (18 per cent), so confirming the tendency in these countries to impose excessive working hours. In the EU, the highest figure is reported in the United Kingdom, where more than 20 per cent of workers were found to work more than 48 hours a week in 1999 and 51 per cent more than 40 hours a week (Eurostat–EC 2001, p. 80). Only 8 per cent of full-time employees in the EU on average were working more than 48 hours a week in 1999, while 20 per cent were working more than 40 hours per week. The gap is thus striking between candidate countries and the EU.

The reality is certainly worse than suggested by official statistics, which largely underestimate the real number of working hours: first, because of the informal economy – much larger in candidate countries than in the EU – where by definition the number of working hours is unregulated and uncontrollable and thus much larger (often above 50 hours a week); second, because employers in the formal economy also have a tendency to under-report total number of working hours, especially in sectors such as construction and other traditionally labour-intensive activities, for example, textiles, clothing, and shoes.

The practices developed in the informal sector not only directly involve a significant number of workers, but also indirectly influence practices in the formal sector by maintaining the pressure for longer working hours. This competition as regards working hours from new member countries could lead to more working hours in an enlarged EU, something which would contrast strikingly with the progress made in the opposite direction by some EU member states to reduce the working week, as in France where new legislation in this field led to numerous company collective agreements on 35 hours. Conversely, other countries, such as the United Kingdom, have opted for total flexibility in respect of working time.

It is this second model that seems to have been applied by many foreign enterprises operating in candidate countries: they impose long working hours, and to make matters worse do not always remunerate extra working time.

More generally, employers in candidate countries were rarely found to make extra payments for work beyond normal working hours. Compared to EU member states, therefore, not only do workers in candidate countries work more hours, but they also are paid less for them.

The raising of the retirement age in most candidate countries has also considerably modified working life. Trade unions, for example in the Czech Republic but also in other countries, have tried to oppose this, or at least to delay it as far as possible, but without success.

2.4.2 Health and Safety: The Heavy Cost of Harmonisation

Health and safety is another area where candidate countries are lagging well behind EU standards. The European Commission is aware of this: 'EC regulations on occupational health and safety must be discussed in depth. This is an area that will require significant investment and adaptation from employers at local level'.[16]

This is a difficult issue for employers: 'The social *acquis* on health and safety at the work place is perhaps the most complex and difficult of the areas with which candidate countries are called upon to harmonise'.[17]

---

16. Opening Speech of Anna Diamantopoulou, Commissioner for Employment and Social Affairs, EC, at the Fourth Round Table of the Industrial and Employers' Federations of the EU and Accession Countries, Nicosia, Cyprus, 22–3 May 2000, p. 5.

17. Welcome Address by Cyprus Employers' Confederation OEB, Michael Zivanaris, at the above Round Table of Employers, p. 3.

In most candidate countries, tripartite sub-committees or councils have been established on health and safety matters – as in Romania, Slovakia, and Slovenia – or on working conditions in general (as in Latvia and Estonia). But most important changes have to be decided at enterprise level, and the assessment within enterprises so far is worrying. Better occupational health and safety requires a significant investment that most employers in candidate countries are not in a position – or are not willing – to make in the short term. They generally tend to focus on other problems considered more urgent – such as finding new markets, carrying out restructuring, avoiding bankruptcy, finding partners, and necessary investment in production, and so on.

Managers – especially of SMEs – also generally fear that upgrading health and safety standards will bring costs that may lower their competitiveness. Such problems have been identified on a large scale in traditional sectors such as construction, agriculture, but also in some high-tech sectors such as engineering (in the Czech Republic for instance). On the other hand, many have also lost, insofar as they ever had them, the overall quality of human resources and production standards that are essential for entering the EU market.

Moreover, this missing long-term view or strategy in health and safety has brought many companies to the brink of industrial accidents. Not surprisingly, fatal accidents as a proportion of the working labour force is found to be much higher in candidate countries. In 1997, for instance, there were 19 877 accidents at work in Poland. While the official figures are already much higher than in the EU, experts in this field report that most work accidents are not declared by the employer and so are not officially registered.

In many candidate countries, however, especially in Central and Eastern Europe, but also in Turkey, public health in general is a problem: 'In the Czech Republic, to some extent it is also caused by insufficient attention to health and safety at work through the educational system. The low level of publicity given to the issues also plays an important role in forming public attitudes to occupational health and safety'.[18] The absence of channels of workers' interest representation within the company is also a factor which obstructs a more transparent and responsible policy on health and safety.

Problems of this kind seem to be present in all types of company. For example, in the public sector 'the knowledge of modern safety and health policy at the workplace is scarce in many accession state companies';[19] as well as in small and medium-size private companies which do not have a health and safety policy:

18. Address by Pavel Prior, Vice-President of the Confederation of Industry of the Czech Republic, at the Fourth Round Table of the Industrial and Employers' Federations of the EU and Accession Countries, Nicosia, 22–3 May 2000.

19. Background material for Third Round Table of the Industrial and Employers' Federations of the EU and Accession Countries, Stockholm, 27–8 April 1999, p. 4.

[T]he situation in small sized companies is significantly worse . . . there is a lack of attention to occupational risks and hazards, and awareness of employers and workers is generally low. This situation is caused predominantly by a lack of knowledge and information about the requirements and possibilities regarding prevention of risks from working activities.[20]

In 1999, the representative of the Estonian employers, Runno Lumiste, summarised the situation in the following terms: 'If Estonia were to join the EU today, half of the country's companies would have great difficulty implementing the EU requirements'.[21]

Paradoxically, there is already significant legislation on health and safety standards in Central and Eastern Europe. These legislative items, however, are generally not applied by enterprises. Moreover, enterprise surveys in different candidate countries have shown that the managers, in agreement with the workers, are distributing a kind of additional risk premium on condition that legislation on health and safety is not applied. This illegal practice has become widespread in Central and Eastern Europe, so much so that it has become a significant source of income for workers, who are consequently among those most opposed to its removal in exchange for improved health and safety practices. In other words, rather than progressing towards better health and safety standards with new legislation, enterprises have evolved towards the payment of risk premiums to avoid the implementation of new legislation in this field. Trade unions are also keen on retaining this type of system, which continues to be widespread in, for example, Bulgaria, Romania, and the Czech Republic. We believe that this system is also prevalent in other Central and East European countries. In this context of collusion between workers and managers in not applying health and safety measures, we doubt that more sophisticated and more restrictive health and safety regulations will be applied at enterprise level. The negotiation process may not change this situation.

Working conditions, including health and safety, are very much related to wages and incomes. Because of the very low wages today characteristic of Central and Eastern Europe, workers are ready to accept lower safety standards in exchange for higher wages through risk premiums. Only wage increases might shift the interest and concerns of workers towards safer working conditions and shorter working time in general. We can already see differences in health and safety between economically more developed countries such as Cyprus and Slovenia, and poorer countries such as Bulgaria and Romania.

20. Address by Pavel Prior, op. cit.
21. Runno Lumiste of the Estonian Confederation of Employers and Industry (ETTK) at the 3rd Round Table of the Industrialists and Employers' Federations of the EU and the Accession Countries, Stockholm, 27–8 April 1999.

But a change of mentality and approach is also necessary. Health and safety must be considered as an investment in the future competitiveness and financial results of the company, rather than merely as a cost. Health and safety problems must also be analysed in a broader perspective, not only in terms of their immediate consequences or causes, but also in terms of other factors in the production process, such as information, training, quality, safety standards and behaviour, work organisation, and management.

2.4.3 Discrimination: The Groups Left Behind

Equal opportunities between men and women
An historical legacy of the Communist period was the high level of educational attainment and the high integration of women into the labour force. These social and educational policies placed women in Central and Eastern Europe in a favourable position in international rankings according to a gender-related development index (GDI), which incorporates gender disparities in terms of income, life expectancy, and schooling (UNICEF 1999, p. 3).

Moreover, on equal opportunities, the principles of equal treatment and equal pay, as well as measures against discrimination, have generally been enshrined in the constitutions and other legal provisions of the candidate countries of Central and Eastern Europe.

However, the enforcement of these principles in the region is not immediately evident, especially during the current transition to a market economy. In several countries, the situation of women appears to have deteriorated rather than improved (UNICEF 1999). In most countries previous policies which facilitated women's labour market participation, such as publicly-funded or enterprise-based child care, have been removed (see Chapter 3 on social protection). Social protection for women with family responsibilities has been reduced by neo-liberal measures aimed at reducing the burden of employers' contributions. At the same time, all the public facilities – such as kindergartens, and so on – which helped mothers to continue to work have also been removed, so obliging them to stay at home. Consequently, women's representation in the labour force has been significantly reduced (see Chapter 4 on employment). Their participation in the labour market is also weaker, since restructuring and unemployment seem to have affected them much more than men. In Bulgaria, as in other Central and East European countries, despite the principle of equality at work, women seem to be more affected by unemployment (see Chapter 4 on employment).

The quality of the work open to those women who have managed to remain in employment is also questionable.

In terms of wages, the gap seems to be widening between men and women. We saw that in the Czech Republic and Hungary, for instance, while in principle men and women are equal under the law and should receive the same pay, in reality women's wages are 25 per cent lower (Clauwaert and Düvel 2000, pp. 15, 30). The difference is 22 per cent in Slovakia. The same situation was observed in Estonia and Poland, although women have a higher educational level on average. We shall see later in this chapter that the emerging profile of new jobs – long working hours, no part-time contracts – is also not convenient and thus discriminatory since it contributes to push women with children out of the labour force.

Transposition of the Community *acquis* in this field may give a boost to candidate countries, especially since, for Irena Boruta, 'on equal treatment, there is a sort of derived right (*droit dérivé*), with a programme of action which is not really taken seriously by the governments of candidate countries'.[22]

We must add that discriminatory practices are reported in the three southern candidate countries, with a lower participation of women in the labour force, as in Cyprus and Malta, and significant discrimination as regards access to employment and at the workplace in Turkey, where women are often considered second-class citizens.

Disabled persons have also been found to be at risk of both unemployment and discrimination at work in many candidate countries. They have often been the first victims of restructuring and thus the first to plunge into long-term destitution. As acknowledged in the EC Regular Report 2001 on Bulgaria, 'access to the labour market remains difficult for ethnic minorities, the disabled and young people' (p. 63).

Protection of minorities

Equal opportunities relate not only to the relationship between men and women, but also to the avoidance of any kind of discrimination based on 'racial or ethnic origin, religion or belief, disability, age or sexual orientation' (Article 13, EC Treaty). The situation of minorities, especially of the largest minority in Central and Eastern Europe, the Roma, is a cause for concern. Roma populations continue to face enormous problems in the region, especially in the seven applicant countries with a high percentage of Roma (see Table 2.5). While most Roma populations played a full part in the labour force during the Communist period, the collapse of the regime led to both economic crisis and

22. Speech of State Secretary of the Polish Ministry of Labour Irena Boruta at the Conference 'The Implementation of the Social Acquis Communautaire in the Candidate Countries', 30 November–2 December 2000, Vilnius, organised by the European Trade Union Confederation (ETUC) for its Network of Labour Law Experts (NETLEX) in both EU and candidate countries.

Table 2.5 Estimated number of Roma in Central and Eastern Europe, 1999

Bulgaria	700 000–800 000
Czech Republic	250 000–300 000
Hungary	550 000–600 000
Poland	50 000–60 000
Romania	1 800 000–2 500 000
Slovakia	480 000–520 000
Slovenia	8 000–10 000

Notes: As reported in EC (1999b). These are estimates only: the real figures are expected to be much higher because of problems in collecting data on Roma (many do not register). For example in Hungary, the real number is reported to be around one million.

a consequent dramatic rise in overt racism. The impact has been dramatic on the living standards – housing, health, education – and human rights of the Roma.

They have been most affected by unemployment – with an unemployment rate of 70 per cent, even more in some areas of Hungary but also in Bulgaria – since they were the first to fall victim to restructuring and layoffs. The only way to survive for most Roma is to work in the informal economy, with its very low skill requirements, uncertain and temporary work, and poor and irregular income, generally in the trading of cars, antiquities, and illegally exported goods (Puporka 1998). Unofficial and very low-paid jobs are also offered to them by companies in construction, agriculture, restaurants, and other traditionally labour-intensive activities.

The Roma suffer discrimination in the education system as well. Roma are often found in separate classes or in so-called 'special schools' used for the mentally disabled (Cahn et al. 1998).[23] This situation is frequent in the Czech Republic, Hungary, and Slovakia. Most children leaving special schools do not continue secondary education: 'Children who finish primary education in special schools are blocked from continuing their education in anything other than remedial technical schools offering vocational training for future low-skilled labour: the so-called "schools for mops and brooms"' (Cahn et al. 1998, p. 4). This situation still prevailed at the end of 2001: 'The under-representation of Roma students in the education system, hand in hand with over-representation in schools for retarded children, continued to exist. The practice of separate classrooms for Roma students was reported in a number of

23. There is a difficulty here however: there is a real phenomenon of 'social–psychological retardation' among Roma children due to family background (poorly educated and not 'school-oriented') and living conditions (no fixed residence, housing and food problems).

Roma adults

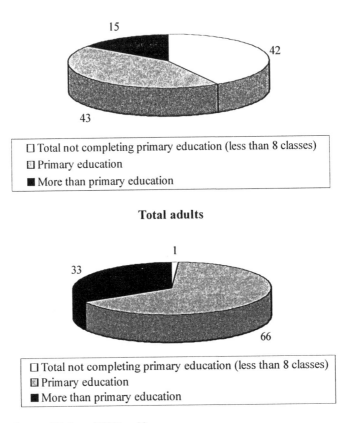

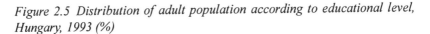

Total adults

Source: Ferge and Tadeusz (2001), p. 23.

Figure 2.5 Distribution of adult population according to educational level, Hungary, 1993 (%)

cases' (EC Regular Report on Slovakia 2001, p. 22). 'There are more than 150 schools in Hungary where special Roma classes are maintained' (EC Regular Report 2001 on Hungary, p. 22). Cases have also been identified in the Czech Republic and Poland. In Romania, where there is a Roma population of over two million, a large number of them are excluded from education entirely, often blocked by segregation and laws demanding that persons show residence permits in order to enrol in school.

> Understandably, many of Romania's educated Roma vigorously deny their ethnic origins; at present, such denial seems, sadly, to be the best strategy for Roma determined to pass successfully through the Romanian education system . . . Roma

throughout Eastern and Southern Europe are also denied education due to the high costs of schooling supplies and an unwillingness among Roma to send their children to school in the shabby clothes of poverty. (Cahn et al. 1998, p. 5)

Discrimination in education reproduces the effects of discrimination across generations, and their level of education continues to decrease. This clearly has direct effects on their ability to find a job, particularly in activities with a better labour contract and working conditions.

According to the pie-charts (Figure 2.5), the percentage of Roma not completing even primary education is high. Moreover, 'less than one per cent get a degree in higher education' (EC Regular Report on Hungary 2001, p. 22).

Surprisingly, most countries of the region remain without effective anti-discrimination legislation, or even if they have it, especially under pressure from the European Commission, there is little willingness to tackle pervasive discriminatory practices seriously.

In Slovakia, 'specific anti-discrimination legislation transposing the EC anti-discrimination *acquis* remains to be adopted' (EC Regular Report on Slovakia 2001, p. 20) and 'the gap between good policy formulation and its implementation on the [ground], as observed in last year's report, has remained' (p. 23). In Romania, 'Roma face difficulties in gaining access to schools, medical care and social assistance . . . and, despite the fact it is illegal, a number of job advertisements explicitly exclude Roma applicants' (EC Regular Report on Romania 2001, p. 30).

Important 'strategic programmes' have been launched, for instance in Slovakia, Hungary, and Romania, and constitute an important step, especially towards the recognition of the problem, but so far without managing to create for Roma workers modern, competitive, and stable jobs that could match the current needs of the labour market. Similarly in Bulgaria, 'the Roma continue to suffer from widespread social discrimination. The political commitment from the government to remedy their problems has still not been matched by concrete action' (EC Regular Report 2001 on Bulgaria, p. 98).

Turkey also remains a problematic country where basic human rights are not respected: 'Turkey does not meet the Copenhagen criteria and is therefore encouraged to intensify and accelerate the process of reforms to ensure that human rights and fundamental freedoms are fully protected in law and practice, for all citizens, throughout the country' (EC Regular Report on Turkey 2001, p. 33).[24] Tough restrictions are also found with regard to the recognition and rights of minorities.

24. 'Since the last Regular Report, the European Court of Human Rights found that Turkey had violated its provisions in 127 cases; it was also found to have breached 14 articles of the Convention with respect to human rights abuses in the northern part of Cyprus' (EC Regular Report 2001 on Turkey, p. 20).

In the regular reports of the EC, discrimination issues have been strongly addressed in the human rights part (among the political criteria for accession). On the Roma problem, the governments of the Czech Republic, Hungary, and Slovakia have been asked to improve the situation (EC Regular Reports 2001 and 2002). Turkey has also been requested to develop human rights and fundamental freedoms.

In the pre-accession phase, we can only regret that discrimination issues have not been addressed with the same emphasis – in contrast to human rights – from the perspective of social rights,[25] and that the same strong messages have not been delivered in the social field. Nothing has been said on minority discrimination at work and in respect of working conditions in Chapter 13 of the Regular Reports, although serious problems are identified in this regard.

Moreover, for some, 'the EC has listened only to the governments, and the National Action Plans for instance were not discussed at all with the social partners', as reported by a Romanian trade unionist. 'As a result, for instance in Hungary, although pre-accession negotiations have been successfully carried out, there is still great discrimination'.[26]

2.5 THE INCREASING CASUALISATION OF WORK

Besides poorer working conditions – along with lower wages – candidate countries have also experienced a radical change in their employment structure: in the course of the transition they have had to endure a total absence of protection at enterprise level due to restructuring and enterprise insolvency. At the same time, this period has been marked by a shift away from life-long employment towards less secure jobs and more atypical forms of work contract. We shall analyse the extent of such changes, especially in comparison with the practices existing in current EU member countries. We shall also see whether the implementation of the Community *acquis* may somehow modify this picture.

2.5.1 Self-Employment: One Way of Avoiding Labour Law

The first major instrument used by employers in candidate countries to employ the labour force in the most flexible manner possible is self-employment, which has become a widespread phenomenon in the course of a few

25. In the pre-accession documents in the social field, the European Commission mainly requested regularly updated information on initiatives in relation to discrimination, particularly on the situation of the Roma minority (CONF-H 8/00).

26. Csilla Kollonay, NETLEX Conference, op. cit.

years. In Hungary, for instance, self-employment has become one major means used by employers to circumvent tax payment and labour legislation: they simply ask their workers to change their status and to work as self-employed, although delivering often the same output or service as before. Their individual labour contracts are thus replaced by a sort of 'contract by assignment', much less constraining for the employer, since they are covered by the civil code rather than by the labour code. They thus escape the payment of social contributions and taxes, whilst the workers do not enjoy the same protection as before, with no trade unions, no right to strike, and no social protection – such as social assistance and pensions. These contracts are also of a short-term character – even if they can be renewed – thus providing maximum flexibility to the employer and leaving the workers with little security.

We must add that this type of 'contract by assignment' also avoids legislation on working time, so that the self-employed generally end up working many more hours than employees on regular labour contracts. This confirms that real working time in candidate countries must be much higher than official statistics suggest.

Nevertheless, employees are tempted to accept this status that obliges them to pay social contributions themselves, but also allows them to deduct certain expenditure (such as fuel for the car, clothing, electricity, or telephone bills) from their income tax. Furthermore, the growth of unemployment does not give the workers much negotiating power.

The self-employed generally declare only part of their income, generally in agreement with their 'employer', in order to limit their income tax – in fact a majority of self-employed are 'officially' in deficit according to Hungarian statistics. They generally declare the minimum legal activity that allows them to continue to be covered by social security and to contribute sufficiently to their pension fund.

The status of self-employment is thus an open door to the informal sector, a path to the informalisation of previously formal activity. For management, it constitutes a permanent reserve of cheap and flexible labour.

Another striking result is that use of this type of contract has been burgeoning not only in those services where freelancers or consultants operate – for instance, interpreting, translation, or consultancy – but also in services that need regular employees, such as banking.

As shown in Figure 2.6, the percentage of self-employed persons is already above the EU average (11.3 per cent in 2000) in almost all the candidate countries. In Poland, Romania, and Cyprus, more than one employee in five are self-employed, a figure matched in the EU only by Greece and Spain. There are therefore already more self-employed in the candidate countries than in EU member states. In Romania, according to Florea (2001, p. 5), there are more than four million self-employed (freelancers, family workers, and so on)

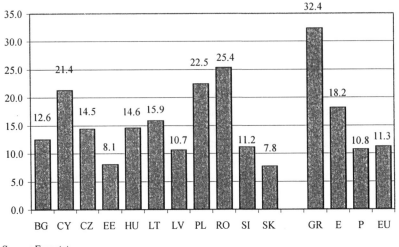

Source: Eurostat.

Figure 2.6 Percentage of self-employed (as % of total employed) in selected candidate countries and EU member states, 2000

among an active population of 11 million; that is, more than one-third of employees. These are Eurostat data for 2000. They are confirmed by recent survey results on working conditions in candidate countries in 2001 (Paoli et al. 2002). The authors find even higher figures for 2001, such as 33.5 per cent self-employed in Poland, 21.9 per cent in Slovenia, 19.7 per cent in Lithuania, 17.4 per cent for Bulgaria and Hungary, 13.7 per cent in Latvia and 12.7 per cent in Slovakia. Their other figures are of comparable magnitude with those presented in Figure 2.6. They present a figure of 15.7 per cent self-employed in Malta.

However, the respective sets of figures do not represent the same phenomenon. In the EU, a large proportion of self-employed in the workforce often reflects the growing number of small new entrepreneurs and businesses, and so represents an important lever for economic and employment growth. In contrast, high rates of self-employed in candidate countries do not illustrate this situation, as witnessed by the very high proportion of self-employed 'without any employees' (see Table 2.6), which can be explained principally in terms of two phenomena:

1. The high number of self-employed in agriculture: more than 50 per cent of those employed in this sector in countries such as Poland, Lithuania, Bulgaria, Romania, and Cyprus. These self-employed are working more on an individual basis, cultivating a piece of land for their own needs, and so represent more an economy of personal survival than organised production.

Table 2.6 *Percentage of self-employed (as % of total employed) with and without employees, by sector, 2000*

	BG	CY	CZ	EE	HU	LT	LV	PL	RO	SI	SK	GR	E	P	EU
Agriculture															
With employees	1.5	5.4	3.0	3.9	4.4	0.5	6.6	2.8	0.0	1.9	1.0	64.1	49.1	60.5	43.8
Without employees	50.8	48.0	13.5	25.8	35.9	59.6	31.8	65.3	48.4	37.6	4.6	–	–	–	–
Industry															
With employees	1.9	7.6	2.9	1.8	4.5	1.1	2.6	4.0	0.9	3.7	2.1	24.9	13.8	4.8	12.2
Without employees	2.9	15.0	8.7	1.8	6.3	2.2	2.2	4.8	2.6	3.2	5.1	–	–	–	–
Services															
With employees	3.1	5.9	5.2	3.8	5.3	2.4	4.3	4.2	2.8	4.0	3.0	26.2	17.0	8.9	10.4
Without employees	7.9	12.6	11.1	4.4	8.7	4.8	2.2	9.9	6.0	5.0	5.5	–	–	–	–
Total economy															
With employees	2.5	6.3	4.2	3.1	5.0	1.7	4.2	3.9	1.1	3.7	2.5	32.4	18.2	10.8	11.3
Without employees	10.1	15.1	10.3	5.0	9.6	14.2	6.5	18.6	24.3	7.5	5.3	–	–	–	–
Total	12.6	21.4	14.5	8.1	14.6	15.9	10.7	22.5	25.4	11.2	7.8	32.4	18.2	10.8	11.3

Source: Eurostat.

Table 2.7 *Percentage of self-employed (as % of total employed) with and without employees, by gender, 2000*

	BG	CY	CZ	EE	HU	LT	LV	E	RO	SI	SK	GR	E	P	EU
Women															
With employees	1.3	1.7	2.2	2.0	3.0	1.0	2.4	2.7	0.5	1.8	1.5				
Without employees	7.4	8.3	6.8	4.4	6.6	11.7	6.2	15.7	16.8	4.6	2.6				
Total	8.7	9.9	9.0	6.4	9.6	12.7	8.6	18.4	17.4	6.5	4.2	21.6	13.3	8.4	6.8
Men															
With employees	3.7	9.5	5.7	4.1	6.6	2.4	5.8	4.9	1.6	5.3	3.4				
Without employees	12.5	19.7	13.0	5.6	12.2	16.8	6.7	21.0	31.0	10.0	7.5				
Total	16.2	29.2	18.8	9.7	18.7	19.2	12.5	25.9	32.6	15.3	10.9	38.9	21.2	12.7	15.0
Total															
With employees	2.5	6.3	4.2	3.1	5.0	1.7	4.2	3.9	1.1	3.7	2.5				
Without employees	10.1	15.1	10.3	5.0	9.7	14.2	6.5	18.6	24.3	7.5	5.3				
Total	12.6	21.4	14.5	8.1	14.6	15.9	10.7	22.5	25.4	11.2	7.8	32.4	18.2	10.8	11.3

Source: Eurostat.

2. The use of self-employment as a tool for managers to engage workers with less protection, as in services, where already more than 10 per cent of the labour force is self-employed without employees in Cyprus, the Czech Republic and Poland. Also to be noted is the significant number of self-employed without employees in industry in Cyprus (15 per cent of employed), the Czech Republic (8.7), and Hungary (6.3). This process involves only a change in individual working status and so does not generate new jobs but rather contributes to reducing the number of employees working under regular contracts. The creation of a new dynamic business should normally provide work for more than one employee.

This phenomenon has been allowed to develop in Central and Eastern Europe on a strikingly large scale. In Hungary, for instance, more than 66 per cent of registered companies were found to consist of self-employed persons without any employees. A majority of them do not declare a good part of their activities, reflecting large-scale operations in the informal sector.

While most of these self-employed work on a part-time basis – but without being included in the statistics as part-time workers – in some sectors many self-employed work full-time, including many bank employees and clerks. Self-employment is widespread not only among men but also among women, even if to a lesser extent than in the EU. Mediterranean countries, such as Greece and Spain, but also Cyprus not only are characterised by a high proportion of self-employed, but also show a much higher percentage of self-employed among male than among female workers.

In addition to self-employment there are many other covert ways in which an imaginative management can introduce more flexible contracts and reduce the protection and rights afforded to workers, particularly as a result of the room left to employers by recent amendments of the labour codes of these countries, paradoxically on the pretext of legal harmonisation with the Community *acquis*. In Poland, employers are trying to deregulate the working relationship, notably by increasing the amount of work done by non-wage-earners.[27] In Bulgaria, 'the amendments to the Labour Code, adopted in March 2001, introduce the concept of "indirect discrimination" but not for the self-employed' (EC Regular Report 2001 on Bulgaria, p. 61); other gaps have also been observed in the new legislation. In Lithuania, the government is also attempting to deregulate all labour provisions: 'there is a general process of deregulation . . . everything is deregulated . . . with this liberal logic, we could also remove the minimum wage [and] minimum working hours'.[28] A similar process has been observed in Estonia, Bulgaria, and other countries of the region.

27. Op. cit., NETLEX Conference.
28. Speech by Lithuanian representative at the NETLEX Conference., op. cit.

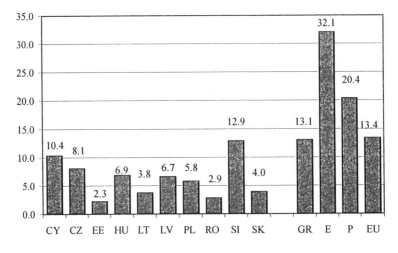

Source: Eurostat.

Figure 2.7 Proportion of employees with a temporary job in selected candidate countries and EU member states, 2000

2.5.2 Temporary Jobs: Life-Long Employment Slipping Out of Reach

The transition process has not only led to employment losses, but also introduced short-term and temporary jobs, another shock for a labour force used to secure and long-term jobs under the Communist regime. The percentage of workers covered by temporary jobs increased from zero in 1990 to 10 per cent of the working population in 2000 in many candidate countries. We can see from Figure 2.7 that in Central and Eastern Europe in 2000 such contracts were more widespread in Slovenia (12.9 per cent), the Czech Republic (8.1 per cent), and Hungary (6.9 per cent), while they are already part of the working culture in countries such as Cyprus (10.4 per cent) and Malta.

These figures are already close to the EU average (13.4 per cent in 2000) and we might wonder whether the upward trend will continue, with the candidate countries developing more systematically their recourse to this flexible but more casual form of labour contract, as in Spain, where approximately one-third of employees – the highest proportion in the EU – are working under such precarious conditions. In 2001, survey results identify 25 per cent of employees on a fixed-term contract in Bulgaria (Paoli et al. 2002).

The increasing use of short-term employment arrangements is clearly intensifying workers' insecurity, with a greater risk of casting them into difficulties due to loss of job and/or income. It thus serves to augment the enor-

Table 2.8 Proportion of employees with a temporary contract, by gender and age, 2000

	BG	CY	CZ	EE	HU	LT	LV	E	RO	SI	SK	GR	E	P	EU
Female															
15–29	19.4	11.3	3.8	10.9	5.7	6.8	9.2	6.1	32.3	6.7		24.4	56.7	38.4	29.1
30+	11.8	8.8	0.8	4.9	1.9	4.0	3.4	1.8	7.1	3.4		12.0	23.3	14.9	9.3
Male															
15–29	13.0	7.9	4.6	10.1	8.8	9.7	9.5	6.3	29.1	6.0		21.1	56.6	31.0	28.4
30+	5.6	6.7	2.6	6.1	3.8	8.5	5.6	2.0	6.7	3.0		8.4	20.4	12.3	7.2
Men + Women															
15–29	16.1	9.4	4.2	10.4	7.3	8.5	9.4	6.2	30.7	6.3		22.6	56.6	34.4	28.7
30+	8.3	7.7	1.7	5.5	2.8	6.2	4.6	1.9	6.9	3.2		9.7	21.5	13.5	8.1
Total															
15+	10.4	8.1	2.3	6.9	3.8	6.7	5.8	2.9	12.9	4.0		13.1	32.1	20.4	13.4

Source: Eurostat.

mous uncertainty that has been thrust upon workers from candidate countries by the transition process, in terms of income, housing, and employment.

Slovenia is already a country where such atypical contracts are used on a large scale. In contrast, there has been little resort to it so far in Estonia, Lithuania, and Slovakia, indicating significant differences between candidate countries. The proportion of temporary contracts seems to be surprisingly low in Romania, too.

This can also be explained by the growth of self-employed contracts, however. In fact, experience shows that most employers in Central and Eastern Europe have recourse to self-employment when they need temporary work, for instance, during peaks of activity: an enterprise that needs extra administrative labour during annual budget reporting and closing will hire a self-employed person to work on the data accounting for a period of a few weeks. The employer does not always declare such temporary assignments, or only some of them, generally in agreement with the contractor (the self-employed).

It is particularly striking that temporary contracts are least used in Romania, which is also the country where self-employment is most widespread, involving around 25 per cent of the labour force. In contrast, temporary contracts are more widespread in countries such as Slovenia, where self-employment is much less significant. Other countries, such as the Czech Republic and Hungary, seem to be developing both forms of casual contract.

In general, temporary contracts are used with young people. Table 2.8 shows that employers, as in the EU, are increasingly using this form of labour contract as a flexible way of employing workers below 30 years of age. In Slovenia, more than 30 per cent of the labour force under 30 is employed under a temporary labour contract. But this is also true in other countries, even those that privilege self-employment, since young people generally do not have the possibility – or rather the knowledge and experience – to be self-employed. Women are as much affected as men by this casualisation of work.

Temporary contracts are also growing in the EU, where 13.4 per cent of employees had a fixed-term contract in 2000 as against only 10 per cent in 1990. In the EU, this form of employment also affects both male and female workers. It should be noted that the EU average is already the result of the neo-liberal wave that has brought more casual working contracts in the last few years. The fact that candidate countries are already close to this average is in this sense a strong sign of the direction they are taking in their employment relations.

The relationship between temporary work and self-employment – and also the informal economy – merits more in-depth investigation and should be more closely monitored.

To summarise, we have every reason to believe that the number of temporary contracts will continue to increase in candidate countries, but not to a large extent, at least not in those countries where employers continue to have the possibility of contracting the self-employed directly for temporary assignments on very advantageous conditions.

We must also emphasise that an increasing number of workers are covered by contracts through temporary agencies. This is the case in Poland, for instance, where it is part of the employers' strategy to 'deregulate the working relationship'.[29] This type of contract allows the employer to hire and fire workers in a much more flexible way. Not only are such workers working on a temporary and uncertain basis, but also they are often not covered by the same social protection as other workers. By definition, they also do not enjoy similar job protection. The development of this type of contract requires specific legislation to protect affected workers. Very few candidate countries have yet introduced such legislation and the absence of EC legislation in this field only serves to encourage their lassitude.

2.5.3 Part-Time Jobs: Driven by a Different Logic

The proportion of employees working part-time has not increased much in Central and Eastern Europe, and they remain well below the EU average (17.7 per cent in 2000). In 2000, this form of employment was more developed in Romania, already close to the EU average with 16.5 per cent of the labour force, but also in Latvia (10.8), Poland (10.6), Lithuania (8.6), and Estonia (6.7). This form is also widespread in Cyprus, especially among women (more than 14 per cent). It is also developed in Malta (12.7 per cent in 2001) (Paoli et al. 2002).

However, this growing percentage of part-time contracts in some candidate countries is mainly due to the prevalence of such contracts in agriculture: part-time work covers approximately one-third of employees in agriculture in Latvia, Romania, Cyprus, and Slovenia. Nearly 50 per cent of women working in agriculture in Cyprus work on a part-time basis. Part-time work on a similar scale is not to be found in agriculture in any EU country.

The prevalence of part-time work in agriculture, generally on a self-employed basis, in countries such as Latvia, Romania, Slovenia, and Poland clearly shows that agriculture remains a means of subsistence for many workers, also those whose main job is not in agriculture but who need a supplementary income.

At the same time, part-time contracts are little used in industry and services, and have even decreased as a proportion of total employed since the mid 1990s, for several reasons. From the employees' perspective low wages push them to work full-time. From the employers' perspective, using part-

---

29. Speech by Irena Boruta at the NETLEX Conference, op. cit.

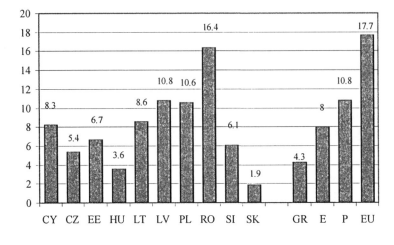

Source: Eurostat.

Figure 2.8 Proportion of employees working part-time in selected candidate countries and EU member states, 2000

time labour is comparatively less beneficial than using full-time labour in terms of taxes and other social contributions. We have seen that the objective of employers is rather to ask their employees to work even more full-time working hours than normal. Moreover, in a context in which working time is highly flexible upwards, the shift to part-time work does not correspond to the current logic of employers. They thus do not offer part-time arrangements. And if there are part-time contracts, these are carried out more informally between employer and worker.

In Slovakia, less than 2 per cent of employees were using available flexible working time patterns; for Cziria (2001, p. 10), 'the employers are not much interested because the implementation of more flexible patterns of work organisation and working time is more demanding administratively'.

We must add that this lack of availability of part-time jobs is a problem for some workers, especially women, since as a result they cannot reconcile working life and family life. It therefore directly affects women's access to or ability to remain in the labour market. Mothers of toddlers often have to choose between giving up their job to stay at home or going back to work full time and putting their children in a nursery for the whole day. It is also a problem for disabled workers who would need to work only part time.

In the EU, the growth of part-time work has often had the positive effect of allowing workers to ensure a better balance between working time and family life. It thus represents a positive step towards more flexible work arrangements, which can be better adapted to the needs of both employers and

Table 2.9 Proportion of employees working part-time, by gender and sector, 2000

		BG	CY	CZ	EE	HU	LT	LV	PL	RO	SI	SK	GR	E	P	EU
Women	Agriculture	–	45.5	6.6	4.4	9.1	17.7	36.0	28.3	35.7	24.6	3.2	–	–	–	–
	Industry	–	13.2	6.9	3.5	4.1	4.8	4.6	5.8	2.1	3.2	2.2	–	–	–	–
	Services	–	12.4	10.6	11.5	5.6	9.3	9.9	11.0	3.5	7.1	3.1	–	–	–	–
	Total	–	14.1	9.5	9.3	5.3	9.6	12.2	13.2	18.6	7.7	2.9	7.4	16.9	16.3	33.3
Men	Agriculture	–	20.6	3.3	9.2	2.1	16.5	47.1	24.4	40.6	21.2	2.5	–	–	–	–
	Industry	–	2.2	1.3	3.5	1.5	4.7	6.9	3.7	2.5	2.5	0.5	–	–	–	–
	Services	–	4.6	3.3	4.4	2.7	7.2	4.6	8.9	4.7	4.4	1.2	–	–	–	–
	Total	–	4.4	2.2	4.2	2.1	7.6	9.5	8.4	14.3	4.7	1.0	2.4	2.8	6.2	6.2
Men + Women	Agriculture	–	27.2	4.3	7.0	3.7	15.6	33.7	23.5	32.3	20.8	2.7	–	–	–	–
	Industry	–	4.6	2.9	3.4	2.4	4.6	5.8	42.0	2.3	2.7	1.1	–	–	–	–
	Services	–	8.1	7.2	8.7	4.3	8.3	7.5	9.8	4.0	5.8	2.3	–	–	–	–
	Total	–	8.3	5.4	6.7	3.6	8.6	10.8	10.6	16.4	6.1	1.9	4.3	8.0	10.8	17.7

Source: Eurostat.

workers. The share of part-time employment increased from 14 per cent of all employment in 1990 to 16.5 per cent in 2000. This rate is higher – above 20 per cent – in Denmark, Sweden, and the United Kingdom, while it is as high as 40 per cent in the Netherlands. Part-time employment is much rarer in the Mediterranean countries of Greece, Spain, Italy, and Portugal, as well as Cyprus.

Finally, we must add that where part-time contracts have been introduced – for instance, 10 per cent of the labour force in services in Poland already work part-time, as do 7 per cent of service employees in the Czech Republic and Latvia – this shift has occurred in a period of restructuring, layoffs, and weakening of workers' protection. They thus have not been introduced on very good terms for the workers, whether male or female, in terms of protection and pay according to working time (generally much longer than it should be in respect of part-time work).

Female workers are affected by part-time work to a slightly greater extent than men. This contrasts with the situation in the EU, where 33 per cent of women in employment are working part-time as against 6 per cent of males. Female part-timers are particularly prevalent in the Netherlands (68 per cent) and the United Kingdom (44 per cent). Cyprus and Malta report a gender difference comparable to EU countries.

This seems to confirm that women in candidate countries – except Cyprus – do not have many opportunities to shift towards part-time contracts, either for financial reasons or because the employer does not allow it.

Women are generally the first to be employed part-time at home, but generally in an informal way, or in the formal sector but under a self-employment arrangement.

We can nevertheless observe a small increase in part-time work for female workers (compared to male workers) in the service sector in Latvia and Estonia. At the same time, the higher proportion of female workers (compared to male workers) who were working part-time in agriculture (it is possible that in the most difficult transition period women had to bring in additional income through part-time agricultural activity) is on the decrease in agricultural countries such as Slovenia, Romania, and Latvia.

2.5.4 Employment without Individual Labour Contracts

There are good reasons to believe that the official statistics underestimate the current usage of atypical forms of labour contract; many employers are operating in the informal economy where, by definition, there is no protection of workers. We shall see in Chapter 4 on employment how extensive the informal sector is in the candidate countries. Many workers are also working in semi-legality with employers offering them contracts that do not respect labour legislation, but which they have no other choice than to accept in a period of restructuring, layoffs, and increased unemployment. Very low living standards are another reason why workers are keen to accept almost any conditions from employers, even if they have to accumulate two or three jobs to be able to achieve a decent income. The decline of unionisation and the absence of social dialogue that we describe in Chapter 5 also provide more freedom to employers, especially in the newly emerging small private enterprises and businesses. In Romania and Bulgaria often no individual labour contracts are given to workers.

In 1999, the two Bulgarian trade unions KNSB and Podkrepa compiled a list of 246 enterprises, mainly held by foreign owners, which had violated the law. Many workers in the textile sector in the region of Sandanski were found to be working without an employment contract and an average of 12–14 hours a day, including Saturdays and Sundays (Clauwaert and Düvel 2000, p. 9). One company was reported to be making its employees work for 30 hours at a stretch with only two short breaks. In Romania, according to a survey carried out in 2001, 32.7 per cent of employees were found to be working without a labour contract (Florea 2001, p. 45).

Similarly, in Lithuania employment without a work contract is widespread, and when a contract does exist it does not mention essential conditions such as working time and wages, a situation evaluated as alarming by some observers (Clauwaert and Düvel 2000, p. 38).

This avoidance of individual labour contracts is also present, though to varying degrees, in all other Central and East European countries, but also in Cyprus, Malta, and Turkey.

2.6 THE COMMUNITY *ACQUIS*: THE RISK OF NON-COMPLIANCE

One of the conditions for candidate countries joining the EU is to fulfil the Copenhagen criteria (presented in Chapter 1 of this volume), including implementation of the Community *acquis*; not only the legal *acquis* – that is, the formal body of all Community laws – but also the institutional *acquis*, represented by the continuously changing institutional terms as enshrined in the different articles of the EC Treaty. This process of harmonisation has two distinct stages: the first, more formal stage refers to the incorporation or transposition of the *acquis* into domestic law; for this, national parliaments generally draft legislation with principles that supersede those of all existing laws that might have contradicted EU law; the second, more practical stage refers to its concrete implementation; it involves the actions of national authorities to ensure policy implementation, for instance through labour inspection, and other monitoring and enforcement mechanisms. New directives and other pro-visions adopted in the course of the negotiations had also to be taken on board by the candidate countries.

2.6.1 The Transposition of Community Labour Law

In light of the developments in terms of working patterns described above, the pre-accession negotiations carried out between the European Commission and the authorities of each candidate country have intervened at an appropriate time. By insisting on the transposition of the Community *acquis* the European Commission has been able to counter some over-flexible or over-liberal work-ing arrangements, and has contributed to redirecting the revisions and amendments of national labour codes towards rules and practices more appro-priate to potential EU members.

Conversely, however, and indeed paradoxically, it is not infrequently the case that governments of candidate countries – under the justification of transposing the Community *acquis* – introduce amendments to their labour code that remove or tone down previous social standards and enact instead labour provisions much less favourable to workers. Not only does this policy contradict both the contents and the principles of EC directives – which are to ensure better protection for the workers – but they may have a catastrophic effect on the population's perception of the accession process, associating it with an erosion of their working conditions and social and living standards. This process has been criticised by several experts and political leaders. For Csilla Kollonay:

> [i]n Hungary, the government has tended to put up a 'façade', sometimes quite cynically, taking advantage of legal harmonisation to introduce a number of new and totally unconnected measures. We must mention the example of new regula-tions on working time that overall lead to an increase and not a decrease in work-ing hours.[30]

Similarly for Poland, Irena Lipowicz, deputy for the Freedom Union (UW), observed in January 1997:

> since 1989, respect for the law in Poland has had its ups and downs, but never has it been flouted so openly as it is now. The government did not have a single regu-lation overturned by the Constitutional Tribunal. Rapid erosion of standards began with the previous coalition and now it is proceeding even faster . . . what we are witnessing today is being done quite shamelessly and out in the open.[31]

30. Speech at the NETLEX Conference, op. cit.
31. Interview in *Politika* (January 1997), and cited in Hausner and Marody (1999), p. 47.

7

This is why the European Commission has insisted that the transposition of the Community *acquis* should not lead to lower standards, but to higher ones in all labour-related fields.

In the negotiation process, the European Commission has also clearly stated that it will not accept derogations or transition periods in the transposition of directives, including those in labour law, and consequently there have not been many such requests. Moreover, any such derogation must be strongly justified and respond to the criteria put forward by the Council of Europe, which stipulates the following:

> The European Union recalls its general negotiating position that transitional measures must be exceptional, limited in scope and accompanied by a plan with clearly defined stages for application of the *acquis*. They must not involve amendments to the rules or policies of the Union, disrupt their proper functioning or lead to significant distortion of competition.

ILO international labour standards have also been presented as complementary tools for progressing on a number of working conditions. Most candidate countries have also ratified the European Charter of the Council of Europe. Already some results can be discerned. Important steps have been taken to harmonise national legislation with EU standards, even if a lot remains to be done.

For instance, on the previously mentioned problem of the delayed or non-payment of wages, implementation of the directive on employers' insolvency has contributed to limiting the extent of the phenomenon. In the Slovak Republic – as in Poland – for instance, a period of delayed wage payments could be halted in late 1999 after a new law was passed on employers' insolvency and guarantee funds to avoid workers being the first victims of their company's bankruptcy. A similar new law was adopted in Cyprus in March 2001.

We can also expect that the transposition of the directives on atypical forms of work will provide the necessary limits to the current uncontrolled development of such contract forms in candidate countries.

Nevertheless, important pieces of EC legislation have not yet been adopted in candidate countries:[32] in 2001, this was the case for instance for the directive on employer insolvency in Bulgaria, the Czech Republic, Latvia, Lithuania, Hungary, and Malta; for the directives on collective redundancies, European Works Councils, and posting of workers for Estonia, Hungary, and Romania (and the last two directives for the Czech Republic and Bulgaria); for the directive on working time for Hungary, Malta, and Cyprus; the directive on part-time work for Bulgaria and Hungary, and many directives on

32. See all 'Regular Reports on Progress towards Accession 2001', 13 November 2001, Sec(2001) 1744 to 1750, and Regular Reports 2002, European Commission, Brussels.

health and safety at work for all candidate countries, especially the Slovak Republic, Bulgaria, Latvia, Romania, and Turkey.

In its Regular Reports, the European Commission has insisted on the proper transposition of directives, even if that leads to delays. At the end of 2001, for instance, the situation in Romania was evaluated as unsatisfactory: 'in the case of social policy, little legislative progress was made over the period and further measures are needed with regard to the adoption of a new labour code' (EC Regular Report on Romania 2001, p. 43). The same for Bulgaria: 'adoption of legislation in the field of occupational safety and health appears rather slow' (EC Regular Report on Bulgaria 2001, p. 63). The EC Regular Report for 2002 did not show much progress either.

Cyprus has also been rather slow in implementing key directives on working conditions, such as on working time, part-time work, fixed-term work, posting of workers, and European Works Councils; the directives on parental leave and equal treatment in employment and vocational training were still not transposed in early 2002. At the end of 2001, Poland was also requested 'to ensure alignment with the *acquis* on anti-discrimination' (EC Regular Report 2001 on Poland, p. 69) on the basis of the recognition that in 'equal treatment there has been almost no progress' (p. 112). Estonia was also encouraged to implement equal treatment to ensure 'transposition of the remaining provisions' (EC Regular Report on Estonia, p. 62). In Bulgaria, 'the EC anti-discrimination *acquis* has not yet been transposed' (EC Regular Report 2001 on Bulgaria 2001, p. 21).

Clearly, the three Mediterranean countries are also far from alignment as regards equal treatment (see EC Regular Reports 2001 on Cyprus; on Malta, pp. 51–2; and on Turkey, p. 70). In Malta 'concerning equal treatment of women and men, only one of the nine EC directives has been fully transposed to date' (EC 2001, p. 51). In Turkey, most elements of EC labour law have yet to be correctly transposed.

Some countries seem to have had problems in the transposition of the directive on working time. Malta in particular has requested a transitional period of four years from 1 January 2003 for the adoption of Directive 93/104 on the organisation of working time. The country seems to be having particular difficulty in applying Article 6 of the directive on the maximum length of working time, fixed at 48 hours per week.

According to a survey carried out in Malta between June and September 2000, a majority of enterprises interviewed – employing 47.2 per cent of workers in Malta – reported working hours well above the weekly maximum length of 48 hours.[33] According to the same survey, the companies that would have the greatest difficulty conforming with Article 6 of the directive would

---

33. Survey carried out by the consultancy firms KPMG, MISCO, and EuropAdvise Ltd.

be those operating in manufacturing in traditional sectors such as textiles and clothing, shoes, leather, and transport equipment, but also those involved in construction and extraction industries. Consultancy firms providing services to enterprises as well as departments of public administration delivering services of general interest were also reporting longer working weeks. This emphasises that the problem in Malta is far from being limited to a few sectors but rather concerns the whole economy, which seems to have based part of its competitiveness on long working hours.

Interestingly, the problem seems to affect mainly large companies (above 200 employees), although we might expect them to be more easily able to manage changes in the organisation of work and the length of working time. Some multinational companies expressed their concerns about the implementation of this directive. According to the trade unions but also local experts, the affiliate microelectronics company of Thomson STM in particular would have put pressure on the government to not implement the directive, and otherwise would even have threatened to leave the country: this major Maltese employer announced that it would relocate its production of electronic chips to countries with more flexible legislation, thus laying off the 2 000 workers it currently employs, a dramatic loss for the island. Similar pressure has come from the American multinational toy company Playmobil. This 'blackmail' clearly emphasises how multinational companies, even from current EU member states, may act against an extension of Social Europe to future member states in order to continue to exploit different social standards to increase competitiveness.

More globally the economic aim of retaining a comparative advantage in respect of labour costs in international markets – especially for export-oriented manufactures – has motivated Maltese companies and authorities to delay the adoption of directive 93/104 on working time. However, this contradicts the social aim of the directive which is to guarantee a higher level of workers' protection within the framework of the single market. Moreover, the directive already includes considerable flexibility, since the reference period (for the calculation of average working time) can be lengthened from the original four to six and even 12 months under certain conditions, including a collective agreement between social partners. From the original demand of a four-year derogation, the European Commission has conceded Malta a delay of 18 months to transpose the directive, and this for a few specific sectors.

If no other candidate country has requested a derogation for the transposition of the working time directive, it does not mean that there are no attempts to implement the directive in the least extensive manner possible, something which will certainly require close monitoring from the European Commission and other actors after accession.

Countries such as Bulgaria had not transposed the entire EU directive on working time as of the end of 2001.

The Hungarian authorities have adopted new amendments to the labour code that correspond to a minimalist interpretation of the directive. Although this is certainly the prerogative of the Hungarian authorities as long as there is no breach of the Community directive, it is revealing as regards the maximum flexibility in working patterns sought by the authorities of many candidate countries, often under pressure from domestic and foreign companies. It confirms the neo-liberal approach being taken by some of these countries.

In the case of Hungary this trend was illustrated by the abolition of the Ministry of Labour in 1998 and the shifting of its previous responsibilities between different Ministries – the Family and Social Affairs, Economics, and Education – thus marking the start of an era of a rather fragmented policy on social affairs and an absence of strong ambitions in this field. The Ministry of Labour was re-established after the new socialist-oriented government came into power mid-2002.

Another sign is that Hungary decided to transpose the working time directive only upon accession, which will make it difficult to assess whether it has been successfully implemented and enforced. The same has been decided for the directives on European works councils and on the posting of workers, and a number of health and safety directives. Late implementation of directives is a strategy that has been followed by a number of candidate countries in the pre-accession negotiations: according to many observers, this strategy has not been countered strongly enough by the European Commission.

For other experts, the adoption of the Community *acquis* has remained too much in the hands of the state: 'Perhaps surprising is the finding that in both Hungary and Poland non-state actors have so far been involved only marginally in efforts to adopt EU social legislation' (Sissenich 2000, p. 6).

In general, candidate countries have requested transition arrangements on employment and social issues only in very specific areas. Poland, for instance, has asked for a transition period until 2006 for two directives: on the use of protective equipment at the workplace and on work with biological agents. The Czech Republic has also requested a transition period for the work equipment directive. Other discussions have taken place with candidate countries (such as Slovakia) on the eventuality of a transition period on occupational health and safety issues. Hungary has requested a transition period until 2006 for the directive on tar yields in cigarettes, which may have implications for public health.[34]

34. For Poland, the directives are 89/655/EEC, 89/656/EEC and 90/679/EEC; see 'Poland's Negotiating Position in the Area of Employment and Social Policy', submitted on 31 May 1999 (<http://www.ukie.gov.pl/cona/snen/13en.pdf>); for Hungary, the directive in question is Dir. 90/239/EEC, especially Art. 2, par. 2; see 'Negotiating Position of the Republic of Hungary on Chapter 13: Social Policy and Employment':
<http://www.mfa.gov.hu/euanyag/SZI/Allaspont/positionpapers.htm>.

Such transition periods have been requested mainly on the basis of cost, in particular in respect of small and medium-size enterprises and smallholders.

2.6.2 The Surprising Neglect of the 'Non-Regression' Clause

For the first time the EC directive on working time incorporated 'non-regression' clause. The aim of this provision was to respond to two types of pressure:

1. The request – within the Council – by some large EU member states (such as France and Germany) which had developed stronger labour regulations, especially on working time, not to be obliged to introduce less favourable EC provisions since this would not only undermine their *acquis* in this field, but drive all more advanced countries towards a sort of 'backwards' harmonisation. Only those countries with standards lower than average would be requested to level them up to EC standards.
2. The extension clause was also made necessary by the EU enlargement to include Austria, Sweden, and Finland, where social standards were also higher than the EU average, and which also wanted to stick to their more generous national provisions. The absence of this 'regression clause' may have motivated some actors in these countries, particularly employers, to request a move backwards towards less advanced legislation.

Since then, the 'non-regression' clause has been incorporated in many directives; this was the case for the directive on young people at work, but also for all the directives elaborated by European social partners through framework agreements, as on fixed-term work, part-time work, and parental leave.

Paradoxically, although motivated by the latest wave of EU enlargement (to Nordic countries and Austria) this 'non-regression' clause has barely been used at all in the current EU enlargement process. Although we have seen that in many areas, such as social protection and working time, the provisions in the 13 candidate countries were higher than the EU average, there has been no systematic checking by the European Commission to ascertain whether new amendments to the labour code introduced in candidate countries were moving backwards compared to their previous regulations. This paradox is even more striking when we realise that most of these new laws and amendments were introduced under the aegis of the need to transpose Community law into national law. The only thing that the EC has checked is whether the new legislation or amendment is in accordance with the contents of EC directives.

Such 'neglect' of the 'non-regression' clause in the current EU enlargement process can be partly explained by a lack of knowledge of legislation and practices in the candidate countries. Many observers and experts from the EC and other national and international organisations still cannot imagine that in some respects, especially in the social area, provisions previously in place in candidate countries – generally considered too often and too systematically as less advanced in every way – may in fact have surpassed EC provisions. It is clear that the governments of candidate countries have taken advantage of this insufficient knowledge.

Another explanation is that the European Commission, which had to negotiate many other chapters – some highly sensitive, such as agriculture or the free movement of persons – was not inclined to make an issue of it in the case of those countries that removed social provisions which happened to be more favourable than the EU average. This is, however, the kind of trade-off which has contributed to diluting the message of the European Commission in the social field, and for which the social price to be paid, once these countries become members, will be extremely high. It is also in this sense that we can say that social matters have been, in a way, 'sacrificed' in the process of a rapid enlargement mainly driven by political expediency.

This is even more astonishing for EC directives which do not promote particularly high standards: this is the case, for example, with the directive on working time, whose legal basis is Article 118a of the Treaty, an article very much used in the area of health and safety, and which leads more to the adoption of an average for the European Community, in contrast to Article 100a which generally leads to a sort of 'upward harmonisation'. In fact, the directive on the organisation of working time – at the time of its adoption – was severely criticised for offering too low an EC average and so being irrelevant for most member states. The possibility of obtaining derogations through collective agreements (for instance, to extend the period of reference of time worked) or even through individual agreements between employer and workers (as stipulated in Article 17) – introduced specifically for the United Kingdom – have also seriously weakened the strength of this directive. This has serious implications in the current EU enlargement process: not only are the provisions on working time already rather undemanding, but in addition candidate countries have, in a way, been allowed – through the EC failure to ask for the implementation of the clause of non-regression – to level their regulations down to this low EC average. This is what happened in Hungary, but also in many other candidate countries, such as the Czech Republic and Bulgaria. We can also predict that employers in these countries will make extensive use of the flexible provisions of this directive, such as the possible extension of the reference period.

2.6.3 Beyond Formal Commitments: Implementation

The transposition of the Community *acquis* clearly entails that its various elements be adopted not only at national, but also at local level, and that the authorities will ensure their proper implementation and comprehensive coverage. However, considering the current failings of candidate countries in terms of labour inspection, judicial system, and also social dialogue – as a way of implementing the directives but also as a complementary monitoring process – there is obviously no guarantee that the provisions accepted today and adopted by candidate countries will be put in place. On the contrary, there are good reasons to foresee that a gap will intervene between the formal commitments made by governments on Community provisions – followed by their formal transposition into national provisions – and their concrete implementation on the ground. We have already observed such a gap in the field of health and safety, and other working conditions.

In Bulgaria and Romania, but also Lithuania, for example, the ineffectiveness of the public administration is a serious barrier to the adoption and implementation of the *acquis*. A significant number of violations have already been registered.

In Bulgaria, the trade unions have complained strongly that the employers do not respect labour law and also violate collective agreements. We have also seen how employers avoid the conclusion of individual labour contracts. Unfortunately, the labour inspectorate is not equipped to provide appropriate answers. In Bulgaria as recently as 2001 there was no independent inspectorate on health and safety standards.

Similarly in Romania, 'A National Action Plan on equal opportunities was adopted in December 2000 . . . however, it does not appear to have been followed by any implementing action and adequate financing . . . other than the National Plan, there has been little progress in improving the position of women on the labour market' (EC Regular Report on Romania 2001, p. 66). Other signs of scepticism about concrete implementation could be reported: 'legislation on preventing and sanctioning all forms of discrimination does exist and contains the basic principles of the *acquis* – equal pay, equal access to employment, training, promotion and working conditions. However, this law is not yet [being] applied due to the lack of implementing legislation' (ibid., p. 69).

In Lithuania, labour law was described in October 1999 as follows:

> Lithuanian law almost corresponds to EU Directives. There does exist a Law on Support of Unemployed People, a Law on Bankruptcy (1997) and a Law on Labour Agreements . . . In reality enterprises manipulate their closure to liquidate or reorganise with the aim of not falling under these laws.[35]

Again in Lithuania, 'several of the directives on health and safety at work are transposed, but they are neither in force nor working in reality. This is due to

---

35. *The Lithuanian Worker*, No. 1 (October 1999), also quoted in Clauwaert and Düvel (2000).

the lack of the needed administrative structure, so that implementation is not possible' (Clauwaert and Düvel 2000, p. 40).

We must add that the Slovak Republic has also been less than exemplary with regard to health and safety directives, as shown by the small number of directives transposed so far, and as emphasised in the various pre-accession reports: 'The focus needs to move now to implementation, with particular emphasis on the enforcement of health and safety at work' (EC Regular Report on Slovakia 2001, p. 91). There was a similar focus in the 2002 EC Regular Report on Slovakia. Similarly in the Czech Republic, 'although some implementing secondary legislation in the field of health and safety has already been issued, a substantial amount of work remains to be done. Harmonisation with the *acquis* will only be achieved once implementing regulations are issued and put into practice' (Regular Report on the Czech Republic 2001, p. 69). This reflects the real difficulties faced by enterprises, most of them small and medium-size and with a very poor technology and financial base, in respect of making the necessary investment to upgrade their safety standards. Similar problems have been identified in Estonia. But this is not only a problem for candidate countries from Central and Eastern Europe. The Regular Report on Malta in 2001 also emphasised the need 'to strengthen the implementation capacity on occupational health and safety' (EC Regular Report on Malta 2001, p. 77).

We have also seen the difficulties that Maltese companies would have to implement the working time directive, and in particular Article 6 which stipulates a maximum weekly working time of 48 hours. According to a recent study (Baldacchino 2001), most employers in hotels and restaurants (36 out of 48 interviewed) claimed that they could easily come to terms with the provisions of the directive. Nevertheless, this sector, like others in services – whose activities are more difficult to monitor than manufacturing – are also known to have regular recourse to informal (or partly informal) work to benefit from more flexible conditions. There could thus be effective compliance on the surface, but a widespread system of longer working hours in reality, something that is also observed in hotels and restaurants in Cyprus.

In Poland, checks in 1998 showed that 48 per cent of employers violated the law on employees' holidays. Some were also taking advantage of holidays to lower wages. This situation does not seem to have improved since then.[36] The EC Regular Report on Poland 2001 (p. 68) concluded not only that 'Poland's labour law is not aligned with the relevant Community *acquis* and will require . . . further amendment to the Labour Code', but also that 'implementation of legislation is frequently scheduled to take place at a much later

---

36. European Social Charter – First Report on the Implementation of the European Social Charter, submitted by the Government of Poland, RAP/cha/POL/I, Strasbourg, 13 January 2000.

stage, and in many cases not until the date of accession. This will make it difficult to monitor implementation and enforcement.' Problems are expected particularly on health and safety (EC Regular Report on Poland 2001, p. 104). This weakness is recognised by the actors themselves. For Irena Boruta, State Secretary of the Ministry of Labour of Poland:

> It is not so difficult to harmonise the law, but it is much more difficult to have similar social services as in the EU, taking into account the differences in wages, GDP, [etc.] something which [strongly determines] implementation . . . in Poland, equality of treatment has been established in many areas such as social security, and other directives have been adopted, for instance on part-time work, and other working time arrangements . . . but there is a clear need to develop monitoring mechanisms and a labour inspectorate, and to render the judicial road more efficient.[37]

The judicial system is often not ready either. In Bulgaria, according to the EC (EC Regular Report 2001, p. 96): 'whilst work on public administration is progressing, the slow pace of the judicial system in enforcing the *acquis* is worrying. Progress on judicial reforms needs to be substantially accelerated'.

A gap also seems to prevail in Turkey between the formal commitments of the authorities and practice at enterprises. Although Turkey ratified ILO Convention No. 182 on the elimination of the worst forms of child labour in January 2001, 'child labour remains widespread and a matter of major concern, particularly during the continuing economic crisis' (EC Regular Report on Turkey 2001, p. 68). Moreover, 'no further transposition can be noted in the area of health and safety at work' (p. 68). Similarly, 'as regards the fight against discrimination, no further progress can be reported' (p. 69), a conclusion that must be seen in light of the serious discrimination in all spheres of work and life suffered by Turkish women every day. As regards social dialogue, 'there are restrictive provisions relating to the exclusion of the right to strike and to collective bargaining' (p. 68), a situation which obviously influences working conditions at enterprises. The assessment is worrying: 'much work remains to be done in order to bring Turkish legislation in line with the relevant *acquis* . . .' Turkish legislation remains very different from that of the European Union, particularly in terms of standards, methods, and monitoring requirements.

All the weaknesses mentioned here in respect of the implementation phase have been recognised by the European Commission itself, and it has emphasised them in the pre-accession reports. The Gothenburg European Council in mid-2001 also emphasised 'the vital importance of the candidate countries'

---

37. NETLEX Conference, op. cit.

capacity to effectively implement and enforce the *acquis*' and added that this 'required important efforts by the candidates in strengthening and reforming their administrative and judicial structures'.

2.6.4 The Risk of a Legislative Armoury of Diminishing Scope

In all these countries, the implementation of the Community *acquis* will be particularly problematic in small enterprises and businesses which are oriented towards making short-term profits during the transition process, regardless of whether this is done by flouting labour standards or by recourse to informal activities. It is worth mentioning in this regard that the life expectancy of most small businesses is only a few years. A human resource culture is also lacking among the new managers of Central and Eastern Europe, except in large enterprises which have to give priority to their long-term survival strategy and thus ensure the quality of goods and services delivered. Growing unemployment and casual labour contracts are also putting managers in a favourable negotiating position vis-à-vis workers and their representatives – if they negotiate at all in a context in which social dialogue and workers' information and consultation are rejected altogether. Finally, even if employers of small units would like to implement the Community *acquis*, they may face much too high a cost to do it in a proper way. This is the case for health and safety requirements which place a heavy burden on small and medium-size enterprises, given the scale on which they operate. As a result of the dominance of small and medium-size private enterprises in these countries, the new legislation adopted by candidate countries may be only poorly implemented.

In some candidate countries there are also some geographical areas, generally free export zones, that avoid normal monitoring and enforcement of labour regulations. While the candidate countries that had such zones have already terminated them, they still exist in, for instance, Turkey. In those business zones, profitability is the key word: not only are trade unions not allowed to enter, but workers often work there without labour contracts, work longer hours, and enjoy less protection in terms of health and safety, and other basic working conditions (holidays, breaks, and so on). By definition EC directives will not apply to zones of this kind, which must be suppressed, as requested by the EC, so far without much success. Some monitoring will also be needed in the 'industrial zones' created in, for instance, the Slovak Republic and other candidate countries.

Finally, candidate countries can adopt some Community directives in such a flexible way that it contradicts their original aims and objectives, even if no breach is apparent. This is the case with the working time directive. We have seen that the Hungarian authorities have adopted it in the most flexible way possible, that is, to allow workers to work long working weeks and months while respecting the overall maximum working time in the reference period (normally four months), which, furthermore, can be extended to 12 months where agreed by way of collective agreements. This outcome was easily achieved in the case of collective agreements concluded which were highly favourable to employers. This should be understood within the context of social dialogue developments in 1998–2002 in Hungary: in 2000 the Government allowed works councils to sign collective agreements in the absence of trade unions – no similar decision has been taken by any other candidate country. We shall see in Chapter 5 on social dialogue that this has led some companies to push trade unions out in order to make industrial relations and collective bargaining more controllable. These developments will obviously influence negotiations on working time. With a works council composed of a few workers' representatives who are on friendly terms with the management it becomes much easier to impose any arrangement in terms of flexible working time. Many companies in, for example, construction and textiles are now making their employees work 48-hour weeks with little rest during peak periods. This situation could also become widespread in respect of other working conditions and for other candidate countries.

We should also add that many new amendments to national labour codes do not take into account all categories of worker, such as the self-employed or workers on a temporary contract. For instance, health and safety should be extended to temporary workers in Estonia and Hungary. At the same time, if the trend towards self-employment was to continue in candidate countries, no doubt it would escape EC legislation, thus reducing its scope of application even further.

To conclude, the Community *acquis*, even if properly adapted and implemented, does not provide all the answers. There is a risk that the Community *acquis* will be transposed but with limited coverage, a growing proportion of workers and enterprises just falling outside it. All the problems mentioned here shed light on possible improvements in current and forthcoming accessions.

2.7 FOR A LONGER-TERM ACCESSION STRATEGY

2.7.1 Extending the Areas of Community Requirements

Wages seems to be one of the only social areas not covered by any of the instruments at EU level (described in Chapter 1) – whether legal provisions, social dialogue or the open coordinated approach – although it continues to represent the principal component in working conditions and the main source of social dumping. Clearly, Community action is needed, for instance, on the minimum wage, going well beyond the ineffectual EC opinion on fair wages.

The minimum wage exists in one form or another in all member states, although they can represent completely different instruments, some being more constraining than others, others completely excluding categories of worker not considered as part of the core labour force. After all, a statutory minimum wage also exists in the United States and Japan. More widely, the minimum wage clearly represents a basic form of protection for workers all over the world.

Nevertheless, there is still no Community instrument – even of a general nature – on the minimum wage and on what it should represent in terms of living standards, coverage, and so on. For instance, should it be fixed at least above the subsistence minimum, or be determined so that it would not go below a certain percentage of the average wage? What categories of worker should it apply to?

EC provisions on the minimum wage could contribute to ensuring its effectiveness in both social – to cover the subsistence needs of all types of worker – and economic (to make it a tool to increase motivation and productivity) terms. This is particularly needed as the accession process is going on. While most candidate countries have introduced a minimum wage, it has often been used as a means of controlling all social expenditure and has been allowed to fall well below any measure of the poverty line, so that it does not perform its proper function. This situation is clearly a source of unfair competition or social dumping (see Chapter 7 in Part II), and will be repeated in other future candidate countries, from the former Yugoslavia, the Balkans, and others. Action is thus urgently needed in this area, which represents a significant flaw in the European Social Model.

This absence of the European Commission from wages and incomes policy is not only a matter of legal regulations but is also reflected in the field, where the EC has, for instance, never attempted to propose a policy alternative to the very restrictive incomes policy imposed by the IMF and the World Bank in candidate countries during the first years of reform. The renunciation of wage policy is obvious in all pre-accession documents, where wages are never mentioned, and basic statistics on average wages are not even presented. One exception to this was a joint ILO–EC project on wage reforms carried out in 1996–7 (see Vaughan-Whitehead 1998). We can thus see the extent to which the non-binding EC opinion on fair wages has been taken into account. In the statistical tables at the end of the Regular Reports, there are no statistics on the average wage or the minimum wage, or even on poverty rates: only the number of cars, telephone lines, and subscriptions to mobile telephone services and to the Internet have been retained as indicators of living standards!

Other areas are excluded from EC competences, such as strikes, where the EC continues not to have any possible right of initiative, despite the fact that strikes continue to represent an important phenomenon in national member states, sometimes even with transnational effects, and the right to strike was included in the Charter for Fundamental Social Rights signed in Nice in December 2001. The promotion of a strong Social Europe requires some progress in this field, with the rights to strike, collective bargaining, and wages being enshrined in the Treaty. EC provisions are also missing on working conditions, such as temporary agency work.

All these missing elements are clearly not being addressed in the negotiation process, and the failings of candidate countries in these areas threaten to create problems in an enlarged EU.

2.7.2 More Binding Provisions

We saw in section 1.4.2 that the European Commission has been developing, in parallel with legislation, other accompanying means, such as the coordinated approach or benchmarking, and best practices. Animated by the same spirit, the progress made by the Commission in developing 'corporate social responsibility' (with a new EC communication and a green book on this issue) is an essential element in developing social responsibility at decentralised levels, and in inducing microeconomic actors to feel committed and responsible with regard to social issues. Undoubtedly, it is much easier to promote elements of social policy in enterprises if employers are convinced of their necessity. In this regard, the whole debate about social elements as positive productive factors has progressively become widespread among employers. Most are now convinced of the need to invest in training to improve their enterprise's human capital and also to involve workers more closely in the decision-making and profitability of the enterprise to boost productivity and economic performance.

At the same time, however, this development can be seen only as a complementary element with regard to other, more binding provisions. In fact, the notion of 'corporate responsibility' is borrowed from the 'liberal' vocabulary, since it leaves the initiative to decentralised levels and actors. It was first used by Jacques Delors in a narrow context when setting up European networks of enterprises to fight social exclusion in the early 1990s, before being progressively invoked in respect of employers' responsibility on a greater number of social issues. This notion has also been developed in the United States in a number of areas, not only social but also environmental. It is relayed in the European Union, however, by other instruments such as the sectoral social dialogue taking place at EU level, as well as the European works councils, which have made possible more rapid results with regard to, for instance, employers' promotion of codes of conduct in one production activity or sector, or the extension of social rights to affiliates or even subcontractors.

Nevertheless, many multinational companies operating in candidate countries, even from the EU, have not implemented the same rules or responsibility there, so showing the clear limits of this approach if significant profits – even short-term ones – are foreseen through the failure to respect EU social standards. This calls for the systematic integration of operations in candidate countries among the criteria for the assessment of 'good social corporate governance'. It also calls for the continuation of binding provisions on working conditions.

2.7.3 Making the Non-Regression Clause an Absolute Requirement

Although the non-regression clause, after its incorporation in the working time directive, was then put in other directives, and thus constitutes 'de facto' a sort of transversal requirement for Community law, it has never been clearly specified as such. It has not been integrated in the Social Protocol (since the directive on working time appeared later on), and it has not been put in the Treaty either. In the prospect of forthcoming EU accessions, it is thus urgent to specify this clause in the Treaty, clearly and unambiguously. It is also crucial to start using such clauses more systematically in the negotiation process to avoid moves backward in their social legislation by candidate countries before they join the European Union. Later on, pressure put on new member states to improve their social standards will not only be more difficult, but also not legitimate, at least not while those countries stick to the application of Community provisions, however lightweight and incomplete these provisions might be.

How the non-regression clause is applied is also not always the same: if it takes place not upon the adoption of the EC directives but only during their implementation phase, applicant countries may have plenty of time, two–three years in most cases, to weaken their armoury of social provisions. The European Commission should be given a mandate to check non-regression clauses as early as the negotiation process, when candidate countries provide their timetable and transposition tables for modifying their legislation according to the Community *acquis*.

Trade unions have a role to play in this regard. We might wonder why they have not fought for non-regression clauses more systematically within the negotiation process. Informed by their national trade union affiliates from candidate countries the European trade unions have the most accurate knowledge concerning backward steps in the social field and could have placed that protection at the core of their strategic policy on enlargement.

2.7.4 For a Bottom-Up Approach

There seem to be three main shortcomings with regard to compliance, related to the actors who can influence the process: the governments of future member states, with their poor administrative capacity; the social partners, and their lack of appropriate structures for social dialogue; and the European institutions, with the limited impact of the negotiation process.

Administrative capacity

First, the administrative capacity of the governments of future member states remains rather poor. Labour inspection is underdeveloped in most future member states and lacks appropriate human and financial resources. Many countries, including the Czech Republic, still have to pass new laws on labour inspection and make it truly operational on the ground. The existence of a large informal economy is the most obvious sign of state weakness in the region. We have seen how harmful informal activities can be for the good application of labour standards. The widespread practice of paying 'risk premiums' for non-compliance with health and safety legislation is a clear indication that labour inspection is not influencing daily enterprise practice. New occupational health and safety acts in accordance with EU standards also require new inspection methods and substantial training both for labour inspectors – this would reduce their very high turnover rates – and the social partners. A financial assessment of the impact of the implementation of health and safety legislation on businesses must be carried out by national authorities. The extension of labour inspection to all types of working conditions, including the payment of wages, should also be progressively ensured.

It is sufficient to have a look at the human resources made available for labour inspection in each country and to compare it with the number of enterprises they are expected to cover, to get an idea of the yawning deficit.

In Romania, for instance, there is 'a serious shortage of qualified staff. The labour inspectorate has been allocated 239 staff at the central level and 2 570 regional staff, but 40 per cent of the central posts and 20 per cent of the regional posts remain vacant' (EC Regular Report on Romania 2001, p. 66).

In Latvia, at the end of 2001 the State Labour Inspectorate was operating with a total of 181 employees. Even if they focus on activities in high-risk branches, industries, and types of enterprise, such an operation is clearly more symbolic than functional. It is not even sufficient to cover the basic assessment of occupational diseases and accidents at work, without even starting on any of the other problems described so far.

Moreover, in most future member states, the enforcement of legislation on working conditions, especially in the field of health and safety, continues to be hampered by the opaque division of responsibilities between different Ministries (Labour, Health, Economic Affairs, and so on) and their respective agencies. More unity and cooperation seems to be required particularly in the Czech Republic, Hungary, Latvia, and the Slovak Republic.

At the same time, specialised courts for labour disputes still have to be created – and even more importantly, put into operation – in many future member states, such as the Czech Republic, Estonia, Latvia, and the Slovak Republic. General courts require a long time to make a decision on cases of labour law: two years in the Czech Republic, and even longer in Bulgaria, where cases are just accumulating without even being processed. The result is that employers have even more incentive to cheat and workers less incentive to go to court in the first place. In Hungary, labour courts exist – they also exist in, for example, Poland and Slovenia – but they are overburdened and proceedings can take several years. Informal practices thus continue to prevail as the only solution for workers. Labour courts should thus represent a priority with a view to changing the current unacceptable situation of workers being unable to exercise their most basic rights.

The lack of administrative capacity will create other problems. In particular, most candidate countries are still not ready to administer the support they will receive through the European Social Fund (ESF), a paradoxical situation when we realise that this fund is aimed precisely at correcting social and regional imbalances and so is crucial for candidate countries in the social field.

This led the European Commission to address the issue in all pre-accession reports and to redirect part of Community assistance – such as the PHARE Programme – to reinforcing administrative capacity to implement the Community *acquis*.[38] This has taken the form of a twinning exercise between similar administrative units in EU and in candidate countries. For some experts, 'the Commission's emphasis on institution-building at the national and sub-national level is remarkable and largely unprecedented in the history of European integration' (Sissenich 2000, p. 26).

To improve administrative capacity in the accession countries, however, effective government structures at all levels are needed and the following priorities should be retained on the policy agenda: reforming law enforcement and the judiciary; improving the functioning and legal framework of the civil service in the direction of greater transparency and accountability; strengthening regional and local government to support necessary decentralisation; implementing cross-sectoral coordination both within and between Ministries; modernising statistical data collection systems and institutes; and more generally increasing the number of staff within and outside government with both a global consciousness of EU enlargement issues and a knowledge of specific technical areas of the Community *acquis*.

---

38. The EU decided in 1998 to allocate a large part of PHARE funding (more than one-third) to 'institution-building' measures.

Social dialogue

The social partners, who could play an active role in the local implementation of directives, have so far been excluded from the negotiation process by the authorities. It has thus remained a top-down affair. This has also been the case for other economic and social actors. In particular, in many candidate countries much of the legal harmonisation is taking place by way of ministerial regulations rather than by way of parliamentary legislation: this leads to more rapid harmonisation, but weakens implementation. While the involvement of the social partners may slightly delay the adoption of new legislative texts – as aggressively claimed by, for instance, the Hungarian government in the course of its labour code revision in 2000 – it ensures their acceptance by those directly concerned at local level, that is, employers and workers, and thus facilitates their concrete implementation and eventual adaptation.

We have seen, for example, that health and safety directives may not be implemented at local level; for the Czech industrialist Pavel Prior, 'the role of employers' organisations in the implementation of directives is crucial; today companies are looking for something more tailored and more stimulating than the old-fashioned approach to occupational health and safety'.[39]

There are good examples in the EU of giving a role to the social partners: in Denmark, there is not much labour law, and all Community directives, including many on health and safety, are implemented through agreements between employers and trade unions. In Belgium, the contents of health and safety regulations are defined by the social partners before being converted into Royal Decrees. In another area, working time, France provides an interesting example of a combination of the legal and social dialogue approaches: a new law on a 35-hour working week was adopted in 1999 and provides the legal framework for managers and workers to conclude collective agreements at local level.

If social dialogue must be clearly developed concerning the nature of working conditions in candidate countries, it must also be ensured that such collective agreements do not bring the workers less favourable terms than labour legislation. Only in this case would it constitute a complementary and adaptable tool for implementing labour regulations.

For the time being, however, collective agreements do not address the most crucial aspects of working conditions. According to a survey in the Slovak Republic carried out in 2000, there were no special provisions in collective agreements on possible flexible ways to reduce or avoid redundancies, despite the fact that the Labour Code and the Law on Employment require employers to discuss large-scale layoffs with trade union representatives. The few cases of appropriate provisions included in collective agreements dealt with the sit-

39. Op. cit., (see footnote 18).

uation only 'ex-post' – that is, in terms of social measures for redundant employees (Cziria and Munkova 2000). Similarly, despite the growth of atypical forms of work, no collective agreements reflected these practices, but rather applied the standard 40-hour working week, a result which also reflects the lack of interest of the social partners. Wage levels and nominal increases remain the main – and nearly the only – issue described in collective agreements.

Moreover, social partners in candidate countries continue to lack the appropriate structures and financial means to ensure through autonomous social dialogue their more active involvement in the implementation of the Community *acquis* at local level, as witnessed by the low number of collective agreements. For instance, if trade unions are not present in new private enterprises, where there are no other forms of information and consultation, this means that workers will not be able to negotiate with their employer about working time and other working conditions. This explains why employers in these countries enjoy maximum flexibility in fixing working standards.

The social partners also lack the elaboration of a clear and well articulated strategy for dealing with specific issues of the Community *acquis* in the social field – for instance, works councils, atypical forms of work, and social security. At the same time, social partners have so far been addressing the issue of wage equalisation although it falls outside EU competence. Neither the social partners nor the governments of candidate countries have so far carried out impact studies of EU enlargement on specific sectors and industries, and the expected costs and benefits for different social groups and categories of worker. We shall address social dialogue issues in Chapter 5.

A more voluntaristic approach from European institutions
Finally, the European Commission will lack sufficient means and the legitimacy to monitor or even demand the appropriate implementation of the *acquis* at local level in candidate countries.

In the past, infringement proceedings have looked not only at transposition but also at the implementation of EU law. We have presented concrete cases where member states had to change their implementation or interpretation of EC labour law after action by the Court of Justice.

In practice, however, such monitoring and infringement proceedings on the implementation side may become more difficult in the future, especially considering the number of future member states and their significant economic and social shortcomings. Moreover, we have seen that there are many ways to circumvent labour law by using covert strategies. The ability of member states to resort to strategies of avoidance may lead to a low degree of compliance with EU law.

On the basis of a comparison between the proportion of EU directives which concern social affairs and the proportion of the number of infringements which are in the social area Sissenich (2000, p. 18) concludes that 'the potential for obstacles to transposition is relatively greater in social affairs than in other areas, particularly in internal market or agricultural legislation'. This may become even more true with the entry of new member states.

This is why the pre-accession period is so crucial. In this process, the European Commission reports on the progress made and further requirements can be influential in determining the speed and quality of implementation. Negotiations on the working time directive with the government of Malta, or on health and safety with other candidate countries, are illustrative in this regard. Although the threat of delaying accession due to implementation lags is a crude enforcement mechanism, it is far more powerful than any other instrument at the Commission's disposal. It is thus essential for the European Commission to push for thorough transposition and implementation of EU legislation while it has the means to do so. However, this approach so far has had three main drawbacks.

First, European Commission policy has regrettably been to allow the late adoption of the Community *acquis*, often only upon accession (entry into the Union), which limits the follow-up monitoring process and thus the pressures on implementation before accession. A more systematic policy of harmonisation well before the date of accession would have reinforced the possibility of monitoring more closely the coverage of directives and eventual problems in their implementation. Such a monitoring policy will be harder – and the problems to be solved perhaps much larger – after these countries have joined the European Union. As an example, despite initial commitments to adopt the EC directive, the number of working hours has not been significantly reduced in the candidate countries. Similarly, the number of casual forms of work contract is increasing, with very unfavourable conditions for workers – despite the armoury of EC legislation in this field – and the latter often have no other choice but to accept if they want to keep their jobs. The current lack of protection in restructuring and enterprise insolvency – a new phenomenon for Central and Eastern Europe – also contrasts with EC provisions. Serious problems with regard to health and hygiene also remain.

More voluntaristic action from the EC before accession is even more essential since employees from applicant countries by definition are not allowed access to the Court of Justice, a situation which can lead to 'unmonitorable' abuses by employers.

The style of the Commission has also been questioned: 'whereas the Commission has relatively clear standards for evaluation concerning the transposition of EU directives, its expectations regarding effective implementation are much less transparent' (Sissenich 2000, p. 35). Similarly: 'the information provided by the Commission in its Regular Reports on Accession 1999 on the aspects in question was not very detailed, not to say quite superficial' (Clauwaert and Düvel 2000, p. 61). Further:

> the message is not clear from the European Commission side, with many regular reports written in a very diplomatic style and not criticising openly the country's policy. And even when the EC has strongly reacted, as was the case against Hungary on social dialogue at the end of 2000, the terminology used, the style of the reports, [was] very diplomatic, too neutral without much contrast between the different country reports, and the overall format – generally only a few paragraphs by topic – finally diluted the message totally.[40]

It is true that despite serious failings concerning social dialogue identified in Hungary, repeated warnings from the EC, and letters of complaint from both social partners, no change in the Government's attitude – driven by the direct aim of watering down social dialogue as soon as possible – has been noted, and the only sentence retained by the EC in the conclusions of its 2001 Regular Report (p. 103) was insipid and almost meaningless: 'as to social dialogue, confidence-building measures are needed to enhance real dialogue'. There was nothing on working conditions.

More generally, we can regret that social issues are not given more space and importance in the Regular Reports; they are often confined to the description of the relevant Chapter 13 but without even being mentioned in all other chapters, and only very rarely in the Conclusions.[41]

As another example, there is not a single reference to strikes and social conflicts due to working conditions or other sources of workers' dissatisfaction in the Regular Reports.

This is surprising considering the European Commission's own policy of considering some social matters, such as social dialogue or social exclusion, and even social protection, as transversal issues that are relevant in respect of other areas.[42] By way of comparison, economic issues such as liberalisation and the market economy are mentioned in all parts of the Regular Reports. As an example, in the case of the Regular Report on Latvia 2001, where a significant proportion of the population below the subsistence level was identified in the discussion on Chapter 13 (p. 73), the final conclusions of the report

---

40. Speech by Csilla Kollonay at the NETLEX Conference, op. cit.

41. As an illustration, social matters are not mentioned at all in the conclusions of the Regular Report 2001 on Cyprus and are very superficially summarised (a few words or one sentence) in the reports on Slovakia, Romania, Estonia, although we have seen that there were still significant shortcomings in the social area in all these countries.

42. Social issues are not addressed – although they probably should be – as examples in Chapter 7 on agriculture (despite the high proportion of the populations of many candidate countries relying on agriculture); Chapter 15 on industrial policy (despite the considerable effects of restructuring on the population); Chapter 16 on small and medium-size enterprises (despite the serious social drawbacks identified in this type of enterprise); Chapter 21 on regional policy and coordination of structural instruments (despite the social implications of regional policies).

completely neglected the issue but rather insisted on macroeconomic issues to emphasise that 'the authorities must continue a policy of fiscal discipline' (p. 114). This clear lack of balance between economic and social matters is contributing to the creation of the wrong sort of image of an enlarged European Union in the candidate countries.[43]

As regards the second main drawback, we have reason to regret the fact that no systematic action has been taken to prevent the authorities of candidate countries from using the opportunity provided by the transposition of EU labour law to adopt amendments to their labour code that introduce much less advantageous and protective provisions for the workers than in their previous legislation. This contradicts the non-regression clauses incorporated in many European labour law directives, for instance on working time. It would make sense to apply such clauses for the current and future candidate countries of Central and Eastern Europe, which formerly benefited from good labour standards in some areas. We must add that these latest changes in the labour code are not aimed at removing the previous labour standards of the Communist regime that were evaluated by some as 'much too generous and financially unsustainable',[44] but rather the final touches after twelve years of transition during which all such higher labour standards were systematically removed.

This downward trend must be stopped, and the Commission must be more active on current changes in national labour law. Still for Csilla Kollonay, 'the EC generally is not aware of the new laws and certainly is not aware of their exact contents'.

This would involve a more in-depth scrutinisation of all current amendments introduced in the candidate countries, however, something that would also require more administrative capacity in relation to the enlargement issue in the Commission.

However, if this is not done, and if previous labour standards continue to be removed or watered down on the pretext of preparing for accession, it will not be surprising if the populations of these countries will come to associate the EU with regression in the social field and so interpret it as a purely economic project without any social ambitions. The situation is even worse if we factor in the very low wages – also decreasing in real terms so far – described

43. It is as if all the comments and suggestions for Chapter 13 concerning the need to develop sound social policies – with the final aim of preserving a European social model in an enlarged EU – prepared by the Directorate General for Employment and Social Affairs were isolated and not taken into account in the general picture of the European Commission, ultimately drawn by DG Enlargement without much internal consultation. In this way, DG Enlargement proves to be much closer to the philosophy of the international monetary institutions and systematically puts the main emphasis on macroeconomic stabilisation programmes and restrictive financial policies without much consideration of social matters (it bears repeating that this is the conclusion of the author in his 'personal' capacity and based on his own experience).

44. Especially by international monetary institutions that have greatly contributed to removing such standards all over the region during the transition period.

in section 2.3. This will increase the risk of an overall rejection of the EU by the populations of these countries who have already had to bear onerous social costs in the transition. It is thus not only the future of Social Europe but the success of EU enlargement as such that is at stake here.

Finally, and for the same reasons, we can regret – and this is the third main drawback – that the European Commission has not made sufficient use of its prerogative to delay the accession process for social issues if and when needed. In the social field, there have been many objective reasons – such as the transposition of labour law on working conditions, such as health and safety and working time, or European works councils – to delay the provisional closure of Chapter 13 on employment and social affairs, or to reopen it eventually (chapters for the time until the end of the negotiation process have been only temporarily closed). Political objectives prevailed, however. The negotiations on enlargement seem so far to have been confined too much to the bureaucratic and diplomatic spheres and too little concerned with substantive issues based on a systematic 'field' evaluation. Here too a bottom-up approach is urgently needed, especially considering other, forthcoming accessions.

At the same time, the Council has not played its monitoring role in the social field. Its members have concentrated their attention on politically more 'sensitive' issues, such as 'free movement of persons' and agriculture, without assessing all the possible implications of shortcomings in the field of working conditions and social standards for all other chapters, including those dealing with labour movement (see Chapters 7 and 9 in this book) and agriculture.

2.8 CONCLUSION

The assessment of working conditions in candidate countries sheds light on the significant discrepancies that continue to prevail with regard to EU standards. Not only are wages found to be much lower in the candidate countries of Central and Eastern Europe, but they represent the variable that has been adjusted the least in the course of the economic reform process, partly because of the restrictive incomes policies imposed by the international monetary institutions. Constrained in periods of economic difficulties, the wages of the majority of the population have yet to benefit from the higher economic growth that most of these countries have enjoyed since the mid-1990s (the second phase of their reform process). Unfortunately, only a small percentage of the population has managed to profit from the privatisation process or become successfully integrated into the market economy, whilst many others have fallen into unemployment or rely on insecure income from the informal economy or token social allocations. Up until now, the outcome of the reform process as far as wages are concerned is therefore rather negative and largely unmonitored: a general fall in real wages over the whole period, minimum wages often still below subsistence levels, increased wage differentials, and in some cases delays in the payment of wages. Not surprisingly, a striking proportion of poverty in the region is accounted for by the working poor.

This is made even more absurd by the fact that wage levels under the old regimes were already artificially low, but extensively supplemented by a wide range of social benefits and services – encompassing education, holidays, housing, and health care – which have been severely curtailed or even eliminated in most countries in the region.

These developments may influence people's perception of their country's accession to the EU: they may associate it with a further decrease in their living standards, and thus reject it altogether. Although we may expect the wage gap to diminish in the years to come – we shall document this in Part II – there is no doubt that such a situation with regard to wages and incomes may influence the EU enlargement process. First, EU enlargement will lead to much greater wage and income differentials than in the current EU15 and reduce average wages and incomes in the EU. More important, however, it may continue to depress economic growth and so retard the social and economic catch-up of future member states, with adverse effects on the enlarged EU as a whole. Wages and incomes must thus continue to be monitored, and more innovative and stimulating wages and incomes policies be progressively put in place. We can wonder in particular whether this rather disappointing picture is not the result of the absence of Community requirements in this field, and whether more binding instruments on wages could not have led to a more desirable outcome. This may lead European institutions to question their absence – and induce them to become more active and determined – with regard to wage policy, especially in view of other forthcoming accessions.

At the same time, we can conclude that differentials between candidate countries and EU member states are not only about wage levels but also about other working conditions. They thus should also be considered as one possible factor in social dumping (Part II). We saw in particular how much poorer is the situation of candidate countries with regard to health and safety at the workplace. Not only is there no appropriate equipment and safety infrastructure, but there is a lack of consciousness and basic knowledge of the economic and social risks of health and safety deficiencies. Far from improving, in many candidate countries the situation is worsening. This is happening alongside the emergence of new small private enterprises and businesses where the managers underestimate and often wilfully ignore all necessary health and safety requirements.

The transition process has also represented an opportunity for the utilisation of 'wild' practices, with no protection of workers in the restructuring process or in case of insolvency. This period has also led to extreme conditions of employment, and clear exploitation of the labour force. Employees in candidate countries are found to work much longer working weeks, with a total number of working hours which in every single candidate country is well above the EU average and any individual national average among EU member states, with the possible exception of the United Kingdom which has, however, chosen in this field a radically different policy in accordance with its neo-liberal ideology. To those who favour long working hours, there is no place for part-time contracts, a situation which does not leave much opportunity – especially for female workers – to reconcile work and family life. Atypical forms of labour contract are also growing rapidly, as witnessed by the rapid increase in temporary contracts. In a period of restructuring, unemployment, and low living standards this merely serves to increase the 'social stress' on workers. While these developments should also be seen in the context of a need for more flexibility, as in current EU member states which are also increasingly resorting to such flexible forms of work, it is worrying to note that almost all candidate countries have already put in place much more extreme working patterns than in EU countries. From a wild transition, future member states in Central and Eastern Europe – or at least many of them – thus seem to be naturally evolving towards neo-liberal capitalism, a process already started in other Mediterranean candidate countries, such as Malta, inspired by the British example. This trend certainly may have an influence on the future of labour standards in an enlarged EU. It may strengthen the arguments of a few EU member states, such as Spain – which makes extensive use of temporary contracts – or the UK (with its upward flexibility of working hours) which have already opted for more flexibility in working conditions despite their obvious drawbacks for workers' security and well-being.

Moreover, the importance of the informal sector in the candidate countries should lead us to conclude that the situation – in terms of working time and labour contracts – is even worse than the statistics show, and that market pressures for downgrading working and social standards will continue in the future.

In this context, we can wonder whether the accession process and its limited time horizon will have succeeded in rebalancing these trends in the direction of greater security for the workers and more EU conforming working standards.

Of course, the negotiations that have taken place – and which continue for Bulgaria, Romania and Turkey – which have the advantage in this field of being based on the Community legal *acquis* and regulations, are putting constant pressure on candidate countries. Nevertheless, these negotiations do not seem to have contributed much so far to changing the trends described above. We might wonder, moreover, whether this Community intervention has not taken place too late: the policy strategies of the region were established in the first twelve years of transition, on the advice of international monetary institutions whose requirements are known to be above all about macroeconomic and economic variables rather than working conditions. Already the way in which some candidate countries have approached the labour law *acquis* – for instance on working time or temporary work – is indicative of the neo-liberal orientation of their governments.

Moreover, beyond its formal adoption, the whole question of the concrete implementation of the Community *acquis* will certainly remain without any answer for a decade. In the area of health and safety, it is well known that enterprises do not have the necessary funds – not to mention the willingness – to fulfil all the requirements of the health and safety directives. It is also foreseen that most new private enterprises will either continue to operate in the informal sector, or if they operate in the formal sector, adopt the most flexible working arrangements possible. Foreign companies are also taking advantage of the situation of flux with regard to national labour law and its enforcement.

Three main shortcomings have to be overcome with regard to compliance. The first is the weak administrative capacity of the governments of candidate countries, which makes it unrealistic to believe that the necessary mechanisms will be in place in the next few years to ensure the proper implementation – or even the monitoring – of the directives at enterprise level. Secondly, social partners and other non-state actors who could play an active role in the local implementation of the directives have so far been excluded from the negotiation process and the transposition of the *acquis* by the authorities; this top-down approach will lead to difficulties in the implementation stage. Social partners must develop the appropriate structures and strategies in this regard. Third, the European Commission will certainly lack sufficient means and the legitimacy to monitor or even request the appropriate implementation of the *acquis* at local level in new member countries. It has so far focused too much on transposition rather than on implementation. We might also wonder whether the current trend of the EC towards other-than-legal instruments in the labour area will be appropriate in candidate countries, and whether on the contrary, the shift back to a focus on more binding provisions, such as directives which have direct coercive force, will not be necessary. When we observe that many EU multinational companies themselves have a tendency to take advantage of differentials in working conditions – although they should be expected to be more receptive in considering labour standards as good for performance – we may conclude that the softer Community policies recently adopted, such as on corporate social responsibility, will have little impact on improving the situation in candidate countries.

We can conclude by saying that the area of working conditions in the EU should continue to be characterised by strong, extensive, and legally binding requirements to avoid the dilution of acquired workers' rights. Areas which have so far been excluded from this process, such as wages, should progressively be included in the legal framework, obviously not with ultimate harmonisation in view, but to ensure minimum requirements for the workers and guarantees on the overall orientation of enterprises. The new Charter on Social Fundamental Rights shows the direction to follow on basic rights to a minimum income, freedom of association, and collective bargaining. The integration of this Charter into the Treaty would constitute an important step forward, and may reduce the risk of competition based on excessive differentials in working conditions identified in this chapter.[45] A deepening of EC instruments on social policy is thus clearly needed. This may also reduce the resistance of EU countries to EU enlargement on the grounds of social dumping. Otherwise, EU enlargement may be achieved in a very tense context with increased fears from EU countries, and disappointments and bitterness on the part of the applicant countries.

At the same time, the administrative capacity of the authorities of future member states to implement EC provisions at local level must be enhanced. A bottom-up approach in this process is also unavoidable in order to match the real capacity of micro actors to implement the necessary standards. This requires more space being given to the social partners and social dialogue, other local actors, and individual company initiatives; in short, it points to the use of the right mixture of the legal provisions and social dialogue which seem to characterise the European Social Model in the field of working conditions.

This increased complementarity between legal provisions and local agreements is particularly relevant in the prospect of EU enlargement. It could represent the right barrier to the wind of deregulation that has been blowing, later in the candidate countries than in the EU but with more strength.

---

45. Interestingly, during their hearing in Brussels before the Convention responsible for the drafting of the Charter of Fundamental Rights, the candidate countries showed complete unanimity in welcoming the Charter, but also near unanimity against its inclusion in the Treaty.

3. Social Protection: Overwhelmed by the Liberal Approach

3.1 INTRODUCTION

As the date of accession comes closer, and most candidate countries are already engaged in substantial reform of their social protection systems, a number of questions can legitimately be asked. Are the social protection systems of the newcomers basically different from those of the EU member states? Have the reforms in this area been carried out according to the basic principles, values, and practices existing in the EU?

A number of questions have also come to the fore within the negotiation process, that has also included social protection. Is there a European model of social protection and social security, or at least some basic common elements that could constitute such a model? If so, what are the main requirements of the EU in the area of social protection?

It seems particularly important to know whether social security and social assistance in Central and Eastern Europe in the first twelve years of transition have developed along the same lines as in the European Union. In this regard, we shall keep in mind that most EU countries are themselves engaged in a process of reform in this area, especially with regard to pensions, in order to adapt to new demographic and economic trends. At the same time, the Community *acquis* and policy in this area is also progressing, a trend that should have a direct effect on the future of EU social protection systems.

We shall thus start with a presentation of the Community *acquis* and EU policies in the area of social protection, with particular emphasis on the most recent developments, made possible by the latest European summits. In this way, we shall briefly describe the diversity, but also the common elements in the different national systems of social protection within the EU.

On this basis, we shall be in a better position to describe and evaluate developments in social protection in the first twelve years of transition in Central and Eastern Europe, as well as in the three Mediterranean candidate countries, and to identify divergent and convergent trends in respect of the EU.

We shall pay particular attention not only to the level of social expenditure, but also to who has access to social protection, and how social services are provided. It will be especially useful to try to identify how the wave of privatisation and liberalisation in social services which has been debated for some time in EU countries could be implemented in countries long characterised by the central role of the state in social protection. This will allow us to discuss the expected effects of EU enlargement on social protection, and whether the arrival of the new member countries will consolidate or endanger the survival of distinctive EU features of social protection.

3.2 A BASIC ELEMENT OF THE EUROPEAN SOCIAL MODEL

Social protection is an area governed decisively in accordance with the subsidiarity principle. As the European Commission has emphasised on a number of occasions (to take the example of pensions): 'it is for the member states to decide what pension system they want . . . As the systems are different in each member state a standard EU-wide response is neither desirable nor appropriate' (EC 2000c).

3.2.1 Social Protection Provisions

There are a number of references to and provisions on social protection. Social protection is one of the fundamentals defined in Article 2 of the Treaty establishing the European Community.

The preamble of the Treaty of Rome (1957) defined the ultimate objective of the European Community: 'a permanent improvement of living and working conditions of European citizens'. Article 117 also mentioned the need to harmonise social protection systems, while Article 118 tasked the European Commission with promoting 'close cooperation between member states . . . notably on matters related to social security'.

The Community *acquis* on social protection will long be confined to the harmonisation of social security, with, notably, two regulations adopted in the early 1990s (1408/71 and 574/72) constituting the foundation, which will later on be adapted and extended to independent workers and their families. They will come to be seen as an important way of eliminating possible competitive distortions with regard to the achievement of the single market.

But other progress will be made in the area of social protection. The Treaty of Maastricht, establishing the European Community, introduced among its fundamental objectives the 'European Union's ability to achieve the promotion of a high level of social protection', but also the improvement of living standards and quality of life, and additionally 'economic and social cohesion, as well as solidarity between member states' (Principles, Article 2). For the first time, '[t]he achievement of a high level of health protection' is also mentioned in Article 3 (Principles) with a Title also on public health, where it is clearly stipulated that 'requirements in terms of protection of human health are a component of the other Community policies'. Social protection, which is enshrined in the Treaty, is thus clearly part of the Community *acquis*.

While the Treaty gives new responsibilities to the Union it also stipulates that the aim is to proceed 'through encouragement, excluding every harmonisation of legal provisions and regulations of member states, or through recommendations by qualified majority'. Since Recommendations do not commit member states, in contrast to Directives, Community action will thus be governed by the principle of subsidiarity in the area of social protection.

Another important element is contributed by the Community Charter of Fundamental Social Rights of Workers adopted by the European Community in 1989 and approved in 1995 by 14 member states (with the exception of the UK). It emphasises the right of all workers to benefit from social security and social services, although it is not binding.

3.2.2 The Main Features of the EU Social Protection Model

Despite the disparities between social protection systems, a number of basic features are shared by EU member states, such as universal social protection (at least to a certain extent), solidarity, combating social exclusion, and so on. It is worth looking in some detail at some of the most distinctive features, especially in relation to social protection systems outside the European Union. These include principles, objectives, and the involvement of different actors.

First, social protection of a universal character, and with a strong solidarity and equity basis, constitutes a basic element of the European Social Model developed by the EU:

* The *principle of universality* is embodied in the Community texts, which emphasise systematically that the goal of improving social protection must be to reach all citizens without discrimination of any kind. This is leading to the development of the principle of equity which also figures among the principles of the European Social Model.
* The *principle of solidarity* must also be ensured between different groups in society, between generations, between people of different ages, between men and women, between those in employment and those out of work. It is the basis for the social cohesion which also occupies an important place in all EC documents.
* Social protection in the EU is also characterised by a *comprehensive approach*: it is seen as a way not only of correcting the effects of economic imbalances or imperfect market functioning, but also as a way of attaining social aims, such as providing safe and adequate incomes and decent

living conditions for every citizen. This comprehensive approach is very much emphasised in, for instance, the recent EC communication on pension schemes. It means also that social protection is very much related to other fields; the well developed systems of social protection we know in the EU are based not only on labour rights, but also on social rights, social partner involvement, and citizen participation.

The roles of the different actors are also specific in EU social protection policy and schemes:

- *The responsibility of the state* is important to guarantee the functioning of and respect for the basic rules and principles. The European model of social protection includes broad public involvement in health care, education, pensions, and other basic services.
- *The involvement of social partners and other social actors* (such as NGOs) in the field of social protection takes place at EU level as well as in individual member states. At EU level, it is stipulated, for instance, that 'long-term stability of pension schemes can only be guaranteed if pension reforms are based on broad social consensus which involves all relevant actors'.[1] At national level, not only are the social partners generally involved in the decisions taken on social protection, but in many EU countries they are directly responsible for the management of the schemes, for instance pension funds.
- Particular importance is given to *gender equality* in social protection. In the recent EC Communication on pension reform, it is emphasised that pension reforms must be conducted 'with a focused effort to restore full employment and raise employment levels, particularly of women and older workers' and with the 'emphasis on reducing inequalities, especially between men and women'.
- The objective of progressively moving towards *cooperation between EU member states* in the field of social protection is also distinctive of the European Union model of social protection.

These common features have been developed by the EC in various documents, reports, communications, and so on, and must be progressively reinforced.

3.2.3 The Latest Significant Steps

Significant steps have been taken at EU level since the late 1990s. On social protection in general, we must mention the Commission Communication of

---

1. Cover note from the Social Protection Committee to the Council, 2001.

July 1999 that has led to a consensus among member states to ensure that social protection system reforms meet four main objectives:[2] (i) to make work pay and provide a secure income; (ii) to make pensions safe and pension systems sustainable; (iii) to fight social exclusion; and (iv) to ensure high quality, sustainable health care. This approach was approved by the Council in its conclusions of 17 December 1999, which also called for equal opportunities for both women and men. A working group on social protection was also created in January 2000, to be converted later on into a committee. This institutionalised the importance of social protection.

More recently, the emphasis has been put on two of the above items: the long-term sustainability of pensions and the fight against social exclusion. On the first topic, the EC submitted a Communication on major principles and objectives of pension reform in the EU, considered to be the reference manual in this field (EC 2000c). Its vision is based on three pillars, without choosing between private insurance or the public pay-as-you-go system. A new and decisive step was taken during the Swedish Presidency (first semester 2001), when the new Committee for Social Protection was established. On the second topic, it was decided to fully implement Article 137 of the Treaty through a large Community programme. The objectives of the new strategy were presented at the Nice European Summit, with four main axes: (i) fighting for the most vulnerable; (ii) ensuring participation in employment and resources; (iii) mobilising social actors; and (iv) preventing exclusion. It was also decided to implement the method of open coordination in the area of social exclusion. For the first time, individual EU member states were requested to submit national action plans in this area by June 2001.

These two approaches led to significant and unexpected outcomes. On pensions, while the Lisbon European Council of 23–4 March 2000 had already given a decisive impetus by calling on member states to develop 'closer cooperation' in the area of social protection, the Stockholm European Council reached the originally defined target by upgrading from 'cooperation' to 'coordination' of social protection policies: 'where appropriate, the potential of the open method of coordination should be used in full'.[3] The implementation of the coordination method is also very significant with regard to the EU fight against social exclusion, previously considered to be covered by the subsidiarity principle and thus entirely left to member states.

This progress has also been supported by the Social Agenda prepared by the Commission and approved by the EU member states at the Nice Summit in December 2000, which outlined the social programme of the EU until 2005

---

2. *A Concerted Strategy for the Modernisation of Social Protection*, EC Communication of 14 July 1999.

3. 'Pensions and the Concerted Strategy for Modernising Social Protection', Introduction, p. 2.

(EC 2000d). In December 2000, common objectives and eighteen indicators were defined in the fight against social exclusion, in relation to which it was decided that the open method of coordination would be applied from 2001 (when the first National Action Plans were implemented). Furthermore, at the European Council of 2 December 2002 it was decided that more precise and focused objectives should be adopted to fight poverty. Social protection also has an important place in the action programme.

The new charter of fundamental rights approved in Nice in December 2000 re-emphasises a number of basic rights in the field of social protection. Although non-binding, it contributes to making more precise the basic principles, values, and rights of social protection in the European Union to which the candidate countries are expected to sign up.

3.3 SOCIAL PROTECTION IN FUTURE MEMBER STATES: THE MINIMALIST APPROACH

Social protection was rather uniform under the previous regimes in Central and Eastern Europe, under Soviet influence. It represented one basic pillar of the system. Central and Eastern European countries generally benefited from a comprehensive system of social protection, with citizens enjoying certain advantages at different levels: they received a wide range of benefits from their enterprise, for instance, holidays and recreation facilities; they also benefited from free services from the state, in basic areas such as education and health care, but also transportation. The prices of basic items such as bread, water, and electricity were also subsidised and kept at very low levels; they could also benefit from low-cost housing. For this reason poverty was limited,[4] as were social inequalities, a situation also facilitated by the guarantee of employment. The policy of full employment and the egalitarian wage system served to ensure a certain minimum standard of living and 'social security' for the whole population in most countries of the region.

This was far from ideal, however, since all these benefits existed largely to compensate for wages kept at artificially very low levels and shortages of goods; at the same time, some categories of people did live in precarious conditions, and there were stark inequalities between ordinary people and party apparatchiks. And this is without even mentioning the sometimes severe curtailment of freedom and personal independence which, rose-tinted hindsight notwithstanding, served to nullify such material benefits as there were.

However, if there is one element of the system that people were relatively satisfied with, and one whose passing they came to regret after the first few

4. For instance in the Czech Republic, the share of households with incomes below half the average income was very small, at 4–5 per cent (Hirsl et al. 1995).

years of capitalism, it was comprehensive social protection. It is worth mentioning that most experts from international monetary institutions immediately wanted to curtail all benefits distributed to citizens, which they considered 'much too generous', thus showing that there was indeed a level of social protection in these countries that may have been above certain standards in Western countries. In this context it is important to examine the extent to which social protection has remained a priority in the region, particularly as a response to the economic and social shocks of the transition.

3.3.1 Downward Plunge after Hasty Cuts in Social Services

The answer to this question is clearly 'no'. Social protection systems in Central and Eastern Europe have not been used sufficiently to soften the consequences of economic stabilisation policies implemented by most governments in the region, and for two main reasons: (i) the social protection systems had to be reformed, not only in order to improve them, but also to adapt them to the new conditions of free market economies; (ii) radical reform of these social protection systems became a basic element of the restrictive macroeconomic policies that most governments in the region implemented – sometimes under strong external pressure – in the first years of transition: significant cuts in social expenditure have been used as a basic means of ensuring a balanced budget, and so of keeping inflation, wages, and exchange rates under control. The international financial institutions have played a central role in this regard by directly 'recommending', under the leitmotiv of financial sustainability and viability, cuts of all kinds in the social protection budget, including social security, social services, and social assistance.

Too many years of communist regimes which claimed to be acting in the name of social justice but inflicted little but misery and frustration on large parts of the population can also explain why these countries have been receptive to blueprint neo-liberal formulae. For some:

> after 40 years of rule by the Communist Party, which claimed that social justice was its aim, but which during the last 20 years had, through its practices, persuaded almost the entire population that it sought only to protect its privileged position, the disillusion with socialist ideas and their compatibility with democracy and human rights was great, and a wave of individualism swept over our society. (Hirsl et al. 1995)

Despite their different political orientations, almost all governments of the region committed themselves to reforms to curtail social benefits as a way of rebalancing the state budget.

In Poland, it was the conservative government which implemented the 'shock therapy' most literally, and was then praised by the World Bank for

such a courageous policy. As a result, social expenditure was drastically curtailed, falling from 22 to 18.8 per cent of GDP, while most social benefits
rapidly lost touch with reality.

By contrast, in Hungary it was the socialist–liberal coalition (with a socialist majority) that introduced the very restrictive Bokros package in 1995.[5]
This was a neo-liberal programme which consisted in reducing the role of the
state by abolishing universal benefits, cutting most other benefits, and making
access to such benefits much more difficult. The liberal-conservative–
Christian Democrat–Smallholders Party government which came to power in
1998 stepped up the process, most notably by abolishing the health and pension boards and renationalising the funds.

In the Czech Republic, the conservative government which was elected in
1992 followed in the footsteps of its Polish counterpart and faithfully followed all the prescriptions of the 'shock therapy' manual, with rapid price liberalisation, restrictive monetary and fiscal policies, and restrictive controls
over wage and income increases, in which the severe curtailment of social
expenditure figured prominently. Expenditure on social security decreased
from 42 to 33 per cent of the budget between 1989 and 1994, and as a consequence all social benefits fell drastically. The maximum pension, for instance,
fell by nearly 50 per cent between 1989 and 1994, so bringing about a rapid
deterioration in pensioners' living standards. Child benefits had lost one-third
of their value by the end of 1994. The share of social benefits in the total net
income of families also decreased steadily from 1992 (Hirsl et al. 1995).
Despite the sharp increase in prices, and the clear deterioration of the social
situation, the Government restricted the income support allowance to the most
needy families by fixing a subsistence income which was allowed to decline
rapidly in real terms. At the same time, many basic social services were terminated as the state withdrew from the social sector.

As a result, social expenditure fell as a proportion of GDP almost everywhere in the region, as shown in Figure 3.1. Unfortunately, very different definitions of social protection and of its different components do not allow
direct comparison, but only a presentation of the evolution of basic social
expenditure in each individual country, such as social security or health.[6] All
Central and East European countries show a significant fall, and are below the
EU average of 28 per cent of GDP.

In Hungary, as a result of the progressive withdrawal of the state from
social policy, the welfare budget has been continuously reduced since 1990.
As a percentage of GDP, social benefits and services had lost 30–40 per cent

5. Minister of Finance Bokros gave his name to this very restrictive incomes and monetary policy advised by international monetary institutions.
6. Some social protection systems do not differentiate between social security and social insurance; health care expenditure is not always included in social security expenditure; and so on.

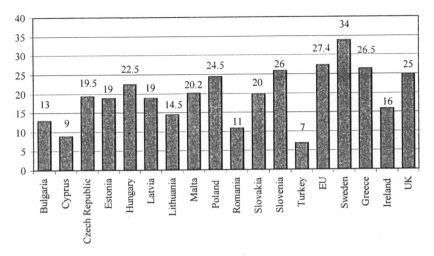

Source: National statistics and Hagemejer (2001).

Note: More recent data for 2000 (EC 2002e) put social expenditure at a slightly higher level: 17.9 per cent for Bulgaria; 19.5 for the Czech Republic; 15.2 for Estonia; 13.9 for Romania; 21.7 for Slovakia; 26.1 for Slovenia; and 11.6 for Turkey. However, these slightly higher percentages are due not to an increase in social expenditure but to a decrease in GDP in 2000. Moreover, social expenditure in all candidate countries remained below the EU average (27.7 per cent in the EU in 2000 as against 13.3 per cent on average in the 13 candidate countries) (EC 2002e).

Figure 3.1 Social expenditure as a percentage of GDP in future and current member states, 1999–2000

of their value by 1998, and have been stagnating since then; from 37.5 per cent of GDP in 1991, they had shrunk to less than 27 per cent by 1999.

Moreover, almost every budgetary item has been affected by these radical cuts. Funding of health and education has fallen by 4 per cent; social insurance, social and care services have been reduced by almost half; while the already very small sums apportioned to housing, the regions, and cultural policy have been curtailed.

In Bulgaria, the situation became acute in 1997 when the country faced a serious economic crisis and had to adopt a currency board policy. Although its social expenditure as a percentage of GDP has increased in recent years Bulgaria remains well below other countries in the region. The government has no room to manoeuvre, however, since this is an issue that comes under the IMF agreement and the currency board.

In Estonia, social protection expenditure (social security and social welfare) accounted for only 17.3 per cent of GDP in 1997, well below the EU average, although social protection expenditure represented nearly 50 per cent of consolidated government spending (Leppik 2000).

Within social security expenditure, the cost of unemployment benefits has rapidly increased in most countries following the increase in unemployment rates, which means that within the aggregate figures on social expenditure, the share of social services has fallen tremendously. Beyond the fall in activity rates, the structure of social funding was also modified over time as a consequence of the increase in the numbers of pensioners and a move away from public funding to insurance funding.

The most important categories of social expenditure are pensions and health care. Pension expenditure is the highest in Slovenia and Poland, and the lowest in Cyprus, Malta, Romania, and Turkey. Health care expenditure is also very poor in the three Mediterranean countries, since they mainly rely on private health insurance (one of the main conclusions of EC 2002e). According to Martin Evans, 'the fight against social exclusion and poverty is a low priority in Cyprus, Malta, and Turkey' (at the conference 'The modernisation of social protection in the candidate countries: new opportunities and challenges for the European Union', organised by the EC in Brussels, 5–6 December 2002, EC 2002e).

Another phenomenon that the figures on social expenditure as a proportion of GDP conceal, however indicative they are in other ways, is the tremendous fall in social expenditure in real terms. Not only has the total package of social expenditure decreased, but the purchasing power of social benefits received by those in need has plunged as prices have soared.

Figure 3.2 on Bulgaria shows that all sources of income have fallen dramatically. While the minimum wage stood at 30 per cent of its 1990 value in 2000 (after falling to 20 per cent of that value in 1997), the basic minimum income, the monthly retirement pension, and the minimum social pensions had all fallen to 40 per cent of their 1990 value. We must also note that all these benefits were already at a very low level in 1990. While there has been a clear improvement since 1997, with some real increases in these benefits, total household incomes fell by a further 6 per cent in 2000, partly due to the effect of the sharp rise in unemployment (up to 17 per cent) on household budgets. Over the period in question it seems that one setback after another has arisen in order to prevent Bulgarian families from enjoying better times.

In Poland, social benefits fell in real terms, and also in relation to the average wage: pensions fell from 63 per cent of the average wage in 1992 to 47 per cent in 1999, a figure which should be placed in the context of a continuous fall in real wages over the same period. According to Gertruda Uscinska (2000), previously 'there was an important social element in pension policy . . . now there is no social element in the scheme, and there is a general trend towards a fall in benefits'.

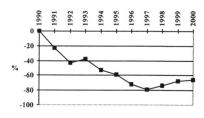

Monthly minimum wage – average

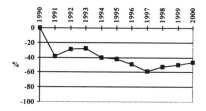

Monthly wage in the non-budgetary sphere – average

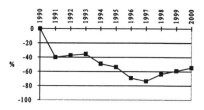

Monthly wage in the budgetary sphere – average

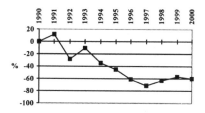

Basic minimum income – average

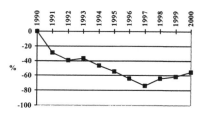

Monthly pension – average

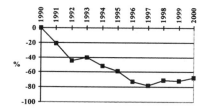

Minimum social pension – average

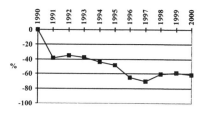

Real total household income per person

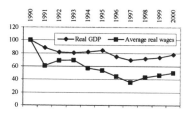

GDP and real wages, 1990–2000

Figure 3.2 Bulgaria – selected indicators, 1990–2000 (index: 1990= 100)

These figures clearly show, particularly in the case of Bulgaria, a reality that is not fully captured by the figures on social expenditure as a percentage of GDP which are systematically used by foreign experts. More data still have to be collected on the erosion in real terms of all sources of social income that has taken place over the twelve years of transition.

In addition, all sorts of previously provided benefits have been curtailed drastically. In Hungary, the IMF and the World Bank requested a cut in family benefits that had traditionally represented a crucial source of income for Hungarian families. This was done in the austerity package of 1995–6, such benefits being reduced from 4 to 1 per cent of GDP. Family allowances in fact lost 30–35 per cent of their real value between 1990 and 1994, and had lost 50 per cent by 1998 (Ferge and Tausz 2001). Despite committing itself to the family and increasing the birth rate the government which came to power in 1998 allowed family allowances to fall further (by 15 per cent since 1998). This may have been partly compensated by a slight increase in the tax allowance for families with a high number of children (three or above), while the fall in maternity benefits was also halted. Nevertheless, the system seems to be increasingly more advantageous for middle-class families, whose benefits are much higher and are improving more rapidly than those of the poor, thus potentially contributing to further division and inequalities.

Contribution rates have also increased in most countries. Particular efforts have been made in some of them to shift the burden of cost from the employer to the employees. The previous government in Hungary aimed to reduce employer contributions by around 10 percentage points by 2002, so as to promote investment and employment. The burden for employees, however, has become increasingly high.

In Poland, following the changes in the social security law in January 1999, significant contributions are demanded from employees (Uscinska 2000).

In Estonia, social protection expenditure has so far been financed mainly from the social tax, that is, from the social security contributions of employers, while employees have not participated directly in the financing of social security, a situation that is changing in the current reform process. Already, employees' contributions have been introduced for the financing of the second pension pillar, as well as for unemployment insurance (Leppik 2000). Despite a relatively higher level of social expenditure, we must add that the general state budget, as well as the pension insurance budget and the health insurance budget, are all in surplus in Estonia, which has followed a prudent policy: under Estonian law a budget cannot be adopted if given items are in deficit. This situation should lead Estonia to envisage the necessary reforms in a more measured fashion, striking the right balance between the sustainability of the system and the ultimate purpose of social protection, to ensure decent standards of living for all.

3.3.2 Keeping Social Benefits Low through the Minimum Wage

The kind of wage policy that has been implemented on the advice of international monetary institutions has also contributed indirectly to cutting or keeping down expenditure on social protection.

Since the calculation of all social benefits is directly related to the minimum wage (often as a multiplier of it) the latter has become a central element in social policy expenditure in the region, often in an unsophisticated fashion. Holding down the minimum wage at artificially low levels has become a means not only of controlling the whole wage scale, but also of keeping down all social benefits, and thus serves as a relatively easy way of limiting public transfers. By linking all social protection expenditure to the level of the minimum wage, governments have sought to give the appearance of not cutting social expenditure. Social benefits are indexed to price increases only if the minimum wage is. As a direct result the minimum wage rapidly became an instrument of impoverishment (Vaughan-Whitehead 1995). Many of the poor have been denied entitlement since in many cases it is only granted if the person's income is below the statutory minimum wage. There is a clear need for a separation of wage policy and social protection.

The figures on Bulgaria show how much social benefits have accompanied the minimum wage in its fall. Similar parallel trends can be observed for all other Central and Eastern European countries (Standing and Vaughan-Whitehead 1995) before they decoupled the minimum wage and social benefits, which did not occur before the late 1990s in most of them. It took more than seven years for Bulgaria to break the connection between the minimum wage and social benefits.

Another way of keeping social benefits down is not to index-link them. In a period of rapidly increasing inflation, the effects on social benefits have been catastrophic. This clearly indicates that social benefits – and their fall in real terms – have been used deliberately, and sometimes cynically, as a stabilisation variable in the transition process. Those who advised this policy probably did not realise how much harm it would do to people, running down 'human capital' in these countries and so harming potential competitiveness.

Still as regards Estonia, there are no automatic indexation mechanisms for social benefits; their levels are reviewed annually and increased in accordance with the available budgetary resources, a system which clearly gives plenty of flexibility to the government to delay or indefinitely postpone indexation at its discretion (Leppik 2000).

There are other perverse effects of a policy of low minimum wages on workers' social protection, not only from the social expenditure and social benefits side, but also from the contributions side. Since many people are paid very low, often merely nominal, minimum wages on which they nevertheless pay contributions, they generally receive extra sums from their employer, generally 'under the table', in order to compensate for this. Because of their lower contributions, however, they often are not building up sufficient entitlements, a phenomenon that may generate severe social difficulties, even if there is no outward sign of them yet.

3.4 REDUCED ACCESS TO SOCIAL PROTECTION

In all Central and Eastern European countries under Communism, social protection was the universal right of all citizens. This universal coverage was generally enshrined in the Constitution (for example Article 28 of the Constitution in Estonia, Articles 26, and 30 to 36 of the Czech Constitution).

Since the start of the reforms, not only has the universal nature of social protection systems been eroded, but the conditions of access have become harder, and most countries have progressively moved towards targeted social assistance.

If most countries have followed exactly the same policy, despite the great variety of circumstances, it may be partly explained by the fact that this policy was already in place in many Western countries, and also because it had been advised by the IMF and the World Bank, which directly applied in these countries their concept of the 'social safety net', aimed at covering only the most vulnerable groups, such as children, the handicapped, and the elderly.

The main way of implementing this policy was to withdraw certain benefits, or to reduce them or the number of those entitled to them by introducing increasingly selective criteria.

At the same time, there has been partial or full privatisation of social services, with a shrinking role for public provision and funding.

3.4.1 Privatisation of Social Policy

As already mentioned, not only has economic activity been privatised, but social policy has too. This applies to all areas, including health care, social care, education, housing, pensions, and employment services. Access to many social services has become market regulated.

In the Czech Republic, for example, funding of the universal health insurance scheme has been left to a new compulsory health insurance system, with private companies offering insurance and collecting contributions from employers, employees, and the state. Although they remain semi-public in nature, and the health insurance scheme continues to be guaranteed by the state, this has led to a proliferation of insurance companies, leading to debates about the need to return to a single insurance company (Macha 2001). Many of these companies are profit-oriented and offer services for fees, while the contributions from the state to this health insurance system have been progressively reduced (Macha 2001). Already in 1993, the share of the state in the health care system had fallen to 10 per cent, while the share of individual health insurance companies had increased to more than 83 per cent.

This 'hidden' privatisation of health services had immediate consequences. The burgeoning of health insurance companies was accompanied by a sharp increase in the costs of public health care, from CZK36.7 billion in 1991 to CZK70.4 billion in 1994; the share of health care in GDP rose from 5.1 per cent to 6.8 per cent in 1994. Effects on patients have not been negligible. Many costs have been passed on directly to the public, for instance for medicines and dental care. The same situation has emerged in the education system, where several non-governmental institutions have emerged to provide educational services, including private schooling. At the same time, the Government has effected large cuts in the construction and maintenance of schools. In a few months in 1993, the share of education costs covered by families had already reached around 10 per cent of household budgets.

The situation in Poland is similar, the curtailment of social benefits accompanying the price liberalisation of basic services and the progressive reduction in the provision of social welfare homes and local social assistance centres.

The privatisation of social protection entails its individualisation; this is inegalitarian, removes the solidaristic element, and creates discrimination. It can also distort the future formation of human capital. Education has traditionally been of a high standard in Central and Eastern Europe so we might ask why international monetary institutions have been so careless about what was considered as the region's main asset, its human capital and skills, and have advised governments to radically cut expenditure in these areas. For one Hungarian sociologist the aim was clear: 'there was a deliberate intention to weaken Central and Eastern Europe, and through this the future potential of an enlarged European Union'.[7]

3.4.2 Means-Testing: The Drift to Selectivity

The main trend of social protection in Central and Eastern Europe has been a drift from insurance-based support to means-tested social assistance. Most governments in the region have integrated in their social protection systems strong selectivity and conditionality criteria. Although similar reforms are being carried out in EU countries, the candidate countries seem to have taken

7. Statements collected directly by the author, Budapest, 1999.

a much more extreme path: 'Central and Eastern European countries are trying to repeat, indeed often exceed, the Western European approach by shifting from universal benefits to means testing of social benefits' (Eatwell et al. 2000, 149).

According to the World Bank (1996), the aim is 'to target the most vulnerable'. Accordingly, means-testing has been introduced for all possible benefits, from child allowances to housing benefits (although rents have increased dramatically).

In the Czech Republic, after the arrival of the conservative government of Václav Klaus, all benefits have been radically reformed to introduce selectivity criteria. In particular, the amount of household income became a key criterion (in proportion to the subsistence minimum) for fixing a number of benefits, including child allowances, social benefits, and transport and housing benefits (Macha 2001). Family allowances were cut again in January 1996 through a complex income-testing procedure which led to the ineligibility of around 10 per cent of children previously covered.

To give an example, the monthly travel allowance which is designed to help Czech families to cover the transportation costs of their children between home and school is now subject to a very bureaucratic procedure (directly under the Ministry of Finance) and the fulfilment of a long series of criteria, including the type of school attended (elementary, secondary, university), daily commuting or otherwise, and distance of commuting.

In general, a distinction has been progressively introduced between those in work and those without work: between the deserving and the undeserving poor (Standing 2000). In Hungary, the most important change in respect of social security was the redefinition of the bases of entitlement, especially for those not in employment. Unless contributions are paid, entitlement is lost to free medical care, pension, sick pay, maternity benefits, and child care provisions. The year 1998 also led to significant changes, including the decision of the new Government to govern the social security funds – covering health and pension insurance – alone, to the exclusion of the social partners, who had previously controlled them.

Again in Hungary, family allowances, which were universal until 1995, became subject to means-testing. Only families under a certain income limit (EUR100 per month, that is, slightly above the minimum wage) were entitled to such allowances. In 1998, however, the government decided to restore universal coverage of this benefit in line with its professed pro-family policy. Benefit levels remained low, however: for example, family allowances in Hungary in 1998 represented between 9 and 30 per cent of the minimum wage (HUF19 500 in 1998, less than EUR80), a gap which was further increased when the minimum wage was nearly doubled at the end of 2000 (from HUF25 000 to 40 000).

As a result of the greater selectivity built into the system, and the austerity package of 1995–6, the scope of social assistance has narrowed dramatically in Hungary. In the case of family allowances, 20 per cent of those previously entitled to them have ceased to benefit.

Even in Slovenia, where social expenditure remains at 25 per cent of GDP, the number of welfare recipients is low – especially among the elderly and those permanently incapable of working – and has been falling over the last few years because of the introduction of selectivity criteria.

In Estonia, the eligibility criteria for the national pension were changed in January 2000. The new State Pension Insurance Act of January 2000 also modified the eligibility conditions and calculation methods of the old-age pension. The same happened in January 2000 for the invalidity pension for those permanently incapable of working (now limited to persons of working age), and also for the survivor's pension, for which a qualification period has also been introduced, along with the requirement that the deceased breadwinner had served a pensionable period in work (Leppik 2000).

In Poland, more selective criteria were also introduced, in particular in 1997 when family allowances were made much more dependent on family income and situation, and in the reforms of the social security system in 1998–9 (Uscinska 2000). As a direct result, the number of beneficiaries was significantly reduced in a few years (by nearly 50 per cent for certain family or child benefits).

More examples of means-testing can be found. In a period of the erosion of already low living standards and rapid price increases, their effects on society have been enormous. According to Ferge and Tausz (2001), 'poor punitive regulations and inadequate levels of social assistance add to the strengthening political division in the country, and have a strong negative impact on social integration'.

This policy has been transplanted without consideration for populations already hard hit by the fall in real wages and incomes and by unemployment; selective child or rental benefits often generate the deepest and most lasting discontent.

For many experts, 'means-testing child benefits is a mistake' (Eatwell et al. 2000, p. 156), and 'the fact that children have been the hardest hit by the transition is an unacceptable long-term risk'. They recommend restoration of the universality of all child and family allowances.

Other economists point to the hypocrisy of this policy:

[those who advocate] means tests, labour tests and discretionary judgments on the deserving and undeserving are little different, although more circumspect and gentle, from those who in the last century were saying that 'poverty and insecurity were needed as incentives to labour, hunger being effective because it was peaceful, silent and continuous'. (Standing 1999)

It is worth quoting here the World Bank's own basic motivation behind the trend toward targeting:

> Such changes are driven more by a need to contain expenditures rather than by a desire to help the poor. Thus the focus is often on keeping individuals off the benefit system rather than ensuring full coverage of the target population. (World Bank 1996)

In this regard, the fulfilment of the 'honourable' aim of 'better cover[ing] the poorest and most vulnerable categories' is certainly the best excuse – and most 'politically acceptable' argument – that the World Bank could find to justify the massive reduction of social expenditure and the progressive shrinkage of the scope of social policies.

The problem, however, is that not only is this selective policy excluding the majority of the population from important social protection rights, but also it has proved to be a failure as regards protection of the most vulnerable groups in society.

Means-tested benefits have the drawback that they do not reach many of those they are supposed to reach because of low take-up rates, which have little to do with need or entitlement. In other words, not only do they exclude many of the poor, but also they cannot even cover the poorest effectively. For the Czech Republic, 'the shortcomings of current social policy in protecting the most vulnerable groups in society have become manifest' (Hirsl et al. 1995, p. 32). We can observe throughout the region how ineffective this policy has been in protecting pensioners, young people, and such socially excluded groups as the Roma (section 3.6).

Twelve years of transition clearly show that such policies have not been effective; although targeted benefits are presented as a means of identifying the truly needy, there is sufficient empirical evidence to show how many of the most needy slip through the 'torn safety net' (Standing 1996).

Apart from fostering further social exclusion, the provision of social benefits via means-testing was also found by the OECD (1997) to have directly detrimental economic effects. First, this system is recognised as creating a sort of 'poverty trap', with households' pre-transfer incomes being reduced to nothing after taxes are paid, and more and more benefits are withdrawn (Standing 1999). Secondly, a targeting approach is very expensive to administer and has an unsatisfactory take-up. 'In fact, the cost of identifying the target population, minimising fraud, and distributing the targeted benefit may well exceed the deadweight losses implicit in untargeted distribution' (Eatwell et al. 2000, p. 151). This is for the simple reason that the targeting approach can be effective when the targeted population is limited and easy to identify; however, this is not the case in Central and Eastern Europe. In economies where the informal sector is very important and represents an important share in economic activity, it is not possible to calculate or even assess people's incomes. Moreover, where a significant proportion of the population is below or not far below the subsistence minimum it is impossible, and socially undesirable, to identify the 'poorest'.

The conclusion of Eatwell et al. (2000, p. 151) is clear: 'where such conditions do not apply, the transaction cost of supplying targeted benefits may well be very high indeed and instead of saving money, targeted benefits may result in substantial waste'.

This assessment should lead us to seriously question the effectiveness and thus the relevance of this type of selectivity in the delivery of social benefits in Central and Eastern Europe, where conditions, including the social costs of transition so far and the high proportion of people in poverty, should rather encourage a return to a more universal type of social protection.

Benefit targeting has been imposed on the advice of the World Bank in order to keep social expenditure at the lowest possible level, without much consideration being given to those who suffer as a result. In stark contrast to this, human capital in the future member states should represent a priority for the EU.

3.4.3 Inadequate and Fragmented Social Assistance

In the face of escalating impoverishment, the development of social assistance takes on an even more urgent character. There is an increasing number of people on social assistance (for example, in Hungary), which must cover new needs and try somehow to compensate for the deterioration of all other benefits. Means-tested welfare assistance has proven to be inadequate to make up for the losses suffered on labour markets, as well as in social insurance.

In the Czech Republic, although the subsistence minimum has been losing significance because it is not indexed on a regular basis, the social care system (as defined by the Social Needs Act) and benefits are aimed at only those citizens whose income is below the subsistence minimum. The importance of the proper calculation and regular adaptation of the subsistence minimum in this context is clear. At the same time, governments are reluctant to introduce more transparency into this field so as not to produce alarming figures on poverty which would cry out for increased social assistance.

In Poland, public authorities in June 1996 also reformed the criteria – in terms of reference income – governing social assistance entitlements. The budgetary capacity of the state is one criterion enshrined in the law which gives us some idea of how likely it is that these basic allowances will be made independent of budgetary arbitration.

The basic necessity of this type of allowance in future member states contrasts with the subjectivity by definition of the budgetary arbitration process.

BOX 3.1 THE SUCCESS OF THE GRADUALIST APPROACH
IN SLOVENIA

Slovenia enjoys a relatively high level of economic development; indeed, it is the highest in the region. Nevertheless, it has experienced the same kind of restructuring and reforms as other CEE countries. Similarly, it has had to address the future of its social security and insurance system, as well as pensions.

The 'shock therapy' option was envisaged in the early 1990s, but finally not adopted; Slovenia's higher level of development helped it to resist external pressures to implement a radical policy of rapid privatisation and cuts in welfare spending. The government has continued its policy of social incomes and family allowances, and has used it to alleviate poverty and reduce inequalities. Although this policy has been criticised as too expensive, as in other countries, the government did not reduce social transfers, although many allowances did become means-tested. The lion's share of government expenditure is earmarked for social security and has risen slightly over the years, from 39.1 per cent in 1993 to 39.4 per cent in 1999. New rights to various forms of social benefits, particularly in child care (introduction of a universal child benefit) and social protection have been introduced. Health insurance remains universal.

This approach has been successful, helping households to absorb the shock of unemployment and the consequent fall in income from work. While income inequalities increased in the period from 1983 to 1993, the trend was reversed between 1993 and 1998, due to other sources of income, particularly social transfers (UNDP 2001). In particular, income from unemployment benefits, but also transfers to families in lower income brackets, increased their share in household budgets. The share of social transfers progressively increased from 16.2 per cent in 1983 to 22.6 in 1993, and to 29.7 per cent in 1999. First-decile households seem to be increasingly dependent on social benefits, grants, and transfers between families. This has led the UNDP to characterise these social benefits as an 'absolute income leveller . . . from which the poorest have benefited more, and without which inequality and poverty would undoubtedly paint a completely different picture' (UNDP 2001, p. 99).[8]

---

8. After calculating concentration coefficients, which show the contribution of one income source to total income inequality, social benefits and in particular unemployment benefits show negative coefficients, indicating that they have played a role in reducing inequalities since the poor have received a larger proportion of that income.

Social indicators, Slovenia, 1983–98

	1983	1993	1998
Share of social benefits in households	16.2	22.6	29.7*
Poverty rate (people under 50% of average expenditure)	–	13.6	11.2
Poverty rate (people under 50% of average income)	–	11.2	9.0
Gini coefficient[9]	0.234	0.272	0.242

* for 1999.

According to Stanovnik and Stropnik (1998), even in 1993 the Gini coefficient was over 0.30, indicating much greater inequalities. We can thus see that Slovenian social policy pursued in the meantime contributed to reducing poverty between 1993 and 1998: according to the measure used by the Slovenian government (people below 50 per cent of average expenditure) poverty decreased from 13.6 per cent in 1993 to 11.2 per cent in 1998. The same decline is observed if we measure poverty from the income side (people below 50 per cent of average income).

Inequalities have thus been limited; nevertheless, responding to an opinion poll in 1998, 90 per cent of respondents believed that inequality was still too great, which shows that it is indeed a national concern (UNDP 2001). At the same time, in an attempt to ensure that households do not come to rely on social benefits more or less permanently, a potential drawback of such a policy, the government has also launched a comprehensive and coordinated strategy – a National Programme – to fight against poverty and social exclusion, to analyse and prevent the causes of poverty (especially in critical groups), and to launch projects for their reintegration into society (UNDP 2001). Slovenia has also reformed its pension system while maintaining a significant public stake.

Slovenia thus seems to have succeeded in progressively upgrading its social protection system while maintaining social cohesion. This should constitute a good basis upon which to hang on to a highly skilled and motivated labour force as a competitive asset in the future.

9. The Gini coefficient measures income or expenditure distribution between persons or households. It shows the deviation from a completely equal distribution; that is, a 0.00 value for the Gini coefficient means that everyone gets the same income or complete equality, while a 1.00 value means complete inequality. Here we measured the inequalities between household incomes.

Unregulated social assistance at local level

In Hungary, responsibility for social assistance was delegated to the local community (according to the 1993 Social Welfare Act and the 1997 Child Protection Act). While this may have theoretically positive aspects – for example, it might make it possible to adapt the regulations on different types of benefits and in-kind social benefits to local needs – it seems to have led in practice to excessive decentralisation and fragmentation. According to Ferge and Tausz (2001, p. 19) it could result in more than 3 000 different local welfare systems; furthermore, it has sometimes encouraged local authorities to give free rein to 'exercising discretion' and discrimination. Since no national minima to orient means-testing were defined, it led to a decentralised and at times even disorderly process of selecting beneficiaries at local level. Local regulations, for example, defined income limits in a very different way from the same type of assistance elsewhere. Far from the principles of universal assistance once ensured by the state this trend seems to be leading in the opposite direction. For Júlia Szalai (1999, p. 25) 'all universal regulations have withered away from programmes for income-maintenance, and the situation of the poor has become dependent on the decision-making bodies of their communities'. Moreover, the poorest regions, where the situation of the poor is the most dramatic, do not seem to have been those benefiting the most from the central budget, contrary to what one might expect, so leading to an increase rather than a decrease in the handling of poor people throughout the country.

In any case, the sums distributed are obviously far from adequate for families to survive on: the average amount of regular assistance was no more than HUF10 000 (around USD40 [23 August 2001]) and housing benefit or crisis assistance around HUF1 000–2 000 (USD4–8), compared with a subsistence minimum or poverty line of (in 1999) HUF30 000 (USD100) for a single person, and HUF70 000 (USD260) for a family of three (HUF85 000 [USD315] for a family of four). The only likely outcome of such a policy is to push a growing number of people receiving social assistance to accept informal work in order to make ends meet. Apart from anything else, this does nothing to generate more revenue to finance social protection and social assistance policy.

3.5 OTHER SOURCES OF IMPOVERISHMENT

We have seen that the level of social expenditure has been declining in Central and Eastern Europe, although state benefits were often little more than symbolic amounts under the Communist regimes, being compensated by other benefits provided by, for instance, enterprises or other social assistance funds; furthermore, many basic goods were heavily subsidised by the state.

3.5.1 Loss of Services Formerly Provided by Enterprises

Enterprises, which under the previous system distributed benefits and provided a wide range of welfare services and even leisure activities for their workers, have progressively abandoned such practices. In Poland, for example, enterprises were considered a key actor for delivering sickness benefits up until 1989; however, their share in expenditure on this type of benefit fell from 91.6 per cent in 1989 to 36.8 per cent in 1999, and will continue to decline in the future.

This marked shift throughout the region has taken place not only because new private enterprises have been understandably unwilling to emulate their socialist predecessors, but also because state-owned companies have abandoned previous practices. Only a few highly-profitable enterprises, generally multinationals, offer so-called 'fringe benefits' to their workers; since the situation of their workers is generally already better in terms of wages and employment security, this has further led to rapid differentiation between different categories of workers according to occupation and place of work.

3.5.2 Prices on Basic Goods Liberalised

Other elements such as rent controls and subsidised utility prices also represented an important anti-poverty measure in many of the countries under consideration. The World Bank and the IMF have pushed for rapid privatisation of public utilities and for price determination based on market forces rather than social considerations. This policy has worsened rather than reduced social problems.

> Undoubtedly, at the beginning of the transition the radical reduction of price subsidies was a legitimate and important element of marketisation because of the former completely distorted price system . . . The cutting of subsidies without compensation was one of the earliest and most stringent loan conditions of the World Bank in quite a few transition countries. (Ferge 2000, p. 8)

In Hungary, price subsidies and housing benefits were removed without compensation, and lost 70 per cent of their real value between 1991 and 1999 (Ferge and Tausz 2001). By the end of 2000 all former public services, such as water, gas, and electricity, price subsidies on which had represented an important service for the poorest categories of the population, had been privatised. Today they constitute a heavy burden for the most vulnerable families whose incomes have not increased in real terms to compensate this loss.

> The abolition of price subsidies was in most cases necessary and rational. Yet the consequences should have been handled carefully in order to avoid the impoverishment of millions. Compensation was firmly and explicitly denied. Particular dif-

ficulties were caused to families by the withdrawal of subsidies for formerly free (almost) public services such as water, sewage, school meals, rent, energy, and pharmaceutical products (Ferge and Tausz 2001).

Similarly, in the Czech Republic the removal of subsidies on food in 1990 and for fuel, energy, and housing in 1994 contributed to a deterioration of living standards, which the universal state compensation benefit provided from 1990 – but which rapidly lost touch with reality – did little to compensate.

Privatisation has also been carried out in accommodation, despite the fact that under Communism people paid moderate rents and eventually were able to buy their flat for a nominal price. For Eatwell et al. (2000, p. 162), 'pervasive and stubborn social exclusion [is the result of] the free working of the market mechanism in the housing area. . . this potential damage is one of the greatest threats to welfare in the transition countries'.

3.5.3 Health Services in Crisis

Shrinking public provision and funding in health care has led to a reduction in the direct public provision of health services, with partial privatisation also making an appearance. Differentiation in the provision of services has also materialised, with some being required to pay while others continue to benefit from free or subsidised provision. This has led to growing discontent.

In Poland, the reform of social insurance and health care systems started in January 1999 and led to widespread industrial action among medical professionals, disrupting the functioning of hospitals and emergency care. The changes radically modified the re-organisation of health services, access to benefits, the definition of the new role of the state, particularly in health care policy, and also imposed new 'responsibilities' on the population in this regard.

In Hungary, the public health system remained almost universal until 1991–2 when it was re-established on a social insurance basis, while the number of medical services that are subsidised or provided free of charge has progressively diminished. Privatisation came on the scene in 1992: for example, the majority of doctors became self-employed. Funding of the health fund has progressively decreased, leading to tremendous problems. Most hospitals accumulated debts, and beds, medical facilities, ambulances, and personnel had to be reduced. The available data are alarming: for example, there are only 90 hospital beds in Hungary for every ten thousand inhabitants, on average, with a much better ratio in Budapest (148 beds) and much worse ones in other counties, such as Pest (43), Fejér (66), Tolna (68), or Komárom–Esztergom (71). The wages of nurses and doctors fell in real terms (from what was an already very low level) and lost ground in relation to increasing average wages in the emerging private sector, thus leading to the general demotivation of those working in this essential sector. Patient contributions, whether official or otherwise (under the table), have become more and more important.[10]

As in other countries in the region, this process has led to social discontent, and a series of demonstrations by health sector workers. In these circumstances, many health care professionals prefer to move to the EU where they will be far better paid and have better working conditions. In Slovakia, this brain-drain phenomenon has already necessitated the employment of health care professionals from Ukraine and Belarus. In Hungary, it has not yet been decided how the health care system will be reformed, whether into a strongly public-insurance-based system, or one based more on private ownership. In the meantime, basic health indicators are among the worst in the region, with a particularly high mortality rate and low life expectancy.

Health indicators are bad in most of Central and Eastern Europe; life expectancy and infant mortality there are far below the OECD level, with the exception of the Czech Republic and Slovenia.

Even in the Czech Republic, however, the first years of transition have had an effect; for some:

the deterioration in the health of the Czech population has been alarming, as can be demonstrated by unfavourable developments in some general health indicators . . . [for example,] the rise in mortality among certain age groups of males, especially those of productive age, has been dramatic. (Hirsl et al. 1995)

Even Slovenia recorded a very high percentage of people not expected to survive beyond the age of 60 (UNDP 2001).

Certainly, some of these poor health indicators can be traced back to developments under the Communist regime, but they also show that the transition period, instead of improving these indicators by giving more weight to health policy, has only made them worse. For some, they also reflect 'the inefficiency of insurance based health systems . . . health care should be a public service' (Eatwell et al. 2000, p. 160). Moreover:

considering the rather low levels and percentages in GDP of expenditure on health, there is no doubt that there is a need in Central and Eastern Europe to continue to improve health services, something for which adequate funding is necessary, no matter what efficiency gains can be realised, or whatever budgetary constraints there are.

10. We know, for instance, that it is a widespread practice in Hungary for every – Hungarian – patient arriving in hospital to start by distributing some money to the nurses and doctors to ensure the best possible treatment. This clearly puts the poorest on an unequal footing, since we might wonder what kind of treatment will be given to those who cannot afford to 'bribe' doctors and nurses. The positive effect that may be expected as regards doctors' and nurses' incomes – compensating their low wages – are also illusory in the long run, since this widespread practice is often used by the government as an argument to justify its refusal to increase their official wages. This system clearly both encourages informal practices and increases inequalities.

The policy of health expenditure reduction and privatisation has gone in the opposite direction: the human cost still requires detailed documentation.

3.6 A SYSTEM GENERATING INEQUALITIES AND POVERTY

As a result of the factors described above – that is to say, the reduction in all social benefits, but also the fall in real wages since the early transition – poverty has escalated in all countries in the region. This contrasts starkly with the preceding period under the Communist regime where poverty was relatively unknown although living standards on average were not high, but where an egalitarian policy made sure there was no exclusion or marginalisation. However, this new phenomenon of rising poverty continues to be terra incognita concerning which we do not have sufficient reliable information.

3.6.1 The Emergence of Poverty as a New Phenomenon

The situation is particularly worrying in Bulgaria and Romania. More than 50 per cent of the population in Bulgaria was found to be living below the national poverty line in 1997 (EC 2002e, p. 27). The poverty rate rose constantly also in Romania to reach 30 per cent of the population in 2000 (EC 2002e, p. 49). Poverty is also spreading in other candidate countries. In Cyprus, the Family Expenditure Survey estimated the average poverty rate as 25.5 per cent in 1997, a figure which dramatically increases – to above 65 per cent – among pensioners (EC 2002e, p. 49). Data are scarce concerning Turkey, although it is the candidate country with the highest incidence of international measures of poverty, affecting around 30-40 per cent of the population.

In Hungary, the percentage of those living below the subsistence minimum or poverty line has tripled since 1992, increasing from 10 per cent in 1992 to more than 28 per cent in 1997, and probably to above 30 per cent in recent years. At the same time, the number of those living in relative poverty – that is, those receiving less than 50 per cent of the average income,[11] and so in danger of falling below the subsistence minimum – has been estimated to have increased from 10 per cent in 1982 to more than 15 per cent in 1998. Their incomes have also been eroded over the years (Ferge and Tausz 2001). This means that close to half of the Hungarian population is either living in poverty or close to it. In fact, according to one survey, more than one-third of

11. 'Relative' poverty (the expression used by Ferge and Tausz 2001) is here to be interpreted with caution since the average wage in Hungary does not provide a decent standard of living. Those receiving less than 50 per cent of this wage can thus be considered to be living in serious deprivation.

Hungarians experience a financial crisis at the end of each month, while only 36 per cent never have such problems (Ferge and Tausz 2001, p. 22).

A survey on living standards carried out in Estonia in 1999 shows that one-third of the population experienced difficulties, and 10 per cent said they were poor; 23 per cent did not say they were poor, but they did have difficulties making ends meet (Leppik 2000).

In the Czech Republic, poverty was estimated at 2.4 per cent in 1996. We should, however, emphasise that the lack of indexation of the subsistence minimum or poverty line meant that in the mid-1990s it represented only a symbolic amount, partly explaining why most Czech citizens appear to be above the poverty line. It is significant that minimum pensions were fixed above this amount. In 1995, the official subsistence minimum was only 35 per cent of per capita consumption, and less than 40 per cent of average household income. It has been increased since then but union leaders have complained that it still does not shield families from deprivation.

Moreover, poverty figures differ radically according to method of calculation and the level of poverty which is retained. For instance, when the subsistence minimum was increased slightly to CZK35 in 1992, the number of people below this level increased by more than 5 per cent. The same phenomenon was observed after the increase in the subsistence minimum to CZK50 in 1996. Slight changes in the calculation method of the subsistence minimum could thus paint a quite different picture of poverty in the Czech Republic.

Even in Slovenia, where poverty has fallen slightly since 1993, critical situations have developed. The minimum level of income intended to ensure survival has fallen gradually since 1993 (its level was fixed in 1992) because of inappropriate indexation mechanisms. This combined with the situation in the labour market to worsen the material and social conditions of marginal groups. This is why the Social Security Act amended in 2001 raised the level of minimum income so that it would suffice to cover minimum living costs. Still, according to Genovefa Ruzic of the Slovenian government, 'the threat of poverty affected 13.8 per cent of the Slovenian population in 2002' (Brussels conference, 5–6 December 2002, EC 2002e). Moreover, when poverty is expressed in terms of a wider and more complex definition – that is, encompassing various other forms of deprivation, such as poor health, lack of social contact, information, knowledge, values, and so on – the situation looks much bleaker: for example, there is 45 per cent functional adult illiteracy in Slovenia (UNDP 2001).

Some population groups have been particularly hard hit. The deterioration of the situation of the Roma minority has been dramatic, a phenomenon which has not been properly documented or received sufficient attention. While Roma living conditions improved in the 1980s, especially after they were compelled to undertake paid regular jobs by the state – with a successful outcome for a majority of them – their situation significantly worsened from the start of the transition, since they often were among the first to be made redundant and to experience social exclusion in terms of employment, income, and housing. While we have seen that the proportion of those below the subsistence minimum may have reached more than 30 per cent in the Hungarian population as a whole, it reached 60 per cent among the Roma (Ferge and Tadeusz 2001): 84 per cent of Roma children under seven years of age, and 70 per cent of children of school age, are poor. Poverty is also extremely high among Roma families in the Czech Republic (Hirsl et al. 1995).

In Hungary, poverty is particularly prevalent among young people (those below 30 years of age): nearly one-third of them are now below the poverty line. Poverty is also a long-term phenomenon for young urban families, while young rural families are particularly hard hit in the agricultural regions of the East and the South, where large-scale industries have disappeared and agriculture does not provide enough to attain a decent standard of living.

Young people are one of the most vulnerable groups in almost every country in the region.

In Poland, relative poverty (measured by the percentage of people earning below 50 per cent of the average wage) was higher among women, at 16 per cent in 1999, compared to 11 per cent for men and 13.4 per cent for the population as a whole. In 1992 less than 6 per cent of the population had been ranked in this lowest income group.

In addition to the destitution resulting from unemployment in the candidate countries, there is also destitution among some of the employed, the so-called 'working poor'. It was found that over 25 per cent of poverty in Hungary, but also the Czech Republic and other countries, was associated with unemployment. Working poverty affects all the countries under consideration here. In Romania 28 per cent of workers were in poverty, while in Latvia and Estonia the rates were close to 20 per cent. However, in Poland and Lithuania working poverty represented more than 70 per cent, while in all other Central and Eastern European Countries the figure was over 40 per cent; 37 per cent of Turkish workers were also found to be in poverty, accounting for 88 per cent of Turkish poverty as a whole (EC 2002e, comparative table on p. 190). One notable source of working poverty, in addition to very low wages, is deteriorating employment conditions – such as increasing recourse to poorly protected self-employment – as described in Chapter 2.

Of course we must temper these figures by mentioning the existence of a generalised reliance on additional incomes earned in the informal economy, which certainly helps many citizens on the verge of deprivation. This is widespread in Hungary, Poland, and elsewhere. At the same time, we do not know how much additional income is earned in this precarious fashion. Moreover, opportunities in the informal economy are very unequal in different parts of the country: naturally, those living in cities are much better off in this respect. Poverty is mainly concentrated – above 60 per cent of the total poor – in rural areas (EC 2002e, p. 208).

Those who cannot rely on such alternative sources of income generally remain in poverty for a long time. As already mentioned, reliance on the informal economy has the added effect of reducing social security contributions even further and so the ability of the budget to provide adequate social protection, thus leading to a vicious circle that must be broken as soon as possible and by all possible means.

3.6.2 Growing Inequalities

Social inequalities have rapidly increased in all Central and Eastern European countries. In Hungary, between 1982 and 2000 the gap between the lowest and the highest paid increased from four times to more than eight times. The Gini coefficient normally used to measure inequality also increased dramatically, from 21 per cent to 34 per cent. Inequalities also increased in the Czech Republic, with economically inactive people being hardest hit by economic 'shock therapy', as pensions and social allowances did not keep up with wage increases. Differentiation has increased considerably in terms of income and living standards, with a much greater risk of social exclusion (Vylitova 2000). Similar trends have been observed in all other candidate countries. The situation can be summarised by the following conclusion by Martin Evans, who stresses the need for an appropriate measure of poverty (not only in relative but also in absolute terms): 'there is no sign of the convergence of candidate countries towards the EU in the area of social exclusion' (Brussels Conference, 5–6 December 2002).

3.7 TOWARDS THE PROGRESSIVE EXCLUSION OF THE SOCIAL PARTNERS?

In the EU, the social partners are traditionally invited to play an important role in the designing of social protection policies, and have even become the main actors in the management of social security funds, as in France. This role of the social partners is reflected in the different policy documents delivered by European institutions in the field of social protection. The recent EC document on pensions, for instance, underlines that 'long-term stability of pension schemes can only be guaranteed if pension reforms are based on broad social consensus which involves all relevant actors'.[12]

12. Cover note from the Social Protection Committee to the Council, 2001.

The involvement of the social partners can thus be regarded as a distinctive feature of the European model of social protection, which should also be considered by the future member states within the framework of the current reform of their social protection systems. The situation in this respect is rather complex and seems to vary greatly in the different candidate countries. Some countries seem to have taken a neo-liberal approach, which requires the progressive exclusion of the social partners from all decision-making bodies, including those concerned with social protection. This seems to have been the case in the Czech Republic in the first period of transition (the Klaus government), and was definitely the case in Hungary between 1998 and 2002 (when the Orbán government was defeated by the Hungarian Socialist Party). Many similarities could in fact be drawn between these two governments.

In 1998 the new Hungarian government decided to fundamentally reform the functioning of the social security bodies by pushing out the social partners hitherto responsible for the management of the funds. This reform reflects that government's strategy of keeping unilateral control of these funds and managing health and pension insurance without interference.

This represented a major step backward for social dialogue, but also for the way social insurance was handled. Social security boards had been regulated since 1991 (by Act LXXXIV of 1991) and had been functioning since 1993 following the election of social security representatives. The last elections of employees' representatives to seats in the so-called 'self-governments of health insurance and pension insurance' took place in 1997. Contribution and benefit levels are decided by legislation, as regulated by Act LXXX of 1997. In a government decree – that is, in a very authoritarian way, without consultation with the social partners – the Orbán government decided to assign control of the health and pension insurance funds to someone in the Prime Minister's Office, after the previous director-in-chief of the National Health Insurance Administration had been relieved of her post. We might wonder whether this type of authoritarian decision-making on such an important – and public – issue as social protection is compatible with the values of the European Social Model, and whether it can generate the type of social protection that we would like to see emerging in the future.

Another major shift took place at the end of 2000 when the government decided to change the one-year national budget into a two-year budget, and this without any prior consultation with the social partners or other social actors. This precluded discussion of social expenditure, despite the significant fall in the levels of social protection and social assistance, a situation which cries out for a public debate and consultation with the social partners and civil society in general (for instance, those NGOs working with the poor). The government would not have had to report back to parliament before the end of 2002. This weakening of the democratic process and democratic institutions is very worrying, especially in a context in which social issues continue to be considered marginal in comparison with economic growth, and inequalities are increasing. The change of government in 2002 may change this trend.

Other examples in the region show that the social partners, despite the existence of tripartite institutions, have rarely been involved in discussions about the budget and social expenditure. Moreover, the social partners have had almost no input in reform of social protection and pensions in Central and Eastern European countries and so there has been no democratic debate. In EU countries, the social partners are direct actors in pension reform. Broad agreement on such reforms has always been reached in countries with long consensual traditions, such as the Netherlands, Finland, and Denmark. National consensus has also been achieved in France, the UK, Italy, Germany, and Spain (Toledo pact). In Ireland, pension policy has been, since the 1980s, the product of wide consultations with the social partners and other interested parties, through both the tripartite Pensions Board and the partnership process. According to the ILO (ILO 2002), the main drawback of social protection systems in the candidate countries has been the lack of consultation of social partners on social protection and of NGOs on poverty issues.

Nevertheless, some positive examples can also be observed in the accession countries. In Slovenia, the social partners are members of most health and social insurance institutions, as well as of the pension and invalidity board, and of the unemployment agency board.

The same imbalance between positive and negative developments can be found in the Mediterranean candidate countries. In Cyprus, the social partners are part of all health and social security institutions, which are all tripartite in nature. Malta also involves the social partners in all the debates and important reforms concerning social protection. By contrast, in Turkey all decisions in this field continue to be taken unilaterally by the government, and the social partners are barely involved in the designing of the national budget, and play no part in the management of health and social security institutions.

3.8 THE RISKS OF PRIVATE FUNDING: THE EXAMPLE OF PENSION REFORM

3.8.1 The Magic Formula of the 'Three-Pillar Pension Funds'

In both the EU and the advanced industrialised countries in general there has been growing concern about the sustainability of pension systems dominated by 'pay as you go' (PAYG) arrangements, and reforms have been carried out to implement so-called 'fully-funded schemes'. The difference is relatively simple. In a fully-funded pension scheme employees' and employers' contri-

butions are used to purchase financial assets that pay for the pensions of contributors (former employees) in retirement. By contrast, in the 'pay as you
go' system, current old-age pensions are paid out from the contributions of
current employees, and are thus directly related to the dependency ratio and the
balance between total current pensions and total current contributions. The system is under growing pressure due to a combination of factors: population
ageing due to declining fertility and increased life expectancy, resulting in a
worsening dependency ratio between pensioners and employees (that is,
more old-age pensioners per employee); growing unemployment; and a disproportion between the level of contributions and the size and length of contributions.

A move away from public pension schemes

International institutions have advised the replacement of the public 'pay as
you go' or 'benefit-defined' system, at least for the most part, by a fully funded private and 'contribution-defined' system, with individual pensions being
the direct product of lifetime contributions and by the yield on the assets they
are used to buy, which in fact represents the privatisation of pension provision, with examples of this policy being found in Chile, Argentina, Mexico,
the USA, and the UK. Since the beginning of the 1990s, there has been a
spread of variants of the Chilean pension system, often recommended by the
World Bank as a model in its campaign to persuade governments to move
towards a multi-pillar or multi-tier system, something that they did systematically in Central and Eastern Europe during the first years of reform.

After having initially strengthened 'pay as you go' schemes in the early
1990s, almost all Central and Eastern European countries then rushed to
implement the magic formula. They put in place multi-tier pension systems in
which the 'guaranteed' state pension – the first tier – was reduced to a rather
modest amount, while the second tier consists of an individualised insurance-
based pension handled by a private pension fund, and the third tier is voluntary, through personal savings or arrangements between workers and
employers.

By 1997, Hungary and Poland had passed laws to cut state pensions and to
establish privately funded schemes. Similar reforms were passed in countries
such as the Czech Republic, Estonia, Lithuania, and Latvia.

In the Polish pension reform of 1997 the authorities, on the direct advice –
and also funding – of the World Bank, devised a three-pillar pension plan in
which the first pillar would be a means-tested minimum pension. In operation
since January 1999, the second pillar involves mandatory participation in
freely chosen, privately managed pension funds, so that the value of the pension will depend on the rate of return on investments made by private insurance companies. The third pillar is a voluntary plan to be worked out between

employers and workers. The main difficulty with this scheme is that the basic 'guaranteed' pension would be very low, at 28 per cent of the average wage. It also makes workers' incomes much more insecure, because it is dependent on the hypothetical success of fund managers. At the same time, the value of the basic state pension is likely to decline further since it will be of concern only to a disadvantaged – and therefore relatively voiceless – minority (Standing 1999).

Hungary was the first country to introduce a mandatory funded pillar, replacing part of the PAYG system, in a move similar to that of Argentina. Since 1 July 1998 all those entering employment for the first time have been legally obliged to pay 25 per cent of their pension contributions, which amount to 30 per cent of their wage, into private pension schemes, with the other 70 per cent going into the public pension plan (those already employed could choose between the two). The World Bank provided a nine-year, USD 150 million loan (with a three-year grace period) to assist this reform (*Financial Times*, 30 January 1998). Among the stated objectives were lower public spending and the enlargement of the private capital market through the development of a pension fund industry. When the second pillar was introduced in 1998, it appeared to be a great success, with 2 700 000 employees entering into it at that time, that is, 70 per cent of active earners: a huge publicity campaign and people's desperate belief that they could obtain a better future are the main explanations of this. Thirty private pension funds appeared, but the bulk of assets are concentrated in only a few (Borbély 2000).

A number of problems have already appeared, above all very high operating costs and a general lack of transparency (particularly difficult for older pensioners who are not very well informed about the complex new private coverage systems). The initial euphoria has now given way to the apprehension, widely debated in the media, that the introduction of the new system might have been in vain. Moreover, the system already appears to be far too dependent on economic and monetary performance, as well as government fiscal policy (Borbély 2000).

The World Bank also had strong requirements about the reform of the first pillar (after reform of the law in 1996); for example, substantial changes were requested in the criteria of eligibility. The age limit was increased considerably: from 60 years of age for women and 62 for men, it became 65 years of age for all. The pension indexation system of the first pillar was also modified under pressure from the World Bank (Borbély 2000). Previously, indexation had taken place according to wage rises and a posteriori. In accordance with the changes introduced in the 1996 law, since 2000 Swiss indexation has been applied, with half of the rise in pensions calculated on the basis of wage rises, and the other half on the basis of inflation. This system is advantageous for pensioners only in a period of high inflation, but since in Hungary the aim is to reduce inflation (since real wages recently began to rise, pensioners are again the most vulnerable group), pensioners will suffer. On the government side, however, considerable savings can be made in this way.

The Slovenian approach was similar to the Hungarian one. Pensions and social allocations in other candidate countries have also suffered from poor indexation mechanisms: 'in Romania, there was little indexation, so that in 2000 pensions stood at only 50 per cent of their 1990 level' (Winfried Schmähl, at the conference 'The modernisation of social protection in the candidate countries').

To summarise, the trend is for the first pillar to be allowed to lose consistency, with the result that it has often fallen below minimum ILO standards (as emphasised at the Brussels conference, 5–6 December 2002), so contradicting the basic principle of pension systems, which should be to guarantee a minimum acceptable pension, however the financial markets might be performing.

We must emphasise that the three-pillar approach was also the one adopted by European institutions, although the importance of the public scheme was also stressed:

> Pension systems comprise both public and private schemes and are usually built on three pillars: basic public schemes, occupational schemes and individual pension plans. Each of these pillars has its specific advantages and drawbacks. However, in all member states, the largest share of older people's income is provided through public pension schemes. (EC 2000c, p. 2)

The ILO, despite its initial opposition, has also rallied to the notion of the three-tier model: 'the ILO, initially critical of the Chilean model and moving away from PAYG pensions because of the insecurities involved, moved to propose a three-tier model (resisting the term "pillar")' (Standing 1999, p. 274), a nuance that might also appear to be more symbolic than anything else in the face of World Bank dominance in this area, although certainly significant differences between the ILO and the World Bank do exist (ILO 1995, 2000, 2002).

An obligatory second private pillar

Mainly inspired by its experiences in Latin America – first in the Chilean pension reforms, and then in a similar exercise in other countries of the region, and variants in Argentina and Bolivia through privately managed pension funds – the World Bank has itself progressively evolved towards more and more reliance on private funding: 'the World Bank has shifted from presenting the public pension as the first and main pillar to presenting the private one as the first of two mandatory pillars' (Standing 1999, p. 274).

Accordingly, in several countries – including Poland and also Estonia – the second pillar has been made obligatory despite the opposition of the general population and also the social partners. In Poland, 'the second obligatory pillar was imposed by the World Bank and was very much criticised' (Uscinska 2000).

These developments contrast strikingly with the situation prevailing in all EU countries, where the second – or 'occupational' – pillar is rarely obligatory. Moreover, in many countries it is the result of a collective agreement between the social partners (at either enterprise or sectoral level); for example, in the Netherlands and Denmark second-pillar occupational arrangements (which cover more than 80 per cent of the working population) are based on sector-wide collective agreements, where nothing can be achieved without the acceptance and support of the social partners. Pension schemes of the second pillar are also based on enterprise or sectoral collective agreements in Italy. Second tiers of the statutory pension system in France, Finland, and Luxembourg are regulated within bipartite or tripartite institutions. Only in France and Finland is the second pillar compulsory, but the social partners are the main actors in the reform and directly regulate the system.

Even in the current process of pension reform in the EU, we are thus far from obligatory private pensions funds imposed unilaterally by the state and then left entirely to the private sector.

To summarise, the problem does not lie in the three-pillar structure itself – especially if implemented in a balanced way. The problem is that the introduction of this 'magic formula' has led to an unbalanced system, with the two so-called 'defined-contribution' pillars, dependent on private investment and financial markets, increasingly being allowed to dominate, while the role of the public pillar has become marginal, below the minimum required to ensure decent pensions.

3.8.2 Social Protection Dependent on Economic Performance

In order to ensure that social expenditure does not exceed economic and financial reserves, one of the World Bank's principal aims – also exported to Central and Eastern Europe – is that social protection should become much more dependent on economic performance; the need to build 'social capital' is also stressed.

The shift to private pension funds was also motivated by the low capitalisation of pension funds in Central and Eastern Europe. In this regard, fully-funded pensions have been presented as a panacea, bringing three main advantages: (i) they would be more sound financially because managed by private entities; (ii) they would bring a higher return on employees' contributions, since they would be invested in the stock markets; and (iii) at the same time, they would contribute to develop financial markets by channelling pension contributions, as well as additional savings, an aspect that has been seen by many as particularly attractive in the context of the emerging capital markets in Central and Eastern Europe.

These arguments, however, seem tenuous. First, the real return on the stock exchange depends very much on the starting situation and the market's potential: for example, the high return obtained on the stock exchange in Chile seems to have been mainly due to fortuitous timing, as the switch to a funded system was implemented at a time when the stock exchange was undervalued. The same market registered negative rates of return in 1995–6, as well as during the crises of 1987 and 1998 (Eatwell et al. 2000). While the stock markets of Central and Eastern Europe indeed have great growth potential their development is unlikely to be uniform: 'in other words, if investment in equities can confer an advantage, they are bringing a parallel disadvantage, which is greater risk and volatility of performance' (Eatwell et al. 2000). After twelve years of transition and falling real wages and pensions, we might wonder whether introducing risk into future pensioners' incomes is the right thing to do. Moreover, an important concentration process in the first few years since the establishment of the pension funds has reduced the range of funds available, with the possible exception of those in the Czech Republic, which offer a very wide range of rates of return, but at the expense of additional exposure to risk; in fact, as could have been predicted, a number of pension funds have gone bankrupt (see section 3.8.3). This certainly requires a more balanced system, and significant government regulation.

The argument concerning the influence of pension funds over the development of financial markets also seems to have been overemphasised because at least some of the savings imposed by participation in pension funds at the expense of PAYG schemes simply goes to replace earlier voluntary savings. Moreover, it is far from sure that additional savings will be matched by additional investments, especially in transition economies where the financial infrastructure required for the successful operation of private pension funds is lacking.

3.8.3 Excessive Reliance on Private Companies

The reliance on private funding is most extreme in the pension system introduced in the Czech Republic in 1997. In supplementary pension insurance the link is clearly made between the contributions of participants and future pensions, and the system is run by private institutions which are profit-based and operating in a competitive environment. In these circumstances, we might wonder what the distribution of earned profits – made on the contributions of future pensioners – will be between shareholders and those taking out the insurance. Moreover, although pension plans are fully funded – that is, they should ensure full coverage of the acquired rights by the fund's assets – this is far from certain in practice since the funds are generally invested in the capital markets. In fact, several insurance companies have collapsed and with them the hopes of pensioners that their pensions will be fully honoured despite years of contributions. Such failures are often the result of corrupt managers; indeed, many of the new private pension funds were fraudulent from the outset. Similarly in Hungary, it is fairly certain that many private funds, whether voluntary or not, will go bankrupt (Borbély 2000). An increasing number of countries in the region are already complaining about their social security systems, dominated by private insurance and a major shift towards market mechanisms.

The system is also a source of inequality. While citizens have the opportunity to choose from various pension plans and insurance companies, as in the Czech Republic and elsewhere, such decisions – which can be very difficult – very much depend on the situation of the individuals concerned; it is clear that some categories of people have all possible information at their disposal on the basis of which to choose the most reliable companies, while others – generally the poorest – are less informed and thus finally bear more risk, although they should bear less.

A new pension system was also introduced in Hungary in 1997. One of its main drawbacks is that funds are often based on the firm or sector (this accounted for around 20 per cent of the whole market in 2000). As a result, many new funds do not have an adequate financial basis to ensure viability and so the payment of pensions in the future.

In Estonia, the government launched its pension reform in 1997, this too based on the 'three-pillar approach'. As a result, there are already eight private life insurance companies operating in Estonia, four of them having been licensed to sell pension insurance policies that give an entitlement to tax deductions. The introduction of the second pillar, also a mandatory funded pension scheme, took place in 2001.

This increasing reliance on the private sector is worrying in countries where there is a lack of private pension provisions as well as other forms of private financial investments.

Still with the aim of improving the balance between contributions and pensions, pensionable ages of men and women have been radically increased in all the countries with which we are concerned. In the Czech Republic, the retirement age has been increased to 62 for men and to 57–61 for women according to the number of children raised. In Estonia, the State Allowances Act of June 1994 (amended in December 1998) will also be modified in order to equalise the pension ages of men and women at 63 years. These changes in the pension age obviously represent a step backwards in terms of working conditions.

3.8.4 The Discretionary Role of the State

Fund management

It is not only the predominant place assigned to the private sector in the pension reform which causes concern, but also – in some cases – the dubious and discretionary role of the state in the management of particular pension funds. For instance, in the Czech Republic the government was severely criticised when, between 1993 and 1995, it used part of a surplus (of 20 billion crowns) amassed from pension contributions to cover other government expenditures rather than to create a reserve fund to cover future exigencies in the obligatory pension insurance system. The idea of managing these contributions through a public social insurance institute external to the government budget was envisaged at that time. Similarly in Hungary, the discretionary management of pension funds by the new neo-liberal government (1998–2002) after the social partners had been expelled from the system may also lead to the discretionary use of contributions. Since 1998 the money has for the most part been invested in government securities and so is very closely tied to the aims of the Government and of the Central Bank, and therefore subject to political instability. For Szilvia Borbély (2000), 'pension funds became a tool for the Government and its policy . . . although a government can come and go, it can still influence the pensions and saving capacity of the population'. The social partners have repeatedly requested that the first pillar be put outside the control of the government to be regulated by a self-governing system composed of the social partners and other economic and social actors.

Supervising private insurance companies

The fact that the establishment of a pension fund must in some countries be generally approved by a state authority which supervises the fund's operations and activities can lead to collusion between government officials and the managers of these companies. Certainly, the hasty shift towards reliance on the private sector in such a vital area as pensions has not taken into consideration the lack of consolidation of the state, especially in newly emerging democracies, and the extensive role of informal or hidden practices in transition economies. The privatisation scandals in Central and Eastern Europe, for instance in Hungary, and the example of the pyramid funds that emerged in Albania, partly with the blessing of the state, should certainly lead to more caution in the implementation of such schemes. Again it must be stressed that the same reforms do not necessarily have the same results in EU member states, that have long decades of experience with social security systems, and in candidate countries, that do not have the same experience and culture, in respect of either social protection systems in free market economies or private entrepreneurship and responsibility.

To summarise, not only has the public pillar become inconsistent, but the state has also failed in many candidate countries to ensure the necessary monitoring of the two other pillars run by private investors. Here the right balance must be found by the state between leaving the necessary autonomy to private investors while monitoring whether their activities do not contradict the basic principles behind pension systems.

3.8.5 Pension Reforms More Extreme than in EU Countries

For many analysts, pension reforms in Central and Eastern Europe so far have been much more extreme than in EU countries: 'despite the fact that a similar trend is also observed in the EU countries, especially towards private schemes, they have been more cautious about pension reform than Latin American and Central and Eastern European countries' (Standing 1999, p. 273).

Nevertheless, transition economies have to face the same demographic and fiscal considerations as those currently afflicting the developed market economies of the EU. The 'multi-pillar' approach has been systematically adopted in Central and Eastern Europe, although with variants, but the trend is definitely towards a progressive reduction of the role of the state in pension schemes. The most worrying trend is undoubtedly towards the provision of a very low base pension by the state, generally on a means-tested basis.

There were other alternatives, however. For instance, one option would have been to implement a financial tightening of the existing ('benefit-defined') PAYG system in order to eliminate the burden on public finances, or at least to reduce it to a bearable level, an approach which is being followed in a few EU countries – such as the UK, Germany and Spain – and which consists mainly in raising the retirement age as well as increasing social security contributions.

At the same time, if a fully funded system is chosen it could also be centralised, that is, promoted by public policy. The usual approach – or at least the one privileged by international monetary institutions – however, is a system run by competing private funds.

However, preserving a strong 'pay as you go' system has been associated with a rapidly mounting fiscal imbalance; for the World Bank, 'they generate a pension burden'. The maintenance of the state as main actor is also considered to be counterproductive. Moreover, many advantages have been presented to justify such a shift in terms of higher rates of return, the development of financial markets and corporate governance, and the promotion of domestic savings.

Many experts have contested the superiority of one system over the other, however: for Eatwell et al. (2000):

the move from a 'pay as you go' system to a fully funded system is politically rather than economically motivated . . . it is a question of the importance attached implicitly to individual choice and risk-taking; to the transparency of individual contributions and entitlements, and to state withdrawal from the economy . . . [Furthermore] the shift is partly unnecessary, to the extent that the PAYG system can be – and should be – reformed so as to be entirely self-financed, and only that part dependent on budgetary financing needs to be converted into open and funded liabilities.

Similarly for the European Commission: 'according to the current state of analysis no type of pension scheme (pay as you go vs. funded, private vs. public, defined benefits vs. defined contributions) can be regarded as inherently superior to another'.[13]

In other words, the move towards fully-funded or even majority private funding – at least until the state system is reformed – is not inevitable, contrary to what is being advised and often imposed on transition countries, not to mention current dominant thinking in the EU.

One can only conclude that pension reform in Central and Eastern Europe, more extreme than in EU countries, was imposed by international monetary institutions at least in great part on political grounds.[14] This would not be a problem if such an extreme shift did not contradict some basic principles of the social protection systems that have been developed, at least so far, in the EU. One might even speculate that the World Bank was using Central and Eastern Europe as a means of shaping the European Union of tomorrow, an aim only half hidden in the following remark on pension reforms made by a senior economist of the World Bank: 'EU countries have a lot to learn from current pension reforms in Central and Eastern Europe'.[15] For the same economist, 'accession countries [have] embraced multi-pillar reforms, as well as more radical approaches in PAYG pillars, more readily than EU members. Accession countries should be assisted in this endeavour by quicker reforms within the EU' (Rutkowski 2000, p. 7).

Such statements contrast with the reality of these reforms, especially with regard to the high risks built into the model due to over-reliance on capital markets and individual companies. Moreover, whilst PAYG pensions tend to involve some redistribution in favour of the poor – of course sometimes to an unsustainable extent – funded schemes could exacerbate the inequality of income distribution among the working population, since the poorer members of society typically make less adequate provision for their

13. Cover note from the Social Protection Committee to the Council, 2001, p. iii.

14. Based on the author's experience over more than eight years advising governments in the region. The term 'imposed' is unfortunately not too strong and describes a particularly sad aspect of the years of transition.

15. Michael Rutkowski, World Bank, at the Conference on Economic and Social Dimensions of EU Enlargement, Brussels, 16 November 2000.

retirement, not having the same access to and culture of understanding financial markets.

To summarise, not only have pension reforms in the candidate countries of Central and Eastern Europe been more radical than those currently being implemented in the EU, but also they have been asked to implement them in a very short time, often only a few months, although normally a shift of such magnitude requires a transitional period so as to avoid any budgetary imbalances.

3.9 A POSSIBLE ALTERNATIVE APPROACH

3.9.1 Recovering the Original Aim of Social Protection

Throughout the transition, changes in social protection systems have been motivated by the need to keep the budget under control, and thus to reduce social expenditure. For Macha (2001, p. 21), 'social reforms in the Czech Republic have focused especially on effectiveness and rationalisation rather than on the fight against poverty or social exclusion'. Similarly for Hirsl et al. (1995, p. 1), 'the content of social policy was determined by a purely fiscal consideration: to keep the government budget balanced'.

Many experts have tried to justify the fall in social benefits in general by the need to increase the funds dedicated to unemployment benefits within the internal redistribution of budgetary lines within welfare expenditure. If unemployment benefits are increased, social benefits should decrease proportionately so that the social expenditure budget remains balanced. This argument is often justified on the basis of the examples of Finland, and Spain, which seem to be characterised by very high unemployment and thus high expenditure on unemployment benefits, but more limited expenditure in other areas of social protection (old-age, sickness, family, and so on).

We believe that the debate on social protection should not be confined to such budgetary and thus automatic arbitration systems, and that the challenges and significance of social expenditure should be discussed more extensively in a wider debate. This sort of implicit budgetary link between employment and social security – or any other budgetary items – must clearly be removed, since social protection, whether unemployment is at a high level or not, and regardless of the level of unemployment benefit, should be used to combat the various forms of social exclusion. Otherwise, social benefits and social protection will be directly dependent upon labour market performance: for example, a household already affected by the unemployment of one of its members would in addition experience a fall in social benefits. As emphasised by Eatwell at al. (2000, p. 156), 'the question is not affordability, but willingness to pay'. Moreover, Slovenia, for instance, has shown that a policy aimed at maintaining both unemployment benefits and social benefits at a high level can serve as a good strategy for improving both economic and social performance: maintaining social protection can be a good way of improving human capital for the sake of future competitiveness.

Despite this, the World Bank continues to assert that 'social protection expenditure and the aim of reducing inequality at any price are unsustainable in Slovenia' (Andrew Rogerson, Brussels conference, 5–6 December 2002).

3.9.2 The Missing Spring

So far, reformers in Central and Eastern Europe have been obsessed with keeping the budget under control, with the result that social expenditure has been dramatically reduced. Little consideration has been given to the fact that the collection of resources (taxes and other contributions) could have been improved in order to maintain the necessary level of social protection. This could certainly be achieved through concrete measures aimed, for example, at reducing the size of the informal sector, reducing capital flight, and widening the tax base. In other words, revenues should be increased to fund social expenditure in contrast to the current policy of cutting social expenditure, which is already very low as a percentage of GDP. The current policy of keeping social benefits low promotes the development of the informal economy, which in turn leads to the further reduction of revenues. This policy, systematically advised by the World Bank in the context of a burgeoning informal economy, the fight against which should become the principal aim of every government in the region, is thus also bad economics since it generates less revenue and continues to leave part of the population outside the economic mainstream in the course of EU accession. The region's economic stabilisation programmes are thus lacking an important spring.

3.9.3 Basing Competitiveness on More Social Protection

Many studies have tried to document the possible effects of the restrictive social protection policies followed in the first years of reforms in Central and Eastern Europe. In the Czech Republic, for example, it has led to 'a deterioration of the crucial conditions for social reproduction, above all in such fields as housing, health care and education' (Hirsl et al. 1995, p. 1). We have also seen in a number of other countries what effects the abandonment of the more universal delivery of such essential services as health and education has had on human capital and labour force skills, essential elements of economic competitiveness. Slovenia's policy in this regard was clearly aimed at preserving a well developed social protection system that would ensure the retention of a highly skilled and motivated labour force. The country's competitive situation depends in large part on this policy.

General recipes must also be avoided. As an example, increasing the pension age has become a leitmotiv in all pension reforms – including those of the current EU – often without much economic foundation. Although longer life expectancy must be taken into account in fixing the pension age, this must be done in a flexible way – that is, with the worker deciding whether to retire or to remain in work – and not be imposed as a universal solution in pension reforms. However, this is precisely what has been done in all candidate countries, where the increase in the pension age has been considered as the first unavoidable element of reform. It was a step backwards with regard to workers' rights, and in many cases has been counterproductive.

As explained by Francis Kessler (Brussels conference, 5–6 December 2002), 'increasing the pension age is far from being a solution because in practice, due to the low labour market demand for older workers, it means that those between 55 and 65, instead of retiring on a pension, either become unemployed or receive such low pay that they have to be supported by the state.' In short, the pension burden is transferred to unemployment or social benefits.

In such a context, it is also amazing that the European Commission – on the cover page of its main social policy publication – strongly presents increasing the pension age as a panacea.[16]

3.10 THE DRAWBACKS OF THE EU'S STRATEGY IN THE FUTURE MEMBER STATES

As early as 1996, the EC Comité des sages (EC 1996) emphasised that:

> Europe was in greater danger than it realised and the 'social deficit' was fraught with menace. Europe cannot be built on unemployment and social exclusion, nor on an inadequate sense of citizenship. Europe will be a Europe for all, or it will be nothing at all.

3.10.1 The Field Left of the World Bank during the Years of Transition

The reforms of social protection systems in Central and Eastern Europe have been promoted and in most cases led by international monetary institutions, and in particular by the World Bank. We have seen that they have been pushing governments to curtail benefits existing under the previous regime, which

---

16. 'Pushing-up the retirement age', cover title of the EC Newsletter *Social Agenda*, Issue No. 1 (April 2002), DG Employment and Social Affairs, Brussels.

they considered much too generous and out of place in modern free-market economies. According to Júlia Szalai (1999, p. 28):

> The IMF and the World Bank have had a dominant role in shaping Hungary's economic and social policy. Different Hungarian governments felt obliged to follow their rigid prescriptions. Considerations of fighting the budget deficit and inflation have guided the reforms in welfare provisions which ultimately concluded in the devaluation of such important benefit schemes as pensions and family allowances.

This view is shared by other observers (Borbély 2000).

It is clear that these institutions represent the principles of the old 'Washington consensus', which are very different from the EU principles of solidarity, public responsibility, and equal rights and opportunities for all citizens.[17] Their policies are therefore not appropriate for countries that will soon join the European Union and apply its basic principles, values, rules, and practices.[18]

The absence of a message from the EU

In light of the activities of the World Bank and the IMF it is particularly regrettable that the EU has not sought to promote its Social Model in the region during the first years of reform, thereby familiarising the candidate countries with what would be expected from them as member states. It was not until the late 1990s that European institutions – within the framework of pre-accession negotiations – started to pay due attention to social protection in Central and Eastern Europe. Moreover, the European Commission did not alert the candidate countries concerning the risks entailed by the shift of emphasis of their social protection reforms and their possible divergence from the social protection model of the EU.

The ILO seems to have been the only organisation during this period to have proposed an alternative to the neo-liberal model supplied by the World Bank, though with little success. Some messages started to come through from different European institutions, and also individual experts, in the late 1990s concerning the potentially high social costs of transition and enlargement. The alarm was raised by the European Parliament (Briefing 39) in 1998 when it requested that 'the applicant countries adjust to the European social model if social peace is to be ensured'; the same request was formulated by

17. We saw in Chapter 1 that international monetary institutions such as the World Bank and the IMF have adopted a policy much closer to neo-liberal theories and views.

18. More fundamentally it means that the World Bank's values and principles differ significantly from those which make up the European Social Model – not only on social protection but also in other areas, as we shall see in other chapters of this book – and advise a different policy. EU countries which are members of these international monetary institutions – which implies some say in the decision-making process – will at one point have to address this issue, while the European institutions themselves will have to evaluate their relations with these organisations.

the President of the European Parliament who 'reminded the governments of the applicant countries to consolidate their social protection models'. However, these broad statements have not been followed by specific requirements.

3.10.2 A Weak and Ambiguous Emphasis

Surprisingly, in the course of the negotiation process so far the European Commission has not emphasised the adverse social developments which we have described. It is paradoxical that almost nothing has been written or said on, for example, poverty and social exclusion in the future member states, worrying trends with regard to major health indicators (life expectancy, infant mortality, health services, and so on), or even on the growth of inequalities. Only in 2002–3 are the first reports on social exclusion to be requested of the candidate countries. Other organisations, such as the UNDP (through its generally excellent Human Development Reports), the ILO, the OECD, and even in some cases the World Bank have all mentioned these problems. Only at the end of 2002 – that is, when negotiations on social issues were already over – that the first reports on social protection in candidate countries were issued by the European Commission and a conference organised on this issue (EC 2002e).

For many external observers, social protection has been neglected in the current negotiation process. The European Commission in particular has been criticised for its lack of strategy or failure to respond in this area, and even for its implicit approval of certain ambiguous social protection reforms. For instance, the Hungarian sociologist Zsuzsa Ferge, who has carefully analysed all the regular reports from the Commission on the progress towards accession (these reports are initially partly prepared by the candidate countries themselves, but are endorsed and also drafted by the EC which puts them into circulation as EC documents), has been very critical of the lack of attention given to social protection. She emphasises that there is no significant chapter on social protection and that the most burning issues have been left out; when the problems of social protection are addressed, it is done very much from a neo-liberal perspective, with the emphasis on financial stability, the level of public expenditure, the liberalisation of prices, and the privatisation of social protection services: 'The main issues of concern for social protection here [for the EC] are financial stability, the level of public expenditure, and the regulation of prices' (Ferge 2000). With regard to pensions, she observes that 'in a majority of the countries under review [9 out of the 10 candidate countries from Central and Eastern Europe] the privatisation of pensions is approved, or encouraged more or less directly' (Ferge 2000, p. 6). She also emphasises that the privatisation of health care has been approved when it has taken place

and encouraged in those places where it has not yet occurred. The privatisation of health care, education, and pensions is 'supported' without mention
being made of the risks of such reform. On the contrary, further steps in this
direction seem to have been encouraged. (See EC Regular Reports 1999, sections on health for Poland and Romania, p. 10, and Hungary, p. 11; for pensions in Slovenia, see Regular Report 1999, pp. 10 and 11.) For instance, on
public expenditure on health care in Hungary – which remains between 4 and
5 per cent of GDP, less than in the EU – the national report mentions that 'the
deterioration of the fiscal deficit needs to be addressed. Priority should be
given to health sector reform which continues to be a major drain in the fiscal
accounts' (Ferge 2000, p. 11). Privatisation is also being encouraged in other
areas connected to social protection (public transport, housing, and other public services, including education).

Zsuzsa Ferge has also found that:

> the Reports make direct or indirect suggestions aimed at the reduction of the level
> of social protection on the grounds of the need for budget consolidation or increas-
> ing competitiveness . . . they also hint at the necessity of changing the structure of
> social protection through the privatisation of pensions, and sometimes of health
> care or other public services. (Ferge 2002, p. 7)

The removal of price subsidies has also been strongly supported, without considering any of the problems that this may imply for many people: 'The
reports urge further cuts in subsidies without mentioning any of the problems
encountered in other [candidate] countries'.

We might wonder whether the European Commission should not have
been more careful before releasing the following statement concerning
Bulgaria, a country in which all incomes and social allowances have fallen in
real terms:

> substantial progress continues to be made in bringing administered prices closer to
> market determined prices. This is particularly true for energy prices, which are
> expected to be liberalised by 2001 as part of the reform of the energy sector. . . . the
> system of monitored prices, which allows the government to influence price set-
> ting, subsists only for two types of goods, namely water and pharmaceuticals.
> (Regular Report for Bulgaria 1999)

Or before endorsing the following judgement on the Czech Republic:

> Price liberalisation in regulated sectors has almost completely stopped under the
> new government, maintaining the market distortions in energy and housing.
> (Regular Report on the Czech Republic 1999)

Thus for external experts, such statements in a context of social crisis – the
Czech Republic included – were made solely on the basis of an economic and

even neo-liberal perspective and were not formed in accordance with the basic social values and principles of the EU.

At the end of her study, Zsuzsa Ferge concludes that 'social protection as a system is not considered to be an integral part of the conditions of accession . . . the reports pay practically no attention to the European model' (Ferge 2000, p. 6). She goes even further: 'in reality there is a clear hidden agenda . . . not far removed from what is usually termed the neo-liberal agenda. It is rather close to what the World Bank stands for in the case of the accession countries.' Furthermore:

> to the question whether social security reform is a different issue for accession countries than for Western countries, on the basis of the accession reports the case seems to be clear-cut: yes, the accession countries are being allowed to reject the European model in this area.

We can of course debate the meaning of such EC statements and reports, as well as the importance that must be attributed to them (the position papers delivered to each individual candidate country, which remain confidential, also represent the position of the European Commission). Moreover, we might also question whether these statements really represent the strategy of the EC as regards social protection or whether they might instead reflect a lack of attention devoted by the EC to such reports. Moreover, other statements closer to EU social values could have been found in the social protection area. On health care, for example, the European Commission has repeatedly requested that the governments of the candidate countries – Hungary included – improve their health service, as well as health and safety conditions at work. A number of important speeches from EC officials underlining the importance of the European Social Model in social protection, also within the EU enlargement process, can be found.[19]

Nevertheless, the lack of a clear message – and sometimes ambiguous statements more due to insufficient consideration of what more than twelve years of transition and reforms have meant for these countries in the social area – from the EC on social protection during the negotiation process may have caused many actors in this field in the candidate countries to wonder what the EC's intentions are as regards social protection, especially after a

19. See, for example, the speech on social protection delivered by G. Clotuche at the conference 'New governance and social dimension of enlargement', organised by the European Social Observatory at the European Parliament, Brussels, 18 October 2000; and the speech by O. Quintin at the conference 'Social policy and EU enlargement', Warsaw, 11–12 May 2000, where important references were made to the enlargement process; see also the more recent (opening) speech by O. Quintin at the conference 'The modernisation of social protection in candidate countries: new opportunities and challenges for the European Union', Brussels, 5-6 December (see EC 2002e).

period during which the EC, as we have seen, has been surprisingly absent in the candidate countries in the field of social protection, and may thus have seemed to give their blessing to the reforms advised – and in many cases even imposed – in this area by the World Bank. The message of the EU has also been very weak because the European Commission, as in the case of current member states, has put the main emphasis on the 'sustainability' of social protection systems and also the need for a 'three-pillar model', without considering the specificities of Central and Eastern European countries and without emphasising all the other distinctive elements of social protection in the EU (as described in section 1). More fundamentally, this policy – or lack of policy – reflects in great part what EU member states currently allow (or in this case do not allow) the European Commission (and European institutions in general) to do in the field of social protection.

3.10.3 The Lack of a Community *Acquis* on Social Protection

This is clearly an area which has been left to be determined by the subsidiarity principle, and so essentially has been made the competence of national governments. As Ms Diamantopoulou, from the EC, has said on several occasions: 'We do not seek to harmonise social policies but to mobilise support towards common objectives' (comments on the adoption of the new Social Policy Agenda).

For Zsuzsa Ferge, 'the adoption of the *acquis* is a necessary condition of accession; the legislation on social protection is [because it comes under subsidiarity] largely left outside the *acquis communautaire*' (Ferge 2000, p. 4). In fact, the Community *acquis* in the field of social security is mainly about the coordination of social security schemes for migrant workers, and indirectly about gender-equality provisions.

As summarised by an expert from Estonia:

> As the binding *Acquis Communautaire* of the European Union is rather limited (equal treatment of men and women; coordination of social security schemes for migrant workers), so are the estimated impacts of the accession upon the social security system in Estonia. (Leppik 2000, p. 14)

Paradoxically, it is in these two areas that the candidate countries should have the fewest problems. The gender-equality parts of social protection systems in Central and Eastern Europe are up to EU standards, and sometimes even better than in some EU member states. Equal treatment in social security is already in place, and there have even been cases of positive discrimination in favour of women, as in Estonia and Slovenia. With regard to social security for migrant workers, equal treatment of nationals and non-nationals is already in place in some countries – as in Estonia – or is in the process of being implemented, so that the relevant EU regulations (1408/71 and 574/72) could directly and rapidly be applied. If problems do emerge in this regard they will be the result of the financial costs. The application of coordination rules will have significant financial implications, especially considering the great difference between the cost of health care and social services in EU member states, and in most candidate countries. For example, candidate countries will have to refund to other member states some of the cost of treating – for example, for the medical care, not only emergency but also regular – the dependent family members of an EU migrant working in a new member (former candidate) country who remained at their original EU residence; or the health costs of those who in other EU countries are insured according to the new member (former candidate) country's legislation. Nevertheless, the progressive improvement of the economic and financial conditions of the new EU members as a result of their joining will progressively help them to overcome these adjustment costs.

It is more in other areas of social protection, where there is no community *acquis*, that significant divergence may occur – for example, as a result of the fragmentation and vulnerability to which an excessive reliance on private companies may subject social protection. This may also be the case with regard to the role of the social partners in social protection policy-making, a feature of the European Social Model concerning which there are no EC requirements, thus giving European institutions very little room to manoeuvre in the current accession process.

The EC would have liked to react more strongly to the abolition by the Hungarian Government of the autonomous and bipartite management – through the social partners – of the Hungarian pension fund. Some emphasis was put on this matter during the negotiations (Regular Report for Hungary 2000), especially within the discussions on developments in social dialogue, but the absence of a legal *acquis* in both the social protection and the social dialogue areas did not motivate the Hungarian authorities to exhibit much concern.

Poverty and inequality is another area in which European institutions should do more. In most candidate countries, especially those of Central and Eastern Europe, the authorities have not yet fixed a threshold of absolute poverty, despite the fact that in most countries in the region – including the Czech Republic, which has the lowest poverty rate – the poverty figures vary radically according to the calculation method and the level of poverty defined. In order to improve – and to obtain a greater knowledge of – the social situation in these countries a specific requirement should be imposed to calculate the level of the subsistence minimum or poverty line. Although this is still not the case even in some EU member states the situation in the candidate countries is more urgent. The recent extension of the open method of coordination to social exclusion (which will lead to the elaboration of guidelines and action plans by national authorities) could greatly help in that direction (extended to current candidate countries as from 2002).

Other international instruments may be used to complement this rather embryonic Community *acquis* on social protection, such as ILO Convention No. 102 (on social security), the 1996 revised European Social Charter, and also the European Code of Social Security.[20] The Council of Europe is also providing some analysis of social protection systems on the basis of Article 163 of the Amsterdam Treaty.

There is also a need to extend the EU requirements imposed on future member states on the basis of a larger concept of Social Europe, based on European social citizenship or the need for more quality in social policy as a key basis for future EU competitiveness. This would allow reconsideration of current reforms in candidate countries from another perspective. Three things are particularly important in this regard:

1. It is not the level of social protection which counts – it is to be reformed in any case – but its mechanisms, something that we should look at carefully because they imply redistribution choices in society as a whole.
2. It is not under the pressure of competition that we should carry out such reforms but with regard to such internal factors as demography, the balance between contributions and expenditure, and so on.
3. Such social expenditure has to be incurred anyway, either in a public or a private form, since it is a more global and coherent vision of social policy which is at stake.

The underlying issue of redistribution within society must equally be taken into account. Economic and Monetary Union, globalisation, new technology, and even enlargement all have distributional implications. Surprisingly, however, this rarely surfaces as a theme of debate.

For the IMF and the World Bank, the choice has been clear, with redistribution focused exclusively on the most needy. This policy approach not only represents a very strong choice about distribution, but also promotes a particular model of society. The question is whether the future member states are already going in the same direction, as witnessed by the excessive liberalisation and privatisation of their social protection systems.

3.10.4 Can Recent EU Developments Influence the Final Outcome in an Enlarged EU?

The basic question is whether it is still possible to help the future member states to shape their social protection systems more in line with the values and

20. European Treaty Series No. 48.

practices of social protection systems in the EU. Naturally, these countries must be helped to promote a more balanced system of social protection, and particularly to guarantee comprehensive systems of social protection while the necessary adjustments to the new circumstances are ensured. A well-developed and rights-based social protection system is a European achievement that should be extended to the candidate countries. Whether this is still possible very much depends on the policy adopted by European institutions over the next few years. It should be marked by a more voluntaristic approach to spreading the values and principles behind the social protection systems of the European Union. The continuation of the policy followed so far would lead only to the perpetuation of unbalanced and precarious systems of social protection in the candidate countries, and even towards the further development of private funding, generating further inequalities and social exclusion.

The European Commission has a key role to play in this process. If it has somehow – and mistakenly – neglected social protection developments in the candidate countries so far, it is because it preferred to emphasise the consolidation and better definition of EU policy and strategy on social protection before accession took place. While this was obviously needed, especially considering the weak *acquis* in this area, it could have led to a situation in which social protection policy is better defined at EU level, but with new members having quite different systems on the ground, something that may affect EU policy in this field in the future.

Recent developments have provided European institutions with an opportunity to do more, and to impose more requirements concerning social protection on the candidate countries. In particular the extension of the open coordination method to social protection, social inclusion, and pensions should make it possible to make significant steps forward also in the candidate countries, but only on condition that such coordination policies take place within a more general framework than that which has dominated social protection reform in Central and Eastern Europe so far – one further from liberal and purely budgetary considerations and closer to the ultimate aims of social protection systems and social policy in general. This would involve the detachment of EU messages and requirements from the kind of social protection policies advised by international monetary institutions in accession countries.

On the other hand, the room for manoeuvre is very small, and we might wonder whether the tools made available by EU membership in respect of social protection will not come too late: Chapter 13 on employment and social affairs has been closed in all future member states, where most social protection systems (social security, pensions, and so on) have already been reformed. Finally, in a context in which a greater percentage of the population is in need, the usual EU social inclusion programmes may be inappropriate.

No doubt substantial assistance from structural funds is also required but here the funds planned for the new member states do not seem to be proportionate to current needs (see Chapter 11).

3.11 CONCLUSION

As a result of the trend towards systematic liberalisation and privatisation, social programmes that once covered the whole population have been limited to those qualifying through means-testing; access to many social services has become market-regulated; and spending on social security and assistance has been drastically curtailed – all in a context in which the number of recipients has substantially increased. These low levels of social protection contrast significantly with social policy in the EU member states. They certainly do not constitute an appropriate response to the general social crisis in the region. There seem to be two main determinants of poverty in candidate countries: first, unemployment, which is of a very long-term nature (see Chapter 4); and second, low wages through which working poverty is a major feature of candidate countries, especially in Central and Eastern Europe. This means that social protection should also aim at covering the 'working poor' and thus be more universal in its redistributive function, an assessment which clearly contradicts the 'targeting approach' promoted by the World Bank in the region.

It might be pointed out that EU member states are also currently engaged in similar social protection reforms – for instance with regard to the sustainability of pension schemes – so that the trends observed in the candidate countries should be viewed as being in line with developments in the EU itself, especially considering the lack of a Community *acquis* in this field. This hasty conclusion does not take into consideration the conclusion of many experts in this field, emphasised in the course of the present chapter, that social protection reforms have been much more radical in Central and Eastern European countries, and also that they have taken place in an environment characterised by much weaker foundations in terms of private pension and insurance funds, state responsibility, and the role of the social partners. Equally important is the fact that these policies have been implemented in extremely fragile societies hard hit by years of transition, in which the extreme shift to neo-liberal models of social protection, rather than offering people relief, has in fact accentuated the social cost of transition, and contributed to increasing social exclusion and poverty, as well as growing inequalities. Such conditions obviously also cast doubt on the economic efficiency – and thus the costs and viability – of the new systems, and on the achievement of their primary objectives.

Of course, no party in the ongoing debate on this topic, in the EU member states as elsewhere, should claim to have the truth all on its side, and there is a significant risk of ideological entrenchment. The purpose of the present chapter is not to pretend that the solution is clear, but rather to alert the reader to the possibility that a single model has dominated in Central and Eastern Europe, with excessive reliance on privatisation and the market, without always measuring the negative effects of this radical shift. We believe that it is important to try to think in less conventional terms about this topic, and to work out a more innovative approach, especially since there is a clear risk that the people in the candidate countries will associate the much contested social protection reforms and selectivity concept – particularly absurd when applied to child and family allowances – with their forthcoming integration in the EU, and as a consequence strongly reject the accession process and European integration as a whole.

The schemes adopted in many countries of Central and Eastern Europe are largely individualistic and inegalitarian, leaving those outside employment or without access to the capital market more exposed to long-term income uncertainty. Moreover, it is basically a risky model, making the income of future pensioners much too dependent on the volatility of the capital markets. These new pension schemes also reward those who have regular, well-remunerated employment.

These policies have been introduced mainly under the influence of the World Bank, which seems to be following its own policy agenda, fostering in accession countries, as in the European Union, social protection systems much less dependent on the state, more related to economic performance and stock market growth, and promoting a much more selective approach – what we have called the 'minimalist approach' – rather than responding to the ultimate aims of social protection and social policy in general, described in Chapter 1 of this volume.

Already some EU observers have tried to attract attention to possible divergence from the EU:

> it is quite clear that the systems imposed by the World Bank and the IMF in accession countries, reflecting the American system, are totally different from EU systems, and therefore lead the social protection systems of these countries very far from the European Social Model.[21]
>
> the influence of the IMF and the World Bank has been decisive in the choices made by these [candidate] countries . . . and one might wonder whether some of the reforms, in some insidious fashion, conceal mechanisms – after whose implementation there would be no turning back – which are at odds with the values, such as solidarity and defence of social cohesion, that bind together EU social protection systems and form the basis of the European Social Model. (Henri Lourdelle 2003)

---

21. Anne Van Lancker of the European Parliament at the conference 'New governance and social dimension of enlargement', organised by the European Social Observatory at the European Parliament, Brussels, 18 October 2000.

European institutions, however, have so far not managed – they have not even made a convincing attempt – to propose an alternative approach to the World Bank policy in the region. The limited Community *acquis* in this field, a lack of voluntaristic policy in the first years of reforms, and rather weak messages in the negotiation process have clearly limited the possible requirements and extension of EU principles in this area. Paradoxically, all future member states will be asked to stick to a given number of principles on social protection – such as solidarity, universality, social dialogue, and so on – while at the same time they have adopted systems which are not based on basic observance of such principles.

A number of issues must urgently be addressed. First, considering the relatively low expenditure on social protection, we believe that a more active policy on social protection is required in these countries. More consideration should also be given to the collection of revenues rather than limiting the debate to cutting expenditure. A larger debate on social protection is also needed on a series of other questions, such as the influence of the informal economy, the redistributional aims of the social protection systems, and the need to consider social expenditure as something more than what is left after all other issues have been dealt with within the framework of budgetary arbitration. Priority should also be given to strengthening the tripartite management of social protection systems (ILO 2002), especially to the involvement of social partners in the formulation of assumptions for long-term projections.

The possible impact on the EU must also be analysed, since we have seen that Central and Eastern Europe seems to have generated an extreme model that EU member states have so far appeared keen on eliminating. There is a danger that the social model sold most aggressively and most successfully in Central and Eastern Europe might return to the EU as it were 'by the back door'. Will the social protection systems of current EU member states, already weakened by neo-liberal policies, survive the wave of liberalisation and privatisation that will soon come from these countries? And will European institutions be able to progress further on social protection when thirteen or more new member countries, all with more extreme welfare systems, join?

Unfortunately, many of these questions have not yet been debated, although the negotiations on social matters have already been concluded with the candidate countries. At the same time, social protection continues to be one of the weakest elements of the Community *acquis*. This leaves our social protection systems with a rather uncertain future in an enlarged EU.

Unfortunately, it is clear that the European Commission arrived too late in the social protection field. In these circumstances, the application to social protection, pensions and social inclusion of the 'non-binding' open method of coordination, while promoting some convergence of new member states with the EU average, may not change the situation significantly since all relevant reforms have already been carried out. As one high official from a future member state has stated, 'we are neither interested in nor willing to reform our reforms'.

New – and perhaps more constraining – initiatives are thus needed at EU level in order to reinforce our common requirements in this area, while a more courageous stance is required on the part of European institutions against neo-liberal recipes and magic formulae to reinforce and extend the main features of EU welfare systems, and to maintain a single European model of social protection.

4. Employment: Towards Unregulated Labour Markets?

4.1 INTRODUCTION

As the candidate countries prepare their economies to join the European Union, employment represents one of the least known areas in the enlargement process. In particular, we still do not know what effects the integration of Central and Eastern European labour markets will have on the shape of labour markets and on employment levels in an enlarged European Union.

One reason for this is that the economies of the former Communist regimes diverged most from the mechanisms of a market economy in this respect: the main features of these economies were planned output levels, centrally controlled decision-making, and artificially low and little differentiated wage levels in order to guarantee employment for all, regardless of economic performance, in sharp contrast to decentralised and risk-taking entrepreneurial decision-making, wage differentials reflecting education, skill levels, and performance, and employment as the result of demand and supply for labour according to results which characterise market economies.

Secondly, the twelve years of transition have profoundly modified the economies and employment systems of these countries. Not only has the shift to market mechanisms been a very difficult and painful exercise, but also the transition process has obeyed its own logic, with macroeconomic stabilisation, reforms such as privatisation and liberalisation, and the setting up of new economic structures all having to be implemented in a few short years. Employment was inevitably profoundly modified by such a heavy policy agenda, whose results have yet to be analysed in all their complexity.

Finally, the accession process will also have its effects on employment, since it represents a unique historical development, with for the first time millions of people joining together in a single market.

The final outcome for employment is thus necessarily uncertain.

The first question we must ask is whether the future member states have at least overcome the economic crisis that followed the collapse of the previous regimes, so that they can look at the employment situation – especially as enlargement looms, together with the economic growth expected to accompany it – with more serenity. Beyond economic results, have the Central and

Eastern European countries abandoned all remnants of the old regime in order to move definitively towards the employment levels and structures, and the labour market systems and practices existing in EU member states? Given the traditional role of the state in the region, does it remain a central actor in labour markets and in employment policy-making, or has it been willing to move away from centralised and over-regulated labour markets towards full deregulation of those markets?

Furthermore, are there distinctive features of employment development in the candidate countries – including the three southern European candidate countries – that diverge fundamentally from the most important principles and policies of the European Union that may perhaps endanger the progress made in this area?

These are some of the questions we shall try to answer in this chapter by means of a description of the main features of employment and labour market developments in the candidate countries. However, before we move on to this it is important to briefly describe some of the elements of the European model of employment or labour markets, especially since the Community *acquis* in this area is not very well known. This is partly because this *acquis* is relatively recent, and partly because it is based less on legal regulations than on a comprehensive set of practices and policies that EU countries – individually but also collectively at EU level – have progressively constructed. The role of the negotiation process on employment will also be addressed.

4.2 HIGHER EMPLOYMENT AS A COMMON EU GOAL

Employment is clearly among the priorities of the EU, and also represents an important part of the European Social Model. However, progress has been long in coming, and it is only in the last ten years that significant steps forward could be achieved.

4.2.1 A Difficult Start

Although employment was mentioned already in the Treaty of Rome, only general references were made, such as the need for 'close cooperation' between member states – to be organised through the European Commission – while no transfer of competences was foreseen to the Community level (Quintin and Favarel-Dapas 1999, p. 17). For years, employment clearly remained the sole prerogative of the member states, in full appliance of the 'subsidiarity' principle. It was only 15 years later, in the mid-1970s, and after the first serious economic tensions and emerging social conflict in Europe following the international oil shocks and world-wide economic turmoil that a first programme for social action was adopted in 1974 by the Council of

Ministers based on three priority objectives: (i) the achievement of full and better employment; (ii) the improvement of living and working conditions; and (iii) the increased participation of social partners and workers in economic and social decision-making. In addition to the significant action for employment of the European Social Fund, the Council during those years adopted several resolutions and recommendations, for instance on preparing young people for working life or on the organisation of working time. These instruments, however, continued to be non-binding. Moreover, the second oil shock and rapid and significant surge of unemployment put a halt to further progress on employment, and on Social Europe in general. The impossibility of reaching unanimous agreement on social legislation at the Council in that period reflected 'national interests' – especially with regard to economic growth and employment – pursued by member states, which limited cooperation in the field of employment, not to mention possible 'coordination'. It is the achievement of the single market, and the modification of the Treaty of Rome provided by the European Single Act, that created a new impetus for Social Europe and employment.

4.2.2 A Sad Assessment: The Imperative to Improve Employment

The Single European Act was ratified in 1986 and came into force in 1987. It confirmed the aim of achieving a single market in economic and trade terms; at the same time, it emphasised the need to promote a social dimension in such a large single market, thus giving a definite push to social policy.

Employment started to appear as a major objective to be tackled at Community level, for a number of reasons: first because of the assessment that other industrialised countries – especially the United States – were performing much better in terms of employment; secondly, the persistence of high levels of unemployment which appeared to threaten social and economic cohesion, as well as long-term European competitiveness; thirdly, the possible contradiction, if not direct opposition, between the objective of economic and monetary union and very high unemployment levels, that is, between the process of economic and monetary integration and the required progress in social policy.

The Treaty of the European Union (ratified in 1992 and coming into force from 1993) reinforced social objectives (Article 2): 'the Community has as its mission, through the establishment of a common market, of a European economic and monetary union, and through the implementation of common policies or actions . . . to promote . . . a high level of employment and social protection, the improvement of the level and quality of life, and economic and social cohesion and solidarity between member states'. In 1993, the then President of the European Commission, Jacques Delors, and his team managed to make employment a major policy priority on the European agenda, notably through their white paper 'Growth, competitiveness, and employment'. A more coordinated approach in this field started to be discussed at successive European summits, and featured prominently in their respective conclusions (notably the European Councils at Essen in 1994, Madrid in December 1995, and Dublin in December 1996).

4.2.3 The New EU Ambition: A Real European Strategy on Employment

A clear upturn in terms of quality was provided by the Amsterdam Treaty (in June 1997, although ratified by all member states in 1999), in which new provisions on employment (new Chapter) were inserted. It marked a new era in EU member states' willingness to coordinate better and to take concrete multilateral action in this field, and to address the issue also at the EU level. Member states committed themselves to ensure 'economic and social progress and a high level of employment' (Title I), but also agreed to consider employment as a 'common concern' (Title VIII) and agreed to put in place a 'coordinated strategy for employment' (Article 3 of the Treaty of the European Community). For the first time, the role of employment as an engine for social policy and 'as the key for social integration' was also recognised (Quintin and Favarel-Dapas 1999, p. 25).

The new title dedicated to employment in the Treaty clearly represented the first attempt to coordinate EU member states' economic and employment policies; in this sense it represented the necessary counterbalance or complementary process to the general economic orientations defined within the framework of monetary union.[1]

This allowed the European Union to move from non-binding Presidency conclusions of European Councils – which had proved inadequate for establishing credible employment coordination – to a requirement of cooperation in the Treaty. This institutional basis was translated into the 'coordinated employment strategy'. The extraordinary European Council of Luxembourg in November 1997 was aimed at operationalising the process.

Although there was still resistance limiting any further delegation of power to the EU, unemployment problems pushed EU member states to move forward,[2] and to put in place follow-up and monitoring mechanisms, that is, a

1. For some observers, the process of monetary union, with its mid-term objectives, indicators and pressure towards convergence, represented the principal source of inspiration for the European Employment Strategy, which in a way 'consisted of mimicking the monetary success story' (de la Porte, and Pochet 2002, p. 2).

2. The new French socialist government, led by L. Jospin, exerted considerable pressure to organise such a special meeting of the Council to address the hot issues of unemployment and job creation, and was supported by other member states, such as Germany, which were initially sceptical. Other member states, such as Spain, Portugal, and the UK were opposed to the setting of quantitative employment targets.

process for the implementation and monitoring of member states' employment policies – also known as the Luxembourg process – which operates on a yearly basis by way of the following:

1. *Employment guidelines*: member states – with the participation of other actors, for instance the social partners – agree on a number of guidelines that are then adopted by the European Council on the proposal of the European Commission.
2. A *National Action Plan* (NAP) drawn up by each member state which describes how these guidelines are to be put into practice.
3. The Commission and the Council examine each National Action Plan and present a *Joint Employment Report* to the European Council. On this basis, the European Commission presents a new proposal to revise the Employment Guidelines for the following year.
4. On the basis of the conclusions by the Heads of State or Government, the Council approves the revised Employment Guidelines for the following years. The Council may also decide, by qualified majority, to issue *country-specific recommendations* upon the proposal of the Commission.

It is thus a peer review process, with a role for member states, but also for the European institutions. Five years after its implementation, and despite the fact that it is not based on binding legal regulations, we can say that it has led to concrete results.

In 1999, the European Commission used the recommendation tool foreseen in the Amsterdam Treaty and, in combination with extensive press coverage, fostered peer pressure among the member states and so rendered the whole process more credible. This new process also made it possible to identify and disseminate good practices in active labour market policies between member states.

In the year 2000, fundamental quantified objectives with target dates were agreed, such as an increase in the employment rate in the EU to 70 per cent by 2010, and in the female employment rate to 60 per cent. New intermediate targets were also defined in 2001: 67 per cent for the overall employment rate and 57 per cent for the female employment rate by January 2005. It was also commonly decided to progressively increase the average EU employment rate among the oldest workers (55–64) to 50 per cent by 2010. Beyond quantitative targets, qualitative objectives were also fixed, for instance on life-long learning, participation of social partners, and quality of jobs in general.

In short, employment became an area commonly addressed in a coordinated way at EU level, making possible some progress in this area. Nevertheless, the willingness of member states has often been called into question, together with the real effectiveness of a non-binding process in this area. In such a context, it is important to analyse how the integration of future member states – with their specific features as regards employment and labour markets – into the EU, and so into the European Employment Strategy, may affect employment in the years to come.

4.3 FULL EMPLOYMENT AS A MIRAGE FROM THE PAST

While capitalist economies are based on risk – including the risk of unemployment – as well as mobility of labour and capital, the former command economies of Central and Eastern Europe provided life-long employment with the same firm; capitalisation was minimal since labour was the priority. In contrast to the significant wage differentiation characteristic of market economies, wages were compressed at a very low level and did not reflect productivity, different levels of human capital, or specific skills. This allowed enterprises to maintain 'full employment' as they achieved the centrally planned output targets. As a result, efficiency in the allocation of labour was poor, while workers had little motivation to improve performance. This could only lead to sub-optimal work organisation, while overstaffing and labour hoarding were widespread in most sectors of the economy.

Another characteristic of the former command economies was the prominence of industry, with large state-owned enterprises dominating the scene, and the lack of a private sector. These economies necessarily fell apart along with the political regimes which imposed them in the first place. The change was abrupt and the employment situation in Central and Eastern Europe will require a long period of adaptation.

4.3.1 The Downward Plunge of Employment Levels since 1990

The most immediate effect of the changes was the dramatic fall in employment levels, as a direct result of the large fall in output that all Central and Eastern European countries experienced, followed by a difficult and long period of restructuring.

Detailed analysis shows the dramatic fall of labour participation rates since 1990 (Burda 1998, p. 5). The decline in total employment between 1990 and 1994 averaged 16 per cent in the four Visegrád countries (Poland, Czech Republic, Slovakia, and Hungary), the absolute figure in Hungary being 26 per cent. By way of comparison, total employment over the same period increased by 1.2 per cent in the European countries belonging to the OECD.

The fall in employment has been particularly severe in industry. The output crisis hit manufacturing first and its share in employment declined dramatically.

In Central and Eastern Europe as a whole, the number of employed is estimated to have fallen by 15–20 per cent between 1989 and 1997, with the largest fall occurring in the early years of transition (1989 to 1993). By 1994–5, conditions had stabilised and in a number of countries employment began to rise, though not nearly enough to compensate for the earlier job losses.

4.3.2 The Latest Trend: A Further Widening of the Gap with the EU

In 1998 and 1999, economic growth slowed down again and employment began to fall in most countries, especially in the Czech Republic, Slovakia, and Estonia. The Baltic countries were also hurt by the Russian crisis in 1998.

Apart from Hungary and Slovenia – which had higher employment levels in 2000 compared to 1999 – employment continued to decrease in 2000 in all countries of the region, though more slowly in Poland, Romania, Slovakia, Estonia, and the Czech Republic than in Latvia, Lithuania, and Bulgaria. This continued in 2001, so that the gap with the EU continued to widen. It has been estimated that raising the region's employment rate to the level reached in the EU in 2000 would require employment to rise by 7 per cent, representing 3 million additional jobs (EC Employment Report 2001, EC 2001b).

While in 1998 the average employment rate was slightly higher in Central and Eastern European countries than in the EU, at around 62 per cent, the sit-

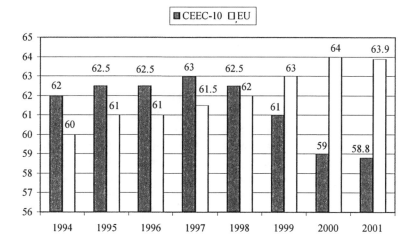

Source: *EC Employment Reports, 2001* and 2002 (EC 2001b and EC 2002b).

Figure 4.1 Employment rates in the CEEC-10 and EU, 1994–2001

uation was reversed in 1999, when the overall employment rate of the ten candidate countries averaged just under 61 per cent of the working-age population (see Figure 4.1). Since then the employment rate has fallen below 60 per cent in Central and Eastern Europe, while it has continued to rise in the EU: in 2000 the two groups of countries were separated by more than 4 percentage points. In 2001, only the Czech Republic and Cyprus had a higher employment rate than the EU average. The employment rate continued to fall in Poland, Lithuania, Romania, and Bulgaria. There was a slight increase in other candidate countries, especially Slovenia (EC Employment Report 2002, EC 2002b). Nevertheless, the gap with the EU may continue to rise in the future, especially because a further fall in employment is to be expected. It is clear that the arrival of new member countries will reduce the EU's current overall employment rate, leading many observers to believe that the target of a 70 per cent employment rate set by the Lisbon European Council will become unattainable. Nevertheless, average figures conceal significant disparities in employment rates between candidate countries which emerged and grew in the 1990s.

4.3.3 Large Disparities between Candidate Countries

Disparities in employment rates widened between countries over the 1990s as employment fell. In 1999, employment rates ranged from 54 per cent in Bulgaria to 66 per cent in Cyprus, and 65 per cent in the Czech Republic.

The scale of the decline in employment in a particular country may also reflect other phenomena, however: employment growth or a lower decline in employment may be due to the success of the transition and to economic growth, but it may equally represent the extent to which jobs have remained protected against market forces or the absence of restructuring. It might also represent the high level of employment in subsistence agriculture. It is crucial to distinguish carefully between these different phenomena since a number of mistakes were made in the evaluation of the first years of transition. The most striking example of this was the Czech Republic, which was praised for its economic growth and low unemployment, while in fact the latter was mainly due to a lack of restructuring in enterprises in the course of the mass privatisation process. Increased unemployment rates in subsequent years confirmed that the Czech Republic was not a success story after all, but rather had accumulated delays in its reform process.

Similarly, while relatively low unemployment rates in Hungary can be partly explained by increased growth and also significant foreign investment, they may also be explained by the large proportion of employees working in the informal economy. The employment rate, moreover, is among the lowest.

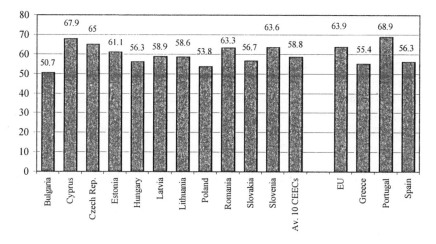

Source: EC Employment Reports, 2001 and 2002 (EC2001b and EC2002b).

Figure 4.2 Employment rates (candidate countries and selected EU), 2001

Labour market developments in Romania in recent years have also been rather exceptional. The decline in urban employment there has led to massive growth in subsistence agriculture, masking rising unemployment. There is every reason to believe that employment and activity rates are inflated and that unemployment is underestimated. This is important because

> given Romania's relative size – accounting for over 20 per cent of the population of the ten Central and Eastern European candidate countries – this has a substantial effect on the labour-market aggregates for the CEECs as a whole. Excluding Romania, the employment rate for the remaining CEECs, at 57 per cent, is now significantly below the EU average. (EC Employment Report 2001, p. 96)

Employment developments in Poland, rather bleak in 2001 (see Figure 4.2), will because of its size (it accounts for half the working age population of the first ten candidate countries) also influence an enlarged EU's future average. In other words, each country has followed its own path and at its own speed.

There have been no success stories with regard to employment and restructuring in Central and Eastern Europe so far, with the result that there is no blueprint that the other countries might copy. In particular, 'shock therapy' did not prove to be more successful,[3] although it was certainly much more costly

3. Despite World Bank assertions to the contrary 'those countries which pursued the boldest economic reforms have benefited the most from the process of EU accession', or even attacks on small-scale reformers: 'CEE countries which are the least corrupt have also made the most progress in structural reforms; countries where reforms are more partial have a greater degree of "state capture"' (World Bank 2000b, pp. 4, 6).

in terms of human capital and social policy, and thus for long-term economic policy. On the other hand, countries that delayed the necessary reforms too long, such as Bulgaria and Romania, encountered more difficulties later on.

Difficulties in defining labour market policies seem to be a particular feature of the new applicants to the EU. It is doubtful that these countries will manage to increase employment levels significantly in the immediate future, even if they continue to register high GDP growth, mainly because there is still substantial overemployment (redundant labour) in many sectors.

4.4 A RADICALLY CHANGING PATTERN OF EMPLOYMENT

In the course of establishing the foundations of a market system, the structure of the economy and thus patterns of employment changed radically in the candidate countries of Central and Eastern Europe, a process which is far from being complete. The main problem for national governments seems to have been to determine which ownership forms, sectors of the economy, and types of enterprise would contribute the most to economic recovery and so help to compensate for employment losses. Profound change has taken place, but this deep restructuring has not been sufficiently thought about and debated.

4.4.1 The Massive Shift to the Private Sector

The main characteristic in the new economic structure is the increased role of private ownership and the shrinking role of the state, a development which is the natural consequence of the privatisation process, but also of the spontaneous emergence of a new private sector. The latter development has been supported by a new philosophy on the part of decision-makers, who have been determined to get rid of the state as a significant actor in the economy. As a result, the private sector dominates the new employment patterns in all candidate countries: by way of an example, in Poland it increased from 45 per cent in 1990 to 71 per cent in 1999, and 63 per cent of GDP is generated by the private sector (Boni 2001).

The restructuring process has often been implemented in a rush and without a long-term vision. For instance, most governments in the first years of transition encouraged the use of pre-retirement schemes to get rid of part of the labour force, so that many people aged between 50 and 60 were given the chance to retire early. This policy, also recommended by the World Bank to accelerate the restructuring process, has proved to be catastrophic: first in economic terms, since these schemes not only led to expensive severance payments, but also turned out to put too heavy a burden on the pension system, all the workers opting for early retirement becoming recipients rather than net contributors to the pension system; secondly, in social terms, because the costs for the workers concerned have been dramatic, many workers suddenly finding that they had to rely on miserable pensions or social allowances, added to the frustration of being considered inactive or non-productive after decades of state propaganda devoted to condemning social parasitism.

Later on, the World Bank recognised its mistake in this regard and advised that it be abandoned in all countries of the region: 'Early retirement in many countries has also reduced incentives for work, which in turn has negative implications for the financing of the pensions system' (World Bank 2000b, p. 58). It continues to advise rapid restructuring through severance pay, however: 'giving generous severance payments to those who lost their jobs as a result of enterprise restructuring would be less fiscally costly than generous unemployment benefits which are difficult to reduce or phase out' (World Bank 2000b, p. 58), although this policy has been shown to be the best way of rapidly increasing poverty without addressing the problem of unemployment in the long run. In Romania, for instance:

> social policy has to be rethought with a view to increasing active measures to promote employment . . . in this regard, the extremely damaging practice of severance payments for workers dismissed from state-owned enterprises, which was not accompanied by active measures of social protection, has been abandoned. (Giurescu 2001, p. 2)

4.4.2 Sectoral Redistribution of Labour

All governments in the region have encouraged the development of the service sector in order to correct another artificial imbalance inherited from the previous regime, the dominance of industry. The latter's share in employment progressively decreased, partly naturally, since many large state enterprises were simply not viable and were closed down or significantly scaled down after first being privatised, and partly through the intervention of the state which cut subsidies or credits, while grants and other incentives were provided for the creation of businesses and employment in services. As a result, employment in services increased everywhere in the region. In 2001, the most developed service sectors could be found in Hungary and Estonia (EC 2002b). In Poland, services already employed half of all employees in 1999 (it was 50.1 per cent in 2001), compared to 36 per cent ten years earlier. Agriculture is still important in countries such as Poland (19 per cent), Lithuania (16 per cent), Latvia (15 per cent), and Romania, which remain over-dependent on agriculture, in which employment has grown in the last years (close to 45 per cent of employment). Its share has decreased in almost all other countries, however, although to different degrees, and with the exception of the countries above

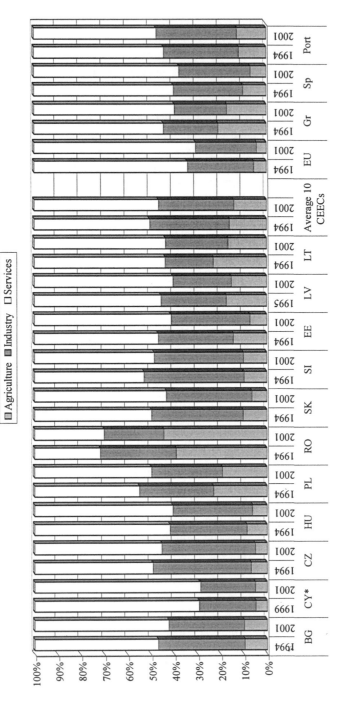

Figure 4.3 *Distribution of employment by main sectors of the economy;
candidate countries and selected EU countries, 1994–2001 (Cyprus 1999)*

Sources: *EC Employment Report, 2001 and 2002* (EC2001b and EC2002b).

where a return to agriculture represented the only possible survival strategy. In many countries, there continues to be significant hidden or unreported employment in agriculture, a phenomenon observed in Romania and Bulgaria, as well as in Poland, where it is estimated to involve nearly one million people (Boni 2001, p. 3). In Lithuania, employment in agriculture has been essentially a coping strategy and even increased in 1996 after land restitution and the restoration of private property in land: 'People preferred hard and not very profitable work in agriculture to unemployment' (Kairelis 2001, p. 1).[4]

Compared to the EU, the ten Central and Eastern European countries as a whole continue to have an underdeveloped service sector (53 per cent of the working-age population as against 69 per cent in the EU), to be overdependent on agriculture as a source of employment (14 per cent as against 4 per cent), while the employment rate in industry in 2001 was also higher (33 per cent against 29 per cent in the EU – EC 2002b). The sectoral allocation of labour, however, is generally shifting towards EU patterns.

4.5 THE UNPLEASANT REALITY: A MASSIVE INFORMAL ECONOMY

The fall in employment rates described above reflects a restructuring process during which many have been forced out of the labour market. At the same time, partly because of this disengagement from the official sector – but also because of its own dynamic – a wave of people have entered the informal sector. As a result, the unofficial economies of Central and Eastern Europe have undergone an unprecedented expansion and become part of everyday experience for large numbers of people.

This is one of the most serious developments in Central and Eastern Europe since it has implications at all levels. Surprisingly, it has received very little attention, partly because many predicted that it should have a rather short life. More than ten years after the transition, the informal economy has not only not lost ground – in many countries it continues to grow – but also seems to have turned into a more permanent feature influencing the functioning of the official economy and labour market.

4.5.1 The Extent of the Disease

The extent of the informal sector is enormous throughout the region: in Hungary, for instance, it has been calculated through surveys that it may well generate little less than half of GDP, although the available statistics estimate

4. Rimantas Kairelis is Vice-Minister of the Ministry of Labour and Social Security of Lithuania.

Table 4.1 The extent of the informal economy as a percentage of GDP, candidate countries, 1990–2001

	1990	1991	1992	1993	1994	1995	1996	1997	1998	1999	2000	2001	2000/2001*
Bulgaria	22.8	25.1	23.9	25.0	29.9	29.1	36.2	–	–	–	20–25	–	36.4
Cyprus	–	–	–	–	–	–	–	–	–	–	–	–	–
Czech Republic	6.0	6.7	12.9	16.9	16.9	17.6	18.0	12.4	12.6	–	–	–	18.4
Estonia	12.0	19.9	26.2	25.4	24.1	25.1	11.8	–	–	–	–	–	39.1
Hungary	27.0	28.0	32.9	30.6	28.5	27.7	29.0	–	–	–	–	–	24.4
Latvia	12.0	12.8	19.0	34.3	31.0	34.2	35.3	–	–	–	–	–	39.6
Lithuania	12.0	11.3	21.8	39.2	31.7	28.7	21.6	–	–	–	–	–	29.4
Malta	–	–	–	–	–	–	–	–	–	–	–	–	–
Poland	15.7	19.6	23.5	19.7	18.5	15.2	12.6	–	15.0	–	–	15–16	27.4
Romania	22.3	13.7	15.7	18.0	16.4	17.4	19.1	–	–	–	24.0	–	33.4
Slovakia	6.0	7.7	15.1	17.6	16.2	14.6	5.8	–	–	–	12.0	–	18.3
Slovenia	–	–	–	–	–	17–21	–	–	–	20–35	–	–	26.7
Turkey	–	–	–	–	–	–	–	–	–	–	–	–	–

Notes:

Most estimates until 1996 are from National Central Statistical offices, EBRD (1997, p. 74); for Estonia and Lithuania also Riboud et al. (2002); for Slovenia, estimates are from Kukar et al. (1995).

Most recent estimates (from 1997–2001) are:
- for Bulgaria, from Kotzeva (2002);
- for the Czech Republic (from 1996) from the Czech Statistical Office, also reported in Belina (2001, table 13);
- for Poland from the Polish Central Statistical Office (GUS), also quoted in Country Report 2001 of US Department of State (February 2002);
- for Romania, from Albu (2002);
- for Slovakia, from the National Bank of Slovakia (NBS), also quoted in the Economist Country Briefing on Slovakia (November 2002);
- for Turkey, estimates from national statistical office and also trade unions; see also Öğünç and Ilmaz (2000).

* data in the last column are an average for 2000-2001 from Schneider (2002): however, these are given only as an indication and should be read with caution - they are only authors' calculations from specific forecast methods (the DYMIMIC method and values using the physical input method) and so are not based on more objective methods, such as employee, employer or consumer surveys, in contrast with the other data in the table.

178

it at approximately 30 per cent of GDP. This sector has more than doubled in Latvia, reaching more than 35 per cent of GDP, a similar figure being observed in Bulgaria. Informal activities in Lithuania and Romania represent more than 20 per cent of GDP, although this is probably an underestimate. Poland is another country where the black economy has expanded enormously; many small and medium-size enterprises have a core of officially reported workers supplemented by a second, unofficial group, enabling them to evade onerous tax and social liabilities, as well as to respond more quickly to demand fluctuations (Burda 1998, p. 10). There is also a significant informal sector in Slovenia, although no data are available on its exact extent (UNDP 2001). Hidden employment is also well developed in Estonia, especially in sectors such as construction, agriculture, trade, hotels and restaurants, and other services (Eamets and Ukrainski 2000).

The shift to the informal sector represents a major structural change in employment in Central and Eastern Europe, alongside the other structural changes described above: the move towards private ownership and the rise of the service sector. The informal economy is also not unknown in the three southern candidate countries, especially Turkey.

It must be emphasised that the size of the informal economy as a percentage of GDP, while serving as an approximate measure of the phenomenon, is not ideal since many informal activities do not generate much added output as regards GDP (small jobs between neighbours, and so on), but rather represent lost opportunities for the formal sector, the time that people dedicate to the informal sector being in effect deducted from the formal economy. The number of people involved in informal activities; the amount of time they dedicate to the informal sector; the share in total income of revenues earned in the informal sector; or even the share of expenditure on informal markets all offer complementary and generally better measures of the extent of the informal sector, and of its importance for households. Information of this kind is generally collected through household surveys of representative samples. So far, however, they remain limited.

4.5.2 The Sources of Expansion

The informal economy is by definition a complex phenomenon, which is subject to many different influences both economic and social, and involves a number of different actors, above all employers, workers, and, indirectly, the state. It is therefore easier to try to analyse the different motivations from both the supply and the demand side.

From the supply side – that is, from those providing the service or doing the work – the informal sector represents a way of obtaining income which avoids taxation, as well as other constraints that come with an official job, such as obligatory working time (which makes it difficult to hold down two or three different jobs), or social security contributions. In general, however, the highest proportion of those working in the informal economy are people who could not find a job in the official economy or were pushed out of the social protection or social assistance system. Long-term unemployment is a phenomenon that leads directly to informal activities: 'discouraged workers withdrawing from unsuccessful job seeking after exhausting income support often turn to some form of informal activity' (Nesporova 2001, p. 4). For unscrupulous employers the high rate of long-term unemployment (see next sub-section) also represents unlimited reserves of cheap and flexible labour. Nevertheless, while many of those officially unemployed are in fact working in the informal economy, they do so under precarious conditions, being excluded from the possibility of unemployment benefits and other social allocations should they lose their job.

For the employer, a central feature of the transition is overtaxation of the labour market, which seems to have stimulated the large underground economy, especially in countries with particularly high taxation, such as Hungary (Laky 1998). The imposition of an increasing number of regulations on the labour market – such as minimum wages, provisions for hiring and firing employees, administrative costs such as the need to have individual labour contracts, and so on – have also been presented as a major cause of employers entering the informal economy. In fact, the informal sector can be seen in general as an unregulated market or as a 'process of labour market flexibilisation on the side of both enterprises and workers' (Nesporova 2001).

The informal sector has also been assimilated to the types of firm which have developed in the course of the transition. The newly established firms are usually small ones trying to exploit emerging market opportunities; however, due to their size and the very unstable environment in which they have to operate, they require more freedom in respect of hiring and firing, and in a number of other areas, so that they feel forced to quit the official sector when labour legislation leaves them no room to manoeuvre (Nesporova 2001). Although the development of myriad small private businesses has contributed to increasing official employment, it has been accompanied by a similar development of small units in the informal sector. We must add that the distinction between the two is often not clear since many small businessmen pursue activities in both sectors, or shift from one sector to the other whenever necessary.

Some countries have tried to implement programmes to combat the informal economy: for example, Slovenia's 'Identifying and sanctioning illegal work' programme in 1997 and the adoption of a new law in 2001 on 'prohibiting illegal work'. Nevertheless, we might wonder whether this type of legal action, although symbolically significant, is sufficient to address the extent and multidimensional nature of the phenomenon.

4.5.3 A Neglected Phenomenon So Far

At the beginning of the transition the informal sector was seen as a temporary phenomenon caused mainly by the transition from a Communist planned economy with 'full' employment to a market economy in which employment is determined by the functioning of the labour market (mainly labour supply and demand). It was thought that it would fade along with economic growth and the expansion of employment. From a social standpoint, the informal economy was viewed as a way of coping with very low wages: again, the envisaged economic growth would increase living standards in the official economy and the black market would die a natural death. In economic terms, informal activities would progressively diminish as sufficient incentives for engagement in the official economy were introduced, including lower taxes, reduction of rigidities related to hiring and firing, and other regulations.

Although we should not give up hope that these developments will emerge in the not too distant future, the informal economy continues to represent an important part of GDP. Moreover, it comprehensively distorts national statistics on economic growth, employment, and unemployment. In light of this, the lack of attention paid to this phenomenon by national governments, but also by international monetary institutions, is extremely surprising. Moreover, its neglect (and even its promotion as a way of deflecting difficulties during periods of restrictive macroeconomic policy) has unfortunately contributed to its tolerance and development at all levels.

The World Bank has taken little account of the informal sector: for example, in a recent 60-page report on labour markets in Central and Eastern Europe, only a single paragraph was dedicated to the informal sector, its main conclusion being that 'the size of the informal sector in CEE countries is not insignificant' (Riboud et al. 2002, p. 279), but without elaborating on what this means for the economy as a whole and also for society. The same neglect can be observed in almost all other documents prepared on labour markets and transition in Central and Eastern Europe (World Bank 2000b and 2002).

Even more surprisingly, the EC has not been particularly keen on raising the issue either. In all the Employment Assessment Reports prepared so far between the EC and the governments of candidate countries, the informal economy is hardly mentioned. The desire to maintain consensus in these joint assessment papers has inevitably influenced their contents, but at what price? The informal economy is perhaps the major problem facing employment in the candidate countries but no one seems to be taking it seriously.

For the World Bank, predictably, the main reason for the burgeoning of the informal economy is the excess of regulations and taxation. This is largely a supply-side (employers) view at the expense of the demand side (employees); other factors, such as the inheritance of the past, cultural elements, and social crisis, are totally ignored, not to mention the possible effects of the restrictive economic policies implemented in almost all Central and Eastern European countries since the beginning of the transition:

> There is the presumption that high taxes on labour create incentives for self-employment and an increase in the informal sector. In this regard the effect of high payroll taxes may add to the effect of employment protection legislation. Available data for CEE are scanty and subject to measurement errors but they suggest that this hypothesis may be relevant . . . in CEE countries. (Riboud et al. 2002, p. 279)

Alternative explanations have been provided for the growth of the informal economy which mainly emphasise the importance of social factors and in particular the growth of unemployment, as well as the spectacular fall in real terms of all sources of income, including wages, unemployment benefits, and social allowances, and the progressive removal of social services previously provided free of charge or for a modest contribution (Vaughan-Whitehead 1998). The increasing reliance on informal employment in subsistence agriculture, especially strong in countries such as Poland, Lithuania, Bulgaria, and Romania, tends to confirm this theory, indicating the strong influence that economic policies implemented in the first years of transition – particularly macroeconomic stabilisation programmes – may have had on fuelling the informal economy.

This may also be one reason why both national governments and the international organisations which influenced their decision-making have sought to deflect attention from the phenomenon, and have even tolerated it for years. The fact that it represents a de facto unregulated market, with implications for diminishing regulation of the formal sector (considered by many to be a condition of generating more economic growth) may constitute an additional explanation.

During the transition, national governments to some extent welcomed the informal sector since it to some extent relieved the social pain of the transition, so avoiding major popular unrest and taking many potential benefit claimants out of the system. Moreover, the spontaneous nature of the informal sector allows government to shrug off responsibility, at least in the short term. The revenue lost as a direct consequence of this policy, however, has been enormous: appropriate and timely tackling of the problem might have provided governments with sufficient budgetary room to manoeuvre to enable them to implement better education, housing, health care, and social protection.

More recently, the lack of attention paid to the informal sector is certainly due to the impact that inclusion of the informal sector would have on the official unemployment statistics, which are already very high.

4.5.4 A Range of Possible Scenarios

A number of scenarios could be elaborated as regards the informal sector. It is possible that economic growth, with a concomitant increase in the demand for labour, combined with the implementation of tougher rules against the informal economy would progressively eradicate the expansion of informal activities. At the same time, EU accession, which will involve the implementation of a series of provisions on working conditions (working time, health and safety, and so on), social dialogue, and workers' participation carries the danger that many enterprises will feel compelled to shift their activities, or at least part of them, to the informal sector. This scenario would be destructive for the implementation of the *acquis*, with the emergence of a dual economic system, and also for the future of social policy in an enlarged EU.

National and international policy-makers alike have a duty to take timely and adequate action on the informal economy. It should also receive more attention from European institutions. In any case, progressive reduction of the informal sector may contribute to increase unemployment.

4.6 UNEMPLOYMENT IN THE FUTURE MEMBER STATES

Unemployment is undoubtedly the worst development that the people of Central and Eastern Europe have had to face since it simultaneously affects income, human capital, social status, living standards, morale (especially in societies in which work has traditionally been highly valued), and, as a result, health. Although EU countries are also confronted by this scourge, the phenomenon seems to be particularly difficult to handle in Central and Eastern Europe. It seems, moreover, to strike there in an even more long-drawn-out and harsh fashion. In the following sections we attempt to explain some of its distinctive features in order to determine what policy implications, especially in prospect of EU enlargement, could be drawn from the first years of transition.

4.6.1 The Inexorable Rise of Unemployment

Unemployment rapidly became a major concern in the candidate countries of Central and Eastern Europe as the transition got under way. The sharp fall in production and employment rates that intervened after the collapse of the Communist regimes (as described above) led to an immediate surge in unemployment which rose in less than three years from virtually zero in 1990 to double-digit levels. For a while the Czech Republic seemed to be the only country to get away with very low unemployment rates, although it turned out that this was probably the result of delayed restructuring in large privatised enterprises rather than better economic performance, as shown by the rapid increase of unemployment rates from 1997.

Conversely, for countries such as Poland and Hungary 1997 represented the year when the long-awaited falls in unemployment finally occurred (in Poland down to 10.4 per cent compared with 13.2 per cent one year earlier; in Hungary down to 10.4 per cent compared with 11.1 per cent in 1996). However, these promising figures did not last for long. A new increase in unemployment occurred in the late 1990s despite more rapid economic growth. In Poland, for instance, unemployment started to increase again after its fall in 1997, a phenomenon described as 'a second wave of unemployment growth' (Boni 2001, p. 5) to reach more than 16 per cent in 2000 and 18 per cent in 2001. Some predict that a context of limited economic growth could bring unemployment rates of more than 25 per cent (Boni 2001, p. 15).

The largest increases were seen in Poland, Slovakia, and Bulgaria, where unemployment went beyond 15 per cent, a similar situation being also observed in the three Baltic countries. Unemployment in these countries is already much higher than the EU average. The remaining countries (Hungary, Romania, Slovenia, and the Czech Republic) have unemployment closer to the EU average. The differences are thus also important among CEE countries, since they vary from less than 6.0 per cent in Hungary in 2001, to nearly 19 per cent in Poland and 20 per cent in Slovakia.

4.6.2 A Poor Response to Economic Growth

The latest figures (for 1999–2001) show that employment does not seem to be responding much to economic recovery: the unemployment figures, in common with the social indicators discussed in the previous chapter, continue to lag well behind economic growth. This conclusion is shared by a number of different observers: 'the recovery in growth has not led to significant declines of open unemployment' (World Bank 2000b, p. 8).

This disconnection seems to underline the complexity of unemployment in the candidate countries, which cannot be reabsorbed merely through better economic performance because it seems rooted in a number of different factors. This casts doubt on the ability of governments to stop the disease; it should also lead us to interpret with greater caution the – seemingly impressive – GDP figures put out by these countries, while trying to address employment issues in more general (other than purely economic) terms. (See Figure 4.4.)

4.6.3 The Misleading Nature of Official Statistics

Unemployment rates in Central and Eastern Europe do not give a full account of the situation of local labour markets. They are often calculated on the basis

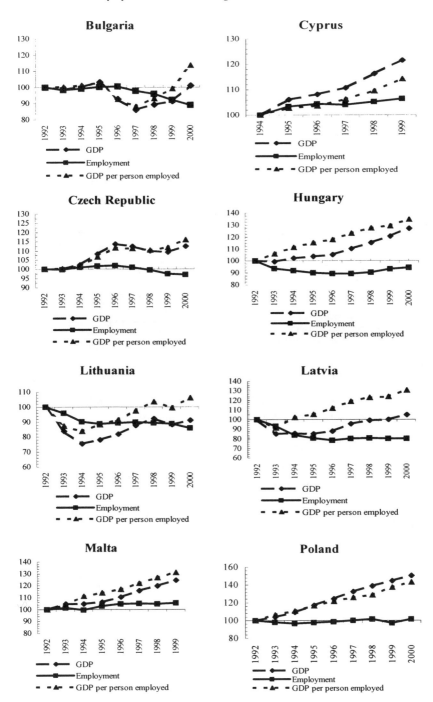

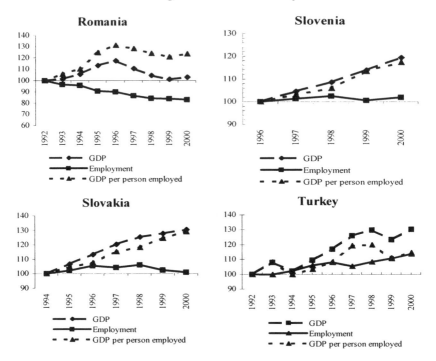

Source: author's esimates; see also Tzanov and Vaughan-Whitehead (1998)

Figure 4.4 GDP growth and employment growth, candidate countries, 1992–2000 (1992=100; otherwise index year indicated)

of questionable methodologies and unreliable data collection by local labour offices,[5] although considerable progress has been made, especially through the implementation of labour force surveys. Moreover, by including only job-seekers they may reflect a trend towards non-registration,[6] and exclude other categories, such as those forced to take early retirement or those in receipt of disability pensions, whose number has sky-rocketed.

5. For instance in the case of Estonia, although official figures were giving a 2.2 per cent unemployment rate in 1998, figures calculated on the basis of ILO methodology estimated unemployment as 9.6 per cent of the working population (see *Economist Intelligence Unit*, Estonia, 1st quarter 1999).

6. Registered unemployment is based on the data generated by local offices and is related to the advantages deriving from this status, such as access to job information, training programmes, and the provision of unemployment benefits. The ineffectiveness of local labour offices and active labour market policies, combined with the introduction of very tight eligibility criteria for unemployment benefits – as part of the new social safety net concept advised by the World Bank – in almost all Central and Eastern European countries, has led to a clear reduction in the number of registered unemployed.

Moreover, unemployment rates also conceal the importance of the informal sector: the large scale of this phenomenon in Hungary is not reflected in
Hungary's low unemployment rate of 5.7 per cent (2001), nor is underem-
ployment, which does not allow workers in the official economy to obtain
enough income. This is the case in Romania where the relatively low unemployment rate of 6.6 per cent (2001) clearly does not reflect the true situation:

> the main issue confronting the Romanian labour market is the prevalence of unde-
> roccupation – employment in activities that produce very little or do not correspond
> to the country's economic necessities – and not of unemployment. (Giurescu 2001,
> p. 2)

Similarly in Estonia, according to Eamets and Ukrainski (2000), low official
unemployment figures (although they have also reached higher levels in most
recent years) are mainly due to high 'hidden unemployment': in 1996 inactive
people constituted 32 per cent of the working population, compared to a 10 per
cent official unemployment rate. Such hidden unemployment was also found to
be hitting some categories of worker more than others, often reflecting a fall in
activity in traditional sectors: young and older people, men, non-Estonians,
and those living in particular regions where restructuring was most severe.

Labour force participation rates are a good complementary measure in this
regard. In the first years of transition, they made it possible to highlight the
dramatic fall of labour force participation since 1990 that was not yet reflected in the unemployment figures. Interestingly, more recently, labour force
participation has continued to decline even in those countries registering a
slight fall in unemployment (for example, Hungary).

4.6.4 Unemployment Rates Already Higher than in the EU

While unemployment is currently declining in the EU (after having increased
rapidly in the late 1990s) due to continuing growth of the economy and labour
market reforms – with an increased rate of net job creation for a given growth
in GDP – unemployment rates in candidate countries are generally following
the reverse trend, with a few exceptions (Hungary and Slovenia, and a few
others from 2001–2).

Unemployment growth has progressively placed candidate countries from
CEE around 13 per cent, that is, above the EU average of 8 per cent in 2000
and 7.4 per cent in 2001. Figure 4.5 shows that there was already a gap of more
than 5 percentage points in 2001 between the ten CEECs and the EU in terms
of unemployment rates.

As a result, in an enlarged EU with the inclusion of the 12 first candidate
countries (excluding Turkey), the EU average would be brought up to more
than 10 per cent (EC Cohesion Report 2001, EC 2001c, p. 19).

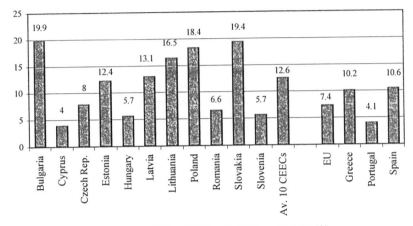

Source: EC Employment Reports, 2001 and 2002 (EC 2001b and EC 2002b).

Figure 4.5 Unemployment rates, candidate countries and selected EU, 2001

Many candidate countries have an unemployment rate of more than 13 per cent, making them comparable only with the EU countries and regions with the highest unemployment: Spain (excluding the Madrid area and the North-East), northern Portugal, Southern Italy and Northern France.

The EU's recent employment performance must be reconsidered in light of poor employment prospects in the candidate countries. While EU analysts recently commented on the better employment performance of EU countries with some self-satisfaction – 'if economic growth can be sustained at its present rate, over the coming decade it could gradually cease to be the major economic problem facing the EU, which it has been for the past 20–25 years' (EC Cohesion Report 2001, EC 2001c, p. 13) – they will now have to integrate the candidate countries in the picture. Future member states will thus contribute to keeping unemployment as part of the policy agenda. While this is an unavoidable consequence of enlargement, we should nevertheless not minimise the risks that this may bring in terms of social policy. Whether we like it or not, the increasing unemployment rates in future member states – especially if unemployment there continues its upward trend – will influence Social Europe and its social policies. We shall see how this phenomenon may contribute, for instance, to social dumping in the second part of this volume.

4.6.5 A Long-Lasting Phenomenon

While unemployment rates have increased in the last few years in Central and Eastern Europe it is long-term unemployment that presents the most marked difference with EU countries, most unemployed remaining so for more than one year. Long-term unemployment rates are much higher than the EU average (3.3 per cent in 2001) in all future member states, with the exception of Cyprus and Malta. It has even gone above 10 per cent of the labour force in Bulgaria and Slovakia, with Poland, Lithuania and Latvia not far behind (see Figure 4.6).

In more than half of the candidate countries, more than 50 per cent of the unemployed are in long-term unemployment, above the EU average (45 per cent), which means that a majority of them are experiencing long periods of inactivity: more than one year, and sometimes even two or three years. In 2000 the proportion of long-term (over one year) unemployed varied between 30 per cent in Cyprus to 63 per cent in Slovenia and 57 per cent in Latvia (Figure 4.7).

It is interesting to note that long-term unemployment is also a problem in Slovenia although the country registers an unemployment rate below the EU average: more than 60 per cent of the unemployed are long-term unemployed. Moreover, those that have registered as unemployed for a very long period, that is more than three years, constitute over one-quarter of all registered unemployed. Official statistics present an average waiting period for the unemployed of 30 months in 1999, which represents a four-month

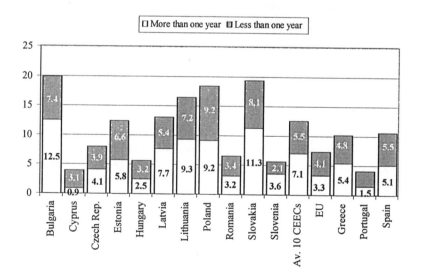

Source: EC Employment Reports, 2001 and 2002 (EC 2001b and EC 2002b).

Figure 4.6 Long-term unemployment (candidate countries and selected EU), 2001

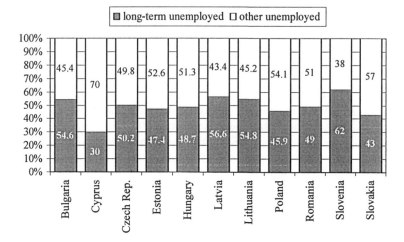

Source: EC Employment Reports, 2001 and 2002 (EC 2001b and EC 2002b).

Figure 4.7 Proportion of unemployed in long-term unemployment, some future member states, 2000

increase compared to 1998, and a six-month increase since 1997 (Rončević 2001, p. 6). These data show the extent of the fragmentation of labour markets in Central and Eastern Europe.

4.7 LABOUR MARKET INEQUALITIES

4.7.1 Enormous Regional Disparities

Regional unemployment differences have also increased: local unemployment in Central and Eastern Europe is now characterised by very high dispersion rates (Burda 1998, p. 8). Over the transition, employment and unemployment have thus become important factors accelerating the – already huge – economic and social differences between regions. Although, unemployment is affecting the regions of candidate countries in a very differentiated way, it seems to be spreading in all the candidate countries according to the same logic and generating factors. Unemployment is generally much lower in urban areas, especially around capital cities, while it is growing rapidly in rural, generally rather isolated and poorly developed areas. Geographical situation also plays a role, for instance, whether a region benefits from a border with an EU country.

In Poland, the situation is much better in Warsaw and environs (Mazowieckie voivodship) than in rural areas and the small towns of the north-east

(Wraminsko-mazurskie) and west (Lubuskie, Zachodniopomorskie), where unemployment rates are 2.5 times higher (above 22 per cent).[7] This situation afflicting rural inhabitants in Poland – they represent 43 per cent of the unemployed – is particularly worrying when we consider that they represent a significant proportion of the Polish population. The high unemployment rates in rural areas are especially difficult to reabsorb since they also concern a less qualified and also less mobile population. Regional imbalances have not been reduced by economic growth:

> The regional disparities in unemployment rates that emerged in the early 1990s have proven to be remarkably persistent. Regions where unemployment was high in 1993 still have high unemployment rates in 2001, despite several years of sustained economic growth. Additionally, the dispersion of unemployment rates between voivodships has been widening. (Rutkowski and Przybyla 2001, p. 2)

A similar situation may be observed in other future member states. For instance in Lithuania, territorial differences have become very large (Kairelis 2001).

Although regional differences are currently slightly smaller than in the EU, at least compared to regional differences within countries such as Italy and Spain (EC Cohesion Report 2001c, p. 20, Figure 5), we can expect the substantial differences already existing to increase even further when economic recovery boosts the already developed regions and leaves the others even further behind. Such regional differences in employment will represent a major social concern in the future, and one which may have an adverse effect on the social situation but also on economic growth.

4.7.2 Low Education the Basic Determinant: The 'Mismatch' Problem

Educational status seems to be the key variable in explaining the varying degrees of unemployment. People with only primary education are the first to lose their jobs; they also have more difficulty finding new ones. In Poland, more than 70 per cent of the unemployed have only primary education, or basic vocational schooling or less (Boni 2001). In Slovenia, 45 per cent of the unemployed are without basic vocational education. In Lithuania, the percentage of unemployed without or having lost their professional skills grew from 25 per cent in 1991 to 60 per cent in 2001 (Kairelis 2001).

People with a lower level of educational attainment also have a greater probability of experiencing long-term (more than one year) or even very long-term (more than two years) unemployment (see Table 4.2).

---

7. These differentials were even larger – four times in 1993 and even eight times in 1998 between Supskie and Warsawskie – before the administrative reform of 1998 modified and reduced the number of voivodships from 49 to 16, so leading to smaller disparities in unemployment rates between them (Rutkowski and Przbyla 2001).

Table 4.2 *Long-term and very long-term unemployment rates of men and women aged 25–54 by educational attainment level in candidate countries (excluding Turkey and Malta), 2000*

	BG	CY	CZ	EE	HU	LT	LV	PL	RO	SI	SK
Women											
Low											
Long-term	7.9	2.2	5.1	4.5	1.8	7.1	8.1	7.1	2.8	3.6	9.7
Very long-term	6.5	0.7	3.2	2.0	1.0	4.3	6.6	3.6	1.7	2.7	7.7
Medium											
Long-term	6.8	1.6	4.2	4.7	1.8	6.1	6.3	6.1	2.9	2.9	7.5
Very long-term	4.4	0.6	2.2	3.1	0.9	4.6	4.5	2.6	1.4	2.3	4.5
High											
Long-term	6.3	1.1	3.0	4.9	1.9	5.3	7.1	4.8	2.1	2.5	5.0
Very long-term	4.1	0.5	0.8	2.7	1.0	3.5	3.8	1.8	1.4	1.8	3.0
Men											
Low											
Long-term	8.3	0.7	4.1	8.5	3.0	10.6	8.1	5.2	3.7	3.9	1.4
Very long-term	6.7	0.2	2.7	3.5	1.7	9.2	6.2	2.3	1.9	3.0	8.4
Medium											
Long-term	7.4	0.4	2.8	7.0	2.9	10.1	7.6	4.6	3.8	3.5	8.1
Very long-term	5.1	0.0	1.3	3.7	1.3	6.8	4.9	2.0	1.6	1.7	4.2
High											
Long-term	7.5	1.0	2.4	4.0	3.6	7.6	9.5	1.8	3.8	2.6	3.7

Source: Eurostat.

These unemployment differences according to qualifications shed light on one of the structural causes of high unemployment, that is, qualifications and skills which do not match new employers' requirements.

This has been observed as a major cause of unemployment in all Central and Eastern European countries, even in Slovenia:

> The increasing mismatch between the newly required skills and the existing skills of the registered unemployed has become the main obstacle in the way of higher employment growth . . . this has led Slovenia, despite its relatively large number of unemployed, to import labour, mainly from former Yugoslav republics, to cover some of its labour market needs. (Kovac et al. 2001, p. 4)

On this basis we can better appreciate the employment implications of the policy advice of the World Bank (described in the chapter on social protection) to curtail expenditure on education, health care, and social services. While continuing this policy of budgetary restrictions in education, however, they recognise the benefits of a good education system for employment: 'to promote growth and reduce unemployment over the long term, reforms of the education system will be needed to provide the population with skills that are more appropriate for a market economy and that enable them to meet the challenge of global competition' (World Bank 2000b, p. 8). However:

> analysis of the (Polish) labour market indicates the importance of the 'educational premium' . . . it should be remembered that 4.2 million young people have not benefited from educational reform, and the bridging forms of education offered them to help adapt their skills to the needs of the labour market were imperfect at best. The adult education network is underdeveloped, and the incentives for adults to join such educational efforts and retraining courses are also quite weak. (Boni 2001, p. 16)

This lack of qualifications, combined with a lack of active employment policies to improve geographical mobility, also contributes to limit the labour mobility of the unemployed. This has been observed in, for example, Slovenia and Poland. Other social policy aspects, such as housing, can also represent an obstacle to internal migration: 'the key factor that inhibits migration within Poland is the poorly functioning housing market. People cannot move to desirable locations due to the very high housing prices in the major cities' (Rutkowski and Przybyla 2001, p. 3).

This confirms our conclusion in Chapter 3 on the need for a comprehensive social protection policy, and again emphasises the linkage between social protection policy and economic matters (such as employment). Poverty as such is often the main reason impeding migration: 'Many people from rural areas consider their farm land as a safety net, which reduces their willingness to migrate' (Rutkowski and Przybyla 2001, p. 4), a situation that has been observed in other countries, such as Lithuania and Bulgaria.

4.7.3 The Situation of Young People

Unemployment in Central and Eastern Europe seems to be hitting young people particularly hard. Those under 24 years of age represent nearly one-third of all unemployed (34 per cent in Poland, for instance) in the candidate countries. Their unemployment rate is much higher – nearly double – than the EU figure (26 per cent against 15 per cent in the EU), which is already considered unacceptably high. Within the EU, such rates can be found only in southern Italy, Greece, and the least developed regions of Spain. The prospects are bleak, since the situation is worsening in many countries. In Bulgaria, Poland and Slovakia unemployment among those under 24 was around 40 per cent in 2001 (see Figure 4.8) and approaching 30 per cent in 2002. Figures for other countries also confirm that the employment situation of this age group continued to deteriorate in 2001–2.

This phenomenon is considered to be particularly dangerous for the future of the candidate countries, since it is striking the first generation of the transition, which might otherwise have been expected to be forging and energising the new market economies. It also represents a tremendous loss in terms of human capital and human resources.

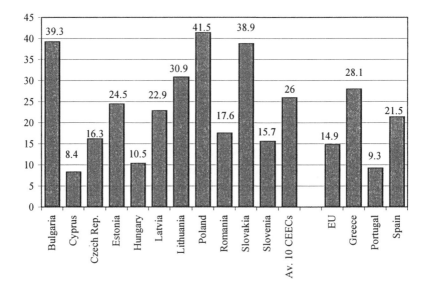

Source: EC Employment Reports, 2001 and 2002 (EC 2001b and EC 2002b).

Figure 4.8 Youth unemployment rate (15–24 years old), candidate countries and selected EU, 2001

4.7.4 Gender Inequalities Brought about by the Market

Under the previous regime Central and Eastern European countries tended to provide women with a central place in the world of work. This situation continues to prevail in most countries in the region. In 2000, for example, and in contrast with the EU pattern, most Central and Eastern European countries had higher male unemployment, with the gap between males and females being greatest in the Baltic countries.

However, the emergence of market economies brought the first imbalances and the first significant signs of inequality in respect of both employment and unemployment. While employment rates continue to be lower for women, as in EU countries (of approximately 20 per cent on average), this difference has started to increase rapidly in some countries of Central and Eastern Europe. Moreover, this is also particularly marked in the three candidate countries of Southern Europe, due to different cultures and traditions.

A significant gap has also started to develop between the unemployment of men and women in some Central and Eastern European countries, particularly in Poland, where it had reached more than 4 per cent (from around zero in 1990) after more than ten years of transition, but also in the Czech Republic.

Women are also at a disadvantage in respect of getting a job, since they seem to experience longer periods of unemployment. In Poland, 53 per cent of them have not been able to find a job for a year and so find themselves plunged into very long-term unemployment, reducing even further their ability to maintain the skills – and motivation – necessary to find a job. In Poland, this percentage also reflects the fact that 65 per cent of unemployed women have no more than – or even less than – primary education or basic vocational schooling (Boni 2001).

In the Czech Republic, empirical evidence shows that female workers and less educated workers have a higher probability of losing their jobs, while at the same time they are less likely to be hired if they are unemployed or have fallen out of the labour force for some other reason (Sorm and Terrell 2000).

The same phenomenon has not been observed, so far, in the other candidate countries of Central and Eastern Europe, where unemployment, including long-term unemployment, continues to be more prevalent among men.

4.7.5 Other Excluded Groups

Among other categories of the excluded we might also mention the disabled whose situation has worsened significantly during twelve years of transition.

In Slovenia, the disabled also represent an important group affected by unemployment (Kovac et al. 2001).

Studies also point to the difficult labour market position of the Roma population, with clear cases of discrimination. Roma people were often found to be excluded from education and employment opportunities. A number of programmes to give them better access to education and training have been implemented. Nevertheless, their situation will not be improved without a more comprehensive policy, aimed also at improving social protection and social assistance coverage, as well as at facilitating their better integration (schooling, housing, and so on), an aspect which the European Commission has emphasised during the accession negotiations (under the sub-chapter 'Human Rights and the Protection of Minorities').

4.8 THE LACK OF SUPPORT FOR THE UNEMPLOYED

4.8.1 New Eligibility Criteria for Unemployment Benefits

Surprisingly, faced with growing unemployment and its social consequences, most national authorities, instead of putting more resources into combating the problem or helping those affected by it, have limited themselves to introducing tougher rules of eligibility for unemployment benefits; many have even reduced unemployment funding overall. The arguments put forward in support of this are often the same: reducing the number of people eligible for benefits is the only way of maintaining a balanced budget and also of encouraging people to make every effort to rejoin the labour market. The World Bank's strong position on the need to implement a strict budgetary policy and to cut social allowances of all kinds, including unemployment benefit, has supported and legitimised government decisions in this area.

It must be emphasized that changes in unemployment benefit eligibility generally have the automatic effect of reducing the number of registered unemployed, but without bringing about a real improvement in the employment situation:

> The number of registered unemployed in Slovenia has been in constant decline since 1998. In spring 2001 it fell to 100 000, the main reason being the adoption of the new law on employment in 1999, when unemployment benefits were reduced and many new active employment measures to assist active job seeking were introduced. (Kovac et al. 2001, p. 4)

Similarly for Lithuania:

> [The year] 1995 was marked by a continual rise in unemployment, related to economic restructuring. In 1996 the unemployment rate began to fall, partly due to

stricter regulations on active and passive labour market measures. (Kairelis 2001, p. 4)

We might wonder whether some might consider this to be a good way of reducing youth unemployment as well:

Where politically possible, eligibility conditions should exclude students and new entrants to the labor force. Benefit duration [for the others] should be limited to six to nine months to reduce work disincentives. (World Bank 2000b, p. 58)

There are, however, different ways of identifying the results of such a policy: for example, by studying the coverage ratio, or even the level of unemployment benefits.

All relevant variables decreased over the period. If we take only one variable into account, for instance the number of unemployed entitled to unemployment benefit – something which can be reduced artificially – it does not reflect a faithful image of reality: for instance, in Poland, the percentage of people entitled to unemployment benefits decreased from 60 per cent in 1990 to 20 per cent in 2000, without a corresponding improvement in the unemployment situation.

4.8.2 Difficulties Reaching and Assisting the Unemployed

The stricter conditions on unemployment registration have clearly discouraged many unemployed persons from registering at local employment offices. Another barrier to registration is the financial costs involved: for instance, for those living in rural areas the distance they have to travel is simply too great. Moreover, the low level of development of local employment offices means that a great deal of time is spent queuing, only adding to the frustration of being without work. Data on several countries show that nearly half of the unemployed do not take the time and trouble to register, also because they have little confidence that they will obtain appropriate assistance. Statistics in Bulgaria, for example, show that only 50 per cent of the unemployed mentioned registration at employment offices as a means of finding a job. In Estonia, the number of discouraged workers was estimated to represent more than 5 per cent of the labour force, and more than 25 per cent of the unemployed (Eamets and Ukrainski, 2000).

The poor state of employment services is mainly the result of high staff turnover, a lack of financial resources, and overly centralised control, suppressing personal initiative. Labour offices are largely seen as institutions which dole out unemployment benefits to laid-off workers; at the same time, their mediation and other services are severely neglected. In Poland, for example:

> Labour market policy . . . is becoming diffused, lending itself poorly to cohesive action programmes. Instead of a cooperative approach involving both government and local authorities, disputes over funding tend to arise. One important side-effect, significant from the point of view of effective management of the labour market, was the high employment turnover (60 per cent in one year) of employment services staff who are paid, for reasons of economy, from the budget for intervention works. This has adverse consequences for the quality and scale of employment intermediation. (Boni 2001, p. 18)

Similarly in Lithuania:

> Employment management structures at all levels lack definite shape. Major state governance and municipal institutions with an influence on employment rates and labour markets do not sufficiently coordinate their activities which impedes timely decision-making . . . with the result that properly considered employment-related decisions are lacking. (Kairelis 2001, p. 8)

In some countries, a series of efforts have been made to introduce private job agencies. The results so far, however, are not conclusive: in Lithuania, for example, a 'lack of professionalism in the activities of private employment agencies gives rise to unnecessary tensions . . . It is necessary to refine the regulation of non-public employment agencies (companies)' (Kairelis 2001, p. 9).

4.8.3 The Lack of Means for Tackling Unemployment

For all analysts, unemployment has become the principal factor in the development of poverty and social exclusion: 'The main cause of poverty is unemployment . . . one of the two population groups at a high risk of poverty are members of households whose heads have lost contact with the labour market . . . CEEC governments would need to address the challenge of reducing unemployment' (World Bank 2000b, p. 8).[8] Similarly in Poland, 'one of the most important determinants of social status is having or not having a job; this factor has become the key determinant of Polish poverty' (Boni 2001, p. 4).[9]

Despite this assessment, expenditure on unemployment benefits has decreased, while less resources are allocated to employment policy in general. We might wonder what the positive effects of such a policy are imagined to be, a point well summarised in the following:

---

8. The second group being households with three or more children.
9. Michael Boni was Minister of Labour and Social Policy, also adviser to the Deputy Prime Minister on employment and accession issues.

Reforms of unemployment insurance should include reduction of high tax rates on contributors to reduce tax evasion and informalisation of the economy; tightening eligibility criteria; reducing the duration of benefits to avoid work disincentives; ensuring consistency of reforms with social assistance programs so that cost savings from reducing unemployment benefits will not be lost because of higher social assistance outlays; and giving one-off severance benefits to those laid off because of industrial restructuring. (World Bank 2000b, p. 9)

The argument that reducing support to the unemployed gives them the incentive to find a job is based on the simplistic assumption that many people prefer to remain in the humiliating state of social exclusion and deprivation than make the effort to find a job. On the other hand, different studies have also shown that a policy of low social protection and social benefits can have adverse effects on the labour market. They can, for instance, induce employees to become risk averse in their employment behaviour, discouraging them from changing jobs: employees are reluctant to look for a better job, even if such a move might give them better wages and working conditions, when they know that, should their change of employment not work out, unemployment benefits and complementary social assistance would be difficult to obtain. This policy thus reduces the labour turnover widely agreed by economists as the best means of allocating labour market resources and so generating economic growth. Once again, we find that a lack of social policy can have adverse implications for the economy.

Nesporova (2001) has clearly identified the relative infrequency of job-to-job moves in Central and Eastern European countries, with the exception of Slovenia (which, as we have seen, has a comprehensive social protection policy), a phenomenon that she explains in terms of the 'lower confidence that people have in labour market and social protection institutions'.

4.8.4 Balance between 'Passive' and 'Active' Labour Market Policies

The removal of unemployment benefits has also been justified by policy-makers and advisers as a sign of the redirection of attention and funding towards active employment policy (labour market training, on-the-job training, business incubators, business clubs, and public works).

While there has been a shift towards active employment policy, some active measures have not proved very successful, such as the extensive and costly use of public works in the mid-1990s in all candidate countries. 'Local government preferences for public works . . . prevent the application of more effective labour market policies' (Boni 2001, p. 18). Moreover, tight central control and strict eligibility conditions for participation in active employment programmes have hindered their wider implementation despite the desperate need to reintegrate the long-term unemployed into the labour market.

4.9 UNCERTAINTY AND INSECURITY

4.9.1 Over-Reliance on Private Small Businesses?

One other major characteristic, probably the most important, of labour markets in Central and Eastern Europe is the increasing role of small and medium-size enterprises. In the course of only ten years small units have become the major actor in the economy in terms of employment; a number of studies have also shown that they have been the main engine of growth. This process has been supported by governments which have tried to facilitate the creation and development conditions of small units. For instance, in Slovenia enormous support was given by the government to promote self-employment, which led to the creation of 23 000 new businesses (Kovac et al. 2001). Small and medium-size enterprises also represented the main source of new jobs.

In most CEE candidate countries, the share of small and medium-size enterprises in employment has increased spectacularly. As an example, in Poland they constitute nearly 60 per cent of total employment, and their contribution to economic growth has been estimated at 45 per cent of GDP in 2000. In Lithuania enterprises of fewer than 50 employees represent 80 per cent of the 128 000 registered enterprises, employing more than 40 per cent of the labour force.

Table 4.3 shows that the percentage of employment in enterprises with less than 50 employees is more than the EU average (52.6 per cent) in most candidate countries, and especially in Estonia (59.7), Slovenia (66.4), and Slovakia (more than 90 per cent). Moreover, most future member states are characterised by a much higher percentage of micro-enterprises – less than 5 employees – as in Slovakia, Cyprus, Poland, Hungary, and the Czech Republic. Future member states are also characterised by a very large number of self-employed people, above the EU average.

More vulnerability
Although they have generated rapid growth, small enterprises are more vulnerable than larger companies. In particular, their life expectancy is lower – although by taking greater risks they can generate higher profits they are also susceptible to incurring more serious losses – so that we cannot be certain that their overall effect on employment (especially on employment security) will remain positive over time. For the Minister of Labour of Poland, 'weak job creation in SMEs pushes up unemployment . . . particularly at a time of disinflationary targets and exchange rate stabilisation, with money and credit becoming very dear' (Boni 2001, p. 15). Similarly, for the state-secretary of the Ministry of Labour of Romania, there is 'insufficient creation of workplaces in small and medium-size enterprises' (Giurescu 2001, p. 3).

Table 4.3 Distribution of employment (% of total employed) by size, candidate countries, 2000

	1–5	1–10	11–49	50+
Bulgaria	–	–	–	–
Cyprus	28.3	41.1	23.4	34.6
Czech Republic	15.9	28.2	26.1	38.1
Estonia	12.8	22.5	37.2	37.4
Hungary	16.3	24.6	28.5	41.7
Latvia	–	–	–	–
Lithuania	–	21.0	22.4	50.2
Malta	–	–	–	–
Poland	–	24.1	26.0	43.2
Romania	–	–	–	–
Slovakia	65.4	80.4	16.8	2.8
Slovenia	32.0	43.9	22.5	33.7
Turkey**	–	27.7	23.7	48.5
EU average*	–	33.6	18.9	47.4

Notes :
* 1998 for EU average
** 1999 for Turkey (Labour statistics, 1999, Ministry of Labour and Social Security)
Total slightly less than 100% in candidate countries because of the answers 'do not know' (between 1 and 8 per cent).

More insecurity

As in EU countries, it seems that employment stability is in direct correlation with enterprise size. Employment in small enterprises in Central and Eastern Europe has been found to be characterised by higher labour turnover and a much shorter period of job tenure (Nesporova 2001).

> the distribution suggests a rather consistent pattern across countries as job tenure clearly increases with enterprise size in almost all the [Central and Eastern European] countries under review. The employees in larger establishments [enterprises with more than 50 employees] have significantly longer job tenure (11.4 years on average in 1999) in comparison with employees in establishments with less than ten workers (7.2 years on average) . . . the pattern by enterprise size may also be partly explained by the fact that employment protection legislation is much less enforced for very small firms, which thus feel less constrained in their layoffs. (Nesporova 2001, p. 27)

Interestingly, divergent results were also found by country. The lowest job tenure was found in Estonia and Lithuania (6.9 years and 7.6 years respectively, and so the closest to the US average of 6.6 years), where more liberal labour market policies have been implemented, followed by the Czech Republic and Hungary (8.2 and 8.8 years), while the longest job tenures were found in Poland and Slovenia (11.9 and 12.0 years, and so closer to EU countries such as Denmark). On the other hand, we have seen that Slovenia is also characterised by the fact that a significant proportion of the labour force is on temporary contracts.[10]

All these results tend to show that job security in the future member states will be influenced by the dominance in the economy of small and very small enterprises, with the concomitant lack of regulation. The combination of high separation rates and high turnover in a context of long-term unemployment (which makes it more difficult for workers to re-enter the labour market) may also have adverse effects and lead to fragmentation of the labour market and more exclusion. Differences will also be observed between those countries which have deregulated their labour market more quickly and more extensively, and those which have followed a more gradual approach. These trends will have to be closely monitored in the future since they may have a direct impact on working conditions and social dialogue at enterprise level.

4.9.2 Overreliance on Services in a Context of Low Consumption

The increased proportion of services in the economies of the candidate countries has been seen by some observers as potentially leading to imbalances, especially since services depend mainly on domestic market prospects and can suffer from a sudden economic slowdown. Moreover, their expansion is directly related to consumption patterns. In Romania, 'the main object of the great majority of small and medium-size enterprises is retail and small-scale production orientated towards consumers' (Giurescu 2001, p. 2).

In a context of widespread social exclusion and poverty, and social developments that do not seem to be following the acceleration in economic growth, small businesses in the service sector may well run into difficulties. This phenomenon has already been observed in some countries. In Poland, 'the lack of a net addition of new jobs in the service sector observed over the past year is a disquieting development, considering that this sector generated over 750 000 new jobs in the years 1994–99' (Boni 2001, p. 8). For Giurescu (2001, p. 2), the poor prospects of small companies in services have the fol-

---

10. As we saw in Chapter 2, Slovenia is the country which makes the greatest use of temporary contracts. This is confirmed by Nesporova (2001, p. 36) who also found a high percentage of workers with a tenure of less than one year (65 per cent). At the same time, there is also a high percentage of workers with job tenure of 10 years or more, which means that the Slovenian labour market is characterised by high fragmentation.

lowing result: 'people who abandon jobs in industry involve themselves in small-scale activities (at family level) in agriculture'.

Nevertheless, the growth of services, especially in relation to industry, continues to be advocated on the assumption that these are the most dynamic and employment creating sectors. For the EC, 'the employment gap in services – three-quarters of the EU average – is important and overall employment growth will depend on job creation in services, particularly financial, business and personal services' (EC Employment Report 2001, EC 2001b, p. 12). While this is certainly true, as can be seen from the impressive growth generated in these countries in recent years, not to mention in the OECD countries, especially the United States, in Central and Eastern Europe this is taking place in a context in which industries and the most potentially profitable activities in this sector have not been consolidated since the collapse of the early 1990s.

Moreover, the employment rate in industry for the ten Central and Eastern European countries as a whole is already nearly at the EU average. If higher rates are recorded in a number of countries, such as the Czech Republic, Slovenia, Estonia, and Slovakia, these are however very much comparable to those in highly developed EU member states, such as Germany and Austria. The European Commission confirms that: 'overall, the data suggest that industrial employment in the CEECs has reached a sustainable level' (EC Employment Report 2001, EC 2001b, p. 96). Further decline should thus be stopped.

In order to motivate growth, the share of services in employment will continue – and should be encouraged – to increase, with important employment prospects emerging in those sectors currently under-employed such as finance and business services, while services such as trade, hotels and restaurants, and transport are already close to the EU average. At the same time, the recovery in industrial production has also played a role in output recovery and economic growth in most Central and Eastern European countries, so this process must be allowed to continue.

> The persistent larger proportion of the secondary sector (industry) in total employment, combined with its internal restructuring, has been decisive for early economic recovery and its sustainability. Consequently, the contribution of services increased there primarily as a result of higher demand of consumers and enterprises. (Nesporova 2001, p. 6)

Industrial policy and specialisation should now be given more emphasis in order to promote the more balanced development of the economy and to give these countries a chance of developing competitive manufacturing activities that could be beneficial both for the trade balance and for economic growth. It should be underlined that industrial policies of this kind are still not in place in most candidate countries despite the need to promote strong industrial sectors and to address the imbalances that an overreliance on services might bring. Most EU member states have defined an industrial policy in response to a need understood since the late 1970s.

Agricultural reform must also be carried out, but gradually, with particular care being paid to all those making a living from subsistence production or employment in agriculture.

4.9.3 Overreliance on Foreign Investment?

Since the beginning of the reforms, almost all candidate countries have multiplied the conditions for attracting foreign investment, through tax incentives, free land, and so on, without selecting much, if at all, the type of investor and in what activity such projects were carried out. Many candidate countries even gave preference to strategic foreign investors in their privatisation process. All opportunities to buy local enterprises for next to nothing, combined with the prospect of the domestic market as well as the possibility of achieving economies of scale and exporting at much lower cost to EU markets, have led to massive foreign direct investment flows. We shall see in Chapter 8 how this has led foreign investment to totally dominate the economies of many candidate countries, in terms of sales, exports, and profits. At the same time, this massive influx of foreign investment seems not to have helped these countries to solve their unemployment problem, especially the long-term unemployment we have discussed so far. We shall explain in Chapter 8 that this is mainly due to the type of labour force, highly skilled and better educated, which is employed by foreign investors, who also do not hesitate to get rid of unskilled workers, the category of workers most vulnerable to unemployment, especially long-term unemployment. Considering the limited effects of foreign investment on employment compared to its contribution to other economic variables such as GDP, sales, and profits, we might wonder whether economic growth entirely led by foreign investment is not too unbalanced and does not generate too much employment insecurity in the long run.

4.9.4 The Call for Less Regulation

Since the late 1990s, voices have been raised advocating less regulation in order to reduce labour market rigidities and to generate more growth and employment. This appears to be a resurgence in the candidate countries of the supply-side theories that marked Western economies in the 1980s and which have given ground to the neo-liberal policies pursued in the USA, the UK, and some other countries.

Such arguments have been advanced particularly by employers' organisations in the course of the revision of the labour code in individual countries. In Poland, for instance, the debate in 2000–1 crystallised around the severance costs to be paid by employers for collective dismissals, and on the removal of obstacles to hiring and firing employees, an issue also discussed in Slovenia in 2000–1. In other countries, proposals to make working time more flexible and overtime less costly for the employer have also been discussed and adopted, as in Hungary and Bulgaria. More freedom to implement atypical forms of employment – which, as we saw in Chapter 2, have not been made much use of as yet but are rapidly increasing – have also been discussed. In Slovakia, revision of the labour code about more flexible labour market measures in late 2002–early 2003 has led to strong disagreements and conflicts between employer and trade union representatives. In Poland, more flexible labour law for temporary or part-time contracts, whose use is particularly sought after by employers in the service sector, have also been proposed. More freedom is also requested for small and medium-size enterprises and for the self-employed. Attacks have already emerged on the minimum wage, which some consider to be the main rigidity impeding more employment growth on the region, although we saw in Chapter 2 that it remains at so low a level that it cannot play any adverse role in the labour market.

> Some of the measures that may help CEE countries reduce unemployment are training and education, ensuring that the minimum wage is not too high, and addressing some non-labour, market-related structural problems . . . in countries where the minimum wage is relatively high, such as Poland where it is above 40 per cent of the average wage, the minimum wage may be binding for certain groups and may have a negative impact on youth employment. This suggests caution in raising the real level of the minimum wage, as well as consideration for a lower minimum wage for young workers. (World Bank 2000b, p. 8)

Interestingly, some countries have proposed replacing some regulations with greater emphasis on social dialogue and collective agreements. This is certainly one promising option which, although certainly not replacing regulations – at least those which are made compulsory within the Community *acquis* – might usefully allow their adaptation to local requirements and conditions through negotiations and agreements between employers and trade union representatives. The social partners' role in employment issues has also been enhanced through the conclusion of tripartite pacts, as happened in Romania with the *Social Agreement* concluded in February 2001 with active measures against unemployment, and in Poland with the *Pact to Create New Jobs* signed in early 2001 and aimed at generating an alternative strategy for tackling unemployment issues and easing the functioning of local labour markets. Progress in involving the social partners in designing and implementing employment policy at national and local level still has to be made in most countries, however, including Hungary and Slovenia.

According to a recent World Bank study on labour market dynamics in some Central and Eastern European countries, the evidence so far is mixed. To the first question addressed by the authors – 'Have candidates for EU accession introduced in their labour markets the same rigidities that exist in EU countries?' – the authors found that 'the answer varies greatly between countries, just as labour markets and institutions in the EU exhibit enormous diversity' (Riboud et al. 2002, p. 283). Moreover:

> compared to EU members, CEE countries fall in the middle of the 'flexibility' scale regarding their employment protection legislation. They have not adopted legislation as flexible as that in the United Kingdom or Ireland, nor have they copied the highly rigid southern European model . . . They also spend relatively little to support the unemployed . . . the CEE average spending in both passive and labour market policies falls below the EU and OECD average, and the behaviour of these countries resembles that of the United States, Japan and Southern Europe, rather than that of Denmark or Sweden in this respect. (Riboud et al. 2002, p. 283)

At the same time, the authors identify much more permissive regulations and thus flexible markets in countries such as Hungary, but also Poland and the Czech Republic which seem to have already moved towards relatively unregulated labour markets. Rules for hiring and firing, including notification, relatively lax in, for example, Hungary where a written statement to an employee is sufficient for dismissal, while in other countries, as in the EU, an employee representative body must be involved, and employers are required to take into account social considerations, to look for retraining, or even to ensure the worker's transfer to another suitable position. At the same time, in Hungary and Poland, the notice period is short and the severance payment small. Czech and Hungarian legislation have the fewest restrictions in two important legislative areas, temporary employment and collective dismissals (Riboud et al. 2002). By contrast, Slovenia seems to have retained more restrictive rules in this regard.

It is too early to assess whether the direction taken by the candidate countries is towards greater or less labour market regulation than in EU countries, which are themselves characterised by marked differences. What is sure is that the trend taken by employers and some governments in the EU towards deregulation is currently also being observed in most candidate countries. The risk is that some future member states may in fact implement more excessive policies than those of the EU – and there are already signs of this in Hungary and the Czech Republic – with clear implications for the balance between 'flexibility' and 'security' that continues to represent a basic principle and aim of EU labour markets and a distinctive feature of the European Social Model.

Already some voices have been raised on the negative effects of such deregulation. In Lithuania 'current legislation regulating restructuring, privatisation
and mass dismissals fails to ensure the timely solution of social problems'
(Kairelis 2001, p. 7). On the other hand, the removal of regulations is demanded particularly by the World Bank in its neo-liberal crusade. They clearly consider the minimum wage, but also 'generous unemployment benefits' as among
the 'rigidities of market policies and institutions' (World Bank 2000b, p. 55).

> The two features low job creation and high long-term unemployment – have often
> been identified as associated with inflexible labor markets . . . in contrast, long term
> unemployment do not represent more than 7 per cent of the pool of unemployed in
> the USA – which has by far the most flexible labor market . . . although the view
> that regulations have no substantial impact also prevail in the literature, one cannot
> dismiss the possible negative impact of regulations on total employment. (Riboud
> et al. 2002, p. 277)

We would like, however, to relocate the debate to where we believe it should
be, in particular by pointing out that it would be unfair – and intellectually dis-
honest – to blame current labour regulations for the high unemployment rates
currently observed in most candidate countries. We have seen that such high
unemployment rates are the result of a complex combination of factors, not
only economic but also social, including the mistakes of employment policies
implemented in the recent past (and advised by the same people or organisations which today put all the responsibility on excessive regulations). In particular, we have seen that the unemployed are currently paying the price for a
lack of appropriate policy in education, training, and active employment measures. They are also paying the price for the absence of a long-term industrial policy – and the identification of promising industries and enterprises – that
should have been implemented since the beginning of the transition to accompany the massive elimination of unproductive jobs and factory closures.

We have also seen how the policy of massive pre-retirement schemes has
been detrimental to social protection funding and for the well-being of the
older population, while the cutting of the budget for unemployment benefits
and employment policy could also restrict labour mobility, both between jobs
and between employment and unemployment.

There must be a serious debate on employment to put it in a more general
context, particularly taking into account its multidimensional nature. This is
what the European Employment Strategy tries to do, by developing a series of
complementary levers – or pillars – for employment growth.

4.9.5 The Lack of Consideration for Demand-Side Economics

In the first years of reform, the strict supply-side policy, with wage controls
and cuts in budgetary expenditure, did not leave much room for consumption

to develop, a process that was deliberately postponed and expected to emerge spontaneously alongside more sustained economic growth. Unfortunately, this does not seem to have occurred. On the contrary, the disconnection we have observed in the last few years (1999–2002) between economic growth and social and living standards – together with widespread poverty – represents a worrying sign not only for society but also for the economy. It not only affects human capital and human resources, so undermining future productivity and competitiveness, but it also has a direct effect on domestic demand, which is being allowed to slowly suffocate. Different studies have documented the direct effects of falling wages and living standards on consumption in the first years of reform (Vaughan-Whitehead 1998), but this process appears to be continuing. Some statistical indicators are particularly telling, such as the consumption of petrol and electricity, but primary food products have also suffered significantly, not only in the countries with major economic difficulties, such as Bulgaria or Romania, but also in those with strong economic growth such as Hungary, the Czech Republic, Poland, and even Slovenia.

In such a context, it seems clear that manufacturing will find it difficult to survive unless a serious boost is given to domestic demand. These economies cannot be sustained by exports alone, because the absence of strong domestic markets will inevitably generate a structural trade imbalance, with imports dominating exports, a scenario already present vis-à-vis the European Union (documented in Part II of this book) that is already stifling some countries in the region. Moreover, producers in these countries – especially after heavy restructuring and difficulties shifting to expensive new technology and modern production techniques, and with product quality still in great need of improvement – require staged industrial development, the local market representing an unavoidable preliminary stage before production for external markets can really take off. Higher domestic demand is also necessary for strong manufacturing, serving as a basis on which to build competitive products. We have also seen that an increase in domestic demand is also a key condition for continuing to sustain the expansion of the service sector, which is already running up against the limits imposed by too low levels of consumption.

A boost in consumption would also help to fight the informal economy, the growth of which is directly related to the fall in incomes and living standards: on the consumption side, low living standards induce households to consume on the black market, where goods are cheaper although of lower quality; on the production side, very low wages in the formal economy, especially in the budget sphere, push an increasing number of people to seek supplementary incomes from second or third jobs in the informal sector. It is time that governments take more careful account of these aspects when defining their wages and incomes (including social benefits) policy. After more than ten years of transition, living standards continue to be below people's expectations, while the promises of successive governments to build a middle class have still to materialise.

4.10 FUTURE MEMBER STATES: A DIFFERENT REALITY?

The foregoing sections have emphasised the rather different features of employment and unemployment in candidate countries. Employment rates appear to be lower, unemployment is on the rise and in most cases already above the EU average; it is dominated by long-term unemployment. The 'mismatch' problem, moreover, seems to be underlining the lack of internal training, mobility, and a personnel and human resources approach within individual enterprises. The fact that very small private enterprises and large multinational corporations are currently driving the economy does not seem to be leading to balanced economic growth, nor to more employment stability.

The progressive shift towards more casualisation of work, with an increased reliance on temporary, part-time, or interim agency work contracts also dramatically increases insecurity for workers.

This means that the situation of employment in future member states may well continue to deteriorate, and potentially change radically the overall picture of employment in an enlarged EU.

4.10.1 A Balance between 'Flexibility' and 'Security'

We have seen in Chapter 2 that working conditions are rapidly evolving in future member states towards extreme casualisation of work, and overreliance on atypical forms of contract and extreme cases of work-flexibility, as with use of working time in Malta, self-employment in Hungary, health and safety sub-standards in the Slovak republic, dismissal rules in the Czech Republic, and sub-contracting and informal activities in Bulgaria or Romania.

For the time being, there is thus a clear imbalance in the future member states, between 'flexibility' – which we have found to be clearly over-used – and 'security', which is lacking for workers.

The transposition of EU directives in this regard represents the best way of preventing the implementation of extreme labour market policies in candidate countries. Nevertheless, the legal *acquis* on the functioning of the labour market is sparse, for instance on the rules concerning entrance and exit from the market. In this context, recent progress on employment policy in the Treaty is a complementary tool. The European Employment Policy fixes an important number of conditions for ensuring a high level and quality of employment.

In particular, all four pillars of the European Employment Strategy are directly relevant for candidate countries.

Candidate countries have started to be involved in a preparatory phase of the European Employment Strategy, through joint assessment reports on employment, commonly drafted by the candidate country with the European Commission. These documents are aimed at carrying out a first assessment of the employment situation, particularly with a view to the forthcoming participation of these countries in the coordinated approach to employment. Follow-up seminars are also organised. No doubt this exercise is useful, if for no other reason than to sensitise the candidate countries to the process in which they will have to participate.

Nevertheless, we should note the generally low interest of candidate countries for this exercise, which they consider more as an obligatory process to please the European Commission before accession than as a key process for improving their employment situation and bringing it into line with other countries.

We could also criticise the style of the so-called JAPs (joint-assessment papers) which are generally written along the same lines and structure, and too rarely address the most sensitive and thus most relevant issues, such as the informal economy, the role of SMEs and of multinational companies in employment growth, the causes of long-term unemployment, and the mismatch problem we described above.

4.10.2 The Social Partners: An Essential Role in the Process

Moreover, the social partners have so far rarely been involved in the inputs for the joint-assessment papers written by candidate countries with the European Commission, although they were expected to be so. While governments did not find much incentive to work with social partners in this area, the European Commission did not always insist as much as it might have done on having the social partners more directly integrated in the whole exercise. This contrasts strongly with the expected role of the social partners in the European Employment Strategy: since 2000, they have been expected to get involved not only in the design of the Employment Guidelines defined every year, but also in the monitoring process at national level with regard to implementation of such guidelines by individual member states. Moreover, social partners have a direct role to play in pillars such as 'employability' – where they are to encourage partnership approaches to ease the transition from school to work, take into account the needs of disadvantaged groups in the labour market, and, more generally, help to develop opportunities for life-long learning – or 'adaptability' (where social partners are invited to negotiate and implement, at all appropriate levels, agreements to modernise the organisation of work, including flexible working arrangements, with the aim of achieving the necessary balance between flexibility and security).

The employment guidelines for 2000 (but also 2001 and 2002) called for a consolidation of the social partners' commitment to this process, emphasising once again the need for their involvement especially in modernising work organisation. The social partners' role in the employment strategy is expanding progressively, as referred to in the mid-term review in the Joint Employment Report:

> Bearing in mind that a number of guidelines are also or exclusively addressed to the social partners, the latter should be invited in future to provide a direct contribution to the National Action Plan implementation reports, in which they should report on their role in implementing the employment strategy. This could imply the setting by the social partners of a joint approach and objectives, enabling them to develop an autonomous process in the context of the Employment Guidelines, including the benchmarking of their contribution at various levels in all relevant pillars, and in particular under the adaptability pillar. (EC 2000b, p. 12)

These increased responsibilities of the social partners in the field of employment, and in particular in the EU coordinated employment policy, contrast strikingly with the situation of employment we have described in candidate countries, as well as with the missing structures of social dialogue and of social partners that we describe in Chapter 5.

4.10.3 The State: Between Policy Coordination and Over-Intervention

The state has a complex task: while it is mainly responsible for the whole employment policy, it should also leave enough flexibility to social partners and also local actors to carry out the most appropriate policies. This balance has rarely been found, not only in candidate countries but also in EU member states.

As an example, it is clear that the state should not have a monopoly on employment services, especially considering the low efficiency and motivation observed. Job seekers should have the possibility to choose alternatives to public employment mediation agencies, as should employers. At the same time, there is a clear need for monitoring and a strong responsibility on the part of the state to ensure that the system works and that the basic principles of the European model in this field continue to be applied (non-discrimination, open to all, and so on). As Eatwell et al. (2000, p. 52) put it, while 'high levels of employment are the foundation of successful social policies', 'successful policies can make an important contribution to the maintenance of high levels of employment in competitive economies'.

In this regard, active employment policy but also more determined policies on social protection, unemployment and social benefits, social dialogue, and labour standards in general could indeed contribute to progressively erase the drawbacks observed in future member states in precisely these areas.

As an example in the labour standards field, the elaboration of an EU directive to regulate the activities of temporary agency work would represent an important step forward to avoid total deregulation in this area. While the European social partners have negotiated for nearly a year on such a directive, their failure to conclude a framework agreement certainly reflects the difficulties of reconciling employers' and trade union representatives' views on the role of private agencies and also the sensitivity of the issue. The preparation of a directive by the EC and its acceptance by the Council would, however, represent a significant step, especially at the moment when future member states are accelerating, often in an excessive way, their implementation of such means of access to the labour market.

4.11 CONCLUSION

Twelve years after the beginning of the transition, while some traces of the distorted mechanisms which governed the economies of Central and Eastern Europe are still visible here and there, all the candidate countries from the region can be said to have introduced not only the basic rules of a market economy, but also all the most important standards in the field of employment which go with it. No doubt the accession process, with the harmonisation to the EU *acquis* in the field of employment, as well as the expectations that rapid economic growth will generate more employment, will further help these countries in their efforts to adopt EU practices and policies. At the same time, as we have seen, the EU has substantial grounds for concern as enlargement approaches.

We have seen that both employment and unemployment figures have started to diverge significantly from the EU average. Moreover, while the employment situation has progressed in the EU in recent years, the prospects in the future member states are somewhat less rosy, with unemployment rates which do not seem likely to fall even alongside higher economic growth and so appear to be disconnected from economic conditions. This situation is already leading to serious problems of economic and social marginalisation.

More fundamentally, employment in the candidate countries seems to have a number of distinctive features: a very large informal sector, but also adverse developments in the formal sector, such as a significant fall in employment, persistent unemployment, often of a very long-term nature and specific categories of people (those with a poor education, those just entering the world of work, women – an emerging phenomenon – the disabled, and also ethnic minorities, such as the Roma and others. We have also seen that employment dynamics seem to be mainly centred around the development of small and micro private enterprises in services, with less priority being given to industrial policy and agricultural reforms.

While the first wave of falling employment – up until the mid-1990s – was clearly the result of the collapse of output and active restructuring, other factors seem to have entered into play subsequently. Our description of the distinctive features of unemployment in the candidate countries has helped us to identify a series of other – non-economic – reasons that may be influencing the employment situation. In particular, we found that the lack of consideration for social issues such as human capital and education, housing, poverty, and social exclusion, which contribute indirectly to the 'employability' of the poor and the low mobility of the unemployed, may help to explain the long-term and exclusive nature of unemployment in the region.

At the same time, we found that support for the unemployed is inadequate; in particular, the policy followed by national governments – for example, tightening eligibility criteria for unemployment benefits – contributes only to pushing the already-excluded deeper into poverty, thus constituting the reserves for long-term unemployment. The absence of social policy may also limit the mobility and entrepreneurial – risk taking – behaviour of those in work.

It seems to us that the major characteristic of unemployment and employment policy in the region is its lack of a social approach, something which prevents these countries from tackling the problem in a sufficiently comprehensive and human way. Also significant is the lack of regional and industrial policies, preventing governments from identifying and so fighting the causes of widespread unemployment. In stark contrast, the different rules and regulations still existing on the labour market have been identified as the main cause of unemployment in these countries. While it is necessary to address these issues it is important to focus – as EU countries have done – on the different ways of improving not only *flexibility* for employers and companies, but also the no less necessary *security* for workers. The debate will thus need to be wider and be opened up to more actors, especially those, such as employers' and workers' representatives, who can play a role in securing the most appropriate balance between these two sets of requirements at local level.

Also striking is the absence of a comprehensive policy to fight the informal sector – and sometimes even of any acknowledgement of the need to do so – a phenomenon whose causes must be sought not only in economic but also in social factors. It is clear that the expansion of the informal sector closely interacts with employment issues. Not only does the phenomenon have roots in the problems of the labour market, but in turn it has serious implications for the labour market. On the employee side, activities in the informal economy became an alternative to unemployment, especially long-term unemployment, and a response to the drawbacks of the unemployment benefit and social assistance policy. On the employer side, the employers of very small companies and the self-employed, who are currently important contributors to economic growth in the future member states, also have the greatest tendency, as well as the most opportunities (because they are less subject to control) to shift part of their activities to the informal economy. We might also observe that the myriad new small and medium-size enterprises in Central and Eastern Europe working in the official economy have a tendency to move towards less regulation, and to avoid social dialogue or workers' participation.

More generally, the new type of enterprise that has emerged during the transition – very small scale, very profitable, but also of short life expectancy – is also a factor leading towards unregulated markets, not only in the informal sector, but also in the formal one.

The existence of such an enormous informal sector should also encourage us to read the official unemployment figures with more caution. The extent of the problem does not seem to have been sufficiently grasped by international organisations, including the European Commission. This phenomenon can also influence EU enlargement, and in particular the future of Social Europe.

To summarise, the future member states, especially those from Central and Eastern Europe, are confronted today by an employment situation characterised by excessive fragmentation on labour markets: between those in and those out of work, and those within the formal economy and those outside it, but also between regions and majority and minority groups. Such fragmentation of the labour market – not comparable to anything in EU countries – has a long-term character, with few possibilities to move from one group to another, with the result that these gaps may even increase.

At the same time, the risk of moving towards totally unregulated markets is real: the persistence and even growth of the informal sector as a large unregulated market, the increased attempts to remove regulations in the official sector, the overreliance on small enterprises that often avoid regulations and social dialogue, the progressive withdrawal of national governments from providing decent benefits and assistance to the unemployed, a limited employment policy (in contrast to a comprehensive and coordinated approach to the problem) are all signs that the future member states may well be moving towards unregulated markets more similar to the American than to the European model. Such fragmentation and lack of regulation should be closely monitored and adequately addressed by policy-makers.

More globally, the features of employment identified in this chapter may well represent sources of differentiation with the EU and generate problems with regard to the implementation of the European Social Model, in which employment figures prominently.

Nevertheless, there are some encouraging signs in a few candidate countries, which seem to be modifying their perspective on employment. Slovenia, for instance, has implemented its employment strategy until 2006 with the main focus on 'strengthening the human capital of the country as the key competitive factor of the Slovenian future', a strategy in line with its social protection policy (described in the Chapter 3), although this policy needs to attain concrete results and a better employment performance.

EU policy in this area can certainly help to address the problems of employment in the future member states from another perspective, one which gives more weight to a series of microeconomic and human-resource factors, as well as to the role of the social partners in the process. In particular the European Employment Strategy aims at addressing many different elements influencing the level and quality of employment, while ensuring, through coordination with all EU countries, that the model is consistent both with global economic developments and with social requirements.

5. Social Dialogue: Why Bother?

5.1 INTRODUCTION

In the current process of enlargement, and perhaps more than in other areas, social dialogue (often capitalised as 'the Social Dialogue') has sometimes given rise to misunderstanding. While grasping the importance attributed by the European Commission to social dialogue, in the course of negotiations the candidate countries have often asked such questions as: 'Why include social dialogue in our long list of priorities?'; or 'Is social dialogue really part of the *acquis communautaire*?'; or 'Do we have to involve the social partners if we want to succeed in "transposing" the *acquis*?'.

While these questions clearly reflect the difficulties the future member states have in identifying what is required as regards social dialogue, they may also reflect differences of culture in terms of industrial relations. The aim of this chapter is to identify basic similarities and differences in this area between future member states and current member states, and to try to assess their implications.

These misunderstandings may also be due to the place given to social dialogue in the whole Community *acquis*, and we shall examine whether this place is appropriate, considering the challenges posed by EU enlargement in this area.

Before doing so, it is important to establish the importance that social dialogue has progressively acquired at the Community level, not only within the Community *acquis*, but also in terms of practices of social dialogue in individual member states. This will serve as a basis for analysing current trends of social dialogue in candidate countries in light of their forthcoming accession to the EU. We shall then try to identify whether all the conditions are being met, by both the EU and the future member states, in order to ensure a perfect match between social dialogue in candidate countries and the values, principles, and practices that prevail in the European Union.

5.2 THE COMMUNITY *ACQUIS* ON SOCIAL DIALOGUE

Social dialogue is certainly one of the most complex issues in the Community *acquis*. In contrast to other, more specialised areas, social dialogue is multidimensional. It is not only an issue in its own right which deserves attention as such, but also, since it involves the social partners, it covers many more areas, social as well as economic and political, in which the social partners may have a role to play. This is why, at the Community level as well as in individual member states, social dialogue not only is an element of social policy, but also over the years has become a means of making progress in other areas.

Moreover, again because of its multidimensional nature, social dialogue is present in many parts of the Community *acquis*, being part of both the legal *acquis* and the institutional *acquis*.

Furthermore, due to the popularity of its basic principle, social dialogue has also become a means of defining a great number of relationships between social and economic actors, and so has acquired many different definitions, some more correct than others, and many concepts have come to be associated with it. We shall try to clarify these in the course of this chapter.

The term 'social dialogue' originally defined the relationship between employers' and workers' representatives, that is, the state was not part of the equation: it is 'a continuous interaction between the social partners with the aim of reaching agreement on the control of certain economic and social variables' (EC Industrial Relations Report 2000, EC 2000a). This is the definition used by European social partners in the European Social Dialogue.[1] However, this definition has been progressively extended – for instance, by the International Labour Office – to cover also tripartite relations between the state and the social partners. In the negotiation process for enlargement the EC has also used the definition of social dialogue in this broader sense.[2] In order to avoid confusion we shall use the same definition in this volume, while trying to distinguish between tripartite consultations with the social partners initiated by the state and direct bipartite relations between employers and trade union representatives that we shall call 'autonomous social dialogue'.[3]

1. In 1989, social dialogue was among the basic rights of workers proclaimed in the Community Charter of Fundamental Social Rights of Workers. In 1996, the Single European Act introduced the notion of 'dialogue between social partners' and of 'social dialogue' in the new wording of Article 118B of the EC Treaty. The concept and functioning of the European Social Dialogue were then incorporated more extensively in the Maastricht Agreement on social policy adopted in 1991 and in the Treaty of Amsterdam in 1997. Two articles of the new Charter of Fundamental Rights of the European Union adopted at the Nice European Summit in December 2000 are related to social dialogue issues.

2. All pre-accession documents use 'social dialogue' to define both the relationship between social partners and the state and between social partners – employers and worker representatives – themselves.

3. Civil society, however, is not part of the definition of social dialogue, although this has also been increasingly used in the last few years. We believe it is important to continue to distinguish between the social partners and representatives of civil society, and between social dialogue and dialogue with civil society.

5.2.1 From Consultation to Social Governance

Social dialogue is a central element of the European Social Model (see Chapter 1), one which has accompanied European integration from the beginning. It has also been progressively strengthened over the years. We can distinguish three main phases:

1. The signature of the Treaty of Rome in 1957 set up a *social partnership between the Commission and the social partners*. Initially established with an advisory capacity (cross-industry advisory committees), tripartite concertation was strengthened in the 1970s (the setting up of the Standing Committee on Employment and the organisation of tripartite conferences), with a particular focus on employment issues.

2. A new process of social dialogue between European social partners started in 1985 in Val Duchesse when Jacques Delors took the initiative to bring the social partners together for a bipartite meeting for the first time so that they could find common ground on economic and social issues. This bipartite cross-industry social dialogue – also known as 'Val Duchesse social dialogue' – henceforth played a major role at European level since it led to intensive cross-industry dialogue between social partners (ETUC [unions], UNICE, CEEP [employers]) on a series of key issues, including the setting up of a cooperation strategy for economic policies and progress towards Economic and Monetary Union, the completion of the internal market, and the implementation of the Social Charter of Fundamental Workers' Rights. On these matters, the European social partners have been able, at summit meetings or through the adoption of joint opinions and recommendations, to influence recent developments and play a role in policy design. This intensified social dialogue prepared the way for the significant steps forward that social dialogue would take a few years later.

3. A new era commenced in the early 1990s, in particular at the 1991 Intergovernmental Conference, when the European social partners (Agreement of 31 October 1991) agreed a joint text on an enhanced role for social partners at European level.[4] The text of this agreement was inserted virtually unchanged into the Social Protocol adopted at Maastricht in December 1991 by all member states – apart from the UK – and became operational in November 1993. This resulting new procedure of social dialogue was then incorporated in the Treaty of Amsterdam in 1997. Social partners acquired new rights to be consulted on propos-

---

4. They proposed not only that consultation be mandatory on relevant legislation, but also that a procedure be established whereby the Council would be given the power to transpose agreements between EU-level social partners into the form of Community law.

also in the social field and also to opt for replacing the traditional leg-islative route (that is, when the EC is preparing a draft directive for sub-mission to the Council) by the negotiation and conclusion of framework agreements, which can also be converted into Council directives. The 'joint opinions' period has thus gradually given way to the negotiation of 'European framework agreements', and the social partners have become key actors in what could be defined as 'shared social governance'.[5]

The 1990s were also characterised by an *increasing emphasis on employment* (see Chapter 4) in which social partners also came to be more extensively con-sulted, in two main ways: (i) they were involved in the implementation, at all stages, of the European Employment Strategy; and (ii) they were invited to make contributions in their own areas of responsibility – through negotiating agreements – on industrial change, modernisation of work organisation, train-ing, and job creation, as well as, more globally, on ensuring the right balance between security and flexibility.

Consultations and dialogue on employment between the Council, the Commission, and employers' and workers' representatives were reinforced within the Standing Committee on Employment, notably through its reform in March 1999.

The 1997 Luxembourg Employment Summit also instituted regular meet-ings between the social partners, the Commission, and the 'troika' of Heads of State or Government of the member states holding the current, most recent, and next Presidencies.

Finally, the 1999 Cologne Economic Summit set up a new '*macroeconom-ic dialogue*' between the social partners, the European Commission, econom-ic and finance ministers, and the European Central Bank, aimed at ensuring economic policy coordination and consistency between the monetary, fiscal, and wage pillars of the 1999 employment pact.

Social dialogue has thus progressed at different levels, ensuring that the social partners can usefully contribute to avoiding gaps between what is dis-cussed at the upper level, in terms of coordination of macroeconomic policies or the European Employment Strategy, and the microeconomic and social realities with which they are confronted on a daily basis.

5.2.2 Social Dialogue as Part of the Legal *Acquis*

Social dialogue is part of the legal *acquis* in a sort of transversal or hori-zontal manner, since the need to consult the social partners is present in the texts of several directives, including areas such as labour law, safety and

5. Compston and Greenwood (2001) call it 'codetermination'.

health, and anti-discrimination. Several of them include references to the principle of workers' consultation. This is the case, for instance, in the Council Directive of 12 June 1989 on the implementation of measures aimed at promoting workers' health and safety at the workplace which stipulates all procedures of information and consultation to be followed by enterprises in this area. Most directives on health and safety make reference to such procedures.

The Directive on European Works Councils, which provides an instrument for social dialogue and workers' representation across borders, is particularly relevant in view of prospective EU enlargement and intensified capital movements in an enlarged Europe. Article 1.1 stipulates the objective of improving 'the right of workers to be informed and consulted in enterprises or groups of enterprises of Community scale', and requires of the management of such enterprises to 'create a European Works Council or an information and consultation procedure, on its own initiative or at the request of at least 100 workers, or of their representatives'.

Social dialogue is also present in the Commission's decision of 20 May 1998 on the creation of sectoral social dialogue committees at EU level, which provides the social partners with a new platform for sectoral social dialogue and thus induces the candidate countries to set up similar structures.[6]

Dialogue with the public authorities also plays an important role, and, as with the dialogue on employment, is enshrined in the EU legal *acquis*, with the new decision of the Council of March 1999 on the reform of the Standing Committee on Employment.[7]

It should also be noted that the Council's decisions have created *consultative committees* on, for instance, health and safety (27 June 1974) and equal opportunities for men and women (9 December 1981), which clearly shows that member states consider that the social partners have a role to play in preparing and implementing legislation in these fields.[8]

During the screening exercise for employment and social affairs (Chapter 13 of accession negotiations), and subsequent negotiations and reports on accession, the European Commission explained each element of the *acquis* to the candidate countries, including on social dialogue, and discussed with them their plans to bring their own legislation and practice into line with Community requirements.

6. Since 1998, these new Sectoral Dialogue Committees (COM(96)448 final) replace the Joint Committees that previously existed in individual sectors.

7. Decision N°99/207/CE of March 1999 which replaces Decision N°70/532/CE of 10 December 1970.

8. Consultative Committees were also created to deal with social security for migrant workers, freedom of movement for workers, the European Social Fund, and vocational training (EC 1998, pp. 6–9).

The role of the European Court of Justice

We must also emphasise that the Court of Justice, through its interpretative role as regards EC legislation, has also contributed to defining the scope of social dialogue provisions. For instance, on several occasions it has had to remind member states of the requirements for the coverage of collective agreements when they are used for transposing European labour law. This happened against Denmark in its implementation of the Equal Pay Directive, as well as against Italy on several occasions since not all workers who should have been were covered under the directives transposed through collective agreements.[9]

5.2.3 Social Dialogue as Part of the Institutional *Acquis*

Recent institutional developments have made it possible for European social dialogue to go even further: as we have seen, the recent breakthroughs in European social dialogue and the treaties of Maastricht and Amsterdam have given new rights and responsibilities to the European social partners. As stipulated in Article 138, there is an obligation to consult them on most legal provisions that the EC intends to adopt, and, if they so wish, the social partners may choose to interrupt the legislative process by initiating negotiations for the purpose of reaching agreement. Furthermore, if such an agreement is reached, they may demand that it be anchored in European legislation. We should also emphasise that the social partners enjoy real autonomy in initiating the process, since they can decide at any time to start negotiations between themselves on a new issue.[10]

This procedure is an innovative and fairly important one, the social partners having become in some way 'legislators' themselves. In fact, they have responded well to this appeal, leading to the most significant breakthroughs of this kind of the last few years, with three agreements concluded, on parental leave (December 1995), part-time employment contracts (June 1997), and fixed-term employment contracts (March 1999) which have been directly converted (following the social partners' request to the EC) into Council directives.[11] A new

9. Respectively case 143/83 ECR 427 for Denmark and case 91/81 (1982) ECR 2133, case 131/84 (No. 2) (1985) ECR 3531, and case 235/84 (1986) 2291 for Italy.

10. We may regret, however, that they have not taken much advantage of this opportunity so far, since they have always decided to negotiate following the initiatives taken by the European Commission. Some experts have also concluded that the final agreements signed by social partners (partly reflecting their 'self-interest strategy', especially on the employers' side) was to a certain extent a toned-down version of what would have been the outcome if achieved by the European Commission (Branch and Greenwood 2001).

11. The three framework agreements were converted into directives approximately 5–6 months later, on 6 June 1996 (Council Directive on Parental Leave 96/34/EC), 15 December 1997 (Council Directive on Part-Time Work 97/81/EC), and 21 June 1999 (Council Directive on Fixed-Term Contracts 99/70/EC), respectively.

agreement was also concluded by European social partners on teleworking in June 2002. Clearly, as we saw in Chapter 1, European social dialogue has become a driving force behind social progress.

Thanks to the new sectoral committees for social dialogue created at European level since 1998 – 27 such sectoral committees have been created since then (EC 2002d) – this EU-level dynamic is also expanding in individual sectors: since the first framework agreement on working conditions in agriculture in 1997, three agreements have been concluded on the organisation of working time in maritime transportation, railways, and civil aviation, which have been translated into European legislation.[12] The multiplication of such agreements shows that such institutionalised autonomous social dialogue at European level is dynamic not only at cross-sectoral level, but also within individual sectors, a dimension closer to the 'coalface' and directly relevant for candidate countries.

The new treaty has also made it possible to progress in the field of employment, one of the key EU priorities. Within the framework of the strategy of Luxembourg, the employment title of the Treaty, and the related European Employment Strategy, open up new avenues for action by the social partners, in particular by inviting them to make proposals on key areas, such as the modernisation of work organisation and life-long training.

Consultations between public authorities and social partners at European level have also become institutionalised, with, for instance, the process of macroeconomic dialogue decided on at the Cologne summit. This was the first time the social partners had had access to such dialogue, which undoubtedly represents a promising structure for social dialogue in the future, considering the importance of macroeconomic issues in economic and monetary union.

All these institutionalised forms of social dialogue represent unavoidable mechanisms of social progress which must be taken into account by the applicant countries and integrated in their national systems and structures. Much is therefore at stake here for the social partners of applicant countries.

Finally, it is particularly important to mention that the Treaty foresees the possibility of social partners transposing EC directives by negotiating agreements rather than by means of national legislation alone. To this end, the social partners have important work to do in most applicant countries to ensure that a genuine structure of social partnership develops.

---

12. The first, on maritime transportation, was enshrined in a new Directive on 21 June 1999 (1999/63/EC). The second agreement, on railways, was included in the general Directive (covering all sectors) on working time (93/104/EC) which was consequently amended by Directive 00/34/EC.

5.3 THE DOMINANCE OF THE STATE IN THE FUTURE MEMBER STATES

5.3.1 Policies in First Years of Reform

After the collapse of the Communist planned economies, in order to avoid strong economic imbalances most countries of Central and Eastern Europe felt the need to engage in a radical economic adjustment strategy – although pursued to varying degrees – in its most radical form being known as 'shock therapy'. This involved a particular sequencing of macroeconomic reforms. It started with price liberalisation and was followed by a stabilisation policy which involved an attempt to impose a tight monetary and fiscal policy in which a restrictive incomes policy always figured prominently. This tax-based incomes policy – which usually relied on an 'excess wage tax' to limit wage increases – was complemented by many other means of intervention in respect of wage and social allowances: the minimum wage, wage tariffs in the budgetary sector, and indexation mechanisms.

In the wake of stabilisation policies governments have also instigated privatisation programmes which have had their own effects on economic and social life, including industrial relations. Strict budgetary arbitration was also unilaterally decided by the powers-that-be.

All these policies were directly decided by national governments, in cooperation with international monetary institutions (IMF, World Bank) and did not lead to any democratisation of the decision-making process of the kind that might have been expected after the collapse of Communism.

5.3.2 Emergence of Unbalanced Tripartism or the 'Authoritarian' Style

There was a clear need to move towards more decentralised policy-making and to carry out restructuring and introduce decentralised practices in the areas of wages, employment, and collective bargaining. Alongside this decentralisation process, most countries of Central and Eastern Europe have started to involve employer and trade union representatives in some policy areas and have promoted social dialogue through tripartite structures.

It is certainly this continuing dominance of the state that explains the success of tripartism in the first years of transition. This type of 'democratic' structure could compensate for the unilateral control of the state over all major economic and social indicators. Moreover, in the wake of the collapse of the Communist regimes, there was no real culture and practice of autonomous industrial relations, and the prevalence of the state in all economic and social matters was such that this form of dialogue became the natural and inherited form of policy-making democratisation after decades of centralisation and totalitarianism. For many, the achievement of independence and/or the formation of a nation has led to nothing more than overcentralised government, a situation that may change with time.

All Central and Eastern European countries have promoted forms of tripartism (but also Cyprus, Malta, and Turkey). They have all created tripartite national councils to which the government could invite employers' and trade union representatives to discuss a number of economic and social issues. This situation contrasts strikingly with industrial relations in western Europe, where formal tripartism is rarely found and social dialogue at national level takes place in a more informal way. Tripartite agreements are generally not based on institutionalised tripartite structures.

Apart from state – which in a way established the 'rules of the game' – dominance, a number of other factors can be brought forward to explain the existence of such structures. In order to impose these rules the state needed other players. In this regard, the success of tripartism in Central and Eastern Europe is undoubtedly due to the social partners themselves. Both for trade unions and employers' organisations, tripartism turned out to be essential: it was necessary to legitimise (particularly for new, alternative trade unions) or to relegitimise (for former Communist unions in particular) their existence and their role in the new society. Particularly because no criteria for representativeness had been developed, obtaining a seat on the tripartite Council represented the best possible way for an organisation to establish its representative credentials, and therefore to consolidate its position among old and potential new members.

But for a game to be played properly, there must also be a referee. In the early transition period, governments in Central and Eastern Europe were influenced by the International Labour Organisation which encouraged the development of tripartite structures as new institutions of stability and democracy, particularly in order to overcome social unrest in the transition. This ensured that the actors adopted the rules and stuck to them. In fact, the ILO has turned out to be more than a referee, having ensured the propagation of the game throughout the region.

Tripartite bodies emerged at different times and in different forms in each country. Hungary was the first to start such tripartite dialogue, as early as 1988, leading to the institutionalisation of the first tripartite body, the Council for the Reconciliation of Interests, in 1990. In the former Czechoslovakia, a national tripartite council, the Council for Economic and Social Agreement, was formed in October 1990, at the federal and republican levels, before giving birth, after the 1993 division of the country, to the Czech and the Slovak National Councils. Other countries in the region introduced formalised tripartite dialogue later on: Bulgaria and Romania in 1993, Poland and Slovenia in 1994, while, for example, Latvia and Estonia waited until the late 1990s (see Table 5.1). Some Polish experts consider that tripartism and social dialogue in

Table 5.1 Tripartite bodies in candidate countries, 1988–2002

Country	Main tripartite body/bodies	Date	Institutional/ legal basis	Composition *	Sub-committees
Bulgaria	- Tripartite Commission for coordinating interests	1991	– agreement	Employers: 4 Trade unions: 2	Yes
	- National Council for tripartite cooperation	1993	– Labour code	Employers: 4 Trade unions: 2	Yes
	- National Economic and Social Council	April 2001	– Law	Multipartite	
Cyprus	– Labour Advisory Body	1960	– Administrative arrangement	Employers: 2 Trade unions: 4	Yes
	– Economic Consultative Committee	1999	– Administrative arrangement		Yes
	– Advisory Committee on Commerce and Industry				–
	– Social Ins. Fund Council	1960	– Law		No
	– Different tripartite training institutes				No
Czech Rep.**	– Council for Social Agreement	1990–92	Tripartite agreement	Employers: 2 Trade unions: 2	No
	– Council for Economic and Social Agreement	1992–95			
	– Council for Social Dialogue	1995–97			
	– Council for Economic and Social Agreement	1997–			
Estonia	– National Economic and Social Council (NESC)	Since 1998	Coll. Agreement Act of April 1993; Law on estab. of NESC of 1998;	Employers: 1 Trade unions: 2 (on a rotation basis)	Yes
	– Council for the ILO	Since 1992	Law on Health Insurance		
Hungary	– Interest Reconciliation Council	1990–98	Government decree, backed by a tripartite agreement ***	Employers: 9 Trade unions : 6	Yes
	– National Labour Council	April 1999–	Government decree	Employers: 9 Trade unions : 6	Yes
	– Economic Council	April 1999–	Government decree	Multipartite	Yes
	– Council for ILO Affairs	May 1999–	Government decree	Employers: 9 Trade unions : 6	No
	– Council for European Integration	June 1999–	Government decree	Multipartite	No
	– New Council for Interest Reconciliation	2002		Employers: 9 Trade unions : 6	Yes
Latvia	National Tripartite Cooperation Council	1998–	Tripartite agreement (30 October 1998) (art. 1)	Employers: 1 Trade unions: 1	Yes
Lithuania	– Tripartite Council of the Republic of Lithuania	1995–	Tripartite agreement	Employers: 2 Trade unions: 4	Yes
	– Commission of Labour Protection				
	– State Social Insurance Council		Law on State Labour Protection		

Country	Main tripartite body/bodies	Date	Institutional/ legal basis	Composition *	Sub-committees
Malta	– Committee on EU Accession		Law on State Social Insurance		
	– Malta Council for Economic Development	1988–	Tripartite agreement	Employers : 6 Trade unions : 2	Yes
	– Malta Council for Economic and Social Development	June 2001–	Law (Malta Council for Econ. and Soc. Development Act XV)	Multipartite	Yes
Poland	Tripartite Commission for Econ. and Soc. Issues	1994– 2001	Government decree	Employers: 1 Trade unions: 9	Yes
		July 2001–	Law on Tripartite Commission and voivodship social dialogue commissions	Employers: 2 Trade unions: 9	Yes
Romania	Tripartite Secretariat for Social Dialogue	1993–97	Under PHARE project	Employers: 8 Trade unions: 5	Yes
	Economic and Social Council	1997	Law on the ESC (No. 109/1997)		
	Social dialogue committees within each ministry	2001	Government Decision no. 314/2001		
Slovakia**	Council for Economic and Social Agreement	1990–	– Tripartite agreement in 1990–1997 Law on Tripartism May 1999–	Employers: 1 Trade unions: 1	Yes
Slovenia	Social and Economic Council	1994	Tripartite agreement (Law under discussion since 1998)	Employers: 3 Trade unions: 4	No
	National Council			Multipartite	
Turkey	– National Labour Council		Tripartite agreement	Not effective	No
	– Minimum Wage Board			Employers: 1 Trade unions: 1	No
	– other tripartite bodies (social security; and unemployment boards; productivity centre, etc.)				No
	– Economic and Social Council	April 2001	Law	Multipartite	Working boards possible

Notes:

* Organisations represented in tripartite bodies; does not mean there are no other organisations.

** In former Czechoslovakia (before the division into two separate Czech and Slovak republics at the end of 1992), there were three tripartite bodies, one for the Federation and two for the Czech and Slovak parts).

*** Government Decree 3240/1990 in an internal, albeit not confidential governmental document. It includes obligations related only to the government.

Poland took its roots from the Agreements from Gdansk, Szczecin, and Jastrzebie in 1980 (Matey-Tyrowicz 2001), which not only indicates the potential importance of tripartism in these countries, but also emphasises that they emerged – and in some places still struggle – under very authoritarian regimes.

Tripartism is also very much developed in southern candidate countries, such as Cyprus and Malta, where state interventionism still plays an important role in the economy. Tripartism in Malta has been promoted since 1988, and was given legal status in the year 2001. Cyprus has also set up a number of tripartite bodies and practices. Tripartism has also been promoted in Turkey, although more recently (since 1995).

The areas covered by such bodies became important. Almost all such main tripartite bodies in Central and Eastern Europe developed specialised subcommittees or commissions to address a number of issues in more detail, such as wages, employment, or privatisation. More recently, some governments have also instituted tripartite councils for discussing ILO matters, as in Estonia and Hungary, or for addressing preparatory steps for EU accession, as in Lithuania and, again, Hungary, where special Councils for European Integration have been created. This wide coverage of tripartite consultations also contrasts with the practice in EU member states where such consultations are often more limited in their content, generally being restricted to dealing with wage restraints in exchange for employment, with the possible – and relatively recent – exception of Ireland, where national pacts include a wide range of areas. The tripartite process in Hungary, for instance (but this is also the case in Poland and Bulgaria) covers a much wider range of economic and social issues, such as the minimum wage and average wages, safety at work, and national training policy, but also labour market and privatisation policies. In most Central and Eastern European countries, tripartite bodies also have the task of proposing and preparing legislative changes.

In sum, tripartite bodies have been very successful in the first years of reform, and have become an important feature influencing industrial relations.

The need for popular acceptance of reforms
For some scholars, no specific conditions in the region encouraged the growth of tripartism; rather it was in the interest of the first democratic governments. In a context of economic and social crisis, with a combination of adverse phenomena – such as the collapse of production, restructuring, emerging unemployment, and very low and falling living standards – tripartite partnership was a pre-condition for governments' survival. Policymakers desperately needed the consent of the social partners on economic reforms and wanted to share with them the responsibility for the sacrifices that such reforms demanded of the population.

At this period most governments in the region looked to sign national agreements on economic and social policies with the social partners. As an example, in January 1991 an Annual General Agreement was introduced in the former Czechoslovakia, as a forum for the introduction of a social compromise package within the framework of a low-wage and low-unemployment policy. In other countries, the signing of a tripartite agreement even preceded the formalisation of a tripartite body, as in Poland, where the Tripartite Commission on Socio-Economic Issues was created in February 1994 in the wake of the tripartite pact signed one year earlier on 'state enterprises in transformation'. Aimed at overcoming resistance to privatisation and free-market measures, this pact well illustrates the compromise pursued in the region in the early years of transition, between guaranteeing minimum security and carrying out economic reforms.

To summarise, most social pacts or agreements were signed in the first period of the transition, with, for instance, two basic social peace agreements in Bulgaria, a social pact in Poland, and annual wage policy agreements and general social pacts in Slovenia. It is also in this period − in 1994 and in 1995 − that some attempts were made to sign a global social pact in Hungary.

Such tripartite agreements were thus generally motivated by political interests − particularly those of the government − to overcome internal difficulties.

The participation of trade unions in the tripartite process clearly helped to rein in trade union protests at the enterprise level. In some cases, the tripartite process even helped to solve particular conflicts, as in Hungary during the taxi and lorry drivers' blockade in October 1990.

In this regard, the disappearance of tripartite agreements or pacts in the second period of transition − that is, for a period of more than six years (between 1993 and 1999) − in most CEE countries is striking. Table 5.2 shows that in the first years of reform (1990–94), there was strong pressure on governments to seek tripartite consensus on a number of reforms that exacted a high toll from the population. Only in Bulgaria was there an agreement also in 1997, which can be explained by the gravity of the situation, when popular consent was urgently requested for the introduction of the Currency Board. The social partners were consulted by representatives of the International Monetary Fund and by the Bulgarian government. This ensured acceptance of the Currency Board and its subsequent restrictions by the Bulgarian population. Significantly, however, such meaningful involvement of the social partners has not been repeated.

It seems that the involvement of the social partners has been regarded as less crucial in the second period of transition, although the reforms have been no less difficult or painful. It is as if the governments felt that they could go ahead without the consent of the social partners. In this regard the trend in

Table 5.2 Tripartite agreements/pacts in candidate countries, 1990–2002

Country	Signing	Title of agreement/pact and contents
Bulgaria	1990	- First tripartite agreement (March)
	1991	- Agreement for social peace
	1997	- Charter for Social Cooperation (consensus for the introduction of Currency Board; October) including a memorandum for Common Priority Action
Cyprus	1977	- Industrial Relations Code
		- Agreements on specific issues: reduction of working hours; declaration for health and safety, etc.
Czech Rep.	1991–94	- General Tripartite agreement (annual)
	1999	- General Tripartite agreement
	2000	- General Tripartite agreement
	2001	- On-going discussions for the conclusion of a long-term social stability pact
Estonia	1990–95	- Few tripartite agreements on the minimum wage fixing
	1996, 1997	- Agreements on industrial democracy
Hungary	Since 1989, except 2000	- Annual agreements on the national minimum wage
		- Attempts to conclude an economic and social pact in 1994 and a price–wage agreement in 1995
		- Tripartite consensus achieved on certain aspects of the state budget, law on taxation, social security contributions, etc.
Latvia	1996	- Agreement on social partnership
	1997–99	- Minimum wages
	1997	- Training in labour safety
		- Many national agreements between social partners
Lith.	1995	- Agreement for solving social, economic and political problems and for social peace
	1999	- Agreement on tripartite cooperation
Malta	1990	- National Agreement on Industrial Relations (incorporating a National Incomes Policy Agreement)
Poland	1993	- Pact on state-owned enterprises in the course of transformation (gave birth to the tripartite committee)
	1995	- Pact on package for social guarantees for citizens
	1995	- Regional pact for Silesia or contract for voivodship of Katowice
	1996	- Regional agreement in voivodship of Zielona Gora

Table 5.2 (cont.)

Romania	From 1992 2000 and	- Unique National (inter-professional) collective labour agreements (yearly) but they are bilateral
	2002	- Social Pact
Slovakia	1990–92	- General agreements (Czechoslovakia)
	1993–96,	- Agreement for 2000 covers 4 policy areas: economy,
	2000	employment, incomes and social affairs
Slovenia	1994	- Agreement on wage policy
	1995	- General agreement on social policy
	1996	- General agreement
	1999	- Agreement on wage policy for 1999–2000
	2000	- Agreement on pension and disability reform
	2001	- General agreement on employment
	2001	- Agreement on wage policy
		- General social agreement
Turkey		- No agreement

Central and Eastern Europe has been in the opposite direction to that in the EU, where tripartite agreements have been experiencing something of a comeback (Industrial Relations Reports 2000 and 2002 – EC 2000a and 2002d).

5.3.3 A Rather Mitigated Assessment after 10 Years

Little social partner influence on decision-making
After more than twelve years of transition, the assessment of tripartite bodies is rather mixed. While they did represent a way of consulting the social partners in many CEE countries the social partners complained that the consultation process remained wholly formal, with major issues sometimes not being discussed. In the first years of transition, the social partners had little influence over decision-making in areas such as the budget, privatisation, employment, and incomes policy. More recently, the lack of social partner involvement in EU negotiations and EU affairs in general is illustrative of the limits of such concertation mechanisms.

In some countries this reflects the whole philosophy of the government and its unwillingness to use the structures of social dialogue in an effective way, as was the case in Hungary between 1998 and 2002 and the administration of the FIDESZ–Smallholders' Party coalition under Viktor Orbán (see Box 5.1).

New political changes after the election of May 2002 are expected to bring new developments with regard to social dialogue, although it is too

BOX 5.1 THE PROGRESSIVE ABANDONMENT OF SOCIAL
DIALOGUE IN HUNGARY?

Hungary was the first country to implement tripartite structures, in 1989. This process was effective since it permitted the social partners to be involved in a number of discussions and on a range of issues, such as incomes policy, labour markets, privatisation, and social protection. The tripartite Council for the Reconciliation of Interests was also given not only consultative but also negotiating rights on the issue of the minimum wage, which was adjusted regularly on the basis of tripartite negotiations and agreements. The coming to power in 1998 of the new Government under Prime Minister Viktor Orbán led to profound changes in social dialogue structures and practices. The aim – barely concealed – of the Government was clearly to ensure that it would act as the only decision-maker, and seek to minimise possible interference from the social partners, a process that was carried out in a number of significant steps. First, existing tripartite structures were modified, above all with the splitting of the previous responsibilities of the National Council for the Reconciliation of Interests – renamed the National Labour Council – into a number of forums (see Table 5.1), with the result that the new tripartite forum would cover only labour issues. Moreover, tripartite meetings became much less frequent and the contents and nature of the involvement of the social partners was changed radically. The Government, after having twice unilaterally modified the level of the minimum wage in defiance of the Labour Code, which gave the responsibility of minimum-wage fixing to the tripartite council, decided to modify even this legal provision. This allowed the Government to unilaterally determine the minimum wage (in case no agreement is reached with the social partners, an outcome that can easily be engineered), as happened in 2000 and 2001.

On other issues, consultations became very formal, and purely informative rather than consultative. Moreover, the social partners have complained that a number of issues were put on the formal agenda for discussion only after the corresponding laws had been introduced in Parliament: this has happened repeatedly since 1998, for instance on minimum wage and budgetary issues. This authoritarian approach to social dialogue has also been reflected in the Government's behaviour as an employer, with the interruption of discussions with the trade unions for more than two years (between 1998 and 2000) in the public sector (despite the fact that such negotiations are enshrined in law), as well as an anti-union policy in public enterprises which has led to a number of major strikes, the most important of which involved the state railway company, MÁV, where workers went on strike for more than two weeks (a total of over 400 hours) in February 2000, and the national airline MALÉV in respect of which government intransigence led to significant discontent among the workforce.

Such a radical deterioration of national consultations with the social partners, and of social dialogue in general, led the European Commission to react on a number of occasions (for example, in all the pre-accession documents, such as the National Plans for the Adoption of the Acquis (NPAA), regular reports, and so on; in the screening process; and at subcommittee meetings), while a number of other institutions emphasised the gravity of the situation.[13] Before summer 2000, the closure of Chapter 13 on Employment and Social Affairs was delayed because of social dialogue and the Hungarian government was asked to explain itself again on developments in this area. Only a few months later, at the end of September 2000, was Chapter 13 provisionally closed on the basis of strong commitments made by the Hungarian Government. At the end of June 2001 a fact-finding mission was organised by the European Commission in order to assess, on the basis of meetings with the Government and all the social partners, whether the social dialogue situation had in fact improved and the Government's commitments in this area duly fulfilled. A few weeks later, the European Commission stated that many of the commitments had not been honoured and that Hungary still had to show significant improvements in this area in the near future (Regular Report on Hungary 2001). The new government that came to power mid-2002, however, has committed itself to the promotion of social dialogue and has already shown promising signs in this direction, perhaps marking the end of the progressive removal of institutions of social dialogue in Hungary.

early to say whether it will bring a new promising era for social partners and social dialogue in the country.

Moreover, in Central and Eastern Europe tripartite structures have remained fora for consultation rather than negotiation (in which the social partners would have a real influence over the decision-making process). Only in Hungary did the original tripartite council – at least before 1998 –

13. See the report of the Economic and Social Committee (ESC 2000), 'Social dialogue has collapsed in Hungary'. Discussions at the ILO, in the Committee on the Application of Standards (8 June 2000), have also drawn attention to the 'ineffective tripartite machinery' and 'total lack of social dialogue' in Hungary.

remain a forum for genuine negotiations, even if it was restricted to determination of the minimum wage and recommendations on wage increases, and did not cover other economic issues. Moreover, its negotiating power on the minimum wage was progressively reduced from 1998. In other countries, tripartite discussions have tended to cover such a large number of issues – from wage to employment policies, including social protection and privatisation – that ultimately they have not amounted to real joint decision-making.

One of the other striking features of the tripartite process in Central and Eastern Europe is the fact that it has not created any linkage between what is discussed or agreed at national level and more decentralised levels of collective bargaining. It thus has little influence over decentralised issues and does not connect macroeconomic policy and local-level industrial relations. We may therefore cast doubt on whether this process has any meaning, and indeed on the whole nature of the decision-making process.

Only in Slovenia has the process been characterised by a strong partnership at national level, although this may reflect the strongly centralised nature of the system. Agreements are made at national level, but within a frame in which collective bargaining and collective agreements continue to be obligatory. It is thus not a spontaneous process and may collapse as soon as obligatory provisions to ensure collective bargaining are removed. A return to free collective bargaining was expected to occur in 2001–2 with a new draft law aimed at removing the previous obligatory bargaining system. Nevertheless, this law was still not passed in mid-2003, mainly because of the opposition of the main actor concerned, the Chamber of Commerce of Slovenia, which is not willing to lose its previous prerogatives, and which is using all its political influence – very important in domestic politics – to block this process of reform. If the situation remains as it is, this would mean that Slovenia would be the only country of a new EU-25 not to have implemented a free collective bargaining system.

A consultative process still directly dependent on the government

A number of examples indicate that the use of tripartite structures is directly dependent on the willingness of governments to make them work. It is interesting to observe that even the names of tripartite bodies have been changed by successive governments depending on their attitude to social dialogue. The election victory of the right Civic Democratic Party under the leadership of Prime Minister Klaus immediately led to the disregarding of the General Agreement of 1993 and the introduction instead of tight wage regulation, while in 1995 the name of the Tripartite Council was changed (see Table 5.1), and its scope narrowed considerably. Only in 1997 was the original name of the Council restored, and with it its original scope. The arrival of a new government in 1998 marked the more regular employment of tripartite consultations.

The same happened in Slovakia: the change of government at the end of 1998 led to a resurgence of the tripartite process in 1999 and the signing of a general pact in March 2000 after three years of interruption (1997–99).

Similarly in Hungary, the evolution of the tripartite process closely followed the willingness of the government to use it. Interest in tripartite negotiations seems to have been on the wane as early as 1996–97, but the arrival of the new 'liberal' government in 1998 marked a period of change and restructuring of tripartite institutions. The belief prevailed that decisions at national level should be taken by the government only, and that social dialogue should be decentralised at local level; as in the Czech Republic, the name of the tripartite Council was modified in 1998 (see Table 5.1) and its competences restricted to purely 'labour' issues, while a new body – the Economic Council – was created to address economic issues, such as privatisation, the budget, and macroeconomic policy previously covered by the Council. The Economic Council had a much wider range of participants: not only the social partners, but also other economic actors, such as representatives of banks and foreign investors. This wider participation had the direct effect of marginalising the social partners. Similarly, one of the first – symbolic – moves of the new government in Hungary in 2002 was to change the name of the tripartite council and to restore its previous name Council for the Reconciliation of Interests.

Tripartism in Turkey also continues to be controlled by the state and remains very much dependent on political influences and changes.

The social partners are also partly responsible for the poor effectiveness and functioning of the tripartite institutions, however, especially when they withdraw from it or prevent newcomers from joining because of rivalries and competition among organisations, as has been the case on the part of both employers' and trade union organisations in Poland over the last twelve years. It may also happen that the withdrawal of one or other of the social partners reflects the impossibility of accepting the only apparently consultative process imposed by the government as the only way of demonstrating disapproval.

Tripartism in Central and Eastern Europe has thus been directly dependent on government willingness to implement or develop it. Its effectiveness often depends on the importance attached to social partnership in the government's political programme and consequently in the decision-making process. It is important to note that the changes in the format of the tripartite councils – despite their original function to promote partnership – in the Czech Republic and in Hungary in recent years have been made unilaterally by government, without consultation of the social partners.

5.3.4 A Permanent Feature of Candidate-Country Policy-Making?

There are a number of indications that tripartite relations may remain a permanent feature of policy-making in the future member states.

1. While all CEE countries have experienced many political, institutional, and economic changes, tripartite structures have remained in place. They thus represent one of the most important features of social partnership in Central and Eastern Europe, surviving political changes.
2. While in most countries in the region tripartite councils have worked on the basis of a tripartite agreement, most recently they have progressively been given a legal basis for their operations. This was done, for example, in Romania in 1997, in Estonia in 1998, in Slovakia in 1999, and in Poland in 2001. Similar laws are under preparation in Slovenia and Hungary. This further confirms that tripartite structures, despite their imperfections and limited effectiveness, will continue to prevail in candidate countries in the future.
3. We can expect that the governments of future member states will make these structures more operational in the future, especially when the conditions and policies associated with European integration – such as economic and monetary union, with its coordination of macroeconomic policy – reduce the room to manoeuvre of national policymakers. In this context, they may again seek the consent of social partners to avoid being blamed for unpopular decisions.

In this regard, we may expect the social partners to become associated with the multiplication of tripartite agreements in a process similar to the one which has emerged in western European countries in the recent past. In fact, after a period marked by the absence of such agreements, in recent times such agreements have been on the rise again also in candidate countries, a process that can be explained by the increasing pressure resulting from the forthcoming EU enlargement and the need to implement a number of preparatory steps.

In February 2001, the Romanian government and social partners signed a general tripartite pact aimed at ensuring social peace and a stable economic framework in order to favour long-term investment. This agreement – directly inspired by Ireland's social partnership – covers a wide number of issues such as wages, employment, the tax system, safety in the workplace, and the grey economy. It was renewed in 2002. Similarly, in 2001 in Slovenia there was a return to incomes policy agreements, and a more general pact was also concluded in late 2001. A social pact was also signed in March 2000 in the Slovak Republic on a number of issues including macroeconomic objectives, employment, and incomes and social policies.

Nevertheless, recent attempts to reach tripartite agreements in candidate countries have continued to leave little room for the social partners, appearing to be even more clearly established within a strategy determined in advance by the government. This tendency is certainly also present in current EU member states, especially in tripartite agreements on wage moderation, but not to the same extent.

As an example, on issues related to the EU accession negotiations, the governments of the region – mostly under neo-liberal influence – have been quite keen to preserve their prerogatives, despite the fact that the social partners' contribution could be crucial in ensuring proper implementation of the *acquis*. For instance, not a single social pact has been signed on the EU accession process. The tripartite systems continue to function with weak trade unions and employers that still have to consolidate their presence. This is all rather different from the philosophy and practice of social dialogue in the EU.

We may also question the effectiveness of the introduction of a legal basis for tripartite mechanisms. The legal anchor introduced in Romania and Slovakia has not radically changed the nature of the discussions and their outcomes. By contrast, experiences of tripartism in Hungary in the early 1990s show that it is possible to have a partnership with social partners and to reach agreements without a legal basis. Experiences of tripartism around the world also show only too well that a legal basis does not help tripartite structures to become more effective if there is no real willingness on the government's part. In the Czech Republic no legal basis has yet been introduced, but the greater attention paid to tripartite mechanisms recently is due to the change of government. Moreover, concluded agreements do not acquire binding status only because tripartite structures are given a legal status; their enforcement will continue to depend on the willingness of the three sides to make them effective, as well as on the representativeness of the social partners to make them operational at local level.

In EU countries, indeed, there is generally no legal basis for tripartite agreements, but respecting such agreements is a way of legitimating social partnership: once a tripartite agreement is signed by the three sides, the expectation is that all the signatories will observe it. We might therefore wonder whether the furnishing of a legal basis does not reflect the weakness of the tripartite process in candidate countries, and the inability of the social partners to obtain the support of their members. In this context, the provision of a legal basis for tripartite consultations may simply render the whole process even more formal than before.

Tripartite agreements might well increase both in number and in effectiveness if pressure from the social partners became more significant. For example, in Slovakia the last tripartite agreement was signed because of the strong pressure of the trade unions – in the form of a general strike and threats of further collective action – which led the government to seek a compromise (Cziria 2001).

However effective their role and basic motivations may be, it is likely that these tripartite structures will remain a basic feature of industrial relations in these countries, something that should be given appropriate consideration.

5.3.5 The Emergence of New Actors

At the same time, multilateral bodies have emerged with the participation of a number of other actors, together with social partners. The Economic Council in Hungary (see Table 5.1), for instance, involves representatives of the chambers of commerce, the Central Bank, and foreign investors; similarly in Bulgaria, the National Economic and Social Council includes representatives of foreign multinational companies. The new Economic and Social Committee in Turkey is also of a multilateral nature.

While the involvement of new actors in the consultative process is not a bad thing in itself, it also has the effect of weakening the social partners. The European Commission has emphasised that, while the involvement of new actors should be seen as positive, it should complement and not substitute the previous tripartite consultative process, in which social partners should remain privileged partners, as in the social dialogue at EU level.

5.4 THE DIFFICULT IMPLEMENTATION OF FREE COLLECTIVE BARGAINING

Since the beginning of the transition most CEE countries have implemented a new legal framework for the conduct of collective bargaining and the conclusion of collective agreements. Although most of these provisions are inspired by industrial relations systems in western Europe, the legacy of previous economic and social systems, as well as the current situation of the social partners, seem to have resulted in differentiated industrial relations development in these countries.

5.4.1 Little Leeway Left by National and International Authorities

The continuous interventions by the state observed in the first twelve years of transition have clearly influenced industrial relations, notably by reducing the room for free collective bargaining. For instance, the very restrictive incomes policies followed by all CEE countries in the first period of reform did not permit any possibility of negotiation on this issue for the social partners or of social dialogue. Social partners had to endure the centralised incomes policy imposed by the governments and international monetary institutions. Given the fact that collective bargaining – in future as well as current EU countries – traditionally concerns wage policy, the serious damage done by this approach to autonomous social dialogue and the preservation of a number of basic pillars of the European Social Model in an enlarged EU can easily be imagined.

Government control still dominates. Even if tax-based incomes policies have been removed in all Central and Eastern European countries – with the exception of Bulgaria – the state still strictly controls wage increases in the economy, although to different degrees depending on the country: first, through wage scales in the public sector, and secondly, through minimum-wage fixing, as exemplified by the recent unilateral fixing of the minimum wage in Hungary in 2000 and 2001. Such unilateral economic decisions by the state do not favour the development of collective bargaining at local level.

In the case of Bulgaria, the collapse of the banking system in 1996 and the adoption of the currency board in 1997 – entailing strict observance of financial and monetary indicators – leave no room for negotiations on working conditions and progressive improvement of wages, working conditions, and social protection at local level.

In other areas, the tripartite process dissimulated the absence of social dialogue at enterprise level: while privatisation was formally discussed in tripartite debates, the issue of privatisation and restructuring in large banks and manufacturing enterprises was decided by the state more in tandem with the World Bank and strategic investors than with the social partners. In such a context, employers and the trade unions at local level were reduced to reacting to decisions taken by others.

Low social-partner involvement in budgetary arbitration at national level has also influenced industrial relations at local level; this explains why free collective bargaining has not emerged in the public sector. With regard to social protection, the abolition in Hungary of the social security boards, which were managed on a bipartite basis by the employers and the trade unions, had suppressed one additional means of strengthening bipartite social dialogue.

5.4.2 Industrial Relations Governed by the Law

Collective bargaining has historical roots in Central and Eastern Europe, existing well before the imposition of Communism. The right of trade unions to bargain in the collective interest of workers was in principle preserved under the Communist regimes, although the establishment of centrally controlled economies was clearly incompatible with basic individual and collective contractual freedom. In such systems, industrial relations were regulated in detail by various labour laws and other legal and sub-legal norms. After the fall of the Communist regimes, most previous regulations were removed, but the tendency to over-regulate industrial relations in one way or another seems to have survived. We can distinguish two main periods in which regulations were modified: (i) the beginning of the transition process, when new regulations governing collective bargaining were introduced in most Central and Eastern European countries, generally to promote free collective bargaining in accordance with ILO international standards; and (ii) the late 1990s and early 2000s when labour codes were renewed in order to permit transposition of the Community *acquis* to national legislation.

In the former Czechoslovakia, a new law on collective bargaining was adopted in 1991, while new regulations on collective bargaining were established in Hungary in the new Labour Code in 1992. Amendments to the Labour Code were also introduced in Poland (in 1994), and in a number of other countries. Only in Slovenia are industrial relations still covered by regulations on collective bargaining in force in 1989 (but a new bill on collective bargaining was drafted in 2001). Despite the differences in timing and in the contents of legal regulations on collective bargaining that characterise Central and Eastern European countries, they seem to share a common basic feature: the implementation of very detailed packages of laws and regulations at the beginning of the transition, which continued – at least partly – to govern industrial relations practices in these countries later on. As a result, industrial relations often have more of a compulsory than a voluntary character.

Moreover, since many such regulations were adopted before the most important economic and social changes took place – at a time when the economy was still dominated by stable employment and large enterprises – they do not always take into account the new property structure and size of enterprises (very small), the new types of labour contract (atypical, seasonal contracts), and the emergence of new trade unions and employers. This has contributed much to the instability of industrial relations systems in the region. It also partly explains the presence of a dual system of industrial relations, with a list of detailed provisions for large-scale enterprises (where a trade union presence and the representation of employees are both ensured by law), while small enterprises largely escape regulation. As an example, we might mention the law on works councils in Hungary – inspired by the German experience – adopted in 1992, which clearly states that works councils should be implemented in enterprises with more than 50 employees. This law was prepared before the privatisation process split large enterprises into small enterprises, and before the emergence of a great number of very small businesses. Similar regulations on works councils implemented in other countries – such as Slovakia – also fail to take into account the prevalence of small enterprises.

In other countries, strict legal provisions also determine to a considerable degree trade union room to manoeuvre in terms of labour dispute settlements and collective agreements. Other provisions are more detrimental to employers, such as a peculiar provision still prevalent in some Central and Eastern European countries with regard to the renewal of collective agreements: in practice, a current agreement, even if terminated, remains valid until a new agreement is concluded (for example, in Poland and, until recently, Bulgaria, where this was modified by the new Labour Code in 2000). This often constitutes a strong incentive for one of the parties – in general the trade unions – not to renew the agreement in order to keep in place the binding provisions of the previous one. In Poland, for example, employers have protested against such regulations which they find contrary to the principle of free collective bargaining that prevails in the European Union.

Such outdated legislative acts represent an obstacle to the introduction of more flexible and voluntary arrangements at the enterprise level. On the other hand, they have pushed many actors in these countries to revise and improve their legislative framework, so providing an excellent opportunity to modify it in accordance with EC directives and recommendations. The social partners in a number of candidate countries – for example, in Estonia, but also in Bulgaria – have been commendably active in this process, proposing concrete labour code amendments.

In general, however, existing regulations have merely been replaced by new ones, so that industrial relations systems continue to be significantly influenced by a number of legislative provisions. For instance, the scope of collective agreements continues to be limited; in both the Czech and the Slovak Republics, a collective agreement may include an issue requested by the social partners only if explicitly permitted by the Labour Code. While this provision was removed in the Czech Republic in 2000, it remains in a number of other countries. Another example of a legal provision recently promoted in many candidate countries concerns sectoral collective bargaining. In order to deal with the limited scope of collective bargaining at enterprise level, a clause extending sectoral collective agreements to all enterprises in the sector has been introduced in many candidate countries. We might wonder, however, if this type of obligation – which can also be found in some EU countries – represents the best way of promoting industrial relations at enterprise level. The prevalence of industrial-relations regulations contrasts sharply with the move towards excessive 'liberalisation' and the removal of existing standards in the field of working conditions (described in Chapter 2), so nourishing the dual aspect of industrial relations in these countries.

5.4.3 The Worrying Absence of Social Dialogue at the Enterprise Level

Since the collapse of the Communist regimes, there have been rapid changes in labour-management practices at enterprise level. Alongside privatisation and the birth of a myriad of new private enterprises, there has been a general decline in trade union membership.

There is also little formal institutionalisation of labour relations in terms of trade union recognition and the signing of collective agreements in newly-created private enterprises, especially in small businesses; the rapid growth of small and medium-size enterprises – for example, in services – has also found trade unions incapable of mustering an appropriate response. This is a worrying trend in a context in which 50–60 per cent of all employees in candidate countries work for small enterprises with less than 50 employees. In Slovakia, more than 97 per cent of workers are employed in enterprises with less than 50 employees; of them, more than 80 per cent work for micro enterprises with less than 10 employees.

Significant differences have also started to appear between property forms with regard to the contents of collective agreements. Not only have private enterprises been found to be signing fewer collective agreements, but these agreements have been less likely to cover particular issues, such as task assignment, job mobility, and work organisation.

Many foreign investors have also been hostile to trade unions and the signing of collective agreements. Considering the weight of foreign investment in the economies of candidate countries, especially those from Central and Eastern Europe, but also in small countries such as Malta and Cyprus, their impact on industrial relations practices are not negligible. Their influence on economic and social reforms has also been important, particularly in Hungary and Poland.

Finally, the high proportion of self-employed people and the growth of a large informal sector are also outside trade union control and state welfare regulations. More generally, the number of collective agreements signed at the enterprise level is very low, even in countries where collective bargaining is most prevalent, such as Hungary and Poland.

Compared to enterprises in the EU, ownership structures are also much more complicated, with a much greater variety of property forms, a situation that has contributed to the instability of industrial relations at the enterprise level. There can be a combination of public capital, domestic private capital, foreign investment, employee share-ownership, and sometimes even vouchers owned by citizens but generally managed by investment funds. Sometimes managements do not know which employers' organisation they should belong to for the purpose of collective bargaining. In such a context, dominated by multiple owners, trade unions also have difficulty in elaborating a clear strategy. This situation can become even more complicated where trade unions coexist with works councils.

As already mentioned, trade unions remain vulnerable as regards small and medium-size enterprises, which account for more than 90 per cent of enterprises in the ten CEE applicant countries. Although many EU member states are also characterised by a large proportion of SMEs, their industrial relations culture and human resource management are more established than in the new market economies of Central and Eastern Europe, where this process can thus be much more detrimental as regards working and employment conditions. This is also important because of the absence of sectoral agreements and the fact that mechanisms and practices of extension still have to be established. Moreover, this casts some doubt on the ability of the social partners to ensure the implementation in SMEs of certain elements of the *acquis*, such as health and safety or other technical requirements that directly depend on the good will of and/or substantial investment by the management.

The governments of the region are often not adequately equipped to deal with these developments. The resources allotted to labour inspection are very meagre. Moreover, these governments do not always register collective agreements, which also reflects their low administrative capacity on social dialogue. As a result, no analysis of the number and contents of collective agreements is possible, a lack of information which also limits the willingness of social partners to engage in collective bargaining. In a plenary session of the National Labour Council in spring 2000, the Hungarian government, on the insistence of the social partners, announced that it would instigate the systematic registration and analysis of the number and contents of these agreements, which it had previously neglected to do. The same situation prevails in other future member states.

5.4.4 The Lack of Autonomous Social Dialogue at Intermediate Level

At the same time, autonomous social dialogue and free collective bargaining are relatively poorly developed at intermediate level in the candidate countries. This means that tripartite consultations are not supported by a strong bipartite relationship between employer and worker representatives at decentralised levels – both at intermediate and enterprise levels – something which casts doubt on the effectiveness of the tripartite process itself and, within it, on the representativeness of the social partners.

In this regard, while social partners in future member states must insist on having tripartite institutions and mechanisms made more effective, they should undoubtedly focus their attention on the promotion of social dialogue at all possible levels, and collective bargaining directly between employers and trade unions' representatives.

Intermediate levels of social dialogue constitute essential elements in developing a coherent system of industrial relations and ensure a bridge between the decisions taken at national level, also within tripartite fora, and the employers' decisions at enterprise level.

There have recently been considerable modifications and simplifications of the labour code in the candidate countries, partly with the intention of leaving more room for the social partners. Candidate countries have also started to promote social dialogue at sectoral level, partly encouraged by the prospect of the sectoral social dialogue that takes place at EU level, and in which their social partners will have to play a role. Nevertheless, both the sectoral and regional levels of social dialogue continue to be poorly developed.

Sectoral dialogue or the missing level

- The very few collective agreements concluded at sectoral level in almost all candidate countries is undoubtedly one significant sign of the weaknesses of the social partners and their structures at intermediate levels of collective bargaining. As shown in Table 5.3, there are less than ten sectoral agreements, on average, in almost all the ten Central and Eastern European countries under study here (Ladó and Vaughan-Whitehead 2003). The number of sectoral agreements has even gone down in the Czech Republic, from 35 in 1995 to 22 in 2001. The same downward trend is observed in Hungary, the number of sectoral agreements falling from 24 in 1992 to 10 in 1996. Their number subsequently increased slightly, with 19 agreements in 1999. Their coverage has decreased by more than 30 per cent in respect of employers and by 75 per cent in respect of employees (Berki and Ladó 1998). In Poland, it was found that in 2001 there were 136 'supra-enterprise' agreements, but only 20 with wide sectoral scope, of which eight represented 'proper' sectoral agreements. In Estonia, Lithuania and Latvia there are fewer than 10 sectoral agreements, covering less than 10 – perhaps less than 5 – per cent of the labour force. Only in Slovenia are all sectors of activity covered by collective agreements, due to the obligatory nature of collective agreements. Enterprises in Slovenia must belong to the chamber of commerce which concludes (now in cooperation with the employers' organisation ZDS) sectoral collective agreements with the respective trade union organisations. Despite repeated attempts by the Government to do away with this system since 1995, there is still no system of voluntary collective agreements in Slovenia.
- The fact that there are hardly any data on the number of collective agreements at the sectoral level is also a sign of the lack of interest in this level of bargaining.
- Moreover, even when such an agreement is concluded, its contents are generally not particularly wide-ranging; for example, it is often confined to wage issues (determining, for instance, a sectoral minimum wage floor, annual wage increases, or wage scales) and does not cover employment issues and other working conditions. The contents of sectoral agreements,

Table 5.3 Number and coverage of sectoral collective agreements, candidate countries and EU member states, 2001

	Number of sectoral collective agreements	% of workers covered
Selected candidate countries		
Bulgaria (2001)	60*	20
Cyprus (2002)	12	–
Czech Republic (2000)	22	–
Estonia (2001)	7	less than 10
	(+10 sub-sectoral)	
Hungary (1999)	19	11
	(+33 multi-employer)	
Latvia (2000)	10	less than 10
Lithuania (2000)	very few	less than 5
Poland (2001)	136*	less than 10
	(20 with sectoral scope but 8 'proper' sectoral agreements)	
Slovakia (2001)	30	up to 60
Slovenia (2001)	38	close to 100
Selected EU countries		
Belgium	1 398	98
France	1 116	94.5
Germany	30 000**	75
Italy	600–700	–

Notes:
* Mainly in the public sector.
** including so-called wage agreements.

Source: National statistics; own sources.

generally speaking, merely reproduce the possibilities offered by the law, so that there are no significant differences from one sector to another. Collective agreements do not show any sign of originality or of progress on the different issues covered. The social partners have reported that such collective agreements are generally 'totally empty'. In Slovakia, for instance, many sectors are covered by a collective agreement whose contents, however, remain very general, all issues relevant for the workers being discussed and negotiated at enterprise level. Similarly in Turkey, while collective agreements are signed in a few sectors, they do not lead to a negotiation process between social partners and merely reassert the general principles already indicated in the previous agreement and also in the law. Sectoral agreements, especially with the coverage we find in most EU countries, are therefore more the exception than the rule.

- In this regard, it is significant to observe that in many countries in the region, the law – generally the labour code – does not even mention or specify the 'sectoral level', but rather refers to other concepts, such as 'multi-employer' agreements, as in Hungary, or 'higher-level' (than enterprise) agreements, as in the Czech Republic and Slovakia. This absence is very meaningful considering the importance of the law in this area, as already discussed. In Hungary, the terminology in the Labour Code is also rather ambiguous since it refers to the 'intermediate level' and does not mention 'sectoral collective agreements', although they should certainly represent one key priority of the government.

Consequently, what we find are generally multi-employer agreements signed between different employers working in the same activity; only a few of them can be considered as representing the whole sector, however. In Hungary, 33 such agreements were signed in 1999; similarly, 56 were registered in 1999 in Slovakia, and 136 agreements in Poland in 2001.

Moreover, as reported by the Hungarian authorities, they are not real sectoral agreements but more 'multi-employer collective agreements, or sub-branch framework agreements providing recommendations only'.

We must add that sectoral social dialogue is also poorly developed in Malta, Cyprus, and Turkey. While the absence of sectoral dialogue may be explained by the relatively small size of the economy and industry in the first two, the dominance of the state and insufficient development of free collective bargaining is the principal explanation in the case of Turkey.

In a context in which sectoral agreements are so few, or are not fully representative of the sectors as a whole, the so-called 'extension clause' (that is, the possibility of extending the provisions in the agreement to other employers in the same sector) takes on particular importance. However, such extension procedures are barely used. In the Czech Republic, for example, resort to extensions has even decreased: while in 1993 the coverage of agreements was extended to 191 employers beyond the scope of relevant employers' federations, by 1995 this had been reduced to only 12, and by 1996 the practice had been entirely abandoned (Pollert 1999). It was retained only in specific sectors, such as construction and textiles on the decision of the Ministry of Labour. Such government prerogatives concerning the extension procedure also exist in other countries, but little use has been made of them so far. In

Hungary, the extension procedure is regulated by law. The use of such extension procedures may increase in the wake of decisions taken by a number of countries – for example, Estonia and Poland in 2000, and Bulgaria in 2001 – to adopt new legislation to promote them and in this way to favour an increase in the coverage of binding collective agreements. Employers' representatives, however, are generally opposed to such an extension mechanism, which they find ill-adapted to the variety of enterprises within a single sector that can be found in these countries.

A number of factors explain the lack of collective bargaining at sectoral level:[14]

The restructuring of enterprise property and organisational forms, with three major combinatory factors:

1. The extreme diversity of enterprises within the same sector: the restructuring and privatisation processes have led to profound changes in the organisational structure, size, and property forms of enterprises. This makes it difficult to regroup enterprises in a single sector, given the major economic, social, and organisational differentials that prevail between them.
2. The growth of private small enterprises: the spectacular growth of such firms makes difficult any attempt to organise a whole industry or branch. The fact that trade unions are not well represented in the sectors dominated by SMEs contributes to this situation.
3. The behaviour of foreign enterprises: new foreign investors also prefer to limit collective bargaining to company-specific economic and financial conditions, and to technological and work organisation.

The structures and strategies of the social partners. The development of such a bargaining level also depends to a large extent on the existence of well-structured organisations on both sides of an industry. This is, however, not yet common in Central and Eastern European countries. The intermediate level is a completely new area for the social partners, at which they have first to find their counterparts and then to learn the ways and means of bargaining. While trade unions are often ready to enter into collective bargaining, the employers generally are not. They prefer the conclusion of individual arrangements at enterprise or establishment level. They often do not allow employers' federations to conclude sectoral collective agreements on their behalf – this happened for instance in the Czech Republic, and also can threaten to withdraw from the organisation if they attempt to do so, as in Poland (Draus 2000). Employers in any case do not have the structures to carry out

14. (For a more detailed analysis of sectoral social dialogue, in both future and current EU member states, see recent EC-ILO joint publication, Ghellab and Vaughan-Whitehead (eds), 2003.)

social dialogue at sectoral level. In contrast, the trade unions can generally draw on existing structures and membership at sectoral and regional level. On the trade union side, it is more usually the existence of a number of trade unions – as in Hungary, Romania, and Lithuania – and competition between them that constitutes an obstacle to trade union representation in individual sectors. In some sectors, trade unions may also be unprepared. In Estonia for instance, while employers' representatives are not ready to negotiate in manufacturing sectors or telecoms, trade unions are particularly weak in trade and construction.

Finally, in a period of economic recession, the room for bargaining is limited, and it is difficult to conduct meaningful bargaining at more than one level. This is particularly so, since in general the principle applied is similar to the one applied in most EU countries: that is, what is determined in a collective agreement at the sectoral or regional level is automatically applied at enterprise level, under similar or more advantageous – and in no case less advantageous – conditions. This is the reason why most employers remain hostile to sectoral collective agreements, while national employers' organisations seem to have understood the need for them within social dialogue structures and for economic and social cohesion more generally.

Practices in regional social dialogue

There are some signs of social dialogue at regional level in some candidate countries, for example, Poland and Bulgaria. In Poland, the restructuring process has been carried out through tripartite committees between the employers' and trade unions' representatives and local authorities. Social dialogue has also been developing in Bulgaria, and also in Romania. There are also some attempts to promote regional social dialogue in other future member states. In Hungary, social dialogue is not well developed at regional level, which is also a result of the fact that the social partners have been ejected from the regional labour councils which played a role in economic and social development in some regions. These councils, which represented a form of institutional involvement in state policy at local level, were important for stimulating a trade union presence – and therefore social dialogue – at regional level.

5.4.5 The Result: The Marginal Scope of Collective Bargaining

Low coverage ratio

To assess the scope and significance of social dialogue, the best indicator is collective bargaining, in both quantitative and qualitative terms. However, despite still insufficient and rather fragmented estimates of collective bargaining in candidate countries so far, we can reasonably state that the vast

Table 5.4 Total coverage of collective agreements (at all levels), selected candidate countries, 2001 (% of labour force)

Cyprus	68
Czech Republic	38
Hungary	40
Latvia	20
Lithuania	15
Slovakia	50
Slovenia	100
Turkey	less than 10

Source: National statistics and self-reported figures for 1999–2001.

majority of workers in these countries are not covered by collective agreements (Table 5.4). In fact, the percentage of employees covered by a collective agreement, either sectoral or even enterprise, is rather low in the future member states; for example, such agreements cover only 20 per cent of Czech employees. Less than 10 per cent of Hungarian employees are covered today by a sectoral collective agreement, and 40 per cent by a sectoral or enterprise agreement. Only one-third of employees are employed in enterprises where basic conditions for meaningful social dialogue – such as local trade union representation, and affiliation to employer and branch trade unions – exist (Ladó 2001). Similarly, micro- and small enterprises are not much covered by social dialogue in Slovenia, which also partly explains why sectoral bargaining has been introduced on an obligatory basis.

The lowest coverage rate is in Lithuania, with less than 15 per cent of employees being covered by a (sectoral or enterprise) collective agreement (Draus 2000), while the highest – excluding Slovenia, where it is obligatory – is in Slovakia (50 per cent of employees covered by a collective agreement).

To summarise, the average bargaining coverage rate for CEE candidate countries, based on the available information, is currently estimated at 25–30 per cent of the labour force. Looked at from the other direction, 70–75 per cent of workers are not beneficiaries of collective agreements. This is precisely the contrary of the general trend in the current EU-15, where currently (2000–2) the coverage rates are as high as (virtually) 100 per cent in Belgium and Austria, above 90 per cent in Sweden, Finland and France, above 80 per cent in Denmark and Spain, with the Netherlands not far behind on 78 per cent and Germany bringing up the rear but still with 67 per cent. Of the future member states only Cyprus has an estimated coverage rate (68 per cent) comparable with the EU average.

We must emphasise that while the existence of clear representativeness criteria can help to promote collective bargaining, too strict criteria can, on the contrary, seriously diminish it. In Turkey, for instance, the existence of two basic conditions for allowing trade unions to sign a collective agreement at enterprise level – that is, having more than 50 per cent of members in the enterprise and representing at least 10 per cent of the workers in the sector concerned – has seriously limited the signing of collective agreements, something which today takes place in less than 10 per cent of enterprises.

The influence of the informal sector

In order to evaluate the scope of social dialogue, we must also take into account the balance between the formal and the informal economy since by definition social dialogue does not exist in the latter. We must also take into consideration how much influence practices in the informal economy have on the formal economy. Certainly the 'wild capitalism' we observe at enterprise level in the new private sector has been influenced by informal practices, especially among small enterprises whose link with the informal sector is generally strong. Small enterprises function without established social dialogue mechanisms, are reluctant to affiliate to employers' organisations, and workplace relations are of a more informal nature (Ladó 2001). Although this situation is also prevalent among SMEs in EU member states, they are certainly less influenced by the – much smaller – informal sector and the alternative solutions it provides, also for the enterprises working in the formal sector which rely on it, for instance through sub-contracting. Central and Eastern Europe is not only characterised by a large informal economy, but also by a more general reluctance to observe established rules, which can partly be traced back to survival strategies inherited from the Communist period (Ladó 2001). Such practices are obviously at odds with social dialogue which promotes further regulation, stricter controls on work related matters, and more transparency on the part of the management.

In this regard, we should also consider the development of social dialogue as a means of curbing informal or underground practices, something that is coming to be regarded more and more positively by employers who wish to protect themselves from unfair competition from their peers. This also underlines why it is so important that the state shows a good example in developing sound practices of social dialogue at national level.

The void in micro- and small enterprises

According to empirical evidence collected so far, the presence of trade unions in future member states is unlikely in micro-enterprises (less than 10 employees) and exceptional in small enterprises (less than 50 employees). Only in medium-size and large enterprises are trade unions generally present.

At present, small enterprises are thus beyond the range of social dialogue, which, as already mentioned, has not been compensated for so far by collective agreements at sectoral level or by extension mechanisms.

Entire categories of employee left out
Experience in the region also shows that there is usually no collective bargaining for civil servants and employees in the budgetary sector. Negotiations hardly take place at all in such sectors as health care, education, transport, communications, and science and research. This leads to general demotivation on the part of civil servants and public employees, whose working conditions, especially in terms of wages, are becoming less and less favourable in comparison with those prevailing in the private sector. It is in these sectors that most disputes and strikes are concentrated, sparked mainly by wages – which remain beyond the trade unions' influence, being determined through imposed budgetary constraints and rigid wage and grading scales, so increasing the wage gap with the private sector – and working conditions.

Moreover, there are numerous legal restrictions and limitations on civil servants' right to strike. This is the source of serious social tensions in most Central and Eastern European countries. Major strikes have taken place in the public sector, especially in health care and education, but also in the judicial field and the police. In the Slovak Republic, tensions in the public sector reached their highest point in 2000 and 2001.

There are also increasing social tensions in large public enterprises whose management tends to follow the tough line of the government, not discussing anything or negotiating with the trade unions. Problems in signing collective agreements have been registered in many public enterprises, which seem to suffer from continuous interference by the state. The companies' trade unions have also complained about infringements of their right to strike. Problems have also been identified in enterprises providing so-called 'services of general interest' (electricity, water, post, and so on) which have been privatised, for instance in the energy sector, where there is also a complete absence of worker involvement in the company or in bargaining, as in Romania or Hungary.

5.5 THE FAILURES OF THE SOCIAL PARTNERS

In order to understand industrial relations developments in Central and Eastern Europe, it is important to briefly describe the main features and trends of the trade unions and employers' organisations. Both have been engaged, since the beginning of the reforms, in profound restructuring, while some have even had to start from scratch, especially on the employers' side.

Privatisation and restructuring have also led to a redistribution of roles among old and new organisations.

5.5.1 Trade Unions: Weakened by Excessive Fragmentation

Rivalry among national organisations
On the trade union side the first years of transition were characterised by strong rivalries between competing organisations and a resulting fragmentation of the trade union movement. While former Communist trade unions involved themselves in a process of democratisation and converted themselves into bodies able to function in a free-market economy, there has been a proliferation of new trade unions. The national trade union organisations have thus often been divided ideologically, but also on issues such as property and trade union asset restitution. Recognition in tripartite bodies has also represented a major challenge for former and new trade union organisations, since it represents a way of obtaining legitimacy from the government, but also of increasing representativeness vis-à-vis individual members.

Internal tensions have characterised the trade union movement in the years of reform, for instance in Bulgaria, where former trade union CITUB and new trade union PODKREPA had to co-exist; in Hungary, where there are a myriad of different trade unions, such as the former Communist trade union MSZOSZ and new trade unions such as the League of Independent Trade Unions (LIGA) and the Federation of Workers' Councils (MOSZ); and in Poland, where the trade union movement is part of political history, with Solidarity, whose activities had been forbidden under the Communist regime, and the trade union OPZZ, originally created as a countermovement in 1981–82 by General Jaruzelski from the original Communist Council of Trade Unions. These historical relationships clearly constituted the basis of later union competition – also often exploited by governments – that weakened the trade unions' position and legitimacy considerably during the transition years, above all making it difficult for them to challenge major restrictive economic policies.

In Poland, for example, rivalry between the two main trade unions has often led to the interruption (or paralysis) of the tripartite commission, each one taking it in turns to quit the tripartite forum for political opposition: Solidarnosc withdrew from the Commission in 1997, only to rejoin later on, while OPZZ decided to withdraw in 2000,[15] thus making it impossible for the Commission to continue its work.

At the same time, too much collusion with official government policy has threatened to jeopardise the trade unions' mandate as voluntary and strategic

---

15. OPZZ also made a complaint about the Polish Government to the International Labour Organisation, which considered it partly justified (Matey-Tyrowicz 2001).

representatives of employees' interests. In Poland, Solidarnosc has experienced a clear tension between its role as a social and political movement – especially when it came to power and implemented restrictive reforms – and its role as defender of workers' interests in the workplace.

The trade union movement is also fragmented between a number of different organisations, as in Romania and Hungary, where five and six, respectively, trade union organisations co-exist. In countries such as the Czech Republic, Slovakia, and Slovenia, there are also a number of organisations, but one major confederation has managed to dominate. Bulgaria and Poland continue to be characterised by dual trade union representation (bipolarism).

Today, after more than ten years of transition, the situation is much better for the trade union movement; the former hostility has progressively been replaced in most cases by mutual acceptance, and sometimes even by the first attempts at cooperation. The question of trade union assets has generally been resolved in all countries, thus reducing the sources of division. New trade unions have generally recognised that the old trade unions have been truly reformed, while the old trade unions have accepted the new ones as part of the social dialogue and collective bargaining scene. Even if progress is still needed in this area, most trade unions have recognised the long-term benefits of being politically non-aligned.

This has led to a new period in which mergers can be attempted between trade union organisations. Nevertheless, old ideological rivalries have been replaced in some cases by rivalries for new members and representativeness, particularly important in a context of falling trade union membership. An increasing number of candidate countries have adopted legal provisions concerning representativeness. Others, such as Estonia in 2000, have also adopted clearer legislative provisions for defining the rights and scope of trade unions, or specific laws on trade unions and on employers' organisations.

The fall in trade union membership
This is a common feature of all candidate countries: in most of Central and Eastern Europe, trade unionisation had fallen below 30 per cent of the labour force by the end of 2001. The fall seems to have been particularly strong in Estonia, down to 12 per cent, but also in Poland and Hungary, with less than 20 per cent trade union membership. The Slovak Republic has done rather better, however, and the highest figure is registered in Slovenia, although here, as already mentioned, the signing of collective agreements has so far been obligatory. Trade union membership is also higher in Cyprus.

The average trade union density for the first 10 candidate countries confirmed by the 2002 Copenhagen summit (that is, all candidate countries,

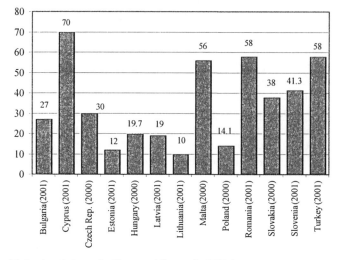

Source: National statistics and self-reported figures for 2000-1.

Figure 5.1 Trade union membership, 2000–1 (% of total labour force)

excluding Bulgaria, Romania and Turkey) is 21.9 per cent, according to a recent estimate (Carley 2002, p. 2). This is already less than the average trade unionisation in the current EU-15, which is 30.4 per cent.[16] This average figure is, obviously, heavily affected by the situation in the CEE accession countries. In contrast, the level of trade unionisation in Cyprus and Malta is comparable to the current EU average.

Obviously, some fall in trade union membership was unavoidable given the 100 per cent rates registered under the previous regime. At the same time, the fall would have stopped after the first years of transition if a number of factors had not combined to provoke a further and continuous decrease.

First, the falling living standards in the first years of transition – which stopped only in the late 1990s for most countries in the region – and growing unemployment contributed to increase workers' disappointment vis-à-vis their trade unions. This trend has often pushed workers to follow individual strategies, such as cumulating second and third jobs in the informal sector, rather than supporting collective action.

This fall in trade union membership also has direct financial implications for the trade unions in terms of membership fees, which weakens them finan-

16. This is the weighted average which takes into account the respective size of the labour force in the different countries. The non-weighted average would give higher figures: 43.8 per cent in the EU-15 and 34.1 per cent in the 10 future member states (Carley 2002).

cially, but also institutionally and politically. In concrete terms, the impossibility for many national trade unions to finance a strike for more than a few days clearly puts into question their mobilisation capacity and thus also their legitimacy.

In such a difficult context, governments are not averse to further weakening trade union organisations. This is why the European Commission has strongly insisted on the need to reinforce the structures of the social partners. In a number of countries, certain developments unfriendly to the social partners were particularly unwelcome, such as the decision of the Hungarian government to modify the way trade union membership fees were collected and accounted, increasing the administrative burden and further discouraging union membership. This is reminiscent of actions taken by Margaret Thatcher in the 1980s to decisively reduce trade union influence in the UK.

A painful absence from new private enterprises

Privatisation has also automatically led to a decline in trade union membership since – along with restructuring – it is often accompanied by the splitting of previously large state-owned companies into a series of smaller establishments, previous trade union structures being destroyed without new ones being created to take their place. Sectoral shifts have also taken place for many enterprises to which trade unions have generally been unable to provide an adequate response. At the same time, trade unions have managed to retain a presence in many privatised enterprises.

By contrast, a trade union presence is often not recognised by employers in the new private enterprises, especially smaller ones. The absence of trade unions in very small and medium-size enterprises remains a major weakness of the trade unions in the future member states. The first generation of entrepreneurs in the candidate countries seems to be more attracted by a neoliberal rather than a human resource style of management. Trade unions still have to find the right strategy to increase their presence in this type of enterprise, while the workers themselves, especially the younger ones, do not seem to have much faith in the ability of the trade unions to defend their interests. High rates of unemployment also render the context particularly favourable to employers.

We must also add that industrial relations are very much influenced by foreign investment, which represents a significant force in those economies. Foreign-owned enterprises generally adopt their own industrial relations systems, with less recognition of national trade unions and even important examples of non-acceptance of trade unions by large EU companies. Their policy in this regard depends also on their basic locational strategy, between, for instance, greenfield or other forms of investment (see Chapter 8).

Table 5.5 *Major strikes, candidate countries, 1990–2001*

Country	Categories excluded (strikes forbidden)	Main sectors	Major strikes
Bulgaria	Limited actions in public services (according to the Law on civil servants of 1999); strikes forbidden in defence, interior affairs, for soldiers, court, prosecutors and judicial investigation Also forbidden in health care, communications, energy, and some other public utilities	Public sector, especially in education; Public enterprises, such as in energy, mining, steel, military-industrial complex, chemicals	Teachers, mining, military-industrial complex in 1999–2001 Major strike in 2000 and 2001 in the company Balkan Airlines, hastily privatised and later on declared bankrupt and closed early 2001
Cyprus	Limited action in public services		
Czech Republic	Judges, procurators, armed forces, police	Public administration, public sector	Railways, February 1997 Public demonstration in 1997 against government Public sector, 1998 Mass media: strike of employees of Czech public television in January 2001
Estonia		Teachers, nurses (warning strikes), mine workers	Teachers' strike in 1992 Metal workers in one enterprise in 1999 Mining and energy (power plants) in June 2000
Hungary	Administrative organs of justice, armed forces, and the police (Act VII of 1989, art 3 (2)) Right to strike in state administration dependent on agreement with the Council of Ministers and the trade unions concerned (Act VII of 1989, art 3 (2)) (above agreement signed only in 1994)	Railways, health sector	Strikes in railways every year, except in 1996 and 1997; most significant strike took place in February 2000, jointly organised by the three representative trade unions: it lasted 329 hours and involved 10–12 thousand workers each day Health sector: major action took place in December 2000, and included 3 demonstrations in 3 different cities and 27 warning strikes all over the country
Latvia	Public administration, police force, judges	Public sectors (teachers, scientists)	Teachers in 1999

Table 5.5 (cont.)

Lithuania	Railways, power engineering, public utilities (water, food, etc.), public administration	Public sector, especially education	Education sector in 2000 and 2001 for wage payment delays Agriculture in 2000
Malta	Employees providing essential services (special appendix to Industrial Relations Act)	Public sector and state-owned enterprises	1998–2000: strike at a state-owned construction company Strike at Malta Freeport in 1998 in protest against higher costs of public utilities Strike at Malta's International Airport in 1999 as a result of inter-union recognition dispute
Poland	Public administration, security and armed forces, police, fire brigade, penitentiary services, courts, prosecutors	Public sector (health, education, culture), industry, transport	Railways in 1998 and 2000 Doctors in 1998 Nurses in 2000
Romania	Crucial services, armed forces		
Slovakia	Civil servants in high positions, in defence, health and public safety and security (firemen, soldiers, etc.)		Railways in January 2003
Slovenia	Police, defence	Public sector (doctors, teachers, judges), textiles, construction, wood, metal and electrical equipment	Metal and electrical equipment, textiles, in 1994–97 Doctors, teachers in 1996 Railways in 1997 (10 days) Air traffic controllers in 2000
Turkey	Rights to collective bargaining and strikes forbidden in public sector (according to new law of 2001)	Public sector, textiles, transport, food, mining 'petroleum, chemicals and rubber', metals	Demonstration against new law in public sector in 2000 and 2001 Examples in 1999 (34 strikes): 9 strikes in transport, 6 in textiles (88 000 work-days lost), 5 in 'petroleum, chemicals and rubber' (71 000), 2 in food and 2 in mining + 10 others

Low mobilisation capacity

This membership weakness finds direct expression in the number and depth of collective disputes,[17] which clearly do not reflect the gravity of the social situation and the burden imposed on workers by the transition; in particular, the sharp fall in real wages in the first years of reform and the use of the minimum wage as a way of controlling both wage increases and social benefits have not led in these countries to major industrial action or a multiplication of strikes. Massive restructuring, with closures and layoffs, has not been translated into industrial action either. The number of days lost due to strikes has remained low. Clearly, an unstable economic environment, with the workers afraid of losing their job or experiencing further wage cuts, does not represent an appropriate context for workers to seek to assert their rights via the trade unions.

Most strikes have been in the public sector, especially among teachers, doctors, nurses, judges, and public administration. The main reason for this was stagnant wage scales, related to a minimum wage that has remained under strict government control. In some countries, however, restrictions on strike action for certain categories of public employee, as in Turkey, limited the multiplication of such strikes.

Major strikes have also taken place in large public enterprises, such as the railways or airlines, as in Poland, Slovenia, Czech Republic, and Hungary. These conflicts often reflect the absence of autonomous social dialogue and collective bargaining in these monopolistic public enterprises where the state acts as the main employer. Strikes have also occurred in sectors subject to harsh restructuring, such as mining and energy in Estonia and Bulgaria, or textiles in Slovenia.

5.5.2 Employers' Organisations: The Weakest Link

Self-evidently, there were no employers' organisations under the former regimes. The only employers were those appointed to run state-owned enterprises, and the only employers' representatives were the chambers of commerce. After the collapse of the Communist regimes, the employers' side had thus to be built up from scratch. In most countries of the region, the workers' side is a much more tangible phenomenon than the employers' side.

This has caused significant problems both at the national level, particularly when governments were trying to build up a tripartite partnership, and at decentralised levels – for instance, sectoral and regional – where employers'

---

17. The fall in membership here corresponds to a low mobilisation capacity. This situation contrasts strongly with, for instance, France where the very low level of unionisation – less than 10 percent – is compensated by a high mobilisation capacity.

representatives were totally absent. This led the state in some cases to provide considerable assistance to the creation of employers' organisations, as in Poland, the Czech Republic, and Slovakia.

Undoubtedly, the most significant weakness in industrial relations since the beginning of the transition is this lack of organised and representative employers' organisations at the national and intermediate levels.

Total lack of representativeness

While employers' organisations have managed to take part in the tripartite process, their lack of representativeness remains a problem. In terms of numbers of members, the representativeness of employers' organisations in candidate countries is rather weak. They represent on average 30–40 per cent of industrial enterprises or between 2 and 5 per cent of enterprises as a whole (Draus 2001). The estimated affiliation rates, measured by share of employees employed in member enterprises, vary considerably between the extremes of 70-80 per cent (Malta) and 15 per cent (Poland). It is also limited in the Czech Republic (30 per cent of employers), Latvia (40 per cent) and Hungary (45 percent) (Ladó and Vaughan-Whitehead 2003).

In many cases employers' organisations did not act on the mandate of their members; even more seriously, they could not ensure that the tripartite agreements they had signed at national level would be implemented at local level, especially by those who are not members of national employers' associations.

Initially, employers' organisations mainly represented the interests of state-owned enterprises. The next stage of development saw a great diversity of employers at the local level – intensified by the privatisation process and the emerging private sector – which also led (as with the trade unions) to a rapid multiplication of employers' organisations. New organisations emerged to represent in particular the interests of private entrepreneurs, and later on of small and medium-size private enterprises.

Fragmentation and poor coordination

Small and medium-size private enterprises are often represented by myriad new employers' organisations, which means that the representation of their interests remains rather dispersed and incoherent: for example, in Poland, as in Slovenia, SMEs are represented by the chamber of crafts; while in Hungary and Romania employers' interests continue to be represented by nine and eight national employers' organisations, respectively.

Since this diversity also weakens the employers' position, in the recent past there have been some attempts to merge, as in Romania. Attempts at coordination have also emerged, as in Hungary where the nine employers' organisations agreed to create an umbrella organisation for international cooperation (CEHIC), especially under pressure from the European employers' organisation UNICE. Other countries, such as Bulgaria, and to a lesser extent Lithuania, Czech Republic, and Poland, are also characterised by pluralism in employers' interest representation. This pluralism often leads to open conflict, as in Poland, where a new actor emerged in 1994, the new Polish Confederation of Private Employers, representing a new competitor for the organisation already in place, the Confederation of Polish Employers, which has so far managed to prevent the new organisation from participating in the tripartite commission.

Other candidate countries are characterised by one major employer organisation, as in Slovenia, Slovakia, and Latvia. In Slovenia, the main national employers' organisation continues to be to dependent – also financially – on the Chamber of Commerce. Similarly in Turkey, the only employer organisation, TISK, represents not only private, but also state-owned enterprises. In Latvia, legislative provisions on employer-organisation representativeness have been conceived so as to ensure the emergence of a single organisation to represent employers' interests.

The ambiguous role of chambers of commerce

Because of the difficulties they have faced in organising themselves, many employers' organisations in Central and Eastern Europe have used the already existing chambers of commerce and industry as a basis. This allowed them to benefit from the start from political recognition as well as already existing institutional resources, in terms of offices, personnel, and members.

The most clear-cut case in this regard is Slovenia, where the chamber of commerce remained for most of the transition the only representative employers' organisation, before it helped to create new employers' organisations, although still on the basis of previous structures. This is the reason why the distinction between employers' organisations and chambers of commerce is generally much more obscure in Central and Eastern Europe than in EU countries.

Moreover, ambiguous situations emerged when the chambers of commerce in a few candidate countries started to participate in national consultations on the invitation of the government, thus increasingly playing the role usually played by national employers' organisations. Furthermore, in some countries they were allowed to engage in collective bargaining and the drawing up of collective agreements. This is the case in Slovenia – where the law says that collective agreements have to be signed by the chamber of commerce – and to a lesser extent in Cyprus and Malta. Attempts to progressively involve the chamber of commerce in social dialogue as alternative partners closer to the government in Hungary have also been made by Prime Minister Viktor Orbán.

In this situation, more must be done in the future member states to make the employers' organisations and chambers of commerce more distinct. The latter also play a role in current EU member countries, but not in connection with collective bargaining. They may also represent the interests of other groups than employers. Only in Austria do the chambers of commerce play such a role, although this due to the obligatory nature of economic chamber membership, a system which does not exist in any other EU member state.

A trend towards (employer) individualism
While most employers' organisations in future member states today benefit from structures and activities which are quite similar to those of their EU counterparts, they continue to be extremely vulnerable for a number of reasons, of which we should emphasise two: (i) the lack of interest of new private employers, and (ii) the difficulties that employers' organisations face in attracting sufficient membership fees and thus general resources for their operations.

Entrepreneurs in Central and Eastern Europe prefer to follow individual strategies rather than being represented by employers' organisations. They thus favour direct contacts with the government or direct relations and collective bargaining with the trade unions or workers' representatives at enterprise level. In most cases, their lack of interest in employers' organisations can be explained by their wish to avoid the signing of collective agreements and recognition of trade unions at enterprise or establishment level. They also complain about the priority given by national employers' organisations to tripartite bodies at the expense of member services. On the other hand, the threat posed by the large informal sector is beginning to push them to seek higher-level representation.

5.6 IMPLICATIONS FOR IMPLEMENTATION OF THE *ACQUIS*

5.6.1 No Favourable Consultative Process

While the social partners have been given an enhanced role at EU level (with the Amsterdam Treaty), in most of Central and Eastern Europe they suffer from a lack of effective involvement in decision-making. We may therefore wonder whether policy in the region is going in the right direction. One of the most important outcomes of this is the likelihood that it will be more and more difficult to inform and mobilise the social partners to the important role they will be called on to play in the implementation of the *acquis*, but also in the European-level social dialogue, as well as in the common European strategies.

This is the case, for example, as regards employment issues where major progress has been achieved at the Community level. While the social partners at EU level are expected to play a major role in defining employment guidelines, as well as in the assessment and monitoring process, also at national level, developments are often in the opposite direction in the future member states.

The lack of social-partner involvement on other economic issues, such as wages and incomes policy, tax laws, and budgetary arbitration, which have direct and indirect effects on employment, is also contributing to weaken the capacity of the social partners to deal with employment strategy issues in the future.

As regards Hungary, for example, in an ILO minute from the June 2000 XIIth session of the Committee on the Application of Standards (p. 7), doubts are expressed about:

> whether the country had effective tripartite consultative machinery that could contribute to the framing of a dynamic employment policy following the dissolution of the Ministry of Labour and the distribution of its previous functions to three separate Ministries, the Ministry of Economy, the Ministry of Education and the Ministry of Social and Family Affairs.

The ILO document also confirms that the 'social partners are currently not involved in the formulation and preparation of the national employment policy' (ibid., p. 10). This clearly also constitutes an obstacle to the future involvement of Hungarian social partners in the coordinated European Employment Policy.

The government of Hungary, but also of other neighbouring countries, must take the need for tripartite consultations more seriously, not only on employment, but also on those economic issues that have an impact on labour and employment.

5.6.2 Difficult Transposition of the *Acquis* at National Level

We have already seen that social dialogue is also a means of implementing Community directives at national level. Many Community directives specify that they may be implemented in the member states by means of legislation or by agreements between the social partners; this option was confirmed by the entry into force of the Amsterdam Treaty.

This clearly requires developed collective bargaining, leading to the signing of legally enshrined or otherwise binding collective agreements. In this regard the Council of Europe, while advocating social dialogue as a way of transposing European legislation, did not specify the need to have mandatory normative effects of collective agreements. It is clear, however (as experiences in EU countries suggest), that this may influence the way chosen by member states to transpose EU labour law. Where mandatory normative effects of collective agreements do exist, as in Belgium, Denmark, Italy, and Sweden, collective agreements as a tool for implementing EC directives have been more frequently used. By contrast, where collective agreements do not have any mandatory effect, as in the UK – where they have the status of a sort of gentlemen's agreement – there is no resort to social dialogue for implementing EC labour law.

Such 'gentlemen's agreements' are also applied in Cyprus and Malta, which have historical links with the UK. The situation is similar in most candidate countries in Central and Eastern Europe, where there are no mandatory collective agreements and collective bargaining is poorly developed. In Poland, for instance, the Constitution (Article 87) does not list collective agreements as legally binding sources, so that it would be impossible to use them as a legal means for the implementation of European labour law within the framework of national labour law (Swiatkowski 2001).

Since member states are ultimately responsible for the transposition of EC labour law, they may be reluctant to allow it to take place on the basis of collective agreements if they know that the adoption of such agreements depends upon weak and poorly representative employers' organisations and trade unions. This means that the appropriate conditions do not yet exist in the future member states for the implementation of one important possibility provided in the Treaty, the use of social dialogue as a means of adopting EC labour law.

5.6.3 The Implementation of the *Acquis* at Local Level

Even if the social partners are not involved in the negotiations for accession with the EC, they must in any case be involved in transposition of the *acquis* at national level, participating in the technical discussions in order to ensure that a strategic policy is adopted in this regard and then playing their part in its implementation at more decentralised levels.

As an example, health and safety is undoubtedly an area where the implementation of the *acquis*, which takes the form of numerous directives, will simply not be possible without involving the employers, who often have to make significant and costly investments, and workers' representatives, since this area is so important for the labour force.

Local-level implementation of the *acquis* also requires social dialogue and the participation of workers' representatives. Clearly the application of EC directives on, for instance, working time requires some sort of social partnership in order to discuss the changes to be introduced in accordance with the economic environment and working conditions of the enterprise. Social dialogue is even more necessary to implement those directives which are directly related to the promotion of social dialogue and workers' participation at enterprise level, such as the European works council directives. Many directives on health and safety, but also on equal opportunities, stipulate the role of the social partners in the implementation of the directive at enterprise level.

In this regard, clearly the low coverage of collective bargaining, combined with the weak development of forms of workers' participation at enterprise level (see Chapter 6), represent serious obstacles to the introduction of Community regulations into the everyday life of enterprises in the future member states. For the candidate countries, the scope of social dialogue will be a key factor when transposing the *acquis*, especially in such areas as labour law, equal opportunities, health and safety at work, employment, and social protection.

5.6.4 Unprepared for Participation in the European Social Dialogue

The trends presented in previous sections have shown that social dialogue in the future member states must be developed at all levels. A lack of consultation at the national level can seriously restrict the emergence of autonomous social dialogue at the branch and enterprise levels by limiting the scope of collective bargaining and collective agreements. At the same time, national consultations will not be effective without strong and representative social partners representing the interests of their branch or enterprise members. In this regard, the poor representativeness of employers and the narrow scope of trade unionisation, with a question mark against even the survival of some social partners, do not represent the best possible conditions for engaging in negotiations and debates at EU level.

Moreover, it will be difficult for representative social partners to emerge without stronger consultation mechanisms at national level and more collective bargaining at local level.

Participation in the European social dialogue also requires representative social partners able to negotiate at EU level on the mandate of their members and subsequently able to ensure that agreements concluded at EU level are implemented at local level.

Such negotiations at EU level also require the social partners being regularly involved in the same issues at national level, not only concerning social, but also employment and macroeconomic matters.

Governments should develop social dialogue in order to make sure that their social partners are able to take part in this European dialogue, and thus protect the national interest, but also in order to ensure that those social partners will be the most representative of workers' and employers' interests according to Community criteria.

The Bulgarian government, for example, should consider carefully whether it could accept an EU framework agreement in the conclusion of which the

Bulgarian social partners have not participated. The Bulgarian social partners must be able to negotiate to the same extent as the social partners in current EU member states. While the European Commission is pursuing a number of activities in order to prepare the social partners of the applicant countries for their future role in this regard, the governments of future member states should promote the emergence of representative social partners, which requires appropriate structures of social dialogue at different levels, as well as political will.

The absence of sectoral social dialogue in candidate countries could undermine the participation of candidate countries in the sectoral social dialogue that takes place at EU level. Moreover, social partners who sign only multi-employer rather than sectoral agreements would not have the legitimacy needed for signing framework agreements covering the whole sector at EU level. This may contribute to halting the autonomous social dialogue started at EU level between sectoral social partners. It would, moreover, contrast with the increasing demand from the social partners in current EU member states for debates on transversal issues, and their willingness to involve their counterparts from future member states in all relevant issues that may be influenced by the EU enlargement process (that is, nearly all issues)..

5.7 INADEQUACIES OF THE COMMUNITY APPROACH

The current trends in industrial relations in the future member states naturally give rise to concerns about what will happen after they join the EU. Are these developments so different from EU practices that they may undermine social dialogue as a basic pillar of the European Social Model? If so, have the European institutions taken them sufficiently into account? What may be required from European institutions to ensure the survival of social dialogue in an enlarged European Union?

It is important to emphasise at the outset that the practice of social dialogue and industrial relations differs significantly from one EU country to the next, precisely because more than any other area it reflects the culture of policy-making, the history of the role of partnership and of the social partners, and the different strategies, but also ideologies behind economic and social policies. This is why social dialogue has always been governed by the subsidiarity principle – that is, member states and their economic and social actors decide on the most appropriate ways of implementing the main principles of partnership and social dialogue defined at EU level. In this regard, the situation is obviously very different in, for example, the Scandinavian countries, which have developed social partnership agreements in many areas of decision-making, and the United Kingdom, which has progressively opted for a very decentralised and liberal approach in which social partners have a less important role to play, especially at central level. The question is therefore not whether the future member states have different industrial relations systems – they obviously do, and indeed they differ sharply among themselves – but whether the main features of their systems are so fundamentally different from those found in most EU countries that they might lead to the drastic modification of the basic features of social dialogue in the EU.

Moreover, although social dialogue is subject to subsidiarity, EU member states have also decided to enshrine social dialogue in the Community *acquis* and to promote it at EU level. This has led to a clearer reference in the Treaty to autonomous social dialogue and collective bargaining, and also to the reinforcement of the social partners' role, not only in EU decision-making processes, but also in coordinated European policies. Despite the subsidiarity principle, this clearly points to the existence of a number of requirements of EU member states in the area of social dialogue that must also be taken on board by candidate countries.

In this regard, we have seen that most candidate countries share a certain number of features, such as the predominant role of the state and the allotting of an important role to tripartite institutions, while autonomous social dialogue is still insufficiently developed, with, as a worrying consequence, very poor collective bargaining coverage, a trend that can seriously undermine other areas, such as working conditions, workers' participation, and the implementation of all necessary EU provisions at enterprise level. Even more fundamentally, we have seen that the culture of industrial relations and human resources is fundamentally different at enterprise level, especially among new private businessmen, who generally adopt a very liberal approach in which social issues do not seem to have a place. While this situation is not surprising after decades of authoritarianism, a lack of independent employers, and a sudden shift to relatively free market economies, it requires more monitoring and more input from the European Union.

In this regard the accession negotiations have constituted an important step, and have certainly played a role in emphasising the extent to which social dialogue is part of the Community *acquis*. We might wonder, however, whether the approach so far has been adequate to deal with the significant gaps, and whether the Community *acquis* can help us to go much further. A number of drawbacks can be identified in the area of social dialogue, especially in light of the developments in future member states already mentioned.

5.7.1 For a Stronger and More Transparent Stance on Social Dialogue

First, a general remark on the place given to social dialogue in the negotiation process, during which it has often been said that social dialogue, however important it may be, is not part of the 'core *acquis*' (that is, the legislative *acquis*), but rather part of the so-called 'soft *acquis*'. This distinction would not have been so essential if the Directorate General responsible for Enlargement at the European Commission had not created it 'as the foundation of' all its pre-accession strategy. It was considered that only the legal provisions should entail serious requirements in the negotiation process, while all the other EC texts, either in the form of communications, decisions, reports, or various (green or white) papers, despite the fact that they contribute greatly to determining EU policy, were left out of consideration. We shall discuss this approach to the whole negotiation process, sometimes rather critically, in the concluding chapter.

This approach has clearly made it more difficult to explain to candidate countries that there are also very strong requirements on social dialogue. Furthermore, the fact that social dialogue is dealt with in many different places, rather than in a single Community directive, reflects the multidimensional nature of the topic. This renders difficult the message outside for EC officials themselves, who must be aware of many directives in the social field before realising themselves that social dialogue is a key precondition for the good implementation of the *acquis* in other important areas. On the other hand, this dispersal of provisions on social dialogue leaves too much leeway to those, also within European institutions, who prefer for ideological reasons not to consider social dialogue as an important matter and thus prefer to forget that there are also EC provisions in this area. This also explains the widespread belief that there is little on social dialogue in the Community *acquis*.

Perhaps the best solution would be to regroup all provisions on social dialogue in a single, comprehensive directive which would explain clearly and without room for misinterpretation why the development of social dialogue is a prerequisite for joining the European Union. A directive on social dialogue would clearly show that social dialogue is an area of the Community *acquis* that must be developed as such, as well as a means of implementing other Community provisions.

5.7.2 Lack of Legal Grounding for Autonomous Social Dialogue

Since the Treaty makes direct reference to the need to promote social dialogue between employers and employees, the European Commission has insisted on the need to promote autonomous social dialogue and collective bargaining. It has also insisted in this regard on the role given to European social partners at the EU level (see section 5.2). At the same time, however, it is worth underlining that there are no legal provisions concerning the right to collective bargaining in the Community *acquis*. We have seen in the chapter on working conditions that this is also true for a closely related area, the right to strike. These shortcomings seriously limit the message being delivered by European institutions and thus the impact they can have on the development of autonomous social dialogue in candidate countries. It means that two of the most important trade union freedoms – to negotiate and reach agreements, and to engage in collective action – are simply not regulated in Community law. If nothing is done to put this right the whole future of social Europe will be undermined.

For instance, the European Commission should take a stronger stance with regard to Turkey which continues to withhold the right to strike and the right to free collective bargaining from most of its public employees. For the time being, the only reference that can be made by the European Commission is to Article 5 of the – non-binding – charter of the Council of Europe and to ILO International Conventions. The same situation exists in other future member states that have still to introduce social dialogue in the public sector (for example, Hungary).

There is thus a contrast between the considerable progress made in autonomous social dialogue at EU level, which is enshrined in the Treaty – and therefore occupies a significant place in the accession negotiations – and the lack of progress made on legal provisions for similar developments within individual countries.

5.7.3 The Absence of Requirements on National Consultation

We have seen that in light of the predominant role of the state and the rather formal nature of tripartism, tripartite partnership must be improved and made more effective in the decision-making process. However, there is no requirement in the Community *acquis* to reinforce consultations with the social partners by the government at national level.

At the same time, many Community policies make reference to the need to consult the social partners – for instance, the European Employment Strategy. It is thus paradoxical that there is no specific requirement for consultations at national level, neither in the legal nor in the institutional *acquis*.[18] What are the implications of this in the face of impending enlargement?

It means in fact that a government of a candidate country that is convinced about the need to develop social dialogue and is doing it in practice will find enough references to social dialogue in the Community documents and in more 'soft' provisions – as EC Communications – for justifying and continu-

18. Not only is there no binding provision, but there is no reference to this need in the Communication of 1998 of the European Commission on Social Dialogue (EC 1998), nor in the new EC Communication on social dialogue (EC 2002f).

ing to promote national social dialogue. On the other hand, it also means that a government which is not convinced about the virtues of national social dialogue and does not want to promote consultations with social partners cannot be constrained to do so, since direct requirements for such consultations do not exist in the Community *acquis*.

We have seen how Hungary between 1998 and 2002 has systematically minimised the influence of the social partners in economic and social affairs, and has turned the consultative process into a meaningless formal process in which the social partners have had little choice other than to rubber-stamp government decisions. Despite the strong reaction of the European Commission, improvements in respect of social dialogue have been marginal. No doubt such indifference to social dialogue would have been more difficult if a clear requirement to consult the social partners at national level had been present in the Community *acquis*.

There is thus a paradox that is becoming more and more evident as EU enlargement draws nearer: the absence of a requirement of national consultations with the social partners despite the fact that such a requirement is essential if social dialogue is to be considered also by the future member states as a basic pillar of European integration.

This serious absence needs to be explained, and two major factors immediately present themselves. First, the United Kingdom has always opposed introducing binding regulations on social dialogue, arguing that this is an area for individual member states. It was only after the majority rule on social issues was introduced that the UK was no longer able to block progress in this area and new responsibilities for the social partners in European social dialogue could be enshrined in the Treaty.[19] At the same time, EU member states apparently have not felt the need to go further on social dialogue at national level, especially after managing to promote autonomous social dialogue at EU level in the Amsterdam Treaty. They seem to have taken it for granted that social dialogue is already well developed at national level, and would thus naturally feed the significant new process of consultations and negotiations in which the social partners were asked to become involved at Community level.

At EU level, it is true that this process makes it possible to replace the previous common positions prepared by the social partners in order to influence EC policies – a sort of tripartism practised at EU level between the EC and

19. We might add that this also motivated the European employers' organisation to sign the social protocol which identifies social dialogue as a way of promoting new social legislation. To some observers, their main motivation was to keep control of developments in this field, notably in the hope that some provisions prepared by the social partners – or under their influence – might be more advantageous to them than legislation directly prepared by the European Commission (Compston and Greenwood 2001).

European social partners – with a more autonomous negotiating process with the direct involvement of the employers and the trade unions. This clearly represents a more advanced stage of social dialogue at EU level. Similarly, at the level of EU member states, tripartism and national consultations have strong traditions in most countries so that the new step towards autonomous social dialogue at EU level has been seen as progress aimed at complementing and not replacing already well-established national consultations.

Nevertheless, EU enlargement offers a different perspective. The problem which has become evident to those involved in the negotiation process is that national tripartite consultations are not yet strongly rooted in these countries, so that the Community *acquis*'s failure to address the issue is a major source of problems and misunderstandings. In such a context, the insistence of the European Commission on autonomous social dialogue – in effect at the expense of national consultations – could be seen by some as an invitation to withdraw from tripartite consultations, leaving the social partners to engage in discussions and negotiations at decentralised levels, and so freeing the state to decide on all national macroeconomic and social issues. In this way, future member states could be tempted to promote bipartism without tripartite consultations at national level, although the two elements are complementary pillars of EU social dialogue. This is a compelling weakness to which European institutions need to respond.

5.7.4 A Better Definition of 'Consultations' with the Social Partners

No definition of tripartite consultations exists at national or Community level. In this regard, there is a need to transpose to national level some of the principles enshrined in the directives on information and consultation at enterprise level. For instance, the directive on collective redundancies stipulates the need to have consultations in 'due time', and that information and consultation must take place with the concrete 'aim of reaching an agreement'. The notion of 'effective' consultations – that is, a process that would provide social partners with a real say in the matter under discussion – should also be contrasted with the mere 'handing down' of information by governments.

5.7.5 Disconnection between Social Dialogue at EU and National Levels

How could the social partners of individual countries contribute effectively to the European social dialogue – in which they are expected to reflect and defend the policies and views of their home country – if they are not consulted on those issues? For example, European social partners have started a dialogue with the European Central Bank and government representatives at EU level concerning macroeconomic issues (the so-called 'macroeconomic dialogue' described in section 5.2). Similarly, the dialogue between social partners and the public authorities on employment is expected to play an important role in relation to employment issues as it is enshrined in the Council decision of March 1999 on reform of the Standing Committee on Employment.[20] But this has turned out to be an inadequate provision for ensuring that individual countries – from EU as well as future member states – implement such consultations at national level.

Without undermining their accession prospects, candidate countries can implement systems that do not foresee appropriate social partner consultations, and may well put in question and even endanger the place of social dialogue in the European Social Model. The speed of the negotiation process (which we address in the concluding chapter) is also allowing them to do so.

The present situation means that there is a disconnection between social dialogue developments at EU level, which are part of the *acquis*, and national social dialogue, which paradoxically is not part of the *acquis*. It is as if EU member states agreed to give some power to social partners at EU level but refused to concede it at national level, thus contradicting the basic principle and commitment to the values of social partnership and social dialogue.

5.7.6 Social Dialogue in the Public Sector

Although the Community *acquis* insists on the need to preserve public services, nowhere does it mention the need to have social dialogue in this sector. Of course, the fact that the *acquis* stipulates that social dialogue is the right of all workers can be interpreted to mean that it should not be restricted to particular categories of employee, or to the private sector. Given the serious drawbacks in the public sector in many future member states with regard to social dialogue, however, a more explicit response is needed in this respect, as, for example, with a number of directives on health and safety where the budgetary sector is mentioned specifically.

5.7.7 Balanced Development of Social Dialogue

The EU is increasingly promoting the involvement of civil society in economic and social life. But here again, enlargement poses a new problem. Where national consultations of social partners have been developing for a long time, as in many EU member states, this move can be seen as complementing the tripartite consultative process, as well as the bipartite relationship between social partners. In most candidate countries, however, where tripar-

---

20. Decision N°99/207/CE of March 1999, which replaces Decision N°70/532/CE of 10 December 1970.

tite consultations have been going on for only a few years and remain limited, the introduction of multilateral dialogue – that is, including representatives of civil society – could serve to substitute rather than complement tripartite consultations in which the social partners should remain privileged partners. Countries such as Bulgaria, Hungary, and Turkey are developing multilateral dialogue, but so far this has had the effect of limiting tripartite consultations even further. At the level of European institutions, by contrast, the existence of the Economic and Social Committee usefully complements the other fora of European social dialogue where social partners play a key role.

5.7.8 Greater Involvement of Social Partners in the Negotiation Process

In the candidate countries the social partners have so far not been seriously involved in the accession process, and dialogue on EU enlargement has been patchy at best. Social partners of most future member states have not been kept informed about the position of their government as the process has developed. Furthermore, governments seem to have purposefully excluded the social partners from seeing important documents related to accession and have decided to pursue their course without consultation. This was the case in many countries with regard to such important pre-accession documents as the government position paper, supplementary information, and the national plans for the adoption of the *acquis*.

Governments were also expected to discuss financial programming with regard to accession, and to have involved the social partners in all the budgetary proposals and figures included in the NPAAs (National Plans for the Adoption of the *Acquis*) and the PHARE programme exercises (in the selection, design, and implementation of projects), but this proved to be more the exception than the rule.

In this regard, it is regrettable that no stronger requirement was imposed on the candidate countries by European institutions to involve the social partners more systematically in discussions on the accession process. This certainly contrasts with EU policy on social dialogue and the latest, more courageous developments related to the Amsterdam Treaty. A more determined policy on social dialogue needs to be implemented in the next rounds of the EU accession process.

5.8 CONCLUSION

Compared to EU practice, social dialogue and industrial relations in the future member states remains much too dependent on the state and too much governed by legal regulations. In particular, most countries in Central and Eastern

Europe have promoted social dialogue through tripartite structures, with discussions between government representatives and the social partners. However, such tripartite structures are often merely formal and therefore do little more than hide the continuing dominance of the state. These structures must be reformed so that they become a more positive element of decision-making and an innovative element in the Social Europe of tomorrow. In this way, national tripartite consultations could provide orientation and so stimulate rather than limit collective bargaining at lower levels, not to mention individual work contracts at local level.

In tandem with this, more independent channels of social dialogue and bilateral negotiations must be developed. There are also shortcomings in collective bargaining and autonomous social dialogue in many of the future member states, although these are priorities in the EU. Entire categories of employee are simply not covered by collective bargaining, such as civil servants and employees of public enterprises.

The most worrying trends are observable at the enterprise level, which often seems to be beyond the control of the social partners and sometimes even the state. Employers' organisations do not seem to have much influence on the myriad small businessmen and entrepreneurs that have emerged in the new private sector. Trade unions on their part have yet to find the right strategy to achieve representation in small private companies. Concerning the state, it has so far failed to promote either provisions that would help trade unions to expand in the private sector, or alternative forms of workers' representation, such as works councils. The state has also failed to ensure the monitoring of labour practices, while the resources dedicated to labour inspection remain disproportionately low compared to the extent of the problem.

In most Central and Eastern European countries the extremely complex and burdensome set of legal provisions governing industrial relations stands in stark contrast with its total lack of influence on the development of industrial relations in the growing private sector, particularly small and medium-size enterprises. Unless this problem is addressed, it may remain a constant feature of industrial relations in these countries in the future.

At the same time – again in contrast to EU experience – there is an absence of collective agreements at the sectoral and regional levels. This means that between the excessively formal tripartite consultations at national level and the poorly developed social dialogue at enterprise level, there is no intermediate level of collective bargaining and social dialogue. This obviously contributes to the very low coverage of collective bargaining currently experienced in all Central and Eastern European countries (not to mention such Southern candidate countries as Turkey). There is currently a significant gap between the culture and practice of social dialogue and industrial relations in the EU and in the future member states, including the balance between tripartism and bipartism, legal regulations and free systems of industrial relations, and different levels of collective bargaining. The negotiation process has so far failed to address these issues.

All of these things are linked. For instance, the dominance of the state through tripartism does not leave much room for the development of autonomous social dialogue and social partners. At the same time, the state can more easily follow this policy since social partners remain weak and trade unions in particular face a fall in membership and low mobilisation capacity. All these trends could easily combine to seriously undermine the social standpoint for the foreseeable future, and thus represent a divergent trend with regard to the policy promoted by the EU. It could also endanger proper implementation of the Community *acquis* in a large number of areas. The European Union must take firm action to strengthen its messages and requirements concerning social dialogue.

6. Workers' Participation: Slipping Away from the Self-Management Tradition?

6.1 INTRODUCTION

In the EU, all member states – to a greater or lesser extent – share the view that workers' participation represents a basic workers' right and as such an essential element of the European Social Model. The Treaty clearly stipulates in Article 137 (Post-Amsterdam consolidated version) that 'the Community shall support and complement the activities of the member states' in the field of 'the information and consultation of workers' with 'a view to achieving the objectives of Article 136 – which is about social rights, the promotion of employment, improved living and working conditions, . . . proper social dialogue, dialogue between management and labour, the development of human resources'. Article 137 adds that 'the Council shall act unanimously on a proposal from the Commission' in a number of fields, including 'representation and collective defence of the interests of workers and employees, including co-determination'.

Workers' participation, however, is a general term that can embrace very diverse and multiple forms of workers' involvement at the workplace, from workers' information and consultation to participation in decision-making, but also participation in enterprises' profits and capital, all of which can be seen as complementary forms of economic democracy at work. Individual member states have emphasised one thing or another according to their culture of industrial relations. For instance, Germany has developed advanced forms of institutionalised codetermination or '*Mitbestimmung*', while the UK has promoted more decentralised systems of industrial relations at enterprise or establishment level while developing workers' participation in enterprise results or profit-related pay.

Workers' participation can also be promoted on a voluntary basis or through more binding, legal provisions. Precisely because of this variety of outcomes at national level, progress at Community level has been rather difficult and slow. Since EU regulations on workers' participation can modify the way an enterprise operates at national and local level, this is an issue on which political consensus among member states has been difficult to reach. As a result, some directives – such as those on European Works Councils and the

European Company Statute – required many years (sometimes 30 years) to be adopted.

Progressively, however, a comprehensive series of legal and other provisions on workers' participation has been promoted at Community level, as we shall report in section 6.2 of this chapter. Since the late 1990s, debates have also identified forms of workers' participation as an essential element in improving workers' motivation and performance and also corporate governance in general, a debate that has contributed to overcoming the initial resistance of some EU member states and national employers' organisations on the issue.

In this rather sensitive and highly debated area, a number of features of particular candidate countries come to the fore as having the potential to influence in one way or another the future of workers' participation in an enlarged EU. Particularly important is to try to assess the story of workers' participation in the first twelve years of transition in the Central and Eastern European candidate countries. Have these countries continued to promote forms of economic democracy and workers' participation at the workplace on the basis of their self-management traditions? Or conversely, have they decided to reject systems from the past and to shift instead towards completely different models? Are these countries today in a position to adopt all EC provisions and frameworks on workers' participation, and even more relevant, to implement them in practice? These are the questions we shall try to answer in section 6.3 of this chapter.

This area, in common with social dialogue, will clearly acquire particular importance in the EU enlargement process since forms of workers' participation, like social dialogue, are expected to facilitate the proper implementation of the Community *acquis* at work, such as health and safety provisions but also other labour standards, which require specific bodies of workers' participation, information, and consultation.

6.2 THE DIFFERENT STEPS FORWARD AT COMMUNITY LEVEL

6.2.1 Information and Consultation in National and Community Law

In the EU, systems for informing and consulting employees, as well as for employee participation on boards of directors, have been promoted by national systems as well as by Community provisions.

At the national level, works councils exist in a majority of EU member states, with the exception of Ireland, Finland, Sweden, and the United Kingdom where representation is solely through trade union delegates. This information/consultation is supplemented by codetermination systems in Germany, the Netherlands, Austria, Finland, and Sweden. The German and Austrian systems are the most advanced, with approval procedures, the right of veto, and joint decision-making.

Provisions exist in Germany, Luxembourg, Austria, and the Nordic countries for staff representation within the supervisory bodies, also in the private sector. These staff representatives usually have the same rights and duties as the shareholders' representatives, except in the matter of industrial disputes. Representation is generally on a minority basis, accounting for a maximum of one-third of the seats, except in Germany which is the only country where, in certain cases, there can be equal representation of employees and shareholders – even with regard to major decisions. In France, work committee representatives are also part of the board of directors, while members can also be appointed to supervisory boards and boards of directors in the Netherlands.

National provisions also comply with the minimum requirements laid down in the Community Directives on the need to inform and consult personnel representatives with regard to certain decisions, such as transfers of enterprises and collective redundancies (see Table 6.1).

In the Directive on Collective Redundancy, a procedure for the prior consultation of workers' representatives is required 'in good time with a view to reaching an agreement'. These consultations 'shall, at least, cover ways and means of avoiding collective redundancies or reducing the number of workers affected, and of mitigating the consequences'. 'All relevant information' shall be provided 'in good time to enable workers' representatives to make constructive proposals'. Provision is made for calling on the services of experts.

The Directive on the Transfer of Undertakings also stipulates that employees' representatives must be informed 'in good time before the transfer is carried out, and in any event before . . . employees are directly affected by the transfer as regards their conditions of work and employment'. Where measures in relation to employees are envisaged, consultations are required 'with a view to seeking agreement'. Information must be provided and consultations take place in good time before the change in the business.

Important provisions also exist with regard to employees' consultation and information for the implementation of all directives on health and safety.

As a first conclusion, we should underline that the information and consultation process has been stipulated in a number of EC directives and thus appear as a transversal or horizontal policy that candidate countries and their enterprises will have to implement. In addition, there are specific directives aimed at promoting workers' participation, described in the following subsections.

Table 6.1 Community legislation on workers' participation, information, and consultation

	Year of adoption	Coverage	Participation
Safeguarding of employees' rights in the event of transfers of undertakings, businesses or parts of businesses (Directive 98/50/EC) (amending Directive 77/187/EEC of 1977) (EC *Official Journal* 17.07.1998 L201/88)	29 June 1998 14 February 1977	Public and private undertakings; all employees under national employment law	(i) right of employee representatives to be informed *in good time* of the transfer (date; reason; implications for the employees, measures envisaged) (ii) right to be consulted *with a view. to reaching an agreement* on the measures envisaged
Introduction of measures to encourage improvements in the safety and health of workers at work (Directive 89/391/EEC) (EC *Official Journal* 29.06.1989 L183/1)	1989	All private and public sectors, excluding only some specific public activities	(i) right of employees to be informed on *risks to safety and to health, risk-prevention, accident reports, etc.* (ii) right to be consulted (subject to national legislation) on questions of *safety and health in the workplace, introduction of new technologies, etc.*
Collective redundancies (Directive 98/59/EC) (consolidated version of Directive 75/129/EEC, amended by Directive 92/56/EEC) (EC *Official Journal* 12.08.1998 L225/16)	20 July 1998 17 Feb 1975 24 June 1992	All employees the termination of whose employment contract by their employer is not related to their behaviour, with the exclusion public employees	(i) right of employees to information, consultation and participation in the event of collective redundancies; (ii) employees' representatives must be consulted 'in good time' in order to 'reach an agreement' on possibilities of 'avoiding or limiting collective redundancies or on measures to mitigate the consequences for employees'

	Year of adoption	Coverage	Participation
Establishment of a European Works Council or a procedure in Community-scale undertakings (or groups thereof) for the purpose of informing and consulting employees (Directive 94/45/ECC) Directive 97/74/EC (extends it to the UK) (EC *Official Journal* 30.09.1994 L254/64)	22 Sept. 1994 1997	(i) undertakings with at least 1 000 employees within the member states and at least 150 employees in each of at least two member states (ii) undertakings with at least 1,000 employees within the member states and at least two undertakings each employing at least 150 employees in different member states	(i) right of employees to information and consultation in Community-scale undertakings and groups of undertakings (ii) right to establish a European Works Council or comparable procedure for informing and consulting employees in order to avoid inequalities in treatment in this respect within the same undertaking created by differences in national laws in the various locations of the establishments in question
Statute for a European Company (Directive 2000) (EC *Official Journal*)	2000	European companies established in accordance with the regulation on the statute for a European company	(i) rights of employees to information and consultation in a European company; (ii) negotiating procedure to reach agreement on the rights of involvement of employees in the planned European company; (iii) on account of differences between national legal systems, no uniform model but at least information and consultation rights, as well as maintenance of existing rights.
Directive establishing a general framework for informing and consulting employees in the European Community (Directive 2001) (EC *Official Journal* 23 March 2002 L80/29)	2001	Public and private undertakings with at least 50 employees which are located in a member state	rights to information and consultation in good time on employment situation, structure, and development; and on decisions affecting work contracts and organisation, etc.

6.2.2 The Transnational Dimension: European Works Councils

The adoption in 1994 of the Directive on European Works Councils represented an important step forward to extend workers' participation, information, and consultation across borders. It reflected the need to inform and consult employees in a transnational framework.

This important directive for the first time lays down that specific procedures for representing, informing, and consulting employees shall be established by agreement in every Community-scale undertaking and group of
undertakings (undertakings or groups with at least 1 000 employees within
member states and at least 150 employees in at least two member states).

However, should negotiations break down after three years, a European
works council shall be established and shall operate in accordance with the
subsidiary provisions laid down in the annex of the directive. Those groups
in which there existed on 22 September 1996 'an agreement, covering the
entire workforce, providing for the transnational information and consultation of employees' shall not be subject to the obligations under the directive
until those agreements expire or are renewed. The vast majority of existing
agreements at the end of 1999 (450 out of a total of 650) were in the latter
form.

We must emphasise that this is a unique framework that clearly represents
a distinctive feature of the European Social Model. It is increasingly being
used by workers' representatives and trade unions, who needed some time to
prepare themselves to make use of this new and powerful participatory instrument.

For instance, this directive allowed trade unionists to take to court Renault
for non-compliance after the decision taken by the French automobile company to close its Belgian factory at Vilvoorde, despite the fact that no significant steps for informing and consulting employees had been taken by the
management. By means of the final Court decision, the 'Renault Vilvoorde'
affair highlighted the requirements for information and consultation of
employees under the directive (Versailles Court of Appeal, judgement No.
308, 7 May 1997, Sté Renault versus CGE Renault, the public prosecutor,
EMF).

6.2.3 Recent Significant Breakthroughs

Directive on the European Company Statute
The adoption of the Directive on the European Company Statute in 2001 also
reinforced the participatory process in EU enterprises.

For 30 years, the stumbling block for this project – aimed at adding a new
type of limited liability company to those existing in the member states in

order to facilitate the constitution of a joint subsidiary or holding between companies in different EU countries – was the issue of employee participation in company bodies.

Brought back into the limelight by the current European economic and financial situation and by the impetus given by the European works councils, in the late 1990s the project was the subject of new discussions and proposals on the question of employee participation. As a result, a directive on the information, consultation, and participation of employees in 'European companies' was adopted at the Council in 2001. The text allows negotiations between partners in constituent companies, the application of reference provisions in the event of the failure of negotiations, and the taking into account of the situation in the constituent companies with regard to participation.

The new Directive on Information and Consultation

While previously – between the 1970s and the 1990s – the development of workers' participation had been taken as an accompaniment to other policy developments, such as management decisions on transfers of undertakings, mass layoffs, or health and safety decisions, in the late 1990s steps were taken to develop workers' information and consultation as such, as an important instrument of dialogue and governance at enterprise level. The development of the European works councils made it possible to develop it in large and multinational companies.

More recently, workers' participation was made possible in smaller enterprises, with the adoption of the new directive on enterprises with more than 50 employees. This European directive 'establishing a general framework for informing and consulting employees in the European Community' was adopted by the Council and the European Parliament on 7 February 2002, after a political agreement had been reached on 17 December 2001.

This represented a major breakthrough since this new directive establishes a general framework containing, in particular, a definition of information and consultation and a non-exhaustive list of the areas covered. Major importance is also given to adaptation at national level and to negotiation of the framework between the social partners at various levels, notably by means of negotiated agreements.

This directive enshrines other important provisions, such as 'the right to permanent information and consultation of employees on economic and strategic developments in the undertaking and on decisions which affect them in all member states'; the right 'to risk anticipation', particularly with regard to employment trends; or to 'ensure that workers are informed and consulted prior to decisions' likely to result in substantial changes in work organisation and employment contracts; and to 'ensure the effectiveness of procedures'.

This new Directive may have important effects not only for future member states but also for current EU members; in fact, for John Monks, General Secretary of the Trades Union Congress in the UK:

> the information and consultation directive opens the door on a whole new era in UK employment relations. The directive will eventually move us forward to a higher skilled and more highly productive workforce. Good employers have nothing to fear from informing and consulting their staff . . . effective consultation helps to enhance competitive performance because employees who are being consulted are far more likely to support management plans. (TUC Press release, 17 December 2001)

6.2.4 Workers' Financial Participation: A Complementary Tool

In the European Social Model, workers' participation in decision-making goes hand in hand with forms of workers' 'financial participation'. In fact, it has been increasingly recognised that it is difficult to imagine workers being involved in decision-making, notably through information and consultation, without having them also share in the financial results of these decisions.

There are two major ways in which employers can distribute the financial results of improved enterprise performance to their employees:

1. Through profit-sharing, part of an employee's remuneration being directly linked to profits or some other measure of enterprise performance. Usually applied to all employees, these bonuses are normally paid in addition to the basic fixed wage and provide a flexible source of income.
2. Through employee share-ownership plans, part of the company's shares being distributed free or sold on preferential terms (at a lower price) to all or a group of employees. Privatisations represent a good opportunity to distribute or sell part of the shares to the employees. Outside the privatisation process, a company can also decide to offer its employees options to subscribe shares of the company.

One specific form of workers' share-ownership is Employee Share-Ownership Plans (ESOPs).[1] Further variants include producer cooperatives, in which all the firm's shares are collectively owned by its workforce, and employee buy-outs, under which the company's shares are purchased exclusively by its workers.

---

1. Widespread in the United States, ESOPs involve a loan to an employee benefit trust, which acquires company stock and allocates it through periodic payments from each employee's ESOP account. The loan may be serviced by payments either from the company or from employees.

Widespread development in the EU

These variant forms of financial participation are combined in some countries and companies. These schemes developed rapidly in the EU in the 1980s and the 1990s, notably under the influence of different legal provisions and fiscal incentives, but also in accordance with the distinctive nature of industrial relations in each country. Financial participation schemes in the 1990s developed mainly in France and the UK. In France, profit-sharing schemes were encouraged very early, with laws in 1959 and 1967, and have been boosted by progressive complementary laws and fine-tuning of the systems operated by enterprises. Voluntary cash-based schemes today cover nearly 15 000 companies and compulsory participation in profits, nearly 20 000 companies and more than five million workers. There have been similar developments in the UK, where a series of new laws on shareholding, most of them introduced during the privatisation of state-owned companies, led to a spectacular increase in the number of workers holding shares, with nearly 5 000 such schemes. France completed its armoury of legislative texts by a new law on savings funds in 2001, notably to extend them to small and medium-size enterprises, whilst the UK adopted the Finance Act in 2000 aimed at providing new fiscal incentives for certain categories of enterprise.

A new dynamic in favour of financial participation has also developed rapidly in other EU countries in the early 2000s, with financial participation schemes rapidly expanding in Greece, Spain, Ireland, the Netherlands, and Finland. It has thus become a feature of industrial relations in most EU countries.

In Ireland, not only is there new legislation providing for fiscal exemptions for these schemes, but also the development of financial participation is enshrined as a priority in the Employment Partnership (pact) concluded between the government, social partners, and non-governmental organisations. Belgium, the Netherlands, Germany, Denmark, Austria, and Spain have also adopted new legislation and fiscal incentives to boost the usage of financial participation systems.

The favourable effects of financial participation on both the social side, as a way of more closely involving employees in their enterprise, and the economic side have motivated the European institutions to promote it more actively.

Initiatives from the European institutions

The European Commission started its initiatives in favour of financial participation at the end of the 1980s, just after the adoption of the Charter of Fundamental Social Rights in December 1989. In a first comprehensive report – the so-called PEPPER Report (Uvalic 1991) – the EC presented all the legislative provisions and practices of financial participation schemes in EU countries, as well as evidence on their possible positive effects: to stimulate employees' collective efforts, to increase productivity, and to ease adaptation to new technologies. Financial participation also appeared 'to make it possible for wages and employment to be more flexible over the business cycle' (EC Industrial Relations Report 2000, EC 2000a, p. 56).

On the basis of the PEPPER report, in July 1991 the European Council adopted a recommendation which represented the first Community text on financial participation. What was also new was the recommendation to EU member states to make increased use of financial participation schemes, to prepare suitable legislation, and to envisage the possibility of granting tax breaks to help the spread of such schemes among companies. It also invited the social partners to take an active part in the promotion of these schemes.

This recommendation was further supported in July 1997 by a second report by the European Commission (PEPPER II), an initiative supported by the Council which was designed not only to further encourage financial participation but also to ensure a more harmonised approach throughout the European Union.

While providing new information about financial participation developments in the EU, the report thus concluded that in many member states the general principles established in the Council recommendation had not been sufficiently applied.

The European Parliament has also contributed to the debate and the initiatives of Community institutions in the area of financial participation by adopting – in 1997 – a resolution on the PEPPER report, with the main purpose of supporting the initiative of the Commission, while also proposing new instruments in this field. The European institutions have thus also been mobilised.

Increased scope
At the same time, the scope of financial participation has progressively evolved. In the early 1990s, financial participation was seen as more of a form of workers' involvement, desirable mainly for social reasons, while its positive effects on workers' motivation and productivity were only beginning to be recognised. Since then, financial participation has been legitimised in a number of areas, not only in its social but also in its economic dimension. First, accumulated empirical research confirmed its positive effects on productivity, profitability, and other measures of enterprise performance. Secondly, the Commission's Communication on Risk Capital of October 1999 underlined the need to develop financial participation in order to boost the risk-capital market, and notably to stimulate the growth of new dynamic enterprises, particularly important for the creation of new jobs. Thirdly, financial participation has also been discussed in the more general context of the modernisation of work organisation. It was mentioned in the Commission's Green Paper of 1997 on work organisation as well as in the Commission's fol-

low-up Communication of November 1998, where the benefits of financial participation with regard to work organisation are presented and where in particular a call is made to the social partners to achieve progress in this field. It is also worth remembering that even the general orientations of political economy (GOPE) adopted by ECOFIN (Ministers of Finance of EU member states) in June 2000 underlined the need to reinforce systems of employee-ownership in order to stimulate capital markets. Financial participation is thus now clearly seen in the EU as stimulating the process of structural reforms aimed at capturing all potentialities of growth, employment, and social cohesion.

It is not by chance that a new impulse was given to workers' financial participation by the Lisbon Summit, which precisely fixed the priority of developing a competitive knowledge economy while developing social policies as productive factors. It led to the Community Social Agenda, adopted at the Nice Summit, in which the need for further development of financial participation was mentioned.

This led in early 2002 to a new Communication of the European Commission on this issue, accompanied by an action plan. The aim is to boost financial participation in terms of three priorities: (i) more pronounced emphasis on the general principles behind financial participation (such as the universal coverage of all employees, the transparency of the formula adopted, or the clear distinction between the basic wage and the flexible wage dependent on enterprise results); (ii) to remove the transnational obstacles to the diffusion of financial participation; and (iii) to launch new initiatives at EU level (pilot projects, exchange of best practices, data collection, and so on) to ensure the wider development of financial participation.

6.3 PARTICIPATORY TRENDS

In view of the above dynamic in respect of workers' participation in the EU, it is essential to assess what developments may be observed in the candidate countries.

We shall focus here on two main forms of workers' participation: (i) works councils, a form of participation in decision-making particularly relevant for Central and Eastern Europe, and one which also represents an important element emphasised by the EU; and (ii) employee ownership as the main form of financial participation, something which has rapidly turned into an important feature of transition in the region.

Although we have seen that they progressed in the EU in a parallel way, interestingly these two forms of workers' participation in candidate countries not only did not follow the same path over the years of transition, but they also evolved independently of each other. This peculiar situation explains why we address the two issues here separately.

6.3.1 Lack of Workers' Information and Consultation at Enterprise Level

In contrast to experience in EU countries, forms of workers' participation, information, and consultation have not been much developed in Central and Eastern Europe, but also in the three candidate countries of Southern Europe. This is the case with, for instance, works councils. By the year 2000, after twelve years of transition, only two countries – Slovenia and Hungary – had introduced legislative provisions for promoting this type of worker involvement in companies. They were therefore the only countries where a dual system of workers' representation prevailed, indirectly through the trade unions and directly through the works councils. More recently, new legislation has been adopted or is in preparation in the Czech Republic, Slovakia, and Lithuania.

Among the factors that explain the poor development of works councils in Central and Eastern Europe, the trade unions' policy towards this form of participation has undoubtedly played a role, though to different extents according to country. Trade unions in Central and Eastern Europe have reacted differently to the development of works councils: from fierce opposition in Poland, Hungary, Romania, and even Slovakia, to more nuanced positions in Bulgaria or the Czech Republic and a clearly positive attitude in Slovenia.

Employers have also played a role in promoting or removing different forms of workers' participation in decision-making. The emergence of small and medium-size enterprises has clearly halted the growth of works councils. Foreign investors have also been found not to be keen on promoting this form of economic democracy in their production units located in candidate countries, as we shall explain later on.

Government policy has also not been neutral towards these forms of workers' participation. Public authorities have influenced the process through the removal of legislation in this field (as in Poland) or through its reinforcement (as in Slovenia) or through peculiar ways of introducing it (as in Hungary).

From concrete examples, we shall see in the following subsections how the development of works councils has been influenced by the strategies followed by the three main actors: trade unions, the government, and employers.

6.3.2 Trade Union Positions Explain Differentiated Routes

Poland: trade unions committed to neo-liberal reforms
In many Central and Eastern European countries, works councils and trade unions have developed an uneasy relationship. In some cases, it evolved over

Table 6.2 Forms of workers' information, consultation, or participation in candidate countries

	Presence of works councils	Law on works councils	Type of workers interest represen-tation*	Works councils can sign collective agreements	Trade unions opposed to works councils	Other forms of workers' partici-pation
Bulgaria	No	Law in preparation (2002)	Single	No	Differing: CITUB: no Podkrepa: yes	No
Cyprus	No	–	–	–	–	No
Czech Republic	Only starting	Accepted in 2000, started operating in January 2001	Single	No, even in new Law; rights limited to information and consultation	Differing: Trade Union Assoc. of Bohemia and Moravia: no CSKOS: yes	No
Estonia	No	No. Only the Law on Shop Stewards of 1993, amended in March 2000	Single	No	–	No
Hungary	Yes	Labour law from 1992; In enterprises with > 50 employees	Dual	Yes, in case of absence of trade unions	Yes	No
Latvia	No	No	Single	No	–	No
Lithuania	No	No	Single	No	–	No
Malta	No	–	–	–	–	No
Slovakia	Only starting	Accepted in 2000	Single	Yes, if no trade unions	Yes	No
Slovenia	Yes	Law on Codetermin-ation from 1993; works' councils in firms with more than 20 employees	Dual	–	No	Codeter-mination (as in Germany)
Poland	No	No	Single	No	Yes	No
Romania	No	No	Single	No	Yes	No
Turkey	No	–	–	–	–	No

Note: * either through trade unions or/and direct workers' participation.

time, as for instance in Poland, where there is a strong tradition of self-management and employee councils, with which trade unions have a very close historical relationship. In the 1980s, when the trade union Solidarnosc was still illegal, many trade union activists utilised these structures to promote free trade unionism. Later on, employee councils clearly provided important institutional support to the trade unions. However, a shift of trade union policy vis-à-vis employee councils appeared in the early 1980s.

Although Solidarnosc's 1980–81 economic reform programme was strongly based on self-management, works councils, self-financing, and autonomy, between 1982 and 1989 the union's leaders committed themselves to an economic reform strategy premised on privatisation and the creation of competitive markets. From 1989, the first Solidarnosc-supported government, led by L. Balcerowicz, implemented a neo-liberal economic reform programme, also known as 'shock therapy'. The message from the government at that time was clear:

> The long-term strategic aim of this government is to return to Poland old and tested economic institutions. Poles cannot afford ideological experimentation. (Tadeusz Mazowiecki, 1989, member of Solidarnosc and close adviser to Lech Wałesa; see Weinstein 2000)

The Solidarnosc leadership supported the basic direction of the government's economic reform strategy, which also included the dissolution of employee councils. In February 1993, both trade unions – Solidarnosc and OPZZ – signed a pact with the government on the elimination of workers' councils in companies going through the privatisation process. The subsequent new law meant that trade unions remain the only representatives of workers' interests at enterprise level, this indirect form of workers' representation replacing direct workers' representation which had developed in the self-management period. However, the trade unions succeeded, as we shall see later on, in promoting employee ownership in the privatisation process.

Polish trade union leaders tried to explain their position with regard to the new legislation on works councils in terms of their fear of seeing workers' councils supplant the trade unions and becoming dominated by the management. But according to Weinstein (2000, p. 61), who studied Solidarnosc's programmes over the years, this position directly reflected the 'conventional conception that Solidarnosc leaders had of property rights'. They believed that co-governance rights would conflict with private management, which was expected to be the only driver of economic growth. This view was confirmed by econometric results from different surveys carried out at different periods among trade union leaders: while they continued to support employee councils in state enterprises, they did not support their establishment in privatised companies (Weinstein 2000).

The new law – and especially the difference it created between the state and private sectors with regard to workers' interest representation – clearly had direct effects at enterprise level. While the presence of workers' councils remained obligatory in state enterprises, where these councils enjoy significant rights – especially with regard to the management of the enterprise, even the appointment of the manager – and its eventual privatisation, the law demands the suppression of works councils once the enterprise is privatised. As a result, a sort of dual system of workers' representation developed in Poland, with (i) works councils with extended rights and strong trade unions in state enterprises, and (ii) the absence of works councils in privatised enterprises where workers' interests can be covered only by their trade unions, whose strength and membership continues to decline. In new private enterprises, the situation is even worse, with the absence of any form of workers' representation (Kulpińska 2002). In this type of enterprise, not only are trade unions not present, but there are no works councils either, partly because national trade unions rejected such participation.

This opposition to works councils, as in the case of many EU trade unions, may well lead in the long term to a growing gap between trade union policy and workers' expectations at enterprise level, and potentially lead to a further weakening of union membership. Trade unions in the future may pay a high price for this policy.

Slovenia: trade unions in the tradition of self-management

By contrast, trade unions in Slovenia, on the basis of a strong self-management tradition, have supported government steps to maintain an extensive framework for workers' participation in enterprise management. Different forms of participation have developed. Workers were first given some influence in decision-making through their participation in supervisory boards and management boards (Law on Worker Participation in Management, 1993). In enterprises with up to 1 000 employees, at least one-third of the members of the supervisory boards – and half in those with 1 000 or more employees – have to be workers' representatives, elected by the workers' council. This law was supported by the trade unions, which also fought to keep all its contents. On two occasions, under pressure from the employers' organisation, the government proposed amendments to the Parliament in order to tone down this law: this failed due to massive trade union protests. The most recent attempt was in September 1999, when the government adopted and sent to the Parliament, without prior tripartite consultation, a proposal for an amendment to Article 264 of the Companies Act, aimed at reducing the percentage of workers' representatives on supervisory boards. It aimed at reducing this participation to 'at most one-third of all members' (Article 45 of the proposal) thus contradicting Article 79 of the Workers' Participation in Management

Act. Once again, the fierce opposition of trade unions, which officially complained and also attracted the attention of international organisations (such as the European Trade Union Confederation and the European Commission) well illustrates the importance that the trade unions currently attach to the preservation of institutionalised forms of direct workers' representation in Slovenia.

Workers' participation was also promoted in Slovenia through workers councils, which were mainly adopted following the main features of the German codetermination model. The system, defined through different legislative items in 1993, mainly the law on codetermination – with other specific issues being covered by the Law on Commercial Companies – was supported by the trade unions from the beginning (Stanojević 2000).

The implementation of the law in the workplace is optional, and is left to the collective initiative of employees. This type of workers' representation exists in around one-fifth of Slovenian companies (Ibid, p. 4).

This may be explained, at least partly, by the tradition of Yugoslav self-management and workers' collectives or works councils, where not only were the workers closely involved in the enterprise, but also trade unions were very close to the workers (Ibid., pp. 9–10). At the end of the 1980s and the beginning of the 1990s, when the old works councils were losing their power, trade unions took over their function of workers' interest representation. They saw the new Law on Codetermination of 1993 as an additional way of stabilising their new role, and in particular of acquiring more control over the privatisation process. For Stanojević (Ibid., p. 12), it is not sure that this strategy has paid off for trade unions since in practice trade unions and works councils are not very close, and often develop separate contacts with the management (Ibid., p. 4). Moreover, works councils would have pushed trade unions to focus primarily on wage negotiations; in a country in which wages are already the highest in the region, and are mainly decided at higher – multi-employer – level, this process would have significantly reduced trade unions and radicalised their position at enterprise level.

It is certain, however, that trade unions have constituted a key factor in the formation of works councils in Slovenian enterprises. Paradoxically, this has led to the double representation of workers' interests in unionised enterprises – that is, mainly state companies – while workers in other, non-unionised companies (all new private enterprises), also because of the optional nature of the law, have suffered from the absence of any form of worker representation.

6.3.3 The Influence of Government Strategy

Czech Republic: Removal of works councils in the reform process
In the Czech Republic, as part of the neo-liberal policy of the government after 1989, works councils were disbanded, while trade unions had to counter

repeated attempts to reduce their influence at national and local level. Similarly to Poland, the maintenance of this form of economic democracy clearly did not fit the 'shock therapy' programme followed at that time by the Czech government.

A good presence at plant level inherited from the previous regime allowed trade unions to protect workers' interests in the transition process, but did not allow them to preserve direct forms of workers' participation. Moreover, this government ideological position against workers' participation was facilitated by two radically opposed positions expressed on workers' participation by the two main national trade unions, the Trade Union Association of Bohemia and Moravia and CSKOS: the first favoured the promotion of works councils, while the second opposed it in order to avoid further deterioration of its influence at enterprise level. The introduction of works councils (new law in 2000), favoured by a change in government, started to erase such contrasts at the local level, both trade unions having to adapt to the new situation. They will have to ensure, however, that the new law is not used by government or employers to circumvent trade unions at the local level.

Playing works councils against trade unions: Hungary and Slovakia
In Hungary, after having been marginalised in the 1970s and 1980s, works councils were promoted by the government at the beginning of the transition and new works councils were defined within the new Labour Code of 1992. Works councils became obligatory in enterprises employing over 50 workers, while workers' representatives could be elected in enterprises employing between 15 and 50 workers. Trade unions first viewed works councils rather suspiciously, as a potential threat to their already weaker position at enterprise level. Nevertheless, after the new law came into force, trade unions and works councils learnt to work together in order to protect workers' rights in the transition.

Employers were for their part rather opposed to any further rights being given to their employees, and repeatedly stated their preference for dealing with the trade unions only, a position that may be explained by the rather weak and fragmented position of trade unions, and the difficulty they had, for instance, in mobilising the labour force and organising strikes.

Trade unions accepted the presence of works councils especially since these new institutions did not have any bargaining rights but only consultation and information rights. Trade unions continued to negotiate and sign collective agreements with the management – on wages and other working conditions – and to play a role in social welfare at plant level. Works councils performed their task of information and consultation, and became particularly active in protecting jobs in the restructuring process, often with the support of trade unions. Trade union representativeness was defined through works council election results. And in many cases, trade unions at enterprise level were interested in setting up works councils in order to initiate council elections, which were held for the first time in early summer 1993. In many cases, works councils helped trade unions to institutionalise their influence at enterprise level, with many works council representatives also being trade union members (Tóth 1997; Ladó and Tóth 1996). This overlapping at the workplace minimised the possible tensions between the two institutions, something which should be viewed as a positive outcome. On the other hand, it also reflects the fact that works councils were dominated by trade unions and therefore did not represent a real alternative – and thus complementary – channel for employee representation and participation.

The relationship between trade unions and works councils became tense again when the new government that came to power in 1998, inspired by neo-liberal theories, decided to give works councils the right to sign collective agreements in enterprises in case of the absence of trade unions, although a similar attempt had failed in 1992. We must note that in a first draft of labour code amendments, the new government, which we have seen has not been much attached to social dialogue (see Economic and Social Committee 2000; see also Chapter 5 on social dialogue in this volume), had even raised the possibility of giving works councils the right to sign collective agreements, even in enterprises where trade unions were already present. The government, however, had to withdraw such amendments due to the strong opposition of trade unions and political parties.

The consequent amendments to the Labour Code, accepted in 1999, brought serious tensions at enterprise level: in many small private or newly privatised enterprises, it gave an incentive to the management to push trade unions out of the enterprise in order to have works councils signing collective agreements, since the latter do not enjoy other trade union rights, especially the right to strike. Similar behaviour was also observed among multinational companies located in Hungary, which tried to circumvent trade unions through the development of works councils. It is in this rather tense context that European works councils will have to be set up in accordance with the EU directive.

Similarly in Slovakia, the government proposed in 2001 that works councils could sign collective agreements where trade unions are not present. This proposal also led to trade union criticism of the law and rejection of works councils altogether. New legislation on works councils was introduced later on but without giving them rights in collective bargaining.

6.3.4 Works Councils as an Employers' Tool

As in the Czech Republic, the two major trade unions in Bulgaria did not follow the same policy with regard to workers' participation, a situation that has been used by individual employers to limit trade union influence at local level. While the national leaders of CITUB generally supported the idea of having works councils, the support of CITUB representatives at industry level was much weaker, while the other national trade union, Podkrepa, clearly rejected works councils and on many occasions emphasised that works councils did not really have a place within the Bulgarian industrial relations system. Despite this rather weak support for works councils on the part of high-ranking trade union leaders, survey results have shown that a majority of trade union leaders at the company level, in both the public and the private sector, favoured the introduction of works councils and saw them as a useful tool to further influence management decisions (ITUSR 1997). Despite this, no law on works councils has yet been promulgated in Bulgaria, where workers nevertheless have a say in the general assembly scheme inherited from the self-management tradition. A new law on works councils should soon be brought before Parliament.

A number of attempts on the part of employer representatives to use works councils as a way of circumventing the trade unions' role, however, may well lead trade unions in Bulgaria to modify their positive position vis-à-vis such councils. The new Union of Employers of Bulgaria (a dissident faction of the Bulgarian Industrial Association), for instance, has clearly expressed a wish to see works councils enabled to sign collective agreements.

Similarly in Romania, national employer organisations have been positive on the introduction of works councils and individual employers have in many cases developed them at local level, partly to bypass the trade unions. Consequently, Romanian trade unions have very strongly rejected this participation form. The leaders of different national trade unions have expressed their fears of progressive erosion of their collective bargaining rights at company level.

6.3.5 European Works' Councils: A Mitigated Impact

In the prospect of EU enlargement and increasing capital movements, the development of European works councils takes on particular importance. At what stage are the future member states in terms of both transposition of the EC directive in this field and concrete implementation at local level?

A slow transposition process
In the negotiation process, all candidate countries have committed themselves to transposing the directive on European works councils. Countries such as Slovenia did so at an early stage, whilst other countries, such as Hungary, have requested implementation only upon accession.

In general, however, the adoption of this directive has so far proceeded very slowly, most candidate countries wishing to gain some time, for a series of reasons, either because they did not consider this as a priority area compared to other more sensitive issues in the social field (free movement, health and safety, working time, and so on), or as part of a general strategy aimed at attracting maximum flows of foreign investment for which the absence of additional constraints on multinational companies – such as works councils – was evaluated as very positive and thus beneficial for the country.

Lack of willingness to involve participants from candidate countries
Moreover, beyond this formal adoption of the EC directive by the public authorities, we may also investigate its implementation in practice. Data available so far provide a first encouraging result, many EU companies with production units in candidate countries having already implemented a European works council. According to Figure 6.1 for eight Central and Eastern European countries, a significant proportion of multinational companies that are covered by the directive and have a subsidiary in one of these countries have implemented a European works council.

More than 73 per cent of companies covered by the directive in Romania and Bulgaria are effectively enjoying this form of transnational workers' representation, a percentage which is slightly lower but represents a much larger number of companies in Poland, the Czech Republic and Hungary – not surprisingly since these countries have attracted most foreign investment flows.

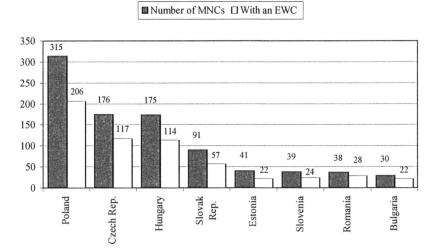

Source: ETUI statistics 2002.

Figure 6.1 European works councils in companies operating in CEECs (covered by the Directive 94/45/EC and 97/45/EC), by country, September 2001

These are certainly encouraging results that will further improve as the date of accession for these countries grows closer.

However, at the same time we observe that the participation of workers' representatives from candidate countries in these European works councils remains very small. According to Figure 6.2 less than one-fifth of European works councils present in companies that operate in applicant countries have taken on board local workers' representatives, either as observers or as full members. In Poland, where there is the greatest number of companies with European works councils – 206 enterprises in total – in only 23 of them (less than 12 per cent) are local representatives allowed to participate. This percentage is even lower – 9 per cent – in Estonia, but also in Slovenia (12 per cent), countries which have attracted large and well known EU multinational companies.

This is a dangerous situation: although European works councils exist, and are also implemented in the host candidate country, they do not involve local representatives. This means that they are not performing their basic function, which is expected to facilitate exchange and discussions between workers' representatives working for the same company in different countries. This also means that workers' representatives cannot get the right information and influence the decision-making process alongside EU enlargement, and thus cannot prevent or limit social dumping attempts by the management.

Different factors can explain this result: first, the management does not wish to see observers from the local production unit participating in order to ease its management strategy, and in particular its differentiated policy – in terms of marketing but also working conditions – between its units at home and in the host country. Secondly, this absence seems also in great part to be coming from the resistance of trade unions and/or workers' representatives from the home country who are on the European works councils, especially when arbitration must be carried out between employment, working conditions, and wages at home and in the host country. There have been cases of representatives of European works councils in Germany, including one works council Director (also a major trade union leader), who refused to have local participants from Central and Eastern European countries in the Council. Examples of this sort of latent conflict between home and host country workers' representatives exist in the metal sector, which is facing difficult restructuring, especially in a context of limiting over-capacity in the EU while newcomers arrive from candidate countries with large potential production capacity, with possible implications in terms of jobs. There would thus be a sort of tacit agreement between the management and workers' representatives of the home country to impose some decisions on the workers of candidate countries.

Differences may be observed by sector, however. The greatest number of companies having at least one seat for representatives from a Central and

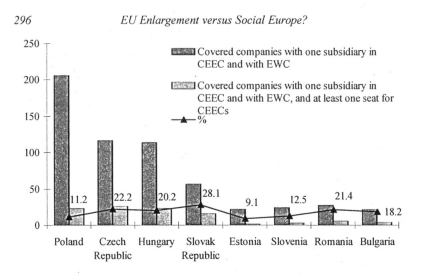

Source: ETUI statistics 2002.

Figure 6.2 Percentage of European works councils with CEEC Members, by country, September 2001

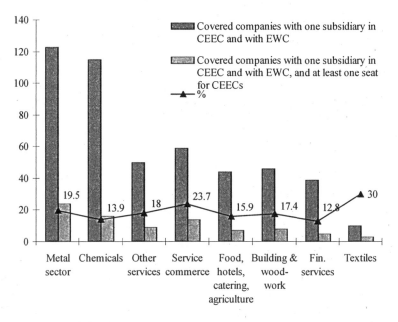

Source: ETUI statistics 2002.

Figure 6.3 CEEC members in European works councils, by sector, Sept. 2001

Eastern European country are in the metal sector, followed by chemicals and services and commerce.

The problems raised above are quite significant: they seem to shed light on the fact that EU enlargement will be the first serious test for European Works Councils. Either they will turn out to be a useful instrument for workers and trade unions as a counterweight to increased capital movements (as in some cases in Poland (Rudolf 2002)), or they will remain a rather formal and empty form of representation, with no real influence on the transnational decision-making process.

6.3.6 Financial Participation: Emphasis on Employee Ownership

Employee ownership on an unprecedented scale

The reform process in Central and Eastern Europe has been accompanied by the widespread introduction of employee ownership. Indeed, in many countries of the region employee ownership has rapidly become a dominant property form, and insider owners – namely employees and managers – have become major owners.

For many, the scope and persistence of the employee ownership phenomenon has been an unwelcome surprise. Employee ownership was never intended to develop on a large scale. For many experts advising governments from this region in their first steps towards a market economy this property form could only lead to bad corporate governance. For instance, for the World Bank:

> employee-owned firms may weaken corporate governance; insiders are generally not able to bring new skills and new capital to the company, and they may deter outsiders with skills and capital from investing. Managers and employees may simply prevent outsiders from buying shares. Moreover, insiders may vote to pay higher salaries even if that reduces profits. (World Bank 1996, pp. 54–55)

In Table 6.3, the World Bank clearly defined employee ownership as detrimental to corporate governance.

Paradoxically, despite this critical – and often ideologically oriented – starting position, employee ownership has rapidly become a predominant property form in much of Central and Eastern Europe (Uvalic and Vaughan-Whitehead 1997). This has taken place extensively, mainly by default, generally because of the difficulties encountered in the course of mass privatisation or other privatisation routes, and the shortage of foreign and domestic capital. The Czech Republic aside, the majority of countries in the region have promoted employee ownership through specific policies and legislative frameworks, bringing Central and Eastern Europe to the forefront in this respect. Enterprises with majority employee-owned enterprises are found to be partic-

Table 6.3 Trade-offs among privatisation routes for large firms (according to the World Bank)

Method	Objective				
	Better corporate governance	Speed and feasibility	Better access to capital and skills	More gov. revenue	Greater fairness
Sale to outside owners	+	−	+	+	−
Management–employee buyout	−	+	−	−	−
Equal access voucher privatisation	?	+	?	−	+
Spontaneous privatisation	?	?	−	−	−

Source: World Bank Development Report, 1996.

ularly prevalent, for instance, in Romania, Poland, Hungary, and Slovenia. In addition, the transfer of minority shares to employees has been a common feature of nearly all privatisation programmes in Central and Eastern Europe.

This process has been observed on a large scale in CIS Republics, mainly in Russia and Ukraine, and in the Baltic countries, especially in Lithuania where nearly all privatised enterprises have had an element of employee ownership and where majority employee ownership was found in more than half of the enterprises privatised (ILO 1998). The same phenomenon, although to a lesser degree, was observed in Latvia. In Romania, most commercial companies have been privatised through the management–employee buy-out method. In Slovenia, no less than 80 per cent of privatised Slovenian enterprises chose the internal buyout as a privatisation method (Prasnikar and Gregorič 2000).

Even in Central and Eastern European countries in which employee ownership is not generally believed to be widespread we can find surprising instances of employee ownership: for example, in Estonia, where foreigners own more than half of private industry, it was estimated that majority insider ownership covered around 36 per cent of newly privatised enterprises. Of these, about half were owned mainly by the management and the other half by a broader group of employees (Mygind 1997, p. 57).

Minority employee ownership has also developed in other Central and Eastern European countries, such as Hungary, Poland, and Bulgaria. In Hungary, it is estimated that there have been nearly 300 cases of privatisation through ESOPs, in which at least 40 per cent of the employees were involved. In Poland, all privatisation routes have included, often to a considerable degree, some form of employee ownership. As a result, there have been a number of employee and management buy-outs there, often taking the form of a lease-purchase agreement. By the end of 1995, 788 enterprises had taken this course, representing 68.8 per cent of directly privatised enterprises (Nuti 1997a, pp. 169–70). By the end of 1998, lease-leveraged employee buy-outs had slightly fallen in number, but still represented about one-third of the completed privatisations, thus representing 'the single most frequently used privatization method' (Kozarzewski and Woodward 2002, p. 3).

This experience in Central and Eastern Europe contrasts with experiences in the West – for instance in the UK and France which have developed employee ownership in the most extensive way – where only a small percentage of the capital of public companies has been privatised through employee ownership. While this development can be explained by the opportunity or necessity to distribute shares in the privatisation process, this undoubtedly reflects a tradition and experiences of employee involvement and self-management in Central and Eastern Europe. Examples of employee-ownership or self-management are also present in Malta, in the shipyard industry (Zammit, 2003).

Social partners played a role in this process. In particular, the employers' aversion with regard to employee ownership was found to be much less prevalent in Central and Eastern European countries. It is significant to note that those employers most suspicious with regard to mixed forms of property including employee ownership were often foreign investors – also from the EU – and not local employers.

Trade unions also played an important role in promoting employee ownership as a property and organisational form, something we document in the next section.

The trade unions' innovative role: helping workers to become owners

Trade unions have contributed to this movement in different ways. In the privatisation process, while foreign experts were mainly advising reliance on private capital – especially through foreign investment – or mass privatisation (through investment funds) trade unions have supported employee ownership as an alternative way of privatisation. Employee share-ownership was often found in the programmes of trade unions (see the example of the Hungarian trade union MSZOSZ in Galgoczi and Hovorka 1998). The promotion of these schemes was generally presented as part of their views in favour of democratic participation, especially in countries with a tradition of self-management, such as Slovenia. In other cases, their support was more pragmatic and represented a means of avoiding the domination of ownership by an external buyer, as well as the restructuring and massive layoffs to be expected in this process. Trade unions have tried to be active at different levels.

At the *national* level, they have often managed to get involved in direct negotiations with the national privatisation agency. In this way, employees have been deeply involved in the privatisation process.

We should mention the essential role that trade unions played, for instance, in Romania or Hungary in encouraging the creation of ESOPs. In Poland, trade unions also contributed to the decision to distribute to employees 20 per cent of capital privatised through trade sales and 15 per cent in companies in the mass privatisation programme. Similarly in Bulgaria, employees were offered 20 per cent of their firm's shares at a reduced price.

Trade unions also succeeded in some cases in resisting the policy of many governments in the region which consisted in privatising through employee ownership only those enterprises on the verge of bankruptcy – also those that did not attract foreign investment – and where heavy restructuring was needed. Trade unions demanded workers' participation also in the best performing enterprises, for instance, in Slovakia and other countries (Brzica 1998, p. 12).

At the *enterprise* level, trade unions have also played a role in helping employees to get involved in the privatisation of their enterprise, and in defending employees' interests in this process. For instance, trade unions in Lithuania have been actively involved in the privatisation process, and have helped workers to become owners of their enterprise. In Estonia, the local trade unions have sometimes used their own resources to help workers buy shares during the privatisation of the company (Laja and Terk 1996).

In Slovakia, where the trade unions enjoy good relations with the banks, lobbying by trade unions also convinced banks to provide credit facilities to employees to buy back their company and operate it. This is particularly important in light of the unwillingness of banks to provide credits to employee-owned enterprises (ILO 1998).

Trade unions have also contributed to influence not only the scale but also the kind of employee share-ownership scheme adopted by the company. In fact, employee ownership can lead to very different – often unfair – distributions of shares among insiders; in some cases, shares can be mainly bought by the management, thus leading to more management buy-out schemes; in other cases, all categories of employee are entitled to participate and decide to acquire shares. By systematically favouring this last scheme, trade unions have helped to safeguard employee share-ownership against management domination. In Slovakia, for instance (Brzica 1998), but also Romania (Munteanu 1997), trade unions often helped workers to prepare a buy-out scheme involving an employee joint-stock company (EBO or Employee Buy-Out) to counter the management's bid to acquire the enterprise through a management buy-out (MBO) and the establishment of a limited liability company.

This promotion of employee ownership has enabled workers to obtain more influence in key policy areas. In Poland, trade unions have contributed to the development of ESOPs in regions in crisis, for instance in the Katowice region, Upper Silesia (Schliva 1997). This allowed workers to have a say in enterprises' restructuring programmes.

In some enterprises in Estonia, trade unions have managed to use the new ownership structure to influence employment decisions and to limit the number of dismissals (Elenurm 1996). In Slovakia, trade unions have seen employee ownership as a way to develop workers' participation in key decisions, and to avoid an increase in unemployment.

The attitude of the trade unions has not been supportive in all countries. In Hungary, despite initial support, different parties and trade unions progressively reduced their enthusiasm not only for employee share-ownership, but also for works councils and self-management principles in general (Cox and Mason 2000, p. 101). In the former Yugoslavia, the unions have opposed employee share-ownership in reaction to the imposition of employee ownership under socialism (Uvalic 1997). In many candidate countries, we shall see that trade unions have done little to develop new institutions to protect employee shareholders, despite their policy intention to support a wide extension of employee ownership.

Encouraging results in terms of corporate governance
The practical economic results are also much more encouraging than the theory predicted, which may be due to the special circumstances of Central and Eastern Europe in transition, especially its initial and dramatic production crisis and fall in living standards. Let us summarise the main results identified through empirical evidence.

In comparison with alternative privatisation options, employee ownership was first found to have net advantages in terms of *speed*. Employee–management buy-outs turned out to be relatively fast and easy to implement, both politically and technically, so contradicting those who believed that the distribution of vouchers to all citizens was the only practical solution for implementing rapid privatisation. Employee ownership schemes also have the advantage over other privatisation methods – particularly the voucher schemes offered to all citizens – of not leading to widely dispersed ownership.

Contrary to theoretical predictions, enterprises with employee share own-ership also appeared to invest in the long-term industrial capacity of the firm instead of systematically seeking to prevent unemployment and restructuring and to force wages up. With regard to the timing and pattern of *labour force adjustment*, while again the available evidence is often patchy, studies of sev-eral countries – including Romania, the Baltic Republics, and Poland – show that employee-owned firms often adjust employment no less than other firms and often more than firms in state ownership. At the same time, the process is often implemented more slowly than in externally-owned firms: before resort-ing to lay-offs, employee-owned enterprises – for instance in Romania – often try to implement alternative restructuring measures, such as product rational-isation, worker mobility, cuts in working hours, and so on.

As with employment adjustment, findings concerning *wages and incomes* indicate that the situation is much more complex than traditional theory would suggest. Average wages in employee-owned firms were often below those earned by workers in other firms, for instance in Estonia (Mygind 1997), but also in Latvia and Lithuania (Mygind 2002) and other countries in the region (ILO 1998). Employee owners, far from taking advantage of their position to pay themselves higher wages, were found to be more likely to accept tempo-rary wage cuts in order to promote enterprise profitability and to avoid employment reductions. The long-term objective of such owners, however, is to ensure better pay and living standards for the workers in line with improved enterprise performance. Workers thus seek to introduce higher wage increas-es and to compensate past wage cuts as soon as enterprise performance improves. This is the reason why employee-owned firms in Central and Eastern Europe have often promoted profit-sharing schemes and other pay-ment systems related to economic performance. All in all, findings thus do not indicate that the behaviour of employees and managers is driven by short-ter-mism, but rather that insiders often manage newly privatised firms prudently.

The existence of a positive link between employee ownership and *produc-tivity* and economic performance is supported by much of the evidence gath-ered in Central and Eastern Europe (Uvalic and Vaughan-Whitehead 1997). Enabling workers and management to purchase ownership led in many cases to more productive and efficient behaviour. Although the evidence so far is not as extensive or as reliable as one might wish, what is available is encour-aging, showing higher worker motivation and productivity, good profitability rates, and lower absenteeism and labour turnover rates in those enterprises. In Hungary, surveys of more than 200 ESOPs reveal that this type of enterprise performed better than the national average. Their profitability was found to be 6 per cent higher, on average, than that of non-ESOP companies (MRP 1997). A similar result was found in relation to 260 management–employee buy-outs in Romania (Munteanu 1997). Results in Lithuania show high profitability and labour productivity levels in employee-owned enterprises (Mygind 1997). Furthermore, econometric evidence for firms in Estonia, Latvia, Bulgaria, and Slovenia points to the beneficial effects of structures that provide for some degree of employee ownership.[2] There are also many cases of exemplary economic performance on the part of employee-owned enterprises. The successful performance of Hungarian ESOPs in traditional activities – for instance, porcelain – has also caught the attention of the media.[3]

But of course the efficiency of employee ownership also depends directly on the form that it takes, and especially whether employees *acquire control of the company* (Nuti 1997b). In general the results present the risks entailed by full employee ownership in terms of corporate governance, while at the same time indicating the great potential of enterprises with mixed property forms, that is, enterprises in which employee share ownership is not the only form of ownership, but is rather efficiently combined with others, such as foreign investment and local private capital.

The results are also very different according to the very different *distributions of shares among insiders* at the enterprise level: in some cases, shares can be bought mainly by the management, thus resulting in more management buy-out schemes – as seems to be the case in Estonia and Hungary – that can be demotivating for the rest of the employees; in other cases, all categories of employee are entitled to participate and to acquire shares.

With regard to *investment*, the evidence seems to indicate a powerful internal funding process in employee-owned firms, with employee owners directing a large part of their profits towards internal capital accumulation and investment activities. In many cases, contrary to theoretical expectations, employees decide not to distribute dividends but to reinvest them in the enterprise. Successful examples were found in the Baltic countries, Bulgaria, and elsewhere.[4]

It also appears, however, that employee buy-outs often have to face the problem of lack of financial capital – generally due to difficulties in obtaining external capital – which can lead to lower investment levels. In Lithuania, results point in the direction of lower investment in both management- and employee-dominated enterprises (Mygind 1997 and 2002). In Hungary, investment in privatised firms with employee share ownership had not increased since privatisation, mainly because of increasing indebtedness (MRP 1997).

2. For the Baltic countries, see Mygind (1997); for Bulgaria, Rock and Klinedinst (1997) and Jones et al. (1997); for the republics of the former Yugoslavia, Uvalic (1997); and for Russia, the World Bank study prepared by Earle et al. (1995), and Lissovolik (1997).

3. See 'Herend now: Hungary's renowned china maker is a model of employee ownership', *Budapest Business Journal* (8–14 September 1997), pp. 1, 6.

4. See Mygind and Noorgard Pedersen (1996), in particular their description of the enterprises Estre, Ester, and Norma in Estonia; Jauda and Dzintars in Latvia; and Sparta in Lithuania, pp. 56, 67, 89, 143, and 327–9. For a similar process in Bulgaria, see Rock and Klinedinst (1997).

Investment in some Polish management–employee buy-outs was also lower than in similar enterprises, mainly due to the burden of lease payments (Nuti 1997a). This lack of fresh capital and lower investment are the greatest disadvantages that the experts have found with regard to employee ownership. But for all these problems it is possible to elaborate concrete solutions, especially through better access to the banking system.

Another aspect often neglected in the current debates on transition, and one to which it is worth attracting attention, is the role of privatisation in providing *social motivation* and in preventing social upheaval. In a context of growing income inequalities, falling real wages – when they were paid at all – and increasing poverty, employee ownership could play an important role in partly compensating the costs that the reforms entailed for a large proportion of employees (ILO 1998), and more generally in promoting economic democracy and creating a new basis for redistributive justice.

Employee ownership survival in danger

Despite the trade unions' initial support for employee ownership in the privatisation process, and encouraging economic performance, a number of obstacles have emerged as this property form has developed.

Lack of share-holders' participation rights. First, the evidence suggests that there has been only a loose relationship between formal structures of ownership, formal structures of control, and real decision-making power (Blasi et al. 1997; Jones and Weisskopf 1996). In general, share-ownership should be accompanied by voting rights on a 'one share–one vote' basis. The more shares that employees have, the more say they should have in company governance. This employee control can be exercised individually by employee owners, with proportional voting on the basis of the number of shares. This system may be considered as the fairest and most efficient.

However, with the exception of the Baltic states – especially Estonia – in several other countries in Central and Eastern Europe, the 'one share–one vote' rule has not been adopted. In Bulgaria, employee ownership was introduced without giving employees any right to participate in decision-making. Non-voting shares were also distributed in Lithuania. But even in the countries where employee ownership was accompanied by voting rights, thus leading to a great number of enterprises with majority worker ownership, in many cases, this did not enable employees to exercise a controlling stake because of dispersed or uninterested employee owners; at the same time, although in theory minority employee share ownership could also lead to control if the remaining shares were dispersed among a number of outside shareholders (Nuti 1997b), in practice outside owners were found to be much less dispersed than the workers.

The absence of real influence in the decision-making process has led many employees to lose interest in ownership and has discouraged them from keeping their shares.

The dilution of employee ownership. In almost all Central and Eastern European countries, employee ownership seems to be evolving along the same lines: after a first phase during which the management succeeded in keeping the enterprise through insider privatisation in partnership with the workers, the management changed behaviour in a second phase, and rather looked for full control of the capital or for a partnership with an external investor. The manager by buying back the shares of the workers generally succeeds in marginalising them in terms of both ownership and decision-making. Dilution of employee-ownership is a general trend in all future member states of Central and Eastern Europe. It has been documented recently in Lithuania (Mygind 2002), Estonia (Kalmi 2002), and Bulgaria (Jones and Klinedinst 2002). In Poland, in employee-leased companies, the share of non-managerial employees in ownership has steadily decreased, from 58.7 per cent immediately after privatisation to 31.5 per cent in 1999. This was mainly due to the high dispersion of insider-owners who did not see any point in keeping their shares, and who retained only minor blocks of shares. As a result, in at least 76 per cent of the companies under review, non-managerial employees could no longer decisively influence the decision-making process. During the same period, managements consolidated their holdings (stabilised at 29.4 per cent of ownership in 1999), while the number of shares in the hands of outsiders (domestic and foreign) increased fivefold (from 7.6 per cent immediately after privatisation to 39.1 per cent in 1999) (Kozarzewski and Woodward 2002, p. 3). In Estonia, from a representative sample of 46 enterprises in which employees were the largest group of owners in 1995, Kalmi (2002) reports that only 12 remained employee-owned in 1999 (75 per cent thus having changed their principal ownership). In another sample of 86 enterprises that had instead implemented only a minor degree of (not majority) employee ownership, in 90 per cent of cases both the absolute number of employee-owners and the stock of shares held by employees had fallen drastically by 1999. This phenomenon is explained, first, by a decline in existing employee shareholders who sold their shares (exit), and second, by the failure to include new employees as owners of the enterprise (no entry) (Kalmi 2002). Another way of diluting employee share ownership consists in issuing new shares in order to allow an external investor to come in. The broadening of enterprise assets has proved to be an easier and quicker way of changing ownership for the management than the repurchase of employees' shares. This is where trade unions as workers' representatives have not always played the monitoring and assisting role they might have. By not playing a more active role in informing the workers of their shareholders' rights and by providing them with little support to keep their shares, they generally did not help employees to maintain a significant degree of employee ownership in the enterprise.

For instance, they did not always oppose augmentation of enterprise capital and did not seem much concerned by the progressive dilution of employee ownership.

Was this a conscious policy on the part of trade unions, in the belief either that external capital would improve corporate governance, or that the dilution of employee ownership would increase trade union power within the enterprise? Or was it only a 'failure' on their side to take into account the possible detrimental effects of this trend on workers as shareholders, but also, by means of an indirect 'boomerang' effect, on trade unions in the long run?

Whatever its reasons, this 'laissez-faire' attitude contrasted with the efforts generally made by the same trade unions to impose employee share ownership in the privatisation process.

For instance, the largest trade union (OK Kovo) in Slovakia has been very active in promoting employee share ownership in the privatisation process – by negotiating with the privatisation agency and the Ministry of Privatisation, and even organising internal training and seminars on employee ownership; between the two waves of privatisation, in 1995–96, they organised meetings with trade union members from enterprises that had already been privatised by employee ownership and employees from enterprises who were starting the same process. Nevertheless, their activity in this field has always focused on the creation and social control of legislation on privatisation. As a result it stopped as soon as the statutory bodies of employee joint-stock companies were created. At that point, trade unions reverted to their traditional role, that is, mainly collective bargaining and in particular negotiating for higher wages (Brzica 1998, 12–13). Other trade unions in the region, after their involvement in the privatisation process, limited their initiatives to the traditional labour–management relationship under the threat of layoffs or real wage decreases without trying to modify the decision-making process through employee share ownership.

In Bulgaria, although trade unions supported MEBO in the the early stages of privatisation, this privatisation technique turned out to be a way of selling state assets to friends (more generous offers from external buyers have often been rejected) on the most advantageous conditions. This privatisation did not induce the new owners to carry out restructuring, but rather led to liquidation or – when the devalued shares of the employees could be bought back by the management at a good price – to the selling of the enterprise or part of it to an external buyer at a much higher price.

As a result of this trend, and despite the fact that employee ownership was found to have a number of net economic advantages, both in terms of speed in the privatisation process and of corporate governance, it has progressively declined in importance over the last few years.

The abandonment of self-management experience in Malta. Another interesting experience has been observed in Malta, where employee ownership has been actively promoted in the shipyard industry. Nevertheless, this experience was abandoned, and with it the belief, it seems, of trade unions in the viability of this form of management and property (Zammit, 2003). By contrast, employee ownership has not been much developed in the other two Southern candidate countries, Cyprus and Turkey.

Far from the EU experience: the total absence of profit-sharing schemes
While employee ownership emerged on an extensive scale in Central and Eastern Europe, no other forms of financial participation, such as profit-sharing, have been promoted. Although enterprises have been found to distribute part of wages in the form of performance-related pay (Paoli et al. 2002), these schemes are used in a very informal way, and are set up and modified unilaterally by the employer without any influence from trade unions and/or workers' representatives. This is different from the institutional and legal framework existing in many EU member states. Such poor promotion of profit-sharing schemes in future member states contrasts with the views prevailing today in the EU in which profit-sharing schemes are considered as part of a new culture of industrial relations based on innovative managerial strategies, more flexible remuneration policies, and more cooperation between labour and capital, which should ultimately result in greater enterprise efficiency. Moreover, one of the conclusions of PEPPER II is that 'the development of financial participation schemes is strongly influenced by government action, in particular by the availability of tax incentives'. This is precisely what the candidate countries have not done: out of the 13 candidate countries none has promoted legislation nor provided fiscal incentives to encourage employers to introduce and develop profit-sharing schemes, a situation that contrasts very much with the current situation in the EU (see Table 6.4). In contrast to the EU, these countries have clearly developed employee share ownership systems rather than profit-sharing schemes.

How could we explain these developments, and this surprising gap with EU member states? A number of different explanations can be provided.

Rejection of 'a scheme from the past'. Before 1989, some socialist countries had adopted profit-sharing schemes. They were usually implemented in the form of bonuses paid to employees and managers, and through indirect com-

Table 6.4 Forms of workers' financial participation in candidate countries

	Employee ownership in privatisation	Law on profit-sharing	Cooperatives
Bulgaria	Yes	No	Dismantled
Cyprus	No	No	–
Czech Republic	Not much	No	–
Estonia	Yes	No	–
Hungary	Yes	No	–
Latvia	Yes	No	–
Lithuania	Yes	No	–
Malta	Yes	No	–
Slovakia	Yes	No	–
Slovenia	Yes, strong	Prepared in 1997–98 but not adopted by the Parliament; discussed again in 2002–3	–
Poland	Yes	No	–
Romania	Yes	No	–
Turkey	No	No	–
EU countries	Some EO during privatisation in France, UK, Portugal	In France, UK, Belgium, the Netherlands, Germany, Denmark, Austria, Spain, Ireland	

pensation for welfare services, such as housing, holidays, and so on. However, although directly financed from enterprise funds, these schemes were not directly related to enterprise results and were difficult to distinguish from fixed wages. Since the start of the transition, such forms of profit-sharing have declined in importance. Workers became opposed to these forms of payment that did not respond to objective qualifications, requirements, or performance. Over the years of transition, almost all the trade union leaders, but surprisingly also the best industrial relations specialists from these countries (with whom the author has had discussions) have always expressed great concern at seeing this type of scheme being implemented again at enterprise level.

Exchange of experiences with EU colleagues and certainly a long time in which to change mentalities seem to be required to change the bad feeling related to the previous regime in this area.

The lack of scope due to centralised incomes policy. The adoption of strict incomes policies – forbidding enterprises to increase their wage fund above a certain percentage – has usually prevented the adoption of profit-sharing. In order to correct the adverse effects of such centralised incomes policies, most governments in the region introduced – from above – productivity as one of the criteria for (centrally) calculating the wage fund – or average wage – norms. Enterprises registering higher sales growth were allowed to translate this economic growth into higher wage increases. Such modification in tax-based incomes policy occurred for instance in Romania, Bulgaria, Poland and many other Central and Eastern European countries on the direct advice of international monetary institutions. This method, however, was little different from past regimes' centralised attempts to relate wages to productivity. Wages turned out not to be better connected to productivity, thus showing the difficulty of installing such a link from the macroeconomic rather than the microeconomic level of the enterprise: a centrally determined formula linking wages to productivity can only reflect an easily observable output measure – such as the ratio sales/number of employees that was adopted by most governments for example – and thus provides only an approximate measure of productivity.[5]

The context of economic crisis. In addition to these central restrictions, the production crisis, combined with high inflation rates, has limited the possibilities for employers to distribute bonuses related to profits. The fall in living standards and growing poverty have also induced the workers to claim higher basic wage increases rather than the distribution of flexible profit-sharing bonuses.

Some aborted attempts. Some attempts have been reported in candidate countries. In the first years of transition in Poland, for instance, although the government also followed a restrictive tax-based incomes policy, known as the '*popiwek*', and abandoned it only in 1995, it also allowed enterprises to distribute part of their profits in the form of profit-sharing bonuses, up to a limit of 8.5 per cent of annual wages. This profit-sharing system was also closely controlled by a progressive tax which was reduced in 1992–94. Despite the possibility of distributing profit-sharing bonuses to employees, this formula has not been much followed by enterprises, especially those in the state sec-

5. The measure of value added per employee, for instance – which can be calculated only from a detailed balance-sheet at the enterprise level – would be much more reliable but much more difficult to apply within a centralised formula of wage controls.

tor which continued to be under strict wage regulations and have encountered serious profitability problems (Chilosi et al. 1995). At the same time, although new private enterprises had full legal autonomy to establish the principles of remuneration, which may include forms of profit-sharing, the first experiences of privatised enterprises tended to indicate that new shareholders, especially in small enterprises, are not really inclined to accept profit-sharing (Chilosi et al. 1995). At the same time, there have been some innovative experiences developed by individual employers (Kabaj 1998).

Slovenia also prepared a profit-sharing law in 1997, partly inspired by the French law on compulsory application of a deferred profit-sharing system. Profit-sharing bonuses would be allocated to the enterprise participation fund, employees being allowed to withdraw such amounts after a retention period of a few years. In the meantime, profit-sharing funds could be used by the enterprise, in consultation with employees' representatives, to fund new investment and employment policies. According to the Ministry of Labour, the main objectives of this law were to fight uncontrolled inflationary wage increases and to replace them by wage increases directly related to productivity and economic performance and possibly placed in the internal investment process of enterprises. For this purpose, the acceptance of a profit-sharing agreement was made directly dependent on the strict following of the wage rules, that is, the indexation of wages limited to 85 per cent of inflation.

However, this was why this draft law was opposed by the trade unions and rejected by the Parliament. Even if profit-sharing schemes should de facto lead to more moderate wage growth – or at least bring wages more in line with productivity increases – introducing a profit-sharing scheme with the direct aim of limiting wage increases is certainly not the best way to get the acceptance of trade unions, as it cannot represent a good method of increasing workers' motivation and productivity. Despite several debates, which could have led to a consensus around an improved proposal – both government and trade unions seem to favour profit-sharing, while the employers would probably show more interest with proper fiscal incentives – the draft law was never revised or reproposed for approval, and the government came to focus on other priorities, especially social security and pension reform. New discussions on a profit-sharing law were expected to take place in 2002–3.

6.4 POLICY CONSIDERATIONS

We have seen that forms of workers' participation have developed in candidate countries, especially in Central and Eastern Europe, in a rather disorganised and unbalanced way, a process for which public authorities but also trade unions and employers, as well as foreign experts and international organisations, share a great deal of responsibility. This trend clearly contrasts with the status and role of workers' participation in the EU, where it is an integral part of the Community *acquis*. Let us try to identify in what specific areas policies and initiatives could lead to more cohesion in participatory policies.

6.4.1 The Survival of Employee Share Ownership

After unprecedented development, employee ownership is progressively disappearing in candidate countries, rarely on the grounds of its effect on corporate governance. The ironic situation might arise in which, by the time Central and Eastern European actors become fully aware of the need to keep employee ownership as part of EU standards, employees will have sold most or all of their shares, depriving these countries of the good start they had made in terms of employee participation.

This should lead us to consider the measures and initiatives that could be taken by the different actors to limit this process.

First, more monitoring is needed from the public authorities. Governments that decided to promote forms of employee ownership in the privatisation process should take additional steps to ensure that this type of enterprise can function properly in the long run, and especially to check that it is not discriminated against as regards access to capital and financial markets. A credit guarantee institution might be created, something that may help to reduce the unwillingness of banks to lend to employee-owned firms. Banks, however, should be asked not to engage in discriminatory lending.

To encourage additional employee ownership and to stabilise current levels there are also a number of fiscal initiatives that might be considered. For individuals these include providing tax concessions to buy shares and more favourable treatment of capital gains. Also, tax concessions might be given to firms which encourage employee ownership. One of the conclusions of EC report PEPPER II is that 'the development of financial participation schemes is strongly influenced by government action, in particular by the availability of tax incentives'.

In addition, as has happened in Hungary (and inspired by legislation in the USA and the UK), ESOP type legislation might be implemented. This would provide a vehicle for employees who wish to form a group and thus enable more effective legal representation of individual employee shareholders.

Our other set of recommendations concerning government actions involves encouraging the establishment of structures which support employee ownership. One key function of such bodies would be informational since we have seen that very limited evidence is available about the economic potential of certain forms of employee ownership.

From the trade unions' side, we have seen that in several transition economies they welcomed employee ownership and played a positive role in its development at enterprise level (ILO 1998). However, they do not seem to have done much to avoid their dilution and progressive disappearance in enterprises. No doubt a more ambitious policy should be designed by trade unions to make it possible for this property form to survive and show its viability in the long run.

Trade unions should organise their action well beyond their traditional mandate. They could, for instance, participate in developing institutions to extend employee share ownership within the enterprise or in designing centres of expertise for employee share ownership. But they could also become much more effective in this area by simply helping workers to behave as shareholders: employees often do not play an active role in shareholders' general meetings because they have yet to acquire a full understanding of their status as owner – they know neither their rights nor their responsibilities. This could help to achieve a better balance between the managerial board and the shareholders' meeting. Furthermore, the lack of interest often exhibited by employees is also frequently related to their lack of information concerning future returns on the company's investments and so their own future dividends; trade unions could redouble their efforts to obtain the relevant information from the management and pass it on to the employees. This could motivate workers to remain co-owners of the firm.

At the same time, the trade unions should in this way seek to extend rather than to abandon their traditional activities in the enterprise. Results have shown that employee share ownership seems neither to lessen trade union influence nor to limit collective bargaining (ILO 1998).

6.4.2 For a More Constructive Stance on Works Councils

We have seen that the relationship between trade unions and works councils can be influenced by different circumstances. We can expect the degree of opposition of trade unions to at first vary according to their strength and situation at enterprise level: the greater their fragmentation, the lower their mobilisation capacity (to call a strike, for instance); and the lower their unionisation, the greater their opposition to works councils because of their fear of seeing their own position marginalised within the enterprise.

It should also be noted that trade union leaders operating at the branch and sectoral level were often found to be the most fiercely opposed to the introduction of works councils at enterprise level. Here trade unions should start a debate among themselves to modify such attitudes, and explain why and how these different types of actor and levels of operation could be complementary rather than exclude each other.

The strategies of the two other main actors – that is, employers and the government – will also influence the trade union position. The management's attempts to use works councils to marginalise trade unions inexorably lead to tensions between the two institutions. On the other hand, it is interesting to observe that employers are less keen on introducing works councils in a context in which trade unions, as in Hungary, find themselves to be relatively weak and thus not in a position to significantly counter management decisions. In this case, trade unions should view works councils as a way of strengthening their influence within the enterprise rather than the opposite.

The way in which the government adopts a law on works councils also influences trade union attitudes, as in Hungary. Trade union involvement in the preparation of the law is crucial, and trade unions should fight to ensure it. The EU should also continue to monitor the way works councils are implemented.

On their side, trade unions should not reject the principle of promoting such forms of worker participation since their reaction could be used by governments to emphasise the 'non-democratic nature of trade unions' and the basic antagonism between trade union policy and the implementation of the Community *acquis* in this area. This situation would certainly give the wrong image of trade unions to the public, and would not be well understood by workers themselves. This policy of 'non-rejection' should also be applied to other participatory forms. For instance, in Slovenia, while trade unions legitimately rejected a first draft of the law on profit-sharing that aimed at constraining wage increases and would have thus interfered with wage bargaining, we may regret that trade unions did not propose an alternative. As a result, there is still no law on profit-sharing in Slovenia.

European works councils: making them work alongside EU enlargement
The mechanism of European works councils does not work properly in candidate countries yet. There have been delays in the transposition of the EC directive, while the involvement of local representatives in these 'transnational' fora has been very limited so far, partly because of the management, but also partly because of the home country representatives of European works councils.

Trade unions should urgently build a strategy around the European works council, especially since European works councils for the time being represent the only transnational tool at their disposal. In this regard, they should help European works councils to extend their scope beyond the purely information and consultation arena and to turn them into a forum where strategic issues are discussed in a transnational context with the management, such as restructuring, employment, and working conditions. Trade unions in this way could start to use European works councils as an essential pillar for the internationalisation of their policy. Conversely, whatever conflict they may have with European works councils would turn out to be counterproductive, and show instead a rather large distance between trade unions and the problems met at company level, that could only lead to a further decline in trade union membership.

Beyond corporate social responsibility

Finally, some monitoring of management's attitudes towards the involvement of participants from host candidate countries in the European works councils should also be monitored by the European Community. In particular, at a time when the European Commission is emphasising the social corporate responsibility of EU enterprises, it should insist on such behaviour also being implemented in future member states, and in particular on ensuring that proper information and consultation mechanisms are put in place in these countries, including Southern countries Malta, Cyprus and Turkey. The lack of proper functioning of European works councils within the framework of the enlargement process could only accentuate the risk of seeing social dumping cases multiply, an issue we address in the second part of this volume.

Moreover, while the adoption of social corporate responsibility is certainly a useful complementary tool to other participatory instruments already promoted in the EU, we should remember that this concept comes from the United States and has also been promoted within neo-liberal models. In this regard, this type of participation, promoted under the sole initiative of the employers, contrasts with the more institutionalised types of participation that we have developed in the EU. The examples of foreign companies already implementing different policies when setting up operations in candidate countries also shed light on the limits of this tool, especially in the negotiation process. It should thus definitely be seen as a complementary tool rather than a 'new way' or form of participation to be promoted in the EU.

6.4.3 For a Better Combination of Participatory Forms

Although candidate countries and their actors have at some point supported one form of direct workers' participation or another, in no country in the region do they seem to have defined a coherent and comprehensive policy on the efficient combination of all the different forms of workers' participation. This means that participatory experiences were rather isolated and did not correspond to a global human resources strategy from the company or public authorities.

We have seen, for instance, that after having promoted employee ownership on a large scale, the progressive dilution of this property form occurred due to an absence or underutilisation of works councils. Despite being share-holders, the workers could not get the appropriate information on enterprise performance, thus rapidly losing interest in keeping their shares and becoming easy victims of management attempts to buy back their shares at a price below their face value. At the same time, works councils or other mechanisms of participation in decision-making have emerged without the development of complementary forms of workers' financial participation.

An overall strategy vis-à-vis these different but complementary forms of workers' participation must be developed not only by public authorities but also employers and trade unions.

Slovenia provides a good example of an efficient combination of employee ownership and works councils. In the 1992 privatisation law (which allocated 20 per cent of shares to the workers, 20 per cent to the Development Fund that auctioned the shares to investment funds, 10 per cent to the National Pension Fund, and 10 per cent to the Restitution Fund) the works council in each enterprise was empowered to allocate the remaining 40 per cent of company shares for sale to insiders (the workers) or outsiders (through a public tender). The proximity between trade unions and the workers obviously often led to common trade union and works council strategies on privatisation and employee ownership, something which also explains the positive attitude of trade unions with regard to direct forms of worker participation such as works councils or employee share-ownership. According to Stanojević (2000) this combination of participatory forms may explain why a higher level of worker–management cooperation was observed in Slovenia compared to Hungary, where similar works councils had been introduced on the basis of the German model.

6.4.4 Extending Workers' Participation to Small Private Enterprises

We have seen that many Central and Eastern European countries are facing the same pattern of participatory practices at enterprise level, strong trade unionisation and workers' participation in state and/or large enterprises, and the absence of any form of worker interest representation in private enterprises, especially in small firms, although a similar outcome was generated by different processes. While in Poland, for instance, the dismantling of workers' participation in privatised enterprises was due to government initiative supported by the trade unions, in Slovenia it is rather the support of works councils by trade unions that led the two forms to coexist in state enterprises where trade union influence was the strongest and led to their absence from small private enterprises. A similar outcome is also observed in Hungary, where the works councils rarely operate in non-union enterprises or otherwise seem to be dominated by trade unions. Only multinational enterprises seem to have clearly pushed out trade unions in order to favour the less adversarial system of works councils.

This shows that there is common ground for trade unions in candidate countries, despite their different ideological positions on worker participation: the urgent need to better represent workers' interests in private enterprises, especially in small businesses. Here, trade unions should see works councils or other forms of workers' participation as effective instruments to reach this goal, and thus influence legislation on works councils to extend it to small businesses.

The absence of workers' participation in new small private enterprises should also induce governments to find appropriate policy measures. This could be campaign awareness or legislative action. The transposition of the Community *acquis* in this area certainly is a good opportunity and should modify the current situation, especially transposition of the new directive on information and consultation in enterprises with more than 50 employees. The presence of this proportion of SMEs could also motivate further legislative steps. In Slovenia, for instance, we saw that provisions on information and consultation have already been extended to enterprises with more than 20 employees.

The situation in candidate countries should also lead the European institutions to move further. The possibility of extending the new directive to enterprises with less than 50 employees (for instance, all those with more than 20 – as initially proposed by the European Parliament – rather than more than 50 employees) has already been requested by the European trade unions. Certainly, this will become more and more needed with the current explosion of new private SMEs in future member states. This would also be required in EU countries where SMEs also predominate, but where the culture of human resources and workers' participation seems to be better rooted than in candidate countries. A threshold of 20 employees instead of 50 employees would double the percentage of enterprises covered by the directive, from 3 to 6 per cent.

6.5 CONCLUSION

The main issue in this chapter is the assessment of whether forms of workers' participation in candidate countries have been promoted and are developing along the same lines as in the EU, where they form an important element of the European Social Model.

Has the tradition of self-management and economic democracy of applicants from Central and Eastern Europe – which involved workers in both their enterprise profits and decision-making – continued in these countries, or has the shift to free market economies brought an end to this type of experience?

Our assessment of workers' participation trends in these countries after twelve years of transition depicts a rather surprising and paradoxical situation.

A first general paradox may be observed: despite a strong tradition of participation in former Communist countries which could have led these countries to develop a strong basis for participatory experiences in line with the Community *acquis*, neo-liberal theories inspired by the Anglo-Saxon model and advisers from international monetary institutions have led these countries in a totally different direction.

Works councils and other forms of workers' involvement in decision-making, considered as 'vestiges' of socialism, have been totally dismantled, together with other self-management forms, such as cooperatives, often with the cooperation of the trade unions.

The second conclusion, or paradox, is that, despite a common past and a similar objective – belonging to the EU and applying its social standards – a rather differentiated situation emerges when we look at experiences country by country. Countries such as Slovenia, in the tradition of self-management in the former Yugoslavia, and the Baltic countries, as in other CIS countries where economic democracy was deeply rooted in enterprises, have developed and combined different forms of workers' participation. Other countries, such as the Czech and Slovak Republics or Poland, have followed a more liberal approach in which little opportunity has been given to employees to participate in the restructuring and privatisation process on the assumption that total distribution to private capital would accelerate the pace of privatisation and enterprise restructuring and lead to the emergence of strong capital markets.

A third paradox can be observed with regard to the two main forms of workers' participation – in decision-making and financial results – which could have been expected to develop in a harmonious way, or at least to follow similar trends. Conversely, workers' participation has developed in a rather unbalanced way, with participatory schemes following radically different trends: while forms of workers' involvement and information and consultation – such as works councils – were poorly developed in the first years of transition but better promoted in recent years, mainly to comply with the transposition of the Community *acquis*, employee ownership was actively promoted in the first stage of privatisation without being allowed to remain a viable property form in the longer run. At the same time, profit-sharing schemes that could have been expected to follow employee ownership and other participatory developments and to be encouraged alongside higher GDP and better economic performance, have been ignored by policy-makers and economic and social actors.

In brief, no coherent policy of workers' participation seems to have been developed so far in future member states, including the three Southern countries: neither by public authorities, employers, nor trade unions.

This situation in future member states is problematic since it means that a form of democracy and social dialogue that exists in the EU is missing at the workplace. Moreover, even where workers' participation has been promoted, it often concentrates in large state-owned enterprises, which also benefit from trade unions and other forms of social dialogue. In the private sector, especially among the new small and medium-size enterprises and businesses, not only is there no social dialogue – as we described in Chapter 5 – but there is no form of workers' information and consultation at the workplace either. This gap certainly represents a problem for the proper implementation of the Community *acquis* in this type of enterprise, which requires an active role by workers' representatives. In this regard, transposition of the EC community *acquis* is crucial and should play a role. Nevertheless, we might also wonder if the Community information and consultation armoury, which has been considerably expanded over the last two years, is fully appropriate to address this issue in enterprises of candidate countries that are dominated by SMEs. Although the presence of small enterprises is comparable in the EU, this is combined in many candidate countries with a total absence of a culture of participation, dialogue, and social standards among new businessmen, in distinct contrast to the EU.

At the same time, although future member states have committed themselves to implementing – and most of them already have – the EC directive on European works councils, large EU companies which have adopted such a transnational participatory framework do not seem to have involved workers' representatives from future member states in them. This means that European works' councils in many cases do not seem to be playing their expected role in protecting workers' interests in the EU enlargement process. This situation should push European institutions, but also European and national trade unions, to improve the functioning of this form of participation and induce EU employers to use it in the desirable way.

To conclude, we might wonder whether the above-mentioned trends – the progressive dilution of employee ownership and the absence of other forms of workers' participation in decision-making and of direct forms of workers' information and consultation at the workplace – will lead in these countries to neo-liberal forms of capitalism. Especially since these trends, combined with the recourse to more flexible working arrangements (Chapter 2), less security of employment (Chapter 4), and poor coverage of social dialogue (Chapter 5) could only contribute to the emergence and extension of more extreme forms of management and working practices than in the EU member states, thus definitely leading these countries away not only from their initial tradition of workers' participation and self-management, but also from the main features of participation in the EU.

PART II

Social Dumping: Myth or Reality?

7. The Social Gap: A Source of 'Unfair' Competition?

7.1 INTRODUCTION

In the EU enlargement process, as with the advent of the single European market in January 1993, fears of 'social dumping' have rapidly multiplied. Although often not based on objective analyses, a series of arguments and statements has emerged concerning the risks that EU enlargement would represent for current EU member states, in terms of jobs, economic growth and social protection.

Capital relocations of EU enterprises to new member states would threaten jobs at home, and lead to closures of production units and massive layoffs. At the same time, a massive influx of migrant workers, drawn by better job prospects than exist in their home countries, would also threaten jobs since current workers could easily be replaced by this new abundant, skilled and cheaper labour force. On the trade side, overall, the opening of the EU market to companies from these countries, which can produce at much lower costs and thus rapidly gain market share, would lead many of our companies to the verge of bankruptcy. These are some of the arguments which have been used so far by many politicians and which have led to suspicion – if not to outright rejection in some circles – of the EU enlargement process and the return of nationalist movements.

Behind all these statements, the notion of 'social dumping' is used in a conscious or unconscious way to vaguely group many totally different possible outcomes which would, however, all have it in common that they would be generated by the 'unfair competition' that would emerge from lower wages and social standards in the new member states.

These fears, crystallised around the EU enlargement process, have been amplified by an international context characterised by greater openness of economies, greater capital mobility and greater international mobility of persons. In this debate, EU enlargement has often been assimilated with globalisation, against which many, from institutionalised organisations to spontaneous movements of civil society, have mobilised their forces and energy.

Since the 'merger' is at risk, it is important to put the debate on EU enlargement in the proper context; to try to respond to ill-thought-out and ideologically driven statements on EU enlargement, while also seriously assessing the situation, including those social and economic differences between current and future member states which may well lead to social dumping, alongside and after EU enlargement.

This is particularly important because the fears expressed so far on social dumping have not been based on any strong empirical studies or forecasting. While being limited in their contents, they have also remained fragmented and selective in their approach, emphasising in general the most controversial, populist and politically advantageous topics, such as 'labour migration'.

Is social dumping a myth or a reality? The aim of the second part of this book is to answer this question and to respond to the fears that increased movements of capital, labour and trade seem to generate. We shall try to address all these issues in both an analytical and a comprehensive way.

The aim of this introductory chapter is to provide a first assessment of the phenomenon by defining social dumping, giving concrete and illustrative examples before discussing the most important sources of social dumping, from wages and labour costs to working conditions and other labour or non-labour – such as environmental – issues. We shall then consider whether there is serious potential for social dumping in the enlargement process, and particularly if substantial movements of capital and labour are to be expected. The importance of social dumping as a possible trade strategy will also be examined. A range of aspects of these three movements – of capital, labour, and goods and services – will be analysed in more detail in the following chapters.

We have already seen in previous chapters that a number of failings can be identified in the candidate countries with regard to social issues. At the same time, we have also identified a number of areas where the Community *acquis* continues to be weak. Certainly social dumping could be fed by an incomplete Social Europe, and by the enlargement of the EU in a context of much lower social standards in the new member countries. A report on social dumping prepared for the French Presidency of the EU Council (Assemblée Nationale, May 2000, p. 68) on the basis of a survey of a number of EU policymakers and economic and social actors concluded that:

> many of the people interviewed for the report have expressed their doubts, even their scepticism, with regard to the European Community's control over the integration by candidate countries of the Community *acquis* in the social field . . . that monitoring would be too formal, that not all aspects of legislation in the social field would be examined, that its respect and application would not be considered as a priority condition for entering the EU . . .

As a result, the report concluded that 'among the future risks of social dumping in Europe, enlargement is among those inducing the most fear' and that 'social dumping risks will be very important in certain candidate countries'.

7.2 WHAT IS SOCIAL DUMPING?

Before entering into the core of the debate and providing examples of past and possible future cases of social dumping in the EU enlargement process, it may be useful to start by giving a definition of 'social dumping' and by examining the issue in more detail.

The absence of a definition despite widespread use of the term

It is surprising to note that social dumping has not yet been defined, either at the Community level and in individual EU member states, or by other international organisations (apart from one rather vague attempt at the 2002 Barcelona European Summit). At the same time, the term has been widely used by many economic and social actors.

The trade unions have often complained about social dumping by employers, but all too rarely provide significant and concrete examples of the problems at issue and why they should be considered as social dumping.

By contrast, the term is not much used by employers, who even have a tendency to reject the term and its different possible meanings altogether, since they generally consider that what is called 'social dumping' by some is just the normal and accepted use of local comparative advantages; on this understanding the term is thus only a slogan behind which there is no concrete form of behaviour or empirical reality. The President of UNICE (Union of Industrialists and Employers Confederation of Europe), George Jacobs clearly states: 'We do not see why the term social dumping is used since it refers to a type of behaviour which is not met in enterprises, and since the risk of seeing such a phenomenon in the EU enlargement process is very marginal'.[1]

Surprisingly, given the sensitivity of the issue, no official definition of social dumping has ever been provided by European institutions, including the European Commission, particularly since the notion of 'social dumping' inspired the founders of the European Economic Community, based on the idea that competition among the economies of the member states would be distorted unless harmonisation of social standards and working conditions was achieved within the Community. The Treaty of Rome partly reflected this worry in Article 117, which stated the need to 'promote improved working conditions and an improved standard of living for workers, so as to make possible their harmonisation while improvement is being maintained', that is, the principle of 'upward harmonisation'. The fears of social dumping remained limited over the 1960s and 1970s, mainly because the six original members of the Community enjoyed similar economic and social conditions, but also

---

1. Statement at the First Conference of European Social Partners on EU Enlargement, Prague, 18–19 March 1999; see also EC (1999a).

because they experienced rapid growth up to the oil shocks of the 1970s (Sapir 1995; Guillen and Alvarez 2000). The debate on social dumping gained momentum with the coming of the single market. First because of the existence of much lower labour costs in Southern countries (Greece, Portugal, Spain) but also because of the fears that the opening of all borders would lead to massive labour movements from less developed to more developed member states, and to massive capital relocations from developed, more capital-intensive member states towards less developed, more labour-intensive member states. The situation was summarised by Mosley (1990) as follows: 'standards of social protection might be depressed, or at least kept from rising, by increased competition after 1992 from states with substantially lower standards'.

A term borrowed from economics

'Dumping' is a term used in economics – and particularly in trade – to define any practice which consists in selling abroad (as exports) products or services below their price on the domestic market. This is the definition used, for instance, by the GATT,[2] but also by European institutions, especially by the Council when determining anti-dumping rights. In some economics textbooks this definition has been extended to include the practice of selling products at prices not only below their domestic level, but also below their production cost. Whatever the reference point is, the aim of such behaviour is generally the same, that is, to gain more market share and/or to acquire a dominant market position. Such behaviour is generally pursued until the desired position is sufficiently consolidated, and also while it is still sustainable for the enterprise in terms of profitability: we can expect a company that attains high profitability through dumping to persist with it as long as possible.

The adaptation of such economic definitions to the social area is difficult, which may explain the current lack of definition in the latter field. The ultimate aim of (social) dumping, however, is the same, to gain more market share through lower prices. In fact, when an enterprise follows an 'economic' dumping strategy, it often does so at the expense of its workers, for instance through much lower wages or working conditions, which represents 'social dumping'. Moreover, just as selling a product below its normal value can be judged unfair in economic terms, similarly any attempt to reduce product prices by failing to respect social legislation or by paying a much lower rate for labour – in terms of both wages and non-wage costs – can be judged unfair in social terms.

2. According to Article VI of the General Agreement on Tariffs and Trade of 30 October 1947, re-stipulated in the General Agreement of 1994.

Towards a basic definition

We would like to define 'social dumping' here as follows:

> any practice pursued by an enterprise that deliberately violates or circumvents legislation in the social field or takes advantage of differentials in practice and/or legislation in the social field in order to gain an economic advantage, notably in terms of competitiveness, the state also playing a determinant role in this process.[3]

Such behaviour can be pursued by domestic or foreign employers. In fact, 'social dumping' often describes a situation in which an employer from one country seeks an advantage by employing labour from another country where social and working standards are lower. There is often a link between the use of social dumping policies and practices by enterprises or governments in one country or part of the world and the erosion of levels or institutions of social protection and working standards elsewhere.

Beyond this general definition, however, it is important to distinguish between a number of different situations.

The distinction between 'illegal' and 'legal' social dumping

First, we would like to distinguish between a very narrow definition of social dumping, limited to respecting or failing to respect the law, and a more general definition based more on the notion of 'unfair competition'.

'Illegal' social dumping would include all situations in which the employer, in order to gain competitiveness, implements working and social conditions that clearly circumvent existing national or international provisions in force in the country where he is operating.

Nevertheless, the existence of legislation is not enough and the fight against illegal social dumping should also be extended to the proper implementation of existing legislation. In many countries, legislated labour standards are strong but their enforcement is very weak. This may be an indirect way of inducing social dumping. We saw in previous chapters that this is precisely what is happening in most candidate countries, with a gap to be expected and already visible between the formal adoption of all EC labour standards and their practical implementation in the field.

The key notion of 'unfair competition'

Although the above definition could include the most obvious and unacceptable employers' behaviour in the social field, it is not sufficient. To limit social dumping strictly to illegal behaviour does not allow us to include other

---

3. I would like to thank Henry Lourdelle of the ETUI for an interesting and lively discussion which allowed us to work out this definition.

types of social dumping, where employers succeed in imposing much lower – and often no more acceptable – working conditions while nevertheless remaining within the law.

We would like to include here cases in which the behaviour of the enterprise in the social field, while remaining within the bounds of legality, is clearly based on exploitative social and working conditions as a source of 'unfair competition'.

While defining the possible cases of 'unfair competition' in the social field, we would, however, like to distinguish between those practices as regards working conditions and employment that rather reflect a difference in comparative advantages and those practices that are more the result of a voluntary social downgrading strategy of the employer. As an example, wage differentials in most cases reflect different productivity levels, and also different economic performance, so that a low-wage policy as practised by enterprises in certain less-developed countries cannot be considered as 'social dumping'.

Nevertheless, if we refer back to the original 'economic' definition of dumping – that is, products being sold abroad at prices below those at home – we could also consider that paying a price for labour abroad which is well below what is the norm at home (that is, paying lower wages abroad) may represent some sort of dumping. Further, if we use the other economic definition – that is, sale of goods at a price below their production costs – we could also consider that the imposition or exploitation of working conditions that are not even sufficient to ensure workforce reproduction or subsistence represent social dumping, even if it does not circumvent legal regulations. This would mean that the term 'social dumping' could be clearly applied to those practices of wages and labour standards that do not ensure survival or proper living conditions.

Compared to the obvious cases in which enterprises do not respect the law in the social field, the cases of 'legal social dumping' are, of course, more difficult to identify, especially in foreign-owned enterprises characterised by multi-country and multi-operational activities, including sub-contracting.

For instance, how should we assess the behaviour of a multinational enterprise that relocates part of its production from an EU country to a candidate or third country in order to take advantage of lower social standards? It is not social dumping in the strict sense if the multinational company does not circumvent local regulations, but it is behaviour that can be assimilated to social dumping, since it clearly circumvents the values that are supposed to be part of the European Social Model and to which all social partners, including employers from the EU, adhere in their own country.

To conclude, it is in many cases very difficult to assess whether an enterprise is following a strategy of social dumping or not. A number of criteria can help us to distinguish the most obvious cases of 'unfair competition' due to lower working conditions, however, on the understanding that this notion – compared to 'illegal social dumping' – can only be based on more subjective considerations.

The employer's degree of intention

One important criterion is the degree of intentionality. To be able to evaluate the level of intent, the following elements should be taken into account:

1. The gap between the legislation in the home country and that in the host country: the greater the gap and the more obvious the willingness or deliberate intent of the foreign company to use this difference as a major source of increased competitiveness, the more appropriate it is to apply the term 'social dumping'. The level of legislation at home is therefore also to be taken into account in evaluating possible intent and thus the probability of social dumping. For example, a multinational enterprise coming from France – where the average working week is limited by legislation to 35 hours – will obviously have more incentive than an enterprise coming from the UK (where the average working week is 48 hours without much by way of legal limits) to relocate production, for instance, to Bulgaria where there is as yet no strict regulation in this field. This situation in turn may lead to pressures in the home country to move existing social standards downward.

2. The 'economic capacity' of the enterprise: the greater the financial means and the better the economic situation of the enterprise, the greater its capacity to progressively assimilate working conditions in the host country to those prevailing in the home country. In this regard, social dumping by a highly profitable multinational cannot be evaluated in the same way as that of a small domestic enterprise which is having problems surviving, and which could not apply better social standards even if it wished. In this way, the degree of intent on the part of the employer to profit from social differences can be captured more easily. The picture becomes even more complicated when the multinational company is using the local company as sub-contractor with full knowledge of the social standards the local company applies.

3. The more or less 'harmful' character of particular practices: the employer generally knows full well what is prohibited, not only by national but also by international law. Even if a country does not have national legislation on a particular issue, and even if it has not ratified the necessary international labour conventions, there are a number of issues – such as child labour, forced labour, freedom of association, collective bargaining, and so on – concerning which the international framework is sufficiently strong to be taken into account in all circumstances. The stronger the international framework, the more flagrant is any attempt to profit from social and labour differences through 'social dumping'. For instance, an enterprise's failure to respect the conventions on child labour, considered to be the worst example of labour exploitation, cannot be assessed in the same way as the failure to respect other conventions, such as wages, concerning which there are much less binding international standards. For the same reason, a multinational company's failure to respect basic international conventions, because it must be much more aware of the international framework, cannot be assessed in the same way as similar non-implementation on the part of a domestic company which may be influenced by local culture and practices. This third aspect is also related to the second criterion, that is, the economic capacity of the company. For instance, if a Romanian employer takes advantage of national legislation which is permissive in terms of working time, thus reinforcing its competitive position and gaining new markets, this can hardly be qualified as social dumping. On the other hand, if a German employer in the same sector produces and employs (in one way or another) workers in Romania in order to benefit from local regulations that permit more working hours than in Germany, it is fair to call it 'social dumping' because the German employer may be expected to apply similar social standards – or at least to upgrade local working conditions in the host country – to those he applies in his own country, even if legally he may not be punished if he does not. This should be considered even more true for basic or core international conventions, such as child labour, collective bargaining, or the right to strike.

The degree of involvement of public authorities

While our basic definition of social dumping mainly refers to enterprises, it also includes the state, which can encourage or discourage such practices, either as an employer in public administration and public enterprises, or as a government through the adoption or not of a legislative or institutional framework in the social field, or alternatively by tolerating a lack of respect for (or non-application of) existing legislation in the social field. These may be defensive moves by governments fearful of incurring competitive disadvantage now or in the future, or just an ideological choice.

For instance, the absence of legislation on a minimum wage or of provisions protecting the existence of trade unions or the right to strike or to collective bargaining may reflect a neo-liberal policy on the part of the government and can create a favourable climate for social dumping, attracting, for instance, foreign-owned companies seeking a lack of social legislation of this kind. The extremity of the social dumping policy of individual governments can probably be best captured in terms of a range of positions between the poles of a passive policy – such as governments abstaining from introducing or expanding social protection legislation – and an active policy (such as decisions to dismantle social protection or social legislation).

An evolving phenomenon

The situation may also change over time. For instance, the use of comparative advantage in respect of labour can turn into social dumping if the national legislation on social issues improves, if it ratifies related international labour standards, and/or if it takes on board the related Community legislation on its way to EU accession. In contrast, a government can decide to remove social regulations that so far limited social dumping, thus creating new incentives to take advantage of differences in social and working conditions.

This evolutionary aspect is important because it shows the implications that any progress in Community legislation and its transposition to candidate countries could have for eradicating the sources of and opportunities for social dumping. For instance, the existence of Community directives on health and safety may directly place enterprises in candidate countries which are not up-to-date in that regard in a situation where they are, almost by default, 'guilty' of social dumping; after a while, it would lead to complaints and possible action from the Community.

It should also be emphasised that recourse to social dumping is itself influenced by economic and social conditions. On the demand side, an economic crisis may induce employers to desperately try to improve their margins through illegal practices or through the running down of social and working conditions. On the supply side, a situation of high unemployment generally generates a labour force which is less demanding in terms of working and employment conditions, whilst increased unemployment in candidate countries may generate more migrant workers in EU member states ready to accept work under conditions much worse than those enjoyed by domestic workers.

7.3 THE DIFFERENT SOURCES OF SOCIAL DUMPING

A social dumping strategy can be followed to take advantage of differentials in a large number of possible areas. Wages have often been designated as the main factor in social dumping. Non-labour costs, including social protection contributions, are also taken into account by employers. They can also try to gain competitiveness through significant differences in working conditions – such as working time, minimum wage, types of labour contract, holidays, health and safety, including compensation for accidents at work or industrial diseases – or other social regulations, such as constraints on layoffs. Widespread informal activities, which by definition escape any form of social and employment regulation, represent the extreme case of – impermissible – flexibility that employers can seek for improving profitability.

All these different areas can become strong sources of social dumping depending on the importance that employers give to these different factors within their production costs. At the same time, we must also try to distinguish whether many of these factors do not in fact reflect comparative advantages. If a country has an abundant labour force, compared to its reserves in capital, it is obvious that cheap labour and low wages represent its main comparative advantage, which in that case should not be mistakenly considered as a source of social dumping (although in some cases, as we have seen, it can). We shall try to distinguish here between borderline cases.

7.3.1 Different 'Tolerance Thresholds' for Black or Informal Activities

The most obvious cases of social dumping are illegal practices: it is obvious that economic activities pursued without paying due heed to social protection legislation are likely to be profitable. By this strategy, many companies – generally small ones, but large ones are not immune to temptation in this regard – can often accumulate substantial profits in a relatively short period. The manner in which the law is applied and respected – including the penalties imposed on 'free riders' – is a key element in this process; we might in fact wonder whether some countries have not tried to increase competitiveness by tolerating different levels of 'black' activity. The size of the informal economy has traditionally been very high in southern economies such as Italy and Greece, and can now be seen on an even larger scale in the future member states of Central and Eastern Europe. We saw in Chapter 4 on employment that the informal economy often represents up to 25 per cent of GDP in these countries, clearly a source of social dumping for both domestic and foreign-owned enterprises. No doubt this type of unfair competition, which clearly corresponds to our case of 'illegal social dumping', although tolerated by the public authorities to a varying degree, can play a role in motivating capital movements, for instance from the EU towards candidate countries or new member states.

7.3.2 Low Wages: An Important Factor in Competitiveness

Wages have always been a central concern of social and economic actors because they represent the most important component of labour costs – even in most developed economies – and thus a key variable of competitiveness.

Social dumping or comparative advantage?
Wage levels, however, have always been determined by factor endowments of labour and capital and other traditional forces. Low wages generally reflect labour-intensive economies, with an abundance of unskilled labour, a small quantity of capital, and low productivity. Low wages have often been considered to be a reflection of low productivity and poor economic performance,

which should thus be seen as a source of national comparative advantage, which may help the country to improve its competitiveness and economic growth. This is why it has always been difficult to qualify wage and income differentials as a source of social dumping.

Many observers, including professional agencies, make the mistake of assimilating social dumping to the existence of cheaper wage costs; this is the case with the European Foundation for the Improvement of Living and Working Conditions in Dublin which defines it as the 'practice adopted by certain countries of offering low wage costs in order to attract foreign investment' (used by the Foundation, for instance, in respect of Spain). Although by 'wage costs' the Foundation probably means all working conditions (including trade unions, health and safety, and so on), this notion is misleading because it tends to narrow the scope of social dumping to wage issues.

Moreover, it is particularly difficult to assimilate lower wages to social dumping as national, EU, and international regulations in this area (apart from minimum wage regulations in many member states and the ILO convention in this regard) are generally quite poor.

The fact that there is no binding Community instrument on the minimum wage limits opportunities to protest against very low wages in some member states, which in fact represent a source of unfair competition as against countries and employers who have adopted higher wage standards. The same applies to candidate countries which benefit from much cheaper labour.

This means that it is perfectly legal and very easy for an employer – for instance from the EU – to relocate part of its production (for instance to candidate countries) to take advantage of lower wages and the absence of minimum wage regulations. Although all candidate countries have implemented national minimum wage legislation, the level of this minimum wage is so low and its implementation so poor that a very low wage policy, sometimes even below those official standards, can be pursued without any legal constraints. The EC recommendation on fair remuneration, even if not binding, should at least induce the future member states to take into account the need for progress in this area.

Nevertheless, although this is legal and seems to be part and parcel of the worldwide game of comparative advantage, we might wonder whether it does not become social dumping when the same company – for instance, again one from the EU – takes advantage of the absence of legal regulations on the minimum wages and/or if it applies wages at the local level that continue to be, for instance, well below any subsistence minimum or poverty line – particularly if the same company could afford wage levels above such symbolic rates without undermining its overall profitability.

Similarly from the government side, while minimum wages or even average wages well below the poverty line may reflect poor economic performance and thus not be considered as social dumping, in reality the absence of regulations or appropriate policies could well correspond to a deliberate policy strategy on the part of the government to maintain a competitive advantage in the labour field to favour enterprises to the detriment of the workers and their living standards (a policy followed by some candidate countries, and described in Chapter 10).

We can thus conclude that, although wage differentials may reflect initial factor endowments and thus comparative advantages, they may be used by enterprises – and this use might be encouraged by governments – in such a way that they amount to social dumping. To distinguish between different examples, we believe that the criteria defined above can be useful; to recap, the intent of the employer, conditions in home and host countries, the enterprise's economic capacity, and the degree of harmfulness of the relevant policies. The list of criteria could also be further developed according to the source of social dumping under analysis (wages, social protection, working conditions, and so on).

To conclude, the borderline beyond which particular business practices can be defined as 'social dumping' is far from clear, even in the field of wages, that should normally be seen as an aspect of comparative advantage. This should encourage us not to generalise in debates on social dumping, but rather to discuss the issue on a case-by-case basis and grounded on solid criteria.

Employers concerned with earnings (labour costs), not wages

Nevertheless, whether or not (according to the particular situation) wage differentials can be considered as a legitimate comparative advantage rather than an illegitimate source of unfair competition and thus of social dumping, it is certain that wage disparities which are already very high between current EU member states will dramatically increase with the integration of new member states from Central and Eastern Europe. We have already discussed the wage differentials between EU and candidate countries in Chapter 2. In order to cast more light on the social dumping argument, consider Figures 7.1 and 7.2 on earnings and labour costs, that is, costs for the enterprise rather than income for the worker, which usually represent the real variable taken into account by the employer for reasons of competitiveness. Unfortunately the latest figures available from Eurostat are from 1998. Nevertheless, they may help us to get an idea of the scale of the wage and labour cost differentials and to foresee the extent to which they may be used by enterprises alongside and after EU enlargement.

Figures 7.1 and 7.2 compare gross average earnings in industry in selected EU and CEE countries for the two main categories of worker, manual and non-manual. They thus represent the cost to the enterprise of employing these two categories of worker.

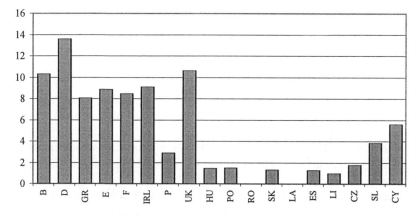

Source: Eurostat.

Figure 7.1 Average gross hourly earnings of manual workers in industry (in euros), CEE and EU Countries, 1998

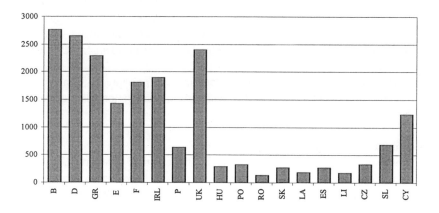

Source: Eurostat.

Figure 7.2 Average gross monthly earnings of non-manual workers in industry (in euros), CEE and EU Countries, 1998

They first show how far wages for manual workers in CEE countries fall short of wages in the EU. Gross hourly earnings in Hungary, for instance, had not by the end of 1998 reached one-quarter of the average earnings of the manual labour force in the UK, Belgium, or Germany. These figures probably underestimate the differences in net earnings, first because workers in Central and Eastern Europe are often not paid – if at all – for extra working time (as they are in the EU), and secondly because income taxes are often much higher in CEE than in EU countries.

Earnings differentials were found to be even greater for skilled employees, although the situation is changing quickly. In most EU countries, non-manual workers were paid in 1998 more than five times the amount that their colleagues in Central and Eastern Europe get. This is not the case for manual workers, for whom a catching-up process has already started. Figure 7.2 shows that manual workers were in 1998 already better paid in Slovenia (EUR3.88 per hour) than in Portugal (EUR2.98). As for manual workers, differences in net earnings for non-manual workers may be even larger, not only because of heavier income taxes in Central and Eastern Europe but also because employees in the EU receive additional benefits and payments (such as profit-sharing, shares, individual bonuses) that are rarely available from CEE companies.

There are large differences among CEE countries themselves, average gross monthly wages for non-manual employees varying from EUR117 in Romania to EUR325 in the Czech Republic, EUR349 in Poland, and more than EUR750 in Slovenia, which has clearly taken the lead among CEE countries in terms of wages and incomes.

These differences, which confirm data for 2000 presented in Chapter 2 but from the employers' side, should be taken into consideration when discussing the possible effects of enlargement.

Non-wage costs or indirect costs
However, the main conclusion here is that differentials between EU and candidate countries are much lower when labour costs rather than wage levels are taken into account. This partly reflects the important share of non-wage costs in total labour costs in candidate countries, generally above the EU average.

For instance, in Hungary extremely high indirect costs to be paid by employers (37.8 per cent, including 31 per cent for social contributions) are often quoted as a factor that reduces the competitiveness of Hungarian enterprises and also limits the attractiveness of the country to foreign investors. This has induced the Hungarian government to reduce charges on enterprises.

The current process of systematically reducing employers' contributions has been described by some analysts as 'social dumping' on the part of

Table 7.1 Comparison of labour cost structures, EU and CEE countries, 1996

	Direct costs	Indirect costs	
		total	employer's social contributions
Hungary	62.2	37.8	31.4
Poland	62.2	37.8	26.9
Romania	73.8	26.2	21.7
Slovakia	71.0	29.0	26.2
Latvia	–	–	–
Estonia	71.7	28.3	–
Lithuania	74.6	25.4	22.6
Bulgaria	–	–	–
Czech Republic	70.8	29.2	25.5
Slovenia	76.4	23.6	11.1
Belgium	67.4	32.6	30.7
Germany	74.3	25.7	23.7
Greece	76.0	24.0	22.9
Spain	73.6	26.4	25.0
France	66.9	33.1	29.2
Ireland	82.7	17.3	14.4
Portugal	75.3	24.7	20.8
UK	84.0	16.0	12.8
EU15	*74.7*	*25.3*	*22.7*

Source: Eurostat.

Central and Eastern European countries. We shall see later that non-wage costs are much more dependent on government policy than wage costs, which reflect more directly the economic situation and the bargaining power of the actors (employers, trade unions).

A race to the bottom or rapid convergence?
In the face of such differentials in terms of both wage and non-wage costs, the first question is whether the competitive advantage of the candidate countries – and especially of those from Central and Eastern Europe – will remain significant for the foreseeable future and so constitute a long-term comparative advantage, and especially whether a 'race to the bottom' to reduce wage- and

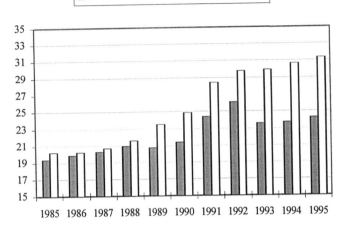

Note: * EU10 excluding Greece for which data are not available.

Source: Eurostat.

Figure 7.3 Catching-up process in average gross earnings between Portugal and the EU, 1985–95 (Portuguese average/EU10* in %)

non-wage costs as much as possible is taking place or, on the contrary, a progressive convergence upward will occur. This may give us some idea of the extent of this source of social dumping and its prevalence over time.

For this purpose, it is instructive to analyse what type of catching-up process operated after the previous accession of less developed economies, for instance, Portugal.

As an indication, Figure 7.3 presents earnings differentials between Portugal and the EU since its accession in 1986. It shows a rather slow adjustment process, earnings in Portugal having increased only from 20 per cent to 30 per cent of the EU average in a period of almost 10 years, although the process seems to have been slightly faster for non-manual employees.
Figure 7.4, which presents the catching-up process of real earnings per employee, also confirms that this process has been rather slow for Spain and Greece, although they are much closer to the EU average.

From this experience, it can be predicted that the earnings catching-up process may also be slow in the candidate countries of Central and Eastern Europe: the delay before the EU average is approached is likely to be around 15–20 years, and there is every reason to believe that they will remain significantly below that average, as is the case with Portugal today. On the other hand, the process may be more rapid for the Central and Eastern European

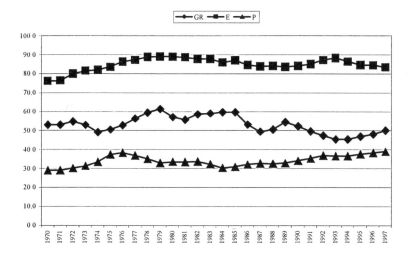

Source: AMECO.

Figure 7.4 Real earnings per employee in Greece, Spain, and Portugal relative to EU average, 1970–97

countries compared to Portugal due to a number of conditions specific to the region. First, starting earnings are much lower in CEE, and the differences with the EU are thus significantly greater; secondly, Central and Eastern Europe achieved price liberalisation within a few years – which continues to have an effect on price increases – and this should lead to a more rapid increase in nominal wages (although experience so far shows much quicker and higher increases in prices than in nominal wages); thirdly, the fact that 10 candidates from Central and Eastern Europe will join the EU may create more interrelations in earnings in countries in the region that may follow the same upward trend. The mass influx of foreign companies – which traditionally pay above the national average – into Central and Eastern Europe, but also new member states from the Mediterranean, will also play a role in wage harmonisation across Europe.

However, even in the case of a relatively faster catching-up process for CEE countries compared to Portugal, there is no reason to believe that the former's comparative labour cost advantage will vanish overnight.

7.3.3 Unit Labour Costs: The Real Source of Competitive Advantage?

Generally speaking, it is not wage or labour costs overall, but rather unit labour costs – defined as labour costs per worker divided by labour productivity – which are normally said to constitute the real variable of competitive-

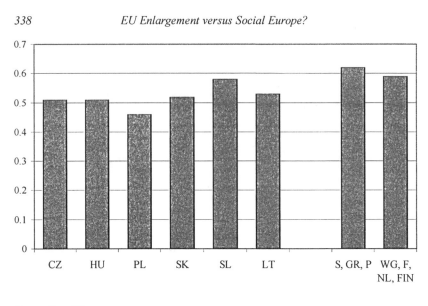

Source: Eurostat.

Figure 7.5 Unit labour costs in CEE countries and EU member states, 1996

ness for an enterprise. The picture on unit labour costs generally presents a different story than the one on wages, with the initial comparative advantage of lower wages tending to be compensated by similarly much lower productivity levels (this in principle tends to have the effect of homogenising unit labour costs across the EU). This is confirmed by Figure 7.5 which compares unit labour costs in Central and Eastern Europe and in the EU. Differences remain between EU and candidate countries, but they are less sharp than hitherto. While unit labour costs in the three Mediterranean countries of Spain, Greece, and Portugal remain above the average in Northern EU countries – for instance, Germany, Denmark, Finland, France, and the Netherlands – all Central and Eastern European countries seem to be benefiting from lower unit labour costs, although not significantly.

Great differences are also observed among Central and Eastern European countries: while Slovenia had nearly reached the level of Northern EU countries as early as 1996, unit labour costs were much lower in Poland and, to a minor extent, in the Czech Republic or Hungary. This is partly due to the higher wage levels in Slovenia. These differences should lead us to analyse wage and unit labour costs country by country rather than by comparing two large regions (EU and CEE) that contain countries at very different economic levels.

The main result, however, is that the differences between member states and candidate countries in terms of unit labour costs are much smaller than differences in wages and earnings suggest. In fact, we saw in Chapter 2 that a comparison of wage levels shows a gap of 1 to 10; this was reduced to 1 to 3 when we took into account earnings, that is, an approximate measure of labour costs for enterprises; the gap becomes marginal when productivity differences are integrated as well. This may prompt us to reassess the importance of wage differentials within the framework of EU enlargement: since lower wages and labour costs seem to be nearly fully compensated by productivity levels, they should in principle not play a crucial role in the relocation strategies of EU enterprises.

However, at this point it is important to nuance this conclusion somewhat since we believe that it would not reflect the real world of relocations by EU multinational companies in candidate countries, which generally count on a rapid increase in productivity through importing to the host country, generally at low cost, the production technology required to attain the same productivity level as in the home country. This is why they take into account mainly current differences in wage levels rather than unit labour costs, which they expect to be reduced quite rapidly in any case. The wage variable is thus the one taken into account – together with the presence of a high-quality labour force – as the main source of competitiveness (an argument that we further develop in Chapter 8).

Clearly, all other working conditions, such as working time, and health and safety, influence labour costs and thus have both direct and indirect effects. They do not necessarily always work in the same direction, however – there are trade-offs. For example, while better working conditions may increase total costs, they may also increase workers' motivation and overall enterprise efficiency, and so contribute to reducing rather than increasing unit labour costs.

7.3.4 Social Protection: Increasingly Used As an Adjustment Variable

Other policies that can have an influence on the reduction of labour costs obviously represent other potential sources of social dumping. We must include here all those practices aimed at enhancing the competitiveness of a national economy by means of reducing or preventing growth of social and employment protection. Employers have always stressed the negative consequences of social charges for their competitiveness in external markets. This can only become more acute when exchange-rate competition becomes non-existent after the adoption of the euro: social contributions of employers will be among the few possible adaptation variables left.

Traditionally, competitiveness has always been closely related to the level of social protection enjoyed by the citizens of a country. The effects of social protection levels may be twofold.

1. On the one hand, the financing of social protection is part of the enterprise's labour costs, so that it may reduce its competitiveness if the enterprise is obliged to raise prices or reduce benefits to cover it. Another way of reducing employer contributions and thus labour costs in the recent past has been the trend to charge workers with social contributions, so diminishing their real income, a practice that can also be assimilated to social dumping. Governments promote social dumping of this kind by enabling firms to reduce their 'non-wage labour costs' by legislation that cuts obligations on employers, or that makes it easier for firms to bypass such obligations, or by changes in labour relations.
2. On the other hand, expenditure on social policy may be conducive to an improvement in workers' motivation and quality of work, and thus lead to increased competitiveness. The good competitiveness in international markets of enterprises from Scandinavian countries, which have also developed the most comprehensive social policies and highest levels of social protection and wealth redistribution, have certainly indicated the possibility of developing a virtuous circle in this regard.

However, this last argument has generally not been emphasised by mainstream, neo-liberal economics, which has placed at the top of most national agendas around the world a progressive reduction in social expenditure and a radical change in their financial structures, something which also reached the Scandinavian countries in the late 1990s.

The evolution of expenditure on social protection generally faithfully reflects such new policy directions. This depends directly on government choices, which thus represent a key agent in fuelling or limiting social protection as a source of social dumping.

While expenditure on social protection grew significantly in all EU member states during the 1950s, 1960s, and 1970s it then stabilised and even started to decrease in many countries. We have seen in Chapter 3 that this shift has taken place even more radically in the accession countries.

This has led to a 'social security dumping' that Albert and Standing (2000, p. 100) define as 'the extent to which transfers and services in social protection schemes are reduced or restructured by shifting the burden of financing. The main tendencies here are shifts from universalism and social insurance to selectivity and "social safety nets"'. We saw that recent trends in social protection in most candidate countries have taken precisely this direction and should thus be expected to lead to more of this type of social dumping in the course of the EU enlargement process and afterwards. We have noticed that these countries have done both, curtailing standards of social protection – with a general decrease in social expenditure ratios – while also changing the financing structures of their social security schemes in a way that shifted the burden from employers and reduced the cost of labour. We must also add that employers' contributions as indirect employers' costs in candidate countries, although high as a proportion of low direct employers' wage costs, are already not as high as in some EU member states, for instance in Italy (45 per cent), the Netherlands (42 per cent), France, and Sweden (32 per cent) (see Leppik 2000, p. 18). Nevertheless, the pension reforms described in Chapter 3 are going in the same direction as in the EU, with the introduction of variations of defined-contribution savings programmes to replace or complement state-sponsored Pay As You Go-defined benefit plans.

Social expenditure also varies to an important degree not only between candidate countries but also between EU countries. Within the EU, the level of social protection is clearly the lowest in the UK and Ireland, and the highest – although also on the decrease – in the Scandinavian countries of Sweden, Finland, and Denmark, relatively high in continental countries such as France, Germany, Belgium, the Netherlands, and Austria, and relatively lower in the Mediterranean countries of Portugal, Spain, Greece, and Italy. Enterprises from countries with relatively high social protection have a tendency to engage most in social dumping and relocations of production to other, more attractive locations, as it seems today to be the case of Scandinavian enterprises investing in the Baltic countries. They can also lead to a larger grey economy, as in Sweden where it represents 20 per cent of GDP according to the OECD (Assemblée Nationale 2000, p. 34).

According to figures on social expenditure, there seems to be a gap, for instance, between Greece, where 16 per cent of GDP is spent on social expenditure and Finland, with a corresponding rate of 35 per cent. We saw in Chapter 3 that social expenditure also varies in Central and Eastern Europe, with rates above 25 per cent in Slovenia, whilst countries like Bulgaria, Romania, but also Hungary remain below 20 per cent, that is, under the EU average.

In the future member states, it is obvious that the radical removal of much social expenditure previously covered by the state or by enterprises represents an important source of social dumping, and often an attempt – sometimes not even concealed by the authorities – to gain in international competitiveness. Our views contradict the conclusion, for instance, of Deacon (2000) according to whom the social dumping argument would be inadequate to explain the situation in Central and Eastern European countries.[4]

A low absolute level of social protection can clearly act as a factor in social dumping, and motivate labour migration in search of better wages and

---

4. Deacon's strong conclusion, however, seems to be drawn from initial data on the transition and does not seem to have incorporated the latest changes that clearly downsized social protection expenditure in these countries.

incomes, but also better social protection systems. At the same time, lower employer social security contributions can also be a factor in attracting foreign investment.

7.3.5 Social Regulations

Gaps in working conditions and social regulations in general can clearly constitute another major source of social dumping. Even within the current EU member states, the differences are sometimes large: for instance in terms of working time, between the 35-hour working week in France and the 48-hour average working week in the UK, Ireland, Germany, and Italy;[5] or in terms of rules for individual layoffs, with strong constraints in Portugal, Spain, and Luxembourg, and the greatest flexibility in the UK, Belgium, and Ireland; or in terms of temporary work contracts, which are widely used in Ireland, the UK, the Netherlands, Austria, and Denmark, and under stricter control in Belgium, Greece, and France.

The integration of candidate countries will obviously increase such diversity. We have seen in previous chapters how some future members are evolving toward greater flexibility as regards working conditions and employment contracts. These differences in working conditions combined with an absence of social dialogue are contributing to leave the ground at local level to individual employers' initiatives; they are also likely to induce them to use lower wages and labour standards as a competitive tool. They may also be used as a source of unfair competitiveness or social dumping.

This is particularly the case since joining the EU, but also after EMU imposed strict economic criteria and limited the possibilities for using macroeconomic variables such as devaluation and exchange-rate policy as competitive tools. This level of constraint may not leave much freedom to enterprises to keep their profitability margins and remain competitive. Labour costs and labour conditions may thus again become the element on which to build flexibility, thus directing enterprises towards a lower level of social policy even if this strategy may not be the most profitable one in the long run.

7.3.6 Social Dialogue and Free Collective Bargaining

We have already documented this in depth in Chapter 5. What it is important to underline here is that the absence of practices of social dialogue or any efforts from public authorities or enterprises to circumvent basic rights in this field may indeed represent social dumping. The absence of social dialogue is generally related to other sources of social dumping, such as working condi-

---

5. 48 hours, that is the maximum level authorised by the EC Directive on working time.

tions, labour contracts, and so on, since it represents a way for the employer to avoid any interference from workers' representatives in its labour practices.

In fact, the law can provide social partners with wider or narrower competences in terms of wage fixing, but also working regulations. Great differences exist between future member states, as between current EU countries, for instance in terms of recognition of the social partners, trade union membership, and so on. On the one hand, in countries such as the UK in the 1980s, the removal of social dialogue and trade union rights was clearly followed as a strategy to improve enterprise flexibility and competitiveness within the framework of a general liberal economic policy. On the other hand, social dialogue differences have not always led to significant social dumping. As an example, we should report that very large differentials in trade union membership – for instance between less than 10 per cent in France and more than 50 per cent in Sweden, Finland and Denmark – did not seem to have motivated significant social dumping within the EU (Assemblée Nationale 2000, p. 28).

Obviously, the transposition of the Community *acquis* on social dialogue may contribute to limiting the possibility of using differentials in the field of social dialogue as a significant source of social dumping and competitive advantage.

7.4 RECENT CASES IN SENSITIVE SECTORS

In recent years, a number of cases of social dumping have caught the attention of the media. Although these cases are just the tip of the iceberg – the rest remain hidden and go unreported by the press – they have helped to reveal the existence of such a strategy among employers within the framework of the EU enlargement process. We present here a few cases that clearly reflect some of the arguments developed earlier.

First, they tend to confirm that social dumping can involve not only illegal practices, but also cases where there is legal employment but under working conditions that amount to unfair competition. The two companies Kralowetz and Betz illustrate this strategy – on different sides of the line separating legality and illegality – as implemented by road transport companies.

Secondly, the cases below also confirm that there is great demand for migrant workers, under worse – and so less costly – working conditions than domestic workers, especially in sectors where there is a ready supply, as in construction, or where competition is particularly tough, as in road or maritime transport and civil aviation, where the differentials between EU and candidate countries can turn out to be highly profitable and are thus particularly attractive. In such activities – especially if their internationalisation increases the difficulty of monitoring them – social dumping may well be pursued on a large scale.

Thirdly, the following examples also show that the role of governments is not neutral with regard to social dumping: by allowing particular practices to develop, providing the appropriate legal framework, or failing to combat unfair competition based on much poorer working conditions, they encourage enterprises to base their operations on social dumping. For instance, it is in the power of governments to demonstrate to companies how important work permits or respect for labour rights are.

7.4.1 Employing Illegal CEE Drivers in the EU: The Austrian Company Kralowetz

The first example provided here is in the road transport sector. In January 2002, a major scandal arose in the press concerning the Austrian company Kralowetz, an international road haulage firm which was found to be employing illegally hundreds of drivers from Central and Eastern Europe. Although the company had its main operations in Austria, and affiliates in eight European countries (including Luxembourg, Germany, Austria, and Spain), it located its head office in the second largest city in Luxembourg, Esch-sur-Alzette, where dispatching was carried out. The evidence suggests that Kralowetz had a fleet of approximately 700 lorries delivering around Europe (most of them with Luxembourg number plates), with 350 white-collar staff and 800 drivers from Central and Eastern Europe who received their instructions from Luxembourg. In other words, the drivers were registered in Luxembourg, but were working elsewhere. The company was operating under the name United Cargo Lines, which was itself made up, as already mentioned, of eight separate enterprises with European subsidiaries, notably Soteco and United Cargolux.

In January 2002, searches were carried out in Kralowetz agencies in eight countries at the request of the Public Prosecutor's Office in Munich, Germany, which was investigating the suspected illegal employment of non-EU nationals. On 23 January 2002, the Luxembourg Criminal Investigation Department arrested one of the company's directors, Karl Kralowetz, on an international warrant, so signalling the end of the company. On February 2002, the two major Kralowetz companies were declared bankrupt (because they had become insolvent) by the Luxembourg Tribunal of Commerce.

'Modern-day slavery'
When the scandal broke, most of the drivers had not been paid for three months, and their only recourse was to drive their vehicles back to Luxembourg. The 164 Kralowetz lorries registered in Luxembourg re-entered

the country and were placed in a large parking area. The drivers, who had been living a precarious existence for weeks with little or nothing to eat, were looked after by the Red Cross and Caritas, which provided them with food and lodging in a variety of centres.

It emerged from the investigation that most of the 800 drivers from Central and Eastern European countries were not registered with Luxembourg's social security scheme: most had only a tourist visa and their had employer required them to enrol in the social security system of their home country. Before hiring them, the company also made them sign undated resignation letters.

The drivers were mainly paid by the kilometre, which is also illegal, for the token amount of euro 0.1 per kilometre (that is, 1 euro per 100 km!). Others reported being paid 5 euros per hour, if they were paid at all. Some drivers had also been required to sign a leasing agreement for use of the lorry, obliging them to work day and night in order to repay the money.[6] Many of them found themselves in debt to their employer. The drivers reported driving 30 000 kilometres a month, working 16–20 hours a day with a total lack of hygiene or safety. No holidays or rest days were allowed. Tachograph discs and other official documentation had allegedly been tampered with. In the case of errors (fines, accidents, delays, overconsumption of petrol, and so on) significant deductions were made from drivers' salaries. At the same time, each lorry was equipped with a computer to allow the drivers to communicate constantly with the enterprise. Between 800 and 1 500 drivers from Central and Eastern Europe (mainly from Bulgaria, Romania, Czech Republic, and Slovakia, but also Ukraine) worked for the company in such conditions. This policy enabled Kralowetz to register an annual turnover of euro 1.24 million.

It is clear that Luxembourg – which has always prided itself on its 'top-of-the-range' social system – has allowed itself to become a 'social dumping zone'.

Public authorities' responsibilities: a permissive policy

The Kralowetz case became a major political controversy in Luxembourg due to the serious shortcomings in the monitoring of international transport companies registered there.

What is most amazing about the Kralowetz case, however, is not the willingness of an EU company to engage in illegal employment practices, since the temptation is always there to take advantage of wage and social differentials, but how the government of Luxembourg could allow this situation to continue for so long. In particular, the Kralowetz case reveals a very permis-

---

6. A Ukrainian driver reported: 'Kralowetz made me sign a leasing contract for the truck. To pay for it, I had to drive day and night. Sometimes even 30 000 km per month. I was drinking five or six litres of coffee per day to keep awake. I was sleeping less than 25 hours a week. And all this for 170 euros. I reckon some slaves were better off.' Reported in *Tageblatt* (3 February 2002).

sive policy with regard to foreign road transport companies, which is likely to be the reason why they attract this type of company.

First of all, conditions are much more favourable in Luxembourg: not only is the transport legislation much more flexible than in other countries, but the vehicle registration taxes are among the lowest in the EU.

Secondly, the lack of requirements (no work visa or work permit requested, transport authorisation easily obtained, and so on) in relation to enterprises locating their head office in Luxembourg is also obvious; in fact, it has been seen as the main reason why the country has become a sort of 'letter box' for European enterprises.

Thirdly, there is evidence that successive governments knew what was going on, yet did not intervene. For the President of the Luxembourg Confederation of Independent Trade Unions (OGB-L), 'for over ten years now, the union has been denouncing abuses associated with enterprises like Kralowetz to successive governments, but without action being taken'. As early as 1998, complaints were being made against Kralowetz, and the Kralowetz file is today several thousand pages long.[7] It has been argued that the Luxembourgian ministers and administrations concerned were aware of Kralowetz's alleged criminal action, but did nothing and passed the matter back and forth on the grounds that the affair should be dealt with exclusively by the Ministry of Justice.

A whole series of ministries and officials seem to have been involved in implementing this permissive policy. For this reason a parliamentary commission of inquiry has been set up and the ministers (both past and present) of labour, of transport, and of small enterprises, traders and agriculture have been interrogated. As far as the Ministry of Transport is concerned, the way in which transport permits are granted is under investigation. Amazingly, the Ministry of Transport was still awarding licences to Kralowetz in late 2001 when the company's managing director was fined euro 10 000 for breaches of EU law; however, the Minister of Transport has always emphasised the good financial situation of the enterprise, as if this should be the only relevant criterion for authorisation.

Furthermore, in relation to the Ministry of Labour, migrant workers seem to have been allowed in without any obligation to acquire a Luxembourg work permit if they stated that they were working beyond the borders.

It is also significant that the whole affair was 'officially' discovered and thus made public because of an official German request rather than on the initiative of the Luxembourgian authorities. The General Secretary of the

---

7. See special coverage of the issue by *L'investigateur*, 'Le Dossier "Kralowetz"', Dossiers <www.gouvernement.lu/gouv/fr/doss/kralowetz>. See also the special issue of *Tageblatt*, 'Routiers: Les routiers de Kralowetz lésés', <www.tageblatt.lu/themes>.

European Transport Workers' Federation (ETF) summarised the situation in the following terms:

> For the Luxembourg government, it is obviously more important to host lots of transport companies than to control what actually happens on their territory.[8]

Many companies have relocated in Luxembourg in order to take advantage of the flexibility which exists there, but without engaging in any economic activity in the country.

According to the main Luxembourgian road transport trade union, there are more than 6 000 foreign companies – most of them Danish, German, Belgian, Austrian, and French – present in Luxembourg.[9]

Other dubious cases have already been identified. A second case of 'social dumping' was uncovered, again by German inspectors, involving another Austrian transport company, Transdanubia, located in the town of Bettembourg. Most of the drivers, almost all from Hungary, seem to have been without any work authorisation and also to be working in terrible conditions. The same seems to apply to the Austrian road transport company Frikus, thus shedding light on the existence of a real 'social dumping connection' in road transport in Luxembourg.

However, this strategy seems widespread in road transport also in other EU countries. According to Georg Eberl, Secretary of the Austrian transport trade union (HTV), '80 per cent of Austrian enterprises in road transport do not pay wages in accordance with regulations'.

According to a report by the Dutch transport inspectorate (Rijksverkeersinspectie) on the use of cheap drivers from Central and Eastern Europe, half of the thirty companies inspected were violating national law. As a result, transport prices had fallen by 30 per cent. The Dutch Hauliers' Federation (TLN) has admitted to the press that between ten and twenty Dutch carriers employed drivers from Eastern Europe to drive vehicles registered in the Netherlands.[10] According to the General Secretary of the European Transport Workers' Federation, 'the situation is replicated all over Europe'.

Following the Kralowetz case, the European Parliament adopted a resolution (7 February 2002 on the 'situation of lorry drivers stranded in Luxembourg'), mainly to harmonise road transport regulations throughout the EU.

---

8. See 'Luxembourg is Everywhere!', European Transport Workers' Federation (ETF).
9. Report prepared by the Conseil National des Transports (CNT – French National Transport Council), *Relocation Activities in the Transport Sector*, Social Committee (Paris: CNT, 2000), 41 pages.
10. See *Verkehrsrundschau* (November 2000).

7.4.2 Using a Candidate Country as a Base: The Expansion Strategy of Willy Betz

Another significant example from road transport, which again hit the headlines, is the German carrier Willy Betz, which managed to implement a social dumping strategy while remaining more or less within the law.

Willy Betz, whose head offices are in Reutlingen, Baden-Württemberg, is an international road haulage company with 7 000 employees, 4 500 vehicles, a large number of subsidiaries across Europe, and a turnover of euro 0.7 billion. Over the years, it seems to have built up its competitive position mainly by employing drivers from Eastern Europe.

The key move for Willy Betz consisted in acquiring a solid basis in Central and Eastern Europe through the purchase in 1997 of Somat, the former Eastern bloc carrier based in Bulgaria, and its subsidiaries (also in Romania), which it had started to acquire in 1994. Capitalising on its links with Mercedes, whose vehicles it imports into Bulgaria, Willy Betz modernised its vehicle fleet. The company retained over 2 000 drivers from Bulgaria, and other countries in which Somat had subsidiaries, to carry goods, also within the EU. How did it pursue such a strategy without breaking the rules?

The letter of the law

Apparently, it is relatively simple: the company uses an Eastern European driver (for instance, from Bulgaria) to work in a country (for instance, France, Italy, or Spain) other than the one where the vehicle is registered (for instance, Germany), under an ECMT licence or a certified copy of the EU licence issued by the country where it is actually registered (in this case Germany). The vehicle is never used in the country where it is registered (Germany), so that inspectors (in France, Spain, and so on) cannot check whether the Bulgarian driver is employed by the German company (in fact, he is employed by the Bulgarian affiliate, with Bulgarian wages and working conditions).

Willy Betz makes most of its vehicles, together with the appropriate permits, available to its Bulgarian subsidiary. These vehicles are driven by Bulgarian drivers for haulage operations outside the country in which they are registered (because otherwise checks could be made in that country), but are none the less chartered by the home establishment, all operations in fact being managed from head office in Reutlingen through modern satellite and internet tracking and communications.

This system – a so-called 'custom-built' operation – which cannot be checked has allowed the German company to employ Eastern European drivers on haulage routes where it is in direct competition with EU carriers employing EU nationals as drivers. In 1999, of Willy Betz's 8 000 drivers, 4 000 were Bulgarians, being paid Bulgarian wages (or slightly above).

It has been calculated that this helps to reduce the (drivers') wage share of total operating costs from 35 to 14 per cent, increasing the profit margin by over 10 per cent.[11] Other EU carriers cannot compete with such a strategy.

In addition to distorting competition between road haulage firms, this strategy clearly has an impact on working conditions. The number of hours each driver is on the road has been reported as being much greater, which apart from anything else entails a clear risk in terms of road safety. The drivers, generally grouped in crews, are divided up and reassembled at the border to avoid checks. Not only their wages but also their working conditions are much worse than those of their EU colleagues: they generally drive the lorries around the clock, one driver sleeping while his colleague drives.

This system at best observes the letter of the law,[12] but takes advantage of the fact that it would be virtually impossible for the police or inspectors to keep a check on its activities or to do anything about them. It also clearly profits from the lack of proper EU regulations in this sector. Other companies have been found to be pursuing the same policy: for instance, RH Transport Services of Nottingham seems to be using Slovakian subcontractors – with drivers mainly from Slovakia and Estonia – to undertake internal EU work.[13] Similarly, the Dutch company Foodtransport (providing transport for the multinational company Amylum) was found to be employing – and to be exploiting under terrible working conditions – Lithuanian drivers through its subcontracting transport firm Hoja.[14]

A possible response
Clearly, it is not possible to control transnational operations or the multinational lorries of road transport companies without more Community harmonisation of legislation and monitoring procedures. This is the reason why in June 2000 the European Commission adopted a communication on the working conditions of road hauliers, particularly the working hours of drivers, the rest periods of long-distance drivers, vehicle spot-checks, vocational training, and employment conditions of third-country hauliers.

More recently, a more powerful Community-wide solution has been drawn up, a driver's certificate, which could represent a simple and effec-

11.   See 'Social Dumping in the ECMT Area', Council of Ministers, European Conference of Ministers of Transport (CEMT/CM(2002)13) (22 April 2002).

12.   Op. cit., p. 5, section 'infringements of regulations'.

13.   See Press Release by the Socialist Truck Drivers, Newsletter Socialist Trucker (June 2002).

14.   See 'Esclaves de la route et du dumping social', Newsletter of the Fédération Internationale des Transports Routiers [International Federation of Road Transport] (15 October 2002, sixth International Road Transport day of action).

tive means of verification. A proposal in this direction has been put forward by the European Commission (OJ/EEC/C096E of 27 March 2001), backed up by a report by the European Parliament (TRAN 501 EN).[15] By means of such a certificate it would be possible to ensure that a driver is legally employed in accordance with the regulations in force in the EU member state where the transport operator is registered (not under the regulations of his home country). This new EC regulation (No. 484/2002) shall apply from 19 March 2003. However, we might wonder whether this will be enough to prevent 'imaginative' transport companies such as Willy Betz from employing cheap labour from Central and Eastern Europe, especially after EU accessions make it legal for companies to pay much lower wages to drivers from new EU member countries, who are ready to accept much lower standards.

The social partners – trade unions and employers in the sector – will continue to have a key role in monitoring and preventing this type of social dumping from becoming the rule in this competitive sector; especially in a context in which manufacturing enterprises will have more and more recourse to road transport within the framework of EU enlargement in order to implement their 'just-in-time' systems (providing the goods at the last possible moment to avoid costly stock maintenance).

7.4.3 Social Dumping in Civil Aviation

Relocation of some activities
Civil aviation is also affected by social dumping. In the late 1990s, an increasing number of companies began to relocate all of their accounting and booking activities: Swissair, Lufthansa, Austrian Airlines and British Airways to India (for accounting activities); British Airways (for aircraft maintenance) and Lufthansa (for call centres and aircraft maintenance) to Ireland.

Moving headquarters
Many companies in this sector have also begun to implement a system of transferring – often fictitiously – to more 'favourable' countries the labour contracts of employees who nevertheless continue to work in their home country. This makes it possible to get away with applying less costly social conditions. Many airline companies have also moved their headquarters in order to apply local conditions to their labour force: for example, companies such as Virgin did not hesitate to relocate their headquarters from Belgium to

15. See also the report 'The Effects on the Road Haulage Business of Social Dumping by Operators from Third Countries', European Parliament, Directorate General for Research (DV/432157 EN.doc) (12 February 2001).

Ireland because of the much lower costs and taxes there, and to prepare labour contracts according to Irish law – more than half of the labour contracts of Virgin pilots are today subject to Irish regulations, which are much more advantageous to the employer than Belgian social regulations.

A decline in working conditions

Western airline trade unions are very worried about the potential multiplication of such cases. A general decline in working conditions is being observed in airline companies, especially under pressure of low-cost operators such as EasyJet, Ryanair, or Virgin, which are well known for their poor consideration for social policy (no trade unions, longer working time, lower health and safety standards).

Employing crew from Central and Eastern Europe

More recently, with the opening of Central and Eastern European countries, relocations involving use of flight crew have been noted.

Many airline companies already hire personnel from Central and Eastern Europe. There are a number of ways of doing this, for instance through the 'freighting' – or 'chartering' – system which consists in subcontracting an activity to a foreign enterprise which applies wage and working conditions much lower than those of the original company; this happens when EU airlines call on other companies, on an occasional basis, which use their own crew (and their own plane), generally with lower wages, longer working time, and less constraining safety and working conditions.

For instance, when Austrian Airlines asks the Hungarian airline Malév to do the Budapest–Vienna flight for them, it involves the use not only of a Malév plane, but also of its crew, naturally with (much lower) Hungarian wages and working conditions. It is clear that this will be much more profitable to Austrian Airlines than the same flight carried out under Austrian conditions. This sort of strategy is also resorted to by the Swiss company Crossair, which is employing a number of pilots from, for example, Bulgaria, so circumventing Swiss regulations (according to which Swiss airlines cannot hire foreign pilots or crew under working conditions worse than in Switzerland). EU companies such as Tyrolean Airlines, and many others, seem to be doing the same.

The current spate of alliances and bilateral agreements between big airline companies could lead to a generalisation of such operations. It is clear that in civil aviation, one of the first economic sectors to liberalise, little or nothing currently stands in the way of social dumping.

It is also clear that this type of behaviour will be even more difficult to monitor when applicant countries become part of the EU; many operations of this kind could become everyday practice, perfectly within the law.

The risk is even greater since there may well be immediate migration of pilots from applicant countries: since all pilots are trained in the same language and under the same international safety and flying conditions, pilots from Central and Eastern Europe would have no problem transferring – overnight – to companies such as Austrian Airlines or British Airways.

7.4.4 Illegal Immigrants in German Public Construction

There have been a few cases of illegal employment of workers from Central and Eastern Europe in the construction sector, for example, in Germany on the construction of the new railway line between Cologne and Frankfurt for the ICE high-speed train (Figure 7.6). Due to the heavy workload (204 km, 26 tunnels, 18 bridges), building delays and lack of human resources, a number of elements of this huge project, publicly financed, have been subcontracted to external companies, including companies located in Central and Eastern Europe. A long subcontracting chain has thus been created, without much control over the working conditions of subcontractors. Nearly half of the workers on the project (4 000 in total) are from Central and Eastern Europe; the proportion is even higher for some parts of the work (tunnel building, metal work, and so on).

Many of these workers were found to be working illegally, or at least not to be employed in accordance with legal obligations. In particular, some

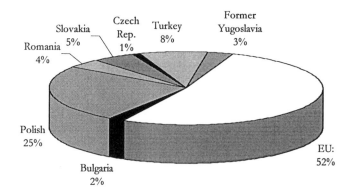

Source: FETBB (2000).

Figure 7.6 Percentage of workers from EU and from candidate countries employed on the project EUROSITE (high-speed train Cologne–Rhine– Main), 2000 (length of project: 21 months)

Romanian and Polish subcontractors were paying only token wages – not remotely comparable with German standards – and also not to be applying the minimum wage regulation (400 such cases have been identified).[16] Specific checks have shown that Central and Eastern European workers were paid less than half of what they were entitled to. The German trade union IG Bau successfully started a legal action against the enterprise POLBAU and others, showing the important role that can be played by trade unions in limiting social dumping practices. All this evidence and multiple cases have been systematically minimised by the German public company Deutsche Bahn. We might also ask how such a large project, supported by public money, did not entail closer monitoring by the German authorities.

7.5 SOCIAL DUMPING AND THE THREE MOBILITIES

Social dumping as a way of gaining competitive ground is clearly intimately related to the different mobilities existing within the European Community: goods and services, capital and labour.[17]

- Social dumping can be generated and have direct effects on the social standards of other countries, first through the trade and movement of goods and services, for instance companies are induced to shift their social standards downward in order to be able to compete.
- Another option for the enterprise is to move its production facilities (to countries with lower standards) in order to produce at lower costs and gain in international competitiveness. Many associate such capital movements with a process of exporting employment – and importing unemployment.
- Another option for the enterprise is to employ at home – legally or illegally – workers from countries which do not have the same requirements in terms of wages and working conditions, thus reflecting from the employers' side a 'demand' for migrant labour. Higher labour standards also attract labour from less developed countries where lower standards prevail, thus creating a 'supply' of migrant labour, or a reserve of workers ready to accept lower working conditions than those prevailing in the more developed country in exchange for conditions that are at least better than those

16. For specific examples of contraventions of the law (in terms of illegal work and working conditions), see the FETBB [European Federation of Building and Woodworking] report (FETBB, 2000), 13 pages.

17. To facilitate the discussion, we present here the mobility of goods and services as one rather than two mobilities, so that, adding the mobilities of capital and of labour, we shall speak in this volume of three rather than four mobilities or freedoms existing in the European Union.

at home. No doubt the matching of the demand and supply of migrant labour from candidate countries may induce EU enterprises to progressively downgrade their existing labour standards.

7.5.1 Capital Movements: Social Standards Motivating Relocation Strategies?

The most common thesis relating to social dumping is that economic liberalisation and structural changes in international and national economic systems have made capital more mobile. This has supposedly increased the power of those in capital markets such that they can exert pressure directly or indirectly on governments to oblige them to roll back social spending and social legislation (Alber and Standing 2000). Governments in particular are trying more and more to adapt their norms to make their economies more attractive to foreign capital investment than those of their competitor countries, something that commentators have called a 'race to the bottom', with countries converging on very low standards of protection.

It is clear that the EU internal market and now the EU enlargement process have amplified the extent and the role of capital movements, including their effects on the social sphere. It is also clear that certain governments from candidate countries have also engaged in a sort of 'race to the bottom' in terms of cuts in 'non-wage labour costs', social spending, but also restricted labour rights, including restrictions on social dialogue and collective bargaining. The example of the request for a derogation in implementing the EC directive on working time from the government of Malta (presented in Chapter 2) mainly under pressure from a few multinational companies is illustrative in this respect. It shows the power of some multinational companies, especially in small economies, that can exert pressure directly or indirectly on governments to oblige them to roll back social legislation or to avoid new provisions intended to give workers and their families protection of one sort or another. Internationalisation of economies and EU enlargement, which will contribute to make capital even more mobile, will not decrease but rather increase the influence of a few large multinational corporations on working and social conditions.

We shall see in Chapter 8 that there were many cases in the 1990s which prove that the relocation threat and social dumping are real and could indeed continue to develop if economic and social gaps are not quickly filled.

The risks of capital relocations pushed the European Parliament to act and to issue a resolution on this issue in 1995.

More recently, a number of questions have been asked in the European Parliament concerning the risks of relocation in the prospect of EU enlargement.

7.5.2 Labour Movements: Abundant and Cheap Reserve Labour Force?

Many economists have pointed out that the most effective way of raising standards for workers in less developed countries would be to allow international migration from low- to high-standard countries (Srinivasan 1995). This argument may also be valid for the current EU enlargement process. Nevertheless, the proponents of harmonising labour standards in the EU have surprisingly been those most fiercely opposed to free migration flows as soon as the candidate countries join the European Union.

It is true that labour migration can lead to many cases of social dumping: if a German company is hiring migrant workers at lower wages and working conditions than German workers, this can be assimilated to social dumping, with a clear objective on the part of the German employer to benefit from the lower demands of migrant workers consequent upon their situation and the much poorer labour standards in their country of origin. This has happened in the past – and is still happening – in the construction sector in Germany, where German unification has given rise to a boom and provoked significant demand for migrant workers moving across the borders. Interestingly, German construction employers have stated on several occasions that they could operate without foreign workers. Early in 1997 there were about 200 000 unemployed German construction workers, and an estimated 500 000 legal and illegal foreign construction workers, including 80 000 British and Irish workers.[18] Since then, there has been a spectacular increase in the number of legal and illegal contracts with workers from Central and Eastern Europe, especially for commuting Polish workers, hired at much lower wages and payroll taxes. The German public railway company was also found to be employing a large number of such illegal workers from Central and Eastern Europe, a case we shall develop in further detail in Chapter 9.

The adoption in March 1996 of the EC directive on posted workers is one answer to social dumping of this kind. EU workers posted to another EU country must usually be paid at least the same wages as local workers from the first day of their employment abroad, with some flexibility during the first month. Trade unions have also been active in preventing social dumping. In the past – for instance during its campaign 'against the World Trade Organisation legalising social dumping in construction' – the European trade union in the construction sector, the IFBWW, has called for ensuring that 'in case of temporary employment higher national labour standards should not be undercut and international labour standards, minimum national labour stan-

18. See Edmund Andrews, 'The Upper Tier of Migrant Labor', *New York Times* (11 December 1996); see also 'Labour Mobility and Social Dumping', *Migration News* 4, No. 1 (January 1997).

dards and existing collective agreements should be respected by all parties to any temporary cross-border movement of workers'.[19]

7.5.3 Movements of Goods and Services: Social Dumping as a Trade Strategy?

If most governments from candidate countries have been particularly active in their negotiations concerning the transposition of many labour regulations, it is mainly because of their fear of seeing their enterprises – through new higher standards – lose competitiveness in international markets, and particularly vis-à-vis EU companies which enjoy high productivity levels and produce high quality products. For instance, we have seen how worried employers from candidate countries are that EU standards on health and safety will be imposed too quickly and too radically, with major implications for their production costs. Lower wage levels, longer working weeks, and lower contributions for social protection continue to represent elements that can help them to partially compensate their lack of productivity and production quality. We shall see in Chapter 10 on trade how far and how differently this strategy has been followed by various candidate countries. One of the key questions we shall try to answer is whether the candidate countries to the European Union have tried – and are still trying – to enhance their international competitiveness above all by reducing the cost of labour, or whether their policies were primarily motivated by the desire to close the gap with other European welfare states and to catch up with the social and working standards attained elsewhere in the EU. We shall also analyse this in terms of trade flows, going into some detail as regards countries and products.

At this stage, however, it is important to conclude that social dumping is indeed motivated by the search for greater competitiveness and that candidate countries today have every incentive to integrate such a policy option, especially in the short to medium term, in order to adapt their production to EU standards in a progressive way, not overnight, and to avoid the emergence of too large a commercial deficit with other countries, especially EU member states.

7.6 CONCLUSION

Fears of social dumping, which emerged with the opening of the single market, have become even more acute with the development of the EU enlargement process to include 13 candidate countries.

---

19. 'IFBWW Campaign against WTO legalizing social dumping in construction'.

The debates over social dumping are symptomatic of a deep 'malaise' within the European Community, due mainly to the fact that European integration has so far been built on an economic policy agenda rather than on a labour and social protection one. Fears increased because of increased differences in the EU with regard to wage costs and social conditions with the addition to the EU of the Southern European countries.

It was thus to be expected that the debate on social dumping would become more and more lively with EU enlargement since the new member states will join with much lower social standards and wage levels. Such huge differentials – by far the largest since the beginning of the European Community – also shed light on the gaps in European social policy and the more general imbalance between the progress made on European integration in the economic sphere and that in the social sphere.

Social dumping is thus crucial to the principal issue addressed in this book: the future of European social policy after EU enlargement.

We have seen that there are many sources of social dumping in both future and current EU member states. In terms of wages, the gap is such that it can only generate significant capital and labour movements, as well as emerging as a key element in the trade of goods and services, particularly because there are good reasons to believe that the catching-up process will take a long time as far as wages are concerned. We have also seen that the differentials are much narrower when non-wage costs are integrated – reducing the gap – and also when productivity is taken into account, the utilisation of unit labour costs reducing the gap even further. Nevertheless, we have also seen that EU companies look rather at wage levels than at productivity – which they can easily increase with new production techniques – in their relocation strategies. Moreover, differences in working conditions, labour practices, and social regulations may also become criteria for enterprise competitiveness in an enlarged EU. Social protection represents another possible source of social dumping, although one very much influenced by the state through its choices on social expenditure, and its structure and form of financing – for instance by employers or increased workers' contributions.

The sources of social dumping analysed here are precisely those seen in previous chapters – wages and other working conditions, social security, forms of employment and labour contracts, social dialogue and workers' participation – in which we have observed serious drawbacks in terms of legislation and practice in candidate countries in comparison with EU member states. Moreover, the difference between formal adoption of the Community *acquis* in the sphere of working conditions and its implementation in practice will undoubtedly represent a major source of social dumping.

All this points clearly to a major risk of social dumping in the years to come.

These social imbalances can only motivate significant capital and labour movements as the date of EU enlargement comes closer. This is probably the reason why many actors and institutions are not at ease with the concept of 'social dumping'. Just as there is no clear definition of social dumping, no systematic information is being collected on it. There is a total absence, for instance, in terms of statistics and studies that may help in assessing the phenomenon of social dumping. There are no precise and up-to-date data on the flows of relocations and transfers of activity between EU countries on the one hand, and between EU countries and non-EU countries on the other. The same situation prevails as regards labour migration and social dumping, and also analysis of the effects of labour migration on employment, and economic and social policies and practices. The European Commission itself has been rather reluctant to address the issues related to social dumping, preferring to ignore the problem and to consider it as an insignificant or marginal phenomenon.

Different perceptions of 'social dumping' among economic and social actors also do not help us to better identify the phenomenon. While, for instance, employers' representatives at EU level generally tend to ignore the problem and present it as non-existent, more radical 'neo-liberal' reformers have a tendency to see social dumping as a healthy force which will oblige countries to lighten the excessive and damaging regulations that they impose on their labour markets. This is an argument that we often meet in future member states. At the opposite extreme, some analysts recommend nearly instantaneous harmonisation of all working conditions, including wage levels.

Certainly, some sort of 'middle way' must be found. While it is essential to fight all forms of social dumping, legal or illegal, enterprises must also be in a position to operate under the best possible conditions in the formal sector, and not forced into relying wholly or in part on illegal or informal activities. They must also be put in a position to remain competitive internationally.

At the same time, we must also analyse the three movements under study here in a more dynamic and long-term perspective, for the economy of an enlarged EU and its individual members, and in a more global perspective. This is what we propose to do in more detail in the next three chapters, dedicated to the movements of capital, labour, and goods and services which we may expect alongside EU enlargement, and their respective effects in both the economic and the social field.

In the next three chapters we address the social dumping question from the perspectives of the three freedoms, and in particular try to answer three basic and related questions:

1. Are the candidate countries being used for social dumping by foreign and local investors and enterprises, especially alongside the EU enlargement process?

2. Are the governments of candidate countries trying to pursue a social dumping strategy or to converge upwards towards EU standards?
3. What are the possibilities and probabilities of social dumping alongside the forthcoming integration of candidate countries into the EU, in terms of capital movements, labour movements, and trade of goods and services? And what will their implications be?

While responding to these questions, we shall try as far as possible to scrutinise the three mobilities together. For instance, capital movements from EU countries to candidate countries may contribute to limiting the labour movement expected from candidate countries to EU member states.

Social dumping and cutting labour costs often reflect the desire of governments and enterprises to increase their trade balance – that is, to boost export competitiveness and their capacity to limit the flood of imported consumer goods. At the same time, trade flows will obviously be influenced by capital and labour movements. Foreign investment, for instance, obviously can improve or deteriorate trade flows depending on whether they increase exports more than imports or the reverse. Conversely, an improved economic situation in future member states also reflected in better trade flows can reduce the incentive for their populations to migrate to current EU member states.

Only an overall vision of different types of mobility and of differentials in the various social areas may help us to provide a coherent vision of the social dumping risks to be expected along with EU enlargement.

8. Capital Mobility: Massive Relocations

8.1 INTRODUCTION

In the EU enlargement process, as happened during the completion of the single European market in January 1993, firms' location strategies are once again in the limelight. Since wage costs and standards of social protection are lower in future member states, this expansion of trade and economic activity may lead to further strengthening of specialisation based on comparative advantage, notably with 'social dumping' to take advantage of lower labour costs by those companies – including from the current EU – operating from the future member states, with a risk of downsizing social policy in all EU enterprises.

On the other hand, the accelerated flows of capital expected – and already observed – with EU enlargement are perceived as a general step that will also help EU firms to achieve competitiveness and profitability gains through channelling resources toward the most productive jobs and, through rationalisation and relocation in future new member states, by fully using economies of scale in an enlarged single market of more than 500 million people. These capital movements are also seen as a key factor in catching up on the part of new member countries, and thus an essential lever for economic growth and so also social standards.

However, trade unions – particularly in current EU countries – are worried about the adjustments that will be required as a result of this process. Does EU enlargement threaten employment in the more highly developed regions? Candidate countries are also concerned about an economic development that would be driven only by foreign investment, especially in already established – and generally lower value-added – industrial sectors.

EU enterprises have not been waiting for the accession of the first candidate countries to relocate part of their production, and this process can only be expected to accelerate after the first accessions.

The aim of this chapter is to try to identify, in accordance with a global picture of direct foreign investment in candidate countries, whether significant relocations are taking place, and if so, to determine their causes, the sectors affected, and also their economic and social implications both for home (EU) and host (candidate) countries. Particular emphasis will be put on the social effects of such capital movements, in terms of industrial relations, social protection, forms of employment, and social standards in general.

8.2 FEARS CONCERNING INDUSTRIAL RELOCATION

Throughout the 1990s there were a number of cases of enterprises transferring or even closing down their activities and shedding jobs for reasons related to social regulations. For instance in 1993, Hoover, which had been producing vacuum cleaners in Longvy, Burgundy (France), decided to move to Scotland, shedding 600 jobs. Working standards accepted by Scottish trade unions, such as a wage freeze, longer working hours, and lower insurance schemes had influenced the management's decision.

More recently, Renault's decision in 1997 to close its automobile factory in Vilvorde (Belgium) sent shock waves throughout Europe, revealing the profound vulnerability of the workers but also the public authorities,[1] to management strategic decisions. Layoffs threatened 3 000 employees, and there was a massive mobilisation of trade unions from different EU countries, with nearly 100 000 French and Belgian people demonstrating in the streets of Brussels on 16 March 1997. The closure of the factory that finally occurred is a good example of a relocation motivated by labour costs, as we shall explain later. It also represented a good example of violation by the management of its obligations in terms of workers' information and consultation.

The EU enlargement process has clearly generated new fears that the same strategies will be followed by EU companies. Compared to the previous accession of Southern countries (Spain and Portugal), the larger differentials, in terms of wages and social standards, and also the much larger potential extension of the EU market, can only lead to much more numerous and systematic relocation strategies.

A few examples have attracted the attention of the media. In October 1999, Philips announced plans to move production of energy-efficient light bulbs from its plant in Terneuzen in the Netherlands to Poland, a relocation of production entailing the loss of 280 jobs out of the total 500 at the plant. The employees of the Terneuzen production plant went on strike and at the end of January 2000, all 6 200 employees of the light-bulb manufacturing division of Philips planned a national protest at Philips's head office in Eindhoven. The management, however, stuck to its decision, stating that relocation of production to Poland was inevitable and that the Terneuzen unit was not sufficiently profitable. Paradoxically, in 1998, the management had announced that the same Terneuzen plant would become 'the Philips knowledge-centre for energy-efficient light bulbs'.[2]

----

1. Both the Belgian and the French Prime Ministers, Mr Dehaene and Mr Jospin, under pressure from domestic public opinion, tried to put pressure on the Director General of Renault to change his decision, without any success.

2. See 'Relocation dispute at Philips', in *European Industrial Relations Review*, No. 313 (February 2000), p. 9.

In 2000, a serious case of social dumping emerged as the press revealed the Europe-wide practices of German transport company Willy Betz, which had created a network of lorry drivers from Central and Eastern Europe – through locating part of its enterprise in Bulgaria – employed at much lower rates and under terrible working conditions (see Chapter 7). In this way the company was able to gain a tremendous competitive advantage vis-à-vis its competitors in the European Union.

These examples illustrate how the social differentials between EU member states and candidate countries could be used as a source of unfair competition or social dumping. Many more examples of this type could be cited. They all show that the problem is real and that this type of behaviour could indeed represent a threat to Social Europe.

The aim of this chapter is to identify whether these few examples presented in the press are only isolated cases or whether they reveal a profound strategic shift of EU companies' operations towards candidate countries, especially those from Central and Eastern Europe.

8.3 DIRECT FOREIGN INVESTMENT IN FUTURE MEMBER STATES

No doubt the fall of the Berlin Wall and the opening up of Central and Eastern Europe led to a new era of investment. Association agreements with the EU and forthcoming EU accession have also boosted capital movements into the region. By the end of 2001, total foreign direct investment in Central and Eastern Europe had reached more than USD 110 billion, with a concentration in three countries: Poland (USD 39 billion), the Czech Republic (USD 25 billion) and Hungary (USD 23 billion). Table 8.1 on cumulative flows shows the distribution by country.

In the 1990s Hungary was the leading location for foreign direct investment in Central and Eastern Europe. Since 1998, however, a declining tendency may be observed, and Poland took the lead. Despite the small size of its market, Estonia has also performed well in terms of foreign investment per capita of GDP (rather than in terms of overall volume), as has the Czech Republic. Other countries, such as Slovakia or Latvia, have yet to attract significant foreign investment. However, in 2001 significant Austrian investment seems to have gone to Slovakia (Hunya and Stankovsky 2002, p. 7).

The situation is not very promising in Turkey, where 'foreign direct investment remained very low, while capital outflows were high, leading to a significant decline in foreign exchange reserves' (EC Regular Report on Turkey 2001, pp. 35–6).

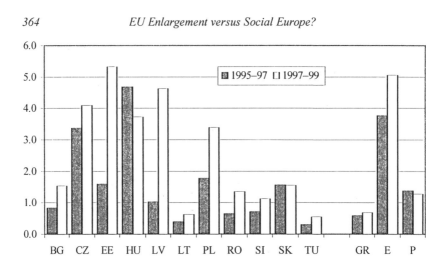

Figure 8.1 FDI flows from the EU to candidate countries, 1995–9 (% of GDP of recipient country)

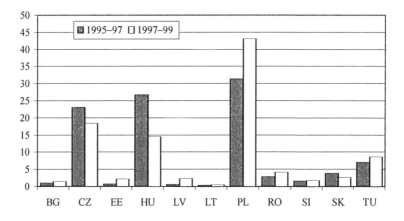

Figure 8.2 Distribution of EU FDI flows by candidate country, 1995–9 (% of total EU FDI in candidate countries)

Table 8.1 Foreign direct investment in candidate countries, 1994–2001

	Per capita GDP in USD (1999)	FDI stock per capita in USD (2001)	FDI Stock as a % of GDP	Cumulated FDI stock (million $, 2001)
Bulgaria	273	494	30.8	4 000
Cyprus	–	–	–	–
Czech Republic	1 508	2 432	44.9	25 000
Estonia	1 170	2 238	58.3	3 200
Hungary	1 764	2 256	45.1	23 000
Latvia	874	1 021	31.8	2 400
Lithuania	569	759	23.2	2 800
Malta	–	–	–	–
Poland	511	1 009	22.1	39 000
Romania	241	339	19.7	7 600
Slovakia	356	1 017	27.7	5 500
Slovenia	623	1 508	16.5	3 000
Turkey	–	–	–	–

Note: '–' means 'not available'.
Source: *Progress towards the Unification of Europe*, World Bank (2000b), p. 24; WIIW–WIFO Database.

8.3.1 The Attraction of Enlargement Prospects to EU Foreign Investors

Most foreign direct investors in candidate countries are from the EU (Figure 8.3): country of origin tends to differ according to candidate country. In Poland, 60 per cent of foreign investment originates from the EU but important investment is also coming from non-EU countries (the USA being the largest source of inward investment; Korea and Japan are also present). In Slovenia, the share of EU countries in foreign investment flows increased strongly in 1994–8, from 62 per cent to 81 per cent. Figures for foreign investment in Estonia have shown that they were up to 92 per cent of EU origin in 2000 (Varblane 2001). The figure is also high (80 per cent) in the Czech Republic. In Bulgaria, more than 70 per cent of foreign investment also comes from the EU, with 91 of the 152 largest investors being EU-based companies. Similar EU penetration was observed in Latvia (68 per cent of foreign investment) in 2000, in all sectors of the economy.

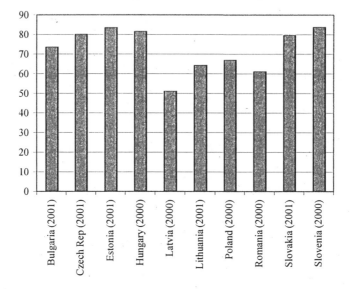

Figure 8.3 FDI flows from the EU to candidate countries, latest figures (2000 or 2001 – % of total FDI flows)

It is clear that forthcoming accession to the EU is a major factor in attracting EU foreign direct investment to candidate countries. For the World Bank (2000b, p. 23):

> the Europe Agreements . . . in addition to preferential access to EU markets . . . also guarantee the right of establishment to EU firms, commit the Central and Eastern European countries to liberalise access to services, and provide for the alignment of the economic regimes . . . as such they increase the flow of direct and portfolio investment into Central and Eastern European countries by reducing the risk that foreign investors face and by improving the business climate . . . EU based firms might consider moving production from the EU into Central and Eastern Europe without fear of deterioration in the conditions of access to their home markets.

It seems to be clear that such incentives will remain and even increase after the integration of candidate countries into the EU.

Geographical proximity seems to be a determining factor: for instance, in Estonia, Latvia, and Lithuania foreign investment is dominated by actors from Finland and Sweden; investment in Slovenia by Austrians, Germans, French, and Italians; in Hungary by Austrians, Germans, but also the Dutch; in Poland by German investors; in the Czech Republic, but also the Slovak Republic, by Germans, the Dutch, and Austrians. Many foreign investors in Bulgaria are also concentrated in the South, especially along the border with Greece and Turkey (where they generally come from).

8.3.2 The Two Main Theoretical Motivations of Foreign Investors

The economic literature distinguishes between two different strategic motivations behind foreign investment: market-seeking and lower-cost-seeking.

In parallel with the enlargement process, no doubt size of market is a determining factor for foreign investment, especially for large countries such as Poland or Turkey: 'the fundamental reason behind the bulk of investment in Poland is the size of its market' (Domański 2001, p. 22). On the other hand, countries such as Estonia or Slovenia are rarely chosen because of the smallness of their markets.

Those seeking vertical or factor-cost advantages seek to profit from lower production costs in the host country. This factor seems to be directly relevant for candidate countries considering the huge economic and social gaps (wages, working standards) with the EU described earlier in this volume. We shall see, however, that this factor is more important in sectors which are more labour-intensive and for which labour costs represent a higher share in total production costs.

While manufacturing is generally following a strategy based on the factor-cost motivation, market-seeking is more relevant for services and public utilities. The factor-cost advantage can also be differently perceived by multinational or small and medium-size enterprises. Reality is generally complex, and companies can be driven by the two motivations, or shift their focus according to restructuring needs and a change in management strategy, as seems to be the case today for foreign investment in candidate countries.

The importance of the other locational factors that we present below is clearly related to the strategy – market-seeking or lower-cost-seeking – followed by the foreign investor.

8.3.3 Other Main Determinants of Foreign Investment

Different factors can explain the differences by country and also by periods of time. Hungary managed to attract most foreign investment because it was already relatively open before the collapse of the Communist regime, with important trade transactions for instance with German partners. It also started its transition process relatively earlier than other countries in the region, and enjoyed better economic growth during the early transition, together with the Czech Republic and Poland. *Economic performance* is thus a key determinant for the confidence of foreign investors, who look carefully at the pace of economic reforms (macroeconomic stabilisation, structural reforms, and institutional development), and are also influenced by decisions and statements from international monetary institutions such as the IMF. For instance, intensive foreign investment started in Bulgaria only after 1997, after the implementation under direct supervision from the IMF of a Currency Board and a comprehensive programme of economic reforms.

There is also a direct relationship between foreign capital flows and the stage of *the privatisation process*: Hungary attracted early attention because its privatisation process gave priority to direct sales, especially to strategic foreign investors. Combined with other attractive incentives (such as a tax free environment and other financial concessions) this allowed (as early as the early 1990s) hundreds of foreign investors to acquire former state enterprises. Countries which favoured other privatisation routes – mass privatisation through vouchers to individual citizens in the Czech Republic, or promotion of employee share ownership in Slovenia and the Baltic countries – or which initially implemented less business-friendly policies towards foreign investors (such as Slovenia and the Czech Republic) attracted less foreign investment.[3] Lithuania managed to attract foreign investment mainly in 1998–9 after the introduction of a privatisation programme involving a number of strategic enterprises (telecommunications, transport).

At the end of the 1990s, the progressive shift away from Hungary can be explained by the fact that privatisation was already almost complete, while in other countries of the region large-scale privatisation had just began. Sectoral distribution of foreign investment also follows the pace of privatisation: important capital flows went into manufacturing in the early privatisation process but their share has been declining in recent years, to the benefit of public utilities, as these sectors have also been opened to privatisation.

The type of privatisation also influences the form that foreign investment takes (acquisition; merger or joint venture; greenfield): participation in the privatisation process induces foreign investors to acquire, or to enter into a merger with a local enterprise. Otherwise they generally favour greenfield investment. The fact that there is little left to be privatised in Hungary has meant that the main form of investment is now greenfield investment, mainly realised by large multinational companies, such as Ford, Opel, Audi, Thyssen, Knorr-Bremse, IBM, Nokia, and Philips. By the end of 1997, greenfield industrial investment carried out by foreign capital already accounted for 22 per cent of total foreign direct investment and covered 296 projects (Ladó 2001, p. 77).

A similar trend is observed in the Czech Republic, with a more important role being played by greenfield investment in the later stages of reform.

This form of foreign investment has generally been boosted by the possibility of establishing industrial free trade zones (IFTZ). These zones, present

3. In the Czech Republic for instance, foreign penetration was restricted to particular economic sectors and public procurement contracts, and was even excluded from certain privatisations. As a result, foreign investors accounted for only 10 per cent of the property privatised within the framework of the large-scale privatisation programme (Zemplinerová 2001, p. 54).

in many candidate countries, such as Hungary, Poland, and Turkey, but also in Latvia, were especially important for foreign investors in the early 1990s when import tariffs were relatively high. In Poland, a regional policy measure of 1995 introduced 17 special economic zones, where domestic and foreign firms received ten-year tax exemptions plus 50 per cent tax relief for another ten years, which induced companies such as Volkswagen, Electrolux, Roca, and Steinhoff to locate their production units there. These zones tend to be associated with distorted economic competition and also social dumping behaviour – as described in Chapter 5 on social dialogue – and thus explain why the European Commission has requested their progressive dismantling.

A third solution for foreign investors, between privatisation and greenfield investment, is the acquisition of local companies, a strategy in current use by foreign investors in Bulgaria (Minchev and Gradev 2001, p. 294).

In some cases, industrial relations can also influence foreign investment. For instance, for Rojec and Stanojević (2001, p. 155), 'the rigidities of industrial relations [*note*: the authors are referring to strong trade unions and the legal existence of works councils] pose a serious barrier to foreign investors in Slovenia and constitute one reason for the small and declining foreign direct investment flows'. Conversely in Estonia, 'weak trade unions are a motivating factor in investment in Estonia' (Varblane 2001, p. 208). We shall investigate this aspect in due course.

Clearly, candidate countries are eagerly seeking even more foreign investment, of all types:

> it is widely hoped that the closer the date of accession to the European Union comes, the more foreign direct investment will flow into the country. Reference is often made to Austria, where foreign direct investment inflow was only ATS 4.2 billion in 1991, but rose as high as 10.3 billion in the subsequent year, and reached 15 billion in 1994, the year of [its] EU accession. (Ladó 2001, p. 79)

8.3.4 The Domination of Candidate Countries' Economies

Foreign investors have moved into key economic actors within national economies. The domination of the Hungarian economy is particularly striking: while foreign capital is present in only 10 per cent of total Hungarian enterprises, it generates 35 per cent of GDP, 75 per cent of Hungarian exports, and one-quarter of total employment (Ladó 2001). There is no branch or sector of the economy that has not been penetrated by foreign capital. This has led some experts to state that 'for better or worse, the behaviour of foreign-owned firms controls the dynamics of Hungarian economic performance' (Kaminski and Riboud 2000, p. 1).

Foreign investment also contributes more than one-third of GDP in Latvia, Estonia, and the Czech Republic. Even in Bulgaria, where there was little for-

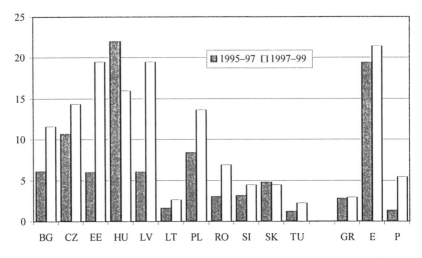

Figure 8.4 EU FDI flows to candidate countries, 1995–9 (percentage of gross domestic fixed investment in recipient country)

eign investment before 1997, foreign direct investment reached 21 per cent of GDP in 2000, compared to only 3.3 per cent in 1998 (Minchev and Gradev 2001, p. 292). By contrast, in other countries, such as Slovenia, although significant, foreign investment is playing a less dominant role, accounting for only 6 per cent of GDP.

The economic weight of foreign investors is most obvious in foreign trade. Foreign investors have been by far the largest exporters, contributing in this way to overall economic growth. Foreign companies account for 47 per cent of Polish exports, with Fiat, Philips, and Thomson now being Poland's top exporters. In Slovenia, foreign investors in 1998 exported 72 per cent of manufactured goods, with even higher rates in specific activities (more than 80 per cent in vehicles and trailers; and machinery and equipment), thus acting as a decisive force behind Slovenian export growth in recent years. In Estonia, not only are 60 per cent of total exports carried out by foreign-owned companies, but a single company, Skoda, is the country's largest exporter (3 per cent of the Czech labour force). Similarly in Slovakia, Volkswagen – which has relocated part of its production of Golfs and Polos there – is the country's largest exporter, accounting for 18 per cent of total exports (Privarova 2001, p. 190). In Hungary, not only are 75 per cent of exports are due to multinational companies, but the driving force in Hungarian exports has been machinery and transport equipment, completely dominated by multinational companies.

This dominance of domestic economies by foreign investors is total in certain sectors. In Estonia, for instance, the share of exports in total sales in foreign enterprises in 1998 reached 93 per cent in furniture, 92 per cent in

Table 8.2 Share of foreign investment in the economies of candidate countries

	% of GDP (in 1999)	% of capital	% of total sales	% of exports	% of employment	% of enterprises
Bulgaria	18.5 (21% in 2000)	43	–	–	–	–
Cyprus	–	–	–	–	–	–
Czech Republic (1999)	29.4	52	41	60 (of manufactured goods)	26 (in manufacturing)	21
Estonia	33.2	–	28	35 (of exports of manufactured goods)	21	9.5
Hungary	37.5	32	50 (1998)	75	27 (1998)	–
Latvia	35.2 (29.4% in 2000)	29 (1999)	39 (1998)	53 (1998)	24 (1998)	–
Lithuania	19.6	–	–	–	–	–
Malta	–	–	–	–	–	–
Poland	12.8	22	38	47	–	–
Romania	15.9	–	–	–	–	–
Slovakia	10.2	–	–	–	–	–
Slovenia	6.3	20	24	33 (of manuf. goods)	9	5 (in manuf.)
Turkey	–	–	–	–	–	–

Note: this table is provided only for indicative purposes, but should not lead to direct comparison or only approximately, especially as regards the share in number of firms, which varies according to the size of the companies selected by official national statistics: for instance, firms above 25 employees for the Czech Republic but slightly larger or smaller for other countries.

leather, 80 per cent in office machinery and electronics components, and 79 per cent in wood products (Varblane 2001, p. 222).

In the Czech Republic, the tobacco industry is wholly dominated by foreign investors, which represent 100 per cent of output, value-added, investment, exports, imports, and employment. The same figures are no less impressive in motor vehicles, with figures of around 90 per cent for the same economic variables (excluding employment, in respect of which the share is 70 per cent). In Latvia, share of foreign investment in employment in tobacco is 100 per cent, 98 per cent in basic metals, and 65 per cent in chemical products (Karnite 2001, p. 270).

8.4 A RELOCATION PROCESS FROM EU COUNTRIES?

Now that we have seen how large EU foreign investment flows have been – and continue to be – in candidate countries, it is important to investigate whether a sizeable proportion of these capital flows represent relocation strategies.

Most studies have tended to conclude that this was not the case, and they have systematically minimised the risk of relocation movements in parallel with the current EU enlargement, mainly on the basis of two arguments: (i) massive foreign direct investment flows currently observed in Central and Eastern European countries are mainly motivated by access to the local market; (ii) even if they were motivated by lower labour costs, the investor would look at unit labour costs rather than wage levels alone – thus including productivity differences – that would thus limit its incentives to relocate. However, empirical evidence so far seems to contradict the above statements.

8.4.1 Multiplication of Examples

The increasing number of companies undertaking large-scale relocations of their production units from the EU to candidate countries is a first basis for concluding that the process of relocation is effectively much larger than had been predicted. The cases are multiplying in all candidate countries, although differences are observed in the sectoral distribution and magnitude of the capital movements involved.

In Hungary, the most prominent and famous examples of job relocation have occurred in the manufacture of motorcars and parts (for instance, Audi and Opel–General Motors), the manufacture of electrical equipment (ABB), household appliances (Philips and Lehel-Electrolux), lighting equipment (General Electric-Lighting-Tungsram), and in the textile and clothing industry.[4]

---

4. Although some of the above mentioned companies are of non-EU origin, for instance from the USA, these have often relocated some of their former production units from the EU to candidate countries.

Similar relocations in the automobile sector took place to Poland, with the large-scale arrival of EU and non-EU companies: Fiat, Ford, Volkswagen, MAN, Scania, Daewoo, General Motors, Opel, and Volvo. We could also include Renault in Slovenia, where the increased activities of its Renault-Revoz factory set up in 1989 in Novo Mesto has undoubtedly replaced part of previous EU production. In the Czech Republic, Skoda is now clearly integrated in the multi-brand strategy of the Volkswagen group. Other multinational companies followed the same strategy by setting up units in the Czech Republic, including ABB, Daewoo, Ford, Motorola, Nestlé, Procter & Gamble, Renault, Siemens, Mitsubishi, and Philips.

For Domański (2001, p. 46), 'relocation from EU countries to Poland is taking place on a large scale . . . Polish factories have become the main producers of certain goods in some corporations or perform a subcontracting role in others'.

In the furniture sector, IKEA has set up no less than 21 production units in Bulgaria (Assemblée Nationale 2000, p. 72).

Swedish's largest textile firm, Boras Wäfveri, also provides a good example of industrial relocation to Estonia, where it bought the biggest Estonian manufacturing company Kreenholm (75.5 per cent during its privatisation in 1994 and then 100 per cent in 1998). This investment, one of the largest Swedish presences in the country, was aimed at producing at lower cost in Estonia to service all Western markets. It was seen by the Swedish management of Boras Wäfveri as the only possible way to remain competitive in EU markets. It clearly involved job losses in Sweden since 83 per cent of its total production is now supplied by its Estonian production unit in Narva (Varblane 2001, pp. 227–9).

Still in textiles, the Italian company Marzotto has also implemented a general relocation strategy in Central and Eastern Europe: after the setting up of a subsidiary (Nova Masiliano) in Brno in the Czech Republic, it relocated part of its production units in Lithuania (closing one factory of 250 employees in Italy) through the acquisition of the Lithuanian–German joint venture Liteksas (Vidickiené 2001, pp. 252–4).

Relocation strategies are clearly based on labour and other cost differentials between the home and the host countries, which can lead to an important competitive advantage, crucial for the enterprise's growth and international expansion: 'these involve in almost every case the manufacture of high-quality products with an established brand name or the parts thereof, sold on higher-value markets the world over' (Neumann 1999, p. 207). As Domański points out:

> the relocation of production from the EU to Poland is occurring as part of the global restructuring and competitiveness strategy of transnational corporations, which are integrating Polish factories into their European or world-wide networks of

plants manufacturing components or final products. Economies of scale and the supra-national specialisation of factories are salient elements of this strategy. (Domański 2001, p. 24)

This policy is obvious among the EU multinational companies that have implemented an overall ambitious strategy in Central and Eastern Europe. This is the case of the Swiss–Swedish Asea Brown Boveri (ABB) multinational, the world's largest electricity generating and distributing company, which employs 215 000 people in 1 100 companies all over the world, in some 140 countries (55 per cent of its sales being in Europe). ABB's move to the East started in 1990, with a shift in the centre of gravity of its manufacturing activities, new production units in the East starting to replace part of the activities it previously carried out in the EU. ABB established new companies in Bulgaria (two companies, ABB Contact and ABB Avangard), in the Czech Republic (seven enterprises in total which then merged into two main ones, ABB Ltd and ABB Lummus Global), Estonia (four companies including a joint venture with cement producer Kunda Nordic Cement in 1998), Hungary (purchase of Láng Gépgyár and joint venture with Daimler-Benz in turbine manufacturing; nine companies in total), Latvia (ABB Latvia and ABB Energoremont, both in Riga), Lithuania (ABB Technika in Vilnius), Poland (takeover of the Zamech turbine company in Elblag and Dolmel generator manufacturing company in Wrocław; also production unit ABB-Elta in Lodz), Romania, and apart from the candidate countries, also in Ukraine, Russia, and former Yugoslavia (Croatia).[5] Its more substantial basic operations started in Poland, and continued in neighbouring countries, mainly the Czech Republic. Today it has more than 70 companies acquired fully or in part in Central and Eastern Europe:

> ABB has followed an aggressive acquisition policy . . . now ABB has eight companies in Hungary, with a total of 2 320 staff, and an aggregate annual turnover of more than USD 100 million . . . all eight Hungarian companies are exclusively owned by ABB . . . at the end of 1995, ABB employed 9 000 in Poland and 7 000 in the Czech Republic. (Ladó 2001, pp. 125–6)

Through this geographical shift towards Central and Eastern Europe, two aims were being pursued: (i) to improve the worldwide competitiveness of company products through a cheap and skilled labour force (the aim being external markets), and (ii) access to the new markets in the region, to compensate for decreasing demand in Western Europe.

Relocations were thus massive. For example, 'ABB's substantial group of operations in Mannheim, Germany has placed numerous orders with ABB sis-

---

5. For the whole list of ABB operations in Central and Eastern Europe, see Pye (1998), pp. 27–9.

ter companies in Poland to take advantage of their low-cost producer position' (Pye 1998, p. 11). From 1990 to 1996, ABB created 56 000 jobs in Central and Eastern Europe and in Asia, while laying off 59 000 in Western Europe and elsewhere in Asia. Expansion of ABB in Central and Eastern Europe, from where it started to supply all European markets, was also accompanied by a further loss of 10 000 jobs in 1997 in the EU and the USA. This gives us a better idea of the scale of capital relocations in a large multinational company such as ABB, with a clear relationship between the production units and jobs created in Central and Eastern Europe, and the production units closed and jobs lost in the EU.

The Dutch multinational company Philips has also massively relocated part of its production in Central and Eastern Europe. Its production formerly located in the Netherlands, Germany, France, and the UK has been taken over by production units in Central and Eastern Europe, notably Poland, with eight production plants. Among those, the production sites of Pila and Kwidzyn have become the largest European Philips factories for lighting and TV sets.

There are many other significant examples of relocations of production activities in other candidate countries: in Slovenia, the Danish Danfoss (compressors), the Italian Saffa (paper mills, paper being the first sector attracting foreign investment in Slovenia), German Bosch-Siemens (small household appliances).

A relocation chain: suppliers follow their customers
We must add that not only is the movement of relocations from EU-based multinational companies in candidate countries of Central and Eastern Europe already massive, but it is also accompanied by a similar relocation process from their suppliers, which often follow them to the host country: to limit transportation costs, to ensure a just-in-time delivery production process (thus avoiding border queues), in short, to ensure that they will not be substituted by cheaper local suppliers. Local supply is an indispensable element in the cost-reduction strategy. This practice of suppliers following customers is common in electronics and cars. As an example, auto components producers followed their customers to Poland: Magneti Marelli, Teksid, Bosch, GKN, Petri, Delphi, Visteon, and Eaton (Domański 2001, p. 41).

Thus a chain of relocation is created, multinational companies dragging their suppliers into their relocation logic and strategy.

8.4.2 Future Member States as a Platform for Exports

Even if the foreign investor is mainly motivated – or claims to be motivated – at least to begin with by the local market, the fact that the same foreign investor after one or two years is dedicating 80 per cent of production to

exports is a clear demonstration that its main strategy was also to use its production capacities in the new host country as a platform for external markets,
mainly those of the EU.

In fact, the EU foreign investor first decides to feed the local market and
for this purpose invests in better human resources and production techniques
in order to reach high productivity levels. If this strategy is successful, and
also leads to high competitiveness also for external markets, the company
passes to a second stage, significantly increasing its production capacity in
order to feed also external markets at low labour costs.

A recognition of this strategy is surprisingly missing from many studies on
foreign direct investment and enlargement, as follows:

> Foreign direct investment in Central and Eastern Europe is mainly taking place to
> obtain market access and to achieve a strategic position in the emerging markets,
> rather than to exploit cheap labour costs . . . Relocation seems to occur mainly
> between parent firms and their subsidiaries in the EU. This suggests that the open-
> ing of Central and Eastern Europe does not pose a threat to job opportunities in the
> EU. (Konings and Murphy 2001, p. 3)

This contrasts with the examples of companies – and the export strategies they
have followed since 1990 – from the countries of the region.

Many examples can be found. In Estonia, Varblane (2001, p. 200) has
explained how 'many foreign firms (mainly from Finland and Sweden) are
relocating the part of their production process that requires skilled and semi-
skilled labour to Estonia, shipping semi-finished products back home for
completion of the production process'. We have already seen the example of
the Swedish textile company Boras Wäfveri, which, after having relocated in
Estonia, is now feeding all its external markets from there: '5 per cent of output is sold in Estonia, while the rest is exported to Western Europe and the
USA . . . One of the largest customers is the giant furniture retailer IKEA'
(Varblane 2001, p. 228).

We might also mention the investment of the Norwegian–Finnish firm
Lindegaard ASA in an Estonian papermill firm: it represented a clear strategic relocation for production at low labour costs and re-export (more than 80
per cent of it) to Scandinavian markets (Sweden, Norway, Finland) (Varblane
2001, p. 230).

This export strategy is also observed in Poland, although foreign investment was primarily attracted by the large size of the domestic market:

> more investors are now coming to Poland as an export platform, and secondly,
> many companies that were originally lured by the local market are expanding
> exports. Hence we find cement plants, paper mills, and tyre factories that sell one-
> third or one-half of their products in Germany and other EU countries. (Domański
> 2001, p. 22)

This is the strategy clearly followed by large multinational companies:

> ABB is rapidly increasingly exports . . . Philips already exports 80–90 per cent of the TV sets, lighting, and batteries manufactured in Poland, and the EU market is crucial for Thomson (TV tubes) and Hoechst (electrodes) as well . . . Fiat exports 50 per cent of its cars. Volvo has decided to make the Wrocław plant its largest bus factory in Europe. Volkswagen erected two export-oriented greenfield plants for electrical wiring (a joint venture with Siemens) and diesel engines. Many other recently-opened automotive component factories are largely geared for export. (Domański 2001, p. 23)

Similarly, ABB units in the Czech Republic export 80 per cent of their production, mainly to the EU (Zemplinerová 2001, p. 54). The President of ABB, Percy Barnevik, summarised clearly its operations in Central and Eastern Europe: 'The build up of low-cost production in these countries is bearing fruit . . . The increase in profits is mainly cost driven' (Pye 1998, p. 20).

Non-EU companies have followed the same strategy, with relocations from their EU production units: Daewoo chose Poland as its new industrial base for feeding the whole EU market, while Opel (GM) has since 2000 produced from Poland the Agila model for all Europe. No doubt this type of relocation as part of an ambitious export strategy will increase after the EU enlargement process, which will erase by definition all trade and customs barriers and also create a unique market of more than 500 million people.

Moreover, as emphasised by several authors (Lankes and Venables 1996; Rojec and Stanojević 2001; Varblane 2001), foreign direct investment projects in Central and East European countries at a more advanced stage of transition are more likely to be export-oriented and integrated into the foreign parent's multinational production process, which is characteristic of factor-cost-advantage-seeking foreign direct investment. This is also the conclusion for Estonia where foreign investment was first motivated by the market, then being more labour-cost-advantage oriented.

Some companies have moved into candidate countries following a combination of the two motivations (market-seeking and low-cost advantage) since they considered the new emerging economies further East also as a sort of 'domestic market' where they could go as a 'first mover' in order to capture demand: this is the case with many multinational companies which feed the Eastern European markets from their new location in one or more of the candidate countries. For instance, the French glass multinational Saint Gobain has located one production unit in Estonia (joint venture Elvex) which is now acting as a production base to feed increasing consumption in the Baltic countries, Ukraine and Belarus (Varblane 2001, p. 228).

In conclusion, we can thus say that even if the domestic market approach represented one of the major factors of foreign investment in the early transition, it has shifted towards a more externally oriented strategy based on lower labour costs, unavoidably involving significant relocations from production units in the EU to newly created ones in candidate countries. Although they generally deny it (pointing to the limited use of managers' surveys in this field), multinational companies have generally been planning such a strategic shift for a long time, which explains why the relocation process has been intense since the beginning.

8.4.3 Wage Costs and Not Unit Labour Costs the 'Reference' for Foreign Investors

The decision to relocate is very much dependent on the productivity levels expected from the new production units in the host candidate country. In fact, a relocation is generally followed by significant investment, and also exports of production techniques and technologies generally from the home country in order to reach higher productivity levels. This means that it is not local productivity levels – of the host economy, and of the former enterprise if it is an acquisition or a merger – that are taken into account by the foreign investor but rather those he can rapidly attain by implementing his own production methods. The foreign investor will thus relocate only on the basis of wage costs and the availability of a skilled labour force which in the new production environment will help to attain higher productivity standards. Contrary to all the literature on foreign investment and enlargement, it is thus not the unit labour costs but rather only the wage levels that are the key variable within a relocation strategy. Low wage rates combined with new production methods will help the foreign investor to dramatically lower unit labour costs. We should add that these productivity improvements do not require significant investment from the foreign investor, since productivity levels in candidate countries were generally so low that even old production techniques from the EU seem to have been sufficient to reach productivity levels that – combined with low wages – have led to the sought-after competitive position.

This situation is well summarised by Rojec and Stanojević (2001, p. 146): 'by moving production facilities abroad, enterprises continue to utilise their existing industry-specific assets, including their production technology, but substitute the home-country labour force with a cheaper one in the host country'. Foreign investors also implement training programmes in order to rapidly increase labour force productivity, as done, for instance, by Volkswagen in its Czech company Skoda (Zemplinerová 2001, p. 56).

Empirical evidence shows that productivity levels have rapidly increased in local enterprises after the injection of foreign capital because of the introduction of new managerial and production techniques (Dörrembacher et al. 2000; case studies in Ladó 2001). In Hungary, labour productivity almost doubled between 1988 and 1994 in FDI enterprises with foreign majority owner-ship (Kaucsek 1996). Similarly, in parallel with massive foreign investment flows, productivity measured in terms of value added per employee more than doubled in the manufacturing sector (Ladó 2001, p. 84).

In Poland, with foreign investment, 'transfer of technological lines and machines dismantled in EU plants is common . . . dramatic progress in pro-ductivity has made it nearly twice as high as in domestic firms' (Domański 2001, p. 27). In Slovenia, a comparison between the performance of domes-tic firms and that of foreign-owned firms reveals a value added per employee 37 per cent higher in the latter; but even more importantly from the compa-ny's point of view, the value added costs/labour costs ratio in foreign manu-facturing firms in Slovenia was found to be much higher than in the manu-facturing sector of any major EU investing country (Rojec and Stanojević 2001, pp. 147–8).

ABB is a good example of high profitability and productivity reached very quickly: not only could they set up a network of production units in Central and Eastern Europe in the first half of the 1990s at very low cost (USD 300 million, corresponding to less than one-quarter of their 1995 profits), but they also rapidly increased productivity through technology and management from the Swiss and Swedish sides (Ladó 2001, pp. 123–9): 'the company has been able to achieve a high level of profitability in almost all its acquisitions with-in a two-year period' (Pye 1998, p. 19).

The fact that foreign investors have been moving to high labour cost coun-tries rather than to low labour cost countries has often been used as proof that low wages are not such a key determinant. But this does not take into consid-eration the fact that wage levels continue to be much lower also in countries like Hungary, the Czech Republic, Estonia, and Poland. These countries have also attracted foreign investment because of their skilled labour force and their economic stability.

For Slovenia, although wage levels are much higher, it is the quality of the labour force which seems to motivate foreign investors, and also industrial relocations:

> motives related to factor-cost advantage seeking – such as technology and know-how, quality of labour, recognized trademarks, availability of raw materials and parts – seem to prevail. The interviews with foreign investors, therefore, seem to indicate that most FDI (from the EU) in Slovenia is of the type favouring reloca-tion/restructuring of the foreign parent company . . . it is the quality of labour which motivates foreign investors in the case of Slovenia. (Rojec and Stanojević 2001, p. 138)

This confirms that relocations can be motivated not only by cheap labour but also by the availability of highly skilled employees who, in addition, continue to be paid below the levels of most EU member states. An illustrative example is provided by the Danish company Danfoss Compressors which invested in Slovenia:

> with a view to accessing relatively inexpensive skilled labour . . . the investment [being] a relocation of part of Danfoss's manufacturing capacity in Germany. Almost all the output is exported, the EU being the major market and Danfoss is grooming its subsidiary to take sole responsibility for the European compressor market. (Rojec and Stanojević 2001, p. 141)

Similarly, 'Bosch-Siemens of Germany took over MGA, which produces small household appliances sold under the various Bosch-Siemens brand names, because it was interested in the lower cost of skilled labour in Slovenia . . . MGA exports its entire output' (Rojec and Stanojević 2001, p. 141).

This means that even a relatively high wage cost country like Slovenia can represent an attractive place for export-oriented relocations.

These conclusions, which are at odds with other literature in this field, are important since they change the expectations we may have in terms of the magnitude of capital relocations: we found first that foreign investment is not only motivated by the domestic market but also, and more and more in the long term, by a low labour cost strategy aimed at reaching external markets; secondly, that it is mainly the wage levels and not unit labour costs which motivate, in combination with the availability of a skilled labour force, foreign investment in candidate countries. We shall see that these conclusions fundamentally modify also the perception we may have of the effects of foreign investment in candidate countries in the long run.

8.5 A FEW 'SENSITIVE' SECTORS?

Another argument that has been used to conclude that the risk of relocation would be marginal was that this process would be limited to a very narrow number of sectors, with generally traditional and very labour intensive activities. Although a relocation strategy will certainly be more deeply investigated by investors in those sectors, we believe that this conclusion is too simplistic and does not really take into account the reality of restructuring in other, more high-tech, sectors also confronted by an increasingly competitive and international environment.

8.5.1 Greater Risks in Traditional Activities

Because social dumping is motivated by the degree of competition in the relevant activity, and is aimed at profiting from differentials in social and work-

Table 8.3 Sectoral distribution of foreign direct investment

	Manufac-turing	Other sectors (share in total FDI stock)	Manufac-turing sectors (within total manufac-turing)	Size of FDI projects
Bulgaria	54.8 (1999) 48.2 (2000)	1999: - Trade (19%) - Financial services (11%) 2000: - Financial services (20) - Trade (16.5)	- Textiles - Furniture	Mainly small and medium- size enterprises (2/3 of FDI) for instance in textiles and clothing, shoes, and wood. Few large-scale projects
Czech Republic	38.7 (1999) 30.4 (2001)	1999: - Financial services (12.6%) Trade (10%) 2001: - Transport and telecoms (24.6) Trade (21)	- Non-metallic mineral products (10% of total FDI) - vehicles, trailers (7% of total FDI) - Food and beverages (6%)	Combination of very large and also many small and medium-size enterprises
Estonia	22.8 (1999) 21.9 (2001)	1999: - Financial services (25) - Transport and telecoms (22) 2001: Financial services (23) - Transport and telecoms (18)	- paper - textiles - non-metallic minerals	Large companies and SMEs
Hungary	38.4 (1998) 36.5 (2000)	1998: - Electricity, gas and water supply (15%) - Trade (12%) - Financial services (11%) 2000: - Real estate (16.1) - Trade (12.5)	- Food and tobacco industry (28.4%) - Engineering (incl. cars) (26%) - Chem. (20%)	Combination of very large and also small-scale
Latvia	17.9 (1999) 15.8% (2001)	1999: Transport and telecoms (24%) Financial services (22.5%) 2001: Fin. services (23) Trade (21.4)	- Timber - Textiles - Glass, chemicals - Metal products	Mainly small and medium-size enterprises

Table 8.3 (cont.)

	Manufac-turing	Other sectors (share in total FDI stock)	Manufac-turing sectors (within total manufac-turing)	Size of FDI projects
Lithuania	32.4 (1998) 28.8 (2000)	1999: - Trade (24%) - post and telecoms (20%) 2000: - Trade (23) - Transport and telecoms	- Food, beverages and tobacco (37%) - Textiles and leather (14%) - Chemical products (11%) - Transport (8%)	Mainly large investors
Poland	50% (1999) 42.5% (2000)	1999: - Financial services (22%) - Trade (10%) 2000: - Financial services (23) - Transport (12)	- Food products and beverages (22%) - Non-metal products (15%) - Motor vehicles (12%)	Combination of very large and also small-scale
Romania	43.8% (1999) 46 % (2001)	1999: Transport (20) Trade (18%) 2001: Trade (18) Services (17.4)	- Food and beverages - Light industry	A few large companies; many small and medium-size ones (9% of FDI)
Slovakia	49.8 (1999) 48.2 % (2001)	1999: - Financial services (21%) - Trade (19) 2001: - Fin. services (19.1) - Transport and telecoms (15.1)		A few large-scale projects, but also small-scale
Slovenia	51.1% (1998) 40.7 (2000)	1998: - Trade (17%) - Financial services (12%) 2000: Fin. services (26) Trade (14)	- Paper (10%) - Chem. (7.6%) - Motor vehicles, trailers (6.6 %)	Large

ing conditions, it is obvious that the probability of social dumping will be much higher in those sectors for which labour and social costs represent a large part of overall enterprise expenditure. EU studies and concrete experience with the 1986 EU enlargement to low labour cost countries Spain and Portugal have shown that relocations have mainly focused on the sectors which have the following features: labour intensive, high share of wages in turnover and value-added, the relatively low skill structure of the labour force, the importance of demand for the product (consumption), degree of international openness (Vaughan-Whitehead 1990). The first type of sector to be affected by relocations was found to be the 'national standard-bearers' that were still relatively protected from intra-Community trade and that also displayed the characteristics of industries at an advanced stage in their 'life-cycle' (low-skill workforce, low demand growth), such as the structural metal products industry or the shipbuilding industry, and where the importance of wage costs encouraged firms to relocate some of their production units in order to revive their competitive position in a saturated market.

Highly sensitive too were those sectors specialising in products accounting for a significant proportion of household expenditure (shoes, sports goods, cotton, wool, cars) or in intermediate goods (glass, ceramics, rubber) where much lower wages in host countries would enable these traditional industries, already open to trade despite barriers, to benefit from the economies of scale that remained to be exploited. This need to exploit wage advantages is all the more pressing with current EU enlargement, since the distribution networks will systematically turn to the least costly suppliers within the European Union.

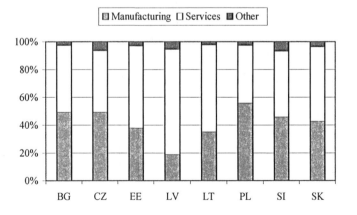

Figure 8.5 Division of FDI in Central and Eastern European countries, by broad sector, 1995–9 (percentage of total FDI)

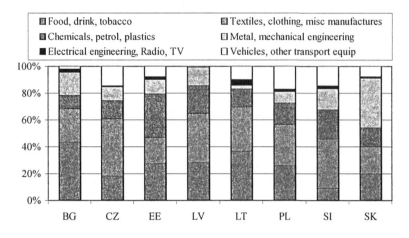

Figure 8.6 Division of FDI in Central and Eastern European countries, by industry, 1995–9 (percentage of total FDI in manufacturing)

Concrete examples of social dumping in candidate countries seem to confirm its higher probability in certain traditional, labour-intensive sectors such as construction, textiles, services (hotels, restaurants, and so on).

Figure 8.5 highlights the fact that manufacturing has been the main target of foreign investors in all candidate countries, although investment in services has been increasing recently. This is an additional element pointing to the presence of a low-cost logic behind such transnational capital movements, something which explains the scale of the EU industrial relocations in candidate countries already described.

At the end of 1999, about half of foreign investment in Poland was in manufacturing, followed by the financial sector (22 per cent) and trade (10 per cent). Similarly in Slovenia, manufacturing, with 51.1 per cent of foreign direct investment stock at the end of 1998 (Table 8.3), was by far the most important recipient of foreign investment, followed by trade (17 per cent) and financial services (12 per cent). Preferred manufacturing sectors are paper and paper products (10 per cent), chemicals and chemical products (7.6 per cent), motor vehicles and trailers (6.6 per cent), rubber and plastic products (5.5 per cent), and machinery and equipment (5.1 per cent). In Estonia, the highest percentage of foreign investment went to manufacturing until 1995, but was then overtaken by the financial sector and also transport and telecommunications, partly because of the end of large privatisation projects in manufacturing.

In Hungary, while at the end of 1998 on average 37 per cent of the subscribed capital of enterprises came from foreign investment, the same ratio was 60 per cent in manufacturing.

Foreign capital participation was highest in the manufacturing of non-metallic minerals, engineering, and food. Foreign investment also exceeded 50 per cent of subscribed capital in textiles, clothing, and leather, chemicals, and metallurgy. In these sectors, an important relocation process had already taken place, from both multinational companies and small and medium-size enterprises. For instance, jeans producers such as the American Levi Strauss and the German Mustang have relocated part of their production to Poland (Domański 2001, p. 44).

Relocation is also taking place on a large scale in the furniture sector, with large EU companies such as the Finnish IKEA and the French Conforama having relocated part of their production of kit-furniture in Bulgaria.

More than two-thirds of all greenfield investment in Hungary was carried out in the engineering sector, especially in the automobile assembly industry, with large-scale investments by General Motors, Audi, Suzuki, and Ford. These new locations in Hungary as we have seen have led to the closure of production units and job losses in the EU. In fact, for Hungary and Poland automobiles is already a sector dominated by massive relocation strategies.

The predominance of foreign investment in certain sectors and the type of actor involved seem to influence the size of foreign investment projects: while the automobile sector attracts the largest multinational companies, a sector like textiles seems to be attracting thousands of small and medium-size enterprises. These sectoral differences also explain why countries like the Czech Republic are characterised by large foreign investors (mainly in automobiles and engineering), while countries like Bulgaria and Romania seem to be preferred by small and medium-size enterprises in the textile, clothing, and food sectors.

Public authorities have tried to promote the entry not only of multinational companies, but also of small and medium-size companies which can create supplier facilities: 'Hungary has smoothly shifted foreign direct investment driven by privatisation to that generated by greenfield investment and is [currently] working towards a more balanced mix of multinational companies and medium-size and smaller foreign companies' (Ladó 2001, p. 78).

Sub-contracting as a major form of relocation

Traditional activities in sectors such as textiles and shoes also clearly have a sub-contracting character. Sub-contracting does not involve a physical move of the EU company but represents in practice a relocation of production activities which henceforth are no longer produced in the EU, but in Central and Eastern Europe and Asia. The prospect of EU enlargement, however, seems to have led to a refocusing of production units in candidate countries, including Turkey, where factories undertake the making-up of brandname products for West European customers which provide both fabrics and design. Such relocation is observed on a large scale in Bulgaria and Romania in textiles, clothing, and leather products, for companies like Adidas, Puma, Neckerman, Quelle, and C&A. The French textile company DIM works intensively with three Bulgarian subcontractors in its underwear production. A recent study carried out for the French Parliament estimated that the extent of subcontracting by French companies in Romania is enormous (Assemblée Nationale 2000, p. 74).

Low fixed capital entry means weak entry barriers and fierce competition with social dumping. 'The operations of such companies are determined by the availability of orders – that is, they are quite irregular and risky, especially for employees' (Minchev and Gradev 2001, p. 304). Certain supplier companies even create a second tier of subcontractors to save even more on wages and other labour costs (especially in the most labour-intensive activities, such as sewing). Piecework and overtime in the form of long hours and Saturday work are often practised, even in an illegal form.

Many work in the shadow economy, with avoidance of invoices and of customs duties for transborder and foreign trade activities, and no protection of employees, with the absence of labour contracts and health and safety standards. In Bulgaria, 10-hour working days, sometimes behind locked doors, with unpaid overtime, are not unusual among this type of subcontractor.

It is clear that the EU customers which sell the final products have a strong responsibility for this process: they are the source of it even if they stand at the end of the production chain. Not only is it leading to employment losses at home, but it contributes to the erosion of social standards in the EU.

8.5.2 A Strategy Also Followed in High-Tech Sectors

In many candidate countries, foreign investment has also been high in more 'high-tech' sectors. In Hungary, significant investment has been carried out more recently in the communications industry (Ladó 2001). According to Neumann:

> the relative cheapness of skilled labour in the traditional sense is also a source of attraction, especially in engineering branches manufacturing individual products for export. The same applies to the spreading R&D sections at Hungarian units of FDI enterprises: highly qualified labour (engineers, mathematicians, and so on) probably offer an even higher profit given the wage gap between West and East. (1999, pp. 198–9)

Foreign investment has been intense in Hungary in the production not only of automotive parts but also of electronics: subsidiaries of Philips and IBM have been mainly responsible for the growth in TV monitors and receivers. The value of exports of these items increased almost thirty-fold between 1990 and 1997 (Kaminski and Riboud 2000, p. 22).

The example of Slovenia also underlines the relocation strategies of EU companies in sectors with more capital-intensive technology.

In the Czech Republic, foreign investment has a share in investment of 91 per cent in telecoms equipment and of 95 per cent in personal computers. In telecoms, it also has 81 per cent of total imports and exports, while it represents 64 per cent of exports in the PC industry (Zemplinerová, 2001, p. 63). Foreign investors in the Czech Republic in fact seem to have been mainly attracted by capital-intensive sectors rather than traditional ones (with low investment in textiles, and so on).

Foreign investors in high-tech sectors were also found to favour greenfield investment, with a higher propensity to export and invest, for instance in TVs, radios, PCs, and electrical equipment, thus confirming the relocation strategy approach in these sectors.

8.5.3 High Risk in the Already 'Internationalised' Transport Sector

Many cases of social dumping have also been identified in road transport (illegal, legal, semi-legal), an activity which is already very much internationalised, with operations which by definition cross borders, well beyond current EU member states. This makes it very difficult to control their operations.

The case of the German road transport company Willy Betz (see Chapter 7) has attracted the attention of the media, and has also led to concrete action from European institutions. The German transport employer, after buying the Bulgarian company Somat with all its trucks, has extended its transportation network all over Europe with Bulgarian drivers, mostly under-paid and working under difficult working conditions, especially in terms of driving-time.

A similar case emerged early in 2002 with Austrian enterprise Kralowetz based in Luxembourg, which was employing drivers from Central and Eastern Europe, something that was presented in Chapter 7 and will also be addressed in Chapter 9 on labour mobility, together with other examples showing how different economic and social standards between countries in parallel with EU enlargement may motivate social dumping.

8.6 LEVER OF ECONOMIC AND SOCIAL EQUALISATION?

Foreign direct investment is generally recognised by the economic literature as an engine of national economic growth. This has also been confirmed by many studies of candidate countries which have highlighted how the injection of foreign capital has boosted all possible factors of economic catching-up (sales, exports, productivity, employment). Nevertheless, we might wonder whether this rosy picture really reflects reality and whether we can make the same assessment when other economic criteria are added (such as trade balance, structure of employment, impact on domestic firms, and local economies) and when social considerations (such as regional balance, industrial relations, working conditions) are brought into the final picture.

8.6.1 A Factor in Economic Growth

In Hungary these enterprises generated almost half of all value added and net sales in 1998, despite much lower employment levels, since they represented only 27 per cent of total employment.

> Foreign direct investment enterprises operated much more efficiently, with much higher productivity than domestic enterprises without foreign participation . . . the per capita value added of FDI enterprises was 78 per cent higher and their sales 74 per cent higher than that of the corporate sector as a whole . . . in the manufacturing sector, where FDI has been by far most widespread, value added increased in real terms by 40 per cent between 1992 and 1997. The contribution of the private sector, and especially that of FDI enterprises, has been decisive. (Ladó 2001, pp. 82–3)

Similarly in Poland, 'as a whole, companies with foreign capital comprise 22 per cent of fixed assets, and 38 per cent of manufacturing sales in Poland' (Domański 2001, p. 27). In Estonia, productivity of foreign investors was in some cases found to be between two and three times higher than in domestic firms, depending on the sector.

In Slovenia, foreign-owned enterprises, on a total sample of 1 200 enterprises, showed higher sales growth (43 per cent against 12 per cent in domestic firms) between 1994 and 1998, a higher propensity to export (growth of 57 per cent compared to 19 per cent), and higher value added (34 per cent against 6 per cent) (Rojec and Stanojević 2001, p. 158). This leads the two Slovenian authors to conclude that 'foreign direct investment has fostered the restructuring of Slovenian manufacturing in an allocative-efficient way' (2001, p. 169).

In contrast to this rosy picture, depicting a better performance by foreign investors, we should also report that in almost all candidate countries the difference in productivity and other economic variables has been found to be progressively narrowing recently, thus showing a catching-up process between domestic and foreign-owned firms (Minchev and Gradev 2001). Unit labour costs were also found to be lower in foreign-owned enterprises (due to higher productivity rather than higher wages), but with domestic firms also catching up in this regard, as for example in Estonia (Varblane 2001, p. 219).

Moreover, we must also point out that foreign-owned enterprises have had a tendency to invest in the best domestic companies, for instance in the Czech Republic (Zemplinerová 2001, p. 65) and elsewhere, a strategy which has certainly led to more rapid restructuring in certain activities and companies but which has also left many other domestic companies out of the picture, with thus limited effect on overall domestic growth.

8.6.2 Impact on Trade Balance

It is clear that foreign investors have brought the most radical changes in trade flows. We have seen that in almost all candidate countries, they dominate domestic firms in terms of export performance. At the same time, they have also been the largest importers, so that the net impact on the trade balance is not clear and requires more explanation. In many candidate countries, at least in the first twelve years of transition, multinational companies seem to have contributed to the deterioration rather than to the improvement of the trade balance. For instance, as far as Hungary is concerned, 'as for the foreign trade balance, the role of FDI enterprises has also been significant: on a five-year average (1994–8), 67 per cent of the negative balance derived from the imports of these companies exceeding exports' (Ladó 2001).

Similarly in Poland, 'foreign-owned plants generate even more imports, adding to the current Polish trade deficit' (Domański 2001, p. 27). The same situation is found in the Czech Republic, where for instance for 1999 the statistics show a higher contribution to imports (share of 64 per cent of total imports in manufacturing) than to exports (60 per cent) (Zemplinerova 2001, p. 61). The gap is particularly high in furniture (share of 72 per cent in exports against a share of 47 per cent in imports), in basic metals (75 per cent against 56 per cent), in printing (53 and 24 per cent), and in traditional sectors such as textiles (49 per cent against 39 per cent) and wood products (77 per cent against 61 per cent), thus contributing to the Czech trade deficit, notably with the EU.

The reasons for such quantities of imports from the multinational companies located in candidate countries is clear: they represent mainly inputs of raw materials and production techniques to be included in the production process. However, there are good reasons to believe that the balance will become more positive in the long run, for a number of reasons: first, because it is not unusual for subcontractors to follow the main multinational companies they are working for, especially if the latter are increasing their production capacity in the new host country, so that it may be expected that part of the imported goods that are today imported will later on be produced and so delivered on the spot and thus not be accounted among trade flows. At the same time, the initial and necessary stage of imports of production and technologies int the new production unit may progressively be reduced, thus also contributing to improving the trade balance. These new techniques are then expected to boost exports in the future. A trend in this direction can already be seen. For Hungary, 'the tendency is promising: while in the mid-1990s FDI enterprises accounted for more than 80 per cent of the foreign trade deficit, their share had gone below 50 per cent by 1998' (Ladó 2001, p. 85).

8.6.3 Differentiated Effect on Employment: Fuelling Long-Term Unemployment?

Considering the proportion of employment provided by foreign investors, the impact is clearly positive. Nevertheless, while greenfield investment is leading to job creation, restructuring and rationalisation of production units bought by foreign investors has led to significant downsizing in order to increase efficiency and productivity. In Poland, foreign investors have been found to carry out significant layoffs and downsizing (Domański 2001).

Moreover, foreign enterprises are generally much more capital intensive than domestic firms, which explains the disproportionately small share of foreign investment enterprises in total employment in candidate countries (compared to their shares in sales or exports) as shown in Table 8.2.

In the Czech Republic, for instance, in all manufacturing sectors the share of foreign investment in employment is 26 per cent of the labour force, while the share in exports and sales are above 60 per cent. This shows that the contribution of foreign investors is less impressive – although clearly largely positive – on the employment side.

In many cases, after the first few years of restructuring, the same foreign companies seem to have created many new jobs, foreign investment producing, in general, a net impact on employment, that varies in the end according to sector, activity, and individual company. In many multinationals, job creations seem to have more than compensated the initial employment losses, whilst in other units the employment loss is significant. In Slovenia, new job creation by foreign investors seems to be already exceeding the initial reduction in employment (Rojec and Stanojevic 2001, p. 158). In Romania, it was found that 'the job-destroying restructuring function of foreign direct investment is stronger than its job-creation function, which finally results in a temporary contribution to increasing unemployment' (Zaman 2001, p. 27).

In Hungary, the impact was found to be already globally positive, with for instance 75 per cent of newly created jobs in manufacturing between 1992 and 1997 being attributed to foreign-owned enterprises (Kaminski and Riboud 2000, p. 13). They have contributed to absorbing a significant proportion of the labour force released by state-owned enterprises, and thus have contributed to taming already high unemployment figures.

Nevertheless, we might wonder whether multinational companies really contribute to reabsorbing unemployment in candidate countries, which as we have seen in Chapter 4 is a long-term phenomenon, due in particular to a mismatch between the education and qualifications of the labour force and labour demand. Unemployment is affecting more vulnerable categories, unskilled workers, or those with out-dated qualifications, and/or those living in remote areas. But multinational companies have mainly required highly skilled or semi-skilled workers for whom market demand is high anyway, which explains why they have felt the need to pay wages above the market rate.[6]

'Foreign-owned private firms have significantly expanded employment opportunities especially for highly skilled labour once their initial restructuring was complete' (Kaminski and Riboud 2000, p. 15). In fact, in the course of restructuring foreign investors were found to get rid of unskilled employees and to retain only the most talented, educated, and skilled employees.

'As a result of downsizing, in most FDI enterprises the skill composition of the workforce has changed for the better' (Neumann 1999, pp. 181, 199); 'redundancies have primarily affected the unskilled and semi-skilled workers, and lower level administrative jobs' (Ladó 2001, p. 104). 'The group of unskilled labourers typical of many socialist factories has largely disappeared' (Domański 2001, p. 36).

In the case of ABB, 'unqualified labour (unskilled and apprentice workers), as well as administrative staff with secondary school qualifications (for example secretaries) has disappeared almost completely from the ABB companies' (Ladó 2001, p. 128).

This means that even if through the restructuring process and the consolidation years there has been a net creation of jobs by foreign investors, with new jobs outperforming job losses, the process seems to have further marginalised the most vulnerable workers, while creating a market for the more skilled labour force.

Foreign investors thus do not seem to be of much help in employing the categories of worker most affected by unemployment; this would explain why there is high and still increasing unemployment – mainly long-term unemployment – in candidate countries despite the dominance of their economies by foreign investment, which is normally expected to create jobs. It can also explain why in many candidate countries, such as Poland and Hungary, the rapid growth of manufacturing output has not been accompanied by an employment increase. We can even conclude here that foreign investment has

6. Those multinational companies which on the contrary are employing unskilled labour force are doing it at very bad working conditions, lowest possible pay, leading to very high turnover and absenteeism, and not providing an adequate answer to long-term unemployment among these categories of worker either (for Hungary, see, for instance, Ladó, 2001, p. 103).

contributed to long-term unemployment, since they do not provide the long-term unemployed with job opportunities. On the other hand, by increasing the demand for skilled workers and increasing their wages, they only contribute to increasing the gap between these two different types of employee, a process that may be even stronger if the foreign investor concentrates its activities in a few geographical areas, something that we investigate below.

8.6.4 Regional Imbalances: Increasing Existing Gaps?

Although the overall economic effect of foreign investment on local economies has been found to be positive, this does not mean that it has led to a balanced development between regions. In particular, do foreign investors tend to reduce regional gaps, notably by helping the remotest and poorest regions to catch up, or do they tend to increase the gap between the most developed areas and the rest? This is an important question for social cohesion as a whole in an enlarged EU, to which the answer is not obvious, since it seems also to depend – similarly to the effects on the foreign trade balance – on the distinction between the short and the long term.

One basic result of all studies on foreign investment in Central and Eastern Europe is that it has so far been concentrated in a few developed areas, generally in the capital cities and surrounding areas.

In Hungary, the clear preference has been first for the capital city, and second for the regions bordering the EU (Fazekas 2000, p. 3): Budapest, together with its surrounding area (Pest county), and the two Austrian border regions (Győr-Sopron and Vas counties) accumulated almost three-quarters of the stock of foreign direct investment inflows between 1992 and 1998. It is familiarly known as the Budapest–Vienna axis, which also includes Tatabánya (Komárom county), and Székesfehérvár (Fehér county) which multinational companies such as Philips have converted into industrial and business centres. Unfortunately, other parts of the country have not been of interest to foreign investors (Ladó 2001, p. 89).

Foreign investment is even more concentrated in Estonia, with more than 80 per cent of it in Tallinn and Harjumaa county, something which confirms the export orientation of foreign investors: Tallinn, one of the most modern ports on the Baltic, represents a key factor for export-oriented investors as shipping by sea is by far the cheapest mode of transportation (Varblane 2001, p. 214). In Bulgaria, foreign investment has also contributed to increase the gap between Sofia and its region and the other, less developed areas of the country (Minchev and Gradev 2001, p. 299).

As part of the explanation for such a concentration of foreign investment, we should mention geographical location (especially areas along borders) for transportation and logistical reasons, infrastructure, economic development, and the educational level of the population (higher in capital cities). Foreign investors do not move into regions with high unemployment rates – also characterised by low educational levels and geographical disadvantages – where their propensity to create new job opportunities would be most welcome.

Similarly in Bulgaria: 'regions with low foreign direct investment are also those with the highest unemployment' (Minchev and Gradev 2001, p. 301); in Lithuania: 'foreign investors have failed to establish businesses in regions with particular unemployment problems' (Vidickiené 2001, pp. 246–7); and in Poland: 'regional distribution of FDI shows that investors are not attracted to areas of low wages and high unemployment' (Domański 2001, p. 28). Foreign capital is concentrated in developed regions and metropolitan areas, such as Warsaw, Posnan, and Upper Silesia.

Certain localities are doing their best to attract greenfield investments by providing generous tax concessions and local facilities.

Table 8.4 Regional concentration of foreign direct investment in candidate countries, 2002

Bulgaria	More than 51.5% in Sofia (41%) and its region (10.5%) and 19% in Verna
Cyprus	–
Czech Rep.	47% in and around Prague
Estonia	81% around Tallinn and in Harjumaa county; 10% in Tartu region
Hungary (1998)	60% in Budapest (49%) and its county Pest (11%); 12.5% on the axis Győr–Sopron (6.6%), Borsod-Abaúj-Zemplén (5.9%)
Latvia	52% in Riga; 7% in Daugavpils
Lithuania	83% concentrated in 3 major cities: Vilnius (60%), Klaipeda (12%), and Kaunas (11%)
Malta	–
Poland	Highest in regions: Warsaw (Mazowieckie, 10%), Poznan (Wielkopolskie: 9%), and upper Silesia (Slaskie: 9%)
Romania	48% in Bucarest, 6% in Timis, and 4% in Prahova
Slovakia	Around 50 per cent in Bratislava and its region; other main areas for investment are Trnava (9%), Kosice (8%), and Trencin (7%)
Slovenia	Mainly around Lljubljana
Turkey	–

The conclusions for Hungary on the basis of all available studies is obvious: 'FDI inflows have been heavily concentrated in particular regions of Hungary, maintaining or even contributing to regional imbalances' (Ladó 2001, p. 89). For better or worse, the actions of foreign-owned firms control the dynamics of Hungarian economic performance.

In Lithuania, 83 per cent of foreign investment is concentrated in three cities, and mainly in the capital Vilnius (60 per cent).

In Estonia, foreign investment has clearly increased wage differentials by region, further increasing already high wages in Tallinn compared to low wages in the rest of the country. Tallinn is characterised by higher inflation, excessive urban concentration, decreasing productivity, and labour shortages, whilst many other regions continue to face high unemployment and very low living standards. For Varblane (2001, p. 214), 'the effect of foreign direct investment on growth may have been reduced by this uneven regional distribution'.

8.6.5 Mitigated Economic Effects on Domestic Firms

Finally, the total employment effect of multinational companies also depends on the spillover effect on domestic firms. Theoretically, foreign-owned companies can greatly contribute to developing domestic enterprises, first directly – through mergers, for instance – by providing them with high technology or integrating them in world markets, and second, indirectly, by involving other domestic firms in their network of suppliers, or by carrying out R&D activities that can also influence the development of domestic firms, or finally by establishing global quality standards that can be beneficial for a whole region or country. While we saw that the direct effects are clearly generally positive, empirical evidence on the indirect effects does not point to a clear positive effect of foreign-owned companies on domestic firms.[7]

In some cases, the multinational company works with a network of local suppliers, so contributing to regional economic growth (see for instance the list of domestic suppliers of Volkswagen in Slovakia in Privarova 2001, p. 193). In many other cases, however, the foreign investors are found to work on their production units in isolation from other local companies, using their own production techniques, importing every single input, and then exporting the bulk of final goods produced. In Hungary:

---

7. While our focus here is on the effects of foreign investment mainly driven by a relocation logic based on low labour costs and aimed at exporting production, we should add that the other type of foreign investor, motivated by access to the local market, can also be harmful to the domestic economy – for instance when it turns into a monopoly, with adverse effects in terms of prices, competition, and local growth.

the indirect (multiplier) employment effect has been rather limited . . . multinational companies are certainly interested in using Hungarian suppliers, primarily because of their lower cost levels, but do not support the necessary development of SMEs very much. Most supplier companies, without investments tailored to given market demand, have difficulties in meeting the quality and time-delivery requirements. (Ladó 2001, p. 98)

The incentives provided by the state to locate production units in Free Trade Zones have further contributed to disconnect foreign investment from the rest of the economy. As emphasised by Kaminski and Riboud (2000, p. 27):

the potential negative impact of export zones on domestic integration of firms is considerable. Firms operating in Free Trade Zones are outside the customs territory. They operate in enclaves, and are devoid of any incentive to develop backward and forward linkages with the rest of the economy. The reliance on a Free Trade Zone usually exacerbates tendencies towards a deformed dual economy . . . hence the most dynamic sector of the Hungarian economy may have potentially weak internal links.

There is another significant element which normally reflects the degree of foreign investor integration into local economies: their research and development activities.

In this regard, all production units of foreign enterprises in candidate countries of Central and Eastern Europe seem to remain in the lower value-added segments of the production chain, with little research and sophisticated design functions being carried out in the host country. 'Only a few of the transnational corporations' research and development (R&D) units are located in Poland' (Domański 2001, p. 36). The same observation can be made for other candidate countries, with several significant examples. For instance, in the case of ABB in Estonia, 'ABB has so far not moved sophisticated production lines. Its strategy of penetration has relied on relatively cheap Estonian labour and expansion of activity has been very fast' (Varblane 2001, p. 227). This was also the case of the Estonian unit of the Swedish textile company Boras Wäfveri. Varblane (2001, p. 228) concludes that 'production in EU countries is now concentrated on high value-added products, which is possible only in cooperation with lower value-added product lines in Estonia'. We can easily foresee the negative effects that such a strategy on the part of foreign investors – which is unfortunately general for all candidate countries – may have in the long term on domestic economies.

Finally, we might wonder why foreign investors have contributed to directing candidate countries towards the development of manufacturing rather than services, which are potentially bigger job creators. This situation is well summarised by Vidickiené (2001, p. 236) for Lithuania: 'Foreign direct investment has been lagging behind the growth of the service sector at the expense of manufacturing, one of the most significant developments in the domestic economy. It should also be mentioned that there were no major green field investments in high technology.'

8.6.6 Uneven Effects on the Social Side

The effects are also far from obvious on the social side: on wages, industrial relations, and working conditions.

Wages higher than the local average, though not reflecting productivity differences

With regard to wages, foreign investors are widely considered to be paying higher rates than domestic companies. Although this is found to be generally true in all studies in candidate countries so far, the size of the gap with local wages is generally also found not to be very large, and certainly not to reflect the productivity differentials between the two different types of company.

For Hungary, interviews have shown that multinational companies paid 30–40 per cent more than domestic wages in the early years of transition, but that wage increases in subsequent years were only just above inflation (Kaucsek 1996). In the machine industry, 'foreign owned firms in general pay 20–30 per cent above average wages to blue-collar workers to keep skilled employees. In the case of professionals and managers the gap between Hungarians and Western Europeans is much more moderate' (Makó 1998, p. 15). In any case, foreign investors are careful to maintain a low-wage policy: 'the main motive of ABB's eastward expansion has been low costs. Therefore, Hungarian ABB companies do not intend, but neither are they being pushed, to pay higher wages' (Ladó 2001, p. 129).

In Poland, although foreign investors were found to vary greatly:

> wages are the main source of dissatisfaction in enterprises with foreign capital. This can be accounted for in terms of greater employee expectations, and by the spectacular growth in output, productivity, worker responsibility, which is regarded as insufficiently remunerated . . . [while] the most common cause of formal disputes started by trade unions in foreign factories in Poland is wage conflicts. (Domański 2001, pp. 34, 38)

A long strike over a pay increase took place at the Lucchini Steelworks in Warsaw in 1994.

The situation is worse in small and medium-size foreign investors, especially in traditional sectors which try to keep wage costs at the lowest possible level. In Bulgaria, 'small and medium-size companies try to squeeze labour costs to the minimum wage level, and in some cases even try to avoid payment altogether . . . or to use "under-the-table" payments' (Minchev and

Gradev 2001, p. 310). The wage policy of foreign-owned enterprises is therefore differentiated, generally in terms of size and sector.

We must add that some conflicts have also occurred between foreign investment and employee-ownership: the workers who own part of a company's shares are often systematically bypassed and ignored by the management, which often does everything possible to buy back shares from the workers (for Romania, for instance, see Zaman 2001, p. 22). Considering the importance of employee-ownership in Central and Eastern Europe, and its importance as a form of economic democracy at firm level – and also as part of the European Social Model (see Chapter 6) – foreign enterprises seem to be imposing a rather different model.

Industrial relation systems often at odds with practices at home

The outcome of industrial relations in foreign companies is also far from obvious, and can greatly vary, according to sector, individual company, and overall context. It also varies according to form of foreign investment: for instance, foreign capital participation in a privatised company generally does not alter the industrial relations form that prevailed in the previous enterprise, thus reflecting the industrial relations of the host country. By contrast, when establishing a greenfield site the foreign investor has more flexibility to transfer its own model of industrial relations from the home country. This flexibility, however – as we saw in Part I – is often used by the foreign investor to implement totally different industrial relations, with for instance no trade unions, no workers' participation, and working standards (for example, regarding working time and temporary work contracts) which are much worse than at home.

Even within the same sector, it is possible to find two different policies from foreign investors (Ladó 2001, p. 103): (i) the 'high road' approach, with wages higher than average, better than average working conditions in return for high quality performance, high flexibility and adaptability from highly skilled employees; but also (ii) the 'low road' approach, with employment of unskilled or semi-skilled workers, preferably young women, on the lowest possible wages, the emphasis being on the continuous search for newcomers ready to join the enterprise temporarily as labour turnover is very high.

These two extreme employment strategies seem to be possible, within the same region, within the same sector, and with foreign enterprises from the same home country. For Ladó (2001, p. 104), in Hungary, 'the available data do not allow us to estimate the dominance of one of the mentioned employment strategies. It is widely assumed, however, that the majority of multinational companies follow the low road strategy'.

In Romania, the many foreign SMEs operating in textiles, food, and light industry 'as a rule have no trade union organisations' (Zaman 2001, p. 11).

This is not only the case in small and medium-size enterprises, but also in the production units of very large and famous EU multinationals. For instance, in the Czech Republic examples can be found of the total absence of trade unions and works councils, even at larger enterprises, where the law requires that works councils be established. In 2001, trade unions sent official complaints to the ILO and the European Commission about the behaviour of Siemens in the Czech Republic which refused to allow trade unions to be created, and also used physical violence to impede trade union meetings. A similar case happened in the Czech affiliate of the German multinational company Boesch. In Poland too, multinational companies often do not recognise trade unions. This is systematically the case for instance with French companies in the agro and supermarket sectors. Other sectors are also affected: 'some pressure is believed to have been put on foremen and supervisors to leave or not to join a union at Fiat' (Domański 2001, p. 37). Still in Poland, unionisation has ceased in some firms where female employees predominate: for example in Henkel as in almost all other foreign textile companies. Moreover, most greenfield plants are still 'union-free': for example, Philips Matsushita in Gniezno (Domański 2001, p. 37). Similarly in Hungary, it is difficult to establish trade unions at greenfield sites, where anti-union attitudes prevail, a situation also found in the Czech Republic (Zemplinerová 2001), Bulgaria (Minchev and Gradev 2001), and indeed in all other candidate countries.

In Romania too, 'in the case of both large and small "greenfield" investments there is a clear tendency to discourage the setting up of trade unions (for example at Metro, Coca-Cola, MacDonald's, and so on)' (Zaman 2001, p. 21).

In Slovenia, although foreign companies seem to recognise trade unions, they also try to use works councils to limit or circumvent trade unions (Rojec and Stanojević 2001, p. 156). In Estonia, according to a survey carried out in 1999 (on 107 firms), only 20 per cent of foreign-owned companies had a trade union, generally among those which had been acquired during the privatisation process, since foreign investors establishing a new venture (greenfield investments) usually do not accept trade unions (Varblane 2001, p. 208). There are also no trade unions at ABB production units in Estonia, Hungary, and other host candidate countries. In Lithuania, very few enterprises with foreign capital are unionised (Vidickiené 2001, p. 248).

For M. Ladó (2001, p. 106) the conclusions for Hungary are clear: 'under the same conditions, local trade unions are less likely to exist at FDI enterprises than at Hungarian ones . . . others have preferred works councils to trade unions, an approach which, in the longer run, might undermine local trade unions, if it does not make them superfluous'.

Even if the foreign owner involves trade unions, these do not have much say in the decision-making process, with less autonomy to negotiate collective agreements, when they are signed at all. In many foreign companies, 'pacts' on wages are signed, rather than collective agreements, which do not enjoy legal protection. This, combined with the absence of collective agreements at sectoral level in all candidate countries, means that these workers are just not protected.

Moreover, the absence of foreign investors from consultation tripartite structures at national level (they prefer personal political contacts with the government, or create alternative channels) and from social dialogue, combined with their dominance of national economies makes social dialogue mechanisms rather empty and meaningless.

This absence of social dialogue is reflected at local level. Collective labour disputes emerged for instance at Polish factories of ABB, Fiat, Philips, and Volvo.

The managements of foreign companies are also found not to share much information on strategic choices. In this regard European works councils could help workers of the host country to have access to more information. We have seen in Chapter 6, however, how local representatives only rarely take part in European works councils, even as observers.

To summarise, we can say that industrial relocations have yet to be accompanied by EU industrial relations.

Working standards: seeking greater flexibility in candidate countries
In terms of working conditions, foreign investment is generally a factor in the improvement of working conditions, especially in terms of new technology, training, and health and safety standards. However, in Chapter 2 we saw that foreign investors have a tendency to introduce in candidate countries much more flexible working patterns compared to local standards, but also often compared to the standards of their home country. In Hungary, Neumann (1999) shows that they have systematic recourse to more flexible working-time arrangements, shift work (also night shifts), week-end work, part-time work, fixed-term contracts, and 'leasing' workers from temporary employment agencies. In a context of unemployment and low living standards, these changes have been accepted by the workers in exchange for higher wages and preservation of jobs, although such casualisation of work forms in the end increases employment insecurity. However, employees in Poland were not found to be paid more or compensated for the introduction of more flexible working patterns, such as more mobility, job rotation, and also often longer working weeks.

It is also not rare to see multinational companies re-employ laid-off people but under the more flexible arrangement of self-employment, thus contributing to the sharp increase of self-employment contracts described in Chapter 2. This phenomenon is observed for instance in Hungary (Ladó 2001, case study

p. 119, and also p. 129). At ABB, collective agreements are not always signed, and where they are, the management has renegotiated the collective agreement to provide more flexibility in the organisation of working time, with longer working periods, especially during peak months, with less use of paid overtime. In Malta, we saw in Chapter 2 how large multinational companies such as Thomson (which threatened to leave the country), and also Playmobil, have fiercely opposed the transposition of the EC directive on working time.

In Poland, Philips employs a significant percentage of its employees (15 per cent) on temporary contracts (usually 7–8 months) to meet seasonal demand. Outsourcing is also a current practice of foreign-owned companies, especially in the clothing sector, which generally implies less security in both employment and social conditions. Outsourcing is also a way of circumventing trade unions, which have then to negotiate the collective agreement with a new employer, generally leading to worse conditions for the workers. For instance in Poland, 'objections to outsourcing were at the root of the dispute at ABB Zamech in 1998 . . . there have been seven collective disputes at ABB Zamech (now Alstom) since 1990' (Domański 2001, p. 38). In Estonia, the management of the production unit of Norwegian–Finnish company Lindegaard ASA took advantage of weak trade unions to avoid signing collective agreements and to introduce the use of labour in three shifts (Varblane 2001, p. 231). There have also been conflicts in Slovenia because of longer working time imposed by foreign investors, as in the case of Renault-Revoz where more working hours were demanded of employees without appropriate overtime payment.

Although on the positive side the introduction of such work patterns may correspond to the necessary flexibility that employers require and have also developed in the EU in the last decade, with potential effects for performance and employment, we might wonder whether this systematic recourse of foreign investors to this form of casualisation of work in candidate countries is not contributing to the unregulated working conditions and also labour markets we described in Chapters 2 and 4. Significantly, in Bulgaria representatives of foreign investors and the largest export producers have created since 2000 an alternative employers' organisation (alongside the existing Bulgarian Industrial Association), aimed at imposing on the government a new version of the Labour Code that would introduce more flexibility in workplace labour relations and working conditions, closer to the position for instance of the American Chamber of Commerce (Minchev and Gradev 2001, p. 314). Foreign investors did the same thing in Romania, creating their own employer organisations (Zaman 2001, p. 20). Similar pressures for more flexibility in the use of temporary work contracts has been exerted by foreign investors in Lithuania, with the support of the International Finance Corporation (IFC) and the World Bank (Vidickiené 2001, p. 247).

8.6.7 Long-Term Risk of Relocations Further East?

Economic growth too much influenced by foreign investment

We saw in section 8.6.3. how the type of employment, and thus of unemployment, is influenced by foreign investors as a result of their weight in the economy. This should lead us to question the strength and viability of national economies which are mainly led by external capital, which by definition will not have – and cannot be expected to have – as one of its principal aims the protection of national interests, that is, of citizens in terms of employment, social protection, and working and living standards in general. Their policy will always be decided from their headquarters, based in another country, following a profitability logic which does not have borders and which will not take into account the possible economic and social implications at local level.

The same imbalance that we found in employment can be generated in many other areas, for instance the trade balance. What if foreign-owned companies decide suddenly to radically modify their structure of imports and exports, or to reduce their investment propensity in the country (for instance by repatriating profits rather than reinvesting them in the local business), or to get rid of a significant proportion of its labour force?

This risk is recognised by several authors: 'the trade policy and actual results of FDI enterprises are of the utmost importance for the whole Hungarian economy' (Ladó 2001, p. 85).

We might wonder, however, whether such direct dependency on foreign investment is a bad thing for a national economy.

We can see that the greater the economic weight of foreign investment, the more limited is the freedom of governments in terms of economic policy and policy in general. The paradox is thus striking in the candidate countries of Central and Eastern Europe, but also of Malta and Cyprus which are also very much economically dependent on a few multinational companies: while foreign investment has helped these countries to overcome their transition production crisis, and has become their engine for growth, the fact of being so dependent on foreign investment may well lead to totally unbalanced and vulnerable economic growth in the future. The implications of this model of economic growth are obviously not neutral with regard to social policy. We have seen in previous chapters how many multinational companies have tried to bypass trade unions, social dialogue, and workers' participation, and have had recourse to the most flexible and casualised forms of employment contract.

The risk of future East–East relocations

In 2001, foreign investment in Central and Eastern Europe showed a small decline, from USD 29 billion to 28 billion. This slump is partly the result of a decrease in privatisation opportunities.

Moreover, major foreign investment projects seem to concern services, notably because of the privatisation of state companies in electricity and gas distribution (in 2001 in Poland and the Czech Republic), or in telecoms (for instance, the sale of the Polish telecom company in 2000 and of Czech Telecom in 2002), whilst foreign investment in manufacturing is already on the decline. In 2001, only about one-fifth of the top deals were in manufacturing, the rest in services (EBRD Transition Report 2001, p. 23).

In Hungary, direct foreign investment has already shown signs of running out of steam, with less new capital arriving in the country in 2000 (although it recovered slightly in 2001). This means that the continuity of Hungarian economic growth will entirely depend on the foreign investors already located in the country, and on their turnover. Only their reinvested earnings can guarantee their continued contribution to the Hungarian economy.

A similar situation seems to characterise other candidate countries, for instance Estonia, since foreign direct investment flows in manufacturing have become much rarer since the end of the privatisation process. Although more relocations are to be expected in the years to come, it is obvious that foreign investment may start to decline.

We can see how such a situation can endanger the national economy of a host country, which can be totally dependent on the decisions of multinational headquarters to maintain or close their affiliates.

We have seen what a wave of indignation was caused by the decision of French company Danone to close a biscuit factory (Győri Keksz) with 660 workers in Győr (relocating it to its other production unit in Székesfehérvár, still in Hungary). Demonstrations were organised, articles were written in the national press, and policymakers tried to intervene (the Prime Minister intensified his contacts and visited the local manager to get him change his decision).[8]

Given that many foreign sub-contractors are following their main multinational client, we can imagine the negative implications that the decision to relocate of a company such as Volkswagen-Audi or Philips would have on national and regional economies. ABB's plans are already to move further East, to Asia but also to Africa and Latin America, and the company will certainly relocate once its status as low-cost producer can no longer be maintained in Central and Eastern Europe.

Moreover, studies of foreign direct investment have shown that the more R&D activities are carried out by the foreign investor in the host country, the longer its commitment to the country will be maintained (Vaughan-Whitehead 1992). In this regard, the fact that most foreign investors have located their

---

8. See the article 'Burnt Cakes: Why Danone wants to close one of its Hungarian plants', in *Business Central Europe* (June 2001), p. 26.

lowest value-added segments in candidate countries, with very few R&D centres, is not an encouraging sign. Most of them could certainly – and would not hesitate to – fly out overnight if new opportunities for high profits and long-term strategic developments appeared further East.

In the textile sector, 'relocations' further East are already taking place, with EU customers looking for new sub-contractors in, for example, Bulgaria, Romania, but also Moldova and Ukraine which not only have a cheap labour force but also have improved their infrastructure and quality of production.

8.7 THE NEED FOR MORE RESTRICTIONS AND MONITORING OF CAPITAL MOVEMENTS

8.7.1 Host Country: The Limits to Be Imposed by Public Authorities

With regard to the host country, the discussions above have emphasised two types of risk that can be associated with foreign investment.

The first is the risk of having a national or regional economy too heavily dependent on the operations of foreign companies. In this regard, public authorities must find the best combination of policy constraints and locational incentives to ensure the balanced development of foreign investment between sectors of activity, and to attract the type of investment which will favour the 'high road approach', with investment in high value-added products and possibly also in research and development activities. There is also a clear need to promote a better regional distribution of foreign investment, and to channel it where it can also help to curb unemployment.

At the same time, public authorities must ensure that the foreign investment will be long term, and minimise the risks of new relocations (for instance further East). Host countries should not hesitate to take the risk of deterring foreign investment that may not contribute to national economic growth. Diverging interests often lead to open conflict. As stated in the EC Regular Report 2001 on Poland (p. 9): 'During the reporting period, there has been a number of high-profile disputes between the Polish administration and investors in Poland'. Karnite (2001, p. 270) summarises how policy with regard to foreign investment should change:

> Foreign direct investment in Latvia is not an unmitigated success story. Several scandalous cases of FDI, as well as ten years' overall FDI experience, suggest that FDI is a complicated issue that must be properly managed, and that conditions must be created such that both parties are satisfied. Up to now work on FDI has focused on the creation of favourable conditions in order to increase FDI inflow. Correspondingly, all assessments were focused on the immediate and unselective attraction of FDI. The current situation requires a more comprehensive assessment of FDI impacts, including qualitative assessments in a long-term perspective.

The second risk is more related to the effects of foreign investment on the domestic economies, in terms of employment, type of economic growth, and also of social and industrial relations developments.

Domański (2001, p. 39) in his case studies reports the words of the representative of the Polish employees on the European works councils of ABB, according to whom industrial relations in particular factories owned by transnational corporations depend by and large on the personalities of local managers and trade union leaders. It is true that even within ABB in Poland, important industrial relations differences can be noted between the different production units. This conclusion however confirms the vulnerability of the workers – but more globally of the whole local community, including public authorities – with regard to the operation of foreign-owned companies. This points to the need to have more binding elements with regard to employment and working conditions in foreign-owned companies.

In this regard, implementation of the Community *acquis* as a precondition of accession – including standards such as those on European works councils, working time, temporary and part-time work – could only contribute to limit social dumping by foreign investors in the host country.

8.7.2 Home Country: Limiting the Social Effects of Relocations

As a first step, actors from home countries should stop denying that a massive relocation process is occurring towards candidate countries, and will certainly continue after the first accessions. According to Domański (2001, p. 47), there is no doubt that 'a further relocation process from the EU to Poland can be expected. One may also anticipate increasing exports of construction materials, paper, chemicals, and rubber and plastic products from foreign-owned Polish plants to the EU, which may substitute part of production in the latter'. This is a process which will continue in all future candidate countries, with obvious implications for EU countries in terms of trade, employment, wages, and labour standards, and should induce public authorities, but also other actors (such as trade unions), to finally address the issue.

Information gathering should be considered a first major priority. Since the managements of multinationals generally try to hide and to deny relocation strategies (because they know the unpopularity of such decisions and the risk of conflicts with the trade unions and local authorities),[9] it is crucial to try to systematically collect information on multinationals which announce the closure of production units in the EU.

For instance, major manufacturers in Poland, such as Philips and ABB, emphasised that they did not come to Poland with the intention of relocating

9. For instance, ABB refuses categorically to provide any information on its investments in Central and Eastern Europe (see Pye 1998, p. 12).

production from the EU, but that relocation decisions were taken later as part of a broader reorganisation of production. The strategy is clear: to carry out relocations in a number of stages, with a few months' delay between the closure of a unit in the EU and the acquisition or creation of new facilities in a candidate country, from which at first only the local market is supplied, followed by the redirection of total production towards external markets.

In this regard, the case of the closure of Renault's production unit in Vilvorde (Belgium) was also remarkable in at least two respects. First, it revealed the total powerlessness of the public authorities of both the host (Belgium) and the home country (France). Despite the personal intervention of the two Prime Ministers, Luc Dehaene for Belgium and Lionel Jospin for France, with the Director of Renault, they could not change of Renault's decision. Second, the closure of Renault's unit in Vilvorde has never been presented as a relocation, but rather explained by the management (and apparently accepted by the media and others) as a normal closure of a non-profitable production unit in Belgium by a large multinational company which was facing financial difficulties and thus carrying out significant restructuring. At the same time, however, Renault was investing in a new production unit in Russia which was justified entirely in terms of direct access to the local market, although the same production unit is today exporting to many other markets. Furthermore, at the same time Renault was also intensifying the operations of its production unit (Revoz) in Slovenia, which was reoriented towards export markets: 'Renault . . . basically changed market-seeking into factor-cost advantage seeking . . . and considered Revoz to be competitive enough to be fully integrated into its business' (Rojec and Stanojević 2001, p. 142). A few years later, Renault were announcing record profits, the highest among the automobile giants remaining on the market. We might wonder whether the closure of Vilvorde was really necessary, or if alternative courses could not have been investigated. Closure of companies and layoffs must be averted if they are not strictly unavoidable and if this does not endanger the survival of the group as a whole. In other words, there are grounds to believe that in many cases relocations could be prevented and limited with better monitoring and control of multinationals' operations.

Considering the ease with which multinational companies can dissimulate relocation strategies and also the difficulty faced by public authorities and trade unions in countering transnational capital movements, especially when motivated by economic reasoning, it is essential that public authorities insist on closures of establishments being accompanied by a comprehensive social plan, with essential measures such as training, labour mobility, and so on, aimed at limiting layoffs.

Monitoring by public authorities at national and EU level of the policies followed by foreign investors is also needed, for instance in terms of information and consultation of workers' representatives, but also social standards and overall transparency. For instance, the profitable retail chain Marks and Spencer's sudden decision to close its stores in France in 2000 led the French government to adopt more restrictive rules in this field.

In sectors such as textiles, more monitoring and regulation are needed to limit the recourse of large EU companies to sub-contractors whose competitiveness is based on watering down existing social standards. More labour inspection is urgently needed, especially in countries such as Bulgaria, Romania, and, on an even larger scale, Turkey. Social partners could also play a regulatory role, as has been shown at EU level through the signing of a code of conduct in the textile sector, which was then extended to the candidate countries.

8.7.3 Trade Union Cooperation: A Tool to Tackle the Relocations Issue

Public authorities are not alone in being powerless in the face of capital relocations: trade unions have also found it difficult to work out a coherent and constructive message, not to mention successfully taking action in this field. They have generally opposed relocations, but without much influence on the final outcome. One important tool that they have learned to use in recent years is international cooperation between national trade unions, particularly in the exchange of information and the acquisition of all the elements of the management's strategy. This is particularly useful when the management is trying to hide the direct relationship between the closure of a company in the EU and the opening of new units in a candidate country. However, the relocations issue can also divide the trade unions: this has happened in a number of cases, and it explains (see Chapter 6) why workers' representatives in the European works councils of multinationals are often reluctant to involve their counterparts from the candidate countries: EU trade unions are trying to preserve jobs whilst trade unions in the candidate countries are also aiming at improving workers' local employment prospects. These are fundamentally divergent interests that can lead to divergent views on almost the whole range of policy. At Fiat in Poland, for instance, 'the confrontation between Italian and Polish trade unions has found expression in interference with the transfer of engine production to Bielsko-Biala' (Domański 2001, p. 40). Similarly, at the Slovenian production unit of the Italian group Bonazzi (producer of polyamide filaments and granulates), there does not seem to have been any cooperation between Italian and Slovenian trade unions (Rojec and Stanojević 2001, p. 166).

In these cases, it is important for trade unions from both sides to enlarge their views and to analyse the problem with regard to the survival of their company in the longer term and in a wider strategic perspective. Communication and exchange of information and ideas, even if divergent, is better than the exclusion of some by others. Full and extensive operation –

that is, including representatives from host candidate countries – of European works councils must be turned into a powerful trade union tool.

Good cooperation is also a precious tool at the disposal of trade unions in avoiding social dumping. For instance, misbehaviour by a local unit of a French retail chain in Poland could be stopped after local trade unions alerted their French counterparts who then put pressure on the French management.

8.7.4 Tools at International Level

In order to limit uncontrollable capital movements and industrial relocations, there is a need for a more voluntaristic approach that should aim not only at consolidating the European Social Model inside the EU, but also at strengthening the respect for fundamental social rights in international trade. There would be no sense in trying to reduce the sources of intra-EU social dumping if the pressures for extra social dumping from lower labour standards outside the EU continue to increase.

However, although the battle over the 'social clause' was lost by the ILO and other international organisations keen on preserving some social standards in commerce, the campaign for fundamental social rights is still going on. In this regard, transnational social instruments for countering or limiting the uncontrolled dominance of capital movements and globalisation certainly represents also one distinctive feature of the European Social Model. If developed, these instruments could progressively represent exemplary developments in international commercial exchanges (see Szell 2001, p. 8).

8.8 CONCLUSION

The above analysis allows us to reach two different sets of conclusions with regard to capital movements and social policy, first about wages and other differentials in working and social conditions as a factor in capital relocations, and second on the social effects of foreign investment.

On the first aspect, analysis of the empirical evidence available so far on capital movements in parallel with EU enlargement leads to a first strong conclusion: although there have been attempts to minimise the risk, it is clear that there is an on-going massive relocation from the EU towards future member countries that may even accelerate after their accession to the EU. We saw how major EU multinationals, but also non-EU companies (located in the EU) have already relocated part of their EU production activities to candidate countries. Surprisingly, despite the large-scale economic and social implications for EU countries, there has been no debate on the issue. It is disappointing to see that painful experiences of the kind which took place at Vilvorde, with famous multinational companies suddenly closing their production units in the EU and relocating them in a candidate country, with dramatic consequences for local workers – and extensive press coverage – may continue to take place before the problem is recognised and hopefully addressed.

However, there is already enough indication that this relocation process will continue: the multiplication of relocation cases, illustrative of a massive movement particularly striking in automobiles, electronics, and machinery and equipment, together with relocations in textiles, which take the form of outsourcing to local supplier companies. In addition, the fact that manufacturing has been the main target of foreign investment confirms the logic of low-cost seeking relocations currently pursued by many EU investors in candidate countries. Even if foreign direct investment may slow down in manufacturing in the next few years, marking the end of the 'golden' privatisation period, we may expect other foreign direct investment and industrial relocations. In early 2002, for instance, there were announcements of new car plants by Toyota-Peugeot for the Czech Republic and Ikarus-Renault for Hungary. No doubt other investors will follow. According to the Commissioner for EU Enlargement, G. Verheugen, 'There will be no further relocations, or they will not be due to EU enlargement'.[10] A few days earlier, though, the *Financial Times* had reported the decision of Peugeot to relocate part of its production facilities to Central and Eastern Europe,[11] and there will be numerous other cases.

A second conclusion can also be reached on the basis of twelve years' experience in Central and Eastern Europe: foreign direct investors seem to be much more 'cheap labour cost-seeking' than the studies in this field have suggested so far. The fact that most foreign investors dedicate the highest percentage of their production to external markets – on average above 75 per cent of production is dedicated to exports, generally to the EU – shows that the importance of the domestic market was just one initial determinant of foreign investment, longer-term policy being oriented much more towards the use of production units with cheap and skilled labour as export platforms to feed the EU and other markets. In this strategy, lower wages – together with the availability of a skilled labour force – were found to be the real variable, rather than lower unit labour costs, targeted by foreign companies in their relocation decision, since they can remodel local productivity levels through transfer of production techniques, technology, and training.

This chapter has also allowed us to counter some over-used and over-simplistic formulae concerning foreign investment in future member states: our analysis concludes for instance that it is not true that 'foreign investment in

10. At 'European Panel 2002: Reforms for a Social Europe – Perspectives on the Work of the European Convention', organised on 5–6 November 2002 in Brussels by the European Trade Union Institute.

11. 'Peugeot chooses Central Europe for new factory', *Financial Times* (29 October 2002), p. 3

candidate countries is mainly motivated by domestic markets' or that 'foreign investment is only market-seeking in Poland', or that 'labour costs are not motivating foreign investors in Slovenia'. On the contrary, we believe that the low-labour-cost approach explains a lot of foreign direct investment and relocation strategies pursued so far, which seems to apply also to large countries such as Poland and to higher wage payers such as Slovenia. These conclusions should induce those working in this field to be more careful before drawing general conclusions, especially considering the complexity of foreign investors' decisions, the different logics by sector, and the great variety of situations among host candidate countries.

A third conclusion concerns the sectoral distribution of the relocation process. Contrary again to the usual inferences about foreign direct investment, the relocation process is occurring not only in the traditional, labour-intensive sectors, but also in some segments of the more high-tech, capital-intensive sectors, such as telecommunications, engineering, and computers. In these internationalised sectors characterised by fierce competition, companies also urgently require low labour costs to succeed in their ambition to create in candidate countries 'export platforms for the EU' before an enlarged EU market is put in place. The presence of relocations in these sectors thus further confirm the extent of current EU relocations in candidate countries.

As regards the second aspect – the effects of foreign investment – our analysis has resulted in a more mitigated image of foreign investment.

On the one hand, foreign investment is undoubtedly a driving force behind candidate country economies, with impressive results on growth, sales, and exports which can only accelerate economic and social catching up. They explain a large part of the future member states' economic performance. Their long-term contribution to candidate countries' trade balances is also expected to be positive – growing exports outperforming high volumes of imports – thus helping them to reduce their trade deficit with the EU. On the EU side, however, this may increasingly reflect a clear substitution effect of previous trade flows from the EU of the same companies that now produce from the candidate countries and no longer from the EU. The effects of this policy on EU economies, especially in terms of employment, have yet to be captured and absorbed by local actors.

On the other hand, foreign investment in future member states has not been found to lead to a spillover effect to domestic firms, notably because of their limited relationship with the network of local suppliers, and insufficient expansion of research and development. Foreign investors thus do not seem to lead local companies to develop higher-value production processes and goods, but rather to develop a 'booming' economy in relative isolation from domestic actors. In this context, massive foreign investment flows represent an element of future instability in the region. Some candidate country economies are already too dependent on foreign direct investors who cannot be asked not to follow a profit maximisation strategy, generally based on lower labour costs and social standards whose progressive increase over the next few years could motivate these companies to relocate again, further East, with significant adverse economic and social effects.

On the social side, contrary to what might have been expected foreign enterprises were not found to be very successful in terms of industrial relations and working conditions: they often do not allow trade unions or local representatives into European works councils. At the same time, they tend to develop highly flexible patterns of employment contract, leading to more 'employment uncertainty' for the workers, with systematic temporary work, interim agency work, part-time work, and longer working time arrangements. We might wonder whether this model of performance enhancement is not taking the opposite direction to the one EU policymakers at the Lisbon summit in 2000 decided to trace for the future, that is, to use social policy and high working standards as productivity and enhanced-competitiveness factors.

The final impact of foreign investment on local employment is also uncertain. While foreign investors implemented significant layoff programmes in the initial restructuring process, their high profitability has led them also to create new jobs at a second stage, so that the net effect on employment may be positive. The picture becomes more complex, however, when we analyse the types of worker employed by foreign investors, mainly skilled and educated employees. The restructuring process has given foreign investors the opportunity to fire the less skilled employees, who have joined the mass ranks of the long-term unemployed. This is being made worse by a concentration of foreign investment in already developed geographical areas, so far totally ignoring poorer and more remote areas, where unemployment rates are highest.

To summarise, and without questioning their positive effect on job creation, we also found that multinational companies do not seem to be contributing much to solving – in some cases they rather seem to be fuelling it – the main employment problem by which future member states are today confronted, namely long-term unemployment. This may partly explain why unemployment in candidate countries remains high despite the fact that their economies are driven by foreign investment. Foreign investment-led economic growth is leaving aside the type of worker it does not need, thus generating further social differentiation.

This model of economic growth mainly based on foreign investment that has developed in many future member states is obviously not neutral with regard to social policy and the features of the European Social Model described in earlier chapters. This requires counterpowers on the workers' side, but also more monitoring of capital movements and the activities of multinational companies, both from national and EU authorities.

9. Labour Mobility: The European Taboo

9.1 INTRODUCTION

Free movement of persons has turned out to be one of the most controversial issues in the current EU enlargement process. The prospect of the accession of ten countries from Central and Eastern Europe has raised fears that low living standards in these countries may lead to increasing migration flows towards the current EU member states as soon as their citizens are granted free movement of labour.

Fears of this kind are not new in the history of 'Europe'. In 1957, when the original European Economic Community (EEC) of six countries – Belgium, Luxembourg, and the Netherlands, Germany, Italy, and France – came into being, the Germans and the French were already afraid of being 'swamped' by Italian guest workers. When in 1981 Greece, and in 1986 Portugal and Spain, joined the European Community (EC), Northern European member countries again worried about potential South–North migration. However, although these fears have not been borne out by experience – migration flows even from Southern countries have remained limited – they have never been as acute as today in face of an EU enlargement process which is proposing to take on board countries which not only have sizeable populations, but also are characterised by much wider economic and social differentials in relation to the EU. If significant labour movements were to take place, it is believed that severe, even unbearable strains would be put on the EU target countries. Such migration would congest already tight EU labour markets and lead to job losses among domestic workers, not to mention increased social security burdens. These fears are particularly marked among countries which have a common border with the future member states, especially Germany and Austria, where political leaders have taken a rigorous stand against immediate freedom of labour, a position also relayed by their national press (although this could also be said of other EU countries). Migration risks have turned out to be one of the most popular arguments against EU enlargement in public debates.

While discussion on this issue seems to have been dominated by either political statements by populist and nationalistic leaders in search of extending their electoral base, or the need to calm fears at the risk of being overoptimistic, the aim of this chapter is to provide an objective assessment, as far as possible, and to present and develop the full range – rather than a relatively narrow selection, as many studies on the issue have done so far – of arguments about expected migration flows, and their possible adverse but also positive effects on both home and host countries.

We shall try to answer two main questions. First, can the estimates – and the related principal conclusions – provided so far concerning potential labour movements from future member states be considered realistic and reliable? Do they point to potential labour movement on a mass scale? Second, have all criteria governing migration, as well as the likely profiles of migrant workers from future member states, been sufficiently taken into account in this analysis?

This first assessment will allow us to evaluate the EU's current negotiating position on freedom of persons, and provide some discussion of alternative policy options. We shall try above all to address the migration issue in terms of the social dimension, and try to identify whether social dumping is already taking place and whether it may multiply once free movement of labour is permitted.

9.2   A BASIC COMMUNITY RIGHT

From the very beginning of the European integration process in 1957, the freedom of workers has been an integral constitutional part of the European Economic Area (EEA). Article 48 of the original EEC Treaty of Rome of 25 March 1957 stipulated that 'freedom of movement of workers' entailed the 'abolition of any discrimination based on nationality between workers of the member states as regards employment, remuneration and other conditions of work and employment'. Consequently, workers with an EU passport are allowed to move without any substantial legal restrictions from one member country to another, in a manner similar to movements within their home country. In the wake of a number of pathbreaking decisions by the European Court of Justice in the early 1990s, the right to free movement within the EEA has been enlarged from 'workers' to 'people' in general.

Moreover, by signing the Single European Act in 1986, the twelve member states of the European Community agreed to establish a single market for goods, services, capital, and persons from 1993. The Treaty thereby enforced the freedom of movement of labour within and between the EU member states.

Since different social security systems may represent an obstacle to labour movement, making difficult the transfer of or access to social security, the European Community has also accompanied such freedom with the mutual recognition of social security regimes.

9.3 TRANSITION PERIOD

Temporary arrangements were utilised in previous enlargements. While the opportunity to migrate to other EU member states in order to find work had been seen exclusively as a positive achievement of the European integration process in the 1960s and 1970s, the perceptions of both the public and policymakers have changed in recent decades.

Already during the accession of Greece, Portugal and Spain into the EU, free movement of persons was restricted and subject to bilateral migration treaties. Greek workers had to wait six years before they were allowed to choose their place of work freely and without restriction within the EU, and the admission of Spain and Portugal was made conditional on the implementation of a seven-year transition period before free movement of persons could be applied (this period came to an end one year early since no significant migration flows had taken place).

'Flexible Transitional Arrangements' for Future Member States
The membership applications of Central and Eastern European countries encouraged the European Commission to propose a transitional period before the free movement of workers would apply. The proposal envisages a general transition of five years, with a possible extension on the part of individual member states for a further two years. After no more than seven years, therefore, free movement of workers would operate fully across all member states.

The aim of this proposal, according to the EC, is to meet concerns where they arise and where they might seem to be justified, while allowing for mobility of workers. These transitional arrangements apply to all candidate countries, with the exception of Cyprus and Malta. Free movement of citizens in general will not be affected by these proposals, which apply specifically to workers.

On the basis of previous policies with regard to enlargement to incorporate Southern countries, the European Commission has argued that the transitional period requested of candidate countries from Central and Eastern Europe is by no means a discriminatory measure but in keeping with EC policy precedents (as a common instrument in community life). Representatives from candidate countries, however, have complained that this decision is profoundly unfair and would lead to an unbalanced distribution of EU enlargement costs, something that we shall discuss in more detail in section 9.9.2.

But are the projections on which this policy stance is based accurate? A number of studies have tried to provide an answer, most notably at the bidding of the European Commission.

9.4 MASSIVE EAST–WEST MIGRATION?

9.4.1 Econometric Studies and Projections

What follows is a summary of the studies carried out so far on migration flows to be expected from Central and Eastern Europe. The main study was commissioned by the European Commission, though there have also been a number of independent studies. Although the aim is generally the same, to forecast possible flows in the next few years, these studies have adopted different methodologies and tested sometimes radically divergent assumptions.

A number of 'empirical' studies have attempted to determine how many immigrants can be expected from candidate countries using two main sources: macro data from previous enlargements to the Southern countries, and data concerning past immigration to Germany, including that from Central and Eastern European countries.

The main variables used to explain variations in migration have typically been income or wage differentials, geographical distance, stock of migrants already in the host country, unemployment, and regional dummies. Income differentials have been found to be the most significant determinant of migration: the greater the difference between the (lower) income of the home country and the (higher) income of the host country, the greater the expected increase in net migration. Unemployment rates also push workers to find a job abroad, whilst distance appears to have a negative effect on net migration. The existence of co-nationals in the host country, constituting a sort of network, was also found to enhance net migration in consecutive periods.

Studies have produced different results according to their basic assumptions in terms of income differentials and other variables, including whether they take into account return migration and other phenomena.

Table 9.1 presents potential migration flows to the EU from the ten Central and Eastern European candidate countries as predicted by the studies available.[1] The table also focuses on the eight countries that are expected to join first, that is, excluding Bulgaria and Romania, whatever reservations we have expressed elsewhere in this volume about this political division. Not all Central and Eastern European countries are included, as in the case of Sinn (2001), Bauer and Zimmermann (1999), Fassmann and Hintermann (1997), and Salt et al. (1999). Romania and Bulgaria, indeed, are rarely included, although the migration risks from these two less developed countries is likely to be higher. An important new candidate country, Turkey, has not been included anywhere, although its inclusion would alone modify all predictions about future migration to the EU.

1. For other studies, see Hönekopp (1999, 2000) and Straubhaar (2001a).

Table 9.1 Synthesis of estimates of migration to the EU from the CEE candidate countries under free movement (main results of comparative studies, 1997–2002)

	CEEC–8 migrants		CEEC–10 migrants	
	Stock	Flow per year over first 10 years	Stock	Flow per year over first 10 years
Fassmann and Münz (2002) – excluding Romania and Bulgaria		3 to 5 million		
Brücker (DIW) **and Boeri** (2000) – only workers – Regression analysis on immigration rate from East Europe to Germany (1967–98)	860 000 (after 10 years)	70 000 declining to 30 000	1.4 million (after 10 years)	120 000 declining to 50 000
Brücker (DIW) and **Boeri** (2000) – all migrants – Regression analysis on immigration rate from East Europe to Germany (1967–98)	1.8 million (after 10 years)	200 000 declining to 85 000	2.9 million (after 10 years)	335 000 declining to 145 000
Sinn et al. (IFO) (2000) – excluding Bulgaria, Slovenia, and the three Baltic states. – Regression model on the basis of past migration (1974–97) of Greeks, Italians, Portuguese, Spanish and Turkish in Germany and projection on CEECs on the basis of wage differentials	2.7 million (after 15 years)	240 000 declining to 125 000	4.2 million (after 15 years) 4–5% of total population of the countries of origin	380 000 declining to 200 000
Hille and Straubhaar (2001)				270 000 to 790 000
Bauer and Zimmerman (IZA) (1999) – excluding Baltic states – econometric simulation based on migration flows after Southern enlargement (and based on unemployment rates and GDP per capita)	2.5 million (after 15 years) 3 per cent of total population of countries of origin	200 000		

	CEEC–8 migrants		CEEC–10 migrants	
	Stock	Flow per year over first 10 years	Stock	Flow per year over first 10 years
Salt et al. (1999) –excluding the Baltic states	2.25 million (3.3 per cent of pop. after 15 years)	140 000		
International Org. for Migration (1999) – micro survey in 11 CEECs on intentions to migrate – sample size of 1 000 respondents per country			7 to 26 per cent interested in migrating permanently 13 to 68 per cent for short-term work 18 to 57 per cent for long-term work	
Walterskirchen (WIFO) and **Dietz** (1998) – excluding commuters – assessment on the basis of extrapolation of expected income (GDP) differentials (correlation found from US data)		160 000 declining to 110 000		
Fassmann and Hintermann (1997) – excluding Slovenia, Bulgaria, Romania and Baltic states – Micro study on the basis of survey of 4 392 people	720 000 (long-term migration) 6 to 18 per cent of respondents with serious intention to leave			
Franzmeyer and Brücker (1997) – excluding Baltic states, Romania and Bulgaria – assessment on basis of extrapolation of expected income differentials			340 000 to 680 000	

Note:
The column '10 CEEC' includes potential migrants from all 10 current candidate countries from Central and Eastern Europe; the column '8 CEEC' includes those whose accession is expected to take place first, in 2004, and thus excludes Bulgaria and Romania.

Source:
European Commission information note, 6 March 2001 (EC 2001), p. 34, and other, more recent studies (Fassmann and Münz 2002).

Moreover, most studies are based on research results from Germany only, as in Brucker and Boeri (2000), and Sinn et al. (2000), or from Austria only, as in Walterskirchen and Dietz (1998), which seriously limits what general conclusions we might draw from them. Most studies also tend to assume that the distribution of citizens from the eight or ten candidate countries from Central and Eastern Europe will remain stable within the fifteen current EU member states, although, as we shall explain later, EU enlargement will create a dynamic that may completely modify this distribution.

9.4.2 Main Conclusion: No Massive Movements to Be Expected

Despite the obvious limitations of these studies, and their different assumptions and statistical models, they surprisingly confirm that East–West migration would involve no more than 3–7 per cent of the population of Central and Eastern Europe within one or two decades after freedom of movement is granted (see Table 9.1). This would represent approximately 3–5 million people for the 10 Central and Eastern European countries or between 300 000 and 600 000 a year. If we consider only the eight countries likely to be allowed in first – that is, excluding Romania and Bulgaria – East–West migration is likely to be around 2 to 2.5 million people. Some studies arrive at higher figures: for instance, the IFO study by Sinn (2001) predicted 4.2 million immigrants by 2015 and by 2030 up to 11 million from the ten Central and Eastern European countries to Germany alone. The more recent study by Fassmann and Münz (2002) predicts that between 4 and 7 per cent of the population of the Baltic states, Poland, the Czech Republic, Slovakia, Hungary, and Slovenia will move to Western Europe by 2020, and could thus reach five million people. Other studies are more modest in their predictions, such as the German Institute for Economic Research (DIW) which estimates that the number of migrants will not exceed 2.5 million by 2030 (Brücker and Boeri 2000). The study commissioned by the EC reported figures – on the not very realistic assumption that free movement of labour would be granted in 2002 – of 2 million people in 2005, 2.9 million in 2010, 3.7 million in 2020, and 3.9 million in 2030 (European Integration Consortium 2000a). In this study the rate of immigration drops quickly after one decade, and the total number of new migrants diminishes considerably. In other studies, the annual flow of migrants remains high over the whole period, thus bringing higher figures (Sinn et al. 2000). Other experts predict higher figures. Blanchard (2001) estimates that 'the estimate given by Brucker et al. of 0.3 million a year is too low . . . and very conservative' and predicts instead an annual net migration rate of 1.75 million.

Other studies insist on the need to take into account return migration, which they predict may be significant, about half the size of gross migration rates, and so between 1 and 2 per cent of the home populations (Straubhaar 2001a). This seems to be confirmed by survey work which shows that about 65 per cent of those surveyed who are willing to migrate do not want to remain abroad for longer than five years (Fassmann and Münz 2002).

Survey studies also tend to conclude that between 1 and 4 per cent of the resident population of Central and Eastern Europe between 15 and 65 is thinking of taking up employment in the EU. According to the study by the International Organisation for Migration carried out in 11 Central and Eastern European countries, between 7 to 26 per cent of the respondents expressed an interest in emigrating to work in the EU on a permanent basis, the percentage becoming even higher – up to 68 per cent – for those interested in working for a limited period (IOM 1999). Survey work based on questions focusing on a serious intention to leave (not only expression of an interest) show a lower percentage, below 20 per cent of respondents (Fassmann and Hintermann 1997).

It is on the basis of this relative convergence of statistical results that most studies, and the European Commission along with them, have concluded that no massive migration is to be expected from Central and Eastern European countries after they are granted free labour access to the EU.

> Concerns that EU labour markets will be swamped by migrants from the CEECs ... seem to be ill-founded. Although Eastern enlargement will not affect wages and employment at the aggregate level, trade and factor movements may well have a non-negligible impact on the regions immediately bordering the CEE countries and on specific sectors that are more exposed to import penetration from the East. (European Integration Consortium 2000a)

Another conclusion on which most studies in this area converge is that there would be stronger migration at the beginning, but the growth rate would diminish in the long run.

These studies confirm that the political argument against enlargement of a massive invasion of foreigners stealing the jobs of domestic workers has been greatly exaggerated for the political profit of nationalistic and populist politicians (such as Haider in Austria).

Nevertheless, it is entirely a matter of speculation as to how far the 3–4 per cent – perhaps even 7 per cent – rule of thumb will be borne out by the realities of the EU's Eastern enlargement.

9.5 METHODOLOGICAL DRAWBACKS

Despite the scientific nature of the above-described studies, their validity for assessing labour migration from future EU member states from Central and

Eastern Europe can be doubted, mainly due to two serious drawbacks affecting their respective starting assumptions:

1. most of them base their forecasts and estimates on past events in a different context, involving countries from Southern Europe which are very different in nature;
2. the current EU enlargement process involving Central and Eastern Europe is unprecedented, and comprises numerous new and unpredictable phenomena (or variables). Studies can therefore rely only on recent and current migration flows from Central and Eastern Europe, which are subject to very different circumstances. The assumption that many variables in the current EU countries will not change, such as stable geographical distribution, unemployment rates, and so on (as in Brücker and Boeri 2000) is unsound, since they will clearly be affected by the EU enlargement process.

9.5.1 Misleading Extrapolation from Past Experience

We shall first examine the validity of applying empirical migration experiences from one area – Southern European countries, mainly Portugal and Spain – to predict movements from an area which is totally different in character, namely Central and Eastern Europe. Most of the studies we have analysed adopted a migration supply function in which a number of variables were tested on the basis of data on Spain and Portugal. Not only do these data refer to a different time, but also the countries diverge radically as follows.

A much larger economic gap
Most importantly, the level of development and the average real per capita income in the 10 candidate countries of Central and Eastern Europe are much lower than in the case of Greece, Portugal, and Spain. At the time of entering the EU in the early 1980s, the Southern countries had attained about two-thirds of average EU per capita income, well above the countries of Central and Eastern Europe, which have reached about one-third of the EU average. This is a substantial difference that could lead to completely different migration behaviour, and in particular to a different scale. In fact, all studies show that individual migration elasticity (an individual's willingness to leave) is greater in the case of larger income gaps but diminishes in the case of smaller income gaps (Straubhaar 2001b, p. 169). This not only means that the numbers implied may be higher, but also that the process may last longer. The large relative economic gap will last for a long decade, as shown by our catch-up scenario presented in Chapter 10.

Greater differences in wages and working standards

We saw in Chapter 2 the large wage differentials that prevail between current and future member states. To the wage or income factor we should add other labour standards that may contribute to migration, such as decreasing social protection, poor prospects on local labour markets, and much more difficult working conditions (as explained in Chapter 2) in terms of working time, health and safety at work, and employment security. Differences in all these standards are greater than they were for the Southern countries at the time of their accession.

Greater number of people involved

The current EU enlargement process involves far more people than was the case with the Southern countries (Spain 39.4 million, Greece 10.5 million, and Portugal 10.0 million in 2000), as Table 9.2 indicates. Poland alone accounts for 38 million people, which should induce us to consider the current EU enlargement process as unique. The populations of the 12 candidate countries represent around 105 million people, nearly one-third of the current EU 15 population of 379 million. This is without counting Turkey, whose population is 65 million.

Table 9.2 Populations of the 13 candidate countries, 2001 (thousands)

Bulgaria	8 149
Cyprus	671
Czech Republic	10 295
Estonia	1 367
Hungary	10 005
Latvia	2 366
Lithuania	3 693
Malta	382
Poland	38 644
Romania	22 430
Slovak Republic	5 402
Slovenia	1 990
Turkey	65 000
Subtotal	170 394
Current EU15	379 400

Source: Eurostat, News release No. 7/2002 (11 January 2002).

Geographical proximity

The distance between country of origin and country of destination is a relevant factor in explaining migration, since distance increases transaction costs and renders it more difficult for potential migrant workers to obtain relevant information on employment prospects and living conditions abroad.

Compared to Greece, Spain, and Portugal, which were always regarded as belonging to the 'periphery' of the European Union, Central and Eastern European countries enjoy a greater geographical proximity to other current EU member states. Many candidate countries of Central and Eastern Europe share common borders with highly developed EU member states. Since distance has been found to be a significant factor in migration, compared to past experience with regard to Southern Europe it may play a greater role in relation to Central and Eastern Europe.

The greater burden of Central and Eastern Europe
There is one major difference that has not been taken sufficiently into account so far, although it should be considered a major element in the enlargement process: Central and Eastern European countries have undergone a painful transformation process from central planning to the free market, an event which is almost unique. This obviously represents an extra burden on these new market economies, from which the Southern countries were mercifully free. This dimension has the further significance that it can not only influence economic behaviour but also drive political changes, including how people from the region – who have borne the main costs of transition – perceive the EU enlargement process (see Chapter 11).

Specific cultural obstacles and incentives to migration
Some studies have tried to show that there would also be a number of cultural obstacles to migration from future member states. For instance, people's social and cultural ties to their local environment, the language problem, and the availability of housing. These factors are indeed very important – more important than for the Spanish and Portuguese who for years had already been fairly well integrated into EU culture – and could limit the willingness of people to move, although differently for different categories of workers, which are not evenly concerned by factors such as language ability. At the same time, other cultural factors could play in the opposite direction: the attractiveness of a new type of society, totally different from the one in which they are used to living, is particularly strong among young workers. Other factors, such as networks of co-nationals already in the host country, are also part of the picture.

All these features lead to the conclusion that factors promoting migration will be much stronger in Central and Eastern Europe than in the case of the Southern countries. This already shows that the simple extrapolation of migration behaviour from the accession of the Southern countries undertaken by almost all studies in this area can represent only a pale reflection – and a clear underestimate – of the real labour movements that will take place.

Moreover, while cultural factors are indeed to be taken into account, we should not forget how much influence the income gap currently prevailing between East and West could have on potential migrant workers.

9.5.2 Movements that Have Yet to Occur

Central and Eastern European countries have no recent historical experience of free migration, first because there was no right to emigrate legally for decades under the previous regime, and second because there has been no right to emigrate legally – or only under very strict conditions – to the EU since these countries started their transition process, over twelve years ago.

The only movement that can be observed so far is illegal migration, which at the same time is governed by a different logic from legal migration and so does not reflect the implications of the forthcoming EU accession process.

The legal labour movements which have been allowed by EU member states so far are limited to particular categories of worker, and also in size, and are of little use in predicting the behaviour of workers in general from candidate countries. Nevertheless, several studies conclude that, since such movements have been limited so far (there were 830 000 registered migrants from Central and Eastern European countries living in the EU member states in 1999, of whom 290 000 were members of the labour force), it is likely that there are no strong incentives for workers from Central and Eastern Europe to come to EU countries.

Generally speaking, these studies take developments in Austria and Germany over the last decade as their point of departure and presuppose that current trends will remain stable. These figures are extrapolated for the EU as a whole.

This extrapolation does not take account of the extraordinary incentive that the opening of frontiers could represent, and on the possible bandwagon effect of EU enlargement. The existence of quotas and related administrative obstacles currently constitute a disincentive to many. Moreover, the forecasting of migration flows to the EU in terms of Germany alone (with some studies extending the analysis to Austria) ignores the fact that in an enlarged EU workers from new member states will be able to move freely from one EU country to another. Again, we can only emphasise the difficulty and very subjective nature of any attempt to predict a phenomenon which is unique in many respects.

9.5.3 The Limits of Opinion Polls

In order to overcome the two drawbacks described above, other studies rely mainly on opinion polls or surveys. It is true that surveys have the merit of addressing questions directly to those concerned and thus undoubtedly give a better estimate – or at least perception – of the possible willingness of citizens from candidate countries to migrate towards the EU. Their object is not to forecast an annual migration flow, but to measure the current stock of people willing to migrate within a certain period of time. However, the methodologies used for such surveys – in terms of survey methods or kinds of questions asked, the sample chosen, and so on – are so varied that it is difficult to draw clear conclusions. As is well known, the type of question asked can directly influence the final outcome. For example, questions are often posed in a very general way – 'Would you eventually envisage going to work in the EU?' – and does not include considerations of time (when the respondent would move) or further information about whether arrangements have already been made by the respondent (which might measure the seriousness of their plans) for such a move. Clearly, the positive response given by many people to such questions often does not represent – and cannot be assimilated to – a strong commitment to migration.

Finally, specific categories or groups of people are rarely interviewed, a method which could lead to more accurate, because more focused, indications of a willingness to move to current EU member states. Finally, it is again inevitable that once a country has joined the EU respondents' perceptions of possible migration to the west may change.

The most reliable survey work can be found in Fassmann and Hintermann (1997) and the IOM (1999), together with country-specific surveys for Latvia (Aasland, 1996) and for Hungary (Berencsi et al. 1995).

The results of opinion polls, despite their considerable variation in quality, have been over-used by the press and some politicians. For example, a study was quoted by the *Neue Krone Zeitung* (2001) which supposedly shows that 17.4 million Poles, 3.9 million Hungarians, and 2.6 million Czechs were planning to work in the EU. The fact that the answers of the survey participants were merely declarations of interest, which say little about actual migration figures in the future, was ignored (as reported by Kunz 2002, p. 7).

However useful they may be, opinion polls have thus to be treated with caution, and should be complemented by other, more scientific analyses and not form the basis of hasty policy decisions.

9.6 THE NEED FOR A 'QUALITATIVE', NOT JUST A 'QUANTITATIVE' ANALYSIS

Most studies on migration and EU enlargement so far have aimed at providing figures on expected migration flows. But estimates of purely quantitative flows do not make much sense in the absence of more detailed analysis.

Paradoxically, attempts to make a more detailed assessment of specific situations in candidate countries are surprisingly rare, probably because they would tend to emphasise the limitations and in some cases the absurdity of merely quantifying East–West migration, especially in terms of the simple extrapolation of past EU enlargement to Southern countries.

In fact, another picture emerges from more detailed analysis aimed at taking into account the different characteristics of candidate countries' labour markets, and in particular the segmentation of the labour force (Heitmueller 2002).

Although the main conclusion may be the same – that massive migrations may not be taking place – such an approach helps us to identify categories of worker in respect of whom such movements may indeed be massive. Moreover, in some cases taking into account the diverse features of migrants and their motivations may indicate that overall flows of migrants may turn out to be even greater than the existing literature predicts.

9.6.1 Significant Migration Potential among Young Workers

Age strongly influences the decision to migrate, since it is more difficult for older workers to move abroad: they are often bound to one particular employer, or have specialised in a certain geographical region, and have employer-specific knowledge, less time to make up transaction costs, and more difficulties adapting to new working and life situations, and are in general less flexible due to ingrained habits.

According to survey results, three-quarters of respondents who are willing to migrate are below 40 years of age (Fassmann and Münz 2002). This accords with observed historical patterns, the first stage of labour migration generally being dominated by younger men, who are later followed by family members.

The majority of migrant workers from Central and Eastern Europe so far – 70 per cent – belong to the 25–44 age group, which is well below the average working age in the EU. Higher migration may certainly be expected from the younger generation, especially because young people often also belong to the most vulnerable categories which have the most incentive to migrate. We have seen for instance that the risks of exclusion and unemployment are greater for younger population groups, which are also more flexible as regards travel abroad, with fewer family links, or language and cultural barriers, and a readiness to work under less favourable conditions than host country workers. It is worth remarking that greater migration of young workers from Central and Eastern Europe may in turn exacerbate the difficulties of their counterparts in the current EU, where very high youth unemployment rates also prevail.

9.6.2 Greater Migration Probability among Skilled Workers?

Migration also depends on the probability of finding a job and information concerning employment possibilities. Skilled workers in this regard are in a better position: higher education, knowledge of foreign languages, better professional and social status, belonging to network of peers of the same profession or having acquired the same skills clearly contribute to the ease with which one is able to acquire the information necessary for making a decision to work in another country. Such workers are also better able to assess the labour market situation at home and abroad.

Modern communications and information technologies (such as the Internet) have also reduced to a minimum, particularly for specialised workers – who have daily access to such technology – the delay in obtaining relevant information, compared to domestic workers. Skilled workers are also more flexible and more open-minded and their qualifications are likely to be recognised abroad.

This is also the reason why skilled workers are generally induced to migrate temporarily rather than permanently, since labour markets at home may change more quickly and more positively than for unskilled labour.

The fact that there is a great reservoir of skilled workers in Central and Eastern Europe on the one hand, and great demand for this category of worker in current EU member states on the other, seem naturally to mark them out as the main candidates for migration. The majority of migrants from Central and Eastern Europe so far have been found to have a significantly higher education than foreign or native employees in the EU.

However, this may not be true across the board. While the demand for skilled labour from EU member states will continue to be high, it is not certain that the supply will continue to be as plentiful because there seems already to be a labour market in candidate countries for this category of worker. We saw in Chapter 8 that foreign investors have already hired most specialists and skilled employees, thus leading to a boom in demand and thus also wages and working conditions for these employees. Domestic companies are also beginning to pay this category of worker better. This is a natural process since, in the coming months and years, future member states will also be confronted by a shortage of skilled labour as they seek to sustain increased economic growth. Better economic conditions will also lead domestic employers to pay more and rapidly to catch up with EU working standards.

In 1999 and 2000, despite great demand from Germany for computer specialists, Hungary was unable to fill its quota of migrant workers in this profession.[2]

---

2. I thank Mária Ladó for this information.

The scenario drawn by Fassmann and Münz (2002) seems to be realistic: 'during an early stage, mainly highly educated and motivated persons would come as pioneer migrants to Western Europe, but during a second stage a larger share of less qualified persons might follow the pioneer migrants'.

9.6.3 The Phenomenon of 'Commuters'

We have seen that geographical proximity is an important element in migration. Proximity lowers transaction costs for migration and makes it easier to obtain relevant information about job opportunities and working conditions.

Cross-border 'commuting workers', who live in the border regions of candidate countries', are a widespread phenomenon, especially in the border regions between Germany and Poland, but also between Austria and Hungary.

The many common borders between EU member states and candidate countries from Central and Eastern Europe should lead to commuting on a large scale. While movement which involves a change of residence is considered as migration, commuters move back and forth between their job and their place of residence on a more or less daily basis.

Mainly motivated by the wage differentials existing between the countries concerned, such workers can combine the higher wages and other benefits provided in the EU member states with the lower living costs in their home country. This means that only the exchange rate rather than purchasing power parities must be considered when comparing wage differentials for this type of migrant worker.

The prevalence of this type of worker is rapidly increasing in some regional labour markets, particularly in the Bratislava–Vienna region and the Western Poland–Berlin area.

Commuting – especially for workers in services – is expected to increase strongly in both directions once new members join the EU.

9.6.4 The Risk of Massive Migration among the Vulnerable

While a good financial background makes it easier to change country of residence, in most cases the pressure to migrate is lower for people who are financially well off. It is for this reason that we believe that the situations of precariousness and poverty – as we saw in Chapters 2 and 3, many people are still living below the poverty line – have not been sufficiently taken into account in the debate on labour migration and EU enlargement. The social situation alone should induce us to reject any possible analogy between Central and Eastern Europe and the Southern countries when they joined the European Community. We saw in the current candidate countries the striking contrast between increasing economic wealth and the situation of ordinary people who often have problems making ends meet. It is from this source that massive migration could eventually come, which should lead us to scrutinise the situation more closely.

9.6.5 Sectoral Patterns

We might expect migration flows to follow sectoral patterns.

Unskilled labour force
Already, a majority of migrant workers from Central and Eastern Europe are found in labour-intensive services (for instance, catering, hotels and restaurants) with a high proportion of unskilled work. Sectors such as agriculture (which employs a majority of seasonal migrant workers) and construction work also traditionally employ migrant workers from these countries. Most workers required by Germany are for construction activities. In Chapter 7, we described how many employees from candidate countries are today employed, legally and illegally, by German construction enterprises, not only private but also public.

We also saw that cases of social dumping exist in transport, citing the examples of Willy Betz and, more recently, Kralowetz. More than in any other sector, wage differentials here are a source of considerable profits for EU companies.

In most of these traditional sectors (services, construction, transport, textiles, and so on), demand is mainly for unskilled or very low-skilled labour, confirming our argument at the end of section 9.6.2 that most massive migration flows may come from these categories of worker rather than from skilled labour. Blue-collar workers are also more likely to become unemployed (Hofer and Huber 2001, p. 14), which may increase their motivation to look for a job abroad.

Workers in the public sector
It is important to consider also the wage levels of those working for the non-profit sector (that is, the budgetary or public sector), even if their productivity (and thus unit labour costs) cannot be easily evaluated. They may well have the greatest incentive to move to EU countries: they cannot enjoy increased wages brought by multinational companies since they continue to work for domestic organisations and institutions, generally dependent on the state, but they have considerable qualifications and skills for which they could earn more in EU countries. While mobility may be limited for certain professions, such as school teachers, it may be very high for doctors, nurses, and so on.

Recently, the demand for foreign nurses and workers in health care has increased in most EU countries, for instance in Ireland, thus showing that for this migrant labour category both demand and supply are high.

On the supply side, however, privatisation tends to limit migration since it can bring competitive price and wage fixing into these sectors, even within national borders. For instance, if health services are partially privatised, doctors can find better paid jobs in private clinics or hospitals.

Nevertheless, a survey carried out in the Czech Republic in May 2002 indicates that almost one-quarter of doctors may be willing to work in current member states after their country enters the EU. The majority were under 34 years of age, mainly specialists working in public hospitals. The strongest willingness was observed among surgeons, while on the other hand private doctors do not wish to leave the country. This could lead to a shortage of doctors after the Czech Republic enters the EU, something which may already be observed in some regions.[3] The same tendency can be seen among public sector doctors in Hungary and other candidate countries.

Skilled labour
In addition to the health sector, there is increasing demand (and supply) of highly skilled employees in very specific activities, for instance, computer software specialists, a category of worker regarding whose immigration countries such as Germany have been very liberal (no age limits, possibility of multiple applications, longer duration of stay, and so on). The UK has also liberalised the rules for IT workers from Central and Eastern Europe. An analysis just carried out for Microsoft shows that the EU economy needs an additional 1.7 million IT workers (that is, both skilled and less skilled employees).[4]

We should also mention civil aviation pilots from candidate countries who are progressively moving to work in EU-based companies. Since there are important common standards in terms of training – particularly universal use of a single language (English) – these pilots have the same skills as their EU colleagues, but at home are paid much less and are employed under more unstable conditions. Tough competition in this sector means that airline companies are actively seeking such pilots who in general are more flexible in terms of wages and working conditions.

9.6.6 Failure to Take Account of 'Non-Working' Categories

The unemployed and inactive have so far not been much considered as candidate groups for migration. However, the unemployed may have a greater incentive than others to migrate, because their opportunity costs are very low: they have nothing to lose since they do not have a job and receive very small,

---

3. 'One-quarter of doctors want to leave for EU countries', in *Czech Happenings* (27 May 2002): www.ceskenoviny.cz.
4. According to Bimal Gosh, 'Why Europe Needs More Immigrants', *Wall Street Journal* (5 January 2001).

often merely 'token' unemployment benefits at home. This is particularly true of the long-term unemployed who represent the majority of those without work in the candidate countries (see Chapter 4). The presence of very low out-flow rates from unemployment, especially in the long run, should clearly be considered as an important factor in potential migration. Higher and growing unemployment, as well as its long-term nature – as described in Chapter 4 – should thus be included in East–West migration studies, something that has not been done so far.

In this context, 'even small differences in the rate of remuneration, com-bined with moderate employment probabilities in the destination region, may be sufficient to trigger migration' (Heitmueller 2002).

There is also a significant number of inactive persons in candidate coun-tries, since a drop in labour force participation rates has been observed over the transition period (Chapter 4). Moreover, significant outflows from unem-ployment into inactivity rather than towards employment have also occurred. Discouraged by unsuccessful job searches, inactive people often get involved in family businesses, contributing to hidden unemployment. Low opportunity costs of migration in terms of forgone wages, combined with poor job prospects in tight local labour markets, seem to endow this category of inac-tive persons with significant migration potential. Workers employed in the informal sector, often under very precarious conditions in terms of both job stability and working conditions, also represent an important migration reser-voir. Moreover, these people are ready to accept illegal work abroad if legal jobs cannot be provided to them, an argument which tends to show the inverse relationship between legal migration – through authorising freedom of move-ment and of work – and the growth of illegal migration.

These aspects have clearly been overlooked in the recent literature on migration and EU enlargement. However, the incorporation of such categories as the unemployed and the inactive may significantly modify our perceptions and predictions of potential East–West migration. More generally, we can say that the features of labour markets in candidate countries that we described in Chapter 4 – their dynamics, weaknesses and potentials – have surprisingly not been taken into account in recent empirical studies about migration after EU enlargement. For instance, Hofer and Huber admit in their study (2001, p. 4) that 'workers who are marginally employed, self-employed, or civil servants are not included'. However, it is also from these missing categories that migration may come on a larger scale.

9.6.7 Social Factors: Downward Trends Pushing Migration

Taking into account the unemployed as a potential category for migration implies that social factors, such as social and unemployment benefits received at home and in the host country, may play a role in the decision to migrate. Available data shed light on a significant gap between benefit entitlements in future and current member states (OECD 1999; Heitmueller 2002). As an example, while a single, unemployed production worker in Poland would receive approximately 38 per cent of his previous working income, a German unemployed would get at least 60 per cent (Heitmueller 2002, p. 6). The gap widens (to 43 and 73 per cent of working income respectively) for a single-earner couple with two children. These different rates, combined with already very different basic wages, are sufficient motivation to seek work abroad, or to prefer being unemployed abroad rather than at home.

Apart from unemployment benefits, other entitlements in the host country can be claimed, such as family benefits, health care, benefits in case of accident, and other transfers.

For Heitmueller (2002, p. 7), 'Relative differences in social benefits become even more striking in the presence of large average wage differentials between Central and Eastern European countries and Western European countries'.

Moreover, once migrants qualify for entitlements, not only the probability of migration, but also length of stay in the host country is a positive function of social benefit differentials. Greater differences in social benefits between home and receiving country also make it less likely that return migration will occur.

Crumbling social protection systems at home (see Chapter 3) can thus increase CEE workers' motivation to migrate, while higher social benefits and unemployment benefits in the host country reward mobility, especially in a home context characterised by long-term unemployment. It is clear that 'the social benefit systems in Central and Eastern European countries fail to provide sufficient cover, particularly for the long-term unemployed, altering their net present value of migration compared to the group of short-term unemployed' (Heitmueller 2002, p. 9).

Sinn et al. (2000) also confirm that not only wage differences but also attractive social security systems are an important reason behind migration. They suggest limiting migration not by restrictions on freedom of movement, but by reducing the social rights and entitlements of migrants from future EU member states in order to make the current EU countries a little less attractive. However, this solution would contradict the basic principle of equal treatment and the antidiscriminatory rules that are part of the Community *acquis*.

In short, although income differences are properly seen as the major driving force of migration, social factors are also important. Not only do these factors provide a direct incentive for particular subgroups, such as the unemployed and the inactive, but also they should be taken into account as an additional motivation to leave as they would reduce the opportunity costs of becoming unemployed abroad.

On the other hand, the social factors behind migration might also cause migration flows to fall as living standards and social conditions improve in new EU member states.

9.6.8 Economic Factors: Migration as Future 'Adjustment' Variable?

Optimistic catch-up scenario

Almost all studies on future labour movements from candidate countries have assumed that, after an initial surge, the propensity to migrate would progressively decrease, and would eventually – together with return migration – lead even to a reduction in the stock of migrant workers in the (current) EU. This optimistic scenario, however, very much dominant in the study commissioned by the EC, depends on very rosy forecasts about economic growth in the candidate countries in the coming years. However, after impressive economic growth – much higher than the EU average – we can reasonably expect these economies to slow down, so that the economic catch-up predicted by migration specialists will occur less quickly. This would totally change expected migration flows, especially in the longer term. In any case, economic catch-up, according to the most optimistic scenario, will take at least 15 to 20 years (see Chapter 10 on trade and economic growth). This means that migration flows will continue to depend directly on the economic performance of the candidate countries, and this may, as in the case of all economies, be disrupted by internal or external factors.

The result of the other two basic freedoms

In Chapter 7 on social dumping we saw that movements of capital, labour, and goods and services are very much interrelated. Significant West–East capital movements and expansion of trade with the EU have so far contributed to boost candidate country local labour markets. Nevertheless, we saw in Chapter 8 that EU foreign direct investment is slowing down in candidate countries, especially as their privatisation processes come to an end, and as wage differentials progressively decrease. This fall in capital movements may well lead to a greater propensity of workers from these countries to find a job in the European Union. At the same time, any slowing down in trade flows from candidate countries, something that may well intervene as a direct implication of a moderation of the activity of EU multinationals, would also constitute a factor pushing labour migration.

To summarise, in marked contrast to the optimistic scenario assumed by many studies, it cannot be excluded that labour movements may emerge as a sort of labour market adjustment variable following an eventual slowing down in economic activity, foreign investment, and trade in candidate countries.

9.7 THE COMMISSION'S DOUBLE MESSAGE

As the accession negotiations have proceeded, the chapter on free movement has been one of the most sensitive issues, causing it to be left among the last to be concluded, together with agriculture and discussions about the structural funds. In the meantime, the European Commission has been active in delivering a number of messages and studies on the issue. Nevertheless, it does not seem to have a clear and transparent policy in this area, as reflected in a sort of 'double message' which candidate countries have found it difficult to understand: although the EC has managed to calm fears related to massive labour movements by means of political statements and a commissioned study showing that such fears are unfounded, at the same time it also decided to adopt a strict policy with regard to the granting of freedom of labour movement to candidate countries. Detailed analysis of the various aims, arguments, and motivations of the EC in this process is therefore essential.

9.7.1 A Commission Campaign Aimed at Calming the Situation

Deliberate underestimation of expected movements?
The EC position on migration has been mainly based on the study it commissioned from a group of researchers (European Integration Consortium 2000a, 2000b). There seems in fact to have been a consensus on the main results: the EU has insisted that there would be no massive migration of labour from candidate countries to the EU, and candidate countries have gone along with this.

This has led to a number of statements and speeches from the EC aimed at calming fears centring on this political 'hot potato', leading some to wonder whether this public campaign was exaggerated and based on a deliberate underestimation of expected movements.

Some experts have been rather sceptical about the study commissioned by the European Commission: 'The partly optimistic basic assumptions of this model are the main reasons for the relatively moderate increase [of migration]' (Fassmann and Münz 2002).

Moreover, it is surprising that the European Commission has neither published nor commissioned other studies and analyses of this issue, despite its political importance and the general difficulty of generating clear and definite statistics in this field, something recognised by the EC itself: 'clearly, estimates of migratory flows should be treated with caution because, amongst other things, they are based on past patterns'.[5]

5. Speech by Odile Quintin, Director General of the DG for Employment and Social Affairs at UNICE, Brussels (7 June 2002): 'European Business Forum: Migration in a Wider Europe', p. 3.

Despite this limited statistical and analytical basis, statements have been rather clear and unequivocal from the EC, which undoubtedly has achieved its ultimate purpose, to dissipate the fears of massive migrations raised by populist political leaders.

More recently, Odile Quintin stated that:

> according to the most reliable studies on the subject, including one published by the Commission last year, enlargement is expected to have only a limited effect on internal mobility . . . potential migratory flows from candidate countries would amount to 335 000 people per year. However, this would include only 120 000 workers as defined by Community law, i.e. those entitled to receive equal treatment as regards employment and to be covered by the coordinated system of statutory social security schemes. Currently around 830 000 EU residents originate from Central and Eastern Europe. It is forecast that this number could rise to 2.9 million in 2010 and 3.9 million in 2030. That corresponds to 1.4 million workers in 2010 and 1.8 million in 2030. These figures are comparable to the current immigrant working population in the EU and are very small when set against the estimated 254 million people of working age who will be in the Union in 2010.[6]

These statements are supported by a number of basic facts and conclusions about past labour movements in the EU.

Limited intra-EU movements so far

In particular, these conclusions are supported by statistics on intra-EU labour movements so far, which show free movement of persons to be the least used EU freedom so far, involving only 2 per cent of EU citizens. In 2000, only 225 000 people, or 0.1 per cent of the EU population changed their residence between two countries. EU citizens preferred to live in their home country, even if wages were higher or employment prospects better in other EU member states, a result which can be partly explained by sociological and psychological factors, such as culture, language and local network of friends and family.

It could thus be concluded that freedom of persons has not led to significant labour movements between EU member states, and that European citizens have reacted little to the opportunity for free movement within a common labour market. They have been reluctant to live and work elsewhere in the EU, despite an encouraging political environment and a series of Commission programmes to promote mobility.

Past experience: no massive migration from Southern countries

Even the significant welfare (and economic) gap that existed between Northern and Southern Europe did not lead to important migratory flows after

6. Op. cit, p. 3.

Greece (in 1981), Portugal and Spain (in 1986) joined the European Union. While in 1988, the year in which free mobility for Greek workers was allowed, the number of migrant Greek workers going to Germany increased, it then decreased over time, to consolidate at around 350 000. Similarly, the number of migrations from Portugal increased significantly (by 26 per cent) in 1993 and greatly in 1994 (by 91 per cent) after free movement was granted, but fell significantly again in subsequent years. The case of Spain is even more interesting, since net migration flows do not seem to have been influenced by the introduction of free mobility of labour. The stock of Spanish citizens moving to Germany, for instance, remained unchanged after free movement of citizens was finally granted in the early 1990s.

Migration risks diminish in parallel with economic growth
Similarly, statistics from 1965 to 1990 show that there is a statistically significant positive correlation between level of economic development and emigration. The less developed a country, the greater the willingness of its citizens to migrate to another EU country, a result that supports the expectation that migration will fall alongside economic integration and catch-up by the candidate countries.

As their living standards have risen, traditional emigration countries, such as Italy, Greece, Spain and Portugal, have progressively become immigration countries.

Increased economic growth also leads to return migration – already observed in the Czech Republic, Hungary, and Slovenia – which helps to balance immigration figures. At the same time, increasing growth also attracts more activity and more citizens from abroad, thus leading to migration in both directions. Already in the ten candidate countries from Central and Eastern Europe, large immigration and not only emigration flows may be observed: for example, currently more Austrians work in the Slovak Republic than vice versa.[7]

It is also expected that increased trade between the EU and Central and Eastern European candidate countries will progressively reduce migration flows (see Chapter 10). Finally, it is expected that a decline in the working age population due to demographic reasons will contribute to reducing migration potential (Fassmann and Münz 2002).

All these factors, which have allowed the European Commission to calm the situation and to play down the migration issue, could also have made possible a compromise that would have satisfied the majority of member

7. See *Kurier*, 'Keine Angst vor Migration' (15 November 2000) (also quoted in Kunz 2002, p. 28).

states and candidate countries. In contrast, the EC decision to propose a transitional period of five years, with the possibility of extending it to seven took many observers by surprise, especially in the candidate countries themselves. We shall try to explain the reasons behind this paradoxical position.

9.7.2 The EC Decision: Under German Pressure?

In its information note of 11 April 2001, the EC proposed transitional periods for free movement of citizens, characterised as 'flexible transitional arrangements for the free movement of workers'.

Nevertheless, however flexible this option might seem, we might ask whether there was a need for such a transitional period if the risks of labour migration were as limited as the experts pretended. To many observers, this seemed to be a political agreement to please the German and Austrian governments, which have been particularly intransigent on this issue, although they seem to have garnered all the benefits of such immigration so far. It is perhaps significant that statements from Germany have often preceded or coincided with statements by the European Commission.

After the European Commission had completed its migration study, which helped to play down the risks of labour migration, statements from Chancellor Schröder seem to have led the EC in a different direction. On 18 December 2000, one week after the European summit in Nice, speaking in Weiden, Bavaria – one of the German *Länder* in which fears of migration are most acute – close to the border (30 km) with the Czech Republic, Mr Schröder said that Germany could not absorb a sudden wave of economic migrants from the East, and called for a seven-year transitional period:

> Many of you are concerned about expansion [of the EU] . . . The German Government will not abandon you with your concerns . . . In view of the fact that we still have 3.8 million unemployed, the capacity of the German labour market to accept more people will remain seriously limited for a long time. We need transitional arrangements with flexibility for the benefit of both the old and the new member states.[8]

Not only did the Commissioner in charge of EU enlargement, Günther Verheugen, react cautiously to this strong statement, evaluating it as 'use-

---

8. For press reactions (on 19 December 2000), see, for instance, 'Schröder wants to restrict workers from new EU states', *Irish Times*; 'Schröder demands restrictions on EU job movements' and 'Chancellor picks border for message', *Financial Times*; 'Germany signals start of endgame to EU expansion' and 'EU member, second class', *The Wall Street Journal*; 'Schröder seeks delay for East bloc workers', *Herald Tribune*; 'Altolà di Schröder ai lavoratori dell'Est', *Corriere della Sera.*

ful',[9] but he has also made several similar statements on the migration issue.

In fact, the proposal by the European Commission in April 2001 included one important point of the 'Schröder formula', that is, the general transitional period of five years, which is subject to automatic review after two years. During this transitional period the member states of the Union can either restrict or open their labour markets to citizens of new member states on a preferential basis, as requested by the German Chancellor.

This similarity between the German and the EC positions has often given rise to indignation in experts and observers:

> The debate is perturbing on grounds of principle. But even more incredible –against the background of the current discussion in Germany on immigration, and the introduction of the so-called 'Green Card' – is that Bavaria's Prime Minister Edmund Stoiber and Germany's Chancellor Gerhard Schröder are among the advocates of a delay before labour can settle freely in border areas, and that the Commission is ready to serve these demands.[10]

Whether the position of the EC has been aligned in accordance with the German position or whether the EC approach is more flexible is not the issue; what is certain is that the German position has very much influenced that of the European Commission, and seems to have led it to a rather strict policy option, whose legitimacy and coherence with the other messages delivered by the EC – at minimizing the migration risks – can be questioned.[11] It is also worth mentioning that less strict views developed by other EU member states have not prevailed. During its Presidency of the EC Council, Sweden proposed to reduce the common transitional period from five to two years, a proposal that was rejected by EU member states, and not taken on board by the European Commission. Generally, EU member states have not opposed the German and Austrian 'imposed position' on migration:

> How sad if Europe's leaders fail to condemn Mr Schroeder's idea unconditionally. While there is nothing particularly objectionable about European countries pursuing additional integration at different paces (the so-called two-speed Europe), Mr Schroeder speaks of something altogether different. His is a two-class system, with Western Europe riding club class and the East Europeans consigned to coach.[12]

---

9. As also reported in the Press, op. cit.; see also 'L'Est polemico con Schroeder', *La Stampa*, 20 December 2000.

10. 'EU enlargement and migration – what's the problem?', Norbert Walter (Deutsche Bank Research), in *Euractiv news* (3 August 2001): www.euractiv.com.

11. See 'Enlarging the EU', *Irish Times* (16 April 2001); 'Bruxelles veut protéger la marché du travail', *Le Figaro* (12 April 2001).

12. 'EU member, second class', *The Wall Street Journal* (19 December 2000).

This policy has been opposed by most candidate countries, whose leaders reacted strongly against the transitional period proposal, and complained of being treated as 'second class' EU citizens. The fiercest opposition came from the Polish government, which has been under strong pressure from its own public opinion.[13] Head of Polish negotiating team Jan Kulakowski said 'we obviously cannot agree with the position taken by Commissioner Verheugen. This integrates almost entirely the Austrian and German proposals with only slight modifications'.[14]

Other countries also complained. The Hungarian government insisted on having such a basic freedom granted immediately to the citizens of new EU member states, even if it was ready to accept a flexible clause envisaging a ceiling on the number of migrant workers: 'Our position is clear: we would like to benefit from free movement from the start' (Gábor Horváth, spokesman of the Hungarian Ministry of Foreign Affairs).[15]

Clearly, 'transitional arrangements reducing the free movement of labour have sent a negative message to citizens of the candidate and future EU member countries' (Fassmann and Münz 2002). In fact, since the transitional arrangements restrict the freedom of movement for a maximum of five to seven years the restrictions will last until 2009–11, with the first candidate countries becoming EU members in mid-2004.

Other reactions have pointed to the dangers of such a policy: 'imposing fortress-type border controls may suit the more developed western states, but at the grave risk of distorting the development of better relations between the candidate countries and their neighbours. In the long term that is a better guarantee of stability and development' (*Irish Times*, 16 April 2001).

On the EU side, the transitional periods seem to have been supported by many, including the EU trade unions. In particular, trade unions in Germany and Austria have been in favour of restrictions banning citizens from future EU member states from EU labour markets.

The German trade union confederation, the DGB, has evaluated as 'necessary' the transition periods due to economic and social differences between the candidate countries and the EU. The Austrian Trade Union Federation has taken an even tougher position on the issue:

> many studies show that after a postponement of ten years the inflow will still be considerably high because the gap in wages decreases slowly. Therefore Austria

---

13. See, for instance, reactions from Polish President Aleksander Kwasniewski, quoted in 'Eastward expansion of EU could be delayed by elections', *The Independent* (4 April 2001).

14. As reported in 'CE propoe sete anos para livre circulaçao de pessoas', *Diario economico* (12 April 2001).

15. See Communication from Agence France Presse of 16 May 2001: 'Budapest insists on free movement of labour with a ceiling'.

would be hardly affected if the freedom of movement of labour is simply postponed by ten years. Experience shows the inflow of migrant workers and cross-border labour ceases once the income gap falls to between 20 per cent to 30 per cent.[16]

The position of the European Trade Union Confederation (ETUC) at EU level seems to be less rigid; although also in favour of a transitional period, especially to limit downgrading of social standards in the EU, the ETUC has also rejected selective freedom of labour, for instance in favour of skilled labour, due to its expected negative influence on candidate countries.

The position of EU employers' organisation UNICE has been more moderate about the need for a transitional period. While accepting the principle, it has emphasised the importance of removing it as soon as possible:

> Freedom of citizens is an integral part of the Community *acquis* . . . transition periods might be needed in some cases, but they should be as limited as possible . . . limited in time and coverage . . . unfounded fears of massive migrations should not lead to unjustified measures.[17]

More fundamentally, not only does the transitional period proposed by the EC contradict their argument according to which migration flows from new member states will be limited, but it also contradicts one of the most fundamental freedoms and principles of the EU. At the same time, the EC has made progress in further strengthening this principle. The European Council of Barcelona endorsed an ambitious Commission action plan designed to eliminate obstacles to mobility by 2005. It includes the elimination of administrative and regulatory obstacles to the recognition of qualifications and occupational skills, the transferability of rights to social protection and especially of supplementary pension rights, and other facilitating measures such as the establishment of a 'European health insurance card', and the setting up of a one-stop Internet site with information on mobility in Europe. Candidate countries, however, will have to wait before getting the right to participate in such an important EU policy area, in terms of both jobs and economic growth. As emphasised by Odile Quintin, 'mobility with fewer restrictions is one of the main tools for promoting the creation of quality jobs, reducing unemployment and improving the competitiveness of the European economy and European business' (Quintin 2002, p. 6). One might wonder why such a policy would not be worth applying to new member states as well, where we have seen that the situation is difficult in terms of unemployment and economic catch-up.

16. 'Position of the Austrian Trade Union Federation on freedom of movement of persons', Meeting of the Working Group 'Enlargement' (11 April 2000), OGB, Vienna.

17. 'Enlargement: freedom of movement of workers and social policy – position of UNICE', UNICE, Brussels (21 June 2001).

9.8 THE HYPOCRISY OF EU GOVERNMENTS

9.8.1 The EU Need for East–West Migration

It is a fact systematically and deliberately ignored or concealed in the debate on labour movements and EU enlargement that current EU member states need more labour mobility. We have seen how low internal EU labour mobility is, and according to experts, 'in order to achieve a "healthy" level of labour mobility and to exploit the job potential of the Single European Market, transnational mobility of European workers would have to be two to three times higher [than today]' (MKW GmbH 2001, p. 240).

Moreover, the general development of EU labour markets points to a greater need for migrant workers in the future. According to the European Commission (EC 2000c), the average age in the EU will increase from 38.5 years in 1995 to 41.5 years in 2015. While the size of the age group 0–25 years will decline, the number of retired people will grow significantly, a trend which will have dramatic effects on labour markets, where less workers will be available to meet demand.

The European Commission has already warned about the implications of this trend: 'Given the intensity of the demographic trends, particularly after 2005, these regions could find themselves in a situation of a contracting and rapidly ageing labour force' (EC 2000c, p. iv).

In Portugal, Italy, Spain, Greece, the United Kingdom, France, Germany and Sweden the average age of the working population has already increased. Further increases are predicted, especially in the case of France, Germany, Ireland and the Scandinavian countries.

A recent European Commission report on the social situation in Europe (EC 2002a) shows that immigration can help alleviate the effects on an ageing population, although it should not be considered as a universal panacea to solve the problem.

The EC report emphasises that immigration alone, even at twice the current rate, will not be sufficient – even if complemented by the doubling of fertility rates – to secure sustainable labour markets and pension systems.

> The population age structure is expected to change more rapidly than the population size, as life expectancy at birth and at retirement age continue to grow and fertility rates are low. In less than 15 years, the number of people aged 80 and over will increase by 50 per cent. By 2015 one-third of those of working age will be 50 and over.

In such a context, it is clear that higher activity rates (for instance, of women and older workers) are needed in order to prevent the collapse of social security systems and to maintain positive growth rates.

It is also clear that immigration from new member states may make a great contribution to relieve the situation in current EU member states, just as past immigration has, accounting for 70 per cent of the increase in the EU population in the last five years (EC 2002a).

In the UK, a lot is expected from immigrant labour, given the current shortages of suitably qualified workers in some areas (especially health and education), and also the Government's pledge to improve public services. There is also increasing demand from Italian enterprises.[18]

Paradoxically, Germany, the country so far most fiercely opposed to granting immediate free movement of labour to candidate countries, will also need a significant number of migrant workers (Kunz 2002, p. 9). The German working population is expected to decline after 2010, from 41 million in 1996 to 25 million in 2040 (Fuchs and Thon 1999).

Der Spiegel recently described Germany as a 'dying nation', an epithet reflected by the statistics: while in 1995 the ratio of working age persons (15 to 64) to pensioners (age 65 and over) was 4.4, from a population of around 82 million, the same age ratio – without immigration – will drop to 1.8 in 2050. During the same period, the population is expected to decrease by nearly 30 per cent, to 59 million people. Immigration is thus a necessity: to maintain a stable population level, Germany would need at least 324 000 net immigrants every year, in which case the age ratio would be 2.3 in 2050 (Kunz 2002, p. 9). Others have put forward a figure of 500 000 working-age immigrants per year to stabilise the working-age population.

To maintain the 1995 age ratio, Germany would have to take in the seemingly incredible figure of 3.4 million immigrants per year net.

An increased average age among the working population would also render unsustainable current social protection systems, and put more pressure on EU governments to reform. Immigration flows in this context could also help to relieve pressures which have in some cases led, we saw in Chapter 3, to too radical downsizing of social protection.

As summarised by Fassmann and Münz (2002):

> expected labour force shortages in Germany, Austria and Switzerland will sooner or later lead to a situation in which the fear of additional migrants and commuters from new EU member states will become irrelevant . . . why should transitional arrangements be introduced now, if they might become irrelevant in the future?

We should add that the countries expressing these fears, mainly Germany and Austria, are also those which are for the moment benefiting most from the EU pre-accession of CEE countries and will continue to benefit from EU enlarge-

18. 'Serve un accordo sugli immigrati: Le aziende li vogliono, la società no', *Corriere della Sera* (4 April 2001), p. 16.

ment, an aspect we shall further investigate in Chapter 10, dedicated to trade and economic developments.

We have already seen that nearly 40 per cent of foreign investment in the candidate countries is from Germany. Trade figures stand at a similar level.

9.8.2 For 'Flexible' Read 'Selective'

In the 1960s and 1970s Germany relied for surplus labour on the signing of bilateral immigration contracts with individual countries – for instance, with Spain and Greece in 1960 and Portugal in 1964 – which did not represent free mobility of workers (foreigners could not come freely to Germany and apply for a job), rather Germany could decide on the number of guest migrant workers to invite, generally for temporary work.

This type of policy, which gives full freedom to the host country, continues to be followed by Germany, as well as by other EC member countries. In particular, the 'green card' policy promoted by Germany recently is part of the same philosophy of selecting the quantity and quality of the labour force to come to work in Germany, generally computer specialists, a category for which there is a labour shortage. In June 2002, German President Johannes Rau signed a law which allows the controlled flow of *skilled* workers into the country, also from candidate countries. Germany also wishes to allow in a number of seasonal workers, and guest workers in the construction industry. The majority of these workers are thus non-skilled workers, showing that there is also a demand for this type of labour. In general, contracts of such short duration put the migrant workers in a very unstable employment situation; experience indicates that returned migrants have difficulty reintegrating in the home labour market. These bilateral programmes have clearly become an instrument for monitoring labour migration and a response to labour shortages.

The Austrian approach is similar. In an interview, Austrian Minister of the Interior Ernst Strasser stressed the need for migrant workers, but in specific areas: 'We will harm jobs and our attractiveness to business if we do not establish the possibility – for a certain period and for certain fields – to hire labour from third countries . . . I believe that people are very open-minded about skilled immigration'.[19]

We must add that the Austrian authorities asked for the application of additional conditions to the transitional period, including the reaching by the new EU member states of at least 80 per cent of Austrian GDP or of EU average

---

19. See 'Austrian Interior Minister Strasser on migration', in *Latest News from the Republic of Austria* (11 January 2001): www.austria.gv.at. See also 'Austrian favours immigration of skilled labour', in *Euractiv News* (19 January 2001): www.euractiv.com.

GDP, a condition that the candidate countries would need more than 50 years to fulfil. The Austrian government relaxed this condition in the course of 2002.

But would a more open policy be so detrimental to the German labour market? After all, Western Germany already experienced migration flows from Eastern Germany, whose workers were ready to work for less, without creating too much disruption in the unified German labour market. We might wonder why Germany feels unable to show some of the solidarity it exhibited on the occasion of German reunification. The situation seems to have been very much influenced by the approach of the general election: 'Immigration is likely to be a dominant theme in September's general election, the conservative opposition to Chancellor Gerhard Schröder's government arguing that Germany can ill afford to take in more foreigners when its unemployment level is so high, currently about 10 per cent'.[20] In fact, this policy seems to have contributed somehow to Mr Schröder's re-election in September 2002.

The European Commission's policy, by leaving the initiative to member states and not providing stricter guidelines on freeing labour movements earlier on, is encouraging such a selective approach. During the general transitional period of five years, member states would continue to operate their own national measures on accepting workers from the new member states; they can thus continue to apply their own restrictions (quotas, green cards, selection of skilled workers, and so on), or decide to go further than others in opening their labour markets according to local needs and circumstances. Similarly, after five years, member states would be able to continue with national measures for an additional two years, despite the fact that the EC will review the situation.

In fact, we might ask whether 'flexible' is the right adjective for the policy option proposed to candidate countries: although current member states could decide individually when to open their markets, what looks flexible in theory may well turn out to be rigid in practice, because countries such as Germany and Austria will obviously not decide to open their labour markets to migrant workers earlier than the maximum seven years, and no other EU member state is likely to take the risk of being the first to open its borders.

In short, we can only conclude that the EU member states, especially those which have common borders with candidate countries, have so far given preference, in terms of freedom of workers, to a selective approach that allows the inflow of highly skilled workers. They have secured their interests instead of carrying out a cost–benefit analysis for both EU and candidate countries.

This conclusion is related to the findings of Chapter 8 on foreign investment: in the enlargement process, EU countries seem to have allowed their

---

20. K. Connolly reporting from Berlin: '5 million eye the west as EU borders expand', *The Guardian* (27 June 2002).

companies at home to employ only skilled immigrant labour, while their affiliates in candidate countries were found also to employ mainly skilled labour. This 'pincer' promotes the exclusion of unskilled candidate-country labour from labour markets both at home and abroad. The cost of such a policy for the candidate countries is obviously high.

We might ask how far these policy positions reflect the democratic values which the EU has so far tried to promote. Do they correspond to the basic philosophy which has led to the promotion of the free movement of people within the EU? Furthermore, what of the generosity and solidarity that apparently motivated the EU to undertake enlargement, helping the post-Communist countries to 'rejoin Europe'?

9.8.3 Supporting Measures – mainly for Germany and Austria

In addition to the transitional period, pressure mainly from Germany and Austria has led to a political decision to assist border regions and vulnerable groups in the current member states, as well as to the provision of support from the structural funds. Considerable assistance has so far been given to border regions. A comprehensive programme and an EC communication on community action for border regions were adopted in July 2001. According to the latter:

> The degree of support available to border regions is considerably higher than the aid given to the Mediterranean regions of the Community prior to the accession of Spain and Portugal in 1986 . . . Germany received by far the largest share of Objective 1 and 2 aid . . . The Commission proposes to dedicate an additional EUR195 million for border regions with applicant countries in the period 2001–2006 . . . there are 23 border regions in the EU, two in Finland, eight in Germany, six in Austria, two in Italy, and five in Greece . . . In Germany, all new *Länder* bordering Poland and the Czech Republic (Mecklenburg-Vorpommern, Brandenburg and Sachsen) are due to receive EUR10.4 billion between 2000 and 2006 . . . Bavaria's Objective 2 programme, which covers the entire length of the border with the Czech Republic, is due to receive some EUR537 million over the period 2000–2006 . . . for the period 2000–2006, EUR889 million have been dedicated to the six Austrian *Bundesländer* bordering candidate countries (Burgenland, Steiermark, Oberösterreich, Niederösterreich, Kärten and Vienna) in the framework of the Objective 1 and 2 programmes . . . some EUR627 million are available for INTERREG cross-border co-operation programmes in Germany during the period 2000–2006 . . . 67 per cent of the German INTERREG IIIA funds (EUR421 million) are dedicated to eligible regions bordering Poland and the Czech Republic . . . As regards the Austrian INTERREG IIIA programme . . . an additional EUR110 million are available.[21]

---

21. *Communication from the Commission on the impact of enlargement of regions bordering candidate countries. Community action for border regions*, EC, COM(2001) 437 final (25 July 2001), Brussels, pp. 10–14.

This massive assistance for EU border regions close to candidate countries is dubious when we know that border regions of candidate countries close to the EU will not be allowed to enjoy similar access to funding, at least for a long time.

Although measures to help less developed EU regions bordering candidate countries are desirable to promote their economic and social catch-up, we might wonder whether they would not be more legitimate if linked to the immediate granting of free movement of labour to neighbouring candidate countries. Conversely, in the context of transitional periods, such heavy assistance looks more like a form of 'protectionism', closing local labour markets in order to give time, through assistance and money, to less developed regions to prepare themselves for the possible effects of the candidate countries' entry.

It appears that an imbalance is emerging between the interests of current and of future member states, one which could have dangerous effects in every sphere, economic, social, and political. This is happening despite the fact that, as recognised by the EC document:

> the available statistics do not suggest that the gradual opening of Community borders to candidate countries during the 1990s has had a negative impact on border regions. For example, per capita income levels in the Austrian border regions increased significantly between 1991 and 1996, while in Bavaria average per capita income remained fairly stable throughout that period . . . the analysis of border regions in this Communication has shown that . . . [EU] border regions will benefit from enlargement in the long term.[22]

9.9 POSSIBLE ADVERSE EFFECTS OF EU POLICY

9.9.1 Fuelling Rather than Stopping Illegal Migration

Freedom of labour would help to limit illegal migration

Public and policymakers' anxiety about EU enlargement can partly be traced back to negative experiences with illicit work and wage dumping by local and foreign companies.

This is the case in Germany and Austria, where in some sectors networks of subcontractors specialise in the supply of legal and illegal manpower from Central and Eastern Europe. This is the case in the construction sector, but also in all big public works. We saw in Chapter 7 that there is significant illegal employment of workers from candidate countries in the construction sector in Germany and also in road transport. Would restrictions on

22. Op. cit., p. 10.

labour movements help to solve the problem or in fact achieve the opposite result?

The prohibition of legal migration would by definition put many migrant workers into the black or illegal economy. The fact that this restrictive immigration policy will certainly allow some labour migration, but only after a selection process which only the best qualified workers will pass, will mean that the rest – mainly the unskilled, but also the long-term unemployed and so the most desperate to emigrate despite the restrictions – will have as their only alternative to work in the black market. Such an increase in the proportion of migrant workers in the black market would lead to social dumping, with obvious implications in terms of labour standards in the formal sector. Moreover, a lack of openness provides the perfect background for the development of hidden illegal networks for East–West migration.

Moreover, instead of distributing the weight of permitted legal migration among all EU countries, restrictions will lead most workers from candidate countries to continue working illegally in the closest EU countries, such as Germany and Austria, which for that reason alone would have every incentive to facilitate rather than restrict the arrival of migrant workers into the EU.

Conversely, the immediate implementation of freedom of labour alongside a strong policy against illegal work, including that from third countries further east, would represent the right combination to transform many illegal jobs into legal ones – with a number of positive effects, including increased social contributions in the host country – while providing the necessary transparency, mainly from the employers' side and their subcontractors, to fight illegal migration and illegal activities. It would also distribute the flows of migrant workers throughout the European Union.

A number of cases seem to confirm this argument. For instance, after the elimination of visa requirements for Romanian citizens travelling in the Schengen area, illegal migration from Romania to the EU seems to have decreased, according to official statistics.[23]

According to R. Münz, 'Illegal immigration should not be fought by barring off parts of Europe . . . this would be a battle of false arguments . . . (in the 1990s the US poured more money than ever into its attempt to barricade its border with Mexico) . . . but at the same time a record number of illegal immigrants entered the country'.[24]

Not only would the granting of freedom of persons limit the sources of illegal migration, but it could also lead to significant return migration after a few years. In a freely accessible labour market, free mobility might in fact

23. 'Less illegal immigrants from Romania to the EU', *Euractiv News* (19 June 2002): www.euractiv.com.

24. '5 million eye the west as EU borders expand', *The Guardian* (27 June 2002); see also Fassmann and Münz (2002).

encourage repatriation of foreigners who would otherwise not dare to leave the host country for fear they might not be able to return.

Closing the borders is far from being a panacea resulting in the reduction of the number of migrant workers, but would instead in many cases convert illegal migrants into potentially legal ones, who become administratively and socially much more vulnerable to every possible form of exploitation.

Confusion of freedom of labour with the fight against illegal migration

We saw that the immediate granting of freedom of labour would help to combat rather than increase illegal migration. However, in public debates the alleged need to postpone the granting of labour freedom to candidate countries has often been assimilated or confused with the general need to fight illegal migration.

However, the two phenomena are distinct, and not contradictory but complementary, involving an integrated policy towards new EU members and a more comprehensive immigration policy and stricter border controls with regard to countries outside the EU.

The general trend in the EU, both at EU and at national level, is towards a stricter policy against illegal immigration.

The Treaty of Amsterdam gave the EU more means to develop a common policy on monitoring borders and controlling migratory flows, sharing the burden with the host countries. The European Commission on 16 November 2001 adopted a Communication on a common policy on illegal immigration,[25] and on 7 May 2002 it proposed an overall package of measures for an integrated policy regarding the EU's external borders, including common principles for border checks, appropriate training of staff, convergence of policies on equipment used by border guards, and, most importantly, the eventual establishment of a European corps of border guards.

The general need for better and tighter controls of flows of illegal immigrants from outside the EU and for a common EU asylum and immigration policy were reaffirmed by the EU heads of state at the European Summit at Seville on 21–22 June 2002.

Stricter immigration measures have recently been implemented by almost all current EU member states, including countries such as Denmark, previously known for their open and flexible policy in this field.[26]

Recently, candidate countries have also started to apply stricter measures in order to cooperate in the war on illegal migration. Within the Central

---

25. The communication identifies six priority areas where measures should be taken to prevent and combat illegal immigration: visa policy; information exchange; border management; police cooperation; laws governing aliens and criminal law; return and re-admission policy.

26. 'Ministers prepare EU anti-immigration plans for Seville Summit', *Euroactiv News* (16 June 2002): www.euractiv.com.

European Initiative (CEI) – the oldest and largest sub-regional cooperation initiative, which emerged in Central and Eastern Europe after the collapse of the communist system – its 17 member countries (including EU countries, such as Italy and Austria) agreed at their last summit in Italy on 22 November 2001 to cooperate more closely in their fight against illegal immigration.[27] This commitment from future member states is important, especially to limit illegal migration from countries such as Ukraine, Russia, and other neighbouring countries.

However, a proper evaluation of the social implications of any new measure to combat illegal immigration would be needed, as sought by Amnesty International in its request to the EU to step back from its 'war on illegal immigration'. Amnesty International also warned that anti-immigration laws in numerous EU countries make it impossible for refugees to lodge asylum claims, thus contradicting an essential commitment to human rights protection enshrined in the Charter of Fundamental Rights.[28]

Moreover, this general move towards stricter rules to control illegal immigration in both current and future EU member countries should in no way become an argument against freedom of labour as a basic EU principle to be preserved in the current EU enlargement process. As emphasised by Odile Quintin from the European Commission:

> Migration has two distinct dimensions . . . the first concerns the exercise of a fundamental freedom that is at the very heart of the European project, that is the free movement of workers, and of people in general. The second is the likely effects of extending the 'Schengen area' eastwards on external border checks and, hence, on our ability to control the flow of illegal immigrants from outside the EU . . . these two aspects of mobility are, of course, very different and are not covered by the same legal framework. However, not everyone necessarily understands this distinction and it is our responsibility to avoid a situation in which confusion, fear and demagogy lead people to reject enlargement.[29]

9.9.2 Delays Too Costly for Future Member States?

Another important issue is the potential loss of young people – that is, of human capital – to the candidate countries. According to Fassmann and Münz (2002), the prosperous Western border regions of Slovenia, Slovakia, and Hungary will be confronted with labour shortages due to emigration to high-

27. See 'Candidate countries vow to combat illegal immigration and terrorism', in *Euractiv News* (23 November 2001): www.euractiv.com.

28. 'Ministers prepare EU anti-immigration plans for Seville Summit', *Euroactiv News* (16 June 2002): www.euractiv.com.

29. Speech by Odile Quintin, Director General of the DG for Employment and Social Affairs at UNICE, Brussels, 7 June 2002: 'European Business Forum: migration in a wider Europe'.

wage regions of the EU. This movement, combined with demographic decline and economic growth in most candidate countries, may well compel them to seek immigrants from third countries, as is already happening from Ukraine.

Ironically, Chancellor Schröder used this argument in a speech of 18 January 2001 to justify transitional periods: 'It is in the interest of the candidates themselves that enlargement does not lead to an abrupt, massive outflow of the best-qualified people'.[30]

New EU member states may also suffer from a fall in social contributions –especially important in a context of demographic tensions, with fewer young people and more pensioners – so leading to reduced social security, and instigating a vicious circle, the lower levels of social protection motivating even more young people to move abroad.

However, it seems that granting free movement of labour immediately would turn out to be less detrimental for the candidate countries than if the process was further delayed. First, the migrant skilled workers who would move to the EU could return later with more experience and thus contribute more to economic growth in the home country. Moving abroad may also allow a proportion of the most vulnerable categories, such as the unemployed, agricultural workers, or public sector employees, who currently have few prospects at home, to acquire skills abroad that may be useful when returning home later on. Secondly, migrations could contribute to economic catch-up through remittances from migrants working abroad:

> immediate freedom of movement for all citizens of new member states would lead to a much quicker reduction of existing migration potential, as well as to a more rapid levelling of underlying structural differences. In any case, the emigrants will transfer capital to their relatives at home. Such transfers will lead to an improvement of the economic situation in the countries and regions of origin. This further reduces emigration pressure and might speed up the closing of the existing economic gap. (Fassmann and Münz 2002)

More generally, delays in granting free movement could play a part in further delaying economic catch-up, an aspect particularly important for less advanced countries like Romania and Bulgaria, but also for large countries like Poland where a large proportion of the population does not seem to have any other labour market prospects – or any financial means of changing their situation – than in unprofitable micro-scale agricultural activities. In the end, a more rapid catching-up process on the part of new member states could only be beneficial for all EU countries.

---

30. As reported in 'Schroeder seeks delay for East bloc workers', *Herald Tribune* (19 December 2000).

9.9.3 Too Narrow an Approach to Labour Movement

The advantages or disadvantages of freedom of labour clearly differ in accordance with the chosen perspective, whether narrow or comprehensive, short-term or long-term, encompassing all EU countries or just a few, including the point of view of candidate countries or limiting itself to that of current EU member states.

The long-term view
Experience of migration in the EU so far has shown, first, that migrant stocks seem to find some kind of long-run equilibrium, and, as studies show, in relation to workers from the ten candidate countries from Central and Eastern Europe this long-term level will be rather low. Secondly, free mobility of labour in the long run generates migration flows which are much more balanced and of smaller size, and with return migration partly compensating emigration. Thus, more integrated labour markets are likely to generate a pattern of mutual exchange rather than of unidirectional migration. This will be increasingly borne out as the economic catch-up of candidate countries progressively reduces migration flows towards the EU.

Given that there is no risk of major imbalances in the long term, we might wonder why EU member states do not show more solidarity in their migration policy also in the short term. Moreover, while in the short run EU enlargement without transitional arrangements would clearly lead to higher East–West migration, in the long term immediate freedom of labour movement could lead to a much more rapid reduction of existing migration potential.

Including all current EU countries and not only 'border' EU countries
EU experience shows that if labour has the right to move freely, although people (especially in border areas) thereby become more internationally mobile, mass migration from one country to another does not necessarily occur. For the time being, alongside restrictions on the movement of migrant workers, it has been estimated that 72 per cent of employed migrants from Central and Eastern Europe are located in Germany and Austria (European Integration Consortium 2000b).

Many studies have emphasised that granting freedom of labour early would help to disseminate labour migration flows among all EU member states, in contrast to their current concentration in neighbouring countries, such as Germany, Austria, and Italy. The freedom to move around the EU would give migrant workers the incentive to seek jobs in other countries and to evaluate the advantages and disadvantages of all EU countries as possible host employers. This should encourage the consideration of all EU member states as potential host countries, not only Germany and Austria, a standpoint which does not seem to have been sufficiently addressed by EC officials in charge of enlargement: 'permanent migrants would be very unevenly distributed as 80 per cent of them would live in Germany and Austria' (Odile Quintin 2002, p. 4).

The number of people involved is another element that should naturally lead to the promotion of greater geographical distribution of migrant workers, a flow that would certainly adapt itself to the prospects of respective local labour markets. Transitional periods could have the opposite effect, and lead to geographical concentration. Faced by the impossibility of legally looking for a job in the EU, migrant workers will have to rely on illegal jobs, often under precarious conditions, in neighbouring countries in order to be close to their country of origin to ensure easy return in case they lose their temporary job. The granting or otherwise of freedom to work everywhere in the EU thus has a fundamental influence on the 'logic' of migration, including the choice of host country. The fears of border countries such as Germany and Austria in the face of immediate free movement thus appear to be alarmist: although freedom would lead to more migration, it would be much more evenly distributed, so relieving pressure on their labour markets.

In favour of a more courageous and solidaristic policy

The right of EU nationals to choose their place of work within the whole territory of the European Union is one of the main principles of the organisation, and one which has been strengthened considerably over the years. Free movement of labour has become a basic right in the Community *acquis*. In a context in which European institutions have insisted upon candidate countries' transposing the Community *acquis* in its entirety (and generally without delay), even putting it among the basic criteria for accession (Copenhagen criteria, as described in section 1.7.2), it is difficult to explain to them why such a basic right should not be granted immediately. The whole credibility of the European Union is at stake here, and, even more seriously, the perception that the citizens of new member states will have of this historic reunification of Europe.

In the European agreements signed in order to help close the gap between Central and Eastern European countries and the EU, and therefore to facilitate their membership, no special rights were granted to CEE nationals to enter the EU labour market. Instead, responsibility was shifted to individual EU member states to decide how to treat migrants from the East. Some of them (Denmark, the Netherlands) applied the same rules as to other third-country migrants, while others (Austria, Belgium, Finland, France, Germany, Greece, Sweden and the UK) relied on the selective approach (through bilateral agreements) to regulate the inflow of guest workers, applying it to special categories such as seasonal workers, project-tied workers, and border-commuter workers.

We can thus again identify a paradox or contradiction here: although free movement of labour represents a basic Community right, whose scope has been extended over the years, especially from the Community level, the responsibility of applying such principles has always been left within the framework of accession to individual EU member countries, thus providing scope for selfish and rather natural nationalistic reactions. For how long will European institutions continue to shift their responsibility regarding such basic rights to individual member countries? Is it in keeping with the universal and comprehensive ambitions to which the EU has always aspired? We believe only a more courageous and solidaristic approach to EU enlargement, carried out in the right (collective) spirit, far from individual interests, could restore the EU's aspirations.

9.10 CONCLUSION

The approach and policy conclusions presented in this chapter contrast with the conclusions reached by the EC and EU member states so far. On the one hand, the EC has concluded through its commissioned study on migration that no massive migration is to be expected, nor will there be adverse effects on EU wages and employment, this has contributed to calm fears. On the other hand, the EC, especially under the influence of German policy, has decided to introduce a transitional period limiting labour movement.

We have tried to provide an alternative picture, leading to two basic conclusions quite contrary to the above listed EC messages.

First, in terms of expectations of labour flows and adjustments, we argued that we simply do not have enough knowledge to be able to draw useful and reliable conclusions since it is by definition very difficult to measure an unknown, forthcoming phenomenon. Since we do not want to fall into the same trap, we have not provided specific figures, concentrating instead on developing the arguments about why the studies conducted so far might be misleading and why the expected movements might be more significant than has been suggested so far. It may well be that the truth lies somewhere in between, but the present chapter will already represent a contribution if it has succeeded in presenting an alternative approach and different policy options from the mainstream and not particularly transparent stance adopted by the European Commission and EU member states.

In particular, we believe, contrary to most studies so far, which tend to be characterised by rather restrictive assumptions, that there is clearly a major risk of migration which, even if not occurring on a massive scale, could significantly affect particular categories of worker, and so seriously affect local labour markets.

Although migration is mainly due to disequilibria between home and host labour markets, specific features of candidate country labour markets have not been taken into account in the identification of potential migration, particularly the presence of long-term unemployment – which particularly affects the unskilled and the young – and a significant number of inactive persons. All migration studies so far were carried out when unemployment rates in Central and Eastern Europe were still not particularly high, and did not take into account the potential migration of 'non-working' categories.

Migration may also greatly depend on the position of other vulnerable categories of people, such as minorities (for example, Roma), women, and so on, who have few prospects in local labour markets.

This represents a link with previous chapters: the difficult labour market situation, especially for the long-term unemployed (described in Chapter 4) and the downgrading of social protection systems, with lower and more restricted unemployment and social benefits (described in Chapter 3) may well induce greater than expected East–West labour migration, and influence not only the decision to migrate but also the length of migration. Significant migration is also to be expected from skilled labour for whom there is increasing demand in current EU countries.

More generally, we believe that migration flows will very much depend on the economic catch-up of future member states. However, while most studies have assumed continuous growth – often above the EU average – we believe that after a few boom years economic growth may turn out to be slower than expected. Our next chapter shows that economic catch-up will in any case take at least 15–20 years. Moreover, labour movements will very much depend on the situation with regard to the other two freedoms, of capital, and of goods and services. In this regard, we have seen in Chapter 8 that foreign investment in candidate countries, after years of rapid expansion, will start to slow down, especially following the ending of privatisation. This lack of foreign capital will induce in home labour markets greater pressure to migrate to the EU. Similarly, a slowing-down in the trade performance of candidate countries may lead to increased labour movements as a sort of adjustment variable.

The effects of the discrepancies in social and working conditions described in Part I will also be important. Very low living standards, impoverishment wages, insufficient social protection, and poorer working conditions (described in Chapter 2) could well push a substantial portion of the labour force to look for work in current EU countries. It is clear that these risks could be progressively minimised if social standards and wage levels in Central and Eastern Europe were generally improved.

Finally, a simple calculation of the populations of the candidate countries (105 million if we exclude Turkey) alone should lead us to conclude that EU enlargement may bring to the current EU member states a significant number of migrant workers. The inclusion of Turkey – although it will be the last – with its 65 million inhabitants and much poorer social and economic conditions, would change our analysis and forecasts entirely. However, the studies published so far have failed to take these considerations into account.

It is probably because they are, in private, well aware of this reality that EU member states have decided to implement transitional periods while continuing to argue that there is no migration risk.

On the other hand, although we foresee greater risks and adjustments than the current literature, it is important that the transposition of the whole Community *acquis* by future member states and the introduction of free movement of capital and goods and services should be immediately accompanied by similar freedom of citizens and workers. First, because it is a basic Community right, and secondly, because denying it would mean that most of the adjustment costs would again be borne by the future member states. Furthermore, liberalising legal migration would be an effective way of combating illegal migration. If economic catch-up is to be achieved progressively, we do not see why short-term adjustment costs should not also be borne by EU member states that are already benefiting from EU enlargement, especially border countries such as Germany and Austria, but also the Scandinavian countries.

This different assessment clearly leads us to different policy options. EU member states tend to privilege a selective approach to migration that would enable host countries to choose the categories of worker they need. This policy would lead to economic, but also social and political costs.

On the economic side, this policy would continue to further aggravate the gap observed in candidate country labour markets between highly skilled and unskilled workers, between those for whom there is strong demand, both from the domestic market and from EU member states, and those who are left out of work, who constitute the majority of the long-term unemployed in candidate countries. As in the case of capital movements – we saw in Chapter 8 that foreign investors in candidate countries mainly hire the most skilled employees – labour movement restricted to skilled labour would thus aggravate rather than ease the labour market and employment problems of candidate countries.

Still on the economic side, there are good grounds for expecting any delay in free movement to slow down rather than to accelerate the catching-up process. All economic adjustments of EU enlargement would thus be placed squarely on the shoulders of candidate countries.

According to Burda (1998), the price of EU membership, even if attenuated by rapid accession, would be much too high for CEE labour markets. While it would yield significant economic advantages, it would entail the additional burden of structural adjustment, as inefficient producers in agriculture, high-tech manufacturing, and services would be squeezed. This would further increase unemployment. In such a context, free movement of labour is an important adjustment mechanism within economic and monetary union, and 'it would be quite absurd to expect the applicants to join a monetary union without allowing them free movement of labour' (Eatwell et al. 1997, p. 55).

Labour mobility could also have economic advantages for the recipient countries. An inflow of young workers likely to pay social security contributions for many years would make a useful temporary contribution to maintaining the level of pensions in countries with rapidly ageing populations, such as Germany and Italy (CEPR and IEWS 1996, p. 9). A new, skilled labour force could also provide dynamism and innovation in the EU's stagnating and ageing economies.

Some economists and businessmen from the EU have tried to emphasise the positive aspects, insisting on the important asset that such mobility could represent for European industry. According to H. Glatz of Daimler-Chrysler: 'Labour mobility is simply a by-product of globalisation, and a particularly useful one in that it supplements the drive for competitiveness'.[31]

On the social side, better distribution of economic costs would contribute to social catch-up, thus reducing social differentials and stopping-up possible sources of social dumping. It seems obvious that immediate free movement of labour may increase social dumping, with workers from future member states coming to work in EU member states and tolerating lower wages and working conditions, leading to downward pressure on current EU standards. But as we argued in Chapter 7, social dumping is mainly associated with illegal working practices, which free movement of labour is likely to reduce through greater transparency. Secondly, immediate freedom of labour would lead to more rapid catch-up in respect of wages and working conditions in future member states and their enterprises, with a consequent upward movement in terms of workers' motivation and productivity, and better quality labour and production.

Moreover, legal migration by definition cannot lead to social dumping, since there are already regulations in the EU that must be respected for all types of worker, including those from candidate countries, for instance the minimum wage. However, certain groups of employees in the EU may directly suffer from East–West migration: it is, for example, unavoidable that cheaper, more flexible skilled – as well as unskilled – workers will enter into direct competition with the same category of worker in the EU. This may lead to increased unemployment for the latter, but the enlarged EU as a whole will be better off. Here the role of social partners, social dialogue, and EU directives within the EU will be important.

---

31. Interview in *The Economist Intelligence Unit*, Briefs (2 December 1998).

More generally, the imposition of a transitional period for labour movement would in general lead to less social cohesion and less solidarity within the enlarged EU. New member states would ask for dispensations elsewhere, such as the social and the environmental areas; some EU member states would also ask for concessions for having supported the German–Austrian approach – for example, Spain has requested special arrangements for its regions with regard to the continuation of structural funds. The current enlargement process would thus see the nationalistic approach progressively dominating the scene.

Finally, the current approach is dangerous above all in political terms. Granting immediate freedom of labour would reinforce the solidarity principle in terms of which EU member states have sought to characterise the EU enlargement process. Transitional restrictions may have catastrophic consequences, such as the integration into the EU of new entrants – with voting rights – who have the feeling they are second-class citizens. In fact, how else could citizens from future member states understand the 'double language' of the EU, with member states on the one hand stating that reunification is welcome as soon as possible and on the other putting their own interests first; on the one hand asserting that there is no major risk of migration or of distorting EU labour markets, while on the other hand restricting such a basic right as labour movement?

To summarise, freedom of labour has become a significant test of the nature of the current EU enlargement process. The whole credibility of the European Union may be at stake here, along with, even more seriously, the perception that the citizens of new member states will have of this historic reunification of Europe. The unique nature of this process should certainly lead current EU policymakers to envisage more open policy options, that would more equally share the costs and benefits of EU enlargement, even if they are politically more difficult.

10. Trade: The Misleading Debate

10.1 INTRODUCTION

Having analysed freedom of capital and labour in Chapters 8 and 9, we address here the last of the freedoms – of goods and services – which underpin the single market. To this end we scrutinise trade between current and future EU member states.

Free movement of goods and services is a basic principle of the Community *acquis*. Several key elements have been developed to ensure its implementation.

The first is *mutual recognition*, which involves accepting products lawfully sold in other member states. Articles 28 to 30 of the EC Treaty establish the principle of free movement of goods and demand that member states do not maintain or impose barriers to trade in areas which have not been the subject of Community harmonisation, except in special circumstances. Every member state is obliged to accept such products on its territory and to acknowledge the standards to which these products conform in the member state of origin.[1]

The second is *harmonisation*, in respect of which current and future member states adopt harmonised European standards and recognise accreditation systems for certification and testing. For the purpose of harmonisation, the European Commission has also developed a new approach which consists not only in imposing technical solutions – this traditional regulatory pattern applies mainly to products such as pharmaceuticals, chemicals, motor vehicles and foodstuffs – but also in establishing the essential requirements which products must meet.

The third important element in the free movement of goods is *protection against defective products*, an area in which important progress has been made since the EC issued its horizontal directive on liability for defective products, and preventive and monitoring policies have been reinforced.

Since the mid-1980s, Community institutions have not limited their requirements to the free movement of goods and services, but also have increasingly insisted on the need to guarantee, throughout the Community, a

---

1. In 1999, the Commission adopted a Communication on the application of the mutual recognition principle. A series of biannual reports (the first was in 1999 and the second in July 2002) have as their objective to assess the progress made in the application of this principle.

regime of undistorted competition; member states recognise that the objectives of the Treaty could not be fulfilled if distortions of competition are allowed to prevail. This development is illustrated by the broader interpretation of the concept of state aid – including, for instance, forms of acquisition by the state of a stake in the share capital of an enterprise, public undertakings and national monopolies, and every national measure that could affect trade and especially imports.

The Maastricht and Amsterdam treaties strongly indicate that EC economic policy is to be based on open market principles. Article 2 of the EC Treaty speaks of a 'high degree of competitiveness and convergence of economic performance'.

While candidate countries have been asked to eliminate barriers to this basic freedom – especially all remaining tariffs and quotas – programmes have also been designed to prepare candidate countries for integration into the EU's internal market and to help them in their process of harmonising their technical regulations with EC law.[2]

The internal market and implementation of competitive policies are also considered to be an essential achievement to be preserved alongside enlargement, because it is expected to continue to extend the vast level playing field, which allows EU actors to exploit the economies of scale which are crucial for a competitive, dynamic, and forward looking EU economy.

According to the EC:

> in retrospect, the merging of fifteen national markets into a single market, open competition and an enlargement with many other countries may well be regarded as the greatest 'supply side' exercise ever in world economics, a huge exercise which stimulates production, increases competition, reduces prices and increases demand within the European Union.[3]

These economic effects could be even more substantial with EU enlargement, since it could open the way for an internal market of over 500 million consumers and thus increase the economies of scale within an open, border-free area.

The EC has emphasised these aspects in the negotiations for accession: 'Alignment to single market rules constitutes not just a sensible economic reform programme for the candidate countries but also a condition "sine qua non" for the proper functioning of the future enlarged Internal Market.'[4]

2. These regulations – constantly updated or enlarged – have considerable scope, since they consist in more than 1,200 regulations, of which roughly 550 are primary and others also include amendments.

3. Speech by Commissioner of DG Internal Market, Frits Bolkestein: 'The internal market: facing the challenge of an enlarged EU', address at Budapest Economics University, 22 March 2002, Budapest.

4. Op. cit.

At the beginning of the reform process in Central and Eastern Europe, many experts and policymakers – particularly in the EU – were reluctant to liberalise freedom of goods and services. A production process based on a much cheaper and skilled labour force in Central and Eastern Europe, as well as much lower working and production standards, was initially expected to outperform the most competitive EU companies, and thus lead to a strong trade deficit for EU countries, with clear losses in terms of jobs and growth. As for the other two freedoms (of capital and labour) studied in previous chapters, social dumping was also feared in relation to the freedom of goods and services, especially in traditional sectors in which illegal and 'black' activities were widespread. Were these fears justified, and did the terms of trade prove to be negative for current EU member states?

In contrast, access to new EU markets was expected to lead to better and higher quality production in candidate countries, stimulated by the need to meet EU standards, while foreign investment in candidate countries would help to improve the technology content of goods exported by candidate countries, so helping them participate in integrated markets with EU partners, leading to overall positive gains for all. Did such integrated markets involving current and future EU members emerge? If so, will they be able to lead to an overall positive cycle in the enlarged European Union, also resulting in the rapid economic convergence of candidate countries? We shall analyse these issues through a comprehensive analysis of both trade statistics and catch-up scenarios.

This will allow us to complete our picture of the various freedoms, and to assess what can be expected in terms of the combined effects of the movements of capital, labour, and goods and services. The present chapter is closely related to a number of other chapters in this volume because the structure, patterns, and speed of trade developments in candidate countries will obviously have direct implications for social standards and social cohesion.

10.2 TRADE LIBERALISATION

At the beginning of the transition, many economists doubted the economic advantages that EU countries could obtain from enlarging the EU to include Central and Eastern Europe, notably in terms of trade. This first debate we address here was clearly dominated by the fear of seeing cheaper goods from these countries suddenly invade EU markets. Was this prediction correct, and could we say, after more than twelve years of transition, that trade has clearly become unbalanced in favour of the newly-emerging free market economies?

10.2.1 Intensified Flows between the Two Regions

The Association Agreements were a first major step towards the integration of Central and Eastern European (CEE) countries in the EU. They provided for the abolition of all quantitative restrictions and tariffs on industrial exports to the EU from the applicants, with the exception of such 'sensitive' products as agricultural produce, chemicals, and steel. These agreements clearly had a marked effect on the geographical and sectoral redistribution of the trade flows of candidate countries.

Before the transition, the bulk of the ten CEE applicants' trade was with the Soviet Union and Eastern Europe, exports being mostly of machinery, and imports mostly of raw materials and fuel. The collapse of these CMEA markets forced a rapid reorientation of trade, to which the Association Agreements with the EU have contributed greatly. The external trade of the Central and Eastern European countries grew faster than GDP and was redirected towards the EU. Since the beginning of their transition, trade with the EU has intensified, more than tripling over the period. The share of candidate countries in EU trade has also significantly increased. Central European countries showed the strongest increase, but trade of the EU with the three Mediterranean countries rose substantially too.

While at the end of the 1980s only 30 per cent of the exports – as well as the imports – of the ten Central and Eastern European candidate countries were to the EU, by the end of the 1990s, the EU's share was above 70 per cent, and is continuing to increase.

10.2.2 A Balance in Favour of the EU

It is important to emphasise, however, that the EU has benefited most from the opening of CEE markets. During the process of transformation, markets were rapidly opened to foreign goods, leading to a sharp increase in imports that also coincided with the fall in domestic industrial production. There was also an understandable boom in consumer demand for 'Western-type' goods which thus led to a trade deficit in all consumer goods, and further aggravated the collapse of local producers.

Later on, deficits occurred in those sectors in which there was most export activity, which was due to the imports (techniques, technologies, components) required by multinational companies to be able to produce and then export on a large scale.

While in 1996 the ten Central and Eastern European countries accounted for about 8 per cent of EU imports, the EU already generated 37 per cent of its total trade surplus from this relationship.

Between 1989 and 1994 EU exports to Central and Eastern Europe

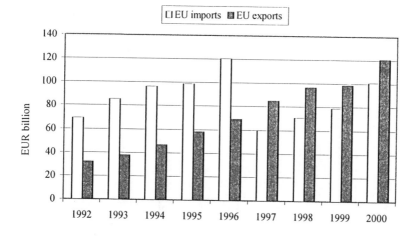

Figure 10.1 Trade flows between the EU and the ten Central and Eastern European countries, 1992–2000

increased by 171 per cent, whereas the growth rate in the opposite direction amounted to only 116 per cent (Inotai 1998). This has continued in recent years (see Figure 10.1).

This excess of EU exports over EU imports in relation to Central and Eastern Europe constitutes an EU trade surplus which is increasing in volume every year, resulting in dangerous trade deficits in almost all Central and Eastern European countries.

This has led economists to the view that trade with the EU has contributed much to the high levels of unemployment in many of the applicant countries (Eatwell et al. 1997, p. 47).

A number of features of this deficit are worth mentioning. First of all, it seems to be a structural – or at least a long-term – deficit that candidate countries will find it difficult to reduce. Figure 10.1 shows that a deficit has been recorded every year since the early transition and that it has significantly increased. The commercial advantage of the EU will continue to grow for the next few years. The calculations of economists point towards a trade potential of between 20 and 50 per cent.

Secondly, a deficit has been recorded in all candidate countries, including the three Mediterranean candidates Cyprus, Malta, and Turkey (see section 10.3.1).

As a result of this increasing flow of exports and imports, the share of Central and Eastern Europe in the foreign trade of the EU has constantly increased since 1992, and by 2000 had already reached 10–15 per cent:

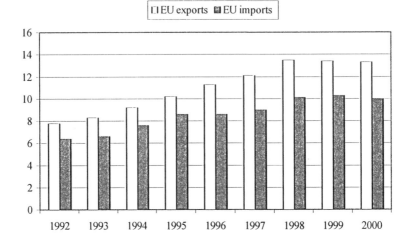

Figure 10.2 EU trade with the ten Central and Eastern European countries, 1992–2000 (percentage of total EU trade)

nearly 14 per cent of EU exports and 10 per cent of EU imports are generated in trade with candidate countries (see Figure 10.2). Although this is not yet comparable with the proportion that trade with the EU represents for candidate countries (between one-half and two-thirds), these transition markets are far from marginal for EU enterprises, especially since they can generate their highest short-term profits there.

No doubt EU enlargement to the East will further contribute to EU trade expansion. These figures tend to show that the advantage in increasing trade with candidate countries has largely been captured by EU enterprises.

10.2.3 The EU Not Always Fair in Opening Markets

During the accession negotiations, the EU has been very strict concerning the principle of freedom of goods and services. It has repeatedly stated that no derogations for transitional periods requested by candidate countries would be accepted, on the grounds that 'they would have a significant impact on competition and the functioning of the internal market'. This, however, should be a mutual process. By August 2002, almost all candidate countries – with a few exceptions, such as Bulgaria and Romania – had finished negotiations on the two chapters 'Free movement of goods' and 'Free movement of services'.

Although on both sides logic dictates liberalisation and opening markets to future partners, the EU has not liberalised such important sectors for future member states as textiles, shoes, and agriculture, but also steel and coal. At the same time, higher value added industries, such as pharmaceuticals, have been lobbying for protectionist policies vis-à-vis new members:

> the European pharmaceutical industry has specific concerns with regard to the operating environment in the Central and Eastern European countries . . . any hesitation shown by Europe's policy-makers to respond favourably to these concerns will constitute a serious handicap for the European pharmaceutical industry . . . When faced with a similar question in 1992 at the creation of the North American Free Trade Area (NAFTA), the United States did not hesitate to maintain the right climate for innovation on its domestic territory by banning the free movement of pharmaceutical products from Mexico, where the level of economic conditions and intellectual property protection were significantly lower . . . therefore, upon accession, an appropriate transition period providing safeguard measures – derogating from the free movement of goods principle – must be allowed for until distortions are eliminated and Central and Eastern European countries' economies and operating environments – via implementation of full and effective legislation and practices – reach EU standards and norms.[5]

While it is clear that a number of guarantees must be made in such a crucial area as health care, it is also clear that the production and sale of pharmaceutical products is one of the most profitable activities in the EU, which in great part explains the very rigid and protectionist behaviour of the EU pharmaceutical giants.

Similarly, EU countries have not been very keen to implement free movement of services, despite the fact that services are clearly underdeveloped in candidate countries: 'The economies of the candidate countries are less heavily weighted towards services'.[6] Furthermore, 'while there are no global transitional arrangements in relation to any provision of services, two member states – Germany and Austria – have negotiated a safeguard mechanism in specific sensitive service sectors on their labour markets'.[7] This is particularly anomalous in light of the fact that a large number of EU foreign investors in candidate countries – among whom German and Austrian investors figure prominently – are in the service sector, largely directed towards supplying the domestic market. This trend is growing in parallel with the privatisation process in public services (energy, telecoms, transport, and so on) which has still not come to an end (it generally started after privatisation in industry).

---

5. *The accession of Central and East European countries to the European Union – Position Paper*, European Federation of Pharmaceutical Industries and Associations (EFPIA), July 1997, Brussels.

6. 'Value added, employment, remuneration and labour productivity in the candidate countries', *Statistics in Focus*, Economy and Finance, Theme 2, 13/2001, EUROSTAT (March 2001), p. 1.

7. Communication from the Commission on the impact of enlargement on regions bordering candidate countries: 'Community action for border regions', COM(2001) 437 final, 25 July 2001, p. 27.

Again, liberalisation and the benefits of EU enlargement do not seem to be shared equally between current EU – especially those with borders with candidate countries – and future EU member states.

EU member states have not always opened their markets despite the fact that the risks for candidate countries seem to have been clearly recognised: 'premature participation in the Single Market may involve risks for the candidate countries . . . for the sometimes relatively underdeveloped and under-capitalised industries of some Central and Eastern European countries, competition from EU industry could be devastating' (EC 1997b, Agenda 2000, p. 4). The importance of services for the economy has also been acknowledged: 'economic growth is essentially driven by services. They account for 70 per cent of GDP and of employment.'[8] So far, however, this seems to have been denied to the candidate countries.

The long-term mutual advantages notwithstanding, the development of trade could involve competitive risks for both groups of countries, but particularly for Central and Eastern Europe; first, because its industries are less competitive and below EU standards, and secondly, because it is much more dependent on trade with the EU than vice versa. Agriculture and coal mining seem to be particularly vulnerable. The only way of avoiding structural imbalances in these sectors would be to open up EU markets as soon as possible. As an experts' report concluded (Eatwell et al. 1997, p. 47), the exclusion of agriculture and other sensitive sectors from the free-trade commitment has had the direct result of increasing the superior competitiveness of EU firms and of contributing to the high levels of unemployment in many of the applicant countries.

According to Polish estimates, Poland's trade deficit with the EU has already meant the loss of 1.2 to 1.4 million jobs, whereas in the EU the trade surplus has resulted in job creation (Kabaj 1997).

10.3 INTEGRATED MARKETS: AN ILLUSION?

During the first years of transition, not only did trade experts predict that the removal of trade barriers between Western and Eastern European countries would mainly benefit the latter, but also that the opening of EU markets to these countries would lead to a fundamental restructuring of trade and production in the candidate countries, especially towards more capital intensive goods with a higher technology content. Was this second prediction accurate,

---

8. Speech by Internal market Commissioner Frits Bolkestein, reported in *EC Press Releases*: 'Internal market: barriers to the free movement of services mean businesses and consumers still get a raw deal', IP/02/1180, 31 July 2002, Brussels.

or was this experts' debate at the beginning of the transition also misleading? We shall answer this question with a careful look at the export and import performance of future member states by sector.

10.3.1 The Traditional Division of Trade Persists

It is clear that the expansion of East–West trade in the 1990s was accompanied by significant shifts in its pattern. While at the beginning of the transition EU exports were essentially of consumer goods, this progressively shifted towards the export of investment goods embodying modern technologies. With regard to EU imports from candidate countries, the picture is less clear, and depends very much on the country concerned and its level of development. Generally, however, early in the transition Central and Eastern European countries were mainly exporting low-skill, labour-intensive – also by way of outward processing – but often also capital-intensive basic products such as fuels, basic chemicals, and metals, that were produced in the oversized industrial conglomerates inherited from the previous regime.

Figure 10.3 indicates that candidate countries from Central and Eastern Europe continue to specialise in labour-intensive products. In 2000, the main surplus of Central and Eastern European countries was still in basic manufactures, while they still have a deficit in chemical products and also in transport and machinery (although the latter is declining, as we shall see).

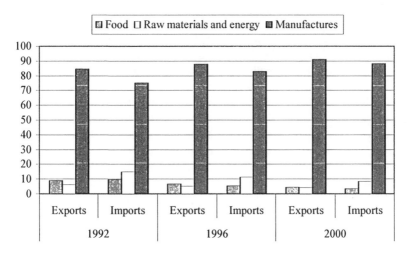

Note: the rates for the three sectors = 100 per cent.

Figure 10.3 The composition of EU visible trade with the ten Central and Eastern European countries, 1992, 1996 and 2000

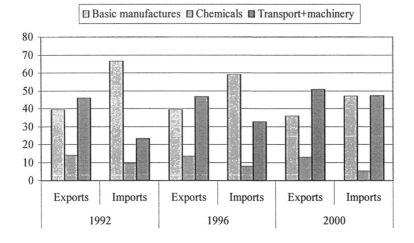

Note: the rates for the three sectors = 100 per cent.

Figure 10.4 The composition of EU trade in manufactures with the ten Central and Eastern European countries, 1992, 1996 and 2000

Leather, textiles, and apparel continue to be among the most important export goods. All the candidate countries have a comparative advantage with regard to clothing and accessories.

Trade in textiles, for instance, seems to be particularly developed for Bulgaria, Romania, Latvia, and Lithuania, where outward processing for EU producers continues to be important. Turkey also specialises in textiles, leather and other traditionally labour-intensive goods. Similarly, Malta and Romania specialise in footwear. EU trade with Malta and Cyprus, however, is more diversified. Poland, Romania, Slovenia and Estonia specialise in furniture. Estonia and Latvia also specialise in cork and wood manufactures.

Due to their strong infrastructure in these areas, some traditional specialisations also persist in infrastructure and heavy industry, as under the previous regime: Slovakia and Bulgaria are strong in metal products, iron and steel manufactured goods; Bulgaria also specialises in non-ferrous metal goods.

A thorough analysis of the individual sectors' contribution to the balance of trade confirms that candidate countries have a comparative advantage for manufactured goods classified in terms of raw materials and miscellaneous manufactured articles – that is, articles that tend to be labour-intensive – and a comparative disadvantage in machinery and transport equipment.[9]

9. 'Specialisation of candidate countries in relation to the EU', *Statistics in Focus*, External Trade, Theme 6, 6/2001, Eurostat (June 2001).

However, some candidate countries have also managed to diversify and to shift towards more sophisticated goods, as shown in Figures 10.5 and 10.6 (general average for the candidate countries) and as explained in the next section. Five countries (Czech Republic, Slovakia, Slovenia, Estonia and Hungary) moved from a situation of comparative disadvantage (imports greater than exports) to one of significant advantage for a group of products in the machinery and transport equipment sector, producing capital intensive goods.

Notably the Czech Republic, Slovakia and Slovenia have managed to increase the proportion of exports in the road vehicle sector, in which they seem to have a definite comparative advantage; between 20 and 30 per cent of their exports are concentrated in this sector.

Hungary has shifted its manufacturing exports towards more sophisticated engineering products, particularly motor vehicles, as well as electrical and electronic equipment. Since 2000, Hungary has also managed to be the only candidate country to register a trade surplus with the EU in office machinery and computers (where others tend to have very large deficits).

Slovenia and Malta seem to have specialised in electrical machinery. Estonia has also switched from a position of comparative disadvantage to one of comparative advantage in telecommunications. Malta was also found to have a comparative advantage in electronic products, which account for about half its exports. It is the only candidate country specialising in professional, scientific and control instruments and apparatus. However, prospects are less rosy in other candidate countries; for instance, in Lithuania, Romania, and Turkey there has been no shift towards the more advanced, higher value added end of the market despite relative growth over the period in electronic engineering and in Turkey in motor vehicles.

To summarise, despite these encouraging trends, we can only conclude that, surprisingly after more than twelve years of transition, the substantial shift towards more value added goods that had been predicted by trade experts has not really occurred: the trade structure of many candidate countries continues to be biased towards raw materials and manufactured goods with low levels of processing. This does not mean that these sectors are not successful, however, and that candidate countries have not managed to register a good performance in them. On the contrary, in recent years the fastest growth rates in Central and Eastern Europe have been registered by export-oriented industries, those that have managed to penetrate new markets in the EU, even if in traditional sectors. For instance, this has been the case for many years for timber-related and textile industries in Latvia.

Even for more economically developed countries such as Slovenia, Poland and Estonia, the trade surplus with the EU comprises basic trade, especially textiles and clothing and metal production; the same countries continue to record significant deficits in more sophisticated trade.

Significant changes may occur in the future, and no doubt more candidate countries will start to diversify their exports.

10.3.2 Foreign Capital 'Integrating' Markets

Integrated markets are developing mainly in a few countries and sectors. It seems that only Hungary, the Czech Republic, Estonia, Slovakia and Poland have managed to develop some specialisation in more capital-intensive products, namely where foreign investment has concentrated. Similarly, it is also precisely the sectors with the highest share of foreign investment, and where exports are driven by foreign investors, that are contributing to some integration of candidate countries into the network of European producers.

Intra-industry trade

The best way to ascertain whether candidate countries are part of integrated markets with the EU is to examine the development of intra-industry trade, which measures the degree to which, increasingly, the same products are imported and exported. Shifts in intra-industry trade generally indicate a deepening of integration, and are also used as a rough indicator of convergence (this is because an increase in the similarity of consumer preferences is one factor in this development). As an example, intra-industry trade has increased between EU member states in parallel with the Single Market (RWI 2001).

According to the available evidence, intra-industry coefficients grew between 1993 and 1998 in all candidate countries except Malta and Cyprus – where such coefficients were already very high – and Bulgaria (explained by the authors in terms of its weaker economic development). The highest coefficients were found in the Czech Republic, Slovenia, Hungary and Poland, that is, the countries whose transformations are most advanced. Nevertheless, these intra-industry coefficients were still found to be lower than those observed in EU countries (RWI 2001).

Trade creation versus trade diversion

A similarity between export patterns on the one hand, and between import patterns on the other can be used to measure trade-creation effects. If EU countries and candidate countries export the same product, they are competitors with a potential for trade diversion. In contrast, if the exports of an EU member fit the import requirements of a candidate country, there is a potential for trade creation.

Generally, studies on coefficients of trade similarity have shown that trade creation effects are the strongest between current EU member states and can-

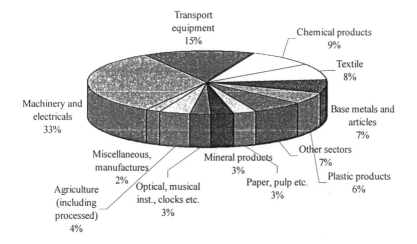

Figure 10.5 EU-15 exports to candidate countries, share by sector, 2000

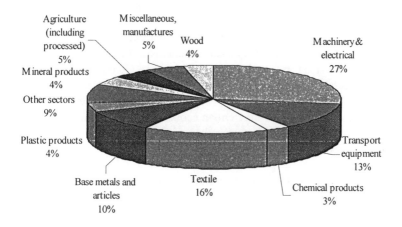

Figure 10.6 EU-15 imports from candidate countries, share by sector, 2000

didate countries (RWI 2001, p. 38). In particular, the export spectrums of Austria, Germany, Sweden, Italy and the Netherlands were found to fit very well with the import needs of the candidate countries.

Trade creation in relation to East–West relations was found to be particularly strong in several sectors: the producers of machinery, electronic products and vehicles, which dominate EU exports to candidate countries, also became exporters from the candidate countries. These sectors are also those dominated by foreign investment, which has thus become the main factor in trade creation, since candidate countries have become an essential part of the integrated production of EU multinationals. Within different production units of the same EU multinational company, components and technologies are being exported to candidate countries, which then export the final product, a strategy that we described in detail in Chapter 8 and which has been followed by EU companies in many sectors.

It is thus clear that producers from current and future member states are trading goods which belong to the same sector of activity, but at different stages of production. Intermediate goods were found to have the highest and growing shares in CEE exports to the EU, especially for electronic products, machinery and vehicles (Freudenberg and Lemoine 1999).

It is significant to observe that in 2000, machinery and electrical goods represented one-third of EU exports to candidate countries and one-third of EU imports from candidate countries, thus ranking first in both directions. Transport equipment ranked second among EU exports (with a share of 15 per cent) and third among EU imports from candidate countries (13 per cent). Such intra-industry trade seems also to have developed in base metals and articles, and in textiles (see Figure 10.5).

More than 70 per cent of trade from candidate countries was found to belong to horizontal, intra-industry trade, especially from the Czech Republic, Hungary and Slovenia. Interestingly, with respect to German trade with the candidate countries, shares of intra-industry trade with the Czech Republic, Slovenia and Hungary were found already to exceed that between Germany and Portugal, indicating that the German economy might be more integrated with the bordering candidate countries than with the peripheral EU countries (Brüstle and Döhrn 2001).

A few multinational companies dominating trade figures

The figures we presented in Chapter 8 show that most exports from the candidate countries originate from foreign-owned enterprises. We estimated that foreign companies account for some 70 per cent of exports in, for example, Hungary, although for only 60 per cent of industrial production, with a similar difference between export shares and output shares; for some countries no more than two or three foreign producers dominate exports. While this is only to be expected in respect of small countries such as Malta – whose exports, not only in electronics, but in general are dominated by one company, Thomson – it is also true of larger countries: for instance, in automobiles, Hungary's exports are dominated by those of Audi-Volkswagen, Slovakia's by those of Skoda-Volkswagen, the Czech Republic's by those of Skoda, and Slovenia's by those of Renault.

Poland and Turkey have increased their intra-industry trade in motor vehicles, with a rise in both imports and exports in this sector, again mainly due to increased operations by foreign companies.

Specialisation in telecommunications equipment in Estonia seems to be directly due to the fact that this country has been selected as a manufacturing and assembly centre by high-tech Scandinavian (such as ABB) and other Western firms. A similar trade performance in telecommunications in Hungary is also due to multinational activities which have given the country a comparative advantage in the two sub-sectors of office machines and power generating machinery and equipment.

It is not by chance that the countries participating in integrated markets are those which have attracted the most foreign investment. The case of Hungary is significant: it does not have a surplus, but rather a deficit in motor vehicles:

> Hungary has the most significant comparative disadvantage for road vehicles. This does not mean that the country is not involved in trade in motor vehicles with the EU – quite the contrary. For Hungary (as for Slovakia and Slovenia), the index at level 3 of the SIT Classification indicates specialisation for motor cars and other motor vehicles and despecialisation (no competitive advantage) for spare parts. This suggests that cars are assembled in these countries using imported parts and exported to the EU.[10]

One exception is Slovenia, which seems to have favourable coefficients in terms of integrated markets despite the relative paucity of foreign investment; this may be due to its success in diversifying production activities and trade.

10.3.3 Specialising in Low Cost Production

The extent of the trade deficit is worrying since it has already motivated many governments in the region to implement deflationary policies. This happened in Hungary in 1995. Successive devaluations – which have the direct effect of rendering exports more competitive and imports more expensive – have helped CEE countries to limit their trade deficits: this was the case, for instance, with the devaluation of the Czech crown in May 1997. The Polish government also devalued in July 1998. Although there are good reasons to assume that CEE governments will wish to continue the policy of competitive devaluation, this will become more and more difficult as Central and Eastern European countries experience the real appreciation of their currencies. This may lead candidate countries to gain competitiveness by reducing wage and labour costs, a strategy which has already been followed in the first twelve years of transition.

10. Op. cit. (Eurostat, June 2001), p. 2.

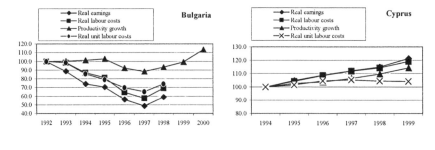

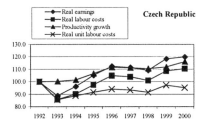

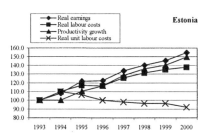

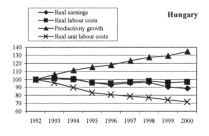

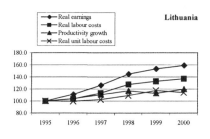

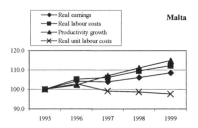

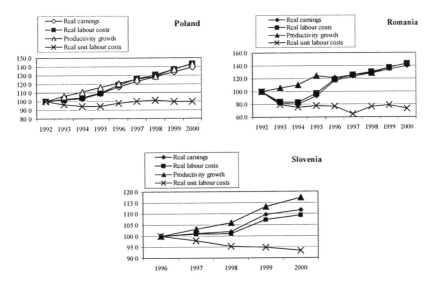

Note: *figures for Slovakia and Turkey not available.*

Figure 10.7 Real earnings, real labour costs, real unit labour costs and pro-ductivity growth in individual candidate countries

The low-cost approach: the example of Hungary

We can see from the series of graphs in Figure 10.7 that some candidate countries have voluntarily adopted the low-cost approach, trying to reduce unit labour costs (calculated as wage costs divided by productivity) by reducing wage costs as far as they will go (and neglecting the productivity effects – for example, by boosting motivation – of higher wages and incomes). *Hungary* provides an illustration of such a policy. It has been systematically following a policy of rapid economic growth based on low costs: a restrictive incomes policy, rare and modest minimum-wage increases, control of wage increases through central incomes policy and tripartite national consultations, very low wages and poor indexation in the public sector and state-owned enterprises. Successive Hungarian governments have managed to keep real earnings and labour costs below their 1992 level, which were already very low, having been inherited from the Communist regime. Only more recently did the right-wing government – mainly under pressure of the 2002 elections (which they lost) – decide to increase wages significantly in order to bring them closer to EU levels (see Chapters 2 and 5).

At the same time, higher productivity rates were achieved through deep company restructuring – rationalisation of equipment, downsizing of labour force – with the result that unit labour costs have been reduced by 30 per cent in less than ten years, an outcome which has attracted more and more foreign investors.

The same policy has been followed by *Bulgaria*, a country with even lower wage levels: a fall in real earnings and real labour costs of more than 40 per cent between 1992 and 1997 (as documented in Chapter 3) has led to a fall in unit labour costs despite poor productivity (caused by a combination of poor motivation and absence of company restructuring). Although earnings were allowed to increase slightly in subsequent years, they remained under the strict control of international monetary institutions (under the currency board policy).

Turkey is also basing its competitive position on very low labour costs, which have continued to fall in real terms over the period: in 1995 they were at 70 per cent and in 2000 at 60 per cent of their 1992 level.

The *Czech Republic* has been characterised by a number of changes in policy over the period. It started to follow a similar low-cost route in the early transition, with a very restrictive incomes policy which led to a sharp fall in real earnings and labour costs. This helped to reduce labour costs even further. A reverse trend is observed between 1993 and 1996 when earnings and so labour costs were allowed to rise above productivity increases (thus leading to a slight increase in unit labour costs), and again in 1996–8 (in the opposite direction) and 1998–2000. However, we should emphasise that if Czech competitiveness in terms of unit labour costs decreased in the second half of the 1990s, it was more due to the absence of restructuring in newly privatised companies – marking the failure of the mass privatisation process – than to an expansionist wages and incomes policy, which on the contrary remained rather moderate.

The higher value added approach: the example of Slovenia and others

Clearly, some countries have followed the higher value added approach. *Slovenia*, for instance, has carried out this policy successfully, managing to reduce real unit labour costs through productivity improvements above increasing real earnings and real labour costs. This has to be considered in a context in which wage levels are already the highest in the region. We have seen in Chapter 3 that this policy was also supported by comprehensive social protection and high-standard working conditions. This example shows how social policies and better coverage of workers could help to develop a productive economic policy: in this case employees could enjoy higher wages while contributing to economic growth through better motivation and higher productivity. The success of Slovenia – which of course was greatly helped by its more advanced starting position – is even more significant in that it is much less based on foreign investment than other candidate countries. We might wonder whether a massive influx of foreign direct investment influences the type of economic policy chosen by the target country: for instance, through their domination of the Hungarian economy, foreign investors have undoubtedly managed to impose the low-cost approach. Foreign investors in traditional sectors in Bulgaria and Romania have also put pressure on the government to keep wages at very low levels, although they themselves pay slightly above the average, precisely to avoid low motivation and to attract the best workers.

Similarly to Slovenia, the two small Southern countries *Malta* and *Cyprus* have opted for a policy aimed at keeping unit labour costs under control through a generous – although still moderate – wage policy (labour costs in real terms increased by 20 per cent in Cyprus in 1994–9 and by more than 10 per cent in Malta in 1995–9) and increased productivity, which rose by 15 per cent in both countries over the same period.

Which strategy pays off?
But is the low-cost policy working? While it has certainly helped Hungary to attract foreign investment and reduce unit labour costs, it has coincided in Bulgaria with no restructuring and low productivity. We can even say that this low wage policy has discouraged companies – which know they can rely on low wage costs – from restructuring and rationalising. A change in policy in *Romania* in 1994–5 seems to show that wages and earnings, after having been allowed to increase, did not lead to higher unit labour costs – which in fact continued to decrease – but instead coincided with a sharp increase in productivity rates (40 per cent) between 1992 and 2000.

At the same time, a balance must be found. It seems that too sharp an increase in real labour costs in *Latvia* – by more than 10 times – since 1992 has led to a significant increase in real unit labour costs – 60 per cent – especially since these higher costs for enterprises were not compensated by a similar increase in productivity. A similar labour-cost increase in *Estonia* – by 50 per cent since 1992 – was affordable due to a sharp increase in productivity, and thus even led to lower unit labour costs (by 10 per cent). *Poland* also managed to maintain unit labour costs at their low 1992 level through a significant increase (by 40 per cent) in both labour costs and productivity.

The same policy had more modest success in *Lithuania*, mainly due to a disproportion between the increase in labour costs (40 per cent in 1995–2000) and the increase in productivity (20 per cent over the same period), which led to increased unit labour costs (by 15 per cent).

Wages not following economic growth
The previous figures are confirmed by Figure 10.8 which presents wages as a share of GDP: it clearly shows that this ratio, far from increasing, in fact fell in Hungary between 1995 and 2000, where wages were not allowed to follow economic growth. The proportion of wages as a percentage of GDP also fell significantly in Estonia, Bulgaria, and, to a lesser extent, Slovenia and

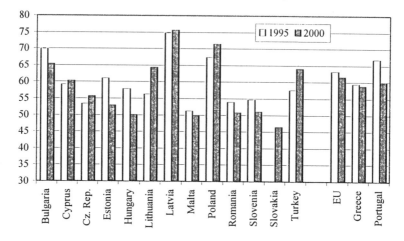

Figure 10.8 Wages (adjusted) as a share of GDP, 1995 and 2000

Romania, a situation which is, however, partly due – especially for Estonia and Slovenia – to a significant increase in GDP. In contrast, wages as a share of GDP increased over the same period in the Czech Republic, Lithuania, Latvia, Poland, and even Turkey, while they remained constant in Malta and Cyprus. Wages constitute the highest share of GDP in Latvia, due to excessive wage increases. Wage costs were also allowed to increase in Poland, but could be partly complemented by productivity rises.

The lowest wages in terms of GDP in 2000 were in Slovakia, Hungary, Malta and Slovenia. In the latter country, however, as in Cyprus and Malta, this is due to the fact that wages are already at a high level – and cannot follow high GDP growth – so that it clearly does not correspond to attempts to implement a low-wage policy.

What the figures generally reveal, however, is that low wages have been used by candidate countries as a tool of specialisation, which also explains why many of them have persisted in traditional labour-intensive activities, as described earlier. Figure 10.8 confirms that Hungary has maintained one of the lowest wage/GDP ratios in the region.

This also means that many candidate countries may well continue in traditional specialisations of this kind if they fail to acquire comparative advantages in other, more capital-intensive sectors and activities. They may also progressively build on this competitive advantage to move towards higher value-added segments in these traditional sectors, following the path that Portugal trod after its accession to the EU.

Integration in the EU and a commitment to Economic and Monetary Union will eventually deprive Central and Eastern European countries of the instrument of competitive devaluation, with clear implications for their competitiveness and trade balances. It may also seriously affect restructuring efforts. These costs for CEE economies must be taken into account by current EU members when formulating the conditions of enlargement. In particular, other economic benefits will have to compensate for this lost flexibility in respect of exchange rates.

10.4 TOWARDS MORE BALANCED TRADE?

Is the current trade deficit in future member states, especially those from Central and Eastern Europe, the healthy reflection of the initial and intermediate stages of economic growth in new market economies, or rather a trend in the wrong direction? For some economists, such persistent trade deficits are not dangerous, since they reflect a combination of EU financial support for the transition process, significant foreign direct investment flows, and increased consumption in Central and Eastern European countries, partly due to higher GDP growth. On the other hand, a persistent trade deficit may also give rise to a number of legitimate concerns. First, it may represent a serious obstacle to generalised economic growth in Europe as a whole by leading progressively to a further deterioration of purchasing power in the future member states, thus limiting import growth and interrupting the potential gains from trade. Without enlargement, which would help Central and Eastern European countries to compensate with other economic and welfare benefits, this second scenario could well become a reality. Secondly, although it is true that current account deficits can be financed by capital inflows, too great a reliance on the latter is dangerous since they may cease in response to changing economic conditions.[11] If enlargement does not take place fairly soon, or if it does not bring the expected economic returns, capital flight may well occur.

10.4.1 Towards a Trade Surplus for the Future Member States?

Nevertheless, a trade surplus with the EU may yet develop in some candidate countries. The series of graphs in Figure 10.9 shows that the deficit seems to have narrowed over the last few years. Slovakia has had a surplus since 1999, although it is not certain that the country will manage to maintain this. Estonia also managed to reduce its deficit and was in balance in 2000, something that

11. Albania represents a good example, since it has relied too heavily on foreign investment since the beginning of the transition: after the political and institutional crisis of early 1997 foreign investment suddenly fled the country, laying bare the extremely underdeveloped domestic production sphere (Vaughan-Whitehead 1999b).

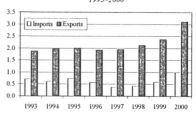

Trade flows between the EU and Bulgaria, 1993–2000

Trade flows between the EU and Cyprus, 1993–2000

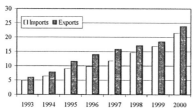

Trade flows between the EU and Czech Republic, 1993–2000

Trade flows between the EU and Estonia, 1993–2000

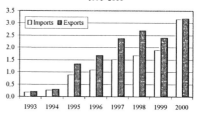

Trade flows between the EU and Hungary, 1993–2000

Trade flows between the EU and Latvia, 1993–2000

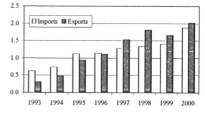

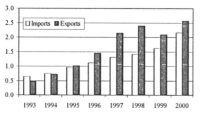

Trade flows between the EU and Lithuania, 1993–2000

Trade flows between the EU and Malta, 1993–2000

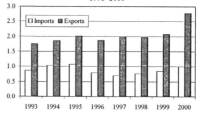

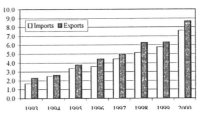

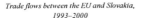

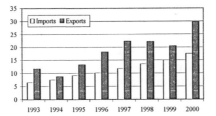

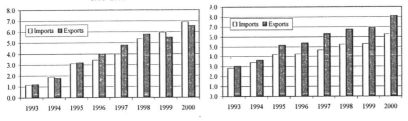

Figure 10.9 Trade flows between the EU and individual candidate countries, 1993–2000 (EU imports and EU exports)

could also happen in the near future for Hungary and the Czech Republic. In most Central and Eastern European countries, the greatest deficit seems to have occurred in the years 1996–8 and started to fall in 1999 (see, for instance, Estonia, Lithuania, Latvia and Slovakia) and 2000 (Bulgaria). The deficit with the EU remains high, however, with no signs of decrease, in, especially, Poland and, to a lesser extent, in Slovenia. At the same time, the deficits with the EU of Malta and Cyprus are also high, but it is Turkey which registers the most significant deficit (see Figure 10.9). The deficit in these three Southern countries, however, is generally offset by a surplus on invisible trade associated with tourism.

10.4.2 Not Always Reflecting Domestic Growth

Nevertheless, if some candidate countries were able to reduce their trade deficit with the EU in recent years it was not always due to better domestic growth, but sometimes to the mechanical effects of a number of other phenomena.

Imports less affordable
First, if candidate countries eventually have a better trade balance it may not be due to higher exports, the sign of healthy domestic industrial growth. On the contrary, it may be due to a general decline in both imports and exports, with candidate countries finding it difficult to maintain import levels because of lower domestic growth. This was the case, for instance, with the Czech Republic, Estonia, Latvia and Romania in 1999 when they experienced a decline in GDP which served to reduce their demand for EU imports. The same happened in Turkey, which experienced a sharp fall in GDP in 1999. On the other hand, significant growth in 2000 led to a sustained rebound in favour of EU imports. In other words, a narrowing of the trade deficit with the EU may be a sign of slowing domestic growth in future member states, so that analysts must be careful not to draw hasty conclusions.

Dependence on EU growth and demand
On the other hand, the narrowing of the trade gap may also reflect in some cases significant export growth from the candidate countries to the EU, as in 2000. This may be the sign of dynamic restructuring and higher productivity from candidate countries. Nevertheless, this again may not always reflect encouraging industrial developments in the candidate countries but increased EU market growth. This is what happened in 2000 when GDP growth in the EU rose from 2.5 per cent in 1999 to an estimated 3.3 per cent in 2000, thus dragging in more imports from candidate countries.

Exports dominated by foreign enterprises
Finally, if the terms of trade have become progressively more rosy for candidate countries, with the deficit narrowing over the years, it may be due to the export performance of multinational companies based in those countries, which contribute to both imports and exports, but whose exports – once technology transfers are over – should, over time, outperform imports. This is clearly positive for the local economy, but, as we have said elsewhere in this volume, the risk is that domestic growth is based on foreign investors alone. In this regard, it is essential to analyse the terms of trade more deeply, particularly the proportions of trade and exports generated by foreign investors and by local companies (in fact, at the moment more than 80 per cent is generated by foreign investors).

These remarks lead to one important conclusion: even if the terms of trade improve in the candidate countries, it may not always reflect higher domestic growth, but rather the growth of EU markets on the one hand and of EU foreign investors on the other. Again, the balance is tipped in favour of current EU actors.

10.5 UNEXPECTED SUBSTITUTION EFFECTS

As we explained in Chapter 7, the three freedoms – labour, capital, and goods and services – are interrelated. The current evolution of trade between candidate countries and the EU thus has a direct influence on expected capital and labour movements in parallel with the accession process. What are the normal relations between these three movements and will future member states follow a similar path in the years to come?

10.5.1 Foreign Direct Investment Normally Boosts Trade

Foreign direct investment creates trade (van Aarle 1996; Döhrn 1996; Brenton et al. 1998). This is particularly true of candidate countries: export growth has been driven by foreign investment (Chapter 8); similarly for other experts, 'exports from [the candidate countries] have until now been driven to a large extent by foreign owned companies' (RWI 2001, p. 37).

At the same time, trade creates economic growth, something that is clearly visible in the candidate countries; in recent years the highest growth rates were registered in the sectors which exported the most – for instance, in road transport, but also electronics, as well as traditional exporting sectors, such as textiles. EU accession has therefore created a virtuous circle in the candidate countries: foreign investment creates trade, thus generating economic growth.

10.5.2 Trade Normally Acts as a Substitute for Labour Movements

This dynamic and virtuous circle – foreign investment helping to boost exports and domestic growth – obviously also has direct positive effects on local labour markets. This situation may progressively contribute to reduce unemployment and so the need to look for a job abroad. Labour migration can thus be limited through better trade prospects (Straubhaar 2001b, p. 170).

Similarly, more trade with the EU, and better terms of trade, could also prevent massive or significant migrations from future to current EU member states (in Chapter 9 we noted that unemployed and inactive persons could represent an important category of migrants to EU labour markets).

10.5.3 The Possibility of a Reverse Movement in Future Member States?

The increase in foreign investment and trade may lead us to believe that candidate countries will experience a similar path in terms of the three mobilities, in a mutually sustainable development of foreign investment, trade, and economic growth. However, there are also signs which point to another scenario, which would have the effect of slowing down the process described above.

Foreign investment flows in candidate countries have slowed down (or dried up) recently, especially in those sectors (industry and now services) in which privatisation has ended (see Chapter 8). At the same time, progressive catch-up in terms of wages and incomes may dissuade foreign investment motivated by lower comparative costs from using the host country as an export platform for EU markets. Already some foreign investment has been vanishing in traditional sectors and moving further East. In economies whose growth and performance – especially on external markets – is mainly driven by foreign investment, this situation may lead to a vicious circle, with less foreign investment, a poorer trade performance, and a slowing down of domestic economic growth. In such a context, companies – domestic as well as foreign – may be tempted to have recourse to social dumping to improve international competitiveness.

Labour movement could also be boosted by such adverse developments, job seekers looking abroad when their prospects are limited in their home country. Obviously, this is a possible alternative scenario which should not be ignored by policymakers and which may have implications for employment and labour movements across borders. In any case, we saw that foreign investment in candidate countries, by systematically absorbing skilled labour, has not reduced, but in fact has increased long-term unemployment in candidate countries, so that whatever the trend in foreign investment and trade, risks of labour migration from those excluded from local labour markets may continue in the next decade.

10.6 ECONOMIC CATCH-UP

For many analysts, a dynamic process has already started in the candidate countries, generating economic growth. After the first difficult years of transition, which required restructuring, re-orientation of trade, and adaptation to EU production and working standards, Central and Eastern European countries definitely enjoy better prospects, especially considering their great potential in terms of consumption, production, and sectoral developments such as in services. Access to EU markets will also boost the already developed economies of Cyprus and Malta, and help Turkey to emerge from economic backwardness. This should lead candidate countries to experience annual GDP growth much higher than the EU average, contributing to a rapid catch-up to EU standards. New opportunities brought by a larger internal market would also attract further capital movements and trade flows, contributing to consolidate these new market economies. At the same time, the potential problems which we have pointed out must be taken into account and integrated in the overall picture.

10.6.1 Catch-Up Not to Be Expected for 10–30 Years

The possible catch-up processes of candidate countries according to different scenarios – 1 to 3 per cent growth above the EU average – are presented in Figure 10.10. They show that convergence of GDP could not take place for most candidate countries, even in the best imaginable scenario, before ten or even thirty years.

When we construct the scenario from 2000 up to 2030, we observe that the countries likely to reach the EU average first – on the forecast that their growth will be one per cent higher than the EU average every year – are

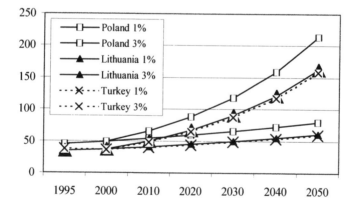

Notes:

[1] data on Malta not available.
[2] data provided by Alphametrics Ltd and already presented in the European Commission Industrial Report 2002 (EC 2002d). I thank Terry Ward for allowing me to reproduce them.

Figure 10.10 Convergence of GDP in candidate countries relative to EU average (assuming 1–3 per cent growth above EU average) (GDP per head in PPP as % of EU average)

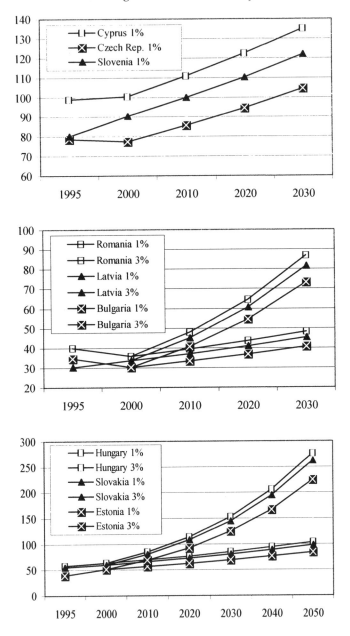

Figure 10.10 (cont.) Convergence of GDP in candidate countries relative to EU average (assuming 1–3 per cent growth above EU average)

Slovenia (though not before 2010) and the Czech Republic (not before 2025) – Cyprus is already at the EU average. Well behind are countries such as Hungary, which with the same GDP performance would reach 85 per cent of the EU average in 2030, while Slovakia would attain 80 per cent, Estonia 69 per cent and Poland 65 per cent by the same date.

At 1 per cent growth above the EU average, it is forecast that countries such as Romania, Bulgaria, Latvia, Lithuania and Turkey would still be below 50 per cent of the EU average in 2030.

Under the more (over-) optimistic scenario of GDP growth – 3 per cent above the EU average – the EU average would be reached by Slovenia before 2005, and by the Czech Republic before 2015. The process would be longer for Hungary, which would reach that level in 2015–20, Slovakia a few years later, and Poland not much earlier than 2025. In the other candidate countries, such as Romania, Bulgaria or Latvia, they could not hope to reach that average before 2040–50.

10.6.2 Catch-Up Slowing Down?

All the above secenarios –with candidate countries' GDP growth above EU average – have generally been based on the expectation of continuous economic growth in these countries, encouraged by their sudden economic jump at the end of the 1990s and afterwards. Nevertheless, we have also seen that such rapid economic development had been for some countries – such as Hungary, Estonia, Poland and the Czech Republic, but also others – mainly driven by massive foreign investment flows. This means that a continuation of their economic growth will depend – at least to a large extent – on the activities of foreign investors. While many of them intend to consolidate their production units in candidate countries, and in some cases even to expand them – we have forecast the continuation of industrial relocation in Chapter 8 – it is not to be excluded that others will rather, after having gained from the privatisation process and a few very profitable years of operation, prefer to progressively shift part of their activity towards countries with better comparative advantages in terms of privatisation opportunities, cheaper labour costs and more flexible working conditions. We can thus predict that foreign investment flows may progressively dry up, at least in those countries where they have been massive so far, as in Hungary. This possible trend, with obvious implications also for trade performance, could modify the catch-up process of candidate countries.

10.6.3 Constant Growth above the EU Rate Unrealistic

The possible scenarios presented here are based on 1 and on 3 per cent annual growth above the EU average because this is generally the hypothesis which is being presented by economists working on EU enlargement; it also gives us a starting basis for our discussion of future prospects. However, our earlier analysis of economic trends and the structure of economic growth in the future member states does not support this hypothesis of a constant annual growth rate superior to the EU average. First, after the initial years of economic boom, during which most candidate countries managed to maintain the forecast growth rate, it is to be expected that there will be a number of years of consolidation, during which annual growth rates will naturally slow down. Secondly, recent experience in some candidate countries has shown that they may face sudden and unforeseen difficulties, as happened in the Czech Republic, where a flawed mass privatisation process had adverse implications for corporate governance and performance which manifested themselves only in the second half of the 1990s. Thirdly, economic growth in almost all candidate countries – with the possible exception of Slovenia – remains too dependent on foreign direct investment and its trade performance. Finally, economic growth – especially in terms of exports – very much depends on the growth recorded in the EU, a close dependence which in itself renders difficult systematic superior growth in candidate countries. We believe it would be more realistic to assume similar economic growth in current and future EU member states, especially since we have seen that current EU countries do not benefit less, but far more, from EU enlargement than candidate countries.

This confirms the need to start working on less optimistic scenarios and to analyse all possible implications, for instance in terms of possible substitution effects between movements of labour, capital, and goods and services, not to mention their possible social ramifications, in terms not only of social dumping, but also of working and living standards.

Another urgent requirement is to develop policy options or routes that may help future member states to strengthen their current model of economic development, and in particular to make it less vulnerable to external shocks and agents.

10.7 POLICY ROUTES FOR MORE SUSTAINABLE GROWTH

In order to avoid a serious deceleration of the candidate countries' economic catch-up, not to mention a number of structural imbalances – mainly due to weaknesses in trade and capital flows – we believe it would be highly desirable for candidate countries to redirect their economic policy towards alternative policy routes that would help to consolidate economic performance, while also positively influencing social developments.

Boosting domestic production through comprehensive industrial policy
For many, industry in the candidate countries – following their production crises of the early transition – would not be worth revitalising and should be allowed to die: other activities, especially services, will be able to sustain their economies in future. In contrast, it is our belief that this would be the surest way to condemn an important part of candidate-country economies to despair. After restructuring, there are promising industries in candidate countries that could emerge as internationally competitive. However, a clear industrial policy should be designed to help the most dynamic industries, not only those which are export oriented, but also those producing for the domestic market. More generally, there is a clear need to move towards more value added products (see below). More selection and monitoring of foreign investment – as described below – could greatly help candidate countries in this upward shift in their specialisation.

However, all the above requires that governments design, at long last, an overall strategy – eventually in concertation with employers' and workers' representatives – and support it with all the appropriate policy instruments (fiscal, commercial, credit and others), while remaining within the limits of EU competition regulations.

A policy more oriented towards higher value added segments would have obvious positive effects in the social field, better working conditions and human resources becoming key elements in implementing such a strategy.

Relying on the growth of services
The service sector has considerable potential in future member states and should thus constitute one of the pillars of economic catch-up. This requires that governments develop the necessary conditions for enterprise survival in this highly competitive sector – for instance, by helping domestic small and medium-size enterprises to operate successfully (by relieving them of such burdens as gross overtaxation, scarce credit, and export difficulties).

At the same time, efforts must also be made by current EU member states. Barriers to service enterprises result in considerable costs for companies doing business between member states. In particular, the ability of small and medium-size enterprises (SMEs) prominent in service industries to grow across borders is currently severely restricted. This limits competition and consumer choice and keeps prices higher than they need to be. In this regard, current EU member states should be required by the EC to open up, for example, with regard to such services as consultancy, engineering, construction, distribution, tourism, leisure and transport. This would not only be fair, given the enormous benefits that EU companies currently obtain from the privatisation of services in candidate countries, but it would also lead to a more competitive European service sector, with positive economic and social implications in terms of GDP, employment, consumption, and local development.

While the growth of SMEs and appropriate incentives for them is a key condition for the growth of services, the authorities will have to closely monitor their practices in terms of working conditions, to ensure that their competitiveness will be based on 'fair' competition and not on 'social dumping'. More open EU markets will also contribute to avoiding such a scenario.

More diversification urgently needed
We have seen how vulnerable most candidate countries – even the most advanced, such as Hungary or Estonia – have become with regard to foreign investment. This dependence is such that any FDI slowdown – and such a slowdown is only to be expected in the natural course of things – over the next few years or any new strategic shift by affiliates of large multinational companies could endanger the economic performance of the country as a whole (especially in terms of exports, trade balance, and GDP growth). We have also seen that this dependence may have detrimental effects on domestic growth and local labour markets. This overdependence must be changed. Slovenia offers a good example of a more diversified economy, based not only on foreign investors but also on a number of competitive domestic operators, and not only on emerging services but also on basic industry.

Other candidate countries must follow a similar policy. The elaboration of a strong industrial policy or appropriate incentives for developing services (as explained earlier) could greatly help this process. In the service sector, the authorities should also try to channel foreign investors not only into tourism and trade, but also other services important for local communities. Obviously, more diversification in production – especially between foreign and local actors – would lead to more diversified industrial relations and working conditions.

For a more selective foreign capital policy
In the first years of transition, the governments of candidate countries seemed to believe that economic growth would best be generated by opening up to foreign assistance and investment. It is true that foreign investment played a crucial role in helping Central and Eastern European countries to redirect their trade from the COMECON market to the EU and to boost their economic growth. At the same time, the great expectations have not always been realised: so far, foreign investors have not given rise to an overall positive trade balance, the growing exports of joint ventures often being accompanied by significant imports of raw materials. The spillover effects for domestic operators and local markets have also been disappointingly poor. In other words, although foreign investment constituted – and will continue to consti-

tute – an important pillar of their economies, it has also shown its limitations, partly due to overexpectations on the candidate countries' side, but also the misbehaviour of many foreign firms.

The elaboration of a clear industrial policy, together with clear targets in the service sector, could help candidate countries to take better advantage of foreign investment, which could then be channelled, within the framework of specific incentives, towards the activities which need it most.

Other specific requirements could be imposed on foreign investors. As is often the case in Western European countries, the government could try to systematically push foreign investors to deal with local suppliers.[12] It is also important to induce foreign investors to help local enterprises to move towards more value added products, for example, in traditional industries such as textiles and clothing, and leather and shoes. Particular emphasis should thus be placed on processing and research and development when signing contracts with foreign companies. This would also be the best way to ensure their longer term operation in the host country.

A better selection of foreign investment would also have a direct effect on the type of commercial strategy and working conditions policy – between the low road or 'social dumping' approach and the high road or 'human resources' approach – that will be followed by foreign investors in future member states.

Favouring the emergence of local producers

A comprehensive economic policy should help to revitalise local production capacity. This is the basic condition for rebalancing economies too much driven by foreign investment. The emergence of a stronger industrial policy would help some local producers to survive in the current restructuring phase and progressively to gain in competitiveness. The growth of small and medium-size enterprises, especially in services, should also be given priority.

It is also important to develop suppliers of raw materials for the most promising industries, something that would also help to rebalance the trade deficit; we have seen that all too often joint ventures of foreign-owned companies import all their basic products, so contributing to trade imbalances.

In many areas, while opening their economy to the EU – and to the rest of the world – it is important that candidate countries develop their own productive capacities and resources.

Towards higher value added products rather than social dumping

Many candidate countries continue to rely on traditional, labour-intensive sectors in which a cheap, but skilled labour force is a definite comparative advan-

---

12. This happened, for instance, in Portugal with the French automobile company Renault, which contributed much to local industrial development.

tage. While this has made possible significant export success and helped these sectors to carry out restructuring, we have also seen that it is not in these sectors that integrated markets and intra-industry trade have the best prospects. It is also not in these sectors, which remain very vulnerable vis-à-vis labour costs in developing countries which are even lower than their own, that technology oriented production – even if a move towards higher value added segments within these traditional sectors would be desirable – will develop. This means that there is more to be gained for the candidate countries from reducing unit labour costs (wages/productivity) and improving working conditions than from keeping wage levels down. Chapter 7 (Figure 7.5 on unit labour costs) showed that wage differentials between current and future EU member states are very large, but also that, for the time being, poor productivity in candidate countries is clearly limiting, and in some countries even cancelling out, the advantage of lower labour costs. Rapid productivity growth is therefore what is required above all in these countries, something which better quality and better use of human resources could definitely help to promote. Such a route would represent the best way for future member states to be fully integrated – and not reliant on affiliates of EU operators – into the European market. It would also correspond best to the current requirements of the EC and the Community *acquis* in working conditions and the social sphere in general.

EU aid for sustainable development

While financial programmes have been made available to candidate countries, no specific concessions have been granted in terms of trade conditions; EU countries have been reluctant to open some sectors to the new competitive market economies of Central and Eastern Europe. This is not giving new operators from these countries the opportunity to become really competitive on EU markets. This is typically the case for agriculture and other basic – and sensitive – forms of production. At the same time, little aid is planned through the traditional structural funds, although this instrument would have greatly helped some of their backward regions to restructure and rapidly catch up. More generally, the assistance provided by the EU seems not to be appropriately channelled, while trade interests – and the most vulnerable regions – of the EU continue to be well protected. Redirection of such assistance would contribute to accelerating not only the catch-up process, but also economic and social cohesion within candidate countries.

Social policy in parallel

GDP convergence, far from developing overnight in the candidate countries, will in fact require many years. During this period, candidate countries may well yield to the temptation to concentrate on economic performance while relegating social issues to the margin. Furthermore, they may even be induced to allow social standards to decline further in order to gain a competitive advantage and to accelerate the catch-up process. We have tried to show how misguided such a policy route would be for practical reasons – and what the elements of an alternative policy might be – not to mention the fact that it would be at odds with the objectives that the EU clearly established at the Lisbon summit, to reconcile economic and social interests with a view to gaining in competitiveness in the long term and evolving into a successful knowledge society. To achieve this objective, all the areas addressed in the present volume – social protection, working conditions, employment, industrial relations, workers' participation – have a significant role to play.

10.8 CONCLUSION

In this chapter we have tried to counter many of the misleading arguments concerning candidate-country trade.

First, contrary to initial expectations, the trade balance seems unequivocally to have benefited current EU member states, whose exports outstrip imports from candidate countries. Although this trade deficit is expected to be progressively reduced in parallel with EU integration and the economic growth of the candidate countries, the latter's economic performance will depend strongly on the good health of the EU as a whole: a sudden crisis would have dramatic consequences. A long catch-up process and the difficulty of maintaining high GDP growth over a number of years also render questionable any marked and long-term improvement in new EU member countries' trade.

Secondly, there is much evidence that the candidate countries' exports still consist to a large extent of labour-intensive low-tech products, which not only have narrow profit margins but also confine candidate countries in low value added specialisations. As a consequence a rather traditional division of labour seems to be emerging in the course of EU enlargement so far, rather than equally developed and fully integrated markets. This is confirmed by the low-wage policy followed by, for instance, Hungary and other candidate countries, aimed at maintaining a comparative advantage in terms of production costs.

Thirdly, it is true that many future member states have already made considerable progress in their integration into the European division of labour. Not only have they significantly increased trade volumes but they have also upgraded the products exported, leading to higher profits. However, we have also seen that the share of intra-industry trade and, more generally, the export performance of candidate countries have been almost exclusively dependent on affiliates of EU companies. Two phenomena seem to confirm this: specialisation in higher technology products has taken place mainly in those countries which have attracted most foreign investment, such as Hungary, the Czech Republic, Poland, Estonia, and, to a lesser degree, Slovakia and Slovenia; secondly, integrated markets with imports and exports within the same sector have been observed in the sectors dominated by foreign investment (in terms of both growth and trade performance) such as motor vehicles and electronics. This could seriously limit the future member states' potential for trade growth in the future, and highlights the risks entailed by the excessive dependence of their trade on external agents.

Foreign investment, after reaching its peak at the beginning of the current decade, may have every reason to slow down, marking the end of the golden era of privatisation and the possible commencement of a rationalisation and eventual further relocation of EU companies in candidate countries. The domination of foreign trade by foreign investment is such that the slightest slowdown in foreign investment could have a direct negative effect on future member states' trade performance.

Fourth, we have tried to moderate the overoptimistic statements about forthcoming economic growth and catch-up in candidate countries, which we believe will require much longer than current studies predict. Even more radically, we mentioned the possibility of adverse scenarios: in strong contrast to a virtuous circle marked by more foreign investment leading to more trade and thus more growth, we saw that the opposite cannot be ruled out in some candidate countries if certain key conditions – such as sustained foreign investment and trade growth – progressively disappear. The social effects could be dramatic in terms of employment and living standards; the combination of reduced trade flows and foreign investment may also encourage labour migration. There could be unexpected substitution effects, the development of trade performance influencing the labour movements presented in Chapter 9. Obviously, we hope that this more pessimistic scenario will not emerge. Nevertheless, some of the arguments developed here are aimed at enlarging the debate and possible outcomes.

The misleading debates and conclusions on the free movement of trade and services should lead us to study this area in a more critical way, and to develop an alternative policy, one that would distribute enlargement costs more equally between current and future member states, so contributing to a more rapid catch-up process. Protectionism of any kind, from both sides, could lead only to the accumulation of enormous overall costs in terms of competitiveness in the newly enlarged EU, despite its great potential, and have dramatic effects, not only in economic but also in social terms.

11. Conclusion: An Uncertain Future after EU Enlargement

11.1 INTRODUCTION

As we have seen, the current EU enlargement to the ten Central and Eastern European and three Mediterranean applicant countries is unique and cannot be compared to previous enlargements: not only because of the number of countries involved and their size (105 million people will join – not including Turkey – the EU), but also because of the huge economic gap and the substantial social differentials. GDP differences are such that one cannot expect economic catch-up to drive social developments. In fact, the contrary is the case, namely that it is difficult to imagine how these countries will be able to achieve high economic growth without promoting more social cohesion alongside it. After twelve years of transition, citizens from these countries are demanding more balanced economic policies that leave more room for social protection. At the same time, EU citizens are demanding more socially-oriented policies in these same countries with a view to helping to prevent or limit social dumping and unfair competition from the soon-to-be new EU member states.

The main aim of this volume is to draw up a comprehensive picture of the social situation in the future member states, and to foresee what implications their integration into the EU might have for EU social policy. Regarding the main question of the book, unfortunately, we have had to confirm that the current EU enlargement may bring serious risks for Social Europe and endanger the survival of the European Social Model.

In this concluding chapter we try to summarise what reasons – some due to the candidate countries, some to the EU itself, others more global in scope – are behind this strong conclusion, before attempting to identify the concrete policy steps that should be taken if such a gloomy future for the newly enlarged EU is to be avoided.

11.2 AN UNHEALTHY BASIS

Part II of this volume presents the imbalances that have emerged between the European Union and the candidate countries during the first years of transition, in terms of the three basic mobilities: goods and services, capital, and labour.

First, as far as trade is concerned, we have seen that, while association agreements with the EU have allowed candidate countries from Central and Eastern Europe to successfully rechannel their trade towards the EU, nevertheless the terms of trade remain generally more favourable to current EU member countries, which are accumulating a net trade surplus in this process.

At the same time, freedom of capital is already operating, since the early transition of these countries has allowed EU companies to establish very profitable operations alongside privatisation. It has also allowed them to establish, at very low cost, a strong commercial basis in candidate countries, leading to the conquest of newly emerging and thus very profitable markets, while progressively developing an impressive platform for exports in an enlarged EU of more than 500 million consumers, something that has for most of them become a crucial element of their overall development and globalisation strategy.

At the same time, we have seen that the last-mentioned freedom, that of labour, has been denied to new EU member states, at least for a transition period of a few years.

On the positive side, all the above developments indicate that the future member states are important for current EU states, and that their EU integration process has created a dynamic movement of trade and capital flows. On the negative side, so far this process is clearly tipped too much in favour of current EU member states, so much so that it may establish EU enlargement on a very unhealthy basis, first, because it is not helping to accelerate the catch-up process but may even be slowing it down. We have seen, for instance, that unbalanced trade flows are not necessarily good for candidate countries. We have also seen the potential vulnerability of economies that are too dependent on foreign investment and do not develop a strong industrial policy of their own. Secondly, such imbalances could create feelings of resentment among citizens and policymakers from candidate countries, that may result in internal functioning and decision-making inside a newly enlarged EU becoming a Kafkaesque process that leads nowhere.

To the above economic imbalances we should add the hesitations and sometimes hypocrisy of the EU in terms of the extension of structural funds to future member states.

In such a context, where a clear advantage is being given to current EU actors in the enlargement process, we do not see why labour mobility could not have been conceded from the start to future member states, especially since those who profess to fear most from these labour movements are precisely those who have so far benefited the most from the EU enlargement process, in terms of trade and foreign investment, such as Austria and Germany.

Germany dominates the scene in terms of economic benefits: it has larger trade flows and the biggest trade surplus with the candidate countries, and has also accumulated more foreign investment. Nevertheless, it has been most vociferous in opposing immediate freedom of labour being granted to future member states.

We might wonder why the European Commission's position in the pre-accession talks has been so much influenced by these countries, which seem to be following a self-interested strategy in Central and Eastern Europe which is far from the solidarity and mutual benefits declared at the beginning of the process.

Similarly, why is it that the current EU member states seem unable to accept some adjustments in respect of their labour markets? In the long run, candidate countries are expected to improve their trade balance, and adjustments on the part of EU member states are likely to diminish alongside decreasing labour migration. Moreover, it is not excluded that such short-term migration flows may even turn out to be beneficial for the EU economy as a whole, especially with the ageing of the EU population and the need for more labour.

No doubt a better balanced policy in terms of trade, including such a sensitive sector as agriculture, but also regarding structural funds, is also required from the EU. On the budgetary side, for instance, it is clear that more funds are needed. After 2006 (that is, after the current EU budget expires in 2006), it will not be possible to continue with this policy and the current member states will have to increase the budget for accession.

11.3 NEW MEMBER STATES: LESS SOCIALLY ORIENTED

In the future EU member states, economic indicators are rapidly improving while social indicators continue to lag well behind. As an example, in Hungary the economy recovered its previous growth and its GDP reached its 1989 level in 2000 and has continued to improve in 2001–3. Social indicators, however, such as wages, social allowances, unemployment benefits, and living standards in general, have yet to experience similar growth. This is the result of insufficient attention being given to social issues in the first years of transition.

Efforts have been made in economic restructuring, but not in social policy; there is a general problem of social cohesion, and adverse developments in specific areas – social benefits and social schemes, pensions, and so on. There is growing unemployment but social protection is becoming less of a priority. At the same time, working and social standards have been allowed to decline in almost all candidate countries.

11.3.1 Working Conditions

Significant discrepancies in working conditions continue to prevail with regard to EU standards. Not only are wages found to be much lower in candidate countries, but the situation is also much worse with regard to health and safety at the workplace, working time, and labour contracts. Candidate countries were also found to be introducing much more extreme working patterns than in the EU. Atypical forms of employment are growing rapidly, such as temporary contracts, interim work, and self-employment. This trend may certainly influence the future of labour standards in an enlarged EU. It may strengthen the arguments of the few EU member states which make more extensive use of such flexible contracts within the framework of more neo-liberal economic policies. In such a context, the accession negotiations concerning the Community *acquis*, with regard to which the EC has not taken up a sufficiently strong position, may not have been very useful, especially since the main problem within the newly emerging free-market economies – beyond the merely formal adoption of EC regulations – will be the implementation of the *acquis* at local level.

11.3.2 Social Protection

The direction of social protection policy in candidate countries is towards more deregulation. As a result of systematic liberalisation and privatisation, social programmes that once covered the whole population have been limited to those qualifying through means-testing; access to many social services has become market-regulated; and spending on social security and assistance has been drastically curtailed – all in a context in which the number of recipients has substantially increased. These low levels of social protection contrast significantly with social policy in the current EU member states, and they certainly do not constitute an appropriate response to the general social crisis in these countries. Reforms of pension schemes have adopted the liberal and capital market–based approach sold with considerable success by the World Bank in all these countries, at a time when the EU was totally absent from the debate in this area. For one observer: 'The implicit model for Central and Eastern Europe is different from the European model. The consequence may be that the countries that would like to join the union may destroy institutions which might ultimately become conditions of admittance' (Ferge 2000, p. 14).

11.3.3 Social Dialogue

While basic legal regulations have been put in place to ensure the development of collective bargaining and social dialogue, and the operations of employer and trade union organisations, in reality the scope of collective bargaining is very poor, generally below 10–20 per cent of the total labour force.

In fact, while tripartite consultations with social partners have been promoted by governments, support has yet to be given to promote bipartite – that is, autonomous – social dialogue between employer and trade union representatives, which is having difficulty emerging, especially at sectoral level. At enterprise level, institutionalised forms of social dialogue are of little help in impeding excessive anti-union and anti-social dialogue practices in a majority of enterprises and sectors of the economy. Social dialogue is often nonexistent in the new small and medium-size enterprises, where employers also do not have much culture of industrial relations and human resources. Such poor scope for social dialogue can only disrupt the proper implementation of the Community *acquis* at local level, especially since it has to be seen in combination with the removal of a number of previously existing workers' rights and social protection.

11.3.4 Workers' Participation

The elimination of works councils and lack of enforcement of the Community *acquis* in this field has also led to the absence of forms of workers' participation at enterprise level, something that could have helped to compensate for the absence of social dialogue structures and practices. At the same time, employee ownership which, after its initial massive development in the privatisation process, was confirmed to be a viable property and organisational form, has progressively been allowed to disappear, rarely on the grounds of economic efficiency and good corporate governance. This is also due to the trade unions, which in many candidate countries have opposed this type of alternative and more direct workers' interest representation, while the institution of European works councils has been characterised by a split between trade union representatives from current and future EU member states.

Other forms of workers' participation, such as profit-sharing, that are widely developed in the current EU, have yet to emerge in candidate countries. This situation contrasts with the strong institutional development of workers' participation in the current EU member states. It may also contribute to undermine the proper implementation of the social *acquis* at enterprise level. Another form of economic democracy is thus clearly missing in the neo-liberal landscape that seems to be spreading in candidate countries.

11.3.5 Employment

The future member states are also characterised by increasing unemployment rates which have reached unprecedented levels already; long-term unemployment dominates, which is a sign of structural imbalances between workers' skills and qualifications and labour market demand. Unskilled labour in particular is being left out of these new free-market economies mainly dominated by foreign investors who require primarily skilled employees. Foreign investment therefore contributes to increase rather than decrease original imbalances and is not helping as much as expected to improve local employment restructuring or to reduce long-term unemployment.

Faced by high unemployment rates, governments of the candidate countries have yet to develop a comprehensive employment policy. Their first reaction has been rather to implement the restrictive policy advised by international monetary institutions, which consists in systematically reducing unemployment benefits and numbers of beneficiaries. As a result, many unemployed have been excluded from receiving unemployment benefits, thus increasing social marginalisation.

Proper institutions able to help job seekers find work have not always emerged, generally because of a lack of human and financial resources.

11.3.6 Informal Economy

The informal economy is a feature of almost all candidate countries which affects all the areas under study in this volume. It adversely disrupts legal employment, wages and incomes, social dialogue, workers' participation, working conditions, and also budgetary expenditure in the social field by reducing budget revenues.

11.3.7 Combining Effects

In light of the above, it is not so much that future member states are so far adrift – although comparison of social protection levels, for instance, shows significant differences – as that they are following the trend characteristic of a number of EU member states, in terms of which social considerations are downgraded in favour of free-market forces relatively unfettered by social elements. In fact, many candidate countries are implementing such neo-liberal theories in a much more radical way that in the current EU, which may represent a risk for the future of Social Europe in the newly enlarged European Union.

In previous chapters we have tried to analyse social developments in specific areas in candidate countries; it is, however, important to consider all these areas in terms of a global picture of social policy in general and their future in an enlarged EU. In particular, the developments described influence each other. For instance, we saw that the presence of a large informal sector influences the coverage of social dialogue (and also participation), which remains low in the economy as a whole. At the same time, the small extent of social dialogue also contributes to adverse developments in terms of working conditions; the informal economy also has direct effects on working conditions. Unemployment also combines with the narrower lower scope of social and unemployment benefits to increase the number of excluded.

The 'wild capitalism' which is apparently emerging in the new private enterprises – leading to less participation and social protection in enterprises – must also be seen in a context in which the state is withdrawing from social protection in favour of economic and social policies of neo-liberal inspiration.

11.4 DILUTING SOCIAL POLICY

The worrying prospects for European social policy are due not only to the situation of the candidate countries in the social field, but also to the trends towards more liberal policies – in which social policy does not figure prominently – in current EU member states. The latter trend – which we present in this section – has clearly also influenced the first, and both combine to increase uncertainties about the survival of the European Social Model in an enlarged EU. A number of different documents or manifestos prepared and co-signed by major political leaders, mainly from the UK, Germany, Spain, and Italy on the occasion of European summits, are a good illustration of the recent policy trend in most current EU countries.

11.4.1 Reducing Social Budgets and Renouncing Redistribution Policies

In the manifesto *The Third Way* co-signed by Tony Blair and Gerhard Schröder, social issues are rarely mentioned, and when they are, it is to declare the need to reform existing systems, the principal objective of which seems to be budget cuts:

> Public expenditure as a proportion of national income has more or less reached the limits of acceptability. (*Europe: The Third Way/Die neue Mitte*, 11 June 1999)

It is striking how similar this policy is to that promoted by the World Bank and the IMF in the first years of reform in Central and Eastern Europe, which advised systematic cuts in public expenditure, especially in sectors such as education, health care, and culture (see Chapter 3), despite the fact that as a proportion of GDP this expenditure was far below that of EU member states.

More generally, the *Third Way* manifesto proposes to remove the policy of redistribution, a basic principle of social policy in the EU so far: 'We must make work pay for individuals and families. The biggest part of income must remain in the pockets of those who worked for it.' This would mark the end not only of the redistribution system, but also of the solidarity principle.

Changes in labour market conditions and in social protection are thus not just about competitiveness, but also turn on fundamental political choices about who receives what in society. Whether it is Economic and Monetary Union, globalisation or EU enlargement that is under review, there are bound to be distributional implications. Surprisingly, however, this rarely becomes a theme of debate, although it is useful to reflect on what is at stake.

For the IMF and the World Bank – and increasingly for EU member states – the choice is clear, with distribution focused on those most in need. Without declaring it, this policy already constitutes a very strong choice concerning distribution, and so a particular model of society.

Seen from this perspective, the 'crisis' of the European Social Model would be less a question of whether EU member states can afford their social protection systems than a deeper debate about how much redistribution there should be in favour of the economically inactive.

11.4.2 Targeting and Workfare

On the rare occasions social policy is mentioned, it is in the narrower perspective of protection of the most vulnerable sections of the population to 'combat social exclusion and poverty'. The targeting approach is visible in all social areas, especially social protection and employment. To cite the *Third Way* manifesto once more, 'this requires adherence to our values but also a willingness to change our old approaches and traditional policy instruments. In the past, the promotion of social justice was sometimes confused with the imposition of equality of outcome.' Furthermore, 'poverty remains a central concern, especially among families with children . . . We need specific measures for those who are most threatened by marginalisation and social exclusion.'

Similarly as regards unemployment: 'we must introduce targeted programmes for the long-term unemployed and other disadvantaged groups to give them the opportunity to reintegrate into the labour market'.

Means testing is also mentioned in the *Third Way* manifesto: 'we must assess all benefit recipients, including people of working age in receipt of disability benefits, concerning their earning potential, and reform state employment services to assist those capable of work to find appropriate work'. This is again very similar approach to the advice given by international monetary institutions in Central and Eastern Europe.

Workfare is also important, that is, employment projects characterised by unskilled work. Public works are part of this scheme, described further in the manifesto:

Successful Welfare to Work programmes raise the incomes of those previously out of work, as well as improving the supply of labour available to employers . . . In Germany the political sector is supporting this endeavour with an immediate action programme for jobs and training that will enable 100 000 young people to find a new job or training place or to obtain qualifications. In Britain the Welfare to Work programme has already enabled 95 000 young people to find work.

In the same spirit, 'public works' have been recommended by the World Bank for the purpose of combating unemployment in Central and Eastern Europe. However, such schemes were found to have a number of drawbacks. Public works have in practice served as a vehicle for subsidising jobs; in many cases they have replaced existing jobs, while pushing down wage levels for the rest of the labour force.

11.4.3 The Wind of Deregulation

With a view to improving the employment situation, especially through the creation of new jobs, a wind of deregulation has been blowing in the European Union for some time. This corresponds to a need for more flexibility in certain activities, sectors, and types of enterprise; it is obvious that the boom in services in the United States – which has yet to be experienced in the EU to the same extent – may have been favoured by better labour market, legal and fiscal conditions for enterprises.

At the same time, such flexibility should not intervene at the expense of the general need for security and protection for workers, which are also key elements in economic growth. Deregulation and liberalisation have become the leitmotiv of political leaders in the last decade, as discussed in Chapter 1. This 'flexibility–security' debate is, however, misleading if it does not take into account the specificities of candidate countries.

As an example, the *Third Way* manifesto insists on the need to reduce regulation in small enterprises; however, considering the trend in SMEs in Central and Eastern Europe, which are characterised by a total absence of social dialogue and social regulations, such a message could be misinterpreted and lead to even 'wilder' deregulation in these countries. The consequences of such a trend have yet to be taken into account by policymakers, even those most in favour of deregulation.

11.5 SOCIAL DUMPING EXACERBATED

We saw that there are certain areas where large differences prevail between most candidate countries and current EU member states. The economic differences in terms of GDP per capita also reflect great differences in the social area, for example, in wages, living standards, and so on. There are also significant differences in terms of working conditions, with health and safety conditions well below EU standards, and also different practices concerning labour contracts – such as increasing temporary and part-time contracts – and conditions of employment.

Although the picture painted in the different chapters of this book seems to be relatively uniform, significant differences can be identified by theme. While the differences in wage levels can look impressive, especially since economic catch-up will not be as rapid as desired, this will progressively disappear and a levelling-up will intervene, so reducing one of the main sources of social dumping in the medium to long term. In other areas, such as workers' participation, the new member states, even if they seem to have rejected the European model in many ways, will progressively have to adapt themselves to the participatory working environment that prevails in the current EU member states. Cooperation and exchanges with other actors from the EU will contribute to this movement. Nevertheless, on other issues the gap already looks too large. In the social protection area, the option chosen by the candidate countries is already in danger of going too far in a particular direction to be modified. All social protection systems have already been more than two-thirds privatised. Moreover, once a reform of pension systems has been carried out, it is very difficult to return to another system since every system requires years to be put in place and its effectiveness assessed. In this area, we can predict that the situation in candidate countries will not change significantly after their membership.

In Part II of this volume, we have seen that trade, foreign investment and labour migration are substitutes, and should thus be studied, analysed and addressed together, something that has not been done so far in the debates and analyses on EU enlargement.

We have seen, for instance, that capital mobility can limit labour movement; free trade also limits capital relocations; and at the same time, foreign investment influences trade flows. Movements of labour can serve as a response to the absence of free trade. This means that inadequate trade liberalisation would lead to more massive migrations, and that the reduction of capital movements would lead to greater demand from EU companies at home for migrant labour. At the same time, the absence of free movement of labour will increase capital relocations and also continue to influence trade flows.

11.6 PUBLIC SUPPORT ERODING

It would not be possible to analyse the future of the newly enlarged EU without a flavour of what citizens of both current and future member states think about the whole process. Considering the unbalanced process we identified above, perceptions of citizens from candidate countries are particularly relevant.

In order to gather information about perceptions of EU enlargement, the European Commission launched a series of surveys in the thirteen candidate countries along the same lines as the standard survey (Eurobarometer) carried out in the EU, which thus allows direct comparison. We present here the results of the survey carried out in October 2001, whose first results were published in March 2002.[1] We shall complement these results provided by the European Commission with the results of survey polls carried out by national institutes in individual candidate countries, in order to provide as faithful an image as possible of the perceptions of citizens from candidate countries of EU enlargement and also of social issues in this process.

11.6.1 An Apparently General Consensus on EU Accession

Results of survey polls show, first, that in general a majority of people are in favour of their country's accession to the EU and would vote for it in a referendum. On average, in October 2001, 59 per cent of those surveyed in the applicant countries regarded EU membership as a 'good thing' for their country. This was much higher than the 48 per cent in favour of EU enlargement in current EU member states. As expected, EU enlargement thus finds broader support in candidate countries than in current EU member states, where citizens feel they may have something to lose from the whole process: 65 per cent on average in candidate countries declared that they would support their country's membership of the EU in any referendum that might be held on this issue. These positive results, however, seem to have led to over-optimism about candidate countries' acceptance of the process as a whole.

We should first direct the attention of the reader to the fact that these opinion polls are generally aimed at building a general and dynamic consensus around the EU enlargement process. One might wonder whether opinion-poll results which suddenly showed a fall in support for the EU enlargement process would be published in full and widely disseminated by European institutions or by national authorities whose aim is to make the process succeed. In fact, opinion polls carried out by independent institutes generally present rather different results, with a general consensus coming out less clearly. In fact, more careful analysis of the results gives reasons for worry concerning the way EU enlargement has been sold and information about it delivered in candidate countries.

1. Results presented here are from: Applicant countries, Eurobarometer 2001 – Public opinion in the countries applying for European Union membership, European Commission (http://europa.eu.int/comm/public_opinion), March 2002, Brussels.

11.6.2 Differences by Country

While support for EU membership is very high in Romania, where 80 per cent consider it a good thing, in Estonia and Latvia the figure is only 33 per cent. Even more worrying, although Malta's referendum on accession – the first in a candidate country – organised on 8 March 2003 came out in favour (53.6 per cent), the small majority, together with a low turnout, reflects concerns about EU enlargement. Moreover, the opposition Labour Party refused to concede defeat and declared that the issue should be decided at the impending general elections (early April 2003). The fact that the referendum result is not 'binding' may mean that a change of government changes the final outcome. The next referenda in 2003 will be in Slovenia (23 March), Hungary (12 April), Lithuania (10–11 May), Slovakia (16–17 May) and Poland (8 June).

In Estonia, only one in four respondents thinks that they would personally benefit from accession, making Estonians among the least optimistic among the thirteen applicant countries. Similarly in Slovenia, only 33 per cent expect that they would benefit from EU membership, against 55 per cent who expect no benefits. Similar results were found in Poland and the Czech Republic.

11.6.3 A Sizeable Proportion Against or Unconvinced

While the majority certainly favour the EU, there is also a high percentage of respondents with a negative image of the EU and who would probably be inclined to vote against membership. Clearly, the whole project does not enjoy unanimous support among citizens of candidate countries. At the same time, the percentage of people without an opinion or neutral is significant – generally not far below one-quarter – meaning that there is a sizeable number of people who can be influenced one way or the other. In Estonia, for instance, nearly half (47 per cent) of respondents reported a neutral image of the EU, followed by Latvia (45 per cent) and Slovenia (42 per cent). Figure 11.1 shows how the outcome of a referendum could be influenced by a campaign aimed at convincing those who are undecided or who say they will not vote.

In all three Baltic countries – and especially Estonia – as well as in Malta, and possibly also in Poland, the Czech Republic and Slovenia, adverse economic and social developments, or any national conflict suddenly emerging against the EU may easily erode the small majority in favour of EU membership while adversely persuading those who are not yet fully convinced or do not have a clear opinion about the EU.

Many national polls carried out in individual candidate countries increasingly point to a high percentage of pessimists about EU accession, which in most of them is little short of one-quarter of the population.

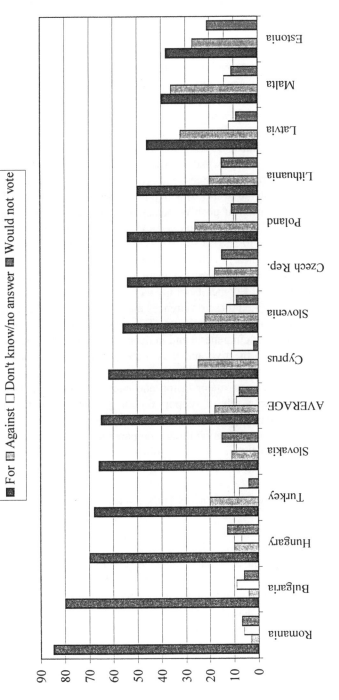

Source: Eurobarometer 2001, European Commission (March 2002)

Figure 11.1 How would you vote in a referendum on EU membership? (% of respondents aged 18 and over)

11.6.4 Population Categories Left Out of the Process

Opinions about EU membership seem also to vary greatly according to social group. In general, young people, especially students, white-collar workers, employees in the private sector, and those with a higher education are found to be more supportive of their country's EU membership than the retired, older respondents, blue-collar workers, employees in the public sector, and those with a poorer education. Men were also found to be more enthusiastic about the process than women.

Sixty-two per cent of students had a positive image of the EU, a similar rate being recorded among the youngest age groups and among managers. A drop was observed among the over-55s, with only 43 per cent with favourable opinions. A lower proportion of positive perceptions was also found among the retired (44 per cent), the self-employed (45 per cent), women (48 per cent), and those between 40 and 54 (49 per cent). Manual workers and the unemployed also ranked clearly below average in terms of support for EU membership. Minorities and farmers too were found to have a very poor image of the advantages of EU membership.

EC reports have explained these differences mainly in terms of the different educational levels of the respondents. The better educated are more informed about the EU both in general and in detail, and would thus be more inclined to have a more objective and thus more positive view about EU membership.

It is true that education is a major factor, and numerous analyses show a clear correlation between levels of support for the EU and education: for instance, only 52 per cent of people who left school aged 15 or younger see their country's membership as a good thing, compared to 67 per cent of people who left full-time education aged 20 or older. However, we believe that other factors may also contribute to explaining these differences.

11.6.5 Educational Differences Not the Only Factor

If level of education was the main or only factor explaining the different perceptions of EU accession, we might wonder why we find differences between, for instance, employees in the public sector – generally no less educated but less supportive of the accession process – and employees in the private sector; and why men should be more supportive of the EU, especially in candidate countries where access to education for women has certainly been more egalitarian than in Western countries? Why should manual workers, including the most skilled, and the unemployed, which are categories that can include all educational backgrounds, be less keen on acceding to the EU?

We believe that the social factors presented in this volume may help to complete the picture. The categories less supportive of the EU are precisely those which have suffered the most from the transition process, and who thus are prone to assimilating the EU with the difficult situation in which they currently find themselves: the unemployed, pensioners, farmers, public employees, unskilled workers, ethnic minorities – and women, although to a lesser degree – are the categories that have suffered the most from restructuring and increased unemployment, reduced social and unemployment benefits, the narrower scope of social and family allowances, and a social policy which is less redistributional at both national and EU level (for instance, for farmers). Employees with higher education, managers, and young people have managed to adapt themselves and improve their situation alongside the transition process, so that they can look to a more rosy future within the EU. At the same time, it is not surprising that farmers feel less confident; they are seen by all respondents as the main category that will lose out from the accession process, in all the applicant countries.

11.6.6 Lack of Information

While the education factor may not be the only one, there is certainly a general lack of information on the process, for all categories of citizen. Most people reported not being well informed either about their country's accession process or about EU enlargement as a whole. Only 28 per cent said they were well informed about enlargement and only 29 per cent feel well informed about their own country's accession process. The differences by country are again strong, with 57 per cent in Slovenia compared to around 20 per cent in Turkey, reflecting different policies with regard to the accession process.

11.6.7 Dissatisfaction about Social Issues

It is significant to observe that satisfaction with life in general continues to decrease in most candidate countries, after more than eleven years of transition. The surveys report a unanimously shared view in the candidate countries that 'the present generations have to sacrifice their interests to some extent to ensure a brighter future for their countries and for the younger generation'.[2]

At the end of 2001, a majority (49 per cent) felt that their present situation had worsened as compared with five years earlier, with 23 per cent reporting no difference – that means their generally unsatisfactory situation of five years ago had not improved – and only one-third reported that their situation was better. We should state that in the EU, where quality of life and individu-

2. Op. cit., p. 62.

al wealth are already very high, a large majority of citizens reported being more satisfied than five years previously. Similarly, confidence in the future is also higher in the EU: to the question about life satisfaction over the next five years, 42 per cent of citizens of the current EU believed that it would further increase, while only 37 per cent responded in a similar way in candidate countries (excluding Turkey, where individual prospects are even worse). The remaining respondents were quite sceptical about rosier prospects, with 26 per cent believing that their situation would get even worse, 26 per cent that it would remain the same, and 11 per cent who could not decide.

In particular, the prospects of households from candidate countries are significantly bleaker than in the EU with regard to their perception of the year to come, the economic situation of the country, their individual financial situation and employment (43 per cent foresee that their employment situation will get worse). If we include Turkey in the picture, where prospects are even worse, the average percentage of people expecting that the situation will deteriorate in the thirteen candidate countries jumps even further for all indicators, up to 50 per cent on the economic situation of the country (74 per cent in Turkey), 37 per cent on the financial situation of the household (54 per cent in Turkey), and 54 per cent on the employment situation (74 per cent in Turkey).

Table 11.1 Perceptions of living standards and economic prospects in the candidate countries

	12 candidate countries (excluding Turkey)	13 candidate countries	EU 15
Past life satisfaction (compared with 5 years ago)	–	Improved = 28% Worse = 49% About the same= 23%	–
Future life satisfaction (over the next five years)	–	Will: improve = 37% get worse = 26% stay about the same= 26%	–
Expectations about economic situation of the country (for the year to come)	Will be: worse: 37% better: 21%	Will be: worse: 50% better: 17%	Will be: worse: 24% better: 24%
Expectations about financial situation of your household (for the year to come)	Will be: worse: 29% better: 22%	Will be: worse: 37% better: 19%	Will be: worse: 11% better: 27%
Expectation about employment situation (for the year to come)	Will be: worse: 43% better: 16%	Will be: worse: 54% better: 13%	Will be: worse: 30% better: 23%

These comparative results do not indicate a strong catch-up process in individual life satisfaction between citizens of current and of future EU member states; they are a sign of significant social problems.

Even more striking, citizens from future member states tend to think that EU policy will not help to improve, but in many cases will exacerbate the poor social situation. When asked what the EU would bring them in ten years' time, only 57 per cent of respondents from candidate countries mentioned 'better quality of life', while 24 per cent expected 'more social problems' and 21 per cent 'higher unemployment'. No less than 54 per cent of Cypriots, and 41 per cent of Maltese and of Estonians expressed the fear that their membership would have a negative effect on their employment possibilities. This confirms their lack of hope that the EU will solve their social problems.

At the same time, they would like the EU to take more initiative. Survey results show that 65 per cent of respondents from applicant countries support not only national action, but also joint decision-making with the EU on the fight against poverty and social exclusion. Sixty-six per cent desire a common campaign against unemployment. It is also significant that social issues were ranked highest in order of importance by citizens of candidate countries: 63 per cent of them selected social issues, well ahead of national politics and the economy (both mentioned by 50 per cent of respondents); 53 per cent of people interviewed also selected social policy among the topics on which they would like more information. This is a clear signal to European institutions, but also national political leaders, to rechannel their policy efforts, especially as enlargement looms ever closer.

11.6.8 Other Issues Influencing General Trust in the EU

Other results are also of some interest in shedding further light on how the EU is perceived in future member states. For instance, one negative answer about the current EU most commonly mentioned was that it is protectionist, reflecting the unbalanced trade flows these countries are currently experiencing with the EU, especially in those areas yet to be opened up. This negative perception was very strongly felt in Malta (by one-third of respondents), but also in Cyprus, Estonia, Latvia, and Slovenia.

Agriculture is another issue that may influence the perception of EU enlargement of citizens from candidate countries; the fear that farmers will find life more difficult was found to be most widespread in Poland, Slovenia, and Latvia, but also in other countries (Czech Republic, Lithuania, Malta, and Slovakia). A more balanced EU policy in this field could thus greatly help to improve the confidence of candidate countries in the whole process.

It is also worth reporting that 'the ability to move freely in the European Union' was reported in all candidate countries as one of the main advantages of EU membership: 61 per cent of respondents said 'freedom of movement' when asked what the EU meant to them personally. Similarly, 71 per cent of those surveyed reported the right to work in any country in the European Union as the main meaning of 'being an EU citizen'. This perception of the EU contrasts strikingly with current EU policy which intends to deny freedom of movement to these new EU citizens for a number of years, to the detriment of their perception of EU membership.

11.6.9 Perception of EU Enlargement by Current EU Citizens

Despite the absence of general support for the EU enlargement process among the citizens of candidate countries, they continue to be more optimistic than those in present EU member states. Over twice as many people in the EU, proportionately, believe that the disadvantages of enlargement will outweigh the advantages. Differences by individual country reveal a similar picture.

This again contrasts strongly with the extent to which the enlargement process is already tilted in favour of current EU member states, something of which current EU citizens seem unaware. The fact that social dumping has not been properly discussed has also played a role: for instance, 60 per cent of respondents from the EU mentioned as one of their main fears 'the transfer of jobs to countries which have lower production costs', that is, a fear of capital relocations which, combined with East–West labour migration, leads many EU citizens to believe that many jobs will be taken away after EU enlargement. The fear of a loss of social benefits was also mentioned by 51 per cent of respondents from the current EU.

It is clear that policymakers, but also the media and all those working on or reporting the enlargement process have a major responsibility to inform citizens, especially about the real advantages and disadvantages, and more generally about the net benefits. However, policymakers should have the courage of their convictions, rather than falling in with scaremongering for electoral purposes. Only 18 per cent of EU citizens feel well or very well informed about EU enlargement, with 78 per cent feeling not very well or not at all informed.

11.6.10 Causes for Concern

These results, which we believe underestimate the true level of disquiet regarding EU enlargement, are worrying, especially with regard to forthcoming referenda on accession in future member states. There is every reason to believe that the lack of information about EU enlargement, combined with social problems, will not be without consequence. The eroding majority in favour of the accession process is significant.

The same lack of information about advantages and disadvantages could also lead to rejection on the part of the citizens of current EU member states, either by way of a 'no'-vote to a particular treaty, as recently in Ireland (at least at the first referendum – the re-run resulted in a 'yes'-vote), or through other means that may turn out to be detrimental for the goodwill required for EU enlargement. Nothing has been done to promote EU enlargement in current member states, although the process is no less important than the adoption of the euro, concerning which there have been a number of significant campaigns.

At the same time, it is worrying that the high percentage of people against or undecided in candidate countries does not seem to have caused much reaction among political leaders, as if a majority in favour of EU accession would eventually be achieved without much difficulty. This is fundamentally the wrong approach. As an example, the following sentence was delivered by the European Commission without much additional comment: 'Attitudinal analyses show that the people who say that the membership of the European Union would be neither good nor bad have currently a net expectation of benefits which is precisely zero.'[3]

However, the fact that there is no sign of enthusiasm, of a dynamic movement around the current EU enlargement process, may cause problems in the future. Policymakers of both future and current member states, as well as the officials of European institutions seem interested only in ensuring that the respective candidate countries join the EU, and are less concerned about how the EU will function thereafter. Furthermore, no account is being taken of the possible implications of the bad feeling and frustration now accumulating among citizens of candidate countries as regards the enlargement process, which will influence the role played by representatives of the new member states in the internal functioning of the newly enlarged EU.

Finally, it is paradoxical that perceptions of the EU, which prides itself on its almost unique emphasis on the social dimension, are worst precisely among those groups most in need and who should expect the most from the current accession process. In other words, the social message of the EU has not reached citizens from candidate countries. What is clearly lacking is an in-depth discussion and action programme regarding the social impact of EU enlargement.

11.7 NEED FOR POLICY REDIRECTION

If EU enlargement could endanger the very survival of the European Social Model, it is not only because adverse developments in many social areas have taken place and continue to take place in future member states, but also

3. Op. cit., p. 63.

because of the absence of a clear strategy on the part of the European institutions, together with their negotiation strategy, which is much too narrow and rigid – with its emphasis only on the 'core *acquis*' – and the too-rapid pace of the process.

It is obvious that the negotiations on the social chapter – which involved discussion of all the issues described in this book – were finished in a very short time. DG Enlargement has never concealed the fact that social issues were among the chapters negotiated first because they were considered as among the easiest to conclude, while considerably more difficulties were foreseen for chapters such as labour mobility, agriculture and structural funds.

This very short period of time, combined with the fact that no single social issue seriously delayed the closure of Chapter 13, calls into question the adequacy of the treatment of social issues; in fact, the failure to systematically include the different elements of the European Social Model in the negotiation process may have encouraged the candidate countries to neglect them. Even a potential new member state such as Slovenia, which entered the transition with a comprehensive social policy stronger than in many current member states and continued to implement it for the first ten years of transition, has been inclined more recently to follow a more liberal approach and to start to cut social expenditure.

The different problems related to divergent developments and problems in the social field described in this book indicate that there was every reason to demand much more of candidate countries in the course of negotiations on a number of issues, such as working conditions, social protection, and employment. At the same time, there are areas on which the European Commission has stood firm, such as health and safety – mainly because of the Community *acquis* – and social dialogue because of its institutional place and its importance for other areas. It is to be hoped that the recent EC progress in these areas, such as social protection and social exclusion, could in one way or another rebalance the process.

The social risks brought by candidate countries have themselves been amplified by more or less covert attempts to undermine the various elements of the European Social Model, both from outside the EU – for instance, we saw how radically different was the international monetary institutions' policy in this area – but also from inside, as exemplified by discussion of the 'modernisation' of the European Social Model, a process which has clearly had an effect also on the negotiation process, something which may transform the nature of the EU in the future. The result is worrying, and requires a thorough redirection and refocusing of EU policy on both enlargement and social policy. More ambitious policies are needed, not only for the newly enlarged EU, but also more extensively to provide an alternative and viable economic system in the new internationalised and global context.

11.7.1 For a Stronger EU Stance on Social Policy

There are enough achievements in the social field in the EU – moreover, sufficiently different from the systems prevailing in other parts of the world – to justify grouping them under the general heading 'European Social Model'. This model has succeeded in providing a minimum set of rights that may be further extended to cover more areas and more categories of people. At the same time, it has to be further improved, so that it represents not only a social achievement, isolated from other developments, but also a key engine of productivity and economic performance. In this regard, the model should be fine tuned, not only in terms of coverage but also in terms of flexibility, its reliance on the subsidiarity principle, and the participation of an increasingly diverse group of actors, such as employer and worker organisations, and representatives of civil society. It is this difficult balance that seems already to have been lost in the current EU enlargement process. In this regard, a few policy issues should be addressed in order to rebalance the whole process.

No sustainable economic growth without social progress
We should not forget that there is currently an ideological struggle in Europe concerning social matters in relation to economic policy. Despite appearances to the contrary, it is not a fight between those in favour of economic growth and those against it, but between those who believe that economic forces alone are able to generate good economic performance, and those who believe that good economic performance not only cannot be sustainable, but also cannot be achieved without social cohesion and sufficient attention to social issues. At the beginning of the European construction process, the project was mainly aimed at building an integrated internal market, with social issues emerging and developing more and more over time. Progressively, the EU has managed to show that it can accompany economic growth and economic integration with strong social policies and social cohesion, a model which clearly contrasts with other economic systems developing in the USA and elsewhere.

Many of the different elements of the European Social Model that we have presented – such as the coordinated approach (on employment), but also social dialogue – are good examples of this mutually sustaining interaction between social and economic forces. The coordinated approach adopted at EU level on employment issues does not merely provide a more humane and cooperative way of coping with employment issues – it is not only aimed at reducing the adverse social implications of unemployment – but above all it aims to diminish the adverse economic effects of unemployment, with positive implications expected for other key macroeconomic variables. If employment issues are to be addressed seriously, it has become impossible to dissociate economic from social and human considerations. The same applies to social dialogue: not only does the development of the role of the social partners represent a key step in addressing social issues, notably through the involvement of the trade unions, but also, since the social partners represent employers' and workers' interests, it coordinates the interests of the main actors in the field and so promotes economic growth. Other social areas – such as social protection, workers' participation, and working conditions – can all make useful and essential contributions to economic growth.

Despite such interaction, the competition between more liberal policies and more interventionist approaches – especially on social issues – will continue. In such a debate, it is important to abandon ideology and to base policy on past achievements. If the EU is to show that it is possible, and even desirable, to implement a comprehensive social policy alongside its economic policy, let us extend these basic achievements to future member states; let us emphasise the economic benefits, especially during the continuation of their reform process, that new member states from Central and Eastern Europe, but also from the South, could obtain from a more balanced social policy, leaving room for such basic principles as equity, solidarity, participation and democracy.

As we saw in Chapter 1, the message of the Lisbon Summit at the political level was important, asserting the need to consider social measures as productive factors. This step is significant since it legitimises politically what a number of empirical studies have found. However, this recognition should now induce member states to implement it in practice, that is, in terms of economic policy. In this regard, economic reforms that depart somewhat from mainstream economics or ready-made recipes from international monetary institutions would be welcome, in both current and future EU members.

11.7.2 Social Policies as 'Productive' Factors: Limits of the Approach

At the same time, it is important to ensure that this message is not abused: the danger is that political leaders could be increasingly tempted to favour measures of social progress when they seem to favour economic performance, but to reject those which do not. For example, in the second half of the 1990s the relative success of the American economy led many to criticise costly labour and social standards in the EU – seen as structural rigidities, sources of inflexible labour markets and an inadequate propensity to innovate – as if they were a major cause of the poorer economic performance and lower employment levels of the European Union. High social charges would make businesses uncompetitive and public spending intolerable.

In 2001, the American economy was no longer growing as much as had been predicted, with zero per cent growth being mentioned by Federal Reserve Bank Chairman Alan Greenspan. Layoffs in 2001–3 are also clear signs of an economic malaise that the US economy still has to overcome. At the same time, the EU economy seems to be achieving higher growth, although lower than expected and with notable differences between member states. Meanwhile, the crisis in Asia in the late 1990s also pointed to the limits and vulnerability of economies that develop rapidly and 'wildly' without any consideration for social protection or workers' rights.

On the other hand, the apparently better prospects of the EU economy, reflected in the improvement of the euro against the US dollar, may lead those in favour of the European Social Model to exaggerate the potential economic effects of social policies. This is also to be avoided.

While social policies can undoubtedly contribute to economic growth – especially in the EU where a high-quality approach in terms of human resources and trade specialisation has been selected – they have to be presented as policies worth developing in their own right, not only on economic and efficiency grounds, but also to achieve society's other objectives in terms of higher living standards. In other words, social policies should not be made dependent on economic growth, coming to the fore when economic performance improves and being sidelined when they are no longer convenient: they must be developed and integrated into a long-term and coherent social, economic, and financial framework.

These remarks should by no means be understood as a criticism of the current emphasis on the contribution of social policies to economic growth – which is right and proper – but rather as a call for clear limits. After all, this new approach has gained a hearing from those previously impervious to persuasion concerning social issues. If international monetary institutions become more receptive to social policy in the design of their stabilisation and growth programmes, even integrating social variables in their macroeconomic models – something that has not happened so far – it would already represent an important step forward.

At the same time, presenting social policies as factors in economic growth must be an argument for reinforcing and deepening social policy, not for modifying it.

It is to be noted, for instance, that the emphasis on 'social policy as a productive factor' has emerged precisely when reform of social security systems has come to the fore in almost all member states, clearly leading to some confusion, as if social security and social protection systems had not played an important social and economic role so far; what is at stake is to improve the funding of these systems and make them viable in the long run, not to make them dependent on economic growth.

11.7.3 Dangers of 'Modernisation' of the European Social Model

It is important to note that the modernisation of the European Social Model represents a key priority also for those more inclined towards neo-liberal theories. It was a priority, for instance, for British Prime Minister Tony Blair before the Lisbon Summit, who identified the key issue as: 'how we modernise the European Social Model; how Europe embraces the enterprise agenda and seeks to match the dynamism of the US, whilst preserving our commitment to social justice.'[4] It is even seen as a key condition for the future: 'The Lisbon Council represents a turning point in Europe's approach to economic and social policy.'[5]

However, this sudden need seems suspect, especially since the 'modernisation of the European Social Model' advocated by Tony Blair is somewhat different from the definition of the European Social Model presented in our introductory chapter. For Tony Blair,

> the way to provide social protection today is not more and more regulation or high business costs and taxes; it is through making our workforce highly adaptable, more employable and better skilled; through encouraging the development of technology; promoting small businesses; and making our welfare systems help people off benefit and into work, with specific measures to combat exclusion. We need a new social model for a new European reality . . . a vision that lets us adapt the European social model to the new realities of global commerce.[6]

This is what Tony Blair has taken up as the 'Third Way' without defining what lies behind the rhetoric, as a result of which numerous different interpretations have emerged. It has been proposed as an alternative to both the Thatcherite–Reaganite project of the 1980s and the state interventionism of the 1970s; an alternative way between neo-liberalism and social democracy, with clear inspiration from the USA.[7] For some analysts, the Third Way could also be interpreted as accepting 'the inevitability of free market capitalism and ask[ing] whether and how a shrunken state should use its residual powers to ameliorate the worst effects of that system' (Gerald Holtham, Director of the Institute for Public Policy Research), whilst for others it would correspond to a fresh application of the principles of social democracy to current circumstances, that is, free markets and globalisation.

---

4. Statement on Lisbon in the House of Commons by the Prime Minister, 27 March 2000.
5. Op. cit.
6. Speech of the Prime Minister in the House of Commons, 23 February 1999.
7. It is interesting that the term 'third way' was also used by President Bill Clinton in his 'State of the Union' speech: 'we have moved past the sterile debate between those who say Government is the enemy and those who say Government is the answer'.

Despite their different objectives, it is amazing how similar – and thus confusing for European citizens – are the formulations of the European Commission on the one hand, and those of political leaders favouring a Third Way in Europe.[8] In particular, both sides recognise a shift – and not a deepening – in the European Social Model, and they increasingly conceive of social policy as an instrument of adaptability and flexibility. This can only be viewed with grave concern.

This is why the debate about the evolution of the European Social Model should focus not on 'modernisation', but rather on 'deepening'. This requires a more profound analysis of the means we have at our disposal to continue making progress on social policy (see Chapter 1) and how to use them in the best possible way in the face of EU enlargement, notably by taking into account what is happening in the candidate countries.

11.8 ENSURING THE SURVIVAL OF THE SOCIAL MODEL ALONGSIDE EU ENLARGEMENT

11.8.1 Reality in the New Member States

Almost incredibly, the 'modernisation' of European social policy seems to have begun without any thought being given to the social dimension of enlargement and without taking into account current shortcomings in candidate countries (they are numerous).

It is significant that EU enlargement has not been mentioned in any recent document on the Third Way. Such documents are not based on an assessment of economic and social trends in Central and Eastern Europe and do not incorporate these countries in the picture, as if neo-liberal values and policies would by definition be good for candidate countries and for an enlarged EU.

At the same time, past and current flexibility concerning the European Social Model can only be detrimental in the future, in a context that will be more and more dominated by markets and economic variables. A comprehensive definition, including its different contents – while leaving room for its evolution – should be attempted before the first new accessions take place.

We should also reassess whether the proposed 'modernisation' has taken sufficient account of the current process of EU enlargement to the countries of Central and Eastern Europe.

8. Within the European Commission – and even within its Directorate for Employment and Social Affairs – a shift within the model is seen as a response to changing economic reality. We can see it in the way in which the European Social Model is being expressed at Community level. For instance for former Commissioner Flynn, 'the European model has to be adapted in order to be preserved'.

A more ambitious social policy is indeed a 'historical necessity' in the prospect of EU enlargement, and the worrying social situation in candidate countries points to the need to reinforce basic minimum social rights and social policy in general in order to ensure that their populations do not reject the EU, that they move towards a more developed, 'knowledge society' in a balanced and smooth fashion, and that social cohesion is preserved in the context of the European and global economies. We have tried to emphasise these aspects on the basis of empirical evidence rather than ideological considerations.

However, fulfilment of such requirements would clearly be diametrically opposed to the kind of modernisation of the European Social Model presented in recent 'Third Way' manifestos issued by European political leaders, which instead emphasise the need to reduce labour regulation.

For Tony Blair and Jose-Maria Aznar, 'Governments should not try to interfere in commercial decisions or impose heavy-handed social and economic regulation . . . in the past, we made the mistake too often of trying to apply social policies that generated obstacles for business growth and job creation.'[9]

These same contrasts can be observed in specific areas: on social protection, according to Tony Blair, 'EU social policy must be modernised to respond to changing employment patterns, increasing life expectancy and deepening social exclusion . . . with member states setting targets in specific areas: unemployment, youth unemployment, overall employment, child poverty and so on'.[10] This vision of social protection, very much focused on social exclusion, particularly very narrow categories of marginalised people, is identical to the recommendations given by the World Bank and the IMF, of which we have seen the direct results in Central and Eastern Europe (see Chapter 3).

The view of labour costs is also very different from what we have proposed: for Tony Blair, cutting labour costs is a clear priority for employment: 'In the last three years, we have created over 800 000 jobs in Britain; in Spain there have been over a million new jobs; and in France, too, employment has risen by over 800 000 in the last two years, in part reflecting new measures to cut the cost of labour'. Similarly in the Blair–Schröder manifesto: 'the labour market needs a low-wage sector in order to make low-skill jobs available'.

This is similar to the incomes policy advised by the World Bank and the IMF in the first years of transition in Central and Eastern Europe, with dra-

---

9. 'The Euro Is Changing the Face of Europe', joint article by Prime Minister of the UK Tony Blair, and Prime Minister of Spain José-Maria Aznar, *Financial Times* (13 June 2000).
10. Statement on Lisbon in the House of Commons, 27 March 2000.

matic social but also economic implications. This policy contrasts with the need 'to improve the living standards and skills of the poorly qualified labour force', as expressed during the Lisbon Summit, and would have detrimental effects if implemented in the candidate countries. The Lisbon agenda would require EU enterprises' strategies not to be driven by lower costs – at least not exclusively so – but also by higher quality human resources, production processes and final products. There is also clearly a need for a more global, coherent and long-term industrial policy, especially in candidate countries where it has yet to develop.

We could multiply illustrations of how little the reality of candidate countries has been integrated in policy views in other areas, such as employment, social dialogue, and labour standards in general.

11.8.2 Imposing More Social Requirements

We have seen in the different chapters of this volume how inadequate the message of the European Commission has been on social policy. This is not new. Already in the association agreements signed with each of the candidate countries, there was no emphasis on social policy.

Alber and Standing (2000, p. 110) emphasise what they call the 'relative indifference of the European Commission in the transition process which contracted out expertise and failed to push a European vision of social policy and a good society'; they insist that 'future developments in the region will depend greatly on the determination with which the Commission demands concessions to European-type social policies as a precondition for EU membership in the coming negotiations on accession'.

Whilst such criticisms are easy and perhaps unfair since they seem to ignore the important work done by the Commission and its specialists in different areas, and also seem not to recognise what the situation would be today if the EC had not emphasised a number of aspects of social policy, we must acknowledge that the European Commission, but also other European institutions, has so far not been convincing on social policy. It is true that the contrast is also high within the European Commission itself, between those working at DG Employment and Social Affairs who have insisted on the social *acquis*, and those in other DGs, including Enlargement and Economic and Financial Affairs, who are themselves barely aware of the Community *acquis* in the social field and seem to be more inclined towards liberal arguments in which social issues do not figure prominently.

It is also true that developments in EU member states themselves, with the neo-liberal wave we have described, have not been favourable to social policy. It is significant that the Blair–Berlusconi–Aznar axis has made converts in Central and Eastern Europe, as in Hungary with (former) Prime Minister

Orbán (1998–2002). This political and ideological evolution contrasts strikingly with the strong Community *acquis* in the social field. The whole problem in the future will be to see how determined EU member states will be in the implementation of such regulations, not only in their own countries, but also in the new member states. What is clear is that developments in candidate countries require a stronger stance and clearer and more comprehensive provisions in all the social areas addressed in this book.

In the end, whether the world moves towards a European or an American type of capitalism – or some other variant – may depend on the pressure exerted by the European Commission, but also by other international agencies, such as the ILO, the World Bank, the IMF, and also transitional institutions.

11.8.3 Preventing Social Dumping

The current phase of European construction has brought social dumping very much to the fore. Those EU member states which participate in Economic and Monetary Union (EMU) will thereby lose national control over exchange rates and monetary policy; at the same time, the Maastricht criteria concerning public deficits and public debt will greatly reduce their room to manoeuvre as regards fiscal policy. Candidate countries will also bear the very heavy burden of adapting almost immediately to these restrictions. In this context, wage costs and social protection may appear to all the new member states – as well as to the old 15 – as the main tool of policy adjustment in conditions of growing competition. We must emphasise that these problems will also affect those European countries that are not part of EMU, such as the UK and Sweden, not to mention Switzerland, since all these states will continue to carry out most of their trade and capital exchange with this area of economic and monetary integration, and will thus experience more competitive pressure (they will also have to define their exchange rate policy in relation to the euro).

In such a context, we may expect even greater risk of social dumping on the part of the new member states. This is, however, a complex issue. As already mentioned, the rapid development of intra-Community trade flows in the 1970s and 1980s, and progressive rises in income have favoured a convergence in social protection in the EU which has acted as an obstacle to social dumping. This means that the economic catch-up process in new member countries will be essential to limit the progression of social dumping. At the same time, economic catch-up will not take place overnight. In this context, it would be inadequate and misleading to expect social dumping to be resolved by economic development alone; comprehensive social policies are also needed. Better coverage and extension of working and social standards within the new enlarged EU would contribute to reducing social dumping. As an example, the two new directives on European works councils in transnational companies and on workers' information and consultation in enterprises with more than 50 employees are clear steps forward. Other measures in the social field are also required.

Of course, some member states would like to go further as regards social legislation, but a number of other countries have persistently used their veto. In order to counter this, we should combine methods according to the objective: while in some areas legislative action is possible, in others a coordinated approach would be more appropriate. However, the policy of open coordination should not be taken to be a substitute for legislation, but more as a complement.

EU enlargement may well lead to more difficulties in implementing and making progress on workers' rights, thus emphasising the need to go forward through more flexible means (such as open coordinated methods, exchange of practices, and so on). At the same time, we have explained why the enlargement process itself requires more binding instruments. In other words, the paradox is that while the situation in candidate countries requires more binding EC instruments, once they have joined the EU the same countries may impede further progress in that direction.

It is for the same reason that the proposed method of 'reinforced cooperation' – that is, progress on that issue but only between a few or a group of member states – that has been much debated at EU level, would not be adapted to a newly enlarged EU. Attempts to reach a qualified majority on important social matters and to fight for it – however difficult it may look – would be more appropriate, in order to avoid the emergence of a multi-speed Europe. It is particularly important not to create further divisions – this time social – on top of the large economic differences prevailing between applicant countries and current EU member states, as well as among the applicant countries themselves.

While the adoption by future member states of the Community *acquis* in the social field must be ensured, it is no less crucial to guarantee its concrete implementation. We expressed serious reservations in this regard in Chapter 2 and subsequent chapters. The inadequate transposition of the Community *acquis* in enterprises of candidate countries will obviously constitute the main source of social dumping in the next few years. Consequently, and according to the European Court of Justice, changing the current European Commission process of monitoring proper implementation of the *acquis* would represent an important first step.

The current system is based on annual implementation reports for each country, compiled by EC officials, generally on the basis of expert groups in the countries concerned. Nevertheless, these reports generally focus on the proper 'legal' implementation of the *acquis*, that is, whether the member state in question has properly transposed EC directives, through either legislation or social partners' agreements, but without any real analysis of their implementation at local level – for instance, within individual enterprises – through surveys, case studies, and so on. This method will clearly not be appropriate for checking the implementation of the *acquis* in the new member states, especially given the fact that most of their governments have blindly transposed all EC community directives, without giving much thought to their implementation, new governments not feeling bound by commitments made by previous governments. To summarise, the more institutionalised – notably through better structures and better coordination between different actors – the European Social Model becomes (both within the Community system and within individual member states), the more influence it will have in shaping policy outcomes.

The lack of data and information on social dumping is also striking given the importance of this phenomenon in the current EU enlargement process and beyond. Not only is there no systematic collection of examples of social dumping (such as enterprises relocating all or part of their production in other EU and non-EU member states), but there is also no analysis of their implications in terms of employment losses, GDP, wages, regional development, and so on. It would be desirable to have a European statistical institution – such as Eurostat – carry out the regular collection of precise data and information on social dumping, obviously in close relationship with national statistical offices.

11.8.4 Available Means

In Chapter 1 we presented all the different instruments currently at the EU's disposal for making progress on social policy. At this point it is worth looking at them from a different perspective, and to try to identify how relevant such tools are in light of particular features of prospective member states, as well as the new configuration of an EU with 27 or more members.

Table 11.2 summarises the different means used so far in the social area, their relevance in the prospect of EU enlargement, and their potential development in an enlarged EU.

We have seen in Chapter 1 that European social policy has made progress by way of different means, from binding legislation to financial aid through structural funds, not to mention European social dialogue and the coordination of national policies (method of open coordination) in new areas such as employment and social exclusion. At the same time, social charters and other, more general declarations have proved useful complementary instruments.

Table 11.2 Means of making progress on social policy: needs and prospects after EU enlargement

Available means	Requirements alongside EU enlargement	Prospects for progress
1) Legislation	Essential need for more binding requirements on social policies	a) increasingly difficult consensus in an EU 27 b) opposition from new member states less keen on social issues c) current EU member states opposed to new binding tools
2) Structural funds	Important aid to be channelled towards backward regions of new member states Concrete assistance required in their most sensitive sectors (agriculture, and so on)	a) difficult to cover new member states in the same way as current EU member states b) opposition from current member states
3) European social dialogue	Would allow progress on local and concrete problems by concerned actors Could provide direct response to social partners' concerns Would help cover transnational issues	a) more difficult with social partners from 27 member states b) social partners and social dialogue structures of candidate countries insufficiently prepared c) will depend on the strength and willingness of European trade union and employer organisations
4) Coordinated policies (open method of coordination)	Useful complementary tool to cover new areas Should not substitute progress through more binding tools	a) monitoring process more difficult in an EU 27 (higher bureaucratic burden, and so on) b) wide scope more difficult to achieve because of less committed member states

5) Reinforced cooperation (among core group of member states)	Risk of two-speed EU Reduced importance of European Social Model (elements made optional) Risks of fragmentation of European construction	a) will be possible among a few member states b) extension to other member states difficult because new and some current member states less socially oriented
6) Social charter	Social charter should cover new areas Should be integrated into the Treaty	a) a few current member states opposed to binding character of the charter; they will be joined by some new member states b) new member states may be opposed precisely in those areas where they are most vulnerable
7) Convention on the future of Europe	May help to establish social issues as a core dimension in the future Europe	Not a single mention of social matters in the Convention so far Final outcome will depend on the Convention's working group on social issues
8) Other	Need for new means, better adapted to the new configuration	Will always depend on member states' willingness Need for proposals from EU institutions and international organisations

What is striking in Table 11.2 is the contrast between the need for and the likelihood of development of means to continue progress on social policy. Although *legislation* is the only truly powerful way of inducing a more pronounced shift among current and future member states towards enhanced social development, the adoption of new EC directives remains highly problematic in an enlarged EU with 27 member states. Candidate countries that seem to be oriented towards economic policies of a more liberal inspiration – that is, less regulation and fewer commitments – will certainly oppose significant progress on that front once they become members, combining with current EU member states which are radically opposed to more regulation in the social field. This calls for legislative action, but would also have required a tougher stance on social issues in the negotiation process.

We have advocated the strengthening of the Community *acquis* on social policy, making it part of the 'hard' rather than the 'soft' *acquis*. Having said that, even if the social *acquis* requires reinforcement, we should also underline that it has always been possible, in legal and institutional terms, as well as in terms of common values and principles – not to mention practices in EU member states – to put more emphasis on social matters, should the willingness have been there on the part of the European institutions (and individual member states through the European Parliament). The reinforcement of the Community social *acquis* should thus be seen as a way of avoiding neglect of important social issues resulting from the discretion of negotiators and their (un)willingness to consider them as part of the European construction.

Similarly, the current negotiation process has shown how little influence solidarity has had on enlargement. Obviously, current member states do not wish to extend to new member states all the *structural funds*. However, those countries currently benefiting from these funds (such as Spain) have insisted on the continuation of such assistance for their most backward regions. At the same time, the lack of willingness to help candidate countries solve the problem of agriculture also contrasts strikingly with the urgent need to provide assistance in this field.

In this context, in the recent past *European Social Dialogue* has shown itself to be an interesting and democratic way of issuing new EC provisions that would help both employers' and workers' representatives to regulate working and employment conditions in the labour market, as exemplified by recent progress on atypical forms of work (part-time, temporary work, and so on) and new forms of employment (such as tele-working). The possibility of European negotiations within individual sectors should also help social partners to address the numerous issues that EU enlargement presents, and help them to ensure the necessary harmonisation in terms of products, trade, and working conditions. At the same time, the increasing number of member states, and so of social partners, combined with the insufficient preparation of social partners and poor structures of social dialogue in new member states, may make it more and more difficult to achieve concrete outcomes through social dialogue. The increasing reluctance of the European employers' organisation to reach agreement in the social field – UNICE has often mentioned the need for a sort of 'moratorium' – and which will only increase with the joining of new employers from future member states with much more extreme attitudes, will be another barrier that trade unions will have to overcome. On their side, workers' representatives at EU level will have to learn to combine the often diverging interests of their old and new members (that is, from current and future member states), something which is particularly acute in relation to such issues as relocation and restructuring (see Chapter 8), as well as in the operation of European works councils (see Chapter 6).

More *direct coordination between member states* is another way of making progress on social policy. In this regard, however, we might wonder whether this strategy would be the most appropriate to the needs emerging from EU enlargement. In particular, the open method of coordination, for instance in the employment field, has undoubtedly been a success so far, which has not only led current member states to develop a coordinated approach – with policy guidelines and a peer-monitoring process – but also has made it possible to make specific requirements concerning employment and labour markets of candidate countries. The extension of this method to new areas, such as social exclusion and social protection, is therefore a step in the right direction, and should also permit such issues to be integrated in one way or another in future accession processes. At the same time, we must also draw attention to the limits of this method. First, doubt can be expressed concerning the operationality and effectiveness of peer-monitoring in an EU with 27, or 30, or 35 member states, and the consequent burden of bureaucracy. This method is already extremely heavy in terms of bureaucratic procedure (both for national and EU administrations) and that could only increase alongside the doubling of the number of member states. After the extension of the open method of coordination to employment, social exclusion and social protection, it is questionable whether other social areas could be convincingly covered in this way. Secondly, as we saw in Chapter 4 on employment, candidate countries are not always keen to follow guidelines that are not binding and rather focus on legal requirements in the negotiation process.[11] Thirdly, this approach is often seen by member states as an alternative to more binding requirements. Its further development could thus act as a substitute rather than a complement to the more binding provisions, although these would be the most effective in respect of successive EU accessions. Moreover, on such important issues for the European Social Model as social protection or social dialogue, should not the European institutions try to go much further?

Other member states may of course wish to go further in extending the social field. This is why the possibility of *reinforced cooperation between a few member states* has repeatedly been mentioned and debated. Nevertheless, it could lead only to an increasing gap between those who follow a more social approach – a relatively homogeneous 'hard core' of countries seeking to go further – and those who would further develop the deregulation approach. This could only lead to a two-speed – or a multiple-speed – Social Europe, leading to a total fragmentation of social policy and perhaps even of the European construction as a whole; especially since the new member states

11. Candidate countries seem to have done what was asked of them by the European Commission (in particular preparing joint assessment papers on employment), but without really considering it as a matter of the Community *acquis*. We might therefore wonder how relevant this exercise was for the elaboration and development of employment policy in candidate countries.

would have the possibility of pursuing the most liberal approach, better fitting their vision of a free-market economy. At the same time, the possibility of opt-outs from new social regulations would impede the European Commission from requesting a strong commitment in this area from new candidate countries (republics from former Yugoslavia, the Balkans, and so on), so making Social Europe a set of optional extras rather than an integral and indissociable part of EU membership.

In this regard, *social charters*, with their more universal character, should be seen as a way of unifying current and future EU member states around basic social values and principles. However, they cannot really contribute to modifying individual member states' policy directions until their provisions acquire a more binding character. This, however, is precisely what member states could not agree on before the Nice Summit, so that the new charter on fundamental social rights was not given any coercive features and did not extensively cover new items such as wages, the right to strike, or a few other basic social rights.

Unfortunately, the latest developments are not much more promising. Within the current work of the *Convention on the Future of Europe*,[12] social matters have not been mentioned at all, the priority being institutional, political, and security issues. Although a working group on social issues, after its initial rejection, has been set up, doubts have been expressed concerning its scope of activity and what it may be allowed to achieve.

The difficulty of making progress with current tools requires that member states and European institutions invent or promote *new means or instruments in the social field*, especially considering current trends in candidate countries. However, progress in this direction will continue to depend on member states' willingness to achieve further concrete progress on social policy, and to go beyond general declarations of intent – made at all European summits – in the social field.

11.9 THE SOCIAL *ACQUIS* IN A GLOBALISED CONTEXT

It would be misleading to believe that the European Social Model could be preserved and even strengthened without extending the debate and action in this field outside the EU. As an example, in order to better monitor and eventually to channel international capital movements and industrial relocations, there is a need for a more voluntaristic approach that should aim not only at consolidating the European Social Model inside the EU, but also at strength-

---

12. This Convention of Europe, chaired by former French president V. Giscard d'Estaing, aims to prepare a Treaty establishing a constitution for Europe. It will also propose reforms of European institutions in order to improve their functioning, especially in an enlarged EU.

ening respect for fundamental social rights in international trade. There would be no sense in reducing the sources of intra-EU social dumping if the pressures for extra-EU social dumping, coming from lower labour standards outside the EU, continue to increase.

Such a policy focus, however, does not seem always to be in accordance with what has been advised by international monetary institutions, which have put the emphasis in Central and Eastern Europe, as in all other transition economies, rather on the flexibilisation of markets and reducing or weakening regulations and institutions, including those dealing with social protection.

In this regard, some social analysts have seen the social policy agenda of the international financial agencies, most notably the World Bank, as geared to a global programme of social dumping:

> there has been a strong tendency to promote a residual welfare state model, based on a very basic 'social safety net' – a 'targeted', selective state floor of transfers and services – coupled with a privatized set of schemes serving mainly the middle class who can afford to pay the required contributions. This agenda suits the commercial interests of major corporations dealing with pensions, health care and educational services. The failures and discrediting of Pay-As-You-Go systems have only been basic first steps in this global agenda. Privatization is the desired global trend . . . it is not too fanciful to depict the rules and strategy of the World Trade Organization as contributing to it. (Alber and Standing 2000, p. 115)

Illustrative of the standpoint of the officials of the World Trade Organisation is the following:

> People in Europe often think that globalisation threatens the European model of capitalism, which tempers markets with government policies that aim to promote social justice. Indeed, it is now conventional wisdom that globalisation sets governments, like companies, in greater competition with each other, and that this will force Europe to remodel itself along American lines.[13]

In a similar fashion, neo-liberal theories and their supporters within the EU are presenting the removal of rigidities in the labour market – such as social standards – as a historical necessity, the 'inevitable march of history' toward free trade and a global market. Policymakers like Blair and Aznar, for instance, have tried to place their views outside the ideological arena and to present their – 'Third Way' – manifesto as a pragmatic response to change:

> In a world of ever more rapid globalisation and scientific changes we need to create the conditions in which existing businesses can prosper and adapt, and new businesses can be set up and grow . . . In this new emerging world people want

13. Speech by Renato Ruggiero, Konrad Adenauer Stiftung, 4 May 2000, Frankfurt (in WTO news; press releases).

politicians who approach issues without ideological preconceptions and who, applying their values and principles, search for practical solutions to their problems through honest, well-constructed and pragmatic policies.[14]

In this regard, the term 'modernisation' is repeatedly used:[15] 'realistic and forward-looking policies capable of meeting the challenges of the twenty-first century. Modernisation is about adapting to conditions that have objectively changed . . . a necessary adaptation . . . The aim of this declaration is to give impetus to modernisation.'

Nevertheless, the neo-liberal approach remains ideologically driven and the need to move towards more deregulation has still to be proved, especially with regard to EU enlargement, but also within a more international context. Numerous researchers in Europe and in the USA have disputed the idea that trade interdependence and increased capital mobility automatically result in convergence on a single model of market capitalism in which the state's policy autonomy is radically curtailed.

After the battle over 'the social clause' was lost by the ILO and other international organisations keen on preserving some social standards in commerce, the debate on fundamental social rights is still going on. The 'race to the bottom' that we described earlier is inducing a global effort to curtail unfair labour practices. It is too early to be confident that this is happening, although pressures on the WTO do seem to be growing, and there may be other initiatives to promote a global social charter.

There are good reasons to believe, however, that the outcome of this debate may influence the direction taken by individual EU member states; at the same time, the direction taken in the EU – and in a newly enlarged EU – may also influence the direction taken at international level. Basically, it is a model of alternative economic development that the EU may succeed in selling outside its borders.

11.10 CONCLUSION

Undoubtedly, the analysis carried out in this volume, in a range of social areas – in an effort to provide an answer to the title of this book *EU Enlargement versus Social Europe?* – has pointed to the high risks that the current enlargement of the EU to future member states could represent for preserving the social *acquis* that the EU has managed to promote alongside European Community construction.

14. 'Joint Statement from Tony Blair and Jose Maria Aznar on Priorities for the Lisbon Strategic Agenda', joint press release of the British and Spanish Embassies, Berlin, 27 October 2000.
15. The term 'modernisation' is mentioned more than 20 times in a ten-page document.

As a conclusion, we must stress that it is not the enlargement to current candidate countries alone which may undermine the European Social Model, but rather the fact that it would take place at a time when a combination of three mutually reinforcing trends could prove fatal:

1. The lack of consideration of social policies in future member states and their move towards more extreme, 'liberal' market economies;
2. The removal of many social provisions in current EU member states, and a similar attempt at EU level, under the heading of the 'modernisation of the European Social Model';
3. At international level, the general trend towards global markets, with more powerful multinational companies, removal of previous public authorities' functions, and a general acceptance of the economic need to move towards more flexible and liberal markets of the American type.

The conjugation of these three trends may well lead to a progressive collapse of social policy in an enlarged EU. The weak demands made of candidate countries by the EU concerning social policy (failing to counter trend 1) reflect the EU's recent movement away from the social (trend 2). Conversely, the integration into the EU of new member states where social policy is poorly developed (trend 1) could only support and accelerate the removal of social policy within the EU (trend 2), especially since it may become very difficult – if not impossible – to make progress on social policy in an enlarged EU with 27 or 30 members, some of which would have little interest in promoting social issues within national economic strategies. At the same time, the trend towards globalised markets (trend 3) might only encourage current and future EU member states to continue moving towards the less social competitive approach (trends 1 and 2). At the same time, the lack of any alternative approach in a newly enlarged EU (trends 1 and 2) would definitely contribute to the development of a global economy and a general trade system in which social issues would not have much priority (trend 3).

The EU would thus lose the opportunity to provide an example to the rest of the world of a system that could efficiently generate both economic competitiveness and social cohesion. This is a challenge which goes well beyond current or future EU borders to encompass the role of social issues in economic developments in the world.

This is what is at stake here and what motivated the writing of this book. The aim is not to end with a pessimistic vision of the future EU, however, but to attract the attention of policymakers and other economic and social actors who could play a role in creating an alternative model of economic and societal development.

We should avoid having to face major social upheavals before we understand that social policy issues must be properly addressed, and try to ensure that social improvements are not implemented too late, when citizens from both current and future member states have lost all their faith and confidence in the EU enlargement process. As recently emphasised by Juan Somavia, Director General of the International Labour Office, 'The social future of the world is in Europe; if Europe is able to maintain its social model, it will be a sign of hope for the rest of the world.'[16]

16. 'L'avenir mondial se joue en Europe' (The world's future is in Europe), *La Libre Belgique* (5 February 2003), p. 7.

Bibliography

Aasland, Aane (ed.) (1996), *Latvia: The Impact of the Transformation*, Fafo Report, NORBALT Living Conditions Project, Oslo: Fafo Institute for Applied Social Science.

Alber, Jens and G. Standing (2000), 'Social dumping, catch-up, or convergence? Europe in a comparative global context', *Journal of European Social Policy*, **10**, No. 2 (May), pp. 99–119.

Assemblé Nationale [French National Assembly] (2000), *Rapport de la délégation de l'Assemblée Nationale pour l'Union Européenne sur le dumping social*, No. 2423 (May), Paris, 155 pages.

Baldacchino, Godfrey (2001), 'Malta and the European Union: a comparative study on social policy, employment and industrial relations', Malta Employers' Association, April, Valletta, 86 pages.

Bauer, T., and K. Zimmermann (1999), *Assessment of possible migration pressure and its labour market impact following EU enlargement to Central and Eastern Europe*, Study for the Department for Education and Employment (United Kingdom), Bonn.

BDA (2001), *Conference Reader of the Fifth Round Table of the Industrial and Employers' Federations of the EU and the Accession Countries*, report of the fifth employers' round table organised on workers' participation, information and consultation in Berlin, 28–29 May 2001, 103 pages.

Bělina, Miroslav (2001), 'Social dialogue in the Czech Republic', mimeo, Brussels, 10 pages.

Bělina, Miroslav, and Kristina Koldinská (2001), 'Social aspects of industrial relations in the Czech Republic', Faculty of Law, Charles University, Prague (February).

Bercusson, Brian (2000), 'The ETUC and the European Court of Justice', paper presented at the conference 'The implementation of the social *acquis communautaire* in the candidate countries', 30 November–2 December 2000, Vilnius, organised by the European Trade Union Confederation (ETUC).

Berencsi, Zsuzsa, and Endre Sík (1995), 'Intentions to emigrate and to work abroad in Hungary 1993-1994', in Fullerton et al. (eds) (1995), pp. 129–40.

Berki, Erzsébet, and Mária Ladó (1998), 'Moves towards free wage bargaining in Hungary', in Vaughan-Whitehead (ed.) (1998), pp. 182–233.

Blanchard, Olivier (2001), 'EU Enlargement and immigration from Eastern Europe', mimeo, 7 pages.

Blasi, J.R., S. Kroumova, and D.L. Kruse (1997), *Kremlin Capitalism*, Ithaca, NY: Cornell, ILR Press.

Boeri, Tito, Richard Layard, and S. Nickell (2000), 'Welfare to Work' (March), London and Milan.

Boni, Michał (2001), 'Labour market in Poland – current trends and challenges', Advisory Team to Deputy Prime Minister, Ministry of Labour and Social Policy, Warsaw, 22 pages.

Borbély, Szilvia (2000), 'Pensions in Hungary and the influence of external players', paper presented at the conference 'New governance and the social dimension of enlargement', organised by the European Social Observatory in Brussels, European Parliament, 18 October 2000, 16 pages.

Branch, Ann, and Justin Greenwood (2001), 'European employers: social partners?', in H. Compston and J. Greenwood (eds) (2001).

Brenton, Paul, Francesca Di Mauro, and Matthias Lücke (1998), 'Economic integration and FDI: an empirical analysis of foreign investment in the EU and in Central and Eastern Europe', CEPS Working Document No. 124, Brussels: Centre for European Policy Studies.

Brücker, Herbert, and Tito Boeri (2000), see European Integration Consortium (2000a).

Brüstle, Alena, and Roland Döhrn (2001), 'Verlängerte Werkbänke? Zur Struktur des deutschen Außenhandels mit den mittel- und osteuropäischen Ländern', RWI-Mitteilungen (2001), 1, pp. 1–21.

Brzica, Dane (1998), 'Privatisation in Slovakia: the role of employee and management participation', IPPRED working paper 12, Interdepartmental Action Programme on Privatisation, Restructuring and Economic Democracy (IPPRED), International Labour Office (March), Geneva, 24 pages.

Burda, Michael (1998), 'The consequences of EU enlargement for Central and East European labour markets', Discussion Paper No. 1881, CEPR (May), London.

Cahn, Claude, David Chirico, Christina McDonald, Viktória Mohácsi, Tatjana Peric, and Ágnes Székely (1998), 'Roma in the educational systems of Central and Eastern Europe', notebook 'Roma and the right to education', ERRC (summer).

Carley, Mark (2002), 'Industrial relations in the EU member states and candidate countries', European Foundation for the Improvement of Living and Working Conditions (EIRO), Dublin.

Carlin, Wendy, Saul Estrin, and Mark Schaffer (2000), 'Measuring progress in transition and towards EU accession: a comparison of manufacturing firms in Poland, Romania and Spain', with the support of the European Bank for

Reconstruction and Development (EBRD), London Business School and University College London, mimeo, 35 pages.

Casale, Giuseppe (ed.) (1999), *Social dialogue in Central and Eastern Europe*, Budapest: International Labour Office–ILO-CEET.

Celin, Mira, and Grigor Gradev (eds) (2003), *The Unity of Europe: Challenges for the Social Dimension*, special issue on EU enlargement, *Transfer*, quarterly of the European Trade Union Institute (spring).

CEPR and IEWS (1996), *Coming to terms with accession*, forum report on the economic policy initiative, No. 2, London: CEPR and IEWS.

Chilosi, Alberto, Anna Krajewska, and Eugeniusz Kwiatkowski (1995), 'Poland: from traditional to new forms of financial participation' in Vaughan-Whitehead et al. (1995), pp. 167–82.

Chlon, Agnieska, Marek Góra, and Michał Rutkowski (1999), 'Shaping pension reform in Poland: security through diversity', *World Bank Pension Primer*, No. 9923.

Chouraqui, Alain, and Kevin O'Kelly (2001), '"Which European social model?" A challenged balance between regulation and deregulation', introduction to the conference 'Which European social model?', 10–11 September 2001, Aix en Provence, organised by the European Foundation for the Improvement of Living and Working Conditions and the LEST.

Clarke, Linda, Peter de Gijsel, and Jörn Janssen (eds) (2000), *The dynamics of wage relations in the new Europe*, Boston–Dordrecht–London: Kluwer Academic Publishers.

Clauwaert, Stefan, and Wiebke Düvel (2000), 'The implementation of the social *acquis communautaire* in Central and Eastern Europe – on the aspects of labour law, equal opportunities, health and safety at work', ETUI Interim Report (September), Brussels: ETUI, 64 pages.

Compston, Hugh, and Justin Greenwood (eds) (2001), *Social Partnership in the European Union*, Basingstoke: Palgrave.

Cox, Terry, and Bob Mason (2000), 'Trends and developments in East Central European industrial relations', *Industrial Relations Journal*, **31**, No. 2, pp. 97–114.

Cziria, Ludovit (2001), 'New challenges for the social partners in Slovakia', mimeo, Research Institute of Labour, Social Affairs and Family, Bratislava.

Cziria, Ludovit, and M. Munkova (2000), 'Zapojenie socialnych partnerov do riesenia problematiky zamestnanosti' [Flexible working time patterns as a means of increasing employment], research report, VUPSVR.

De la Porte, Caroline, and Phillipe Pochet (2002), 'A two-fold assessment of employment policy co-ordination in the light of economic policy co-ordination', paper prepared for the ETUI/SALTSA/HBS Conference, 13 May 2002, Brussels, 25 pages.

Deacon, Bob (2000), 'Eastern European welfare states: the impact of the politics of globalisation', *Journal of European Social Policy*, **10**, No. 2 (May), pp. 146–61.

DGB (Deutscher Gewerkschaftsbund) (1999), 'Comments on migration policy – EU enlargement: freedom of movement for workers and services and cross-border employment', Migration Unit, International Department, DGB (German Trade Union Federation) (May), Düsseldorf, 10 pages.

Döhrn, Roland (1996), 'EU enlargement and transformation in Eastern Europe: consequences for foreign direct investment in Europe', *Konjunkturpolitik*, **42**, Essen: Rhine-Westphalian Institute for Economic Research (RWI), pp. 113–54.

Domański, Bolesław (2001), 'Poland: labour and the relocation of manufacturing from the EU', in Gradev (ed.) (2001), pp. 21–49.

Dörrembacher, C., Michael Fichter, László Neumann, András Tóth, and M. Wortmann (2000), 'Transformation and foreign direct investment: observations on path dependency, hybridisation, and model transfer at the enterprise level', *Transfer*, No. 3, Brussels: ETUI.

Draus, Franciszek (2000), *Les organisations patronales dans les pays de l'Europe Centrale et Orientale – Pologne, République tchèque, Hongrie* (February), Brussels: ETUI and MPIFG.

―――― (2001), 'Social dialogue in the European Union candidate countries – synthesis report', prepared for the conference 'Social dialogue in the European Union candidate countries', organised by European social partners in Bratislava, 16–17 March 2001; see also in ETUC–UNICE–UEAPME (2001).

Eamets, Raul, and Kadri Ukrainski (2000), 'Hidden unemployment in Estonia: experience from the early years of transition (1989–1996)', *Post-Communist Economies*, **12**, No. 4, pp. 463–84.

Eamets, Raul, Epp Kallaste, Jaan Masso, and Marit Room (2003), 'How flexible are labour markets in CEE countries? Macro-level approach', in Celin and Gradev (eds) (2003).

Earle, John. S., Saul Estrin, and L. Leshchenko (1995), 'Ownership structures, patterns of control and enterprise behavior in Russia', Working Paper (November), Central European University.

Eatwell, John, Michael Ellman, Mats Karlsson, Mario D. Nuti, and Judith Shapiro (1997), *Not 'just another accession' – the political economy of EU Enlargement to the east*, London: Institute for Public Policy Research (IPPR).

―――― (2000), *Hard budgets and soft states. Social policy choices in Central and Eastern Europe*, London: Institute for Public Policy Research (IPPR).

Economic and Social Committee (2000), 'Social dialogue has collapsed in Hungary' (February), Brussels: ESC.

Elernum, Tilt (1996), 'NORMA: an employee owned company in the metal industry', in N. Mygind and P. Norgaard Pedersen (eds) (1996), pp. 89–102.

Estrin, Saul, Kirsty Hughes, and Sarah Todd (1998), *Foreign direct investment in Central and Eastern Europe*, London: Cassell.

EBRD (European Bank for Reconstruction and Development) (1995–2001), *Transition Report*, London: EBRD.

European Commission (1993), *Growth, competitiveness and employment*, White Book (December), Brussels.

———— (1994), *European social policy. A way to follow for the European Union*, White Book (COM (94) 333) (July), Brussels.

———— (1996), *Report of the Comité des Sages: For a Europe of civic and social rights*, report presented at the European Social Policy Forum (March), Brussels.

———— (1997a), *Agenda 2000*, vol. 1: *For a stronger and wider Union*, DOC/97/6, Strasbourg; vol. 2: *The Challenge of Enlargement*, COM(97) 2000 final, Brussels; vol. 3: *The opinions of the European Commission on the applications for accession – summaries and conclusions*, Strasbourg and Brussels.

———— (1997b), *Agenda 2000 and the Single Market: a bridge to Central and Eastern Europe*, October 1997, Brussels.

———— (1998), *Adapting and promoting the social dialogue at Community level*, EC Communication (COM(98) 322), Brussels.

———— (1999a), *Social dialogue for success – the role of the social partners in EU Enlargement*, conference of the social partners on EU Enlargement, Warsaw, 18–19 March 1999, Directorate General for Employment and Social Affairs, Brussels.

———— (1999b), *EU Support for Roma communities in Central and Eastern Europe* (December), Brussels: EC, Directorate General for Enlargement.

———— (1999c), *Forum Special – five years of social policy*, Brussels: EC, DG Employment and Social Affairs.

———— (2000a), *Industrial relations in Europe – 2000* (July), Brussels: EC, DG Employment and Social Affairs, 90 pages.

———— (2000b), 'Preparing for Enlargement', *European Social Dialogue*, special issue (September), Brussels: EC, Directorate General for Employment and Social Affairs, 24 pages.

———— (2000c), *The future evolution of social protection from a long-term point of view: safe and sustainable pensions*, COM(2000) 622 final (October), Brussels.

———— (2000d), *European Social Agenda*, included in the conclusions of the European Summit in Nice: 'Presidency Conclusions: Nice European Council Meeting, 7, 8 and 9 December 2000', EN SN 400/00, ADD1.

European Commission (2000e), *Glossary – Institutions, policies and enlargement of the European Union*, Brussels: Directorate General for Education and Culture, 79 pages.

———— (2000, 2001, 2002), regular reports on progress towards accession for each candidate country.

———— (2001a), *European governance – a white paper*, COM(2001) 428 final (July), Brussels: EC, 35 pages; other version also available at the Office of Official Publications of the European Communities, Luxembourg (2001), 69 pages.

———— (2001b) *Employment in Europe 2001 – recent trends and prospects*, Brussels: Directorate General Employment and Social Affairs, European Commission, 91 pages.

———— (2001c), Second Report on Economic and Social Cohesion Report, European Commission (January), Brussels.

———— (2001d), *The free movement of workers in the context of enlargement*, Information note (March), Brussels

———— (2001e), *The impact of eastern enlargement on employment and labour markets in the EU member states*, prepared for the European Commission by the European Integration Consortium (DIW, CEPR, FIEF, IAS, IGIER), Final Report, Brussels: EC, Directorate General for Employment and Social Affairs, 240 pages.

———— (2000f), *Social Trends: Prospects and Challenges*, EC Communication, (COM(2000)82 final), Brussels.

———— (2001g), *Communication from Mr Verheugen in agreement with Ms Diamantopoulou – essential elements for the draft common positions concerning 'freedom of movement of persons'* (July), Brussels: EC, 11 pages.

———— (2001h), *Eurobarometer survey*, No. 54 (autumn).

———— (2001i), Promoting a European framework for corporate social responsibility, Green Paper, DG Employment and Social Affairs, European Commission (July), Luxembourg: Office for the official publications of the European Communities, 28 pages.

———— (2002a), *Social situation report 2002*, Brussels.

———— (2002b), *Employment in Europe 2002 – Recent Trends and Prospects*, Directorate General Employment and Social Affairs, Brussels: European Commission, 206 pages.

———— (2002c), *Report of the High Level Group on Industrial Relations and Change in the European Union*, Directorate General for Employment and Social Affairs (January), Brussels.

———— (2002d), *Industrial Relations Report 2002*, Brussels.

———— (2002e), 'The modernisation of social protection in candidate countries: new opportunities and challenges for the European Union', Synthesis Report (248 pages); and National Reports on candidate countries, presented at the Conference organised on this issue (same title) on 5-6 December 2002 in Brussels.

European Commission (2002f), *The European Social Dialogue, a force for innovation and change. Proposal for a Council decision establishing a Tripartite Social Summit for Growth and Employment*, Communication from the Commission COM(2002) 341 final; 2002/0136 (CNS), 26 June 2002, Brussels.

European Council (1994), 'The perspectives of European social policy: a contribution to economic and social convergence within the Union' (94/C 368/03), Brussels.

European Economic and Social Committee (2001), 'Opinion on the employment and social situation in the CEEC', CES 533/2001 (April), Brussels.

European Integration Consortium (DIW, CEPR, FIEF, IAS, IGIER) (2000a), *The impact of eastern enlargement on employment and wages in the EU member states*, Part A (Analysis), 141 pages, and Part B (Strategic Report), 195 pages.

———— (2000b), *The impact of eastern enlargement on employment and labour markets in the EU member states*, prepared for the European Commission, Final Report, Brussels, 240 pages (also reference as EC 2000e).

European Trade Union Confederation (ETUC) (2000), *Resolving labour disputes in accession-country companies*, Brussels, 89 pages.

ETUC–UNICE–UEAPME (2001), *Social dialogue in the European Union candidate countries*, report of the conference 'Social dialogue in EU candidate countries', organised in Bratislava, 16–17 March 2001, Brussels: ETUC–UNICE–UEAPME, 95 pages.

European Trade Union Confederation (2001), Press release of the Nice European Summit, ETUC, Brussels.

European Trade Union Institute (ETUI) (1995), 'Labour markets, wages and social security in Central and Eastern Europe' (April), Brussels: ETUI.

———— (2000), 'Enlargement as a trade union issue, *Transfer*, special issue, **6**, No. 3 (autumn).

Eurostat–European Commission (1999, 2000, 2001, 2002), *Employment and labour markets in Central European countries*, three numbers per year, Studies and Research, Theme 3 (population and social conditions), Luxembourg.

———— (2000), *Patterns and trends in international migration in Western Europe*, Studies and Research, Theme 3 (population and social conditions), Luxembourg, 195 pages.

———— (2001), *The social situation in the European Union 2001*, Luxembourg, 127 pages.

Fassmann, Martin (2002), 'Shadow economy', Ceskomoravska Konfederace

Odborovych Svazu [Czech Confederation of Trade Unions], Department of Education (January).

Fassmann, Heinz, and Christiane Hintermann (eds.) (1997), 'Migrationspotential Ostmitteleuropa: Struktur und Motivation potentieller Migranten aus Polen, der Slowakei, Tschechien und Ungarn', ISR Forschungsberichte (Research Reports), No. 15, Vienna: Verlag der Österreichischen Akademie der Wissenschaften, 70 pages.

Fassmann, Heinz, and Rainer Münz (2002), 'EU enlargement and future east–west migration in Europe', Chapter 4 in IOM (2002).

Fazekas, Károly (2000), 'The impact of foreign direct investment inflows on regional labour markets in Hungary', SOCO Project Paper No. 77c, Programme on 'Social Consequences of Economic Transformation in East-Central Europe' (SOCO), Vienna: Institute for Human Sciences, 22 pages.

Fazekas Károly, Jenő Köllő, László Neumann, and András Tóth (1999), *Relokáció: a munkahelyek áttelepülése Nyugat-Európából Magyarországra* [Relocation: the transfer of workplaces from Western Europe to Hungary], *Európai Tükör*, **59**, Budapest: MEH–ISM.

Ferge, Zsuzsa (2000), 'Social security reform: is it a different issue for accession countries?', paper presented at the conference 'Economic and social dimensions of EU enlargement', organised by the French Ministry of Economics and Industry, CEPS, ENEPRI, and CEPII, Brussels, 16 November 2000.

Ferge, Zsuzsa, and Katalin Tausz (2001), 'Social security in the transition countries of south-east Europe – the case of Hungary', prepared for the regional project of the FES (January).

FETBB (2000), *Projet EUROSITE – Nouvelle ligne de train ICE Cologne-Rhin/Main*, Fédération Européenne du Travail du Bois et du Bâtiment [European Federation of Building and Woodwork], Brussels (March), 13 pages.

Florea, Anca (2001), 'Non-payment/delay in payment of wages in Romania', research paper presented at the ILO conference 'Non-payment of wages', organised in Sofia (Bulgaria), November 2001, mimeo, ILO–CEET, Budapest.

Franzmeyer, F., and H. Brücker (1997), *Europäische Union: Osterweiterung und Arbeitskräftemigration*, DIW, Berlin Wochenberichte, **5**.

Freudenberg, Michael, and Françoise Lemoine (1999), 'Central and Eastern European countries in the international division of labour in Europe', Working paper, CEPII Resarch Centre (Centre d'Etudes Prospectives et d'Informations Internationales) (May), Paris.

Fuchs, Johann, and Manfred Thon (1999), 'Nach 2010 sinkt das Angebot an Arbeitskräften', in *IAB-Kurzbericht*, **4**, 1–6, Institut für Arbeitsmarkt- und Berufsforschung der Bundesanstalt für Arbeit.

Fullerton, Maryellen, Endre Sik and Judit Tóth (eds) (1995), 'Refugees and migrants: Hungary at a crossroads', Budapest: MTA PTI.

Fultz, Elaine (ed.) (2002), see ILO (2002).

Fultz, Elaine, and Markus Ruck (2000), 'Pension reform in Central and Eastern Europe: an update on the restructuring of national pension schemes in selected countries', International Labour Office Central and Eastern European Team (ILO–CEET), Report No. 25, Budapest, 23 pages.

Galgóczi, Béla (2002), 'Wage formation in the Central and Eastern European candidate countries', paper presented at the Seminar on Wage Formation in Candidate Countries, in Gdansk, 26–27 April 2002, working paper prepared for the European Trade Union Institute (ETUI), Brussels, 59 pages.

Galgóczi, Béla, and János Hovorka (1998), 'Employee ownership in Hungary: the role of employers' and workers' organizations', IPPRED working paper 11, Interdepartmental Action Programme on Privatization, Restructuring and Economic Democracy (IPPRED), International Labour Office (March), Geneva, 19 pages.

Ghellab, Youcef, and Daniel Vaughan-Whitehead (eds) (2003), *Sectoral Social Dialogue in Candidate Countries*, ILO in cooperation with the European Commission, Budapest : ILO-CEET.

Gill, Colin, and Hubert Krieger (2000), 'Recent survey evidence on participation in Europe: towards a European Social Model?', mimeo.

Giurescu, Ion (2001), 'Developments and current labour market issues in Romania', presented at the conference 'Labour, employment and social policies in the EU enlargement process: changing perspectives and policy options', organised in Baden, Vienna, 28–30 June 2001.

Goetschy, Janine (2001), 'The future of the European Employment Strategy', in Mückenberger (ed.), 2001, pp. 151–75.

——— (2002), 'The European Employment Strategy, multi-level governance and policy coordination: past, present and future', in Zeitlin and Trubek (eds), *Governing work and welfare in a new economy: European and American experiments*, Oxford: Blackwell.

Golub, Stephen (1997), 'International labour standards and international trade', IMF Working Paper 97/37 (April), International Monetary Fund (IMF), Washington.

——— (2002), 'Are international labor standards needed to prevent social dumping?', *Finance and Development*, Washington: World Bank, 8 pages.

Góra, Marek (2001), 'Polish approach to pension reform', in OECD Series 'Private Pensions and Policy Issues', 13 pages.

Gradev, Grigor (ed.) (2001), *CEE countries in EU companies' strategies of industrial restructuring and relocation*, Brussels: ETUI.

Greenwald, B., and Joseph Stiglitz (1986), 'Externalities in economies with imperfect information and incomplete markets', *Quarterly Journal of Economics*, **101**, No. 2, pp. 229–64.

Guillén, Ana M., and Santiago Alvarez (2000), 'Southern European welfare states facing globalization: is there social dumping?', presented at the Year 2000 International Research Conference on Social Security 'Social Security in the Global Village', Helsinki, 25–27 September, International Social Security Association (ISSA) Research Programme, Geneva.

Hagemejer, Krzysztof (2001), 'Challenges facing financing of social security systems from the European Union enlargement and opening the inner borders in Europe: Results of simulations with a simple model', ISSA Working Paper, Geneva: International Social Security Association, 12 pages.

Hausner, Jerzy, and Mirosława Marody (eds) (1999), *Three Polands: the Potential for and Barriers to Integration with the European Union*, Warsaw: Friedrich Ebert Foundation.

Heitmueller, Axel (2002), 'Eastern enlargement, social benefits, and migration incentives', working paper, Centre for Economic Reform and Transportation, Heriot-Watt University, Edinburgh (January), paper presented at the 2002 Methodology Conference in Crieff.

Hille, H., and T. Straubhaar (2001), 'The impact of EU enlargement on migration movements and economic integration: results of recent studies', in OECD (2001).

Hiršl, Miroslav, Jiří Rusnok, and Martin Fassmann (1995), 'Market reforms and social welfare in the Czech Republic: a true·success story?', Innocenti Occasional Paper EPS 50, UNICEF Innocenti Research Centre (August), Florence: Monee publications, 17 pages.

Hofer, Helmut, and Peter Huber (2001), 'Wage and mobility effects of trade and migration on the Austrian labour market', Economic Series No. 97 (February), Vienna: Institute for Advanced Study.

Hönekopp, Elmar (1999), 'Central and Eastern Europeans in the member countries of the European Union since 1990: development and structure of migration, population and employment', Background Report for the European Integration Consortium report (2000) (December), Nuremberg, 43 pages.

——— (2000), 'Auswirkungen der EU-Osterweiterung auf die Arbeitsmärkte der Mitgliedsländer der Europäischen Union', Friedrich-Ebert-Stiftung, Bonn.

Hunya, Gábor, and Jan Stankovsky (2002), 'Foreign direct investment in Central and East European countries and the former Soviet Union', WIIW–WIFO Working Paper (February), Vienna.

ICFTU (1998), *Annual Report on the Violation of Trade Union Rights*, International Free Trade Union Organisation (ICFTU/CISL).

ILO (International Labour Office) (1995–2000), *The cost of social security*, yearly report, Geneva: ILO.

———— (1998), *Employee ownership in privatization – lessons from Central and Eastern Europe*, Experts' Policy Report, ILO Central and Eastern European team and ILO Action Programme for Privatization, Restructuring and Economic Democracy, 1998, Geneva: ILO, and Budapest: ILO–CEET, 46 pages.

———— (2002), *La réforme des pensions en Europe Centrale et Orientale*, 2 vols (coordinated by Elaine Fultz), ILO–CEET (Bureau International du Travail – Equipe d'Europe Centrale et Orientale), vol. 1: 224 pages; vol. 2: 164 pages.

———— (2002), *Pension Reform in Central and Eastern Europe*, ed. Elaine Fultz), Volume 1: *Restructuring with Privatization: Case Studies of Hungary and Poland*; Volume 2: *Restructuring of Public Pension Schemes: Case Studies of the Czech Republic and Slovenia*, Budapest: ILO-CEET.

IMD (International Institute for Management Development) (2000), *World Competitiveness Yearbook*, Lausanne: IMD.

Inotai, András (1998), 'Economy', in Bertelsmann Foundation, Research Group on European Affairs (eds), *Costs, benefits and chances of Eastern enlargement for the European Union*, Gutersloh: Bertelsmann Foundation Publishers.

Institute of Macroeconomic Analysis and Development (IMAD) (2000), *Slovenian Economic Mirror* (April), Ljubljana.

IOM (International Organization for Migration) (1999), *Migration in Central and Eastern Europe: 1999 Review*, Geneva: International Centre for Migration Policy and Development (ICMPD), 195 pages.

———— (2002), *Migrations Challenges in Central and Eastern Europe – 2002 Review*, Geneva: International Centre for Migration Policy and Development (ICMPD).

ITUSR (1997), 'Survey results on workers' participation in Bulgaria', mimeo, Sofia: CITUB.

Jecchinis, Chris (2001), 'Promoting civil society and workers' participation in the EU', *European Review*, No. 20.

Jobert, Annette (2001), 'Le système: un modèle social européen multi-niveaux', presented at the Conference 'Which European Social Model?', Aix en Provence, 10–11 September 2001, organised by the European Foundation for the Improvement of Living and Working Conditions and the LEST.

Jones, Derek, and Mark Klinedinst (2002), 'Bulgarian ownership patterns in transition', preliminary paper presented at the 11th conference of the International Association for the Economics of Participation (IAFEP),

'Participation Worldwide', held in Brussels, 4–6 July 2002, 11 pages (available at http://ocean.st.usm.edu/~mklndnst/index.html).

Jones, Derek, and Jeffrey Miller (eds) (1997), *The Bulgarian economy: lessons from reform during early transition*, Aldershot: Ashgate.

Jones, Derek, and Tom Weisskopf (1996), 'Employee ownership and control: evidence from Russia', *Proceedings of the 48th Meeting of the Industrial Relations Research Association*.

Jones, Derek, Mark Klinedinst, and Charles Rock (1997), 'Productive efficiency during transition: evidence from Bulgarian panel data', *Journal of Comparative Economics*.

Kabaj, Mieczysław (1997), 'Jobless or employment-oriented growth strategy: searching for a dual model of development of the Polish economy (1996–2000)', mimeo, Warsaw.

———— (1998), 'Searching for a new results-oriented wage negotiation system in Poland', in Vaughan-Whitehead (ed.) (1998), pp. 234–71.

Kairelis, Rimantas (2001), 'Labour market trends and issues in Lithuania', presented at the conference 'Labour, employment and social policies in the EU enlargement process: changing perspectives and policy options', Baden, Vienna, 28–30 June 2001, 12 pages.

Kalmi, Panu (2002), 'Employee ownership and degeneration evidence from Estonian case studies', paper presented at the 11th conference of the International Association for the Economics of Participation (IAFEP), 'Participation Worldwide', held in Brussels, 4–6 July 2002, 33 pages (available at http://ocean.st.usm.edu/~mklndnst/index.html).

Kaminski, Bartloliej, and Michelle Riboud, (2000), 'Foreign investment and restructuring – the evidence from Hungary', World Bank Technical Paper No. 453, Europe and Central Asia Poverty Reduction and Economic Management Series (March), Washington DC: World Bank.

Karnite, Raita (2001), 'Latvia: assessment of the situation and major trends', in Gradev (ed.) (2001), pp. 263–89.

Kaucsek, György (1996), 'A multinacionális vállalatok szervezeti–vezetési viszonyai és az emberi erőforrással kapcsolatos viselkedése' [Organisational–managerial patterns of MNCs and their human resource approach], mimeo, Budapest: Institute for Labour Research.

Kavar Vidmar, Andreja (2000), 'Social exclusion and poverty in Slovenia', presented at the conference 'New governance and the social dimension of enlargement', organised by the European Social Observatory in Brussels, European Parliament, 18 October 2000, 14 pages.

Kester, Gerard, and Henri Pinaud (1996), *Trade unions and democratic participation: a scenario for the 21st Century – Scenario 21*, Aldershot: Avebury.

Konings, Jozef, and Alan Murphy (2001), 'Do multinational enterprises sub-

stitute parent jobs for foreign ones? Evidence from firm level panel data',
LICOS Discussion Paper 100/2001, Katholieke Universiteit Leuven:
LICOS Centre for Transition Economics.

Kovac, Zdenka, Franci Kluzer, and Alenka Kaiser (2001), 'The main challenges of the Slovenian labour market: completing the transition from a
socially owned economy, joining the EU, and facing the globalisation of
the economy', presented at the conference 'Labour, employment and social
policies in the EU enlargement process: changing perspectives and policy
options', Baden, Vienna, 28–30 June 2001, 13 pages.

Kozarzewski, Piotr, and Richard Woodward (2002), 'Firms privatized by
employee buyouts in Poland: enterprise performance and the evolution of
ownership structure', paper presented at the 11th conference of the
International Association for the Economics of Participation (IAFEP),
'Participation Worldwide', held in Brussels, 4–6 July 2002, 26 pages
(available at http://ocean.st.usm.edu/~mklndnst/index.html).

Kukar, S. et al. (1995), 'Siva ekonomija v Sloveniji' [The grey economy in
Slovenia], Ljubljana: Institute of Economic Research.

Kulpinska, Jolanta (2002), 'Employee participation in Poland: conditions for
development in the 1990s', paper presented at the 11th conference of the
International Association for the Economics of Participation (IAFEP),
'Participation Worldwide', held in Brussels, 4–6 July 2002, 8 pages (available at http://ocean.st.usm.edu/~mklndnst/index.html).

Kunz, Jan, (2002), 'Labour mobility and EU enlargement – a review of current trends and debates', ETUI Working Paper DWP 2002.02.01
(February), Brussels: ETUI.

Ladó, Mária (2001), 'Hungary: FDI and its impact on industrial relations', in
Gradev (ed.) (2001), pp. 73–136.

Ladó, Mária, and Ferenc Tóth (1996), *Helyzetkép az érdekegyeztetésről.
1990–1994* [Overview of interest reconciliation, 1990–4], Erdekegyeztető
Tanács Titkársága–Phare Társadalmi Párbeszéd Projekt, Budapest.

Ladó, Mária, and Daniel Vaughan-Whitehead (2003), 'Social dialogue in candidate countries: What for?', in Celin and Gradev, special issue of *Transfer*
on EU enlargement.

Laja, R., and E. Terk (1996), 'ESTRE: ownership dominated by a core group
of employees', in Mygind and Pedersen (eds), pp. 49–58.

Laky, Teréz (1998), *Main trends in labour demand and supply*, Annual Labour
Market Report (April) Budapest: Labour Research Institute.

––––––– (2001), *Main trends in labour market demand and supply*, Annual
Labour Market Report, National Employment Service, Budapest: Public
Employment Service.

Langewiesche, Renate (1999), 'EU enlargement and the free movement of
labour', ETUI Yearbook 1999, Brussels: ETUI.

Langewiesche, Renate, and András Tóth (eds) (2001), *The unity of Europe – political, economic, and social dimensions of EU enlargement*, Brussels: ETUI, 303 pages.

Lankes, H.P., and N. Stern (1998), 'Capital flows to Eastern Europe and the former Soviet Union', EBRD Transition Working Paper No. 27.

Lankes, H.P., and A.J. Venables (1996), 'Foreign direct investment in economic transition: the changing patterns of investment', *Economics of Transition*, **4**, No. 2, pp. 131–347.

Leahy, Dermot, and Cati Montagna (2000), 'Temporary social dumping, union legalisation and FDI: a note on the strategic use of standards', *Journal of International Trade and Economic Development*, **9**, No. 3, pp. 243–59.

Leppik, Lauri (2000), 'Poverty situation and policies to fight social exclusion in Estonia', paper presented at the conference 'New governance and the social dimension of enlargement', organised by the European Social Observatory in Brussels, European Parliament, 18 October 2000.

Lissovolik, Bogdan (1997), 'Rapid spread of employee ownership in the privatised Russia', in Uvalic and Vaughan-Whitehead (eds) (1997), pp. 204–49.

Lourdelle, Henri (1999), *Livre Blanc sur la Protection sociale dans les pays d'Europe Centrale et Orientale* (October), Brussels: ETUC.

———— (2003), 'Social protection and EU enlargement: challenges for the candidate countries and for the European Union', in Celin and Gradev (eds).

Mácha, Martin (2001), 'Le système de sécurité sociale en République tchèque', *Revue Belge de Sécurité Sociale*, special issue on EU enlargement, **43** (July).

Makó, Cs. (1998), 'FDI and restructuring business organisations in Central Eastern Europe: lessons from sector and region focused projects in the transformation economies', Institute for Economic Research, Hitotsubeshi University, Kunitachi, Tokyo.

Marsden, David (ed.) (1992), *Pay and employment in the new Europe*, Cheltenham: Edward Elgar.

Martin, Roderick, and Anamaria Cristescu-Martin (2001), 'Employment relations in Central and Eastern Europe in 2000: the road to the EU', *Industrial Relations Journal*, **32**, No. 5, pp. 480–93.

Matey-Tyrowicz, Maria (2001), 'Reflections about social dialogue in Poland and in Europe', mimeo, Brussels, 15 pages.

Minchev, Vesselin, and Grigor Gradev (2001), 'Bulgaria: FDI and labour relations', in Gradev (ed.) (2001), pp. 291–329.

MKW GmbH (2001), *Exploitation and development of job potential in the cultural sector in the age of digitalisation. Obstacles to mobility for workers in digital culture in the European Union*, study commissioned by the

European Commission, Brussels: Directorate General for Employment and Social Affairs.

Mosley (1990), 'The social dimension of European integration', *International Labour Review*, **129**, No. 2, pp. 147–63.

MRP (Employee Stock Ownership Plan, Hungary) (1997), 'Figures on ESOPs in Hungary', Budapest: MRP.

Munteanu, Costea (1997), 'Employee share-ownership in Romania: the main path to privatization', in Uvalic and Vaughan-Whitehead (eds.) (1997), pp. 182–203.

Mückenberger, Ulrich (ed.) (2001), *Manifesto for Social Europe*, Brussels: ETUI.

Mygind, Niels (1997), 'Employee ownership in the Baltic countries', in Uvalic and Vaughan-Whitehead (eds) (1997), pp. 49–79.

———— (2002), 'Ownership, control, compensation and restructuring of Lithuanian enterprises – preliminary results from a manager survey', paper presented at the 11th conference of the International Association for the Economics of Participation (IAFEP), 'Participation Worldwide', held in Brussels, 4–6 July 2002, 36 pages (available at http://ocean.st.usm.edu/~mklndnst/index.html).

Mygind, Niels, and Peter Noorgard Pedersen (eds.) (1996), *Privatization and financial participation in the Baltic countries: case studies*, Centre for East European Studies (March), Copenhagen: Copenhagen Business School.

Nacsa, Beáta, and László Neumann (2001), 'The system of collective bargaining in Hungary', presented at the conference organised by the National ILO Council of Hungary and the ILO in Budapest, 20–21 September.

Neal, Alan C. (1998), 'Regulating health and safety at work: developing European Union policy for the millennium', *International Journal of Comparative Labour Law and Industrial Relations*, **14**, No. 3 (autumn), pp. 217–46.

Nesporova, Alena (1999), *Employment and labour market policies in transition economies*, International Labour Office, Geneva, 105 pages.

———— (2001), 'Changing patterns of job stability and labour market flexibility in transition economies: the case of Central and Eastern Europe', mimeo, ILO: Geneva, 40 pages.

———— (2002), 'Why unemployment remains so high in Central and Eastern Europe', Employment Paper No. 2002/43, Geneva: ILO, 38 pages.

Neumann, László (1997), 'Circumventing trade unions in Hungary: old and new channels of wage bargaining', *European Journal of Industrial Relations*, **3**, No. 2, pp. 183–202.

———— (1999), 'Munkahelyek áttelepülése (Esettanulmányok magyarországi multinacionális vállalatokról)' [Relocation of jobs (Occasional case studies on MNCs in Hungary)], in Fazekas et al. (1999).

Nuti, Domenico Mario (1997a), 'Employee ownership in Polish privatiza-
tions', in Uvalic and Vaughan-Whitehead (eds.) (1997), pp. 165–81.
——— (1997b), 'Employeeism: corporate governance and employee share-
ownership in transition economies', in Mario I. Blejer and Marko Skreb
(eds.), *Macroeconomic stabilisation in transition economies*,
Budapest–London–New York: Central European University Press, pp.
126–54.
——— (2000), 'Employee participation in enterprise control and returns: patterns, gaps and discontinuities', presented at the 10th Conference of the
International Association for the Economics of Participation (IAFEP),
'Participation in the twenty-first century: new opportunities, new perspec-
tives', at University of Trento and Arco, 6–8 July 2000.
OECD (1997), 'Relations between the Central and Eastern European
Countries and the European Union in the field of international migration',
Note by the Secretariat, prepared by L. Barros, Working Party on
Migration (June), Paris.
——— (1999), 'Benefit systems and work incentives in OECD countries',
Background information, Organisation for Economic Co-operation and
Development, Paris.
——— (2001), *Migration policies and EU-enlargement – The case of Central
and Eastern Europe*, Paris: Organisation for Economic Co-operation and
Development.
Ögünc, Fethi, and Gökhan Yilmaz (2000), 'Estimating the underground econ-
omy in Turkey', discussion paper for the Central Bank of the Republic of
Turkey, Ankara (September).
O'Leary, Christopher, Alena Nesporova, and Alexander Samorodov (2001),
Manual on evaluation of labour market policies in transition economies,
Geneva: International Labour Office (ILO), 153 pages.
Palacios, Robert, and Rafael Rofman (2001), 'Annuity markets and benefit
design in multipillar pension schemes: experience and lessons from four
Latin American countries', Washington DC: World Bank.
Paoli, Pascal, Agnès Parent-Thirion, and Ola Persson (2002), *Working Conditions
in Candidate Countries and the European Union (in 2001)*, Dublin: European
Foundation for the Improvement of Living and Working Conditions.
Pollert, Anna (1999), *Transformation at work in the new market economies of
Central and Eastern Europe*, London: Sage.
Pöschl, Josef et al. (2002), 'Transition countries face up to a global stagnation:
Is it catching?', WIIW Working Paper No. 283, Vienna Institute for
International Economic Studies (WIIW) (February), Vienna, 93 pages.
Poutsma, Erik (2001), *Recent trends in employee financial participation in the
European Union*, Dublin: European Foundation for the Improvement of
Living and Working Conditions, 113 pages.

Prasnikar, Jan, and Aleksandra Gregorič (2000), 'Workers' participation in Slovenian enterprises ten years later', presented at the 10th Conference of the International Association for the Economics of Participation (IAFEP), 'Participation in the twenty-first century: new opportunities, new perspectives', University of Trento and Arco, 6–8 July 2000.

Privarova, Magda (2001), 'Slovakia: FDI, industrial relations, and development of the economy', in Gradev (ed.) (2001), pp. 173–95.

Puporka, Lajos (1998), 'La situation économique des Tsiganes en Hongrie', *Etudes Tsiganes*.

Pye, Robert B. K. (1998), 'From West to East: ABB Asea Brown Boveri in Central and Eastern Europe and the former Soviet Union', paper presented at the fourth annual CREEB conference 'Convergence or divergence: aspirations and reality in Central and Eastern Europe and Russia', Buckingham College, Chalfont St Giles, 23–24 June 1998.

Quintin, Odile (2002), 'European Business Forum: migration in a wider Europe', contribution to the second UNICE European Business Forum, 7 June 2002, Brussels, 6 pages.

Quintin, Odile, and Brigitte Favarel-Dapas (1999), *L'Europe Sociale – Enjeux et Réalités*, Paris: La Documentation Française (Collection Réflexe Europe).

Riboud, Michelle, Carlos Silva-Jauregui, and Carolina Sánchez-Páramo (2002), 'Does Eurosclerosis matter? Institutional reform and labor market performance in Central and Eastern European countries' (June), in World Bank (2002), pp. 243–311.

Rock, Charles, and Mark Klinedinst (1997), 'Employee ownership and participation in Bulgaria, 1989 to mid-1996', in Uvalic and Vaughan-Whitehead (eds.) (1997), pp. 80–119.

Rojec, Matija, and Miroslav Stanojević (2001), 'Factor-cost-seeking FDI and manufacturing', in Gradev (ed.) (2001), pp. 137–71.

Rončević, Borut (2001), 'The social situation and the state of reforms in Slovenia', report prepared for the Friedrich Ebert Foundation, University of Ljubljana, Institute of Social Sciences.

Rudolf, Stanisław (2002), 'The Polish Employee Representation in European Works Councils', paper presented at the 11th Conference of the International Association for the Economics of Participation (IAFEP) 'Participation Worldwide', held in Brussels, 4–6 July 2002, 23 pages (available at http://ocean.st.usm.edu/~mklndnst/index.html).

Rutkowski, Michal (2000), 'Social security reform: is it a different issue for accession countries?', presented at the conference 'Economic and social dimensions of EU enlargement', organised by the French Ministry of Economics and Industry, CEPS, ENEPRI, and CEPII, Brussels, 16 November.

Rutkowski, Jan, and Marcin Przybyla (2001), 'Poland – regional dimensions of unemployment', mimeo, Washington DC: World Bank, 18 pages.

RWI (Rheinisch-Westfälisches Institut für Wirtschaftsforschung) (2001), *The impact of trade and FDI on cohesion*, Final Report to the European Commission, Directorate General for Regional Policy (April), Essen, 46 pages.

Salt, J., J. Clarke, S. Schmidt, J. Hogarth, P. Densham, and P. Compton (1999), *Assessment of possible migration pressure and its labour market impact following EU enlargement to Central and Eastern Europe*, Migration Research Unit, Department of Geography, University College London.

Sapir, André, (1995), 'The interaction between labour standards and international trade policy', *World Economy*, **18** (November), pp. 791–803.

Schliva, Rainer (1997), 'Enterprise privatization and employee buy-outs in Poland: an analysis of the process', ILO Working Paper, Interdepartmental Action Programme on Privatization, Restructuring and Economic Democracy, ILO, Geneva.

Schneider, Friedrich (2002), 'The size and development of the shadow economies of 22 transition and 21 OECD countries', IZA Discussion Paper No. 514 (June), Bonn.

Sinn, Hans-Werner (2001), 'Social dumping in the transformation process?', NBER Working Paper No. 8364 (July), National Bureau of Economic Research (NBER), Cambridge, MA, 36 pages.

——— (2002), 'Germany in the world economy – "hope springs eternal"', presentation given at the annual meeting of the IFI Institute, 25 June 2002, Supplement to *CESifo Forum*, **3**, No. 2 (summer).

Sinn, H.-W., G. Flaig, M. Werding, S. Munz, N. Düll, and H. Hofman (2000), *EU-Erweiterung und Arbeitskräftemigration: Wege zu einer schrittweisen Annäherung der Arbeitsmärkte,* in cooperation with the Max-Planck-Institut für ausländisches und internationales Sozialrecht, Federal Ministry of Labour and Social Affairs, Berlin.

Sissenich, Beate (2000), 'The diffusion of EU social and employment legislation in Poland and Hungary', mimeo, Cornell University (December).

Schneider, Friedrich (2002), 'The size and development of the shadow economies of 22 transition and 21 OECD countries', IZA Discussion Paper No. 514 (June), Bonn.

Smith, Adam (1776), *An Inquiry into the Nature and Causes of the Wealth of Nations*, reprinted in W.B. Todd (ed.) (1976), *Glasgow Edition of the Works and Correspondence of Adam Smith*, vol. 1, Oxford: OUP.

Sorm, V., and K. Terrel (2000), 'Sectoral restructuring and labor mobility: a comparative look at the Czech Republic', *Journal of Comparative Economics*, **28** (3), pp. 431–55.

Spear, Roger, Jacques Defourny, Louis Favreau, and Jean-Louis Laville (eds) (2001), *Tackling social exclusion in Europe – The contribution of the social economy*, Aldershot–Burlington: Ashgate.

Srinivasan, T.N. (1995), 'International trade and labour standards' in Peter Van Dyck and Gerrit Faher (eds), *Challenges to the new World Trade Organization*, Amsterdam: Martinus Nijhoff/Kluwer.

Standing, Guy (1996), 'Social protection in Central and Eastern Europe: a tale of slipping anchors and torn safety nets', in G. Esping-Andersen (ed.), *Welfare states in transition. National adaptations in global economies*, London: Sage.

————— (1999), *Global labour flexibility: seeking distributive justice*, Basingstoke: Macmillan.

————— (2000), 'Globalisation and flexibility: dancing around pensions', Geneva: ILO (June), 20 pages.

Standing, Guy, and Daniel Vaughan-Whitehead (eds) (1995*), Minimum wages in Central and Eastern Europe: from protection to destitution*, Budapest: Central European University Press.

Stanojevic, Miroslav (2000), 'The German model of industrial relations in post-communism: workplace co-operation in Hungary and Slovenia', presented at the 10th Conference of the International Association for the Economics of Participation (IAFEP), 'Participation in the twenty-first century: new opportunities, new perspectives', University of Trento and Arco, 6–8 July 2000.

————— (2001), 'Industrial relations in Slovenia', mimeo, Brussels, 15 pages.

Stanovnik, Tine, and Nada Stropnik (1998), 'Vpliv socialnih transferjev na revšèino in dohodkovno neenakost v Sloveniji' [Impact of social transfers on poverty and income inequality in Slovenia: a comparison between 1983 and 1999], *IB revija*, 8–10, pp. 69–82.

Stiglitz, Joseph E. (2002), *Globalization and Its Discontents*, New York: W.W. Norton and Company, 282 pages. French translation (2002), *La Grande désillusion*, Paris: Fayard, 324 pages.

Straubhaar, Thomas (2001a), 'Migration and labour mobility in an enlarged European Union', paper prepared for the Fortis Bank Chair at the Catholic University of Leuven, Centre for Advanced Legal Studies (March), Leuven.

————— (2001b), 'East–West migration: will it be a problem?', *Intereconomics* (July/August).

Swiatkowski, Andrzej Marian (2001), 'Are the post-socialists' current collective bargaining procedures effective as a means to implement European labour law in Poland?', mimeo, Warsaw.

Szalai, Júlia (1999), 'The social security system in Hungary and some of the problems in view of adhesion', mimeo, Budapest.

Szamuely, László (1997), 'The social costs of transformation in Central and Eastern Europe', Discussion Paper No. 44, Kopint-Datorg (January), Budapest.

Szell, György (2001), '15 questions with regard to the European Social Model', paper presented at the conference 'Which European Social

Model?', held on 10–11 September 2001 in Aix en Provence, organised by the European Foundation for the Improvement of Living and Working Conditions and the LEST.

Tang, Helena (ed.) (2000), *Winners and losers of EU integration – policy issues for Central and Eastern Europe*, Washington DC: World Bank, 326 pages.

Tóth, András (1997), 'The invention of works councils in Hungary', *European Journal of Industrial Relations*, **3**, No. 2, pp. 161–81.

Tzanov, Vassil, and Daniel Vaughan-Whitehead (1997), 'Macroeconomic effects of restrictive wage policy in Bulgaria: empirical evidence for 1991–1995', in Derek Jones and Jeffrey Miller (eds), *The Bulgarian economy: lessons from reform during early transition*, pp. 99–126.

—— (1998), 'Republic of Bulgaria: for a new incomes policy and strategy', ILO–CEET, Report No. 23, Budapest.

Tzanov, Vassil, and Temenuzka Zlatanova (2001), 'Non-payment/delay in payment of wages in Bulgaria', research paper presented at the ILO Conference on the 'Non-payment of wages', organised in Sofia (Bulgaria) (November 2001), mimeo, Budapest: ILO–CEET.

UNDP (2001), *Human Development Report – Slovenia 2000–2001*, ed. Matjaz Hanzek and Marta Gregorčič (March), Ljubljana: UNDP and IMAD, 135 pages.

UNICE (2000a), *Occupational Safety and Health – A Priority for Employers* (August), Brussels: UNICE.

—— (2000b), UNICE Position Paper on Enlargement (October), Brussels, 14 pages.

—— (2001), 'Enlargement: freedom of movement of workers and social policy – position of UNICE' (June), Brussels.

UNICEF International Child Development Centre (1993, 1994, 1995, 1996, 1997, 1998), Regional Monitoring Reports, Nos 1–5, Florence.

—— (1998), *Education for all?*, MONEE Project CEE/CIS/Baltics, Regional Monitoring Report, No. 5, Florence.

—— (1999), *Women in Transition*, MONEE Project CEE/CIS/Baltics, Regional Monitoring Report No. 6, Florence.

Uni-Europa Graphical (2001), 'Extending European Works Councils to Central and Eastern Europe in the graphical sector – an introductory study', undertaken by Lionel Fulton, Labour Research Department, London, for Uni-Europa Graphical (December), Brussels, 19 pages.

United Nations (1999 and 2000), *World Investment Report*, New York–Geneva: United Nations.

Uscinska, Gertruda (2000), 'Pension systems in Poland after reform', presented at the conference 'New governance and the social dimension of enlargement', organised by the European Social Observatory in Brussels, European Parliament, 18 October 2000.

Uvalic, Milica (1991), 'The PEPPER Report: Promotion of employee participation in profits and enterprise results in the member states of the European Community', *Social Europe*, Supplement 3/91, Luxembourg.

—— (1997), 'Privatization in the Yugoslav successor states: converting self-management into property rights', in Uvalic and Vaughan-Whitehead (eds) (1997), pp. 266–300.

Uvalic, Milica, and Daniel Vaughan-Whitehead (eds) (1997), *Privatization surprises in transition economies – employee ownership in Central and Eastern Europe*, Cheltenham: Edward Elgar.

Van Aarle, Bas (1996), 'The impact of the single market programme on trade and foreign direct investment in the European Union, *Journal of World Trade*, **30**, No. 6, pp. 121–37.

Varblane, Urmas (2001), 'Estonia: strategic objectives of foreign investors', in Gradev (ed.) (2001), pp. 197–233.

Vaughan-Whitehead, Daniel (1991), 'Investissements directs dans le sud de l'Europe – Science, technologies et cohésion économique et sociale', FAST Occasional Paper No. 238, MONITOR–FAST Programme (June), European Commission, 112 pages.

—— (1992), 'The internal market and relocation strategies', in Marsden (ed.) (1992), pp. 42–98.

—— (1995), 'Minimum wages: the slippage of the anchor', in Standing and Vaughan-Whitehead (eds) (1995).

Vaughan-Whitehead et al. (1995), *Workers' Financial Participation: East–West Experiences*, Labour–Management Relations Series, No. 80, Geneva: ILO.

—— (ed.) (1998), *Paying the price – the wage crisis in Central and Eastern Europe*, ILO Studies Series, London and New York: Macmillan.

—— (1999a), 'Employee ownership on the policy agenda: lessons from Central and Eastern Europe', *Economic Analysis*, **2**, No. 1, pp. 37–55.

—— (1999b), *Albania in Crisis – The Predictable Fall of the Shining Star*, Cheltenham: Edward Elgar.

—— (2000), 'New hidden borders: economic and social gaps in an enlarged European Union', Robert Schuman Policy Paper No. 2000/29 (June), Florence: European University Institute.

Vidickiené, Dalia (2001), 'Lithuania: foreign investors' strategies – the views of labour market actors', in Gradev (ed.) (2001), pp. 235–61.

Vidovic, Hermine (2001), 'Labour market developments in the CEECs', Vienna Institute for International Economic Studies (WIIW) (June), Vienna.

Vylitova, Marketa (2000), 'Using social benefits to combat poverty and social exclusion: opportunities and problems from a comparative perspective. The Czech Republic', mimeo, Country Report for a Research Project of the Council of Europe.

Walterskirchen, E., and R. Dietz (1998), *Auswirkungen der EU-Osterweiterung auf den österreichischen Arbeitsmarkt*, Vienna: WIFO.

Weinstein, Marc (2000), 'Solidarity's abandonment of worker councils: redefining employee stakeholder rights in post-socialist Poland', *British Journal of Industrial Relations*, **38**, No. 1 (March), pp. 49–73.

World Bank (1996), *World Development Report. From Plan to Market*, Washington DC: World Bank.

——— (2000a), 'Balancing protection and opportunity: a strategy for social protection in transition economies', Social Protection Team, Human Development Sector Unit, Europe and Central Asia Region (May), Washington DC: World Bank.

——— (2000b), *Progress towards the unification of Europe* (September), Washington DC: World Bank, 70 pages.

——— (2002), *Labor, Employment, and Social Policies in the EU Enlargement Process – Changing Perspectives and Policy Options*, ed. Bernard Funck and Lodovico Pizzati, conference report, conference organised in Baden-Vienna, 28–30 June 2001, Washington DC: World Bank, 406 pages.

Zaman, Gheorge (2001), 'CEE countries in EU companies' strategies of industrial restructuring and relocation – the case of Romania', in Gradev (ed.) (2001).

Zammit, Edward (2003), 'Efficiency versus democracy at the workplace: a post-mortem on self-management at Malta drydocks', presented in an informal seminar of the Scenario 21 network, ETUI, Brussels, December 2000, revised in 2001, forthcoming in Michael Gold (ed.), *New frontiers of participation at work* (Scenario 21 – vol. 2) (2003), Ashgate.

Zemplinerová, Alena (2001), 'Czech Republic: FDI in manufacturing, 1993–1999', in Gradev (ed.) (2001), pp. 51–71.

Zilvere, Ruta (2001), 'Searching for solutions to reduce social exclusion', mimeo, Ministry of Welfare, Riga, 7 pages.

Index